T0178429

# Lecture Notes in Artificial Intelligence 10948

Subseries of Lecture Notes in Computer Science

More information about this series at http://www.springer.com/series/1244

Carolyn Penstein Rosé · Roberto Martínez-Maldonado
H. Ulrich Hoppe · Rose Luckin
Manolis Mavrikis · Kaska Porayska-Pomsta
Bruce McLaren · Benedict du Boulay (Eds.)

# Artificial Intelligence in Education

19th International Conference, AIED 2018
London, UK, June 27–30, 2018
Proceedings, Part II

 Springer

*Editors*
Carolyn Penstein Rosé
Carnegie Mellon University
Pittsburgh, PA
USA

Roberto Martínez-Maldonado
University of Technology
Sydney, NSW
Australia

H. Ulrich Hoppe
University of Duisburg-Essen
Duisburg
Germany

Rose Luckin
UCL Institute of Education
London
UK

Manolis Mavrikis
UCL Institute of Education
London
UK

Kaska Porayska-Pomsta
UCL Institute of Education
London
UK

Bruce McLaren
Carnegie Mellon University
Pittsburgh, PA
USA

Benedict du Boulay
University of Sussex
Brighton
UK

ISSN 0302-9743     ISSN 1611-3349   (electronic)
Lecture Notes in Artificial Intelligence
ISBN 978-3-319-93845-5     ISBN 978-3-319-93846-2   (eBook)
https://doi.org/10.1007/978-3-319-93846-2

Library of Congress Control Number: 2018947319

LNCS Sublibrary: SL7 – Artificial Intelligence

Printed on acid-free paper

This Springer imprint is published by the registered company Springer International Publishing AG
part of Springer Nature
The registered company address is: Gewerbestrasse 11, 6330 Cham, Switzerland

# Preface

The 19th International Conference on Artificial Intelligence in Education (AIED 2018) was held during June 27–30, 2018, in London, UK. AIED 2018 was the latest in a longstanding series of (now yearly) international conferences for high-quality research in intelligent systems and cognitive science for educational computing applications. The conference provides opportunities for the cross-fertilization of approaches, techniques, and ideas from the many fields that comprise AIED, including computer science, cognitive and learning sciences, education, game design, psychology, sociology, linguistics, as well as many domain-specific areas. Since the first AIED meeting over 30 years ago, both the breadth of the research and the reach of the technologies have expanded in dramatic ways.

For the 2018 conference on Artificial Intelligence in Education, we were excited to have a co-located event, the "Festival of Learning," together with the International Conference of the Learning Sciences (ICLS) and "Learning at Scale" (L@S). The festival took place in London (UK) during June 24–30. Since the days of landmark tutoring systems such as SCHOLAR and WHY decades ago, the fields of artificial intelligence, online learning, and the learning sciences have grown up side-by-side, frequently intersecting, synergizing, and challenging one another. As these fields have grown and matured, they have each experienced trends and waves, and each has seen a recent renewal that we celebrate in this year's conference. In artificial intelligence, the most recent renewal is in the emerging area of deep learning, where advances in computing capacity both in terms of memory and processing speed have facilitated a resurgence of interest in neural network models, with greater capacity than in the last neural network revolution. In the learning sciences, a recent emphasis on scaling up educational opportunities has birthed new areas of interest such as massive open online courses, which are also an important focus for the L@S community. In this year's conference we considered these recent renewals together and asked how advances in artificial intelligence can impact human learning at a massive scale. More specifically we asked how the fields of artificial intelligence and learning sciences may speak to one another at the confluence, which is the field of artificial intelligence in education. Thus, the theme of this year's conference was "Bridging the Behavioral and the Computational: Deep Learning in Humans and Machines."

There were 192 submissions as full papers to AIED 2018, of which 45 were accepted as long papers (12 pages) with oral presentation at the conference (for an acceptance rate of 23%), and 76 were accepted for poster presentation with four pages in the proceedings. Of the 51 papers directly submitted as poster papers, 15 were accepted. Apart from a few exceptions, each submission was reviewed by three Program Committee (PC) members including one senior PC member serving as a meta-reviewer. The program chairs checked the reviews for quality, and where necessary, requesting that reviewers elaborate their review or shift to a more constructive orientation. Our goal was to encourage substantive and constructive reviews without interfering with the reviewers' judgment in order to enable a fair and responsible process. In addition, submissions underwent a discussion period to ensure that all reviewers' opinions would be considered and leveraged to generate a group recommendation to the program chairs. Final decisions were made by carefully considering both scores and meta-reviews as well as the discussions, checking for consistency, weighing more heavily on the meta-review. We also took the constraints of the program into account and sought to keep the acceptance rate within a relatively typical range for this conference. It was a landmark year in terms of number of submissions, so the acceptance rate this year was lower than it has been in recent years, although the number of accepted papers was substantially higher. We see this as a mark of progress – something to be proud of as a community.

Three distinguished speakers gave plenary invited talks illustrating prospective directions for the field: Tom Mitchell (Carnegie Mellon University, USA), Paulo Blikstein (Stanford University, USA), and Michael Thomas (Birkbeck, University of London, UK). The conference also included:

- A Young Researchers Track that provided doctoral students with the opportunity to present their ongoing doctoral research at the conference and receive invaluable feedback from the research community.
- Interactive Events sessions during which AIED attendees could experience first-hand new and emerging intelligent learning environments via interactive demonstrations.
- An Industry and Innovation Track intended to support connections between industry (both for-profit and non-profit) and the research community.

AIED 2018 hosted one full-day and nine half-day workshops and tutorials on the full gamut of topics related to broad societal issues such as ethics and equity, methodologies such as gamification and personalization, as well as new technologies, tools, frameworks, development methodologies, and much more.

We wish to acknowledge the great effort by our colleagues at the University College London in making this conference possible. Special thanks goes to Springer for sponsoring the AIED 2018 Best Paper Award and the AIED 2018 Best Student Paper Award. We also want to acknowledge the amazing work of the AIED 2018 Organizing Committee, the senior PC members, the PC members, and the reviewers (listed herein), who with their enthusiastic contributions gave us invaluable support in putting this conference together.

April 2018

Carolyn Rosé
Roberto Martínez-Maldonado
Ulrich Hoppe
Rose Luckin
Manolis Mavrikis
Kaska Porayska-Pomsta
Bruce McLaren
Benedict du Boulay

# Organization

## Program Committee

| | |
|---|---|
| Lalitha Agnihotri | McGraw Hill Education |
| Esma Aimeur | University of Montreal, Canada |
| Patricia Albacete | University of Pittsburgh, USA |
| Vincent Aleven | Carnegie Mellon University, USA |
| Sagaya Amalathas | UNITAR International University, Malaysia |
| Ivon Arroyo | Worcester Polytechnic Institute, USA |
| Roger Azevedo | North Carolina State University, USA |
| Nilufar Baghaei | UNITEC |
| Ryan Baker | University of Pennsylvania, USA |
| Nigel Beacham | University of Aberdeen, UK |
| Gautam Biswas | Vanderbilt University, USA |
| Ig Ibert Bittencourt | Federal University of Alagoas, Brazil |
| Nigel Bosch | University of Illinois Urbana-Champaign, USA |
| Jesus G. Boticario | Universidad Nacional de Educacion a Distancia |
| Jacqueline Bourdeau | TELUQ |
| Kristy Elizabeth Boyer | University of Florida, USA |
| Bert Bredeweg | University of Amsterdam, The Netherlands |
| Paul Brna | University of Leeds, UK |
| Christopher Brooks | University of Michigan, USA |
| Tak-Wai Chan | National Central University |
| Mohamed Amine Chatti | University of Duisburg-Essen, Germany |
| Weiqin Chen | University of Bergen, Norway |
| Wenli Chen | National Institute of Education, Singapore |
| Min Chi | North Carolina State University, USA |
| Sherice Clarke | University of California San Diego, USA |
| Andrew Clayphan | The University of Sydney, Australia |
| Cristina Conati | The University of British Columbia, Canada |
| Mark G. Core | University of Southern California, USA |
| Scotty Craig | Arizona State University, Polytechnic, USA |
| Alexandra Cristea | The University of Warwick, UK |
| Mutlu Cukurova | UCL Knowledge Lab, UK |
| Ben Daniel | University of Otago, New Zealand |
| Chandan Dasgupta | Indian Institute of Technology Bombay, India |
| Barbara Di Eugenio | University of Illinois at Chicago, USA |
| Vania Dimitrova | University of Leeds, UK |
| Peter Dolog | Aalborg University, Denmark |
| Hendrik Drachsler | The Open University |
| Artur Dubrawski | Carnegie Mellon University, USA |

# Abstracts of Keynotes

# What if People Taught Computers?

Tom Mitchell

Carnegie Mellon University, USA
tom.mitchell@cmu.edu

**Abstract.** Whereas AIED focuses primarily on how computers can help teach people, this talk will consider how people might teach computers. Why? There are at least two good reasons: First, we might discover something interesting about instructional strategies by building computers that can be taught. Second, if people could teach computers in the same way that we teach one another, suddenly everybody would be able to program. We present our ongoing research on machine learning by verbal instruction and demonstration. Our prototype Learning by Instruction Agent (LIA) allows people to teach their mobile devices by verbal instruction to perform new actions. Given a verbal command that it does not understand (e.g., "Drop a note to Bill that I'll be late."), the system allows the user to teach it by breaking the procedure down into a sequence of more primitive, more understandable steps (e.g., "First create a new email. Put the email address of Bill into the recipient field."...). As a result, LIA both acquires new linguistic knowledge that enables it to better parse language into its intended meaning, and it learns how to execute the target procedure. In related work with Brad Meyers we are exploring combining verbal instruction with demonstration of procedures on the phone, to achieve "show and tell" instruction. In work with Shashank Srivastava and Igor Labutov, we are extending the approach to general concept learning (e.g., in order to teach "if I receive an important email, then be sure I see it before leaving work." one must teach the concept "important email."). This talk will survey progress to date, implications, and open questions. This work involves a variety of collaborations with Igor Labutov, Amos Azaria, Shashank Srivastava, Brad Meyers and Toby Li.

# Time to Make Hard Choices for AI in Education

Paulo Blikstein

Stanford University, USA
paulob@stanford.edu

**Abstract.** The field of AI in education has exploded in the past ten years. Many factors have contributed to this unprecedented growth, such as the ubiquity of digital devices in schools, the rise of online learning, the availability of data and fast growth in related fields such as machine learning and data mining. But with great power comes great responsibility: the flipside of the growth of AIED is that now our technologies can be deployed in large numbers to millions of children. And while there is great potential to transform education, there is also considerable risk to destroy public education as we know it, either directly or via unintended consequences. This is not an exaggeration: in recent months, we have indeed learned that the combination of social media, technological ubiquity, AI, lack of privacy, and under-regulated sectors can go the wrong way, and that AI has today a disproportionate power to shape human activity and society.

On the other hand, most schools of education around the world are not equipped – or not interested – in this debate. They either ignore this conversation, or simply attack the entire enterprise of AI in education—but these attacks are not stopping wide dissemination of various types of AIED projects in schools, mainly driven by corporations and fueled by incentives that might not work in the benefit of students (i.e., massive cost reduction, deprofessionalization of teachers, additional standardization of content and instruction).

In this scenario, the academic AIED community has a crucial responsibility— it could be the only voice capable to steering the debate, and the technology, towards more productive paths. This talk will be about the hard choices that AIED needs to face in the coming years, reviewing the history of AI in education, its promise, and possible futures. For example, should we focus on technologies that promote student agency and curricular flexibility, or on making sure everyone learns the same? How do we tackle new learning environments such as makerspaces and other inquiry-driven spaces? What is the role of physical science labs versus virtual, AI-driven labs? How can AIED impact— positively and negatively—equity in education?

I will review some of these issues, and mention examples of contemporary work on novel fields such as multimodal learning analytics, which is trying to detect patterns in complex learning processes in hands-on activities, and new types of inquiry-driven science environments.

The AIED community is strategically placed at a crucial point in the history of education, with potential to (at last) impact millions of children. But the way forward will require more than technical work—it will require some hard choices that we should be prepared to make.

# Has the Potential Role of Neuroscience in Education Been Overstated? Can Computational Approaches Help Build Bridges Between Them?

Michael Thomas

University College London/Birkbeck University of London, UK
m.thomas@bbk.ac.uk

**Abstract.** In the first part of this talk, I will assess the progress of the field of educational neuroscience in attempting to translate basic neuroscience findings to classroom practice. While much heralded, has educational neuroscience yielded concrete benefits for educators or policymakers? Is it likely to in the future? Or is its main contribution merely to dispel neuromyths? In the second half of the talk, I will assess the role that computational approaches can play in this inter-disciplinary interaction. Is neuroscience best viewed as a source of inspiration to build better algorithms for educational AI? Or can neurocomputational models help us build better theories that link data across behaviour, environment, brain, and genetics into an integrated account of children's learning?

# Contents – Part II

**Industry Papers**

**Young Researcher Papers**

**Workshops and Tutorials**

# Contents – Part I

# Posters

# Ontology-Based Domain Diversity Profiling of User Comments

Entisar Abolkasim[1]([✉]), Lydia Lau[1]([✉]), Antonija Mitrovic[2]([✉]),
and Vania Dimitrova[1]([✉])

[1] School of Computing, University of Leeds, Leeds, UK
{scl0ena, L.M.S.Lau, V.G.Dimitrova}@leeds.ac.uk
[2] Intelligent Computer Tutoring Group, University of Canterbury,
Christchurch, New Zealand
tanja.mitrovic@canterbury.ac.nz

**Abstract.** Diversity has been the subject of study in various disciplines from biology to social science and computing. Respecting and utilising the diversity of the population is increasingly important to broadening knowledge. This paper describes a pipeline for diversity profiling of a pool of text in order to understand its coverage of an underpinning domain. The application is illustrated by using a domain ontology on presentation skills in a case study with 38 postgraduates who made comments while learning pitch presentations with the Active Video Watching system (AVW-Space). The outcome shows different patterns of coverage on the domain by the comments in each of the eight videos.

**Keywords:** Diversity analytics · Ontology · Semantic techniques
Video-based learning · Active video watching · Soft skills learning

## 1 Introduction

Despite the growing importance of modelling diversity, there is limited computational work on user-generated content in learning context. Despotakis et al. [4] developed a semantic framework for modelling viewpoints embedded within user comments in social platforms to understand learner engagement with situational simulations for soft skills learning [5]. Hecking et al. [9] adapted network-text analysis of learner-generated comments to capture divergence, convergence and (dis-)continuity in textual comments to characterise types of learner behaviour when engaging with videos. In both approaches, domain differences across learner groups were studied; visualisations to illustrate engagement with learning content. While visualisations were used to reveal interesting patterns, their adoption for automated profiling is not feasible.

This paper presents a novel computational approach to *automatically* detect the domain coverage in user comments by deriving *diversity profiles* for the learning objects. Our work adapts an established diversity framework developed in social science [13]. The domain knowledge is represented by an ontology [7, 8]. By using semantic techniques and metrics for diversity measurement, the coverage of concepts from the interaction between the learner and the learning material is explored. Such an approach

© Springer International Publishing AG, part of Springer Nature 2018
C. Penstein Rosé et al. (Eds.): AIED 2018, LNAI 10948, pp. 3–8, 2018.
https://doi.org/10.1007/978-3-319-93846-2_1

can provide useful insights for learning environment designers and, most importantly, it generates diversity profiles that can be used to broaden learner's domain knowledge.

## 2 Diversity Properties: Variety, Balance and Disparity

Stirling's diversity framework [13] with three basic properties (variety, balance and disparity) is used. A more thorough discussion of the model can be found in [1]. **Domain diversity** of the comments is the focus here. An ontology is used to represent the domain. Each comment is linked to a set of ontology entities (e.g. through semantic tagging). Given an ontology representing the domain $\Omega$, a pool of comments linked to a set of entities $E$ from $\Omega$, and a class in the ontology taxonomy $T$ providing the entry category for which diversity will be calculated as follows.

**Variety** is the number of sub-categories of $T$ which have at least one entity from E (i.e. mentioned in the user comments). The higher the number, the higher the diversity.

$$Variety(\Omega, E, T) = |K| \tag{1}$$

where $K$ is set of sub-categories for T, i.e. ontology classes that are sub-classes of $T$; each of the classes in K has at least one entity in E.

**Balance** calculates how much of each sub-class of $T$ is covered by the user comments, using the set of entities $E$. The formula is based on Shannon Entropy Index [12]; we use only the number of distinct ontology entities covered by the comments. The higher the number, the better the domain coverage; higher diversity.

$$Balance(\Omega, E, T) = \frac{1}{n} \sum_{i=1}^{n} p_i ln(p_i) \tag{2}$$

where n is the number of sub-categories of $T$ and $p_i$ is the proportion of distinct entities in $E$ that belong to the taxonomy headed by the sub-category against the total number of entities in that taxonomy.

**Disparity** is the manner and degree to which the elements may be distinguished. We consider *within disparity*, which is calculated by measuring each sub-category's dispersion, i.e. how scattered/dispersed the entities from $E$ that belong to each sub-category of $T$ are. The formula uses Hall-Ball internal cluster validation index [2], which gives the mean dispersion across all the sub-categories that are covered by the comments. The higher the number, the higher the disparity.

$$Disparity(\Omega, E, T) = \frac{1}{n} \sum_{i=1}^{n} dis(c_i) \tag{3}$$

where $n$ is the number of sub-categories $c_i$ of $T$. Dispersion $dis(c_i)$ is the shortest path between each of the entities in $E$ that belong to sub-category $c_i$ and the medoid of $c_i$.

# 3   The Ontology-Based Diversity Profiling Pipeline

The steps in the pipeline are: (i) Input preparation for the **S**emantic-**D**riven **D**iversity **A**nalytics **T**ool SeDDAT [1]. This includes getting the domain ontology $\Omega$ and annotate the comments with the ontology entities $E$. (ii) SeDDAT execution to calculate the diversity properties for specified pool of comments. (iii) Analysis to interpret the diversity characteristics. (iv) When potential interesting patterns are spotted, the analyst can specify the next level to run SeDDAT for more fine-tuned diversity profiles.

# 4   Case Study – Comments on Videos for Learning

Earlier work in AVW-Space indicated that constructive learners who wrote comments while watching videos were more likely to increase their knowledge [10, 11]. This paper explores the relationship between diversity patterns and video usage for learning. In particular: *How do the learner comments on the videos cover the domain, and are there any diversity patterns that can be related to the learning of presentation skills?*

**Videos Used.** Four tutorials (T1–T4) on presentations and four examples (E1–E4) (two TED talks and two 3-min PhD pitch presentations) [6].

**Participants.** The comments were collected from 38 postgraduate students in a study conducted in March 2016. These students can be classified as constructive according to the ICAP framework [3].

## 4.1   The Domain Ontology – PreSOn (Presentation Skills Ontology)

A semi-automatic ontology engineering approach [9] was used to convert an initial taxonomy (extracted from surveys in study) into an ontology, then extend with the Body Language Ontology from [4]. Refinement was made after 3 presentation skills trainers (from the University of Leeds) inspected the initial ontology. This resulted in a Presentation Skills Ontology (PreSOn) with four top level categories – three related to core presentation skills (*Structure, Delivery, VisualAid*) and one to include terms describing quality of presentations (*Presentation Attribute*). The next level of core subcategories and number of entities in each are as follow: (i) *Stucture: StructureApproach* (5) and *StructureComponent* (62); (ii) *Delivery: SpeakerEmotion* (10), *SpeakerAura* (5), AudienceEmotion (1), *VerbalCommunication* (18), *NonVerbalCommunication* (55) and *Preparation* (10); (iii) *VisualAid: VisualAidArtefact* (71) and *VisualAidDevice* (22).

## 4.2   Domain Diversity for Videos

**Domain Variety Patterns.** When the entry point was '*Thing*', all videos had variety 4 (i.e. all top categories were covered). We created profiles using each of the main categories of presentation skills (*Delivery, Structure, VisualAid*) as the entry point. An example of outcome: Video E4 has the highest variety for *Delivery* '5' out of a maximum '6' – this gives an indication that this video may be useful to learn about delivery.

**Domain Balance Patterns.** Top half of Fig. 1 shows the overall balance and the proportions of the top four categories for every video. Overall, we can identify T1 as a good tutorial for *VisualAid,* T2 and T3 for *Structure,* and T4 for *Delivery.* For E1–E4, concepts relating to *Structure* seems to be most readily noticed in the comments.

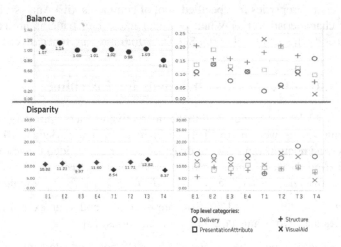

**Fig. 1.** Domain balance and domain disparity for *Thing* (left) and the proportions of the four categories (right).

**Domain Disparity Patterns.** Disparity indicates the spread of entities within a category – the higher the disparity, the broader the coverage, while low disparity indicates concentration on a small area. The bottom half of Fig. 1 shows the dispersion of all the videos at the level *Thing.* Drilling down one level: *Delivery* scores are consistently highest (except for T1), whilst *Structure* tends to be lowest – i.e. a broad range of domain entities related to *Delivery* whereas comments on *Structure* are concentrated on the narrow area around *StructureComponent* (opening, body, closing).

**Combining Domain Balance and Domain Disparity.** Separately, balance and disparity yield interesting patterns for some videos only. Table 1 summarises the possible patterns and their interpretations by combining them to provide further insight into the usefulness of the videos for informal learning.

**Table 1.** Possible interpretations of a combination of balance and disparity

|                 | Low balance               | High balance             |
| --------------- | ------------------------- | ------------------------ |
| High disparity  | *Lack of focus*           | *A good diverse coverage* |
| Low disparity   | *A niche or poor coverage* | *A good focus*           |

Looking at the tutorial videos on the right of Fig. 1, several observations can be made: T1 has a good focus on *VisualAid* and T3 on *Structure* (high balance and low disparity); T2 somewhat lacks focus on *Delivery* (low balance and high disparity); T4 has a diverse coverage on *Delivery* (high balance and disparity). Observations can be made for examples, though not as prominent as in tutorials: E1 has a niche/poor coverage on *VisualAid* (low balance and relatively low disparity); E2 lacks focus on *Delivery* (low balance and high disparity; E3 gives a good focus on *structure* (low disparity and relatively high balance); and E4 does not show any pattern.

# 5  Conclusion

The contribution of this paper is a novel computational approach for detecting domain coverage automatically. The demonstrated benefit of diversity profiling for understanding learner engagement with videos indicates that the approach can be applied to other scenarios of video-based learning (e.g. MOOCs, flipped classroom, informal learning). Modelling diversity is especially valuable in soft skills learning, where contextual awareness and understanding of different perspectives is crucial.

# References

1. Abolkasim, E., Lau, L., Dimitrova, V.: A semantic-driven model for ranking digital learning objects based on diversity in the user comments. In: Verbert, K., Sharples, M., Klobučar, T. (eds.) EC-TEL 2016. LNCS, vol. 9891, pp. 3–15. Springer, Cham (2016). https://doi.org/10.1007/978-3-319-45153-4_1
2. Ball, G.H., Hall, D.J.: ISODATA, A Novel Method of Data Analysis and Pattern Classification. Stanford Research Institute, Menlo Park (1965). (AD699616)
3. Chi, M.T., Wylie, R.: The ICAP framework: linking cognitive engagement to active learning outcomes. Educ. Psychol. **49**(4), 219–243 (2014)
4. Despotakis, D.: Modelling viewpoints in user generated content. Ph.D. Dissertation, University of Leeds (2013a)
5. Despotakis, D., Dimitrova, V., Lau, L., Thakker, D., Ascolese, A., Pannese, L.: ViewS in user generated content for enriching learning environments: a semantic sensing approach. In: Lane, H.Chad, Yacef, K., Mostow, J., Pavlik, P. (eds.) AIED 2013. LNCS (LNAI), vol. 7926, pp. 121–130. Springer, Heidelberg (2013). https://doi.org/10.1007/978-3-642-39112-5_13
6. Dimitrova, V., Mitrovic, A., Piotrkowicz, A., Lau, L., Weerasinghe, A.: Using learning analytics to devise interactive personalised nudges for active video watching. In: Proceedings of the 25th Conference on User Modeling, Adaptation and Personalization, pp. 22–31. ACM (2017)
7. Gruber, T.: A translation approach to portable ontology specifications. Knowl. Acquis. **5**, 199–220 (1993)
8. Gruber, T.: Collective knowledge systems: where the social web meets the semantic web. Semant. Web Web 2.0 **6**(1), 4–13 (2008)

9. Hecking, T., Dimitrova, V., Mitrovic, A., Ulrich Hoppe, U.: Using network-text analysis to characterise learner engagement in active video watching. In: Chen, W., et al. (eds.) Proceedings of the 25th International Conference on Computers in Education ICCE 2017, Christchurch, 4–9 December 2017, pp. 326–335. Asia-Pacific Society for Computers in Education (2017)
10. Lau, L., Mitrovic, A., Weerasinghe, A., Dimitrova, V.: Usability of an active video watching system for soft skills training. In: Proceedings of the 1st International Workshop on Intelligent Mentoring Systems, ITS 2016 (2016). https://imsworkshop.files.wordpress.com/2016/03/ims2016_paper_7_lau.pdf
11. Mitrovic, A., Dimitrova, V., Lau, L., Weerasinghe, A., Mathews, M.: Supporting constructive video-based learning: requirements elicitation from exploratory studies. In: André, E., Baker, R., Hu, X., Rodrigo, M., du Boulay, B. (eds.) AIED 2017. LNCS (LNAI), vol. 10331, pp. 224–237. Springer, Cham (2017). https://doi.org/10.1007/978-3-319-61425-0_19
12. Shannon, C.E.: A mathematical theory of communication. Bell Syst. Tech. J. **27**, 379–423 (1948)
13. Stirling, A.: A general framework for analysing diversity in science, technology and society. J. R. Soc. Interface **4**(15), 707–719 (2007)

# ROBIN: Using a Programmable Robot to Provide Feedback and Encouragement on Programming Tasks

Ishrat Ahmed[✉], Nichola Lubold, and Erin Walker[✉]

Computing, Informatics, and Decision Systems Engineering,
Arizona State University, Tempe, AZ, USA
{iahmed7,nlubold,eawalke1}@asu.edu

**Abstract.** LEGO Mindstorms robots are a popular educational tool for teaching programming concepts to young learners. However, learners working with these robots often lack sufficient feedback on their programs, which makes it difficult for them to reflect on domain concepts and may decrease their motivation. We see an opportunity to introduce feedback into LEGO Mindstorms programming environments by having the robot itself deliver feedback, leveraging research on learning companions to transform the programmable robot into a social actor. Our robot, ROBIN, provides learners with automated reflection prompts based on a domain model and the student's current program, along with social encouragement based on a theory of instructional immediacy. We hypothesize that by having the robot itself provide cognitive and social feedback, students will both reflect more on their misconceptions and persist more with the activity. This paper describes the design and implementation of ROBIN and discusses how this approach can benefit students.

**Keywords:** LEGO Mindstorms · Feedback · Immediacy

## 1 Introduction and Background

Learning through building and programming robots can lead to improvements in a learners' computer science (CS) skills and motivation [1,2]. LEGO Mindstorms is a programmable robotics kit that is widely used as an educational tool. Programs written in this kit provide visible results, giving the learner hands-on experience to understand the fundamentals of abstract CS concepts like loops and conditional statements. Watching the direct effect of their coding on the robot provides a motivating learning environment for participating students [2].

While there is some evidence that LEGO Mindstorms can be used to improve domain learning and motivation [2,3], the lack of feedback in the rapid compile-run-debug cycle is considered to have a negative impact on students. When a learner tries to load a program into the robot and the program does not behave as expected, several issues may lead to frustration and inhibit learning.

© Springer International Publishing AG, part of Springer Nature 2018
C. Penstein Rosé et al. (Eds.): AIED 2018, LNAI 10948, pp. 9–13, 2018.
https://doi.org/10.1007/978-3-319-93846-2_2

For example, the learner may be unaware of an error they made or may not be motivated to explore the cause of the error, and repeated failed attempts may further discourage the learner. In such scenarios, feedback which can draw the learner to a correct problem-solving path could greatly influence students' CS skill and motivation.

A great deal of educational research has focused on designing effective prompting and feedback for various learning environments [4,5]; however, feedback delivered by programmable robots is still under-explored. In this work, we introduce a feedback system into the LEGO Mindstorms programming environment using a learning companion paradigm. Learning companions are based on the framework of peer learning, where a learner and an agent work together to solve problems [6]. We design a feedback model for ROBIN based on a learning-by-doing approach [7], where reflective feedback is provided by the programmable robot itself, transforming it into a learning companion. Learning companions have direct interaction with the learner, so behaviors that enhance interpersonal communication, such as immediacy [8], can affect the nature and quality of the learning environment. By leveraging social behavior like immediacy into the reflective feedback provided by the programmable robot and encouraging a dialogue, we expect the learner to develop rapport with the robot. Due to this rapport, when students receive feedback from ROBIN, they may be more motivated to reflect on their misconceptions and solve encountered errors.

In this paper, we discuss the design and implementation of ROBIN, proposing a novel type of learning companion where the agent is (i) a programmable robot that is (ii) responsible for providing feedback, and (iii) socially engages with students. Future work will evaluate the use of ROBIN in order to investigate the potential of a feedback system delivered by a programmable robot.

## 2   System Description

ROBIN consists of an iPhone mounted on a Lego Mindstorms EV3 robot, and a desktop application written in Java. To program ROBIN, the student uses the EV3 development environment that comes with the LEGO Mindstorms robotics kit, a graphical interface that models programming as a process where the user drags and drops different sets of blocks (representing programming steps) on a screen to complete a program. For example, if the user adds a *Move Steering* block, ROBIN can go forward, backward, turn, or stop depending on the input parameters (i.e. speed, power). Once done, the finished program is downloaded to the robot via a connection cable. ROBIN executes the program independently and initiates a spoken-language interaction based on the correctness of the program. Primarily, simple programs are used, for example, moving forward, backward or picking an object; but more complicated programs can be used as well. Figure 1 shows an image of ROBIN and Fig. 2 shows a sample program.

In the desktop application, the user selects the file location of the EV3 program that they are modifying. A *filewatcher* program continuously monitors whether the selected file is being modified and saved. Once saved, the

**Fig. 1.** ROBIN

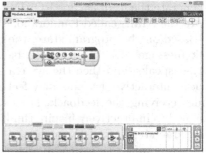

**Fig. 2.** Sample block program

EV3 file is unzipped to create an XML file containing program instructions. For example, if the rotation parameter in the block is set as 3, the XML file contains $< ConfigurableMethodTerminal\ ConfiguredValue = "3">$. This XML is parsed using a *parser* and information pertinent to the correctness of the program, such as which blocks were used, number of blocks used, and input values, is extracted.

Next, ROBIN uses a domain model to compare these extracted values and assess the correctness of the program. The domain model consists of several constraints, specific to each problem, that outline the parameters of the correct solution. For example, the first problem asks students to program ROBIN to go 80 cm forward. The program requires a *Move Steering* block to go forward, and a rotation parameter within the range 6.2 and 6.5. A *problem analyzer* checks for several different kinds of errors based on the domain model, including choice of an incorrect block, and incorrect input parameters for a block. Based on the number of errors, the student program is then labeled as being in one of three states: Correct (C; 0–10% incorrectness), Partially Incorrect (PI; 10–50% incorrectness) and Incorrect (I; more than 50% incorrectness). For example, to verify if ROBIN was correctly programmed to move 80 cm forward, we use the following conditions:

*IF (($6.2 \leq rotation \leq 6.5$) & block = Move Steer) THEN program = C*
*IF (($5 \leq rotation \leq 6.2$) & block = Move Steer) THEN program = PI*
*IF (rotation < 5 || rotation > 6.5) THEN program = I*

The program state and identified errors are used by a *Dialogue Manager* which runs as an iOS application on the iPhone mounted on ROBIN. The iOS application utilizes the accelerometer on the iPhone to detect when ROBIN has finished executing the learner's program. Once executed, the dialogue manager retrieves the identified errors for the program and determines an appropriate response using AIML or Artificial Intelligence Markup Language (AIML) [9]. The basic building block of AIML is a *category* containing a *pattern* and a *template*. The *pattern* is matched with a system/user input and ROBIN responds with the *template* as its answer. AIML has a collection of *pattern-template* pairs that help to generate the feedback for ROBIN. Our system utilizes a web-based service to create the AIML called Pandorabots [10].

Based on the program state, the dialogue manager generates the first feedback message of a two-turn feedback exchange (i.e., the system speaks, the learner speaks, and then the system speaks one more time). Because this feedback is interactive, learners may feel a greater sense of connection with ROBIN while receiving the feedback. For example, in the *incorrect* state feedback is designed to interactively inspire thinking. If the learner entered the "wrong rotation parameters", ROBIN might say *"We are almost there but I think one of the parameters might be wrong! Which parameter do you think?"* Feedback for the *partial incorrect* state might provide encouragement along with a prompt to try again; *"Great job! I went half-way, why don't you try again?"* If the learner tries again and the program remains in the *partial incorrect* state, similar feedback is provided again by ROBIN; *"Any thoughts on why I am only going half-way?"* This ensures variability in the feedback. Finally, a *correct* program might generate feedback with praise; *"Keep up the good work!"*

ROBIN outputs the response through the built-in microphone on the iPhone. The initial feedback response is designed to initiate a dialogue with the learner. After ROBIN speaks, the dialogue manager captures the learner's response using automatic speech recognition (ASR) and generates a feedback using AIML. All the dialogues reflect the following verbal immediacy behaviors to foster rapport: praising the students, addressing them by name, and using "we"/"our" instead of "i"/"your" during conversation. These behaviors should further foster social engagement and rapport with the system [11,12]. A complete dialogue-based interaction between ROBIN and a fictional student, Melissa, in the context where ROBIN did not go 80 cm forward due to a rotation parameter error follows:

> ROBIN: We are almost there but I think one of the parameters might be wrong! Which parameter do you think Melissa?
> Melissa: Ha, I see! Do I change the rotation parameter?
> ROBIN: Wow, you got that right. Let's do it!

We designed the templates with a randomized list of relevant responses to avoid repetition and support variation in the feedback. We also designed the dialogue to handle ASR errors or failed interpretations of the user dialogues.

## 3   Conclusion

We introduce a novel approach for a social feedback system in programmable robots based on the concept of the learning companion. In this paper, we discuss our initial step towards the investigation of the design, implementation, and evaluation of ROBIN. In the future, we plan to run experiments exploring the effects of our design of social interaction and feedback on student motivation and CS learning gains.

**Acknowledgments.** The authors gratefully acknowledge Nicholas Martinez for his assistance in developing the initial version of the system. Support for this work was provided by NSF CISE-IIS-1637809.

# References

1. Lawhead, P.B., et al.: A road map for teaching introductory programming using LEGO mindstorms robots. ACM SIGCSE Bull. **35**(2), 191–201 (2002)
2. Lykke, M., et al.: Motivating programming students by problem based learning and LEGO robots. In: 2014 IEEE Global Engineering Education Conference (EDUCON). IEEE (2014)
3. Alvarez, A., Larranaga, M.: Using LEGO mindstorms to engage students on algorithm design. In: 2013 IEEE Frontiers in Education Conference. IEEE (2013)
4. Lazar, T., Možina, M., Bratko, I.: Automatic extraction of AST patterns for debugging student programs. In: André, E., Baker, R., Hu, X., Rodrigo, M.M.T., du Boulay, B. (eds.) AIED 2017. LNCS (LNAI), vol. 10331, pp. 162–174. Springer, Cham (2017). https://doi.org/10.1007/978-3-319-61425-0_14
5. Johnson, A.M., Guerrero, T.A., Tighe, E.L., McNamara, D.S.: iSTART-ALL: confronting adult low literacy with intelligent tutoring for reading comprehension. In: André, E., Baker, R., Hu, X., Rodrigo, M.M.T., du Boulay, B. (eds.) AIED 2017. LNCS (LNAI), vol. 10331, pp. 125–136. Springer, Cham (2017). https://doi.org/10.1007/978-3-319-61425-0_11
6. Chou, C.-Y., Chan, T.-W., Lin, C.-J.: Redefining the learning companion: the past, present, and future of educational agents. Comput. Educ. **40**(3), 255–269 (2003)
7. McKendree, J.: Effective feedback content for tutoring complex skills. Hum. Comput. Interact. **5**(4), 381–413 (1990)
8. Mehrabian, A.: Silent Messages, vol. 8. Wadsworth, Belmont (1971)
9. Marietto, M.d.G.B., et al.: Artificial intelligence markup language: a brief tutorial. arXiv preprint arXiv:1307.3091 (2013)
10. Pandorabots. https://www.pandorabots.com
11. Frisby, B.N., Martin, M.M.: Instructor-student and student-student rapport in the classroom. Commun. Educ. **59**(2), 146–164 (2010)
12. Gulz, A., Haake, M., Silvervarg, A.: Extending a teachable agent with a social conversation module – effects on student experiences and learning. In: Biswas, G., Bull, S., Kay, J., Mitrovic, A. (eds.) AIED 2011. LNCS (LNAI), vol. 6738, pp. 106–114. Springer, Heidelberg (2011). https://doi.org/10.1007/978-3-642-21869-9_16

# Conversational Support for Education

Damla Ezgi Akcora[1], Andrea Belli[2], Marina Berardi[1], Stella Casola[2],
Nicoletta Di Blas[2(✉)], Stefano Falletta[1], Alessandro Faraotti[3],
Luca Lodi[2], Daniela Nossa Diaz[1], Paolo Paolini[2], Fabrizio Renzi[3],
and Filippo Vannella[1]

[1] Politecnico di Torino, Turin, Italy
[2] Politecnico di Milano, Milan, Italy
nicoletta.diblas@polimi.it
[3] IBM Italia, Segrate, Italy

**Abstract.** This paper describes the development of chatbots that can help
learners make the most appropriate use of a large body of content. The purpose
of a COntent-based Learning Assistant, COLA, is to suggest optimal educational paths, along with a persuasive and empathic coaching. COLAs are supported by a novel technology, iCHAT, based on the cognitive engine Watson
(by IBM).

**Keywords:** Chatbots · Education · Virtual teaching assistant
Virtual learning assistant · Learning companion · Interactive tutoring system
Knowledge representation and reasoning

## 1 Introduction

In recent years, several bodies of digital content have been developed, for all school
grades and higher education: libraries of learning objects, online courses, MOOCs, etc.
Despite the fact that millions of users are actively using them, we can still observe that
millions of potential users are lost. This is due, in part, to the difficulties for a user to
find an (effective) way across several content items. Most libraries either provide
predefined pathways or something equivalent to a traditional index or an analytical
index where the user has to choose what she wants: a difficult operation for a learner
who may not know the subject, let alone that specific body of content.

Our proposal is to build a conversational COntent-based Learning Assistant
(COLA), not as an expert on a subject, but *on a body of content* covering that subject,
so that it can suggest optimal paths across the content items. Conversations, if properly
designed, can combine guidance (across the various items), with adaptivity (to the
learner's profile) and flexibility (dynamically steering paths).

## 2   The Case-Studies

The approach is developed through 2 case-studies. The first is about an online course on equations; the second is about a MOOC on "Recommender systems" to be offered on Coursera (in July 2018). The equations' course had a twofold goal: to support struggling students in the $9^{th}$ grade, or well-performing students in the $8^{th}$ grade. The 4-weeks course was created by harvesting learning objects from the web (educational videos, interactive resources, PDFs, eBooks, …), with other resources created on purpose. The whole body of content included more than 150 "learning objects".

The second case is about a MOOC ("Recommender Systems" by prof. Paolo Cremonesi of Politecnico di Milano), developed with an innovative methodology, "iMOOC" (Casola et al, 2018), for designing customizable MOOCs that support different kinds of learners. iMOOC acknowledges that many users of MOOCs may have goals that do not imply going through the whole set of materials, in the sense that some learners may want to get an overview of a topic, others may already have a good background and therefore aim at accessing only advanced materials, etc. The chatbot is meant to support the learner in choosing the most appropriate path.

## 3   Organizing Content

The first step to develop a COLA is to create "topologies", i.e. colored graphs representing possible interconnections among content items, to build adaptive paths. A topology can take into account various aspects: (i) quality of the background of the learner, (ii) commitment of the learner (time to spend), (iii) goals of learning (e.g. concepts, skills, …), etc. Table 1 is a (simplified) example of topology.

Each content item has a node ID and a DB ID (that univocally identifies the item); the length (in minutes) and the media (e.g. "video") are also specified. The color of the item represents the level of difficulty (e.g. a red item is an "advanced" content); the color of the arrows instructs on the possible paths among the items taking into account the difference between first time visitors (blue) and second time visitor (violet). The strong/light hue of the arrows represents strong/low motivation.

## 4   Content-Based Learning Assistant

We can imagine 3 main directions for an application supporting learning:

A. Helping by providing knowledge about **the specific subject matter.** Intelligent Tutoring Systems that are "experts" on the specific subject matter.
B. Helping by providing a **predefined body of content** and **interaction mechanisms** to access it. Most (if not all) online courses or MOOCs or libraries of learning objects (e.g. Khan Academy, Brainpop) fall in this category.
C. Helping by providing a **predefined body of content** (like A) and providing **intelligent mechanisms** to access it (like B). **This is the approach of COLAs.**

**Table 1.** Excerpt from a topology of content for a learner with a low background

| Node ID | Item ID | Item title | Media | Minutes | Color | Arrows |
|---|---|---|---|---|---|---|
| 1 | cc1001 | Course Overview | Video | 05:00 | Black | → 2 blue<br>→ 2 light blue<br>→ 3 violet<br>→ 3 light violet |
| 2 | cc1002 | Introduction | Video | 03:32 | Black | → 3 blue<br>→ 3 light blue<br>→ - violet<br>→ - light violet |
| 3 | cc1003 | Taxonomy of Recommender Systems | Interactive presentation | 04:03 | Black | → 4 blue<br>→ 4 light blue<br>→ 4 violet<br>→ 4 light violet |

Useful learning assistants can be developed using the approach "C", i.e. providing a well-organized body of content and using modern AI to build conversations on it. Under which conditions can COLAs improve a learning process?

(a) **The intrinsic quality of content**, i.e. quality of the learning objects.
(b) **Optimal (dynamic, adaptive, flexible) paths across the content items,** that facilitate the learning process taking into account (i) the teacher's plan, (ii) the learner's static profile and (iii) the dynamic situation of the learner.
(c) **Empathic, friendly and persuasive conversation**, not just offering the right items in the right sequence, but also generating a feeling of "being taken care of".

B and C are the aspects where AI may help. In the next section, we describe iCHAT, the AI-based technology that supports the development of COLAs.

## 5   iCHAT: The Technology

iCHAT is an innovative technology being developed as a joint effort by Politecnico di Milano (HOC-LAB) and IBM (the Italian research division). iCHAT allows developing (at a reasonable cost/time) a chatbot that can support a user in her effort to access a body of content. The execution of an iCHAT application is supported by the architecture shown in Fig. 1. A user interacts with "iCHAT Conversation manager"; she can start several streams of conversations: at the end of the session, they can be saved to be resumed later (via the "iCHAT long-term memory manager").

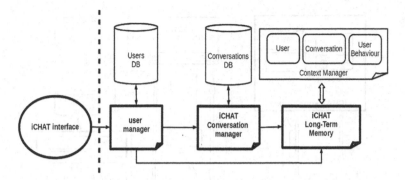

**Fig. 1.** Overall architecture of iCHAT

The user chats with the chatbot, alternating turns; sometimes (not always) a new content item is offered to the user, consisting of a variety of media: video, images, audio, text, etc. We use, at the moment, a combination of chat-line and multimedia player; in the future, we could add a text-to-speech or speech-to-text interface or house robots. The technology of the interface can be replaced with different interfaces. The conversation module of WATSON (Fig. 2) is used to implement the linguistic aspects of the conversation. One of the goals of the conversation is also to collect information about the user's situation (e.g., is she tired? Did she understand?). All the current information about the user and the "usage" of the topology define the **current context**. Whenever a user takes a turn, a "user intent" is detected (by the conversation module) and interpreted. The interpretation may lead to 3 possible situations: (i) the conversation does not need a new item of content and therefore it continues along a traditional line; (ii) the conversation (implicitly) needs a new item of content and the intent interpretation engine is activated; (iii) the user explicitly asks for a piece of content and the entity interpretation engine is activated.

The style/wording of the conversation is different for each family of applications (Education vs. Cultural Heritage) and within the same family for each "genus" (school education vs. higher education). Training the chatbot to a specific pair of <style, wording> is done (via WATSON) at family (or genus) level and does need to be redone for each specific chatbot: this is one of the main advantages by iCHAT.

The Intent-Interpretation Engine is a new piece of SW. A user intent defines what the situation of the user is (e.g. is she understanding?); a "transition intent", instead, defines a more objective intent, that can be considered a requirement for identifying the next item of content to be offered to the user. The transition engine translates a user intent into a transition intent. When the chatbot replies to the user, the opposite translation occurs: the motivation of the chatbot for selecting that specific content item is translated into a motivation that makes sense for the user. The **Entity-Interpretation Engine** is activated when the usernames a specific subject of interest, which must be translated into a proper entity that makes sense for the chatbot. The engine performs its job using Vocabulary_DB and the vocabulary-mapping developed using WATSON learning capabilities.

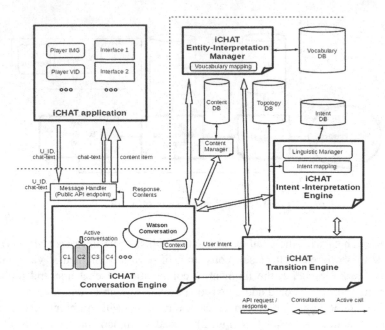

**Fig. 2.** iCHAT conversation manager

## 6 Conclusions and Future Work

We have discussed, in this paper, a number of issues:

(a) Introducing the idea of COLA: a COntent-based Learning Assistant specialized in helping the user to make an "optimal use" of the items of a specific body of content. It is important to note again that, differently with respect to other AI applications, the expertise of a COLA is about a body a content, not a subject.

(b) The proposal of using the **semantic organization of content in order to drive the conversation** (see the example of topology in Sect. 3). This approach promises two advantages; to allow non-technical experts of the subject to optimize the conversation (via optimization of the organization of content), to make the effort of development and maintenance scalable and sustainable.

(c) Proposing that a valid learning assistant, besides reacting to the user's interaction, should also reflect the **point of view of the teacher**. The teacher, defining metadata and topologies, implicitly determine which paths are offered to learners.

(d) Putting forward the idea that a **conversational interface** has several advantages over a more traditional point-and-click interface. First of all, it can establish a friendly and empathic relationship with the learner, secondly, it can be used to collect information about the current situation of the user.

(e) The proposal of a **novel architecture, ICHAT**, to support the development of COLAs.

We are currently improving the organization of content for the two real-life case-studies described in Sect. 2. Teams of teachers are involved in this effort and for the linguistic training of the conversation engine. The user testing of the COLAs should start in the late spring of 2018. Using control groups of students, we will verify if, how, and under which conditions COLAs effectively improve the quality of learning.

# Reference

Casola, S., Di Blas, N., Paolini, P., Pelagatti, G.: Designing and delivering MOOCs that fit all sizes. In: Proceedings of Society for Information Technology and Teacher Education International Conference 2018 (2018), (accepted)

# Providing Proactive Scaffolding During Tutorial Dialogue Using Guidance from Student Model Predictions

Patricia Albacete[1(✉)], Pamela Jordan[1], Dennis Lusetich[1],
Irene Angelica Chounta[2,3], Sandra Katz[1], and Bruce M. McLaren[2]

[1] Learning Research and Development Center, University of Pittsburgh,
Pittsburgh, PA, USA
palbacet@pitt.edu
[2] Human Computer Interaction Institute, Carnegie Mellon University,
Pittsburgh, PA, USA
[3] Institute of Education, University of Tartu, Tartu, Estonia

**Abstract.** This paper discusses how a dialogue-based tutoring system makes decisions to proactively scaffold students during conceptual discussions about physics. The tutor uses a student model to predict the likelihood that the student will answer the next question in a dialogue script correctly. Based on these predictions, the tutor will, step by step, choose the granularity at which the next step in the dialogue is discussed. The tutor attempts to pursue the discussion at the highest possible level, with the goal of helping the student achieve mastery, but with the constraint that the questions it asks are within the student's ability to answer when appropriately supported; that is, the tutor aims to stay within its estimate of the student's zone of proximal development for the targeted concepts. The scaffolding provided by the tutor is further adapted by adjusting the way the questions are expressed.

**Keywords:** Dialogue-based tutoring systems · Scaffolding · Student modeling
Zone of proximal development

## 1 Introduction

Tutorial dialogue systems typically implement a framework called "Knowledge Construction Dialogues" (KCDs), which guide all students through the same pre-scripted "directed line of reasoning" [10], regardless of the student's ability level. KCDs only deviate from the main path in the script to issue "remedial sub-dialogues" when the student answers incorrectly, then pop back up to the main path (e.g., [3, 9]). This approach can be frustrating and inefficient for some students because they are forced to go through long, repetitive and unnecessary discussions due to the dialogues' lack of adaptation to students' knowledge level.

One possible way to overcome this limitation is to incorporate a student model in the tutorial dialogue system that would emulate how human tutors construct and dynamically update a normative mental representation of students' grasp of the domain

© Springer International Publishing AG, part of Springer Nature 2018
C. Penstein Rosé et al. (Eds.): AIED 2018, LNAI 10948, pp. 20–25, 2018.
https://doi.org/10.1007/978-3-319-93846-2_4

content and use this representation to adapt the tutor's scaffolding to meet students' needs [5].

Additionally, a tutorial dialogue system needs policies for how to adaptively structure a discussion. Research on human tutoring (e.g., [17]) shows that tutors use their assessment of student ability to target scaffolding to the student's "zone of proximal development" (ZPD) [15]—"a zone within which a child can accomplish with help what he can later accomplish alone" [2]. This work suggests that automated tutors should ask challenging questions which the student can answer with adequate support and, eventually, be able to answer without assistance. The tutoring system described herein implements a decision-making process that attempts to emulate this aspect of human tutoring with the support of a student model.

## 2  The Adaptive Tutoring System: Rimac

Rimac is a dialogue-based tutoring system that engages high school students in conceptual discussions after they solve quantitative physics problems (e.g., [1, 13]). When using the tutor, students typically start by taking an online pretest; they then solve problems on paper, such as the one presented in Fig. 1. After working on a problem, students use the tutor to watch a video of a sample correct solution and then engage in several reflective dialogues, which focus on the concepts associated with the quantitative problem. An example of a reflection question is shown in Fig. 1.

---

**Homework problem statement:** Suppose you aim a bow horizontally, directly at the center of a target 25m away from you. If the speed of the arrow is 60 m/s, how far from the center of the target will it strike the target? That is, find the vertical displacement of the arrow while it is in flight. Assume there is no air friction.

**Reflection Question:** During the arrow's flight, how does its horizontal velocity change?

---

**Fig. 1.** A sample homework problem statement and reflection question

Rimac's reflective dialogues were designed so that the tutor could provide domain and instructional contingency [16] depending on the student's level of performance. To achieve domain contingency—that is, to decide what content to address next—different versions of the dialogues were developed, each corresponding to a line of reasoning (LOR) at different levels of granularity. These LORs, when embedded in dialogues, can be visualized as a directed graph, where nodes are concepts that the tutor queries the student about and arrows are the inferences needed to go from one node to the next. (See Fig. 2 for a sample segment of a discussion about the reflection question shown in Fig. 1. $P0 \rightarrow P1$ would represent an expert LOR and $P0 \rightarrow S1 \rightarrow S2 \rightarrow P1$ a LOR with intermediate reasoning steps.) The system captures such inferences as knowledge components (KCs) which will be used to predict if the student can answer the next question correctly. To implement instructional contingency—that is, to vary the way tutor questions are expressed—authoring rules were developed to guide how much support to embed in a question. For example, node S1 in Fig. 2 can be expressed directly as, "What is the value of the acceleration in the horizontal direction?" or with more support as, "Given that the horizontal net force on the arrow is zero, what is the horizontal acceleration of the arrow?" (see [12] for a detailed description of these authoring rules).

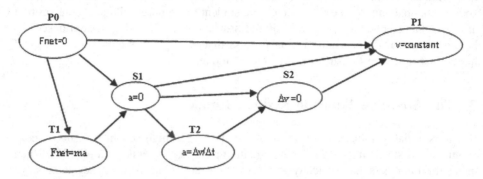

**Fig. 2.** Graphical representation of the line of reasoning Fnet = 0 → v = constant with different levels of granularity. Nodes represent questions the tutor could ask. Arcs represent the knowledge (KCs) required to make the inference from one node to the next.

Rimac incorporates a student model which enables it to predict the likelihood of a student answering a question correctly [6, 7]. An individual student model is built in two steps: first, using the results of the student's pretest, a clustering algorithm classifies the student as low, medium, or high. Second, the student is assigned a cluster-specific regression equation that is then personalized with the results of the student's pretest. The regression equation assigned to the student represents an implementation of an Instructional Factor Analysis Model (IFM), as proposed by [4]. This student model uses logistic regression to predict the probability of a student answering a question correctly as a linear function of the student's proficiency in the relevant KCs. Additionally, as the student progresses through the dialogues, his student model is dynamically updated according to the correctness of his responses to the tutor's questions.

Once the tutor engages the student in a reflection dialogue, it needs to decide at what level of granularity it will ask the next question in the LOR (or in a remediation if the previous question was answered incorrectly), to proactively adapt to the student's changing knowledge level. The tutor will always aim for mastery by selecting the question at the highest possible level that the student can likely answer correctly with adequate support. In other words, the tutor will choose a question in the highest possible LOR that it deems the student will respond correctly or that it perceives to be in the student's ZPD. To make this choice, Rimac consults the student model which predicts the likelihood that the student will answer a question correctly. The tutor interprets this probability as follows: if the probability of the student responding correctly is higher than 60% then the student is likely to be able to respond correctly, and if it is lower than 40% the student is likely to be unable to respond correctly. However, as the prediction gets closer to 50%, there is greater uncertainty since there is a 50% chance that he will be able to answer correctly and a 50% chance that he will not be able. This uncertainty *on the part of the tutor* about the student's ability could be indicative that the student is in his ZPD with regards to the relevant knowledge. Hence the tutor perceives the range of probabilities between 40% and 60% as a model of the student's ZPD [6, 7]. Thus, the tutor will choose to ask the question in the highest possible LOR that has a predicted probability of at least 40% of being answered correctly. The expression of the question within the LOR is adapted to provide increased support as the certainty of a correct answer decreases [12].

As an example of how the tutor proactively adapts its scaffolding during a dialogue, suppose the student has correctly answered the question at node S1 in Fig. 2. The tutor will consult the student model to estimate the likelihood that the student would be able to answer P1 (the highest possible node in the LOR) correctly. If this estimate is at or above 40% it will ask the corresponding question because this would indicate that the student is at or above the tutor's model of the student's ZPD for that question. However, if the probability is below 40% the tutor will try to pursue the discussion in a simpler way and examine S2 in the same manner as with P1. This process is repeated until a question can be asked or a leaf is reached in which case the question is asked at the highest level of support. As described previously, the tutor further adapts the support it provides by adapting how the question at the selected node is expressed.

## 3 Discussion and Future Work

In this paper we described a tutoring system, Rimac, that strives to enhance students' understanding of physics concepts and their ability to reason through "deep reasoning questions" [8]. Rimac presents a novel approach to the use of a student model by incorporating the idea of modeling the tutor's estimate of the student's zone of proximal development which it then uses to guide scaffolding during reflective tutorial dialogues. The system takes a proactive approach by anticipating students' needs and presenting a question at each step of a LOR that challenges the learner without overwhelming him, and by expressing the question with adequate support.

The tutor's scaffolding adheres to the main tenets of contingency, fading, and transfer of responsibility [14]. This is accomplished by proactively varying the level of complexity of the knowledge discussed and the way it is expressed and by adapting, step by step, to the student's changing ability. The tutor reduces the support it provides (i.e., it fades) as the learner becomes more competent and gradually provides the intermediate steps on his or her own (transfer of responsibility).

An evaluation of the effectiveness of the tutoring system is currently being conducted. The version of Rimac described herein is being compared with a control version that embeds a poor-man's student model which assigns students to a fixed LOR level in each reflection dialogue based solely on their pretest scores [11].

**Acknowledgments.** We thank Sarah Birmingham and Scott Silliman. This research was supported by the Institute of Education Sciences, U.S. Department of Education, through Grant R305A150155 to the University of Pittsburgh.

# References

1. Albacete, P., Jordan, P., Katz, S.: Is a dialogue-based tutoring system that emulates helpful co-constructed relations during human tutoring effective? In: Conati, C., Heffernan, N., Mitrovic, A., Verdejo, M.Felisa (eds.) AIED 2015. LNCS (LNAI), vol. 9112, pp. 3–12. Springer, Cham (2015). https://doi.org/10.1007/978-3-319-19773-9_1
2. Cazden, C.: Peekaboo as An Instructional Model: Discourse Development at Home and at School. Stanford University Department of Linguistics, Palo Alto (1979)
3. Chi, M., Jordan, P., VanLehn, K.: When is tutorial dialogue more effective than step-based tutoring? In: Trausan-Matu, S., Boyer, K.E., Crosby, M., Panourgia, K. (eds.) ITS 2014. LNCS, vol. 8474, pp. 210–219. Springer, Cham (2014). https://doi.org/10.1007/978-3-319-07221-0_25
4. Chi, M., Koedinger, K.R., Gordon, G.J., Jordon, P., VanLehn, K.: Instructional factors analysis: a cognitive model for multiple instructional interventions. In: Pechenizkiy, M., Calders, T., Conati, C., Ventura, S., Romero, C., Stamper, J. (eds.) EDM 2011, pp. 61–70 (2011)
5. Chi, M.T., Siler, S.A., Jeong, H.: Can tutors monitor students' understanding accurately? Cogn. Instr. **22**(3), 363–387 (2004)
6. Chounta, I.-A., Albacete, P., Jordan, P., Katz, S., McLaren, Bruce M.: The "Grey Area": a computational approach to model the zone of proximal development. In: Lavoué, É., Drachsler, H., Verbert, K., Broisin, J., Pérez-Sanagustín, M. (eds.) EC-TEL 2017. LNCS, vol. 10474, pp. 3–16. Springer, Cham (2017). https://doi.org/10.1007/978-3-319-66610-5_1
7. Chounta, I.A., McLaren, B.M., Albacete, P., Jordan, P., Katz, S.: Modeling the zone of proximal development with a computational approach. In: Hu, X., Barnes, T., Hershkovitz, A., Paquette, L. (eds.) EDM 2017, pp. 56–57 (2017)
8. Craig, S.D., Sullins, J., Witherspoon, A., Gholson, B.: The deep-level-reasoning-question effect: The role of dialogue and deep-level-reasoning questions during vicarious learning. Cogn. Instr. **24**(4), 565–591 (2006)
9. Graesser, A.C., Lu, S., Jackson, G.T., Mitchell, H.H., Ventura, M., Olney, A., Louwerse, M. M.: AutoTutor: a tutor with dialogue in natural language. Behav. Rese. Methods Instrum. Comput. **36**(2), 180–192 (2004)
10. Hume, G., Michael, J., Rovick, A., Evens, M.: Hinting as a tactic in one-on-one tutoring. J. Learn. Sci. **5**(1), 23–49 (1996)
11. Jordan, P., Albacete, P., Katz, S.: Adapting step granularity in tutorial dialogue based on pretest scores. In: André, E., Baker, R., Hu, X., Rodrigo, Ma.Mercedes T., du Boulay, B. (eds.) AIED 2017. LNCS (LNAI), vol. 10331, pp. 137–148. Springer, Cham (2017). https://doi.org/10.1007/978-3-319-61425-0_12
12. Katz, S., Albacete, P., Jordan, P., Lusetich, D., Chounta, I.A., McLaren, B.M.: Operationalizing Contingent Tutoring in A Natural-Language Dialogue System. Nova Science Publishers (2018, submitted)
13. Katz, S., Albacete, P.: A tutoring system that simulates the highly interactive nature of human tutoring. J. Educ. Psychol. **105**(4), 1126–1141 (2013)
14. van de Pol, J., Volman, M., Beishuizen, J.: Scaffolding in teacher-student interaction: a decade of research. Educ. Psychol. Rev. **22**, 271–296 (2010)

15. Vygotsky, L.S.: Mind in society: The Development of Higher Psychological Processes. Harvard University Press, Cambridge (1978)
16. Wood, D., Middleton, D.: A study of assisted problem-solving. Br. J. Psychol. **66**(2), 181–191 (1975)
17. Wood, D., Wood, H.: Vygotsky, tutoring and learning. Oxford Rev. Educ. **22**(1), 5–16 (1996)

# Ella Me Ayudó (She Helped Me): Supporting Hispanic and English Language Learners in a Math ITS

Danielle Allessio[1(✉)], Beverly Woolf[1], Naomi Wixon[2],
Florence R. Sullivan[1], Minghui Tai[1], and Ivon Arroyo[2]

[1] University of Massachusetts, Amherst, MA, USA
`allessio@umass.edu`, `bev@cs.umass.edu`,
`{fsullivan,mtai}@educ.umass.edu`
[2] Worcester Polytechnic University, Worcester, MA, USA
`{nbwixon,iarroyo}@wpi.edu`

**Abstract.** Many intelligent tutors are not designed with English language learners (ELL) in mind. As a result, Hispanic ELL students, a large and underserved population in U.S. classrooms, may experience difficulty accessing the relevant tutor content. This research investigates how Hispanic and ELL students perceive the utility of and relate to animated pedagogical agents based on evaluating two theories of learning: students will be more attracted to a learning companion (LC) avatars that matches their personality and will regard a LC as a substitute self-construction. Results indicate that ELL students find LCs more useful and helpful than do Caucasian students and ELL students purposely design LCs that look more like themselves than do the non-ELL students.

**Keywords:** Intelligent tutoring system (ITS)
Animated pedagogical agent (APA) · Learning companion (LC)
English language learner (ELL)

## 1 Introduction

Intelligent tutoring systems (ITSs) and animated pedagogical agents (APAs) enhance learning [1–3], show learning gains of approximately .70 SDs for deep levels of comprehension [4], and lead to improved student self-efficacy and learning outcomes [5]. One limitation of past empirical work is that the visual representations of APAs is often chosen by researchers rather than students and lack social cues (e.g., gender, identity) with which students could identify themselves [6]. This research explores issues of race, gender and identity and asks how tutors can reach more Hispanic and English language learners (ELL) based on two learning theories. **Similarity-Attraction Hypothesis** (SAH) posits that people like and are attracted to others who are similar to themselves; thus, students will be more attracted to learning companions (LCs) that match their own personality than LCs that don't [7]. Research has shown that attraction leads to increased interaction and attention [8, 9] and similarity-attraction effects have been found in computer interactions [10, 11], counseling, and in classrooms,

© Springer International Publishing AG, part of Springer Nature 2018
C. Penstein Rosé et al. (Eds.): AIED 2018, LNAI 10948, pp. 26–30, 2018.
https://doi.org/10.1007/978-3-319-93846-2_5

particularly for students of color. **Identity Construction Theory** (ICT) states that the construction of an individual sense is achieved by learners' personal choice regarding with whom and what they associate; thus, LC construction enables individuals to experiment with identities and to express multiple aspects of themselves [12, 13]. Students will regard LCs as substitute self-construction and tend to reproduce either their real self or an improved or idealized self [14–17].

## 2   Experiment and Results

This mixed-method research was conducted with a math tutor called MathSpring (MS) that includes a student model, which assesses individual student knowledge and effort exerted [18]. MS also adapts the problem choice accordingly and provides help using multimedia. Additionally, LCs deliver messages focused on student effort and growth mindset to support student interactions (see Fig. 1). An avatar design activity[1] was followed by a mixed quantitative and qualitative survey, questions (Tables 1 and 2). Two studies were conducted with seventy-six ($N = 76$) middle-school aged students: thirty-nine ($N = 39$) sixth-grade students in an urban school district in Southern California, and thirty-seven ($N = 37$) seventh-grade public-school female students in New England, many of whom will be first generation college applicants. All of the ELL students were Hispanic and their first or primary language was Spanish.[2] There were fifty-six females ($N = 56$) and twenty males ($N = 20$); these numbers are skewed because all of the participants in the New England class were females. Additionally, sixty-one students in the study were Hispanic ($N = 61$) and fifteen were white ($N = 15$) while twenty-four students were ELL students ($N = 24$) and fifty-two were non-ELL students ($N = 52$).

**Fig. 1.** The LC shows high interest (left) and encourages the student (right).

---

[1] Conducted with My Blue Robot (mybluerobot.com) an avatar design application.

[2] The term Hispanic refers to the people, nations, and cultures that have a historical link to Spain. ELL refers to a person who does not speak English at home and is learning the English language in addition to their native language.

**Table 1.** Item Means and Standard Deviations

| Factor Subscales | | All Students (N = 76) | Hispanic (N = 61) | White (N = 15) | ELL (N = 24) | Non-ELL (N = 52) |
|---|---|---|---|---|---|---|
| | | Mean (S.D.) | Mean (S.D.) | Mean (S.D.) | Mean (S.D.) | Mean (S.D.) |
| I liked using the Learning Companion, Jane, in MS because she helped me understand. (*Me gustó usando el Compañero de aprendizaje, Jane, en MS porque ella me ayudó a entender.*) | JaneHelpful 3.48 (1.14) | | 3.54 (1.14) | 3.5 (1.12) | 3.11 (1.19) | 3.9 (.88) | 3.2 (1.0) |
| Jane was not that useful to me, so I did not use her. (*Jane no era tan útil para mí, así que no usamos ella.*) | | | 3.32 (1.31) | | | | |
| I think Jane was a very helpful part of MS. (*Creo que Jane era una parte muy útil de MS.*) | | | 3.59 (1.22) | | | | |
| The Learning Companion/Avatar that I created looks a lot like me. (*El compañero de aprendizaje/Avatar que creé se parece mucho a mí.*) | AvatarLooksLikeMe 3.22 (1.23) | | 3.12 (1.47) | 3.2 (1.14) | 2.9 (1.57) | 3.6 (1.0) | 3.0 (1.2) |
| The Learning Companion that I designed looks nothing like me. (*El compañero de aprendizaje que diseñé parece en nada a mí.*) | | | 2.96 (1.50) | | | | |
| The Learning Companion that I created has a lot of my characteristics. (*El compañero de aprendizaje que he creado tiene un montón de mis características.*) | | | 3.59 (1.16) | | | | |

The survey measured two constructs on a 5-point Likert scale from 1 (strongly disagree) to 5 (strongly agree): do students find Jane the LC useful and are features in student-created LCs similar to students' features. The JaneHelpful subscale ($\alpha = .92$) and the AvatarLooksLikeMe subscale (a = .87) each consisted of 3 items.

The first question, about whether the LC was helpful, did not show a significant difference between scores for the Hispanic and White student conditions. There was a significant difference between ELL ($M = 3.9$, $SD = .88$) and non-ELL ($M = 3.2$, $SD = 1.0$) student conditions. An independent-samples t-test $t(74) = -2.2$, $p < .028$ suggests that there is a difference between how useful ELL students and non-ELL students found the LC. Examples of qualitative results that support the quantitative findings: "She was helpful due to me not knowing a decimal problem she gave me an example." "I thought Jane was helpful because she encouraged me and congratulated me when I got something correct." and "she gave hints if you were struggling."

The query about whether Hispanic and ELL students designed LCs with characteristics similar to themselves used an independent-samples t-test to show that there was not a significant difference between the Hispanic and White student conditions. There was a significant difference between the scores for ELLs ($M = 3.6$, $SD = 1.0$) and non-ELL students ($M = 3.0$, $SD = 1.2$); $t(74) = -2.0$, $p < .046$, suggesting that ELL students design their LC more similarly to themselves than do non-ELL students. Qualitative results from open-ended survey questions support the quantitative findings, Table 2.

LC design images and images of the students are also in Table 2. Image analysis was conducted to determine whether the student-designed LCs were similar to or different from the student image. The student designs were analyzed by eye, hair and skin color selected and compared generally to students' actual features. A significant difference existed between the scores for the ELL student ($M = 3.1$ $SD = .58$) and

**Table 2.** Sample qualitative ELL Open-ended survey results, LC designs and student image.

| Why did you design your Learning Companion the way you did? (¿Por qué el diseño de su compañero de aprendizaje de la manera que lo hizo?) | Student LC Avatar Design | Student Image |
| --- | --- | --- |
| "I disigned it this way because I wanted it to look like me." | | |
| "I wanted it to look like me." | | |
| "I wanted him to look like me and I will make him have all my personalities and my characterisics." | | |
| "I gave her hair similar to mine and glasses cause most of my family members have glasses and a blue shirt because my favorite color is blue." | | |
| "I designed my avatar the way i did because he looked a lot like me and he also looks cool." | | |

non-ELL student ($M = 2.8$, $SD = .47$) conditions; $t(20) = 2.92$, $p < .008$, suggesting that the ELL designs and the non-ELL designs were different.

## 3 Discussion

We provide evidence that ELL students designed LCs that looked more like themselves than did the non-ELL students. Results demonstrate LC design for ITS is important for building student-tutor rapport and for certain students, the design correlates with improved engagement, performance and learning. These finding substantiate that the stronger the relationship between the student and their LC (identification with the LC), the more likely the learner will engage with the environment and have a positive experience thus, we suggest that ITSs should incorporate functionality for students to design their own LCs.

Future work includes inviting more non-Hispanic (White and African American) students to compare how they relate to their LCs. We also intend to examine whether ELL students perceive the utility of and relate to a bilingual LC. We predict that ELL students will be more engaged and have a more favorable experience if they can identify and connect with a bilingual LC that is similar to themselves.

**Acknowledgement.** This research is supported by the National Science Foundation (NSF) #1324385 IIS/Cyberlearning DIP: Impact of Adaptive Interventions on Student Affect, Performance. Any opinions, findings and conclusions, or recommendations expressed in this paper are those of the authors and do not necessarily reflect the views of NSF.

# References

1. Arroyo, I., Royer, J.M., Woolf, B.P.: Using an intelligent tutor and math fluency training to improve math performance. Int. J. Artif. Intell. Educ. **21**(1–2), 135–152 (2011)
2. Domagk, S.: Do pedagogical agents facilitate learner motivation and learning outcomes? J. Media Psychol. **22**(2), 84–97 (2010)
3. Moreno, R., Mayer, R., Spires, H., Lester, J.: The case for social agency in computer-based teaching: do students learn more deeply when they interact with animated pedagogical agents? Cogn. Instr. **19**(2), 177–213 (2010)
4. Graesser, et al.: AutoTutor: a tutor with dialogue in natural language. Behav. Res. Methods Instrum. Comput. **36**(2), 180–192 (2004)
5. Baylor, A.L., Kim, Y.: Research-based design of pedagogical agent roles: a review, progress, and recommendations. Int. J. Artif. Intell. Educ. **26**(1), 160–169 (2015)
6. Moreno, R., Flowerday, T.: Students' choice of animated pedagogical agents in science learning: A test of the similarity-attraction hypothesis on gender and ethnicity. Contemp. Educ. Psychol. **31**(2), 186–207 (2006)
7. Byrne, D., Nelson, D.: Attraction as a linear function of proportion of positive reinforcements. J. Pers. Soc. Psychol. **1**(6), 659–663 (1965)
8. Berscheid, E., Walster, E.: Physical attractiveness. Adv. Exp. Soc. Psychol. **7**(3–7), 157–215 (1969)
9. McCroskey, J.C., Hamilton, P.R., Weiner, A.N.: The effect of interaction behavior on source credibility, homophily, and interpersonal attraction. Hum. Commun. Res. **1**(1), 42–52 (1974)
10. Isbister, K., Nass, C.: Consistency of personality in interactive characters: Verbal cues, non-verbal cues, and user characteristics (2000). https://doi.org/10.1006/ijhc.2000.0368
11. Nass, C., Isbister, K., Lee, E.: Truth is beauty: researching embodied conversational agents. In: Cassell, J., Sullivan, J., Prevost, S., Churchill, E. (eds.) Embodied Conversational Agents, pp. 374–402. MIT Pres, Cambridge (2000)
12. Turkle, S.: The Second Self. MIT Press, Boston (1984)
13. Turkel, S.: Life on the Screen: Identity in the Age of the Internet. Simon and Schuster, New Yorek (1995)
14. Taylor, T.L.: Living digitally: embodiment in virtual worlds. In: Schroeder, R. (ed.) The social life of avatars: presence and interaction in shared virtual environments. Computer Supported Cooperative Work, pp. 40–62. Springer, London (2002). https://doi.org/10.1007/978-1-4471-0277-9_3
15. Bessière, K., Fleming, A., Kiesler, S.: The ideal elf: identity exploration in world of warcraft. CyberPsychol. Behav. **10**(4), 530–535 (2007)
16. Tisseron, S.: L'ado et ses avatars. Adolescence **27**(3), 591–600 (2009)
17. Jin, S.A.: Parasocial interaction with an avatar in second life: a typology of the self and an empirical test of the mediating role of social presence. Presence: Teleoper. Virtual Environ. **19**(4), 331–340 (2010)
18. Arroyo, I., Mehranian, H., Woolf, B.P.: Effort-based tutoring: an empirical approach to intelligent tutoring. In: Educational Data Mining, pp. 1–10 (2010)

# VERA: Popularizing Science Through AI

Sungeun An[1]([✉]), Robert Bates[1], Jennifer Hammock[2], Spencer Rugaber[1], and Ashok Goel[1]

[1] School of Interactive Computing, Georgia Institute of Technology, Atlanta, GA 30308, USA
sungeun.an@gatech.edu
[2] National Museum of Natural History, Smithsonian Institution, Washington, DC 20002, USA

**Abstract.** Citizen scientists have the potential to expand scientific research. The virtual research assistant called VERA empowers citizen scientists to engage in environmental science in two ways. First, it automatically generates simulations based on the conceptual models of ecological phenomena for repeated testing and feedback. Second, it leverages the Encyclopedia of Life biodiversity knowledgebase to support the process of model construction and revision.

**Keywords:** Citizen science · Conceptual modeling · Ecology
Encyclopedia of life · Simulation

## 1 Introduction

General public scientists, sometimes called citizen scientists, participate in scientific research in part to contribute to and expand the impacts of any study [1–3]. Yet, the role of citizen scientists is often limited to data collection [4,5]. We seek to develop computational techniques and tools to empower citizen scientists to play a more active role in scientific research, especially in environmental science and policy [6].

The scientific process often starts with the identification of an atypical or abnormal phenomenon such as unprecedented movement of a biological species into a new geographical region [7]. The scientist may then propose, elaborate, evaluate, revise/refine, and accept/reject multiple hypotheses for explaining the phenomenon. Professional scientists widely use multiple kinds of models of the system of interest including conceptual models and simulation models [8,9]. Conceptual models are abstract and declarative representations of a system with components, relations, and processes. Simulation models can be executed to evaluate a hypothesis by calculating the real effects and courses of action under certain conditions of the system. Thus, a conceptual model can help express hypotheses that can then be evaluated and revised through simulations. The construction of a conceptual model requires relational knowledge that involves relationships between two species (e.g., predator-prey relationships), whereas

C. Penstein Rosé et al. (Eds.): AIED 2018, LNAI 10948, pp. 31–35, 2018.
https://doi.org/10.1007/978-3-319-93846-2_6

model simulation requires quantitative information about a species (e.g., population, birthrate, lifespan). These are two areas in which many citizen scientists need much support.

Thus, our research question is how to develop a virtual research assistant that can help citizen scientists construct, test and revise their hypotheses about ecological phenomena. The Virtual Ecological Research Assistant (VERA; http://support.dilab.gatech.edu/okuwiki/mantis/virtual_ecological_research_assistant_vera/start) empowers citizen scientists in two ways. First, it automatically generates simulations based on the conceptual models of ecological phenomena for repeated testing and feedback. Second, it leverages Encyclopedia of Life (http://eol.org/) biodiversity knowledgebase to support the process of model construction and revision. A couple of pilot studies show promising results.

## 2    VERA

Conceptual models of ecological phenomena in VERA are expressed in the Component-Mechanism-Phenomenon (CMP) language [10,11]. CMP modeling of natural systems is an adaptation of the Structure-Behavior-Function modeling of technological systems [12,13]. A CMP model consists of components and relationships between components. A component can be one of four types: biotic, abiotic, base population, and habitat. A relationship relates one component to another in a directed manner (e.g., component X consumes component Y). The allowed relationships vary based on the source, and destination components selected, but always are a subset of the relations ontology supported by EOL. The sixteen types of relationships presently implemented in VERA including "consumes," "destroys," "infects," and "spreads." Figure 1 illustrates the VERA system that includes MILA-S [10,11] for automatic generation of agent-based simulations and EOL for retrieving traits of species.

### 2.1    Automatic Generation of Agent-Based Simulations

Following our earlier work on the ACT [14] and MILA-S system [10,11], VERA uses an artificial intelligence compiler to automatically translate the patterns in the conceptual models into the primitives of agent-based simulation of NetLogo [15]. The running of the simulation enables the user to observe the evolution of the system variables over time, and iterate through the model-simulate-refine loops [16]. In this way, like MILA-S, VERA integrates both qualitative reasoning in the conceptual model and quantitative reasoning in the simulation reasoning on one hand, and explanatory reasoning (conceptual model) and predictive reasoning (simulation).

### 2.2    Integration with Encyclopedia of Life

VERA integrates MILA-S with EOL [17] to provide the user with access to knowledge about biological species, for example, data about the traits of a

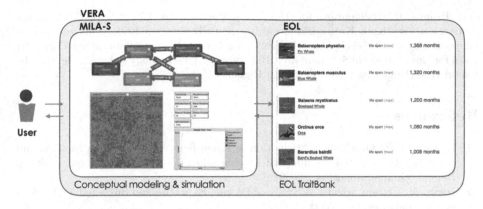

**Fig. 1.** The overall structure of VERA. VERA includes MILA-S to let users create conceptual models about the problems in ecological systems and execute simulations. In the meantime, VERA uses EOL TraitBank to scaffold the process of model construction.

species. In particular, once having built a conceptual model of an ecological phenomenon, the user may need quantitative data about the biological species in the model to set up the agent-based model simulation. VERA enables the user to look up this kind of data in EOLs TraitBank [18]. For example, when creating a model that explains why a specific kind of starfish is dying off the west coast of USA, the user can search EOLs TraitBank for the birthrate and lifespan of the starfish and set the simulation parameters accordingly.

We are presently constructing additional tools for accessing knowledge from EOL to support citizen scientists. For example, when adding predator-prey relationships of starfish, a user may not know what starfish eat or what might eat starfish. To facilitate looking up this kind of information, we seek to use IBMs Bluemix services to search the EOL for an answer by entering a question such as "What do starfish eat?"

## 3 Conclusion

The VERA system helps citizen scientists in constructing and testing models of ecological systems in two ways. First, it automatically generates simulations based on the conceptual models of ecological phenomena for repeated testing and feedback. Second, it leverages the Encyclopedia of Life biodiversity knowledgebase to support the process of model construction and revision. Initial pilot studies indicate promising results. To contribute to environmental sustainability, citizen scientists can use the VERA system to model, analyze, explain, and predict problems in ecological systems.

**Acknowledgement.** At Georgia Tech, we thank David Joyner and Taylor Hartman for their contributions to MILA-S, and Abbinayaa Subrahmanian, Christopher Cassion and Pramodith Ballapuram for their contributions to VERA. At Smithsonian Institution, we thank Katja Schulz for her contributions to EOL. This research is supported by an US NSF grant #1636848 (Big Data Spokes: Collaborative: Using Big Data for Environmental Sustainability: Big Data + AI Technology = Accessible, Usable, Useful Knowledge!) and the NSF South BigData Hub.

# References

1. Bonney, R., et al.: Public participation in scientific research: defining the field and assessing its potential for informal science education. A CAISE Inquiry Group Report, Online Submission (2009)
2. Irwin, A.: Citizen Science: A Study of People, Expertise and Sustainable Development. Routledge, New York (2002)
3. Hand, E.: People power. Nature **466**(7307), 685–687 (2010)
4. Brossard, D., Lewenstein, B., Bonney, R.: Scientific knowledge and attitude change: the impact of a citizen science project. Int. J. Sci. Educ. **27**(9), 1099–1121 (2005)
5. Cohn, J.P.: Citizen science: can volunteers do real research? AIBS Bull. **58**(3), 192–197 (2008)
6. Couvet, D., et al.: Enhancing citizen contributions to biodiversity science and public policy. Interdisc. Sci. Rev. **33**(1), 95–103 (2008)
7. Nersessian, N.J.: Model-based reasoning in conceptual change. In: Magnani, L., Nersessian, N.J., Thagard, P. (eds.) Model-Based Reasoning in Scientific Discovery, pp. 5–22. Springer, Boston (1999)
8. Clement, J.: Creative Model Construction in Scientists and Students: The Role of Imagery, Analogy, and Mental Simulation. Springer, Dordrecht (2008). https://doi.org/10.1007/978-1-4020-6712-9
9. Nersessian, N.J.: Creating Scientific Concepts. MIT Press, Cambridge (2010)
10. Joyner, D., Goel, A., Papin, N.: MILA-S: generation of agent-based simulations from conceptual models of complex systems. In: Proceedings of the 19th International Conference on Intelligent User Interfaces, pp. 289–298. ACM (2014)
11. Goel, A., Joyner, D.: Impact of a creativity support tool on student learning about scientific discovery processes. In: Proceedings of the Sixth International Conference on Computational Creativity, Park City, Utah, June 2015
12. Goel, A., Gomez, A., Grue, N., Murdock, J., Recker, M., Govindaraj, T.: Towards design learning environments - exploring how devices work. In: Proceedings of the International Conference on Intelligent Tutoring Systems, Montreal, Canada, June 1996
13. Goel, A., Rugaber, S., Vattam, S.: Structure, behavior and function models of complex systems: the structure-behavior-function modeling language. AIEDAM **23**, 23–35 (2009)
14. Vattam, S., Goel, A., Rugaber, S., Hmelo-Silver, C., Jordan, R., Gray, S., Sinha, S.: Understanding complex natural systems by articulating structure-behavior-function models. J. Educ. Technol. Soc. **14**(1), 66–81 (2011)
15. Wilensky, U.: NetLogo: Center for Connected Learning and Computer-Based Modeling, Northwestern University, Evanston, IL (1999). http://ccl.northwestern.edu/netlogo/
16. White, B., Frederiksen, J.: Causal model progressions as a foundation for intelligent learning environments. Artif. Intell. **42**(1), 99–157 (1990)

17. Parr, C., Wilson, N., Leary, P., Schulz, K., Lans, K., Walley, L., Hammock, J., Goddard, A., Rice, J., Studer, M., Holmes, J., Corigan, R.: The encyclopedia of life v2: providing global access to knowledge about life on earth. Biodivers. Data J. **2**, e1079 (2014)

18. Parr, C., Wilson, N., Schulz, K., Leary, P., Hammock, J., Rice, J., Corrigan, R.: TraitBank: practical semantics for organism attribute data. Semant. Web Interoperability Usability Appl., 650–1860 (2014)

# Modelling Math Learning on an Open Access Intelligent Tutor

David Azcona[1](✉), I-Han Hsiao[2], and Alan F. Smeaton[1]

[1] Insight Centre for Data Analytics, Dublin City University, Dublin, Ireland
david.azcona@insight-centre.org
[2] School of Computing, Informatics and Decision Systems Engineering,
Arizona State University, Tempe, USA

**Abstract.** This paper presents a methodology to analyze large amount of students' learning states on two math courses offered by Global Freshman Academy program at Arizona State University. These two courses utilised ALEKS (Assessment and Learning in Knowledge Spaces) Artificial Intelligence technology to facilitate massive open online learning. We explore social network analysis and unsupervised learning approaches (such as probabilistic graphical models) on these type of Intelligent Tutoring Systems to examine the potential of the embedding representations on students learning.

**Keywords:** Machine learning · Intelligent Tutoring Systems
Social network analysis · MOOC

## 1 Introduction

Massive Open Online Courses (MOOCs) are revolutionizing education by giving students around the world open access to first-class education via the web. Lectures, readings, exercises and discussion forums are now one click away to anybody, anywhere. In 2016, Arizona State University (ASU) launched the Global Freshman Academy (GFA) where they provide first-year university courses through the edX platform allowing students to earn transferable ASU credits from anywhere. ASU currently offer 13 courses and our analysis will focus on two Math modules: College Algebra and Problem Solving, and Precalculus. These courses leverage the Assessment and Learning in Knowledge Spaces (ALEKS) technology, which is a web-based artificially intelligent assessment and learning system. ASU's GFA Math courses combined with ALEKS technology is ASU's effort to get students ready for college-level mathematics. The effectiveness and adaptiveness of this Artificial Intelligence (AI) tutoring systems have the potential to motivate and help students acquire these skills.

## 2 Related Work

ALEKS leverages AI to map student's knowledge. ALEKS is based on knowledge spaces, which was introduced in 1985 by Doignon and Falmagne, who describe

© Springer International Publishing AG, part of Springer Nature 2018
C. Penstein Rosé et al. (Eds.): AIED 2018, LNAI 10948, pp. 36–40, 2018.
https://doi.org/10.1007/978-3-319-93846-2_7

the possible states of knowledge of a learner [4]. In order to develop a knowledge space, a domain like Algebra or Chemistry is modelled and divided into a set of concepts and feasible states of knowledge where the student's knowledge is at any given time. This technology adapts and navigates the students by determining what the student may know and may not know in a course and guides her to the topics she is most ready to learn. It assess the student's knowledge periodically to ensure topics are learned and retained [5]. Recent research has shown using ALEKS for learning Math has a positive learning impact on an after-school program for more than 200 sixth graders [2,3].

Recent research has shown that Social Network Analysis (SNA) measurements can be predictive features for machine learning models in addition to generic content-based features [1]. Moreover, sequential modelling (i.e. Hidden Markov Models (HMMs)) can be useful to uncover student progress or students' learning behaviours [6–8]. We hypothesise that by modelling the evolution of large amount student's working behaviours with social network features, will allow us to uncover student's progression and the possibility to enhance student experience with further personalized interventions on these Intelligent Tutoring Systems as it gathers rich information about concepts, topics and learning states.

## 3  Data Collection

An anonymized data of 15,000+ students learning on the two Math courses in edX with the ALEKS technology was collected between April 2016 and October 2017. Students are assessed continuously while navigating through ALEKS and daily aggregates of the topics learned and retained are generated. We tracked 40,000+ assessments and 8+ million daily aggregates. In addition, 5+ million transactions of students navigating through the concepts have been extracted from the edX logs. Each timestamped transaction contains the student, the concept being studied and a learning state. The learning states are the following and final states are determined by the system:

- **L**: Initial state for each concept where a student reads the **L**esson
- **C**: Intermediate state where a student gets an exercise **C**orrect
- **W**: Intermediate state where a student gets an exercise **W**rong or Incorrect
- **E**: Intermediate state where a student asks for a working **E**xample
- **S**: Final state where a student has **M**astered a particular concept
- **F**: Final state where a student has **F**ailed to master a particular concept.

## 4  Methodology

Through the ALEKS platform, we then observe the learning states students go through. We analysed how students transition from one learning state to another and in between concepts and slices (higher-level representations of concepts). The data has been stored and indexed in a non-relational database and made available using a web application where they can explore individual students

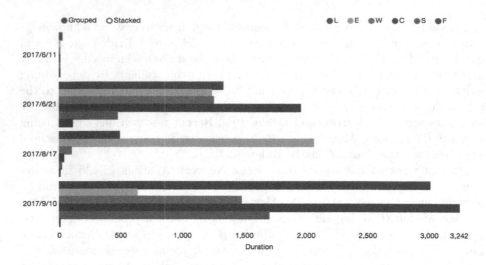

**Fig. 1.** Grouped transactions for a particular student

and how they are redirected through the material, concepts and their underlying difficulty based on completion and likely sequence patterns around concepts and slices. Figure 1 shows the time distribution for each learning state for a particular student with respect to the other states.

## 4.1 Network Analysis

We follow a social network analysis approach to investigate the structure of the student's learning on these systems by leveraging networks and graph theory. Network analysis can give us insights into the properties of these learning states. A network of the observed learning states is developed for each student and each topic and posted on the web application. Figure 2 shows two very different learning paths from students working on similar topics, a linear learning path versus a student who failed to master the concept in the beginning but was brought back to the concept and mastered it. Considering these learning states as nodes

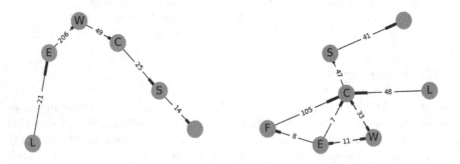

**Fig. 2.** Networks of learning states where students are navigated

of a network enables us to analyse their centrality and measure their importance in the learning of these concepts and disciplines. By creating a network for each topic with all student data, we are measuring the degree centrality of the learning states and finding out where students are most likely to struggle or succeed by looking at the final states. Moreover, we are developing a network with all the learning states and their corresponding topics and analysing the students' progression; looking for centrality hubs; hypothesizing whether further interventions may be added; measuring eigenvector centrality and how important are the neighbors of the nodes; using the geodesic distance to measure the closeness and betweenness between topics for each slice, which slices take more effort from students and how to help them succeed. In addition, we will cluster the nodes and see if the groupings correspond with the sections of the topics.

### 4.2   Summary and Future Work

The learning states extracted from the transactions and the underlying navigation through the course can be modelled using a Markovian procedure by assuming the future learning states depend only on the current learning state. This could be further developed by looking at sequences of learning states and topics learned in order to model the likelihood of future learning states. In our case we consider the learning states as observable states and are modelling their learning using an HMM, the unobserved or hidden states are estimated from the sequence of learning states students follow and are navigated on the system. On the other hand, based on the large number of transactions gathered, another higher-level representation of this sequence of learning states can be learned using embeddings. We are learning these embeddings by inputting the sequence of learning states to a supervised machine learning algorithm, a Recurrent Neural Network, that take the time constraint into consideration. This is a promising avenue of research that has successfully been applied to Computer Vision to learn high-level features using Deep Learning approaches.

**Acknowledgements.** This research was supported by the Irish Research Council in association with the National Forum for the Enhancement of Teaching and Learning in Ireland under project number GOIPG/2015/3497, by Science Foundation Ireland under grant SFI/12/RC/2289, and by Fulbright Ireland. The authors are indebted to the Action Lab at EdPlus in Arizona State University for their help.

## References

1. Chen, W., Brinton, C.G., Cao, D., Mason-singh, A., Lu, C., Chiang, M.: Early detection prediction of learning outcomes in online short-courses via learning behaviors. IEEE Trans. Learn. Technol. (2018)
2. Craig, S.D., Anderson, C., Bargagloitti, A., Graesser, A.C., Okwumabua, T., Sterbinsky, A., Hu, X.: Learning with ALEKS: the impact of students' attendance in a mathematics after-school program. In: Biswas, G., Bull, S., Kay, J., Mitrovic, A. (eds.) AIED 2011. LNCS (LNAI), vol. 6738, pp. 435–437. Springer, Heidelberg (2011). https://doi.org/10.1007/978-3-642-21869-9_61

3. Craig, S.D., Hu, X., Graesser, A.C., Bargagliotti, A.E., Sterbinsky, A., Cheney, K.R., Okwumabua, T.: The impact of a technology-based mathematics after-school program using aleks on student's knowledge and behaviors. Comput. Educ. **68**, 495–504 (2013)
4. Doignon, J.P., Falmagne, J.C.: Spaces for the assessment of knowledge. Int. J. Man Mach. Stud. **23**(2), 175–196 (1985)
5. Doignon, J.P., Falmagne, J.C., Cosyn, E.: Learning spaces: a mathematical compendium. In: Falmagne, J.C., Albert, D., Doble, C., Eppstein, D., Hu, X. (eds.) Knowledge Spaces, pp. 131–145. Springer, Heidelberg (2013). https://doi.org/10.1007/978-3-642-35329-1_8
6. Hsiao, I.H., Huang, P.K., Murphy, H.: Uncovering reviewing and reflecting behaviors from paper-based formal assessment. In: Proceedings of the Seventh International Learning Analytics and Knowledge Conference, pp. 319–328. ACM (2017)
7. Piech, C., Huang, J., Nguyen, A., Phulsuksombati, M., Sahami, M., Guibas, L.: Learning program embeddings to propagate feedback on student code. arXiv preprint arXiv:1505.05969 (2015)
8. Piech, C., Sahami, M., Koller, D., Cooper, S., Blikstein, P.: Modeling how students learn to program. In: Proceedings of the 43rd ACM Technical Symposium on Computer Science Education, pp. 153–160. ACM (2012)

# Learner Behavioral Feature Refinement and Augmentation Using GANs

Da Cao[1]([✉]), Andrew S. Lan[2], Weiyu Chen[1], Christopher G. Brinton[1,2],
and Mung Chiang[3]

[1] Zoomi, Inc., Malvern, USA
da.cao@zoomiinc.com
[2] Princeton University, Princeton, USA
[3] Purdue University, West Lafayette, USA

**Abstract.** Learner behavioral data (e.g., clickstream activity logs) collected by online education platforms contains rich information about learners and content, but is often highly redundant. In this paper, we study the problem of learning low-dimensional, interpretable features from this type of raw, high-dimensional behavioral data. Based on the premise of generative adversarial networks (GANs), our method refines a small set of human-crafted features while also generating a set of additional, complementary features that better summarize the raw data. Through experimental validation on a real-world dataset that we collected from an online course, we demonstrate that our method leads to features that are both predictive of learner quiz scores and closely related to human-crafted features.

## 1 Introduction

Online learning platforms, such massive open online courses (MOOCs), have the capability of collecting large-scale learner behavioral data at low costs. Examples of such data include content usage patterns [7], social interactions [16], and keystroke/clickstream events [1]. The existence of behavioral data has motivated research on identifying non-assessment-related factors that contribute to learner performance, e.g., engagement [15] and particular sequences of actions [5].

These factors in turn have the potential of providing effective learning and content analytics to instructors, with research having shown that learner behavior is highly predictive of learning outcomes. For example, [10] found that learner activity patterns are predictive of certification status and early dropout, respectively. Further, [1,14,16] found that learner discussion forum, assignment submission, and keystroke pattern activities are predictive of test performance, exam scores, and essay quality respectively.

Despite its predictive power, behavioral data is itself often massive and highly redundant. [6,12], for example, showed that a single learner can generate thousands of clickstream events even in short courses. When extracted carefully, however, even small sets of features have been seen to sufficiently characterize learner behavior in a manner that is predictive of learning outcomes [4].

© Springer International Publishing AG, part of Springer Nature 2018
C. Penstein Rosé et al. (Eds.): AIED 2018, LNAI 10948, pp. 41–46, 2018.
https://doi.org/10.1007/978-3-319-93846-2_8

Existing approaches to finding such representations can be divided into two categories: model-driven features extraction and human-crafted features. Model-driven features will by definition capture even the most subtle nuances in the raw learner data, and lose the least amount of variance in the process; examples include principal component analysis (PCA)[2], matrix factorization [3], and variational autoencoders [11]. The features resulting from these approaches, however, exhibit little to no interpretability, and do not offer strong learning and content analytics for instructors. Human-crafted features are based on human knowledge of education and are highly interpretable as a result [4,12]. However, they often have significantly lower predictability [13] and require human effort to formulate.

In this paper, we develop the first model-driven approach for analyzing behavioral data that generates features with both high predictability and interpretability, in the sense that they are more human-like as they possess strong similarity to human-crafted features.

## 2   Feature Generation Method

Let $U$ denote the number of learners, indexed by $u \in \{1, 2, \ldots, U\}$, and let $D$ denote the number of raw features, indexed by $d \in \{1, 2, \ldots, D\}$. We represent learner $u$'s data as the feature vector $\mathbf{x}_u^r \in \mathbb{R}^D$.

We also leverage a set of $G \ll D$ given, human-crafted "gold standard" features. Letting $\mathbf{x}_u^g \in \mathbb{R}^G$ denote the vector containing learner $u$'s gold standard feature values, our goal is to produce a set of refined features and an additional set of $A \ll D$ complementary features that satisfy two conditions: a) the refined features are similar to the gold standard features, but better resemble the raw data, and b) the additional complementary features, together with the refined features, form a low-dimensional representation of learner behavior that is able to reconstruct the raw data with high fidelity.

We denote learner $u$'s refined and complementary feature vectors as $\mathbf{x}_u^f \in \mathbb{R}^G$ and $\mathbf{x}_u^a \in \mathbb{R}^A$, respectively. In order to satisfy these conditions, we make use of the GAN framework [9]. Our model consists of three parts: (i) a **generator** that outputs a vector $\mathbf{x}_u^{gen}$ for each learner, consisting of each refined feature $\mathbf{x}_u^f$ and each complementary feature $\mathbf{x}_u^a$, given the learner's raw data features $\mathbf{x}_u^r$ as input; (ii) a **discriminator**, which seeks to classify whether a learner's gold standard feature vector $\mathbf{x}_u^g$ and refined feature $\mathbf{x}_u^f$ vector each are human-crafted or generated, and (iii) a **reconstructor**, which takes each learner's refined and complementary features and reconstructs the raw data features from them.

## 3   Experiments

### 3.1   Course

To evaluate our feature generation method, we employ a dataset collected by Zoomi Inc. hosting a particular online corporate training course. Total enrollment in this course was about 3,000, and the content was a roughly 40-slide slideshow presentation, with some slides containing quiz questions. Recall that our model requires two sets of features for each learner as input: raw data features $\mathbf{x}_u^r$, and human-crafted gold standard features $\mathbf{x}_u^g$. The raw data features for this course consisted of four quantities measured at the individual slide level: time spent, expected time spent, number of views, and engagement score [6]. The set of gold standard features, on the other hand, consisted of the same four quantities aggregated at the course level, and two additional features: the number of times a learner switched away from the course platform, and the number of visits to the course.

## 3.2 Training Procedures and Metrics

Our model parameter training procedure seeks to minimize the generator, discriminator, and reconstructor losses. In each training epoch, a batch of 50 learners is used to infer the model parameters. In a round-robin fashion [9], we train the generator twice before training the discriminator once, whereas the reconstructor network is trained in every epoch. The number of additional complementary features, $A$, is tuned by sweeping over values as $A \in \{0, 1, \ldots, 15\}$. We quantify the ability of the generator and discriminator to classify hand-crafted and generated features using the standard cross entropy loss metric [8], while we use the $R^2$ score to quantify the reconstructor's ability to reconstruct the raw learner data.

## 3.3 Predicting Quiz Performance

We compare the generated features $(\mathbf{x}_u^{gen})$ to features generated by baseline methods in terms of their ability to predicting learner quiz scores. Since the overall quiz score for each learner in this course took a value in the discrete set $\{0, 0.8, 0.9, 1\}$, we formulate this as a multi-class classification problem. We consider the following baselines: (i) high-dimensional raw features $(\mathbf{x}_u^r)$, (ii) low-dimensional, human-crafted gold standard features $(\mathbf{x}_u^g)$, (iii) low-dimensional features constructed by principal component analysis (PCA) on raw data features, denoted as $\mathbf{x}_u^{PCA}$, and (iv) low-dimensional features constructed by training a one-layer autoencoder [8], denoted as $\mathbf{x}_u^{ae}$. We use tanh for the GAN encoder nonlinearity, while specifying no nonlinearity for the GAN decoder. For a fair comparison with the latter two baselines, we ensure that the number of features is equal to the total number of features in our GAN (*i.e.*, $A + G$).

**Method and Metrics.** In predicting the quiz performance class from features, we employ several classifiers: Logistic Regression (LR), Multi-layer Perceptron (MLP), and Linear Discriminant Analysis (LDA). We report the performance of our model generated features and baseline features on two standard evaluation metrics: (i) accuracy and (ii) cross entropy loss. In each case, we perform 5-fold cross validation and report the average metric values.

**Classification Performance.** In Table 1, we show the prediction results for each algorithm on the features constructed by proposed GAN model compared

**Table 1.** Accuracy and Cross entropy values for quiz response prediction with $A = 15$ using different classifiers. The refined and complementary features from the generator achieves the highest performance.

| Features | LR | | MLP | | LDA | |
|---|---|---|---|---|---|---|
| | Accuracy | Cross entropy | Accuracy | Cross entropy | Accuracy | Cross entropy |
| Raw, $\mathbf{x}_u^r$ | 0.604 | 0.948 | 0.596 | 0.937 | 0.585 | 1.203 |
| Gold, $\mathbf{x}_u^g$ | 0.540 | 0.972 | 0.539 | 0.971 | 0.543 | *1.121* |
| PCA, $\mathbf{x}_u^{PCA}$ | 0.624 | 0.934 | 0.618 | 0.988 | 0.617 | 1.163 |
| Auto-encoder, $\mathbf{x}_u^{ae}$ | 0.579 | 0.949 | 0.552 | 0.964 | 0.563 | 1.157 |
| GAN, $\mathbf{x}_u^{gen}$ | *0.627* | *0.923* | *0.631* | *0.917* | *0.624* | 1.157 |

with the baseline features ($\mathbf{x}_u^r$, $\mathbf{x}_u^{ae}$, $\mathbf{x}_u^g$, and $\mathbf{x}_u^{PCA}$), for $A = 15$. We have highlighted the entries in the table that have achieved the best performances when compared to the other feature types. We observe that features constructed from our proposed GAN model, $\mathbf{x}_u^{gen}$, outperform other feature types, regardless the choice of the classifier. Also, prediction quality is reasonably invariant to the choice of classifier.

**Varying the Number of Complementary Features $A$.** We also analyze the effect of the number of complementary features on prediction quality. Figure 1 shows the results. While PCA compressed features outperform all other feature types when $A$ is small, $\mathbf{x}_u^{gen}$ shows a continuous trend to increase while $A$ increases. When $A$ is larger than 10, the classifier built on $\mathbf{x}_u^{gen}$ outperforms $\mathbf{x}_u^r$, $\mathbf{x}_u^{ae}$, $\mathbf{x}_u^g$, and $\mathbf{x}_u^{PCA}$ in most cases.

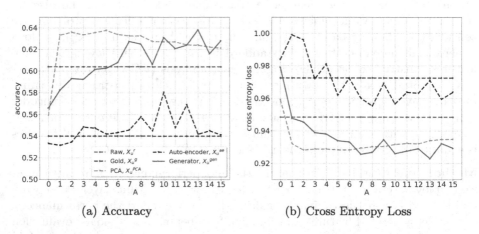

(a) Accuracy     (b) Cross Entropy Loss

**Fig. 1.** Comparison of accuracy and cross entropy loss in predicting quiz score versus the number of complementary features ($A$). The refined features and additional features from the generator outperform other compressed features at large $A$, while PCA features achieve the best performance at small $A$.

# 4   Conclusion and Future Work

In this work, we developed a method for generating low-dimensional features to summarize high-dimensional, raw learner behavioral data using the generative adversarial network (GAN) framework. Avenues of future work include: (i) incorporating content-specific features that enable us to extract learner interactions with various types of content, and (ii) using other neural network architectures, such as recurrent neural networks (RNNs) to learn time-varying representations; this information will enable us to model the dynamics of learner behavior.

# References

1. Allen, L., Jacovina, M., Dascalu, M., Roscoe, R., Kent, K., Likens, A., McNamara, D.: ENTERing the time series SPACE: uncovering the writing process through keystroke analyses. In: Proceedings of International Conference on Educational Data Mining, pp. 22–29, June 2016
2. Beheshti, B., Desmarais, M., Naceur, R.: Methods to find the number of latent skills. In: Proceedings of International Conference on Educational Data Mining, pp. 81–86, June 2012
3. Bergner, Y., Droschler, S., Kortemeyer, G., Rayyan, S., Seaton, D., Pritchard, D.: Model-based collaborative filtering analysis of student response data: machine-learning item response theory. In: Proceedings of International Conference on Educational Data Mining, pp. 95–102, June 2012
4. Brinton, C., Chiang, M.: MOOC performance prediction via clickstream data and social learning networks. In: Proceedings of IEEE Conference on Computer Communications, pp. 2299–2307, April 2015
5. Brinton, C., Buccapatnam, S., Chiang, M., Poor, H.V.: Mining MOOC clickstreams: video-watching behavior vs. in-video quiz performance. IEEE Trans. Signal Process. **64**, 3677–3692 (2016)
6. Chen, W., Brinton, C., Cao, D., Chiang, M.: Behavior in social learning networks: early detection for online short-courses. In: Proceedings of IEEE Conference on Computer Communications, pp. 1–9, May 2017
7. Gelman, B., Revelle, M., Domeniconi, C., Johri, A., Veeramachaneni, K.: Acting the same differently: a cross-course comparison of user behavior in MOOCs. In: Proceedings of International Conference on Educational Data Mining, pp. 376–381, June 2016
8. Goodfellow, I., Bengio, Y., Courville, A., Bengio, Y.: Deep Learning. MIT Press, Cambridge (2016)
9. Goodfellow, I., Pouget-Abadie, J., Mirza, M., Xu, B., Warde-Farley, D., Ozair, S., Courville, A., Bengio, Y.: Generative adversarial nets. In Advances in Neural Information Processing Systems, pp. 2672–2680 (2014)
10. Halawa, S., Greene, D., Mitchell, J.: Dropout prediction in MOOCs using learner activity features. In: Proceedings European MOOCs Stakeholders Summit, pp. 58–65, February 2014
11. Klingler, S., Wampfler, R., Kaser, T., Solenthaler, B., Gross, M.: Efficient feature embeddings for student classification with variational auto-encoders. In: Proceedings of International Conference on Educational Data Mining, pp. 72–79, June 2017

12. Lan, A.S., Brinton, C.G., Yang, T., Chiang, M.: Behavior-based latent variable model for learner engagement. In: Proceedings of International Conference on Educational Data Mining, pp. 64–71, June 2017
13. Lee, K., Chung, J., Cha, Y., Suh, C.: ML approaches for learning analytics: collaborative filtering or regression with experts?, December 2016. http://ml4ed.cc/attachments/LeeLCCS.pdf
14. McBroom, J., Jeffries, B., Koprinska, I., Yacef, K.: Mining behaviours of students in autograding submission system logs. In: Proceedings of International Conference on Educational Data Mining, pp. 159–166, June 2016
15. Slater, S., Baker, R., Ocumpaugh, J., Inventado, P., Scupelli, P., Heffernan, N.: Semantic features of math problems: relationships to student learning and engagement. In: Proceedings of International Conference on Educational Data Mining, pp. 223–230, June 2016
16. Tomkins, S., Ramesh, A., Getoor, L.: Predicting post-test performance from online student behavior: a high school MOOC case study. In: Proceedings of International Conference on Educational Data Mining, pp. 239–246, June 2016

# Learning Content Recommender System for Instructors of Programming Courses

Hung Chau[✉], Jordan Barria-Pineda, and Peter Brusilovsky

School of Computing and Information, University of Pittsburgh, Pittsburgh, PA, USA
{hkc6,jab464,peterb}@pitt.edu

**Abstract.** In this paper, we present a course-adaptive recommender system that assists instructors of programming courses in selecting the most relevant learning materials. The recommender system deduces the envisioned structure of a specific course using program examples prepared by the course instructor and recommends learning content items adapting to instructor's intentions. We also present a study that assessed the quality of recommendations using datasets collected from different courses.

**Keywords:** Course authoring · Learning content recommendation

## 1 Introduction

Over the past twenty years, most of the intelligent tutoring Systems (ITS) focused their personalization efforts on helping students to find an "optimal path" through learning content to achieve their learning goals. A range of personalization technologies (course sequencing, adaptive navigation support, and content recommendation) can take into account the learning goals and the current state of student knowledge and recommend the most appropriate content (e.g., a problem, an example, etc.). However, in the context of real courses, students are expected to work on course topics in the order determined by the instructor's plan. The personalized selection of learning content should account for both a student's prospects (i.e., current knowledge levels) and the instructor's prospects (the preferred order of topics or learning goals). These considerations are especially important when learning programming, where almost every instructor and every textbook introduce a unique course organization [1,2].

The work presented in this paper expands the functionality of a course authoring tool that supports instructors in selecting *smart learning content* for students of an introductory programming courses. Smart content could be selected by instructors from a large pool of parameterized problems [3] or annotated examples [4]. Our work with instructors revealed that the assistance provided by the current course authoring tool is not sufficient. While defining a sequence of topics is an easy task, selecting the most relevant content for each topic is a real challenge. The instructors need to carefully review a large number

© Springer International Publishing AG, part of Springer Nature 2018
C. Penstein Rosé et al. (Eds.): AIED 2018, LNAI 10948, pp. 47–51, 2018.
https://doi.org/10.1007/978-3-319-93846-2_9

of problems and examples in order to select those that fit their learning goals for the topic. This is a time-consuming and error-prone process [5–7].

To assist instructors in the authoring process, we developed the *Content Wizard*, a content recommender that suggests learning activities that are most appropriate to instructors' intended model of the course. The following sections present the Content Wizard and its evaluation with real course data.

## 2   The Content Wizard

The Content Wizard is developed for a typical course authoring approach where the course structure is defined as a sequence of *topics* and a set of learning items of different types is provided for each topic. This course structuring approach is supported by every major learning management system and textbook.

The goal of the Content Wizard is to help instructors in selecting learning content for each topic. To provide help, the Content Wizard ranks all content items of the selected type by their match to the selected topic. It also assigns "star" relevance rating to all content items. This support is based on Wizard's understanding of fine-grain course structure and prerequisite relationships on the level of domain concepts. The instructor is not expected to define the fine-grain structure as required by some earlier approaches [8,9]; instead, the course structure is automatically derived from the order of course topics and set of code examples that instructor prepared for each topic (i.e., a lecture or a book chapter). The next section explains this approach in details.

## 3   The Course Model and Content Representation

To offer recommendations, the Course Wizard builds a *course model* as a sequence of concept sets. Each set corresponds to a topic and includes the concepts instructors aim to introduce at that topic. For example, Unit 2 is the unit of the course where the concepts *Array Variable* and *Array Data Type* are introduced for the first time. The concepts introduced in the earlier units become prerequisite concepts for the later units. This deeper level concept-based course modeling has been used in many ITS and Adaptive Hypermedia authoring systems [8–10], however, it was assumed that course or system authors create this model manually. The difficulty of manual modeling is a known bottleneck of fine-grain course structuring approach. The Content Wizard, however, is able to derive this model automatically using *code examples* provided by the course authors.

Code examples are extensively used in teaching programming. For each lecture, an instructor usually prepares several code examples that illustrate newly introduced concepts. To build a deep course model that follows instructor's preferences, the Content Wizard uses the code of these examples. First, it uses the Java parser [11] to extract programming concepts associated with each code example. Second, for each unit, it forms a set of *covered concepts* merging concepts from all unit examples. Finally, it sequentially processes the units to find target concepts for each unit (i.e., concepts that are first introduced in the unit).

To identify a match between a unit and an activity, the Wizard considers a set of concepts associated with a candidate activity and the course structure. Since all types of learning activities available in the system (i.e., examples or problems) include code fragments, we use the Java parser [11] to represent each activity as a "bag" of Java programming concepts (Fig. 1a). This "bag of concepts" representation could be used by a number of traditional recommendation algorithms. A match to a specific unit, however, depends on the position of the target unit in the course. Using the course model, the Wizard classifies each concept appearing in an activity into one of three categories (Fig. 1b):

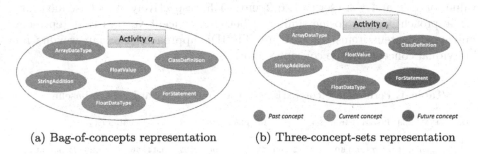

(a) Bag-of-concepts representation      (b) Three-concept-sets representation

**Fig. 1.** Demonstration of representing learning content as programming concepts.

- *Past concepts (P):* Concepts covered in the previous units.
- *Current concepts (C):* Concepts covered in the current unit (and thus not been covered in any previous unit).
- *Future concepts (F):* Concepts have not been covered up to the current unit.

This representation reflects instructor's preferences and supports our recommendation idea that recommended activities should *focus* on current concepts, *consider* past concepts, and *avoid* future concepts.

## 4   The Recommendation Method

For each learning activity $a_i$ consisting of three concept sets $C_i$, $P_i$ and $F_i$, the Wizard calculates its ranking score using Eq. (1):

$$score_{a_i} = \alpha|C_i| + \beta|P_i| + \gamma|F_i| \qquad (1)$$

where $\alpha$, $\beta$, and $\gamma$ are the parameters controlling the importance of the three categories. The values for these parameters might be different for different domains and even for individual instructors, depending on how much they focus on current and past concepts and how much they want to avoid future concepts. Indeed, [2] revealed differences among the proportions of reinforcement, recombination and introduction of concepts of two Japanese Textbooks and two online learning tools (Duolingo and Language Zen).

## 5 Evaluation

To evaluate our recommendation method, we collected three data sets from University of Pittsburgh, USA and University of Helsinki, Finland. Each dataset encapsulated instructor preferences in content selection (i.e., "ground truth").

We estimated parameter values in Eq. (1) using an expert analysis (we can't learn it from the same data that we use to evaluate the approach). The estimated values of $\alpha$, $\beta$, and $\gamma$ are set to $1$, $0.2$ and $-1.5$, respectively. As a baseline ranking approach, we use cosine similarity between concept vectors that represent units and content items [12]. We use TF*IDF approach to assign weights for individual concepts in the concept vector.

**Table 1.** Performance comparison of the Content Wizard vs. the baseline

| Dataset | Method | Precision@top (%) | | | | Recall@top (%) | | | | F1@top (%) | | | |
|---|---|---|---|---|---|---|---|---|---|---|---|---|---|
| | | 3 | 5 | 10 | 15 | 3 | 5 | 10 | 15 | 3 | 5 | 10 | 15 |
| 1 | wizard | 62.74 | 50.59 | 34.7 | 25.09 | 51.26 | 63.36 | 77.51 | 80.44 | 56.42 | 56.26 | 47.94 | 38.26 |
| | baseline | 21.57 | 18.82 | 15.29 | 15.68 | 21.57 | 18.84 | 29.14 | 42.33 | 15.57 | 18.84 | 20.06 | 22.89 |
| 2 | wizard | 47.05 | 37.64 | 32.94 | 26.66 | 34.23 | 41.91 | 66.32 | 76.86 | 39.63 | 39.66 | 44.01 | 39.59 |
| | baseline | 21.57 | 17.65 | 14.11 | 14.11 | 17.63 | 23.05 | 33.33 | 43.08 | 19.40 | 20.00 | 19.83 | 21.27 |
| 3 | wizard | 96.3 | 88.89 | 75.76 | 64.44 | 41.45 | 52.79 | 73.32 | 83.90 | 57.96 | 66.24 | 74.42 | 72.89 |
| | baseline | 81.48 | 73.33 | 66.67 | 57.04 | 37.24 | 44.97 | 64.34 | 73.18 | 51.12 | 55.75 | 65.48 | 64.10 |

As shown in Table 1, the Content Wizard outperforms the baseline for all datasets. On the dataset 1 and 2, the performance of the Wizard is much better (2–3 times!) than the baseline while in the dataset 3 the relative difference is smaller. In addition, the precision of both approaches is considerably higher for dataset 3. We believe that both differences stem from the differences in the nature of the datasets. The ranking tasks for the dataset 3 was much easier than for datasets 1–2. First, for dataset 3, recommender approaches had to rank only the actual items used in the course (and no "spares"). The number of units to match was also much smaller (10 vs. 18). Recommendation for datasets 1–2 required ranking or all content items in the repository out of which only a part was used in the course.

## 6 Discussion and Future Work

While our work indicates a strong potential of the suggested approach, it has several problems, which we plan to address in the future work. Most importantly, our work revealed that the examples provided by instructors for a topic might not be exhaustive (i.e., using all intended concepts). While a group of related concepts is usually introduced in the same topic, only some of these concepts are usually illustrated in the code examples. In our future work, we are planning to extract the relationships between the programming concepts from Java ontology and assume that a group of closely related concepts is added as a whole to a unit once at least one concept is used in the examples.

# References

1. Moffatt, D. V., Moffatt, P. B.: Eighteen pascal texts: an objective comparison. SIGCSE Bull. **14**, **2**, 2–10 (1982)
2. Wang, S., He, F., Andersen, E.: A unified framework for knowledge assessment and progression analysis and design. In Proceedings of the 2017 CHI Conference on Human Factors in Computing Systems, pp. 937–948. ACM, New York (2017)
3. Hsiao, I.H., Sosnovsky, S., Brusilovsky, P.: Guiding students to the right questions: adaptive navigation support in an e-learning system for Java programming. J. Comput. Assist. Learn. **26**(4), 270–283 (2010)
4. Brusilovsky, P., Yudelson, M.V.: From WebEx to NavEx: interactive access to annotated program examples. Proc IEEE **96**, **6**, 990–999 (2008)
5. Murray, T.: Authoring intelligent tutoring systems: an analysis of the state of the art. Int. J. AIED **1**, **10** , 98–129 (1999)
6. Murray, T.: An overview of intelligent tutoring system authoring tools: updated analysis of the state of the art. In: Murray, T., Blessing, S.B., Ainsworth, S. (eds.) Authoring Tools for Advanced Technology Learning Environments: Toward Cost-Effective Adaptive, Interactive and Intelligent Educational So ware, pp. 491–544. Springer, Dordrecht (2003). https://doi.org/10.1007/978-94-017-0819-7_17
7. Sottilare, R.A.: Challenges to enhancing authoring tools and methods for intelligent tutoring systems. In: Sottilare, R.A., Graesser, A.C., Hu, X., Brawner, K. (eds.) Design Recommendations for Intelligent Tutoring Systems, pp. 3–7. U.S. Army Research Laboratory, Orlando, FL (2015)
8. Cristea, A., Aroyo, L.: Adaptive authoring of adaptive educational hypermedia. In: De Bra, P., Brusilovsky, P., Conejo, R. (eds.) AH 2002. LNCS, vol. 2347, pp. 122–132. Springer, Heidelberg (2002). https://doi.org/10.1007/3-540-47952-X_14
9. Brusilovsky, P., Sosnovsky, S., Yudelson, M., Chavan, G.: Interactive authoring support for adaptive educational systems. In: Proceedings of the 2005 Conference on AIED: Supporting Learning Through Intelligent and Socially Informed Technology, pp. 96–103. IOS Press, Amsterdam, The Netherlands (2005)
10. Brusilovsky, P., Eklund, J., Schwarz, E: Web-based education for all: a tool for developing adaptive courseware. In: Ashman, H., Thistewaite, P. (eds.) Proceedings of Seventh International World Wide Web Conference, Brisbane, Australia, 14–18 April 1998, pp. 291–300 (1998)
11. Hosseini, R., Brusilovsky, P.: JavaParser: a fine-grain concept indexing tool for java problems. In: The First Workshop on AI-supported Education for Computer Science, pp. 60–63. Springer, Heidelberg (2013)
12. Medio, C.D., Gasparetti, F., Limongelli, C., Sciarrone, F., Temperini, M.: Course-driven teacher modeling for learning objects recommendation in the Moodle LMS. In: Adjunct Publication of the 25th Conference on User Modeling, Adaptation and Personalization (UMAP 2017), pp. 141–145. ACM, New York (2017)

# Human-Agent Assessment: Interaction and Sub-skills Scoring for Collaborative Problem Solving

Pravin Chopade[1(✉)], Kristin Stoeffler[2], Saad M Khan[1], Yigal Rosen[1],
Spencer Swartz[1], and Alina von Davier[1]

[1] ACTNext, ACT Inc., Iowa City, IA, USA
pravin.chopade@act.org
[2] ACT Inc., Iowa City, IA, USA

**Abstract.** Collaborative problem solving (CPS) is one of the 21st century skills identified as a critical competency for education and workplace success. Students entering the workforce will be expected to have a level of proficiency with both cognitive and social-emotional skills. This paper presents an approach to measuring features and sub-skills associated with CPS ability and provides a methodology for CPS based performance assessment using an educational problem solving video game. Our method incorporates K-Means clustering to evaluate and analyze the feature space of the CPS evidence that was gathered from game log-data. Our results illustrate distinct participant clusters of high, medium and low-CPS skills proficiency levels that can help focus remediation efforts.

**Keywords:** Collaborative problem solving (CPS)
Human-agent interactions · Sub-skills · Performance assessment
Artificial intelligence · Machine learning

## 1 Introduction

Many 21st century skillsets have been identified as critical competencies for success across the Kindergarten to Career continuum. These skills include a broad range of cognitive and non-cognitive (social-emotional) skills such as creativity, communication and collaborative problem solving (CPS). Students entering the workforce will be expected to have a level of proficiency with these skills, but authentic insights for learners about their proficiency with these skills remain elusive [1, 2]. CPS consists of multiple skills, such as sharing resources, assimilation of knowledge and maintaining communication, which must be simultaneously present for successful outcomes [3–5]. This paper focuses on collaborative problem solving, a broad range of cross-cutting capabilities, which is part of an even broader Holistic Framework (HF) proposed by Camara et al. [6].

We present results from a study that utilized a game-based prototype, "Circuit Runner," to measure CPS facet abilities (five sub-skills) such as Problem Feature Analysis (PFA), Persistence (P), Perspective Taking (PT), Reaching the Goal (G) and

© Springer International Publishing AG, part of Springer Nature 2018
C. Penstein Rosé et al. (Eds.): AIED 2018, LNAI 10948, pp. 52–57, 2018.
https://doi.org/10.1007/978-3-319-93846-2_10

Establishing Strategy (S), as participants seek to solve challenges presented within the game. In the game a participant navigates a series of rooms/hallways in a 3-D circuit board maze (first person perspective) and is required to solve the challenges by collaborating with a "bot" (computer agent) via a chat panel [7]. We designed the dialog elements of this game in alignment with the CPS construct inspired by HF constructs in order to elicit skill evidence with a range of performance level options per facet. In our study, we recruited 500 participants using Amazon's Mechanical Turk (AMT) during the July/August 2017 timeframe to play the CPS game. Out of 500 study participants 355 provided complete and quality log data, we used these 355 participants' data (mean age: 34, median: 31) for the following research analysis.

## 2 Scoring Methods for CPS Skills

### 2.1 CPS* Score (Sub-skills Score)

In the "Circuit Runner" game, the human/computer agent dialog consists of pre-defined responses derived from dialog trees designed to align with sub-skill performance levels outlined in the CPS framework. Sub-skills (CPS*) scores are derived from dialog tree responses tagged to specific sub-skill levels as well as telemetry scoring from tasks designed to identify a range of performance levels for specific sub-skills. Figure 1 shows the CPS "Circuit Runner" game User Interface (UI) and a sample of the different game components [7].

**Fig. 1.** CPS "Circuit Runner" game components-user interface and conversation flow (CF).

In the game, data logs were generated through specific interactions. The Conversation Flow (CF) is the record of the dialog between the participant (player) and the bot (computer agent). To explore these skills, in the chat panel, the computer agent presents an initial prompt (the prompt is derived from the dialog tree) and then a set of response options from which the player must select, aligned with the four levels (0, 1, 2, 3) of the sub-skills presented in the CPS framework. The CPS* score is given by Eq. (1),

$$CPS^* = \frac{1}{m}\sum_{i=1}^{m}\left(\frac{1}{n}\sum_{1}^{n}G, \frac{1}{n}\sum_{1}^{n}P, \frac{1}{n}\sum_{1}^{n}PFA, \frac{1}{n}\sum_{1}^{n}PT, \frac{1}{n}\sum_{1}^{n}S\right) \qquad (1)$$

Where, $n$ is the number of common nodes within the dialog tree per sub-skill (may vary across sub-skills); $G, P, PFA, PT$ and $S$ are sub-skills; $m$ is number of sub-skills (five sub-skills are measured in the current version of the game). Response levels (the four levels) are based on the dialog in which the response appears, as well as the context of game-play and previous dialog (prompt/response) set.

## 2.2 Interaction Score (IS)

Interaction scores are calculated based on the player and bot (agent) conversation flow (CF). Interactions are measured with parameters such as effective conversation flow (between human-agent), the distance travelled in an attempt to complete game tasks, and time spent in collaborative interaction. The conversation flow data log is arranged in rows, and records all of the dialog response selections, with a prompt row followed by a transition row, which generates the conversation flow frames. Using these game interaction elements (obtained from telemetry data) user-agent interaction scores are calculated. Sub-components of the interaction score are listed below:

*Effective Conversation (EC)* The conversation which led to a selection of a response initiating a player to engage in successful game activities. EC led participants to follow pathways through common dialog tree nodes with minimum time.

*Conversation Flow Scores (CFS)* were calculated based on conversation flow frames.

*Interactions Count (IC)* is the total number of interactions between the participant and the bot throughout the entire game play. IC indicates the participants' level of interaction with the computer agent as the player attempts to complete the required game tasks. IC is also an important indicator for minimum and maximum time spent in successive game interactions. Minimum and maximum response times (while interacting through prompt and response session) are useful indicators for deciding or evaluating the participants' sub-skill levels.

Based on these (above listed) interaction sub-components, the interaction score (IS) is calculated using Eq. (2) below:

$$SP_i = \left(\frac{CFF_i}{DI_i} * TI_i\right) \qquad (2)$$

Where, $SP_i$: The interaction score for user '$i$'; $CFF$: Conversation flow frames (prompt/response sets) per interaction; $DI$: Distance travelled during interaction. The distance travelled in the game at the time during which the score event was generated; $TI$: Time spent during interaction. Total interaction time in second(s); $i$: Game participant/player/user.

In order to mitigate time as controlling factor for the interaction score, we modified Eq. (2) and used log of TI. The modified interaction scoring is given by Eq. (3), and normalized interaction score is given by Eq. (4),

$$SP_i = \left( \frac{CFF_i}{DI_i} * \log(TI_i) \right); \tag{3}$$

$$IS_i = 1 - \frac{SP_i}{\sum_i^N SP_i} \tag{4}$$

This set of equations helps us map the participants' collaborative interactions and its relation to the participants' skill levels (skill matrix) which in turn contributes towards the participants' overall CPS performance.

## 3   Interaction and CPS* (Sub-skills) Score Analysis

In this study, we used 355 AMT participants' data for research analysis. Data collected as part of the study includes in-game data such as object clicks, communicative exchanges, distance, duration, time stamp, location and dialog tree node choices. Using the IS and CPS* scoring methods, we carried out different machine learning analyses using MATLAB [8] for the above listed in-game data. The outcomes consist of manifold clustering analyses of the evidence delivered over a series of game plays that is based on approaches defined by the Artificial Intelligence (AI)/educational data mining communities [9–11]. We performed cluster analysis using CPS* and IS as features. For IS we used the K-Means clustering algorithm and varied the 'k' value from 1 to 10 clusters and used the average Silhouette method [12] for selection of the optimal 'k' value. With the optimal value, k = 3, we obtained three clusters as shown in Fig. 2. Clustering analysis found that the data was largely a continuous normal distribution and provide evidence about the participants' high, mid and low performance levels.

Results indicated a high degree of usability, with a reasonable ability of challenges to detect differences in performance across small groups of individuals, suggesting that further use of the game for additional and larger experiments to explore targeted relationships between game play, personality variables, and achievement.

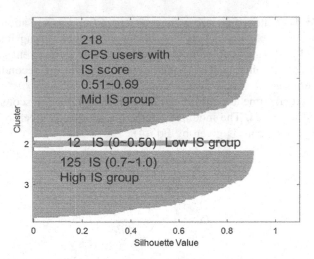

**Fig. 2.** Game participants clusters using K-Means for k = 3 based on IS.

## 4  Discussion

In this paper we presented an approach to identify evidence and subsequently score individuals on CPS skills using a custom designed interactive game called 'Circuit Runner'. We developed measures of collaborative interaction skills CPS* and the IS scores that can be used to compute the users' CPS overall performance index. The CPS performance index will be an important indicator for 21st century education and workforce success. Our future work will target comparing clusters obtained through the CPS* method with the IS based clusters and validating IS scores for a multi-user environment.

**Acknowledgements.** The authors would like to thank Andrew Cantine - ACTNext Technical Editor for editing this work. We are also thankful to ACT, Inc. for their ongoing support as this paper took shape.

## References

1. OECD: PISA 2015 results in focus, Paris, France (2016)
2. Fiore, S., Graesser, A., Greiff, S., Griffin, P., Gong, B., Kyllonen, P., Massey, C., O'Neil, H., Pellegrino, J., Rothman, R., Soulé, H., von Davier, A.: Collaborative problem solving: considerations for the National Assessment of Educational Progress. In: IES, National Center for Education Statistics (NCES), April 2017
3. Rosen, Y.: Assessing students in human-to-agent settings to inform collaborative problem solving learning. J. Educ. Meas. **54**(1), 36–53 (2017)
4. Care, E., Scoular, C., Griffin, P.: Assessment of collaborative problem solving in education environments. Appl. Meas. Educ. **29**(4), 250–264 (2016)
5. von Davier, A., Zhu, M., Kyllonen, P. (eds.): Innovative assessment of collaboration. Springer, Cham (2017). https://doi.org/10.1007/978-3-319-33261-1

6. Camera, W., O'Connor, R., Mattern, K., Hanson, M.: Beyond academics: a holistic framework for enhancing education and workplace success. In: ACT Research Report Series no. 4 (2015)

7. Stoeffler, K., Rosen, Y., von Davier, A.A.: Exploring the measurement of collaborative problem solving using a human-agent educational game. In: Proceedings of the Seventh International Learning Analytics & Knowledge Conference (LAK 2017), pp. 570–571 (2017)

8. Mathworks Inc.: MATLAB - Statistics and Machine Learning Toolbox

9. Polyak, S., von Davier, A.A., Peterschmidt, K.: Computational psychometrics for the measurement of CPS skills. Front. Psychol. **8**, 20–29 (2017)

10. Bauckhage, C., Drachen, A., Sifa, R.: Clustering game behavior data. IEEE Trans. Comput. Intell. AI Games **7**(3), 266–278 (2015)

11. Khan, S.M.: Multimodal behavioral analytics in intelligent learning and assessment systems. In: von Davier, A.A., Zhu, M., Kyllonen, P.C. (eds.) Innovative Assessment of Collaboration. MEMA, pp. 173–184. Springer, Cham (2017). https://doi.org/10.1007/978-3-319-33261-1_11

12. Rousseeuw, P.: Silhouettes: a graphical aid to the interpretation and validation of cluster analysis. J. Comput. Appl. Math. **20**, 53–65 (1987)

# Investigation of the Influence of Hint Type on Problem Solving Behavior in a Logic Proof Tutor

Christa Cody[✉], Behrooz Mostafavi, and Tiffany Barnes

North Carolina State University, Raleigh, USA
{cncody,bzmostaf,tmbarnes}@ncsu.edu

**Abstract.** Within intelligent tutoring systems, hint policies are needed to determine when and how to give hints and what type of hint is most beneficial. In this study, we focus on discovering whether certain hint types influence problem solving behavior. We investigate the influence of two hint types (next-step hints and more abstract high-level hints) on students' behavior in a college-level logic proof tutor, Deep Thought. The results suggest that hint types can affect student behavior, including hint usage, rule applications, and time in-tutor.

**Keywords:** Tutoring system · Hint type · Data-driven

## 1 Introduction

Intelligent tutoring systems (ITS) provide adaptive instruction to students and have significant effects on learning [1]. Data-driven methods, where actions within the tutor are based on analyzing historical data, have been used to great effect to individualize computer-aided instruction [2–4]. Within an ITS, hint policies are needed to determine when and how to give hints and what type of hint is most beneficial [5]. The most minimal hint type is error-specific feedback, which provides a hint regarding an error the student has made [5]. However, research has suggested that goal-directed feedback leads to better performance by providing students with direction in solving the problem [6]. A common approach is to provide a sequence of hints beginning with a more general hint then transition to more specific and directive hints (e.g. Point, Teach, and Bottom-out [7]). However, students may benefit from receiving a certain hint type over another, so providing hints in a strict sequence might limit the effectiveness of receiving hints. Some research has created individualized hint policies based on student behavior and ability, allowing the student to receive the appropriate hint without stepping through strict levels of hints [8,9]. Additionally, research has shown that high ability learners benefit from lower amounts or more abstract guidance while low ability learners benefit from higher amounts or more concrete guidance [10,11]. The goal of this work is to determine if hint type influences student's performance and behavior.

© Springer International Publishing AG, part of Springer Nature 2018
C. Penstein Rosé et al. (Eds.): AIED 2018, LNAI 10948, pp. 58–62, 2018.
https://doi.org/10.1007/978-3-319-93846-2_11

## 2    Method

We tested our two hint types in a propositional logic proof tutor, Deep Thought [2,12], as assigned homework in a two sections of a college-level discrete mathematics course taught by the same instructor in Fall 2016. The tutor presents worked examples and problems consisting of logical premises and a conclusion to be derived using logical axioms, and is divided into 6 levels. At the end of each level, the student is presented with a final problem with no hints, which serves as a level posttest. Hint type was randomly assigned for Next Step Hints (NSH, n = 48) or High Level Hints (HLH, n = 47) before tutor use. Students who collaborated or dropped out of the tutor were removed (NSH n = 12, HLH n = 11), because their data would skew time and step features. Therefore, the following analyses were based on data from 36 NSH and 36 HLH students. To analyze the specific influences hint type has on student problem solving, each condition provided one of two hint types: **Next-Step Hints (NSH)** or **High-Level Hints (HLH)**. Next-step hints suggest the next step of a logic proof that can be immediately implemented in the student's current proof – providing more explicit instruction. Whereas, high-level hints represent hints that can be 2 or 3 possible rule applications ahead of the current proof state [13]. High-level hints are aimed at helping the student develop a strategy. There is a significant problem regarding help avoidance where students may avoid asking for hints even when they might need them [14], so we implemented proactive hints by providing a hint when the student is taking longer than the median time to correctly complete a single step.

### 2.1    Description of Metrics

To examine the effects of hint types, we focused on behavior- and performance-related features. In Level 1, all students receive the same set of problems and are not given any worked examples. Therefore, the student's performance on Level 1 is used as a **pretest** to measure their incoming knowledge. The average performance of Levels 3–6 is used as a **posttest** to measure their post-training performance. Additionally, all students were evaluated using two proof problem questions as part of a mid-term examination. **Total Correct/Incorrect Steps** are the number of correct/incorrect rule applications over the course of the whole tutor. **Mean/Median Correct Step Time** and **Mean/Median Incorrect Step Time** represent the mean/median time between steps (correct and incorrect, respectively) for each student. **Total Time to Complete** is the total time spent solving a problem in minutes. **Final Solution Length** is the number of derivations made to reach the conclusion in the final solution. We also analyzed the number of hints requested, proactive hints, and total hints received.

The data is positively skewed so we transformed it using a log transform then applied ANOVA to find significant differences between the groups. We examined the metrics for the end of level problems (containing no hints) to discover differences in problem solving that may be affected by the hint type.

## 3   Results and Discussion

First, we looked at the performance metrics, which did not show any significant differences between the groups. Next, we analyzed the differences between students behavior using the end of level problems, which allows a view of how the hints may be shaping the behavior of a student's problem solving. For the sake of space, we selected representative problems and only report behaviors that are indicative of differences between the two groups. In Table 1, the HLH group took significantly less time solving the problem and with significantly less incorrect steps. However, the HLH group spent approximately the same amount of time (p = 0.641) on Level 1, which means that they spent longer during the initial few problems before speeding up in the end of level problem.

**Table 1.** Stats and significant ANOVA results for the end of level problem for Level 1

| End of level problem - Level 1 | | | | | |
| --- | --- | --- | --- | --- | --- |
| Metric | NSH (n = 36) | | HLH (n = 36) | | |
| | Mean(SD) | Median | Mean(SD) | Median | p-value |
| Total incorrect steps | 5(5) | 1 | 2(2) | 0 | 0.296 |
| Total correct steps | 6(5) | 4 | 5(1) | 4 | 0.200 |
| Time to complete (min) | 7.3(12) | 2.3 | 3.2(4.2) | 1.6 | .0365* |
| Median correct step time (s) | 63(122) | 26 | 34(39) | 23 | 0.067 |

In Table 2, the NSH group has significantly more correct steps (p = 0.007) and marginally more incorrect steps (p = 0.062). Due to the nature of the tutor and solving proofs, students may make as many derivations as they want; however, having higher correct and incorrect steps is indicative of gaming behavior. The NSH group also spent significantly longer on this problem (p = 0.002).

**Table 2.** Stats and significant ANOVA results for the end of level problem for Level 3

| End of level problem - Level 3 | | | | | |
| --- | --- | --- | --- | --- | --- |
| Metric | NSH (n = 36) | | HLH (n = 36) | | |
| | Mean(SD) | Median | Mean(SD) | Median | p-value |
| Total incorrect steps | 16(25) | 6 | 5(7) | 2 | 0.062 |
| Total correct steps | 13(9) | 8 | 9(3) | 7 | 0.007* |
| Time to complete (min) | 26.2(69) | 4 | 4.5(4) | 3 | 0.002* |
| Mean incorrect step time (s) | 80(101) | 45 | 48(29) | 37 | 0.089 |
| Mean correct step time (s) | 72(115) | 29 | 33(33) | 23 | 0.015* |

In Table 3, the NSH had significantly more incorrect steps (p = 0.042), took longer to complete the problem (p = 0.021), took longer to correctly apply rules (p = 0.042), and had a longer final solution (p = 0.058). These metrics indicate that the NSH group has less knowledge or strategy to solve the problem as compared to the HLH group.

**Table 3.** Stats and significant ANOVA results for the end of level problem for Level 5

| End of level problem - Level 5 | | | | | |
|---|---|---|---|---|---|
| Metric | NSH (n = 36) | | HLH (n = 36) | | |
| | Mean(SD) | Median | Mean(SD) | Median | p-value |
| Total incorrect steps | 24.05(44) | 8.5 | 11.2(14) | 5 | 0.042* |
| Total correct steps | 20.15(18) | 13.5 | 16.15(12) | 12.5 | 0.687 |
| Time to complete (min) | 36.1(60) | 11.5 | 13.2(22.8) | 6.7 | 0.021* |
| Mean incorrect step time (s) | 466(2060) | 54.4 | 61(64) | 43.6 | 0.066 |
| Mean correct step time (s) | 124(262) | 33.7 | 37(24) | 28.6 | 0.042* |
| Final solution length | 10.5(3) | 10 | 9.5(2) | 9 | 0.058* |

During the course of the tutor, there is a widening gap between NSH and HLH group with respect to the time it takes to complete the problem, the amount of incorrect steps made, and final solution length. One possibility for this difference in behavior is HLH are promoting strategy-oriented behavior, which, if so, we would expect the students to make fewer mistakes and less steps because they would be planning out a few steps ahead thus less likely to go down an incorrect path. Another possibility is the NSH students could have been using the hints to directly discover what to do next, which could have led to gaming behavior [15].

## 4    Conclusion and Future Work

In this study, we compared two test conditions of Deep Thought, HLH and NSH hint groups, to further the understanding of the impact of hint type on the behavior of students during problem solving. We found that students receiving HLH seem to produce more positive in-tutor behavior resulting in less incorrect steps and less time spent during end of level problems, while students in the NSH group seemed to have less desirable in-tutor behavior, including larger amounts of incorrect steps. Even though there were no significant differences in the performance metrics, longer time spent solving a problem and learned strategies are a large concern due to possible transfer of behavior outside of the tutor. Large amounts of incorrect steps, especially occurring closer together, are indicative of gaming the tutor to finish a proof.

To further explore the influences of hint type, we will be conducting a more in-depth study of the behavior surrounding hints, including how long it took the student to derive a hint, and what type of behavior indicates when each type of hint is beneficial. This can be further analyzed by looking into how and which hints are followed. A more formal posttest will be used in future evaluations to provide more insight to the students' learning over the course of the tutor.

# References

1. Murray, T.: Authoring intelligent tutoring systems: an analysis of the state of the art. Int. J. Artif. Intell. Educ. **10**, 98–129 (1999)
2. Mostafavi, B., Barnes, T.: Evolution of an intelligent deductive logic tutor using data-driven elements. Int. J. Artif. Intell. Educ. **27**, 1–32 (2016)
3. Stamper, J., Eagle, M., Barnes, T., Croy, M.: Experimental evaluation of automatic hint generation for a logic tutor. Int. J. Artif. Intell. Educ. **22**(1–2), 3–17 (2013)
4. Fossati, D., Di Eugenio, B., Ohlsson, S., Brown, C., Chen, L.: Data driven automatic feedback generation in the ilist intelligent tutoring system. Technol. Instr. Cogn. Learn. **10**(1), 5–26 (2015)
5. Vanlehn, K.: The behavior of tutoring systems. Int. J. Artif. Intell. Educ. **16**(3), 227–265 (2006)
6. McKendree, J.: Effective feedback content for tutoring complex skills. Hum.-Comput. Interact. **5**(4), 381–413 (1990)
7. Hume, G., Michael, J., Rovick, A., Evens, M.: Hinting as a tactic in one-on-one tutoring. J. Learn. Sci. **5**(1), 23–47 (1996)
8. Stern, M., Beck, J., Woolf, B.P.: Adaptation of problem presentation and feedback in an intelligent mathematics tutor. In: Frasson, C., Gauthier, G., Lesgold, A. (eds.) ITS 1996. LNCS, vol. 1086, pp. 605–613. Springer, Heidelberg (1996). https://doi.org/10.1007/3-540-61327-7_160
9. Anohina, A.: Advances in intelligent tutoring systems: problem-solving modes and model of hints. Int. J. Comput. Commun. Control **2**(1), 48–55 (2007)
10. Arroyo, I., Beck, J.E., Woolf, B.P., Beal, C.R., Schultz, K.: Macroadapting animalwatch to gender and cognitive differences with respect to hint interactivity and symbolism. In: Gauthier, G., Frasson, C., VanLehn, K. (eds.) ITS 2000. LNCS, vol. 1839, pp. 574–583. Springer, Heidelberg (2000). https://doi.org/10.1007/3-540-45108-0_61
11. Luckin, R., Du Boulay, B., et al.: Ecolab: the development and evaluation of a Vygotskian design framework. Int. J. Artif. Intell. Educ. **10**(2), 198–220 (1999)
12. Mostafavi, B., Eagle, M., Barnes, T.: Towards data-driven mastery learning. In: Proceedings of the Fifth International Conference on Learning Analytics and Knowledge, pp. 270–274. ACM (2015)
13. Eagle, M., Johnson, M., Barnes, T.: Interaction networks: generating high level hints based on network community clustering. International Educational Data Mining Society (2012)
14. Aleven, V., Koedinger, K.R.: Limitations of student control: do students know when they need help? In: Gauthier, G., Frasson, C., VanLehn, K. (eds.) ITS 2000. LNCS, vol. 1839, pp. 292–303. Springer, Heidelberg (2000). https://doi.org/10.1007/3-540-45108-0_33
15. Baker, R.S., Corbett, A.T., Koedinger, K.R.: Detecting student misuse of intelligent tutoring systems. In: Lester, J.C., Vicari, R.M., Paraguaçu, F. (eds.) ITS 2004. LNCS, vol. 3220, pp. 531–540. Springer, Heidelberg (2004). https://doi.org/10.1007/978-3-540-30139-4_50

# Modeling Math Success
# Using Cohesion Network Analysis

Scott A. Crossley[1]([⊠]), Maria-Dorinela Sirbu[2], Mihai Dascalu[2],
Tiffany Barnes[3], Collin F. Lynch[3], and Danielle S. McNamara[4]

[1] Department of Applied Linguistics/ESL, Georgia State University,
Atlanta, GA 30303, USA
scrossley@gsu.edu
[2] University Politehnica of Bucharest, Splaiul Independenței 313,
60042 Bucharest, Romania
maria.sirbu@cti.pub.ro, mihai.dascalu@cs.pub.ro
[3] North Carolina State University, Raleigh, NC 27607, USA
tiffany.barnes@gmail.com, cflynch@ncsu.edu
[4] Institute for the Science of Teaching & Learning, Arizona State University,
Tempe, AZ, USA
dsmcnama@asu.edu

**Abstract.** This study examines math success within a blended undergraduate
course using a Cohesion Network Analysis (CNA) approach while controlling
for individual differences and click-stream variables that may also predict math
success. Linear models indicated that math success was related to days spent on
the forum and by students who more regularly posted in the online class forum
and whose posts generally followed the semanticity of other students.

**Keywords:** Math success · Cohesion Network Analysis
Online learning · NLP

## 1   Introduction

Recent research linking math success and linguistic productions indicate that students
who produce language that is more syntactically complex and less cohesive do better in
math college-level classes. In addition, click-stream findings suggest that students who
are more active in on-line classroom discussion forums are also more likely to receive
higher math grades [1]. This research helps to link language production and on-line
activity to math performance.

The current study builds on these finding by examining the linguistic properties of
the online discussion forums using Cohesion Network Analysis (CNA; Dascalu et al.
[2]) metrics. CNA metrics can be used to estimate cohesion between text segments
based on similarity measures of semantic proximity and enable the analysis of discourse structures within collaborative conversations such as those found in online
discussion forums [3]. In practice, CNA metrics can examine student language productions within educational tutoring systems to investigate whether forum posts are on
topic, are more related to other student posts, are more central to the conversation, or

© Springer International Publishing AG, part of Springer Nature 2018
C. Penstein Rosé et al. (Eds.): AIED 2018, LNAI 10948, pp. 63–67, 2018.
https://doi.org/10.1007/978-3-319-93846-2_12

induce higher collaboration. Our goal is to examine links between CNA metrics and final scores in a discrete math class to better understand how collaboration can influence success as well as parse out differences between cohesion and on-line forum activity reported in earlier studies [1].

## 2 Method

### 2.1 Classroom Data

We use the same data as reported Crossley et al. [1]. Briefly, the discrete math course was offered to undergraduate students in a computer science department. The course was blended and included standard lectures, office hours, and support from online tools. The tools included a standard question-answering forum for students, teaching assistants, and instructors. Data for this study was collected in 2013 from 250 students (a number of whom were peer-tutors within the class). Click-stream data included how many times students made, or answered posts, and how many days students visited the forum. Forum post data was extracted at the end of the course. Of the 250 students, 157 made posts on the forum.

### 2.2 Cohesion Network Analysis

In CNA, cohesion is computationally represented as an average value of similarity measures (or an aggregated score) between semantic distances resulting in a *cohesion graph* [3] that represents a proxy for the semantic content of discourse and active engagement within discourse. This approach differs from measuring cohesion in language produced by a single participant (e.g., number of connectives produced in a writing sample) because it focuses on cohesion within a community of participants. The cohesion graph is a multi-layered structure containing different nodes and the links between them. A central node, representing a conversation thread, is divided into contributions, which are further divided into sentences and words. Links are then built between nodes in order to determine a cohesion score that denotes the relevance of a contribution within the conversation, or the impact of a word within a sentence or contribution. Other links are generated between adjacent contributions, which are used to determine changes in topics or in the overall conversation thread. These changes are reflected by cohesion gaps between units of texts.

From the links within the cohesion graph, longitudinal analyses following weekly timeframes in terms of social knowledge-building (KB) processes and CNA indices (e.g., in-degree, out-degree) are derived and quantified [2]. Social KB relates to the dialog between at least two participants supporting collaboration, while CNA indices reflect Social Network Analysis metrics applied on the sociogram (i.e., an interaction graph among all participants). Our longitudinal analysis was performed by taking into account the distribution of each participant's level of CNA involvement within the imposed timeframe, followed by the usage of global CNA metrics (e.g., average CNA scores, standard deviation, entropy, recurrence, degree of uniformity) to describe participant's evolution within the time series.

## 2.3    Statistical Analyses

Linear regression models were computed to assess the degree to which CNA features in the students' forum writing, along with other click-stream and individual difference variables (i.e., was the student a peer tutor in the class) were predictive of students' final math scores. Assumptions of linear modeling were checked prior to analysis (i.e., normality and multicollinearity) leaving seven CNA variables and six click-stream and individual difference variables for the final models. Model selection and interpretation was based on $t$ and $p$ values for fixed effects and visual inspection of residuals distribution for non-standardized variables. We developed and compared two models: (a) a baseline linear model including click-stream and individual difference variables (i.e., non-linguistic effects) and (b) a model including both CNA and non-linguistic features. We compared the strength between the two models using Analyses of Variance (ANOVAs).

# 3    Results

## 3.1    Click-Stream and Individual Differences Data

Our first model examined the potential for click-stream data to predict math success. During initial analyses, four outliers had to be removed to ensure the assumptions of the linear model were met ($N = 153$). A final model using these 153 students revealed significant effects for whether the student was a tutor or not, the number of days on the forum, and the number of forum posts answered. Table 1 displays the coefficients, standard error, $t$ values, and $p$ values for each of the significant click-stream and individual difference variables. The model was significant, $F(4, 148) = 7.354$, $p < .001$, $r = .407$, $R^2 = .166$. Post-hoc analyses indicated no multicollinearity in the model, normally distributed residuals, and no homoscedasticity. The non-linguistic variables explained around 17% of the variance and indicated that higher math scores were best predicted by students who acted as peer tutors, students who spent more time on the forum, and students that answered more forum posts (i.e., were more engaged).

**Table 1.** Click-stream model for predicting math scores

| Fixed effect | Coefficient | Std. error | $t$ |
|---|---|---|---|
| (Intercept) | 86.237 | 1.061 | 81.314*** |
| Is a peer tutor | 3.881 | 1.400 | 2.772** |
| Is not a peer tutor | 4.401 | 1.484 | 2.967** |
| Days on forum | 0.024 | 0.009 | 2.655** |
| Forum posts answered | 0.174 | 0.115 | 1.516 |

Note * $p < .050$, ** $p < .010$, ***$p < .001$

## 3.2  Full Model

Our full model examined the potential for click-stream, individual difference, and CNA variables to predict math success for the 153 students in our final dataset. The linear model for this analysis revealed significant effects for days on forum, average recurrence for the CNA indegree metric, and degree of uniformity for the Social KB metric. Table 2 displays the coefficients, standard error, $t$ values, and $p$ values for each of the significant CNA variables. The model was significant, $F(3, 149) = 12.120$, $p < .001$, $r = .443$, $R^2 = .196$. An ANOVA comparison between the full model, and the non-linguistic model demonstrated significant differences ($p < .001$) in variance explained for both. Post-hoc analyses indicated no multicollinearity in the model, normally distributed residuals, and no homoscedasticity. The click-stream and the CNA variables explained around 20% of the variance and indicated that higher math scores were best predicted by students who had lower recurrence (i.e., distance expressed as number of weeks between two consecutive timeframes with non-zero values) of postings that generated collaborative effects (both Social KB and CNA indegree) with other participants. If participants regularly contribute in each consecutive timeframes from the longitudinal analysis, their corresponding recurrence score is zero; in contrast, if additional successive weeks are skipped, their recurrence scores increase. In contrast to CNA scores that denote active involvement, recurrence quantifies unbalance and inconsistent participation over time.

**Table 2.** Full model (click-stream and CNA variables) for predicting math scores.

| Fixed effect | Coefficient | Std. error | $t$ |
|---|---|---|---|
| (Intercept) | 83.994 | 3.257 | 25.793*** |
| Days on forum | 0.024 | 0.008 | 2.819 |
| Average recurrence scores (In Degree) | –0.566 | 0.219 | –2.589* |
| Degree of uniformity Social KB | 9.497 | 3.992 | 2.379* |

Note * $p < .050$, ** $p < .010$, ***$p < .001$

Moreover, social KB quantifies whether a participant's post generated follow-up contributions from other course participants (i.e., collaboration perceived as a CNA outdegree effect targeted at different members), whereas indegree reflects the in-edge relations produced by a post in a specific timeframe. Thus, social KB can be also perceived as a more refined measure for quantifying the value of students' forum posts by measuring the influence each post has on subsequent contributions.

## 4  Discussion and Conclusion

This study analyzed success within a blended undergraduate math course using a CNA approach. Linear models demonstrated that math success was predicted by the number of days spent on the forum and by the regularity of forum posts that generated collaborative effects (i.e., posts that precipitated discussion among other students). The results indicate that language collaboration is an important component of success in blended math courses such that students who linguistically encouraged greater collective efforts among students generally received higher final scores.

All CNA metrics are fully automated and the results from this study may have important implications for increasing student involvement in online systems through feedback provided in near real-time. However, it is important to remember that CNA mostly reflects behavior traits in terms of online active participations that differentiates between highly and less performant students.

**Acknowledgements.** This research was supported in part by the National Science Foundation (DRL-1418378). Ideas expressed in this material are those of the authors and do not necessarily reflect the views of the National Science Foundation. In addition, this research was partially supported by the 644187 EC H2020 *Realising an Applied Gaming Eco-system* (RAGE) project and by the FP7 2008-212578 LTfLL project.

# References

1. Crossley, S.A., Barnes, T., Lynch, C., McNamara, D.S.: Linking language to math success in a blended course. In: Proceedings of the 10th International Conference on Educational Data Mining (EDM), pp. 180–185, Springer, Wuhan (2017)
2. Dascalu, M., McNamara, D.S., Trausan-Matu, S., Allen, L.K.: Cohesion network analysis of CSCL participation. Behav. Res. Methods, **50**(2), 604–619 (2017). https://doi.org/10.3758/s13428-017-0888-4
3. Crossley, S., Dascalu, M., Baker, R., McNamara, D.S., Trausan-Matu, S.: Predicting success in massive open online courses (MOOC) using cohesion network analysis. In: 12th International Conference on Computer Supported Collaborative Learning (CSCL), pp. 103–110. International Society of the Learning Sciences, Philadelphia (2017)

# Amplifying Teachers Intelligence in the Design of Gamified Intelligent Tutoring Systems

Diego Dermeval[1(✉)], Josmário Albuquerque[1], Ig Ibert Bittencourt[1],
Julita Vassileva[2], Wansel Lemos[1], Alan Pedro da Silva[1], and Ranilson Paiva[1]

[1] Center of Excellence for Social Technologies,
Federal University of Alagoas, Maceió, AL, Brazil
diego.matos@penedo.ufal.br
[2] Department of Computer Science, University of Saskatchewan,
Saskatoon, SK, Canada

**Abstract.** Researchers are increasingly interested in using gamification along with Intelligent Tutoring Systems (ITS) to motivate action, promote learning, facilitate problem-solving, and to drive desired learning behaviors. In fact, although the desire of teachers to be active users of gamified ITS, these systems are not personalized according to teachers' preferences. Several research problems might arise when trying to empower teachers in the design of gamified ITS, for instance, the high complexity and variability of features to manage, the need to consider theories and design practices, and the need of providing simple and usable solutions for them. In this work, we propose a gamified ITS authoring tool that supports authoring (fully or partially) of the domain, gamification and pedagogical models of gamified ITS by teachers. We investigate how different versions of the tool are perceived by users assuming the role of teachers. Our results indicate a positive attitude towards the use of the authoring tool, in which participants agreed that they are easy to use, usable, simple, aesthetically appealing, have a well-perceived system support and high credibility.

**Keywords:** ITS Authoring tools · Gamification
Intelligent Tutoring Systems · Gamified intelligent tutoring systems

## 1 Introduction

To enhance student motivation and engagement during instruction, researchers have been increasingly using gamification along with Intelligent Tutoring Systems (ITS) [1–4]. The use of gamification in ITS target achieving better results and to create enhanced solutions and experiences [5].

However, teachers are interested in actively using adaptive educational systems. For example, recent surveys of trainee teachers in the US [6] identified access to adaptive technologies as a key determinant of future teaching success,

C. Penstein Rosé et al. (Eds.): AIED 2018, LNAI 10948, pp. 68–73, 2018.
https://doi.org/10.1007/978-3-319-93846-2_13

while a survey of 1,000 public middle-school teachers in Brazil [7] found that 80% were interested in the potential of adaptive learning. Teachers also say that games enable them to differentiate instruction (60%) and to create classrooms that are more learner-centric (44%) [6] and that by using gamification they can motivate their students [8].

Moreover, as argued by Baker [9], we probably need tutors that are designed intelligently, and that leverage human intelligence (e.g., teachers), rather than relying only on artificial intelligence. But, to amplify the active participation of teachers in the design of gamified ITS combining teachers and artificial intelligence, we must face several research problems [10]. For instance, designing these systems include dealing with a huge variability [11] and all feature combinations might not be necessarily effective for learners [12]. Gamification, ITS theories, and design practices should also be considered to constrain the design space of gamified ITS [13] to aid designing more effective tutors. In addition, assuming that a teacher intends to customize such a complex system, it is imperative to make the design process simple, usable and not demanding advanced technical skills, e.g., on programming, artificial intelligence and/or software engineering [14].

In this work, we propose an authoring tool to design gamified ITS for teachers. It implements a process that leverages teachers intelligence in the domain, pedagogical and gamification models of the gamified ITS development process as well as supports extra configurations (e.g., reports presented, evaluation methods, and so on). It also allows the customization of gamified ITS features in two alternative flows, one creating a gamified tutor from scratch and the other applying a configuration template.

## 2 Authoring Gamified Intelligent Tutoring Systems

A gamified ITS development process was defined considering the four classic ITS components as well as a gamification model and extra ITS features. The activities are abstract enough to allow gamified ITS designers to use whatever sub-activities they need to develop their systems. This flexibility might be important since there is no agreement in the literature regarding the types of ITS, features to consider, and technologies to use in the development of ITS [10].

The gamification model should consider all the features related to the inclusion of gamification in the ITS. For instance, game design elements (i.e., dynamic, mechanic and components [15]) to include in a gamified ITS and how these elements are connected (e.g., gamification design, i.e., activity loops [15]) to the learning contents, instruction and student knowledge behavior in the domain. Moreover, this model might also take into account strategies for personalizing the gamification and/or the tutor according to student characteristics (e.g., player type [16]).

An ontological model connecting gamification theories, frameworks and design practices to ITS concepts (e.g., the Gamified Tutoring Ontology [4]) aids the customization of gamified ITS by constraining the design space for the teachers. Additionally, the role of such ontology for interoperating our authoring tool and a third-party gamified ITS (e.g., based on the architecture proposed by Dermeval et al. [17]) is twofold. First, it contains the knowledge about the domain model created by the teacher, which can be reasoned by a gamified ITS. Second, it also contains the decision on which a gamification target behavior is selected by a teacher which can be used by a gamified ITS to activate several activity loops in the system.

In the gamified ITS authoring tool, we incorporate features that allow reuse of previous ITS configurations (e.g., apply a template, reuse curriculum, and reuse educational resources) to decrease the effort required from teachers to author gamified ITS. We also include features that allow teachers to select a pre-configured set of game design elements by choosing a target behavior or to select particular game design elements to be included in the authored gamified ITS. Figure 1 illustrates the prototypes on which teachers may choose if they want to configure a tutor from scratch or apply an existing template configuration in the system (in the left). Figure 1 also shows how a teacher may select a gamification target behavior during the authoring process (in the right).

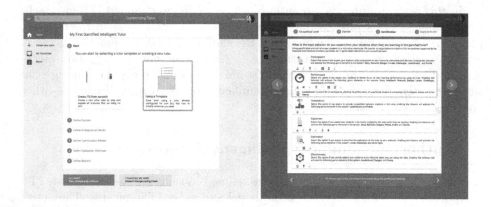

**Fig. 1.** Prototypes of the gamified ITS authoring tool

## 3   Experiment Design

Our experiment intended to analyze the prototypes combining two ways for authoring (template or scratch) vs. two ways for gamification authoring (selecting target behaviors or game design elements) to evaluate them with respect to several metrics such as perceived ease of use, perceived usability, complexity, aesthetics, novelty, unity, intensity, attitude towards use, perceived system support, and credibility from the viewpoint of teachers in the context of graduate students and researchers, from two research groups in Brazil and Canada, analyzing the prototypes and answering a survey[1]. A $2 \times 2$ between-subjects design

---

[1] Available at https://fluidsurveys.usask.ca/s/agits-survey/.

was used, on which 57 participants were shown only one of the four possible versions of the prototypes. Note that the version in which a participant evaluated the prototypes were randomly allocated. Participants were asked to answer questions regarding the prototypes and a Likert scale was used for measuring the variables.

We identified that there is statistical significance for stating that the aesthetics (adjusted p-value of 0.0333912) and perceived system support (adjusted p-value of 0.0208950) of the version 1 (template and behavior) are better than of the version 2 (scratch and behavior). These results might suggest that the prototypes that present customization by template and gamification authoring by selecting a behavior (version 1) may be more aesthetically appealing as well as give more support to aid performing the task required than version 2, which includes prototypes for customizing features from scratch and authoring gamification by selecting a target behavior.

Although we could not identify statistical differences for the comparison between the four versions (regarding the other metrics), the scores received for all response variables might be considered positive. The median of all variables collected for the versions are above 5 (except for novelty in version 3), which might suggest that participants, in general, have a positive attitude towards the use of the authoring tool prototypes and somehow agreed that they may be ease to use, usable, simple, novel, unique and intense. Moreover, among the four versions, three versions (1, 3 and 4) present in terms of median a credibility with score 8, whereas version 2 presents a median credibility of 7. In addition, both prototypes for authoring gamification have a 6 score as the median for the understandability, information load and perceived system support metrics, which also suggest that participants are likely to agree with the designed prototypes regarding these metrics.

## 4 Conclusion

In this paper, we designed a gamified ITS authoring tool allowing teachers to co-design the domain, pedagogical and gamification models of gamified tutors. To empirically evaluate our solution, we conducted a controlled experiment varying some features of our authoring proposal. The experiment intended to analyze prototypes investigating four combinations of activated or deactivated features (authoring using or not template and gamification authoring by selecting target behaviors or game design elements) in the authoring process with respect to ten metrics in the context of students and researchers from two research groups in Brazil and Canada.

The results of this work might be of utmost importance to improve the authoring tool presented in this paper. In future works, we intend to conduct other empirical studies with teachers and to develop an integrated infrastructure that includes the authoring solution proposed in this work and a third-party gamified ITS system that may reason on teachers' decisions to be reconfigured. We also intend to investigate the use of authoring tools to amplify the participation of teachers by using artificial intelligence throughout the gamified tutor life-cycle, from the beginning of an ITS design (pre-instruction) and at later stages of the execution of the tutor (i.e., during instruction and post-instruction).

# References

1. González, C., Mora, A., Toledo, P.: Gamification in intelligent tutoring systems. In: Proceedings of the Second International Conference on Technological Ecosystems for Enhancing Multiculturality, TEEM 2014, New York, NY, USA, pp. 221–225. ACM (2014)
2. Andrade, F.R.H., Mizoguchi, R., Isotani, S.: The bright and dark sides of gamification. In: Micarelli, A., Stamper, J., Panourgia, K. (eds.) ITS 2016. LNCS, vol. 9684, pp. 176–186. Springer, Cham (2016). https://doi.org/10.1007/978-3-319-39583-8_17
3. Shi, L., Cristea, A.I.: Motivational gamification strategies rooted in self-determination theory for social adaptive E-learning. In: Micarelli, A., Stamper, J., Panourgia, K. (eds.) ITS 2016. LNCS, vol. 9684, pp. 294–300. Springer, Cham (2016). https://doi.org/10.1007/978-3-319-39583-8_32
4. Dermeval, D., Bittencourt, I.I.: Authoring gamified intelligent tutoring systems. In: Proceedings of the Workshops of the Brazilian Congress on Computers and Education, vol. 6, p. 1 (2017)
5. Kapp, K.M.: The Gamification of Learning and Instruction: Game-based Methods and Strategies for Training and Education. Wiley, New York (2012)
6. ProjectTomorrow: Speak up 2014 research project findings - the results of the authentic, unfiltered views of 41,805 k-12 teachers nationwide (2014). http://www.tomorrow.org/speakup/pdfs/SU2014_TeacherTop10.pdf Accessed 5 Feb 2018
7. Lemann, F.: Class council: the teachers' view on education in brazil (2015). http://fundacaolemann.org.br/novidades/a-visao-dos-professores-sobre-a-educacao-no-brasil. Accessed 23 July 2015
8. Martí-Parreño, J., Seguí-Mas, D., Seguí-Mas, E.: Teachers' attitude towards and actual use of gamification. Proc. Soc. Behav. Sci. **228**, 682–688 (2016)
9. Baker, R.S.: Stupid tutoring systems, intelligent humans. Int. J. Artif. Intell. Educ. **26**(2), 600–614 (2016)
10. Dermeval, D., Paiva, R., Bittencourt, I.I., Vassileva, J., Borges, D.: Authoring tools for designing intelligent tutoring systems: a systematic review of the literature. Int. J. Artif. Intell. Educ., 1–49 (2017)
11. Silva, A., Costa, E., Bittencourt, I.I.: Uma linha de produto de software baseada na web semântica para sistemas tutores inteligentes. Revista Brasileira de Informática na Educação **20**(1), 87 (2012)
12. Woolf, B.P.: Building Intelligent Interactive Tutors: Student-centered Strategies for Revolutionizing E-learning. Morgan Kaufmann, Boston (2010)
13. Nacke, L.E., Deterding, S.: The maturing of gamification research (2017)
14. Sottilare, R., Graesser, A., Hu, X., Brawner, K.: Design Recommendations for Intelligent Tutoring Systems: Authoring Tools and Expert Modeling Techniques (2015)
15. Werbach, K., Hunter, D.: For the Win: How Game Thinking Can Revolutionize Your Business. Wharton Digital Press (2012)

16. Nacke, L.E., Bateman, C., Mandryk, R.L.: BrainHex: a neurobiological gamer typology survey. Entertainment Comput. **5**(1), 55–62 (2014)
17. Dermeval, D., Leite, G., Almeida, J., Albuquerque, J., Bittencourt, I.I., Siqueira, S.W., Isotani, S., Silva, A.P.D.: An ontology-driven software product line architecture for developing gamified intelligent tutoring systems. Int. J. Knowl. Learn. **12**(1), 27–48 (2017)

# Where Is the Nurse? Towards Automatically Visualising Meaningful Team Movement in Healthcare Education

Vanessa Echeverria[1,2]([✉]), Roberto Martinez-Maldonado[1],
Tamara Power[1], Carolyn Hayes[1], and Simon Buckingham Shum[1]

[1] University of Technology Sydney,
PO Box 123 Broadway, Ultimo, NSW 2007, Australia
Vanessa.I.EcheverriaBarzola@student.uts.edu.au
[2] Escuela Superior Politécnica del Litoral, ESPOL,
PO Box 09-01-5863, Guayaquil, Ecuador

**Abstract.** Providing immediate, effective feedback on team and individual performance in healthcare simulations is a challenging task for educators, such is their complexity. Focusing on emergency procedures on patient manikins, our prior work has demonstrated the feasibility of using multimodal data capture and analysis to generate visualisations of student movement, talk and treatment actions. The limitation to date has been the need for manual steps in the analytic workflow. This paper documents how we have automated several key steps, using new technologies, which were piloted during a nursing simulation. Combining role-based nurses' movement data with high fidelity manikin logs, we have implemented a zone-based classification model, and are able to automatically visualise movements within an emergency response team, providing the data needed to design near real-time feedback for both educators and students.

**Keywords:** Teamwork · Collaboration · Analytics · Movement
Localisation

## 1 Introduction and Related Work

Healthcare simulation scenarios are commonly utilised in undergraduate nursing education. They expose students to real-world scenarios using a variety of technologies and modalities within a safe environment [4]. *Debriefing* with an educator after the simulation is critical for learning and improvement [3]. Although it is commonplace to video record simulations, video's utility is often constrained by the tutor's ability to document, in real time, key moments s/he wants to return during debriefing. One key feature of high performance teams attending to a patient is their ability to position themselves correctly at critical points. Currently, the educator has limited capacity to track each participant's positions along with other aspects of a team's performance.

Previous work on indoor location analysis in healthcare scenarios has shown the potential of these systems to monitor and model patients' behaviours with the purpose of providing better assistance [2, 9]. For example, a recent study showed the potential of visual representations of participants' movement and location during healthcare

© Springer International Publishing AG, part of Springer Nature 2018
C. Penstein Rosé et al. (Eds.): AIED 2018, LNAI 10948, pp. 74–78, 2018.
https://doi.org/10.1007/978-3-319-93846-2_14

simulations, as they can augment the post-simulation debriefings and foster workflow management changes [7]. However, there has been little research concerning the automated analysis of indoor location in healthcare simulations and in *educational* contexts in general. Tracking movement may be particularly critical to carry human factors analysis in situations where teams are developing clinical and/or teamwork skills by engaging in activities that involve the psychomotor realm and reflecting explicitly on the scope for improvement. Our prior work has demonstrated the feasibility of using multimodal data capture and analysis to generate visualizations of student movement, talk and treatment actions [5, 6]. The limitation to date has been the need for manual steps in the analytic workflow. This paper reports progress in the challenge of using multimodal analytics and Internet of Things (IoT) sensors to capture and analyse teamwork activities by tracking individuals to potentially identify pitfalls regarding clinical procedures, towards providing near real-time feedback.

## 2  Pilot Study

Nine second and third year undergraduate students from the UTS Bachelor of Nursing program volunteered to participate in a simulation scenario. We randomly organized students into three teams (of 2, 3 and 4 students each; Teams 1, 2 and 3 respectively). A cardiac-arrest scenario was designed by a teacher in the context of caring for a deteriorating patient requiring basic life support. The simulation scenario ran for approximately 12 min and involved five sub-tasks that students were meant to perform sequentially (see Table 1, column 1). Each student had a specific role (RN1-4) with an associated set of subtasks (Table 1, columns 3 to 6). Depending on the number of students, the subtasks associated which each role were distributed among the team members (e.g. RN2 and RN3 were merged into one single role for the team with two students).

Students' movement data was logged through wearable badges[1]. We automatically recorded *student-id, x-position, y-position, timestamp* or each student every second. Since the data gathered contained noise from the positioning system, we applied a Kalman filter [1] to improve further calculations. Some student actions (*timestamp, action-name*) were automatically logged by the high-fidelity manikin[2] (for reference see Table 1, Column 2). In addition, all the simulations were video-recorded for further analysis.

## 3  Indoor-Location Analysis

Following the methodology proposed in [5], we performed the following steps to generate team's and individual's movement visualisations:

---

[1] Indoor localization system: *Pozyx* (https://www.pozyx.io).
[2] Simman 3G: Laerdal (http://www.laerdal.com).

**Table 1.** Sub-tasks and actions logged by the manikin given specific roles.

| Sub-tasks | Actions logged by the manikin | RN1 | RN2 | RN3 | RN4 |
|---|---|---|---|---|---|
| ST1: Oxygen therapy | Place oxygen mask<br>Set oxygen level | x | | | |
| ST2: Assessment of chest pain (PQRST) | Attach NIBP<br>Measure blood pressure | x | | | |
| ST3: One dose of anginine | Administer medicine | x | x | | |
| ST4: Connection to a 3-lead monitor and heart rhythm identified | Attach 3-lead ECG | | | x | |
| ST5: Life support according to the DRSABCD protocol | Start CPR<br>Stop CPR | x | x | x | x |

**Clustering.** From the educator's perspective, we coded 4 meaningful locations that students usually cover around the room: (1) head of the bed, (2) bedside, (3) bed-footer, and (4) far away from the bed and (5) by the trolley (which contains an automated external defibrillator). These physical areas are often associated with meaningful tasks that nurses commonly perform. For example, a nurse located at the head of the bed is usually there to hold the patient's head during a CPR intervention. Nurses at the bedside are commonly interacting with the patient directly; while nurses closer to the bed-footer are there commonly to read the notes about the patient or discuss the case. With this information, we assigned a location (from 1 to 5) to each logged position in our dataset.

**Visualisations.** We generated a set of network graphs to the nurses' space usage around the patient's bed. Figure 1 shows how the meaningful locations became the nodes of the network graph. The links between the nodes represent the movement of each nurse from one area to another. In case the nurse spent time in the same area, it is represented with a lasso. Each nurse is assigned with a different a colour (RN1-brown, RN2-blue, RN3-red and RN4-green). The width of the links represents the time the nurse spent in that area.

**Segmentation.** We divided the dataset into meaningful segments from the manikin actions. This helped us into to understand roles and team performance by stages. Table 1 shows the manikin actions according to each subtask. Since the manikin actions did not log starting points (except for CPR), we manually set the starting point of the sub-task by watching the videos. The timestamp from the manikin's logs served as the ending point of the sub-task.

**Making Sense of Location Patterns.** Our analysis explored how each individual and team movement data could support educator's insights and how these relate with the learning activity. Due to space limitations, we describe one possible way to make sense

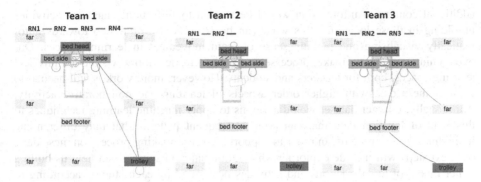

**Fig. 1.** Network graph representing team and individual locations (coloured lines) from the beginning of the simulation until patient received *oxygen therapy* (ST1). (Color figure online)

of this information. In a post-hoc interview, an educator expressed that Team 1 and Team 2 were high-achieving teams, whereas Team 3 was a low-achieving team.

**Overall performance and team movement.** We observed that each team occupied the room in different ways, yet we can see some similarities. It seems that all three teams moved around *bed sides*, *bed head* and the *trolley* more often. This behaviour is appropriate for the task, given that participants had to provide basic life's support near the patient (e.g. oxygen therapy, vital signs).

**Individual performance and role movement.** From the examples depicted in Fig. 1, we observed that role **RN1,** often occupied the *bed head* and *bed sides* areas, to assist the patient. Mapping the role movement with their assigned task, we can see that, RN1 have been assigned the communication with the patient. Thus, we expected that RN1's presence would be associated with areas in close proximity to the patient (e.g. at the *bed head* and *bed sides* areas). Regarding **RN2**, in teams 1 and 3 this role showed a similar trajectory: both nurses occupied the *trolley* area at some point. However, the nurse in Team 2 spent most of the time in *bed sides* area. From the commentaries made by the teacher about Team 2 performance, we could say that both RN1 and RN2 shared the same locations because RN2 was helping RN1 to provide basic life support. Finally, observing **RN3**, we can appreciate that RN3 in Team 1 covered the *bedsides*, *bed-footer* and *trolley* areas. By contrast, RN3 in Team 3 only occupied one *bed side* and a *far* area. This is in line with the comments made by the teacher, which expressed that RN3 in Team 3 should be more aware and responsive.

## 4    Conclusions and Further Work

In this paper, we have presented an approach to track and visualise how teams of students occupy the physical learning space in the context of healthcare simulation. Drawing from the learning design, we segmented our dataset by giving meaning to the locations in the space. We explored the potential of visualising the location data in helping explain the behaviour of teams from a teacher's point of view. Whilst additional contextual information would be needed to fully understand the activities unfolding in those locations, this work can be seen as an initial step towards automatically visualising and making sense of team movement in learning spaces. Our overarching aim is to make processes and performance more visible in physical learning spaces, both for teachers and students. However, more work is still needed to connect these data with higher order aspects of learning and collaborative activity. Additionally, a larger dataset would allow us to apply machine learning techniques to this kind of location data that can point at frequent patterns that may differentiate individuals, roles or teams. In order to support the sense making process on these data, our next steps will include exploring what additional data sources can help us build a richer model of team's actions and activities performed by each student according to their role. As our ultimate goal is to provide feedback to teachers and students, we are planning to validate an improved version of these visualisations with prospective users. Currently, we are involving teachers and learners into the design of such visual representations using participatory designed techniques [8] tailored to data-intensive educational scenarios.

# References

1. Bishop, G., Welch, G.: An introduction to the Kalman filter. Proc. SIGGRAPH Course **8**, 41 (2001)
2. Fernández-Llatas, C., Benedi, J.-M., García-Gómez, J.M., Traver, V.: Process mining for individualized behavior modeling using wireless tracking in nursing homes. Sensors **13**, 15434–15451 (2013)
3. Fey, M.K., Kardong-Edgren, S.S.: State of research on simulation in nursing education programs. J. Prof. Nurs. **33**, 397–398 (2017)
4. MacLean, S., Kelly, M., Geddes, F., Della, P.: Use of simulated patients to develop communication skills in nursing education: an integrative review. Nurse Educ. Today **48**, 90–98 (2017)
5. Martinez-Maldonado, R., Pechenizkiy, M., Buckingham-Shum, S., Power, T., Hayes, C., Axisa, C.: Modelling embodied mobility teamwork strategies in a simulation-based healthcare classroom. In: 25th Conference on User Modeling, Adaptation and Personalization, Bratislava, Slovakia, pp. 308–312. ACM (2017)
6. Martinez-Maldonado, R., Power, T., Hayes, C., Abdiprano, A., Vo, T., Axisa, C., Shum, S.B.: Analytics meet patient manikins: challenges in an authentic small-group healthcare simulation classroom. In: 7th International Conference on Learning Analytics and Knowledge, LAK 2017, pp. 91–94. Association for Computing Machinery (2017)
7. Petrosoniak, A. et al.: Tracking workflow during high-stakes resuscitation: the application of a novel clinician movement tracing tool during in situ trauma simulation. BMJ Simul. Technol. Enhanc. Learn. (2018)
8. Prieto-Alvarez, C.G., Martinez-Maldonado, R., Anderson, T.: Co-designing in learning analytics: tools and techniques. In: Lodge JCH, J.M., Corrin, L. (eds.) Learning Analytics in the Classroom: Translating Learning Analytics Research for Teachers (In press) (2017)
9. Yassin, A., et al.: Recent advances in indoor localization: a survey on theoretical approaches and applications. IEEE Commun. Surv. Tutor. **19**, 1327–1346 (2017)

# Exploring Gritty Students' Behavior in an Intelligent Tutoring System

Erik Erickson[1]([⊠]), Ivon Arroyo[1], and Beverly Woolf[2]

[1] Worcester Polytechnic Institute, Worcester, MA 01609, USA
eerickson@wpi.edu
[2] University of Massachusetts Amherst, Amherst, MA 01003, USA

**Abstract.** This research focuses on determining whether a student's grit impacts their behavior within an intelligent tutoring system, towards developing better student models and feature sets that can help tutors predict student behavior and determine whether tutors might foster improvements in students' grit, perseverance and recovery from failure. We use rare Association Rule Mining to explore how students' grit may be associated with students' behavior within MathSpring, an intelligent tutoring system, as a first step.

**Keywords:** Grit · Perseverance · Student models · Association rule mining

## 1 Introduction

Studies have shown that grit is more predictive of life's outcomes compared to the "Big Five" personality model, a group of broad personality dimensions (e.g., conscientiousness, extraversion, agreeableness, and neuroticism [9]). Unlike IQ, the previous gold-standard predictor for life outcomes, grit may not be a static quality but one that can be developed [7]. Grit has become ubiquitous in the lexicon of public schools across America [10]. Educators look for answers to some lingering questions: *"Can students increase their grittiness?"* and *"How do students go about doing so?"* Gritty individuals can maintain high determination and motivation for a long time despite battling with 'failure and adversity'. Students can increase their grittiness through classroom activities [10]. Educators are interested in fostering growth in children, and would be interested in fostering grit in their students.

Our research focuses on how a student's grit and perseverance might impact behavioral patterns in a tutoring system, towards understanding how digital tutors might foster gritty-like behaviors, and in turn, grit assessments. We move research on grit forward as a tool to refine student models in intelligent tutoring systems, by answering the following questions:

RQ#1. *Can we predict if a student is gritty or not by looking his/her behaviors? Here, grit is a target to predict, or a consequence.*
RQ#2. *Does the grit of a student influence student behavior inside a tutor? In which way(s)? Here grit is a cause or antecedent.*

© Springer International Publishing AG, part of Springer Nature 2018
C. Penstein Rosé et al. (Eds.): AIED 2018, LNAI 10948, pp. 79–83, 2018.
https://doi.org/10.1007/978-3-319-93846-2_15

## 2  Method

Grit has typically been assessed using Duckworth's instrument of the Grit Scale [8], asking students to report on twelve Likert-scale questions. Some examples of questions are, *"I often set a goal but later choose to pursue a different one"* and *"Setbacks don't discourage me."* Our testbed is MathSpring, an intelligent tutoring system (ITS) that personalizes problems by assessing students' knowledge as well as effort and affect as they engage in mathematics practice online [3–5]. Students used MathSpring during class time over several days, as part of their regular mathematics class, and solved many math problems, while the system captured detailed event-level and problem-level information on their performance. These students also filled out a grit scale survey [6] that produced in an aggregate grit score. Seventh grade students from two school districts participated. After combining the two datasets, there were 456 rows of Grit survey responses representing thirty-eight students. Sixty-eight students used Math-Spring, producing 3,012 rows of data, each representing a student-math problem interaction. Variables were discretized into Booleans, indicating high/low or true/false. The negation of each variable was created (e.g., for GUESS, we also created NoGUESS). Along with Guess, other variables included Hi/Low Grit, is/is not Solved, Hi/Low Mistakes, Hi/Low Hints, Yes/No Finished, Not/Likely Read (the problem).

Association Rule Mining, a non-parametric method for exploratory data analysis, was used to find association that occur more frequently than expected from random sampling. The four critical parameters and minimum thresholds used are the following: Support 0.05, Confidence 0.84, Lift 1.15, Conviction 1.75. Last, we subjected the most important rules to a Chi-Square statistical test, those with solely "High Grit" or "Low Grit" as a consequent or antecedent.

## 3  Results

The mean Grit Score for the N = 38 students in the sample was $M = 3.07$, $SD = 0.51$, $Median = 3$, $Range = [1, 5]$. This means the student grit assessment had some variability but the distribution is centered on a neutral grit value. A median split was done, classifying students as low or high grit, so that half of the students were considered gritty or not. Interestingly, we found that HighGrit students produced much more activity, 71% of the student-problem interactions in the dataset vs. 29% for the Low-Grit students. Table 1 shows the number and percent of cases for notable variable in detail, after the discretization process. Due to a low support threshold of 0.05, thousands of rules were created. Only a selected subset of rules was chosen for interpretation; rules with a single consequent or antecedent, and those which met thresholds and had highest values for the metrics of confidence, conviction and lift.

A notable finding was that no rules with *LowGrit* as a consequent appeared at all according to our criteria specified in the parameter thresholds. This led us to realize that, due to the much lower number of math problems seen by LowGrit students, the *confidence* for any rule with *LowGrit = 1* as a consequent would be at chance level at 0.288 (as opposed to 0.5). We realized that the *confidence* metric is not very reliable in this case due to the imbalanced dataset. On the other hand, the metric that balances the

**Table 1.** Name, number of Cases and Percent Cases for all Variables in the final dataset

| Variable name | N cases | % High (or True) | Counterpart variable | N cases | % High (or True) |
|---|---|---|---|---|---|
| HiGrit | 2146 | 71.25% | LowGrit | 866 | 28.75% |
| GUESS | 368 | 12.22% | NoGUESS | 2644 | 87.78% |
| DNFINISH | 261 | 8.67% | FINISHED | 2751 | 91.33% |
| NOTREAD | 86 | 2.86% | LIKELYREAD | 2926 | 97.14% |
| isSolved | 1655 | 54.95% | NotSolved | 1357 | 45.05% |
| HiMistakes | 1343 | 44.59% | LowMistakes | 1669 | 55.41% |
| HiHints | 822 | 27.29% | LowHints | 2190 | 72.71% |

rarity of the premises of a rule and their confidence is the *'conviction'* parameter. We thus set conviction as our first priority for selection of rules.

Table 2 shows rules with the highest conviction, confidence and lift. These rules also are the most complete rules (as generally subsequent rules that met the parameter thresholds had similar premises, but combined subsets of the propositions). **Rule A** is the rule with highest confidence, conviction and lift, and states that *if a student made a high amount of mistakes in a math problem, and asked for many hints as a way to help them solve the problem, then the student will report a high level of Grit*. This joint condition happened in 19% of the total student-problem interactions examined. The significance of the effect for each rule was verified with a Chi-Square test by computing cross-tabulations between the premise being true/false vs. High/Low Grit (p < 0.0001 for rules 1, 2, and 3).

**Table 2.** Grit as a Consequent: Association Rules with highest Conviction, Confidence, Lift

| Rule | Confidence | Conviction | Lift | Support |
|---|---|---|---|---|
| **Rule A.** HiMistakes ∧ HiHints → HiGrit[*] | 0.89 | 2.56 | 1.25 | 0.19 |
| **Rule B.** LowMistakes ∧ isSolved → Low Grit[*] | 0.45 | 1.29 | 1.56 | 0.10 |

[*]Significant difference at p < 0.0001, $\chi^2$ (1, N = 3012)

On the other hand, no rules were found that met the thresholds of confidence, lift and conviction for *LowGrit* as a **consequent**. Still, we show the rule that has the best outcome for those metrics. The implication *LowMistakes ∧ isSolved → Low Grit* has a confidence level of 0.45, which is low, however, it is higher than chance as stated earlier (chance level for any *LowGrit* row is 0.288). The rule suggests that if a student solves problems and makes a low number of mistakes, then the student will report NOT gritty. Table 3 summarizes the found rules with Low/High Grit as a premise. This time, it was easier to find rules with *LowGrit* as an antecedent that met the thresholds of confidence, lift and conviction but not for *HiGrit*. Rule C is the main rule found for Low Grit as an **antecedent** (other similar rules are variations of this same effect), suggesting that if students have low grit, they will likely ask for few hints in a problem.

The rule that contains *HiGrit* as an **antecedent** is Rule D. While Rule D does not meet the lift and conviction thresholds we had set, it does meet the confidence threshold, and has the highest values of confidence and conviction. This rule captures the fact that *if a student is gritty, then the student will not quick-guess the correct answer to a problem.* Remember that guessing implies that a student entered many answers incorrectly and did not ask for help/hints, until they manage to solve it. We consider that students who guess are avoiding help when they should instead be asking for it, as they are answering incorrectly, as stated in previous research [1, 2]. These students rush to get the right answer without fully understanding why, and avoid seeking help.

**Table 3.** Grit as an Antecedent: Association Rules with highest Conviction, Confidence, Lift

| Rule | Confidence | Conviction | Lift | Support |
|---|---|---|---|---|
| **Rule C.** Low Grit → Low Hints[*] | 0.88 | 2.27 | 1.21 | 0.18 |
| **Rule D.** Hi Grit → NoGUESS[*] | 0.89 | 1.16 | 1.02 | 0.7 |

[*]Significant difference at p < 0.0001, $\chi^2$ (1, N = 3012)

## 4 Discussion

This research starts to unpack how grit may be expressed in student behavior inside an intelligent tutor, and how fostering gritty-like behavior might eventually improve a students' grit. In general, the results suggest that there are differences students' behaviors depending on their assessed level of grit. Apparently, students who are gritty tend to neither quick-guess answers to problems, nor make lots of mistakes while avoiding help. At the same time, rules found with grit as a **consequent** suggest that if a student is in a situation of conflict, making mistakes but resolving them by asking for hints (or videos or examples), we can predict that the student will record high grit. This is a desirable behavior when facing challenge in interactive learning environments, as specified by research on help seeking and help provision in interactive learning environments [2].

It was harder to find Association Rules that associated students with low grit with behaviors (there are not as many systematic behavior patterns that could be associated with students of low grit). Still, the few rules found suggest that when students record low levels of grit, they will seek fewer hints. Conversely, the behavior that a student is NOT gritty is that he/she makes a low number of mistakes and eventually solves the problems correctly. While MathSpring provides relatively high student agency, this does not necessarily mean that low-grit students tend to solve problems correctly (otherwise solve-on-first would have been part of the rules found). Students who skip problems or give-up will receive easier problems in an adaptive tutor. Also, students can select material that is easier, or already mastered, to guarantee higher levels of success. Further analyses could help discern if this is the case, by analyzing the level of difficulty of the problems students received. Grit is a construct that will predetermine students to have different kinds of self-regulatory behaviors while learning in interactive learning environments.

**Acknowledgements.** This material is based upon work supported by the National Science Foundation under Grants #1551594 and #1324385. Any opinions, findings, and conclusions or recommendations expressed in this material are those of the authors and do not necessarily reflect the views of the National Science Foundation.

# References

1. Aleven, V., McLaren, B., Roll, I., Koedinger, K.: Toward meta-cognitive tutoring: a model of help-seeking with a cognitive tutor. Int. J. Artif. Intell. Educ. (IJAIED) **16**(2), 101–128 (2006)
2. Aleven, V., Roll, I., McLaren, B., Ryu, E.J., Koedinger, K.: An architecture to combine meta-cognitive and cognitive tutoring: pilot testing the help tutor. Artif. Intell. Educ. Support. Learn. Through Intell. Soc. Informed Technol. **125**, 17 (2005)
3. Arroyo, I., Beal, C., Murray, T., Walles, R., Woolf, B.P.: Web-based intelligent multimedia tutoring for high stakes achievement tests intelligent tutoring systems. In: Proceedings of the 7th International Conference on Intelligent Tutoring Systems (ITS 2004), Maceo, Brazil, pp. 142–169 (2004)
4. Arroyo, I., Woolf, B.P., Beal, C.R.: Addressing cognitive differences and gender during problem solving. Int. J. Technol. Instr. Cogn. Learn. **4**, 31–63 (2006)
5. Arroyo, I., Woolf, B.P., Burelson, W., Muldner, K., Rai, D., Tai, M.: A multimedia adaptive tutoring system for mathematics that addresses cognition, metacognition and affect. Int. J. Artif. Intell. Educ. **24**(4), 387–426 (2014)
6. Corno, L., Snow, R.E.: Adapting teaching to individual differences among learners. In: Wittrock, M.C. (eds.) Handbook of Research on Teaching. MacMillan, New York (1986)
7. Duckworth, A.L., Peterson, C., Matthews, M.D., Kelly, D.R.: Grit: perseverance and passion for long-term goals. J. Pers. Soc. Psychol. **92**(6), 1087–1101 (2007)
8. Duckworth, A., Quinn, P.: Development and validation of the Short Grit Scale (GRIT-S). J. Pers. Assess. **91**, 166–174 (2009). https://doi.org/10.1080/00223890802634290
9. Eskreis-Winkler, L., Shulman, E.P., Beal, S.A., Duckworth, A.L.: The grit effect: predicting retention in the military, the workplace, school and marriage. Front. Psychol. **5** (2014)
10. Saltman, K.J.: The austerity school: Grit, character, and the privatization of public education. Symploke **22**(1), 41–57 (2014)

# Characterizing Students Based on Their Participation in the Class

Shadi Esnaashari[(⊠)], Lesley Gardner, and Michael Rehm

University of Auckland, Auckland, New Zealand
{S.Esnaashari, L.Gardner, M.Rehm}@auckland.ac.nz

**Abstract.** With the increasing number of students in class, it is very important to give insights to the lecturer about how students are learning. In this study, clustering has been applied to the students' class participation data to group them based on similar performance and scores. Participants were 102 second-year undergraduate students at a New Zealand university. The data include students' responses to the regular quizzes and at the end of online modules questions, internal test, and tournament questions. Applying K-Means, four different groups of students have been identified. The results revealed that students who were more active and participated more in activities achieved better scores on their final exam.

**Keywords:** Students' participation · Audience participation tool
Clustering

## 1   Introduction

The importance and effects of active participation in group activities have been emphasised by scholars [4, 9]. However, maintaining the participation of students in class is not an easy task. Different technology tools have been used by researchers in classroom environments to improve participation and engagement of students [12]. These tools could collect engagement data from students, and therefore, it would be possible to recognise disengaged students [10]. Even though the importance of tool use in learning has been emphasised [16], it is the students' choice of whether or not to use the tool. Learners decide for themselves what tool to use and to what extent to use the tool. In axiom 2 of Winne [15] it is mentioned that learners are agents and they have the capability to exercise choice. In this study, we were motivated to understand, when the lecturer provides a variety of tools for the students, how students engage with different tools and how it affects the performance of students. We have used the digital footprint from students whenever they engaged with the tools. There are studies using learning management systems' data to identify the students who are at risk of failure [2, 3, 5, 11]. To the best of our knowledge none of these studies uses data from in-class participation in order to identify at-risk students. Therefore, this study addresses the gap by collecting data from TechSmith and TopHat tools while students were participating in class activities. Then we applied K-Means clustering algorithm to cluster students based on their participation in classes. Based on students' participation in class, four clusters of students have been identified. The results proved the theories of participation by showing that students who participated more eventually achieved the highest scores. In the following sections of the paper, an overview is given on the related work in the area, study design, data collected and how the data were analysed. Finally, the conclusion is presented.

## 2 Related Work

Different techniques have been applied to the students' data to distinguish between their learning strategies [1]. Clustering technique is used as one of the many techniques utilised by different researchers to cluster the students based on the learner profile. Romero et al. [14] used data from students' activities on the Moodle (assignments, messages, forums, tutorial and quizzes) and applied a variety of data mining techniques including clustering, classification, and associate rule mining to identify those students who are likely to fail or pass. They cluster the students to 3 and classified them into two groups of those who fail or pass the course. Hung et al. [6] used a time series clustering approach to find students who are at risk of failure based on the extent they used learning management systems. Their model found that the best performing model identifies one successful and one at-risk pattern. Lopez et al. [8] used forum data and used classification via clustering approach to predict final marks. Their model showed that student participation in the course was a good predictor of the final marks. Jiang et al. [7] used clustering technique to cluster students based on the duration of different tool uses and how it relates to their course outcome. They clustered the students into four different groups.

## 3 Study Design

102 second-year undergraduate students from a New Zealand university participated in this study. The lecturer used a TechSmith platform to upload the recorded video lectures of the class and quizzes at the end of each online module. In addition, TopHat has been used by the lecturer in class to increase the participation of students. At the end of each video module, the lecturer set a quiz. Students needed to attempt the quizzes if they wanted to get participation marks. The students were also required to participate in the tournaments which were run through Top Hat at the end of each session of the class.

## 4 Methodology

In this study, the aim is to find a pattern in the data without having prior knowledge about that. Clustering is a famous method for this purpose. In clustering, the goal is to find the data which can be grouped naturally together. This study clustered the students based on the amount of participation they had in the activities run in the class and the number of correct answers to the questions. We mapped students' participation data from the quizzes and tournament questions data to their internal tests and final course outcome. For the purpose of this study, we used K-Means clustering learning algorithm. K-Means [14] is one of the simplest unsupervised learning algorithms.

## 5  Data Analysis

After data collection, we started to pre-process and clean the data so that we can do the analysis. The data about 102 students were sorted for 12 weeks. The final grades of students have been classified into different categories of, A+, A, A−, B+, B, B−, etc. Since we had the detailed data for each session of the class, we started to aggregate the questions for each session of the class so that we identify the attributes, which have the largest effects on the clustering of the students. For the first round of analysis, we used the data regarding each question and each session of the class during the 12 weeks of the course and clustered the students. Even though we had a high accuracy in our clustering analysis (81.2% accuracy), our model was over fitted. Therefore, for the next round of analysis, we used just three weeks of data and applied the clustering. In this section on top of students' answers to the quizzes, we used tournament data. The tournament has been run twice in each session. In each round of our analysis, we just used data from one round of running the tournament. We used students' data from three sessions of the course and the tournament data from the first run of the tournament. We applied the K-Means clustering algorithm (Fig. 1). We used elbow method to identify the number of clusters for K-Means algorithm. The class of cluster evaluation showed 2.94% incorrectly clustered which was the best result out of all the clustering that we applied. For the next round, we used data from the second round of running the tournament and applied the clustering. But the accuracy decreased (incorrectly clustered was 8.82%).

The clustering in Fig. 1 helped us to understand the characteristics of each cluster. Learners in Cluster 0 participated in very few quizzes. Cluster 0 performed poorly in all activities. There were a few numbers of learners in this cluster 7/102. The students in Cluster 0 did not participate in any tournament. They only participated in two sets of quizzes at the end of two online modules. They also did not participate in the exam. Students in Cluster 0 were the minimum achievers among the groups. Students in Cluster 1 did not participate in the first tournament but participated in three online quizzes and the next two tournament questions. It is interesting that they did not

```
Final cluster centroids:
                                 Cluster#
Attribute         Full Data         0         1           2           3
                   (102.0)       (7.0)     (17.0)      (24.0)      (54.0)
===========================================================================================
Student.ID
Session.1           1.5554      0.2727    0.7807       1.803      1.8554
Tournament.1    0.571428571          0         0 0.571428571 0.571428571
Session.2           1.3091           0    1.4052      1.1296      1.5284
Tournament2.1       0.4374      0.0649    0.3904      0.2727      0.5738
session.3           1.6426           0    1.7706      1.5417        1.86
Tournament3.1       0.5124           0    0.6029      0.2552      0.6646
Exam           74.66666667        #N/A 82.66666667 70.66666667          96
```

**Fig. 1.** Clustering of students based on their answers to the quizzes and the first round of the tournament

participate in the beginning but they may have seen the result and amount of fun involved and then they continuously participated in the tournaments and quizzes at the end of modules. There were 17/102 learners who belonged to this group. The students in this cluster could get good scores.

Cluster 2 students had a higher participation rate compared to Cluster 1 students and a less effective participation rate compared to students in Cluster 3. This cluster was the second largest cluster of students with 24 students in the group. The participation rate was similar to Cluster 3, but they had different effective participation. Since they had different effective participation rate, they got different scores. Students in Cluster 3 also participated in all the quizzes and tournaments, but the level of effective participation and the scores they got were different. The students who were in Cluster 3 performed better on the exam and got the highest scores of all, and these students had the highest participation and scores in the tournament questions and quizzes at the end of online modules. The majority of students belonged to this cluster (54/102).

The clustering of students could help the lecturer to find the students who were at risk of dropout. In this way, the teacher could keep an eye on those special students who may not have been motivated to participate in class activities. Through appropriate intervention, the lecturer can help the students.

## 6  Conclusion

We used K-Means clustering algorithm to cluster 102 undergraduate students in a New Zealand university based on their amount of participation in their class activities. The data was gathered through two tools; Techsmith and TopHat. Four different clusters of students have been identified. The results of clustering showed that students who participated more in the activities got better results at the end of the course. This study reaffirmed the previous studies that showed participation would be important in achieving a better course outcome.

## References

1. Baker, R.S., Inventado, P.S.: Educational data mining and learning analytics. In: Learning Analytics, pp. 61–75. Springer, New York (2014)
2. Campbell, J.P.: Utilizing student data within the course management system to determine undergraduate student academic success: an exploratory study. ProQuest (2007)
3. Cocea, M., Weibelzahl, S.: Can log files analysis estimate learners' level of motivation? (2006)
4. Dearn, J.: Enhancing the first year experience: creating a climate for active learning. In: Proceedings of the Second Pacific Rim Conference on the First Year in Higher Education Transition to Active Learning, University of Melbourne (1996)
5. Hecking, T., Ziebarth, S., Hoop, H.: Analysis of dynamic resource access patterns in online courses. J. Learn. Anal. JLA **1**, 34–60 (2014)
6. Hung, J.-L., Wang, M.C., Wang, S., Abdelrasoul, M., Li, Y., He, W.: Identifying at-risk students for early interventions—a time-series clustering approach. IEEE Trans. Emerg. Top. Comput. **5**(1), 45–55 (2017)

7. Jiang, L., Elen, J., Clarebout, G.: The relationships between learner variables, tool-usage behaviour and performance. Comput. Hum. Behav. **25**(2), 501–509 (2009)
8. Lopez, M.I., Luna, J., Romero, C., Ventura, S.: Classification via clustering for predicting final marks based on student participation in forums. International Educational Data Mining Society (2012)
9. Mcconnell, J.J.: Active learning and its use in computer science. ACM SIGCSE Bull. **28**, SI, 52–54 (1996)
10. Mining, T.E.D.: Enhancing teaching and learning through educational data mining and learning analytics: an issue brief. In: Proceedings of Conference on Advanced Technology for Education (2012)
11. Pistilli, M.D., Arnold, K.E.: In practice: purdue signals: mining real-time academic data to enhance student success. About Campus **15**(3), 22–24 (2010)
12. Ravishankar, J., Epps, J., Ladouceur, F., Eaton, R., Ambikairajah, E.: Using iPads/Tablets as a teaching tool: strategies for an electrical engineering classroom. In: International Conference on Teaching, Assessment and Learning (TALE), pp. 246–251. IEEE (2014)
13. Romero, C., López, M.-I., Luna, J.-M., Ventura, S.: Predicting students' final performance from participation in on-line discussion forums. Comput. Educ. **68**, 458–472 (2013)
14. Romero, C., Ventura, S., García, E.: Data mining in course management systems: moodle case study and tutorial. Comput. Educ. **51**(1), 368–384 (2008)
15. Winne, P.H.: A metacognitive view of individual differences in self-regulated learning. Learn. Individ. Differ. **8**(4), 327–353 (1996)
16. Winne, P.H.: How software technologies can improve research on learning and bolster school reform. Educ. Psychol. **41**(1), 5–17 (2006)

# Adaptive Learning Goes to China

Mingyu Feng[1(✉)], Wei Cui[2], and Shuai Wang[1]

[1] SRI International, Menlo Park, CA 94025, USA
mingyufeng@gmail.com, sam.wang@sri.com
[2] Shanghai Yixue Education Technology Inc., Shanghai, China
cuiwei@classba.cn

**Abstract.** Adaptive learning, by definition, adjusts the content and guidance offered to individual learners. Studies have shown that adaptive systems can be effective learning tools. This paper introduces an adaptive learning system, "Yixue," that was developed and deployed in China. It diagnostically assesses students' mastery of fine-grained skills and presents them with instructional content that fits their characteristics and abilities. The Yixue system has been used by over 10,000 students in 17 cities in China for learning 12 subjects in middle school in 2017. The hypothesis is that the Yixue adaptive learning system will improve student learning outcomes compared to other learning systems. This paper describes major features of the Yixue system. A learning analysis of 1,355 students indicates that students learned from using the Yixue system and the results can generalize across students and skills. We also report a study that evaluates the efficacy of the Yixue math program in 8th and 9th grade.

**Keywords:** Adaptive learning · Mastery-based learning
Diagnostic assessment · Efficacy

## 1 Introduction

Through machine learning algorithms and data analytics techniques, adaptive learning systems offer learning personalized to students' characteristics and abilities. The intent is to determine what a student really knows and to accurately, logically move the student through a sequential path to prescribed learning outcomes and skill mastery. Many learning products with adaptive features have been developed, such as Cognitive Tutors®, i-Ready®, DreamBox® Learning, Achieve3000®, Knewton®, RealizIt®, ALEKS®. Such systems constantly collect and analyze students' learning and behavior data and update learner profiles. As students spend more time in it, the system knows their ability better and can personalize the course to best fit their talents (Triantallou, Pomportsis, & Demetriadis 2003; van Seters et al. 2012)

Studies have shown that such systems can be effective learning tools (VanLehn 2011) and can promote student engagement. An analysis of learning data from 6,400 courses, 1,600 of which were adaptive, revealed that the adaptive courses were more effective in improving student performance than the 4,800 nonadaptive courses (Bomash & Kish 2015). In general, meta-analyses have found positive impacts from technology-based interventions for mathematics and other subjects (e.g., Cheung & Slavin 2013; Steenbergen-Hu & Cooper 2013, 2014). Recent large-scale studies (Pane

© Springer International Publishing AG, part of Springer Nature 2018
C. Penstein Rosé et al. (Eds.): AIED 2018, LNAI 10948, pp. 89–93, 2018.
https://doi.org/10.1007/978-3-319-93846-2_17

et al. 2014, 2017) also found positive evidence of intelligent tutors and personalized learning in support of student mathematics performance.

Online education has developed rapidly in China in recent years. According to the China Internet Network Information Center (2017), by December 2016 the number of online education users in China had reached 138 million, accounting for 19% of total Internet users. Yet the development of learning systems, especially systems that adapt to students' needs, is still in the early stages in China, and little empirical evidence exists on their promise in improving learning outcomes.

Yixue Inc. was one of the first organizations to develop an adaptive learning system in China. With the objective of introducing effective learning systems to China, an initial version of the Yixue was created and tested in 2016. Yixue Inc. has developed instructional materials for middle school mathematics, English, physics, Chinese, and chemistry and is working on expanding content coverage to the whole spectrum of K–12 education settings. In 2017, Yixue was used by over 10,000 students in 17 cities in China, representing a broad range of student populations with respect to socioeconomic status, urbanicity, and performance levels.

## 2   The Yixue Adaptive Learning System

The Yixue intelligent adaptive learning system is a computer-based learning environment that adjust the content and guidance to individual students at both macro- and micro-levels (VanLehn 2006). It provides many opportunities for practice and feedback (Martin, Klein, & Sullivan 2007).

As a **macro-adaptive strategy** supported by psychometric measurement models and artificial intelligence, the system implements competency-based learning and tracks students' mastery of knowledge over time. In competency-based, or *mastery-based*, learning (Park & Lee 2003), students advance to a new learning objective only when they demonstrate proficiency in the current one. In Yixue, students are first given a pre-assessment that diagnoses which knowledge components they have mastered and which ones they have not, according to the predefined hierarchical knowledge structure map. Thus, the system identifies the student's position in the domain model, and the student model is updated accordingly. Then students enter a learning-by-doing stage. The knowledge they demonstrated mastery on during the pre-assessment is skipped during the instructional phase, while knowledge components they were weak on are arranged in an optimal order for learning. As students work, the system simultaneously updates (a) estimates of their competency on each individual knowledge components using a Bayesian statistical model and (b) estimates of overall student proficiency level using an item response theory (IRT) model (van der Linden 2016) and delivers individualized learning content to each student, such as instructional videos, lecture notes, worked examples, embedded practice problems, or unit tests.

The **micro-adaptive strategy** in the Yixue design has to do with provision of just-in-time feedback to students. After a student submits his/her solution to a problem, the system provides immediate feedback on the correctness of the answer. Students may attempt a problem multiple times and request an elaborated explanation of the solution processes step by step if they encounter difficulty. To increase learning efficiency and prevent students from wasting time in over attempting (such as taking a guess-and-check approach and repeatedly entering incorrect answers), the system stops students from trying after three failed attempts and displays the explanation. For selected subjects where misconceptions are common (e.g., physics), if the system detects a student repeatedly making the same kind of error after a number of practices, it automatically plays an instructional video addressing the misconception associated with the error.

Fundamental to the Yixue design is automatic collection of student performance data and provision of feedback and reports to students and teachers. As students work, the Yixue system automatically collects their responses to questions. Students are constantly presented with summary information on the screen. At the end of each session, the system presents students with a summary report on how they performed with direct links to problem solutions and instructional videos on each topic.

# 3  Analysis of Data to Determine Learning Effects

We looked at data from Yixue to see if students demonstrated better performance after using the system. In Yixue, each item is tagged with a focal skill. Learning was assessed by comparing students' performance on the first item they were given with their later performance on the second, third, and forth items on the same skill. If students tend to perform better on later opportunities at a skill, this indicates that they may have learned from the instructional assistance the prior items in the group provided. To see whether learning occurred and was generalized across students and skills, we conducted both a student-level analysis and a skill-level analysis. The data came from student use of Yixue mathematics programs in 2017 across multiple grade levels.

For the student-level analysis, we set the criteria to include students who had worked on at least 10 skills and had at least four opportunities on each skill. A total of 1,355 students fit the criteria. We calculated average percentage correct on the four opportunities for all the sets of similar skills that they participated in and then conducted a t test to see if their performance was better at later opportunities. The results showed that the percentage correct increased significantly from students' first opportunity ($p = 0.03$) to the second opportunity and then continued to increase from the second to the third and the forth opportunities ($p < 0.01$).

For the skill-level analysis, we included only skills that had been studied by more than 20 students, with each student completing four problems addressing the skill. There were 662 different sets of skills that met the criteria for this analysis. We conducted $t$ tests and saw the average percentage correct per skill increased significantly from each opportunity to the next ($p < 0.01$).

Overall, results from the student-level and item-level analyses suggested that students learned from using Yixue math products, and learning generalized across skills and students.

## 4 A Quasi-Experiment to Examine Efficacy of Yixue System

In Oct 2017, we conducted a study, aiming at comparing efficacy of Yixue with whole group instruction provided by expert teachers. 78 students from two grade levels (grades 8 and 9) were sampled from local schools and were assigned to treatment condition (38) or control condition (40) based on geographic convenience. Students in the control condition were then split into three groups that received whole group instruction from three experienced teachers from local schools[1]. The study lasted for 4 days, during which each student received about 5 h of instruction each day. The content covered during the instructional sessions included the Pythagorean theorem and its application, rational numbers, expressions, properties of a triangle, and line symmetry. These are representative of content covered in the grade 8 curriculum in local schools. Students in the treatment group were assigned user accounts in the Yixue system and worked on topics above individually during the study with no teacher assistance. In the control group, teachers taught the topics according to learning standards of the province. Students in the control group were not supported by any online learning programs. Math pre- and post-test were administered to both group of students before and after the instructional sessions. Items in the tests were constructed by an experienced math teacher in a local school (not a part of the research team) and reviewed by two independent, experienced subject matter experts. Each test composed of 14 multiple choice, short answer, or constructed responses problems, with a total score of 100 points. Students were given 60 min to complete the test.

First, we looked to see if students learned during the study by comparing their scores from the posttest to the pretest. Across all students, pretest scores were highly correlated with posttest scores ($r = 0.67$). A paired t test showed that students' posttest scores were significantly higher than pretest scores ($p < 0.01$), suggesting that math achievement improved significantly. We confirmed the pretest total score was balanced between the treatment group and control group for grade 8 ($g = 0.13$) and grade 9 ($g = 0.24$). We then used generalized linear modeling to analyze student achievement, with the student posttest scores as the outcome variables, adjusting for pretest score, and treatment condition as a predictor at the student level. The results showed that when student prior achievement was controlled, grade 8 Yixue students ($M = 69.96$, $SD = 22.34$) had significantly higher posttest scores than control students ($M = 61.40$, $SD = 20.99$) ($b = 10.56$, $F (1, 32) = 3.35$, $p = 0.08$, $R^2 = 53.08$, $g = 0.48$).

## 5 Conclusion

The Yixue adaptive learning system was launched in 2016 and presently has over 100,000 users. In this paper, we introduced features of the system, its implementation model, and theoretical basis. Promising evidence was found that students learned during their use of the system, and a small-scale quasi-experiment demonstrated the efficacy of the system.

---

[1] No students received instructions from their regular math teachers in school.

The study has limitations; it was quasi experiment with relatively small sample. The study was conducted during a short time (4 days), focused only on selected math topics, and no external measure used. Thus, further research is warranted to examine the efficacy of the Yixue adaptive learning system.

As the technology infrastructure continues to develop in China, there are an increasing number of learning systems developed and there is broad interest in how to select and use such systems. With these studies, we have the opportunity to contribute to much-needed knowledge about adaptive learning in K–12 instruction in China.

# References

Bergan, J., Sladeczek, I., Schwarz, R., Smith, A.: Effects of a measurement and planning system on kindergartners' cognitive development and educational programming. Am. Educ. Res. J. **28**(3), 683–714 (1991)

Bomash, I., Kish, C.: The improvement index: evaluating academic gains in college students using adaptive lessons. Knewton, New York (2015)

Cheung, A.C., Slavin, R.E.: The effectiveness of educational technology applications for enhancing mathematics achievement in K-12 classrooms: a meta-analysis. Educ. Res. Rev. **9**, 88–113 (2013)

China Internet Network Information Center (2017). Statistical survey report on Internet development in China. Accessed 15 March 2017. http://www.cnnic.cn/hlwfzyj/hlwxzbg/hlwtjbg/201701/P020170123364672657408.pdf

Martin, F., Klein, J., Sullivan, H.: The impact of instructional elements in computer-based instruction. Br. J. Edu. Technol. **38**(4), 623–636 (2007)

Pane, J., Griffin, B.A., McCaffrey, D.F., Karam, R.: Effectiveness of cognitive tutor algebra I at scale. Educ. Eval. Policy Anal. **36**(2), 127–144 (2014)

Pane, J., Steiner, E., Baird, M., Hamilton, L., Pane, J.: How Does Personalized Learning Affect Student Achievement? RAND Corporation, Santa Monica (2017). https://www.rand.org/pubs/research_briefs/RB9994.html

Park, O., Lee, J.: Adaptive instructional systems. In: Jonassen, D.H., Driscoll, M. (Eds.): Handbook of research for educational communications and technology, 2nd edn., pp. 651–684. Laurence Earlbaum, Mahwah (2003). http://www.aect.org/edtech/ed1/25.pdf

Steenbergen-Hu, S., Cooper, H.: A meta-analysis of the effectiveness of intelligent tutoring systems on college students' academic learning. J. Educ. Psychol. **106**(2), 331–347 (2014)

Subban, P.: Differentiated instruction: a research basis. Int. Educ. J. **7**(7), 935–947 (2006)

Triantallou, E., Pomportsis, A., Demetriadis, S.: The design and the formative evaluation of an adaptive educational system based on cognitive style. Comput. Educ. **41**, 87–103 (2003)

VanLehn, K.: The behavior of tutoring systems. Int. J. Artif. Intell. Educ. **16**(3), 227–265 (2006)

VanLehn, K.: The relative effectiveness of human tutoring, intelligent tutoring systems, and other tutoring systems. Educ. Psychol. **46**(4), 197–221 (2011)

van der Linden, W.: Handbook of Item Response Theory. Chapman and Hall/CRC, Boca Raton (2016)

van Seters, J.R., Ossevoort, M.A., Tramper, J., Goedhart, M.J.: The influence of student characteristics on the use of adaptive e-learning material. Comput. Educ. **58**, 942–952 (2012)

# Ontology Development for Competence Assessment in Virtual Communities of Practice

Alice Barana[1]([⊠])(iD), Luigi Di Caro[2]([⊠])(iD), Michele Fioravera[1]([⊠])(iD),
Marina Marchisio[1]([⊠])(iD), and Sergio Rabellino[2]([⊠])(iD)

[1] Department of Mathematics, University of Turin, Turin, TO, Italy
{alice.barana,michele.fioravera,
marina.marchisio}@unito.it
[2] Department of Computer Science, University of Turin, Turin, TO, Italy
{luigi.dicaro,sergio.rabellino}@unito.it

**Abstract.** This paper presents an ontological model for defining competency paths in STEM education, designed for the implementation of an adaptive system integrated in virtual communities. The model is applied for clustering materials for automatic assessment and the results are discussed.

**Keywords:** Automatic assessment · Competence · Ontology
Virtual community

## 1 Introduction

The present work is part of a research whose aim is to enhance competency-based education. To foster learners' formative assessment and to support instructors in extending teaching strategies, a new system is proposed. Development and experimentation are conducted in Technology Enhanced Learning Environments (TELEs), ideal tool for managing large amount of data. Semantic-capturing methods are considered for automatically structuring resources by intended in-and-outcomes.

A methodology for preparing materials for automatic assessment is discussed considering results from ontology-based clustering of resources shared within the virtual community of a national-wide project for Secondary School.

## 2 Methodology

To enable automatic organization of any kind of resource, the system provides for natural language descriptions about intended in-and-outcomes. Models are applied for clustering a collection of resources produced and shared by instructors. The comparison between the original grouping and generated clusters are exploited for gathering insights about the applicability of the models.

© Springer International Publishing AG, part of Springer Nature 2018
C. Penstein Rosé et al. (Eds.): AIED 2018, LNAI 10948, pp. 94–98, 2018.
https://doi.org/10.1007/978-3-319-93846-2_18

## 2.1 Models

The new model of Measurable Learning Object is designed and proposed as essential authoring guide to explicate learning intentions and success criteria the materials are designed for. This model is linked to an ontological one, designed for extracting information about competences from free-texts. The Virtual Learning Community model specifies the context where the system can be implemented as integrated resource.

**Virtual Learning Community**

The feasibility of the system relies on the existence of a common framework of competences expected to be achieved by learners at the end of the learning process, which instructors agree upon. Such framework can be efficiently explained and maintained in a Virtual Learning Community (VLC) [1, 2]. It is a "community of communities": the community of instructors who collaboratively learn new methodologies supported by tutors in the use of advanced tools; the community of the online courses held by a teacher for his students; the global community of students.

The system is proposed to be experimented in national [3] and transnational [4, 5] scale, as integration of the Learning Management System hosting the VLC.

**Measurable Learning Object**

This study focuses on the 'atomic' components of the products of Computer Aided-Assessment [6], referred to as Measurable Learning Materials (MLO): digital resources containing one (only one) response area dedicated to automated assessment, associated to the "PRO" triple of descriptors:

- P – Performance ("instructional", "behavioural" or "learning" objective) is a specific statement about the observable behaviour required to the learner.
- R – Requisites ("pre-requisites") states the necessary and sufficient objectives that the learner is able to fulfil to successfully perform the MLO.
- O – Objectives (or "goals") specifies what the learner is required to be able to do as result of the educational activity the MLO was created for.

**Ontology**

To extract knowledge from the descriptors' textual description, this research involves the use of an ontological version of Anderson and Krathwohl taxonomy integrated with the domain-specific OntoMathPRO ontology (translated in Italian). OntoMathPRO is a bilingual (Russian/English) ontology of mathematical knowledge, shared with the Semantic Web community [7]. Anderson and Krathwohl's classification organizes types of knowledge and thinking processes into categories [8].

Considering the ontological model, a MLO can be linked to a set of concepts' couples referring to a matrix: the first dimension of the matrix represents the types of knowledge while the second dimension represents the cognitive processes involved. The connection between a MLO and a matrix's element is established by identifying cognitive processes and knowledge type from its content or metadata.

## 2.2    Experimentation

The models are applied for clustering a collection of MLOs by different features: the MLO's surface text and two versions of the MLO's Performance (P), Requisites (R) and Objectives (O) authored separately by two experts. On each MLO's feature – which consists in an input string representing a descriptor or the surface text – the clustering process is performed by following 4 main phases.

- Tokenization, stop words removal, stemming, bag-of-words representation. Maple, the ACE on which Maple TA is based, is used for parsing surface text's formulae. To enhance the influence of semantically relevant concepts, this phase is repeated with tokens' filtering using the ontology:
  - Words that appear in less than 2 input strings are filtered out.
  - Words that appear in more than the half of the input strings are filtered out.
  - Words recognized as ontological concepts are kept regardless the previous rules.
  - After the previous rules, only the first n most frequent words are kept, with values of n between the average lengths of vectors.
- The 'transformation model', initialized from the corpus of bag-of-words vectors, is used to convert any vector to the tf-idf representation.
- Mini Batch k-Means clustering algorithm [9] is executed on each feature's similarity matrices, constructed by calculating cosine similarity for each pair of vectors: each MLO is labelled with one out of k clusters, where k is equal to the number of "natural" MLOs' groupings by 'Disciplinary area' and by 'Response area type'.

V_measure homogeneity metric enables to estimate correlations between different clusterings [10]. Mean and standard deviation of the v_measure values from 10 process's repetitions are calculated. To evaluate whether clusterings correlation depends on the number of clusters generated, this is performed for different values of k. Clustering analysis is conducted by using tools from Gensim [11], nltk [12] and scipy [13].

## 3    Results

196 MLOs, produced with the Automatic Assessment System Maple TA [14] of the PP&S VLC [15], were selected from problems shared by secondary school teachers.

Figure 1 shows the mean of the v_measure values obtained comparing each of the 6 clusterings generated from the MLOs' descriptors of each given author (1P, 1R, 1O, 2P, 2R, 2O) to respectively the labelling by disciplinary area (D) and by response area type (A), in case of k = 8 clusters to be generated, both without and with filtering considering values of n between 7 and 15 in steps of 2. The standard deviation values are about two orders of magnitude smaller than the means. Correlation values slightly increase/decrease with the increase/decrease of k from the number of D (and A) groupings, confirming the hypothesis of 8 clusters to be expected. Results highlight that clusterings generated by the descriptors highly reflect both D and A groupings, since the v_measure mean value is higher than 0.5. These results align with the expectation that a MLO can be composed in potentially infinite modalities: the descriptors express concepts of mathematical problems referring to the mathematical model covered by the problematic situation. Filtering influences the descriptors accordingly with their respective average lengths of the generated vectors: it might enable to generate clusters which express concepts slightly different from those implicit in D or A.

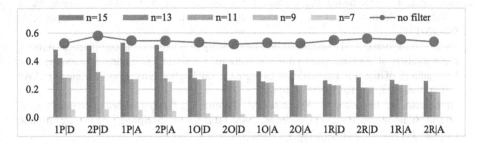

**Fig. 1.** Mean values of the *v_measure* comparing 1P, 1R, 1O, 2P, 2R, 2O to D and A, in case of $k = 8$ clusters to be generated and values of $n$ between 7 and 15 in steps of 2.

Correlation is less strong in comparison with the clustering generated by the surface texts: on average, the v_measure mean is less than 0.3. To guarantee the quality of the clusterings obtained, 1P, 1R, 1O, 2P, 2R and 2O are compared to randomly generated clusterings: the v_measure mean values are significantly less than 0.1.

Some correlation between descriptors is expected. Figure 2 shows the mean of the v_measure values between different combinations of 1P, 1R, 1O, 2P, 2R and 2O. Results suggest significant correlation among Performance and Objectives of the same author, while Requisites appears to be highly independent.

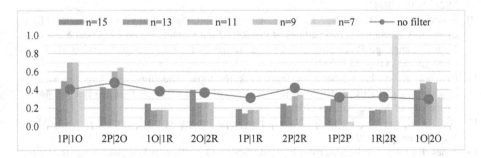

**Fig. 2.** Mean values of the *v_measure*, for combinations of clustering from authors' descriptors, in case of $k = 8$ clusters to be generated and values of $n$ between 7 and 15 in steps of 2.

Only Objectives evidence stable inter-annotation agreement between the authors. Adopting ontologies as semantic-proxies would enable to capture semantically related concepts expressed with distinct words which generate differences between authors. Semantic measures based on ontologies will be the subject of further research towards the implementation of a system for adaptively providing learning resources. Ontology development will grow by activating projects at national and European scale.

# References

1. Ellerani, F., Parricchi, M.: Ambienti per lo sviluppo professionale degli insegnanti. Web 2.0, gruppo, comunità di apprendimento (2010)
2. Demartini, C., Marchisio, M., Pardini, C.: PP&S100 - una comunità di comunità di collaborative learning attraverso le nuove tecnologie. Atti Didamatica Pisa 2013, pp. 989–998 (2013)
3. Barana, A., Fioravera, M., Marchisio, M.: Developing problem solving competences through the resolution of contextualized problems with an Advanced Computing Environment. In: Proceedings of the 3rd International Conference on Higher Education Advances (HEAd 2017), Valencia, pp. 1015–1023 (2017)
4. Brancaccio, A., Esposito, M., Marchisio, M., Pardini, C.: L'efficacia dell'apprendimento in rete degli immigrati digitali. L'esperienza SMART per le discipline scientifiche. Mondo Digitale 15, 803–821 (2016). ISSN 1720-898X
5. Brancaccio, A., Marchisio, M., Meneghini, C., Pardini, C.: Matematica e scienze più smart per l'insegnamento e l'apprendimento. Mondo Digitale XIV(58), 1–8 (2015)
6. Barana, A., Marchisio, M.: Ten good reasons to adopt an automated formative assessment model for learning and teaching Mathematics and scientific disciplines. Procedia: Soc. Behav. Sci. 228, 608–613 (2016). https://doi.org/10.2016/j.sbspro.2016.07.093
7. Nevzorova, O.A., Zhiltsov, N., Kirillovich, A., Lipachev, E.: *OntoMath$^{PRO}$* Ontology: a linked data hub for mathematics. In: Klinov, P., Mouromtsev, D. (eds.) KESW 2014. CCIS, vol. 468, pp. 105–119. Springer, Cham (2014). https://doi.org/10.1007/978-3-319-11716-4_9
8. Anderson, L.W., Krathwohl, D.R., et al.: A Taxonomy for Learning, Teaching, and Assessing. A Revision of Bloom's Taxonomy of Educational Objectives. Addison Wesley Longman, New York (2001)
9. Pedregosa, F., Varoquaux, G., Gramfort, A., Michel, V., Thirion, B., Grisel, O., Blondel, M., Prettenhofer, P., Weiss, R., Dubourg, V., Vanderplas, J., Passos, A., Cournapeau, D., Brucher, M., Perrot, M., Duchesnay, E.: Scikit-learn: machine learning in python. JMLR 12, 2825–2830 (2011)
10. Rosenberg, A., Hirschberg, J.: V-measure: a conditional entropy-based external cluster evaluation measure. In: Proceedings of the 2007 Joint Conference on Empirical Methods in Natural Language Processing and Computational Natural Language Learning (EMNLP-CoNLL), pp. 410–420 (2007)
11. Řehůřek, R., Sojka, P.: Software framework for topic modelling with large corpora. In: Proceedings of LREC 2010 Workshop New Challenges for NLP Frameworks, pp. 46–50. University of Malta, Valletta (2010)
12. Bird, S., Edward, L., Ewan, K.: Natural Language Processing with Python. O'Reilly Media Inc., Sebastopol (2009)
13. Jones, E., Oliphant, E., Peterson, P., et al.: SciPy: Open Source Scientific Tools for Python (2001). http://www.scipy.org/. Accessed 29 Jan 2018
14. Barana, A., Marchisio, M., Rabellino, S.: Automated assessment in mathematics. In: IEEE 39th Annual Computer Software and Applications Conference (COMPSAC), pp. 670–671 (2015). https://doi.org/10.1109/compsac.2015.105
15. Brancaccio, A., Demartini, C., Marchisio, M., Palumbo, C., Pardini, C., Patrucco, A., Zich, R.: Problem posing and solving: strategic Italian key action to enhance teaching and learning of mathematics and informatics in high school. In: IEEE 39th Annual Computer Software and Applications Conference (COMPSAC), pp. 845–850 (2015). https://doi.org/10.1109/compsac.2015.126

# How Gamification Impacts on Vocational Training Students

Miguel García Iruela[(⊠)] and Raquel Hijón Neira

Universidad Rey Juan Carlos, Calle Tulipán, s/n, 28933 Móstoles, Spain
{miguel.garciai, raquel.hijon}@urjc.es

**Abstract.** Gamification in educational context has been the subject of many studies in the last few years. There are studies for primary, secondary and higher education, which evaluate the effect of gamification on learning, motivation, engagement, concentration and enjoyment. Although vocational training is very important for training professionals, a few researches study gamification as a learning method in this type of education. Students in vocational training classes are most heterogeneous due to the difference in age among the students and their previous training. This paper focuses on how gamification affects the motivation and learning in a group of students of vocational training. Our results indicate that students using gamification as a means of learning improved slightly more than the rest. Most students enjoyed the gamified experience and they showed a great interest in continuing using this methodology.

**Keywords:** Gamification · Kahoot! · Game-based learning
Educational games

## 1 Introduction

Games have been part of our Society throughout history; typically, they intended to have fun and entertaining. A game can be a physical or mental activity in which one or more players compete to achieve goals following some established rules. The aim of gamification is to improve learning in non-ludic environments using game mechanics [1].

This idea can be applied in different areas such as marketing [2], encouraging healthy habits [3] or education [4]. Researchers suggest that this methodology increases motivation and engagement of users [5]. If so, it can help to archive a goal beyond entertaining.

Game-based learning has proved effective for enhancing results of the students when compared with conventional methods [6–8]. A search in published papers, reveals plenty of information about gamification applied to secondary and higher education. In this paper, we focus on the existing gap in gamming applied to vocational training.

There are two main relevant differences with teachings analysed in previous studies. On the one hand, the great heterogeneity of the students, both because of the difference in previous training and in age, and on the other hand, the more practical approach focused mainly to the employability of the students. In this case, the

© Springer International Publishing AG, part of Springer Nature 2018
C. Penstein Rosé et al. (Eds.): AIED 2018, LNAI 10948, pp. 99–103, 2018.
https://doi.org/10.1007/978-3-319-93846-2_19

gamification could help to adapt theoretical contents to this diversity of students in a more informal way.

For this experience, we choose Kahoot! to perform the gamified activity, because it is a simple tool which allow integrate gamification components such as the management of scores, the leader-board and provides an instant feedback to students [9, 10].

## 2   Methods

Participants. 24 first-year students of 'Computer Network Systems Administration' of vocational training took part on this experience. The sample consisted of 3 women and 21 men, averaging 25 years in age (SD = 5.75). The data analysed in this paper were collected from an activity in the 'Fundamentals Hardware' course.

The experience used Kahoot!, a web application to generate multiple-choice quizzes. "Kahoot! is a free game-based learning platform for teachers of awesome, classroom superheroes and all learners. Play, learn, have fun and celebrate together!" [11].

To begin with, the teacher generates a questionnaire in www.kahoot.com. Each question has an assigned response time. In class, the teacher access the web via a computer connected to a projector and activates the test (Fig. 1 left). The students log in www.kahoot.it with a code given by the teacher. Once all the students are logged, the teacher runs the quiz (Fig. 1 right).

**Fig. 1.** Kahhot! initial screen with logged students (left). A sample question used (right). In Spanish: a communication system consists at least of: emissary, receptor, message and channel.

A "Kahoot" consists in showing students multiple-choice questions with a projector and letting them answer using either computers, tablets or smartphones. Students have a limited time for each question before the App shows the answers (Fig. 2 left) and a temporal ranking. Points awarded in each question depend on the time consumed by every student to input an answer. Finally, Kahoot! yields the ranking of the students (Fig. 2 right).

Procedure. To examine the impact of gamification in the learning process the students were divided in two groups: control and test. The control group worked on the same topics as usually, revising material and exercises during a 2-h session. The test group used kahoot! as a learning medium for the same period of time and topics. All participants took a previous test (pre-test) and a post-test to compare their respective

**Fig. 2.** Screen of a question answer (left). Final ranking of a questionnaire (right).

knowledge acquisition for both groups. After the post-test, the control group was allowed to use Kahoot! as well, since they were willing to do so. Finally, the students answered a questionnaire compiling their impressions.

## 3 Results

Table 1 presents the results of pre-test and post-test. The control group started with a grade average lower than the average of the gamified group. Therefore, the control group had (at least in theory) more room for improvement; however, the post-test statistics reveals a meagre progress for this group. In contrast, the gamified group experienced a marked improvement. Standard deviations of both groups are similar in the pre-test and in the post-test, although the value in the post-test is lower.

**Table 1.** Pre-test and post-test results.

| Group | Avg pre-test | SD pre-test | Avg post-test | SD post-test |
|---|---|---|---|---|
| Control | 6.54 | 1.85 | 6.57 | 1.41 |
| Gamification | 7.55 | 1.75 | 8.27 | 1.49 |
| All students | 7 | 1.84 | 7.32 | 1.66 |

The impressions survey, consisted on five questions to value from one to 7 and an extra question to express the opinion. Table 2 displays the results of the survey in percentages, and the average value of the five questions. The majority of students valued the experience positively, with only a few exceptions. They found Kahoot!

**Table 2.** Impressions survey results (valued from 0 to 7).

| Question | 1 | 2 | 3 | 4 | 5 | 6 | 7 | Avg |
|---|---|---|---|---|---|---|---|---|
| Did you find Kahoot interesting? | 5% | 5% | 0% | 0% | 10% | 40% | 40% | 5.85 |
| Did you have fun? | 0% | 0% | 10% | 0% | 10% | 40% | 40% | 6 |
| You have learned something? | 5% | 0% | 0% | 10% | 25% | 40% | 20% | 5.5 |
| Would you repeat the experience? | 5% | 0% | 0% | 11% | 21% | 16% | 47% | 5.79 |
| Are you more prepared in the subject? | 5% | 5% | 10% | 5% | 20% | 30% | 25% | 5.2 |

funny and very interesting and they considered that, thanks to it, they had improved, and felt better prepared. With regard to the open question, the general opinion was that the experience was entertaining and Kahoot! a funny method to learn. As expected, several students objected the short time to respond, something very easy to modify.

## 4   Conclusions

Currently, gamification is not widely used in vocational training. The differences between the type of students of our research with other previous studies keep us in a state of uncertainty. Nevertheless, the results of this experience prove that this kind of students achieved a remarkable improvement in a short time thanks to using gamification components.

We can observe that gamification methodology has worked better than conventional methodology in this group of vocational training. We are aware that the time allowed to the experience was not long enough and that the sample of the experience is not broad enough either, but the information drawn from the experience is a good reason to reaffirm our points of view, and to persevere in this line of research. It was rewarding to see that not only most of the participants felt motivated and comfortable with this activity, but that they were willing to proceed working on this methodology throughout the year.

This experience about the impact of gamification on education covers a poorly evaluated spectrum. Consequently, we plan to continue evaluating the impact during a full academic year (next year) to obtain data that are more robust and prevent the novelty effect [12].

**Acknowledgment.** This research received financial support from Ministerio de Economía y Competitividad (TIN2015-66731-C2-1-R), Comunidad Autónoma de Madrid (S2013/ICE-2715), and Rey Juan Carlos University (30VCPIGI15). We are thankful to IES Clara del Rey and Lisbon University for giving us all facilities to carry on the experiences.

## References

1. Stetina, B.U., Kothgassner, O.D., Lehenbauer, M., Kryspin-Exner, I.: Beyond the fascination of online-games: probing addictive behavior and depression in the world of online-gaming. Comput. Hum. Behav. **27**, 473–479 (2011)
2. Hamari, J.: Transforming homo economicus into homo ludens: a field experiment on gamification in a utilitarian peer-to-peer trading service. Electron. Commer. Res. Appl. **12**(4), 236–245 (2013)
3. González, C.S., Gómez, N., Navarro, V., Cairós, M., Quirce, C., Toledo, P., Marrero-Gordillo, N.: Learning healthy lifestyles through active videogames, motor games and the gamification of educational activities. Comput. Hum. Behav. **55**, 529–551 (2016)
4. Hanus, M.D., Fox, J.: Assessing the effects of gamification in the classroom: a longitudinal study on intrinsic motivation, social comparison, satisfaction, effort, and academic performance. Comput. Edu. **80**, 152–161 (2015)

5. Jang, J., Park, J.J.Y., Yi, M.Y.: Gamification of online learning. In: Conati, C., Heffernan, N., Mitrovic, A., Verdejo, M.F. (eds.) AIED 2015. LNCS (LNAI), vol. 9112, pp. 646–649. Springer, Cham (2015). https://doi.org/10.1007/978-3-319-19773-9_82
6. Clark, D.B., Tanner-Smith, E., Killingsworth, S.: Digital games, design, and learning: a systematic review and meta-analysis. Rev. Educ. Res. **86**(1), 79–122 (2015)
7. Wouters, P., van Nimwegen, C., van Oostendorp, H., van der Spek, E.D.: A meta-analysis of the cognitive and motivational effects of serious games. J. Educ. Psychol. **105**, 249–265 (2013)
8. Hamari, J., Koivisto, J., Sarsa, H.: Does gamification work?—a literature review of empirical studies on gamification. In: Proceedings of the 47th Hawaii International Conference on System Sciences (2014)
9. Fotaris, P., Mastoras, T., Leinfellner, R., Rosunally, Y.: Climbing up the leaderboard: an empirical study of applying gamification techniques to a computer programming class. Electron. J. E-Learn. **14**(2), 94–110 (2016)
10. Varannai, I., Sasvari, P., Urbanovics, A.: The use of gamification in higher education: an empirical study. Int. J. Adv. Comput. Sci. Appl. **8**(10), 1–6 (2017)
11. Kahoot! http://www.Kahoot.com/what-is-kahoot/. Accessed 6 Feb 2018
12. Wang, A.I.: The wear out effect of a game-based student response system. Comput. Educ. **82**, 217–227 (2015)

# Classifying Educational Questions Based on the Expected Characteristics of Answers

Andreea Godea$^{(\boxtimes)}$, Dralia Tulley-Patton, Stephanie Barbee,
and Rodney Nielsen

University of North Texas, Denton, TX, USA
AndreeaGodea@my.unt.edu, draliatp@gmail.com, barbeesteph@gmail.com,
Rodney.Nielsen@unt.edu

**Abstract.** Question classification is an important part of several tasks, especially in educational systems. In this paper, we present a system that classifies questions asked in an educational context based on the expected characteristics of answers, with a future goal to facilitate the analysis of student responses. To this end, we propose an approach that employs a deep neural network together with features tailored to each question type (expected answer characteristic), word embeddings and inter-class dependency features. To demonstrate the effectiveness of the proposed method, we use a corpus of questions collected from real science classrooms and augment it with data from online resources from the same domain. Our approach achieves a weighted $F_1$-score of 0.678, outperforming the baseline by 56%.

**Keywords:** Question classification
Expected characteristics of answer · Educational questions
Question dataset and taxonomy · Neural networks

## 1 Introduction

The classification of questions with respect to expected answer characteristics is important in an educational application that does not rely on pre-authored questions. For instance, the classification can be used to facilitate the analysis of student responses with respect to the question's requirements. Given a question, if the student fails to provide a complete answer, this can imply that the concepts elicited were not entirely understood. As can be seen, identifying the characteristics of the expected answer will help improve assessment and analytics by facilitating the interpretation, comparison and contrasting of corresponding components of student responses. Characterizing the expected answers to questions can also be effectively leveraged to improve teachers' question asking strategies or to help them construct more complex or diverse student assessments.

Previous works in the educational domain analyzed questions based on the *subject* [2,3], *difficulty level* [8], *educational objective* [1] or *expected answer types*

© Springer International Publishing AG, part of Springer Nature 2018
C. Penstein Rosé et al. (Eds.): AIED 2018, LNAI 10948, pp. 104–108, 2018.
https://doi.org/10.1007/978-3-319-93846-2_20

[5]. In this paper, we present a novel approach to classify questions based on the expected answers' characteristics using the dataset from [5]. Our approach employs deep artificial neural networks, tailored features, word embeddings (WEs) and inter-class relationships. The longer term aim of this work is to use the characterizations of expected answers to improve the analysis of student responses.

## 2 Related Work

Previous research has proposed various question classification schemes and methods that rely on the correlation between a question and the expected answer. However, they were mainly developed for automated question answering (QA) and question generation systems [4,11]. Question classification has been integrated as a core component in QA systems, where question taxonomies and approaches were highly influenced by QA shared tasks [6,7,9,11]. In the educational field, [5] proposed the first taxonomy and approach to classify questions based on expected answer characteristics, intended to facilitate the analysis of student responses. In contrast with their method that relies only on WEs, we propose a higher performing approach which employs features tailored to the domain and task, inter-class correlations, and domain-independent WEs.

**Table 1.** Number of instances per class in the web data.

| Data | Sents | Clarif | subjC | sel1 | selN | T/F | List | MultiP | shrtA | OtCR | Proc | Eq | soln | Draw | Cntxts | AnsV | Order |
|------|-------|--------|-------|------|------|-----|------|--------|-------|------|------|-----|------|------|--------|------|-------|
| Train | 1251 | 89 | 70 | 85 | 109 | 53 | 112 | 57 | 269 | 201 | 22 | 85 | 102 | 94 | 85 | 102 | 59 |

## 3 Data Description

The data was introduced by [5] and contains science questions asked by teachers in middle school classrooms. Each sentence in a question was annotated using 16 categories based on the expected answer types: *Clarification, SubjectiveConcept, Select1, SelectN, TrueFalse, List, Multi-Part, VeryShortAnswer, OtherConstructedResponse, ProcessProcedure, Equation, Drawing, ContextSensitive, AnswersWillVary* and *Ordered*. A sentence can have one or more labels. Several class pairs are highly correlated, a fact that will be leveraged in this paper. The authors split the questions into two separate sets – 66% for *train* and 34% for *test*. Since several classes have less than 50 examples, we augmented the training set with 811 science questions from various online resources[1]. We annotated the web data and show the distribution per class in Table 1.

---

[1] biology-resources.com, louisianabelieves.com, ets.org, nysedregents.org, doe.mass.edu, timss.bc.edu, vcaa.vic.edu.au, neptune.k12.nj.us, ed.gov, tea.texas.gov.

# 4   Question Classification Approach

We utilized a supervised approach that employs a deep feedforward artificial neural network to classify questions based on the expected characteristics of answers. For experimental purposes, we split the training data into two sets – 66% for training and 34% for validation. We use the *validation* set to tune the parameters and identify the best set of features per class. Finally, we train a classifier on the full training set and use it to classify the held out test instances.

| | |
|---|---|
| **Clarification** – mainVerb (200d) - *interrogQ, imperQ, qHasHint, qHasEnum, (max/avgMax/minMax)PMIWithPrevSent, (max/avgMax/minMax)SemSimWithPrevSent, imperQInBrackets, cosSimNormSumWEmbdsWithPrevSent, maxCosSimWEmbdWithPrevSent* | **ProcessProcedure** – verbs, whWords (100d) – *interrogQ, imperQ, properNounSubj, qAsksWhatHappens(To), qNeedsExplanation, procWords, maxPMIVbsWithProc, maxPMIVbsNearHowWithProc, maxPMIWithProc, maxPMINounsWithSci, actionVbs, maxCosSimWEmbdsAnd(Proc/Action), maxCosSimNounsEmbdAndSci, maxCosSimVbsEmbdAnd(Proc/Action), qHasHowAndModal.* |
| **SubjectiveConcept** – verbs, whWords (100d) – *interrogQ, imperQ, qHasSecondPersPron, #opinionWords, #sciWords, subjLinkedByYour, whWords, #nouns, qHasWordWithNumVals, qAsksForAPreference, #preds, avgPMIWithSci, avgSemSimWith(Sci/Person), maxCosSimWEmbdWithSci, maxCosSimVbAdjAdvEmbdsWithSci, onlySubjIsYou, aSubjIsYou, qAsksYouAboutSmthing, subjectivity.* | **Equation** – verbs (100d) – *interrogQ, imperQ, whWords, eqWords, maxCosSimWEmbdsAndEq, maxSemSimOfWordsWithEq.* |
| | **Solution** – verbs, subject (200d) – *interrogQ, imperQ, whWords, qHasWordWithNumVals, subjHasNumVals, qHasAdverbialWithHow, maxSemSimWithQuantity, qHasWordRelToQuantity, #sciWords, qHasUnitsOfMeasure, maxCosSimWEmbdsAnd(Sci/Sol/Quantity), maxCosSimVbsEmbdAndSol, maxCosSimSubjEmbdWith(Sci/Quantity), #wordsWithNumVals, qHasNumbers, solWords.* |
| **Select1** – conjunctions, whWords (100d) – *interrogQ, imperQ, whWords, qHasEnum, qIsEnum, nextSentHasEnum, nextSentIsEnum, qHasEnumWithOr, qHasOr, subjWithDet, singularSubj, subjWithDetOrWhWord, optionsListInPrevSent, qFollowedByOptionsList.* | |
| **TrueFalse** – mainVerb, whWords (200d) – *interrogQ, imperQ, whWords, interrogQStartsWithVerb, trueFalseWords, parseTreeHasSQ, qStartsWithAuxVerb, qHasOr, mainClauseStartsWithVerb.* | **Drawing** – verbs (200d) – *interrogQ, imperQ, drawWords, whWords, maxCosSimWEmbdsAndDraw, maxSemSimWithDraw, maxPMIWithDraw.* |
| | **ContextSensitive** – contentWords, whWords (100d) – *interrogQ, imperQ, allQHasNoun, CSWords, maxCosSimWEmbdsAndCSWords, qHasThisThatEach, minPMINounsAndSci, qHasNounWithDetNearSubj, qHasTemp, prevSntHasCSWord, (max/min)CosSimNounWithDetEmbdAndSci, (max/min)CosSimNounEmbdAndSci, maxCosSimNounEmbdAndCSWords, minCosSimPrevSntNounEmbdAnd(Sci/CSWords), minPMINounWithDetAndSubj.* |
| **List** – mainVerb, subject, whWords (100d) – *interrogQ, imperQ, whWords, qHasNumbers, qHasNumberWithDet, pluralNounWithDet, pluralSubj, qHasQuantifierModif, subjWithDetOrWhWord, pluralSubjInMainClause, subjWithNumberInMainClause, subjWithDetOrWhWordInMainClause, qHasNounWithNumberQuantif, maxCosSimWEmbdsWithList, qHasWordList, qMainClauseHasNounWithNumberQuantif, maxCosSimDetsAdjsEmbdsWithQuantity, qHasEnum, subjWithNumber.* | |
| | **AnswersWillVary** – verbs, pronouns, adjectives (200d) – *interrogQ, imperQ, qHasNumberWithDet, qHasNumbers, qHasExample, subjectivity, #opinions, explanationWords, qHasQuantifierModif, whWords, qHasNounWithNumberQuantifier, pluralSubj, qAsksYouAboutSmthing.* |
| **Multi-Part** – conjunctions, whWords (100d) – *interrogQ, imperQ, qHasEnumWithAnd, subjsLinkedByAnd, posTagsLinkedByAnd, qHasAnd, #fillInTheGaps, prevSentHasAnd, oneWordInQ, qHasEnum, whWords, qHasClausesLinkedByAnd, clausesStartWithWhWordOrAdverbial.* | **Ordered** – verbs, whWords (200d) – *interrogQ, imperQ, orderWords, qNeedsExplanation, qHasHowAndModal, actionVbs, qHasAntonyms, #fillInTheGaps, dobjsLinkedByAnd, vbsLinkedByAnd, subjsLinkedByAnd, clausesLinkedByAnd, actionVbs, maxCosSimWEmbdsAndProc, maxCosSimWEmbdsAndAction, maxCosSimWEmbdsAndSci.* |
| **VeryShortAnswer** – verbs, whWords (200d) – *interrogQ, imperQ, whWords, solWords, qHasExplanWhWord, qAsksWhatHappens(To), qHasNounWithWhWordOrDet, qEndsInColon, qHasExample, #preds, qHasSpecificWhWord, maxCosSimWEmbdsAndSolution, #fillInTheGaps.* | **SelectN** – conjunctions, whWords (200d) – *interrogQ, imperQ, whWords, qIsEnum, nextSentHasEnum, nextSentIsEnum, qHasEnumWithOr, qHasEnum, pluralSubj, qHasPluralNouns, qFollowedByOptionsList.* |
| **OtherConstructedResponse** – verbs, whWords (200d) – *interrogQ, imperQ, whWords, #qAsksForDef, qEndsInColon, subjWithDet, #preds, qAsksWhatHappens(To), maxCosSimWEmbdsAnd(Procedure/Action).* | |

**Fig. 1.** Feature sets per classifier with WE POS and dimension (d).

We use tailored features, WEs and inter-class correlations. The WE features are derived from [10]. For a given sentence, these WE features are the sum of the keyword embeddings normalized to a unit length vector. We experimented with different WE dimensions and keyword types (based on POS tags). Figure 1 shows the tailored features, word types and dimension.

We leveraged inter-class correlations to boost performance. Specifically, we used the training data to sort the classes in increasing order of the maximum information gain of each class given the labels of all the other classes. The ordered set of class types is: *ContextSensitive, Clarification, Drawing, Equation, Select1, TrueFalse, Multi-Part, SelectN, OtherConstructedResponse, Solution, VeryShortAnswer, List, AnswersWillVary, SubjectiveConcept, ProcessProcedure* and *Ordered*. We trained separate binary-label artificial neural networks [12] for each class, using the gold standard labels of all less dependent classes. At test time, the classification of a question progressed from the least dependent through the most dependent class and each of the prior classes' *predicted* labels were included in the feature set of subsequent classes.

**Table 2.** Test Set $F_1$-score results per class using *All* features.

| Training | Clarif | SubjC | Sel1 | SelN | T/F | List | MultiP | ShrtA | OtCR | Proc | Eq | Soln | Draw | CntS | AnsV | Order |
|---|---|---|---|---|---|---|---|---|---|---|---|---|---|---|---|---|
| Orig | 0.273 | 0.091 | **0.778** | 0.00 | 0.867 | 0.596 | 0.580 | 0.62 | 0.81 | 0.471 | 0.667 | 0.400 | 0.750 | 0.55 | 0.526 | 0.472 |
| Orig + Web | **0.296** | **0.270** | 0.705 | 0.00 | **0.968** | **0.617** | **0.602** | **0.66** | **0.85** | **0.629** | **0.800** | **0.500** | **0.889** | **0.56** | **0.588** | **0.574** |

# 5   Results

We employ a supervised approach using artificial neural networks to classify questions based on the expected characteristics of answers. We tuned the parameters of the networks for each feature set using the validation data. Finally, we used 2 hidden layers and 3000 epochs. The number of nodes in a hidden layer ranges from 3 to 10 and the learning rate has values between 0.01 and 0.1.

In Table 2, we present the $F_1$-score using *All* our features (tailored features, WEs and labels of less dependent classes) based on two training datasets, the first using the training from [5] (labeled *Orig*), the second including the web data (labeled *Orig + Web*). As the table shows, when training on *All* features, adding the web training data to the original training set (*Orig + Web*) results in better performance on all but one class (*Select1*). In this setting, the three best performing classes are *TrueFalse*, *Drawing*, and *OtherConstructedResponse* with $F_1$-score = 0.968, 0.889, and 0.85, respectively. Disregarding *SelectN* (with only a single example in the test set ), the three worst performing classes are *SubjectiveConcept*, *Clarification*, and *Solution* with an $F_1$-score = 0.270, 0.296, and 0.500, respectively. All other classes had an $F_1$-score $\geq$ 0.56. Considering the results obtained using the two different training sets (*Orig* versus *Orig + Web*), we conclude that the web data played an important role in our task, helping the classifier learn better patterns across question types.

We provide the overall results of our classification approach when training on *Orig + Web*, in terms of the weighted $F_1$-score over all the classes, in Table 3. The results show that our best feature set *All* provides a substantial improvement compared to other studied feature versions. Using *All* features outperforms the baseline (*WE*) by 56% relative to the weighted $F_1$-score. Compared to the tailored features (*T*) and their combination with WEs (*TWE*), our full feature set achieves a relative increase in the weighted $F_1$-score of 16% and 4%, respectively. The best performance is achieved using all features and training on *Orig + Web*, with a weighted $F_1$-score = 0.678, while training only on *Orig* using all features yields a weighted $F_1$-score = 0.633.

**Table 3.** Weighted $F_1$-score over all classes

| Features | WE | T | TWE | All |
|---|---|---|---|---|
| **Weighted $F_1$-score** | 0.434 | 0.582 | 0.653 | 0.678 |

# 6   Conclusions

We proposed a new approach to classify questions based on the expected characteristics of answers that aims to facilitate the analysis of student responses. We employed fully-connected deep neural networks and assessed the value of typical WE features, tailored features and inter-class correlations. Our approach achieves a weighted $F_1$-score of 0.678, outperforming the baseline by 56% in a relative sense. The experimental results demonstrate the effectiveness of the system, which has a variety of potential applications.

**Acknowledgements.** This research was supported by the Institute of Education Sciences, U.S. Department of Education, Grant R305A120808 to University of North Texas. Opinions expressed are those of the authors.

# References

1. Bloom, B.S.: Taxonomy of Educational Objectives: The Classification of Educational Goals: Cognitive Domain. Longman, New York (1956)
2. Conner, M.: What a reference librarian should know. Libr. J. **52**(8), 415–418 (1927)
3. Crews, K.D.: The accuracy of reference service: Variables for research and implementation. Libr. Inf. Sci. Res. **10**(3), 331–355 (1988)
4. Curto, S., Mendes, A.C., Coheur, L.: Question generation based on lexico-syntactic patterns learned from the web. Dialogue Discourse **3**(2), 147–175 (2012)
5. Godea, A., Nielsen, R.: Annotating educational questions for student response analysis. In: 11th Edition of the Language Resources and Evaluation Conference (2018)
6. Harabagiu, S.M., Moldovan, D.I., Paşca, M., Mihalcea, R., Surdeanu, M., Bunescu, R., Gîrju, C.R., Rus, V., Morărescu, P.: FALCON: Boosting knowledge for answer engines (2000)
7. Hovy, E., Hermjakob, U., Ravichandran, D.: A question/answer typology with surface text patterns. In: Proceedings of the Second International Conference on Human Language Technology Research, pp. 247–251. Morgan Kaufmann Publishers Inc. (2002)
8. İnce, İ.F.: Intellegent question classification for e-learning environments by data mining techniques. Ph.D. thesis, Institute of Science (2008)
9. Li, X., Roth, D.: Learning question classifiers. In: Proceedings of the 19th International Conference on Computational Linguistics, vol. 1, pp. 1–7. Association for Computational Linguistics (2002)
10. Pennington, J., Socher, R., Manning, C.D.: Glove: global vectors for word representation. EMNLP **14**, 1532–1543 (2014)
11. Radev, D., Fan, W., Qi, H., Wu, H., Grewal, A.: Probabilistic question answering on the web. J. Assoc. Inf. Sci. Technol. **56**(6), 571–583 (2005)
12. Team, D.D.: Deeplearning4j: open-source distributed deep learning for the JVM, apache software foundation license 2.0. (2017). http://deeplearning4j.org

# On the Learning Curve Attrition Bias in Additive Factor Modeling

Cyril Goutte[1(✉)], Guillaume Durand[2], and Serge Léger[2]

[1] National Research Council Canada, Ottawa, ON, Canada
{Cyril.Goutte,Guillaume.Durand,Serge.Leger}@nrc-cnrc.gc.ca
[2] National Research Council Canada, Moncton, NB, Canada

**Abstract.** Learning curves are a crucial tool to accurately measure learners skills and give meaningful feedback in intelligent tutoring systems. Here we discuss various ways of building learning curves from empirical data for the Additive Factor model (AFM) and highlight their limitations. We focus on the impact of student attrition, a.k.a. *attrition bias*. We propose a new way to build learning curves, by combining empirical observations and AFM predictions. We validate this proposition on simulated data, and test it on real datasets.

**Keywords:** Learning curves · Attrition bias · Additive factor model

## 1 Introduction

Artificial Intelligence in education offers increasingly advanced models to help understand complex learning mechanisms and improve learning environments, experiences and efficiency. The Additive Factor Model (AFM) [1] is an effective model of student performance, used in PSLC-Datashop [5]. It characterizes learners and skills (a.k.a. knowledge components) through dedicated model parameters. Learning curves are an essential tool to improve learning systems. By plotting performance versus opportunities to practice, they help us measure how learning takes place [9], and allow practitioners to understand, compare and improve a cognitive model [8,10,11]. A steeper curve reflects faster skill acquisition.

However, over time and increasing number of opportunities, more learners master the skill and stop practicing it, or simply drop-out. The amount of observations per number of opportunities drops, so that empirical learning curves quickly degenerate and providing incorrect visual guidance. This problem is known as the *attrition bias* in the literature [10,11], an example of *censoring*: it under-estimates the amount of learning, among other issues [4]. This paper proposes to use the Additive Factor Model to address the student attrition bias.

## 2 Methods

The Additive Factor Model (AFM) is a cognitive diagnostic model proposed by Cen [1,3] and implemented in the PSLC Datashop [5]. It models probability of

© Her Majesty the Queen in Right of Canada 2018
C. Penstein Rosé et al. (Eds.): AIED 2018, LNAI 10948, pp. 109–113, 2018.
https://doi.org/10.1007/978-3-319-93846-2_21

success of student $i$ on item $j$ as a mixed-effect logistic regression:

$$P(Y_{ij} = 1 | \alpha_i, \boldsymbol{\beta}, \boldsymbol{\gamma}) = \frac{1}{1 + \exp\left(-\alpha_i - \sum_{k=1}^{K} q_{jk}\left(\beta_k + \gamma_k t_{ik}\right)\right)} \quad (1)$$

with $\alpha_i$ the *proficiency* of student $i$, $\beta_k$ the *easiness* and $\gamma_k$ the *learning rate* of skill $k = 1 \dots K$; the *Q-matrix* $\mathbf{Q} = [q_{jk}]$ represents the mapping of items to skills, and $t_{ik}$ is the number of opportunities student $i$ had on skill $k$.

**Performance curves** offer a convenient way to show how skills or knowledge components are acquired as students practice.[1] Ideally, if students do learn, learning curves will increase, which is enforced in AFM by constraining $\gamma_k \geq 0$. For an individual student with proficiency $\alpha = 0$, the learning curve is:

$$\mathsf{LC}_k(t) = \text{logit}^{-1}\left(\beta_k + \gamma_k t\right) = \frac{1}{1 + \exp\left(-\beta_k - \gamma_k t\right)}. \quad (2)$$

The **individual learning curve** is disconnected from actual observations and does not account for averaging performance across students. **Empirical learning curves** address this: with $p_k^{it} \in [0,1]$ the underlying probability of success for student $i$ at opportunity $t$, and $o_k^{it} \in \{0,1\}$ the observable binary outcome, let us denote $\mathcal{S}_k(t)$ the subset of students who practiced skill $k$ at opportunity $t$. The empirical curve averages success over students who practiced the skill:

$$\mathsf{LC}_k^{\text{Emp}}(t) = \frac{1}{|\mathcal{S}_k(t)|} \sum_{i \in \mathcal{S}_k(t)} o_k^{it}, \quad \text{while} \quad \mathsf{LC}_k^{\text{AFM}}(t) = \frac{1}{|\mathcal{S}_k(t)|} \sum_{i \in \mathcal{S}_k(t)} \widehat{p}_k^{it} \quad (3)$$

is the **model curve** produced by using AFM model estimates $\widehat{p}_k^{it}$ (Eq. 1) in lieu of $o_k^{it}$ to smooth the curve.[2] $\mathsf{LC}_k^{\text{Emp}}(t)$ and $\mathsf{LC}_k^{\text{AFM}}(t)$ are the red and dashed blue curves in Fig. 1. Observations are typically *censored* due to attrition bias: students move on to practice other skills after several success, so averages in Eq. 3 are on diminishing student bases as $t$ grows. We illustrate this impact by comparing with averages over all students, without censoring:

$$\mathsf{LC}_k^{\text{All}}(t) = \frac{1}{N} \sum_{i=1}^{N} o_k^{it}, \quad \text{and} \quad \mathsf{LC}_k^{\text{Ref}}(t) = \frac{1}{N} \sum_{i=1}^{N} p_k^{it} \quad (4)$$

$\mathsf{LC}_k^{\text{All}}(t)$ is typically only available for simulated data when all $o_k^{it}$ are available, and $p_k^{it}$ is known. In real situations, some $o_k^{it}$ are missing and $p_k^{it}$ is unknown. However, AFM provides[3] estimates $\widehat{p}_k^{it}$ (Eq. 1), so that we can impute the missing data and compute the *completed* learning curve:

$$\overline{o}_k^{it} = \begin{cases} o_k^{it} \text{ if } i \in \mathcal{S}_k(t) \\ \widehat{p}_k^{it} \text{ otherwise} \end{cases} \quad \text{and} \quad \mathsf{LC}_k^{\text{cmp}}(t) = \frac{1}{N} \sum_{i=1}^{N} \overline{o}_k^{it} \quad (5)$$

---

[1] *Error curves* show probability of error, *Learning curves* probability of success.
[2] Both curves are shown in the PSLC Datashop platform diagnostics.
[3] Using parameters $\widehat{\beta}$ and $\widehat{\gamma}$ estimated on observations outcomes $o_k^{it}$ only.

**Table 1.** Validation on various learning conditions (easy, medium hard skill; fast, slow and no learning): mean absolute distance (in %) to ideal (not observable) error curve.

| $\gamma$ | $\beta$: | | | | | | | | | | | |
|---|---|---|---|---|---|---|---|---|---|---|---|---|
| | $-1.5$ (hard) | | | | 0.0 (medium) | | | | 0.7 (easy) | | | |
| | $LC^{Emp}$ | $LC^{AFM}$ | $LC^{All}$ | $LC^{Cmp}$ | $LC^{Emp}$ | $LC^{AFM}$ | $LC^{All}$ | $LC^{Cmp}$ | $LC^{Emp}$ | $LC^{AFM}$ | $LC^{All}$ | $LC^{Cmp}$ |
| .05 (no) | 5.25 | 3.97 | 3.32 | **3.28** | 12.58 | 10.28 | 2.99 | **2.65** | 14.61 | 12.98 | 4.46 | **4.12** |
| .30 (slow) | 8.82 | 7.65 | 3.55 | **3.09** | 12.15 | 9.62 | 3.04 | **2.74** | 13.07 | 10.06 | 3.04 | **2.47** |
| .75 (fast) | 6.12 | 2.99 | 2.36 | **2.33** | 5.36 | 2.28 | **0.89** | 0.90 | 6.43 | 1.79 | **0.75** | 0.77 |

## 3 Experiments

We first use artificial data simulating various conditions to validate our approach. We simulate hard, medium and easy skills with $\beta \in \{-1.5, 0, 0.7\}$ and fast, slow and no learning with $\gamma \in \{.75, .3, .05\}$. For each learning condition ($\beta$, $\gamma$ pair), we sample 100 students by drawing their $\alpha_i$ from a Gaussian distribution with zero mean and unit variance. To reflect attrition, we assume students stop practicing a skill after four consecutive successes. We then compute four learning curves: empirical $LC_k^{Emp}(t)$, model-smoothed $LC_k^{AFM}(t)$, completed using model imputation $LC_k^{Cmp}(t)$ and empirical over all outcomes $LC_k^{All}(t)$ (unobservable, but useful for comparison). Table 1 measures the quality of each curve by computing the mean average error to the reference learning curve $LC_k^{Ref}(t)$, again only available for simulated data. Our proposed completed learning curve $LC^{Cmp}$ is the closest to the reference curve in seven out of nine cases. In the remaining two cases, it is not significantly different from $LC^{All}$, which uses non observed outcomes and is therefore not available in practice. Visual inspection (not included here for lack of space) shows the over-estimation bias caused by attrition. With *no* learning, the empirical curves actually *increase*, causing large error w.r.t. reference.

For our experiments on real data, we use the "Geometry Area (1996-97)" dataset (a.k.a **ds76** henceforth) from DataShop [5]. It contains 6778 observations for 59 students on 139 items from the "area unit" of the Geometry Cognitive Tutor course (school year 1996–1997). This classic datasets has been used and studied extensively [1,2,6,7]. From the several cognitive models available, we selected one generated by LFA [1], "hLFASearchModel1_context-single", with 19 skills and 5104 observations. This cognitive model shows good predictive abilities (according to Datashop metrics) and interesting learning curves.

Using the dataset exported from Datashop, we estimated the AFM model $(\widehat{\alpha}, \widehat{\beta}, \widehat{\gamma})$ for the chosen cognitive model, and used it to obtain the $\widehat{p}_k^{it}$ needed to build $LC^{AFM}$ and $LC^{Cmp}$. Figure 1 shows the impact of our proposed learning curve on the diagnostics of four knowledge components from this cognitive model:

**parallelogram-area_context** (No learning) Low but flat error rate; Erratic.
**radius-from-area** (Still high) High error rate with no apparent learning; The empirical curves even seem to increase.

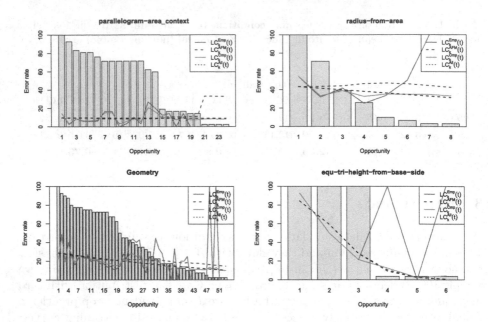

**Fig. 1.** Error curves for Datashop `ds76`. Two problematic KC on top, two "Good" ones below. Gray bars show student attrition as #opportunities increase.

`Geometry`: (Good) Slow but steady decrease in error; many opportunities.
`equ-tri-height-from-base-side`: (Good) Quick reduction in error over few opportunities; Extreme fluctuations in empirical error above 4 opportunities.

**Top left:** All curves show no learning (AFM estimate $\gamma \approx 0.00$). $\mathsf{LC}^{\mathrm{Cmp}}$ is similar to $\mathsf{LC}^{\mathrm{Emp}}$ for low opportunities, but better behaved as attrition kicks in. **Top right:** $\mathsf{LC}^{\mathrm{Emp}}$ and $\mathsf{LC}^{\mathrm{AFM}}$ show *increase* due to student attrition, but the completed learning curves shows slow learning, consistent with an estimated $\gamma = 0.08$ in AFM. **Bottom left:** Erratic behavior of $\mathsf{LC}^{\mathrm{Emp}}$ after $\sim 20$ opportunities is completely smoothed out: $\mathsf{LC}^{\mathrm{Cmp}}$ shows slow but steady learning, again consistent with an estimated $\gamma \approx 0.03$. **Bottom right:** As all but a few students stop practicing, $\mathsf{LC}^{\mathrm{Emp}}$ fluctuates from 100% to 0%. On the other hand, $\mathsf{LC}^{\mathrm{Cmp}}$ reflects the fact that this skill is learned quickly ($\gamma = 1.38$).

## 4  Summary

Learning curves are an essential tool to analyze cognitive models and improve learning systems. We described various ways to compute learning curves with AFM, show and discuss limitations of usual curves (used e.g. in Datashop). We confirm that student attrition is as a major source of bias and propose a new way to build learning curves by imputing missing data with AFM estimates. We validated our approach on simulated data, then showed how it improves diagnosis and interpretation of learning curves for a real-life cognitive model.

**Acknowledgement.** M. McLaughlin, C. Tipper for help with Datashop ds76.

# References

1. Cen, H., Koedinger, K., Junker, B.: Learning factors analysis – a general method for cognitive model evaluation and improvement. In: Ikeda, M., Ashley, K.D., Chan, T.-W. (eds.) ITS 2006. LNCS, vol. 4053, pp. 164–175. Springer, Heidelberg (2006). https://doi.org/10.1007/11774303_17
2. Cen, H., Koedinger, K., Junker, B.: Is overpractice necessary? – improving learning efficiency with the cognitive tutor through educational data mining. In: Luckin, R., Koedinger, K.R., Greer, J. (eds.) Proceeding of the 2007 Conference on Artificial intelligence in Education: Building Technology Rich Learning Contexts that Work. Frontiers in Artificial Intelligence and Applications, vol. 158, pp. 511–518. IOS Press, Amsterdam (2007)
3. Cen, H., Koedinger, K., Junker, B.: Comparing two IRT models for conjunctive skills. In: Woolf, B.P., Aïmeur, E., Nkambou, R., Lajoie, S. (eds.) ITS 2008. LNCS, vol. 5091, pp. 796–798. Springer, Heidelberg (2008). https://doi.org/10.1007/978-3-540-69132-7_111
4. Chen, L., Dubrawski, A.: Learning from learning curves: discovering interpretable learning trajectories. In: Proceedings of the Seventh International Learning Analytics & Knowledge Conference, LAK 2017, pp. 544–545, New York, NY, USA. ACM (2017)
5. Koedinger, K., Baker, R., Cunningham, K., Skogsholm, A., Leber, B., Stamper, J.: A data repository for the EDM community: the PSLC Datashop. In: Romero, C., Ventura, S., Pechenizkiy, M., Baker, R. (eds.) Handbook of Educational Data Mining. CRC Press (2010)
6. Koedinger, K.R., Cunningham, K., Skogsholm, A., Leber, B.: An open repository and analysis tools for fine-grained, longitudinal learner data. In: EDM, pp. 157–166 (2008). www.educationaldatamining.org
7. Koedinger, K.R., McLaughlin, E.A., Stamper, J.C.: Automated student model improvement. In: EDM, pp. 17–24 (2012). www.educationaldatamining.org
8. Linehan, C., Bellord, G., Kirman, B., Morford, Z.H., Roche, B.: Learning curves: analysing pace and challenge in four successful puzzle games. In: Proceedings of the First ACM SIGCHI Annual Symposium on Computer-Human Interaction in Play, CHI PLAY 2014, pp. 181–190, New York, NY, USA. ACM (2014)
9. Martin, B., Mitrovic, A., Koedinger, K.R., Mathan, S.: Evaluating and improving adaptive educational systems with learning curves. User Model. User-Adap. Inter. **21**(3), 249–283 (2011)
10. Murray, R.C., Ritter, S., Nixon, T., Schwiebert, R., Hausmann, R.G.M., Towle, B., Fancsali, S.E., Vuong, A.: Revealing the learning in learning curves. In: Lane, H.C., Yacef, K., Mostow, J., Pavlik, P. (eds.) AIED 2013. LNCS (LNAI), vol. 7926, pp. 473–482. Springer, Heidelberg (2013). https://doi.org/10.1007/978-3-642-39112-5_48
11. Nixon, T., Fancsali, S., Ritter, S.: The complex dynamics of aggregate learning curves. In: Proceedings of the 6th International Conference on Educational Data Mining (2013)

# The Impact of Affect-Aware Support on Learning Tasks that Differ in Their Cognitive Demands

Beate Grawemeyer[1](✉), Manolis Mavrikis[2], Claudia Mazziotti[3],
Anouschka van Leeuwen[4], and Nikol Rummel[3]

[1] School of Computing, Electronics and Maths, Coventry University, Coventry, UK
ac7655@coventry.ac.uk
[2] UCL Knowledge Lab, Institute of Education, University College London,
London, UK
m.mavrikis@ioe.ac.uk
[3] Institute of Educational Research, Ruhr-Universität Bochum, Bochum, Germany
{claudia.mazziotti,nikol.rummel}@rub.de
[4] Faculty of Social and Behavioral Science, Utrecht University, Utrecht, Netherlands
A.vanLeeuwen@uu.nl

**Abstract.** This paper investigates the effect of affect-aware support on learning tasks that differ in their cognitive demands. We conducted a study with the iTalk2learn platform where students are undertaking fractions tasks of varying difficulty and assigned in one of two groups; one group used the iTalk2learn platform that included the affect-aware support, whereas in the other group the affect-aware support was switched off and support was provided based on students' performance only. We investigated the hypothesis that affect-aware support has a more pronounced effect when the cognitive demands of the tasks are higher. The results suggest that students that undertook the more challenging tasks were significantly more in-flow and less confused in the group where affect-aware support was provided than students who were supported based on their performance only.

## 1 Introduction

It is well understood that not only cognitive factors but also students' affective states play a major role for learning. In recent years some studies have been undertaken to shed more light on the relation between learning and emotion [1,2,4]. However, previous research has missed investigation of how characteristics of learning tasks (e.g., difficulty level) are linked to students' affective states. Therefore, the first goal of our study is to investigate whether and to what extent students differ in their emotional response to different kinds of tasks. Since we know from [2,6] research and our own research that affect-aware support has the power to promote or keep students in a 'positive' affective state, the second goal of our study is to investigate what role the affect aware support plays when students engage with different kinds of tasks.

© Springer International Publishing AG, part of Springer Nature 2018
C. Penstein Rosé et al. (Eds.): AIED 2018, LNAI 10948, pp. 114–118, 2018.
https://doi.org/10.1007/978-3-319-93846-2_22

We report results from a user study which investigated the hypothesis that affect-aware support has a more pronounced effect when the cognitive demands of the task are higher. In Grawemeyer et al. [3] we describe the development of affect-aware support and the effect of the support across fraction learning tasks. In contrast, in this paper we report on the impact of affect-aware support on tasks that differ in their cognitive demands.

## 2    The iTalk2Learn Platform

iTalk2learn is a learning platform for children aged 8–12 years old who are learning fractions.

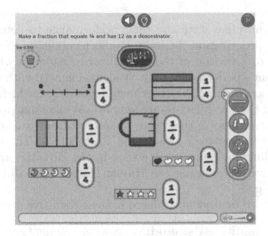

**Fig. 1.** Exploratory learning environment.

Figure 1 shows the *Fractions Lab* interface of the exploratory learning environment. The learning task is displayed at the top of the screen. Students are asked to solve the task by selecting a representation (from the right-hand side menu) which they manipulate in order to construct an answer to the given task.

## 3    User Study

To investigate our research questions we conducted a user study in which students were aligned to either the affect-aware support condition or the non-affect aware support.

47 students took part in this study. These participants were all primary school students, aged between 8 and 10 years old, recruited from two schools in the UK.

Students were randomly allocated in either of the groups. In the affect condition (N = 25) students were given access to the full iTalk2Learn system, which

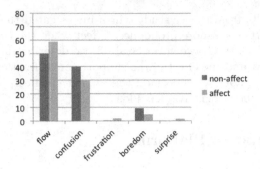

**Fig. 2.** Affective states of low/medium cognitive demanding tasks from the affect or non-affect condition.

uses the student's affective state and their performance to determine the feedback type and its presentation. In the non-affect condition (N = 22) students were given access to a version of the iTalk2Learn system in which feedback is based on the student's performance only. Students engaged with the iTalk2Learn system for 40 min according to the experimental condition, which included either the affect-aware or the non-affect-aware support. While students were engaging with the iTalk2learn platform they were monitored from two researchers using the Baker-Rodrigo Ocumpaugh Monitoring Protocol [5]. The researchers who undertook the coding, and who were trained in the BROMP method, recorded the student affective states using the Human Affect Recording Tool (HART) Android mobile app.

The tasks provided to students differed in their cognitive demands as follows:

- **low/medium cognitive demand:** tasks where students are asked to create one or more fractions and check if they are equivalent in the compare box. Students can complete these tasks without performing any fraction calculation.
- **high cognitive demand:** tasks where students create a particular fraction as well as an equivalent fraction with particular constraints (e.g. a specific representation or a different denominator).

## 4    Results

To investigate our research questions we conducted a multivariate ANOVA using Pillais trace for the different affective states that occurred within the groups for the different learning tasks.

**Tasks with Low/medium Cognitive Demand.** The affective states of students while performing low/medium cognitive demanding tasks can be seen in Fig. 2. It shows that students in the affect and non-affect condition were mainly

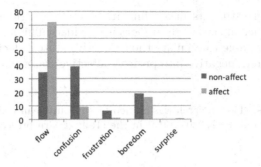

**Fig. 3.** Affective states of high cognitive demanding task from the affect or non-affect condition.

in flow (affect mean: 58.91; non-affect mean: 49.91). There was no significant statistical difference in students' affective state based on which condition they were in V = 0.086, F(5, 67) = 1.26, p > .05.

**Tasks with High Cognitive Demand.** The affective states of students in high cognitively demanding tasks can be seen in Fig. 3. It shows that in the affect condition students were mainly in flow (affect mean: 72.12; non-affect mean: 35.78). While students in the non-affect condition were mainly confused (affect mean: 9.21; non-affect mean: 39.08;). There was a significant statistical difference in students' affective state based on which condition they were assigned to V = 0.29 F(4, 64) = 6.55, p < .05. Follow-up t-tests between the different affective states and the conditions, revealed a significant difference in students being in flow and the affect and non-affect condition (t(55.42) = 3.92, p < .05). Also, there was a significant difference between the groups and students being confused (t(45.52) = −4.12. p < .05).

## 5   Discussion and Conclusion

We developed a system that is able to provide intelligent support that takes into account students' affective state. The aim of the affect aware support is to move students from negative into positive affective states and hence tries to regulate a students' affective state by tailoring its feedback [3].

The intelligent affect-aware support (affect condition) was compared against support that was based on students performance only (non-affect condition). The results show that in low/medium cognitive demanding tasks no difference between the affect and non-affect group in students affective state was detected. However, on high cognitive demanding tasks there was a significant difference between students who received the affect-aware support and the students who received the support based on their performance only. Students in the affect condition were significantly more in flow and less confused than students in the non-affect condition. This may imply that when the cognitive demands of the task are high, students might find it difficult to regulate their affective states. However, when affect-aware support is provided in high cognitive demand tasks, students were able to regulate their affective states effectively and might have been moved from negative into positive affective states via the affect-aware support.

**Acknowledgments.** This research was funded by the European Union in the Seventh Framework Programme (FP7/2007-2013) in the iTalk-2Learn project (318051).

# References

1. Baker, R.S.J.d., D'Mello, S.K., Rodrigo, M.T., Graesser, A.C.: Better to be frustrated than bored: the incidence, persistence, and impact of learners cognitive-affective states during interactions with three different computer-based learning environments. Int. J. Hum. Comput. Stud. **68**(4), 223–241 (2010)
2. D'Mello, S.K., Lehman, B., Pekrun, R., Graesser, A.C.: Confusion can be beneficial for learning. Learn. Instruc. **29**(1), 153–170 (2014)
3. Grawemeyer, B., Mavrikis, M., Holmes, W., Gutiérrez-Santos, S., Wiedmann, M., Rummel, N.: Affective learning: improving engagement and enhancing learning with affect-aware feedback. User Model. User Adap. Inter. **27**, 119–158 (2017). Special Issue on Impact of Learner Modeling
4. Kort, B., Reilly, R., Picard, R.: An affective model of the interplay between emotions and learning. In: IEEE International Conference on Advanced Learning Technologies, pp. 43–46 (2001)
5. Ocumpaugh, J., Baker, R., Rodrigo, M.: Baker-Rodrigo observation method protocol (BROMP) 1.0. training manual version 1.0. Technical report. EdLab, New York. Ateneo Laboratory for the Learning Sciences, Manila (2012)
6. Porayska-Pomsta, K., Mavrikis, M., Pain, H.: Diagnosing and acting on student affect: the tutors perspective. User Model. User Adap. Inter. **18**(1), 125–173 (2008)

# Mitigating Knowledge Decay from Instruction with Voluntary Use of an Adaptive Learning System

Andrew J. Hampton[1]([✉]), Benjamin D. Nye[2], Philip I. Pavlik[1],
William R. Swartout[2], Arthur C. Graesser[1], and Joseph Gunderson[3]

[1] Institute for Intelligent Systems,
University of Memphis, Memphis, TN 38152, USA
{jhmpton8,ppavlik,graesser}@memphis.edu
[2] Institute for Creative Technologies,
University of Southern California, Los Angeles, CA 90007, USA
{nye,swartout}@ict.usc.edu
[3] California State Polytechnic University, Pomona, CA 91768, USA
jrgunderson@cpp.edu

**Abstract.** Knowledge decays across breaks in instruction. Learners lack the metacognition to self-assess their knowledge decay and effectively self-direct review, as well as lacking interactive exercises appropriate to their individual knowledge level. Adaptive learning systems offer the potential to mitigate these issues, by providing open learner models to facilitate learner's understanding of their knowledge levels and by presenting personalized practice exercises. The current study analyzes differences in knowledge decay between learners randomly assigned to an intervention where they could use an adaptive system during a long gap between courses, compared with a control condition. The experimental condition used the Personal Assistant for Life-Long Learning (PAL3), a tablet-based adaptive learning system integrating multiple intelligent tutoring systems and conventional learning resources. It contained electronics content relevant to the experiment participants, Navy sailors who graduated from apprentice electronics courses (A-School) awaiting assignment to their next training (C-School). The study was conducted over one month, collecting performance data with a counterbalanced pre-, mid-, and post-test. The control condition exhibited the expected decay. The PAL3 condition showed a significant difference from the control, with no significant knowledge decay in their overall knowledge, despite substantial variance in usage for PAL3 (e.g., most of overall use in the first week, with fewer participants engaging as time went on). Interestingly, while overall decay was mitigated in PAL3, this result was primarily through gains in some knowledge offsetting losses in other knowledge. Overall, these results indicate that adaptive study tools can help prevent knowledge decay, even with voluntary usage.

**Keywords:** Mobile learning · ITS · Electrical engineering · Life-long learning

© Springer International Publishing AG, part of Springer Nature 2018
C. Penstein Rosé et al. (Eds.): AIED 2018, LNAI 10948, pp. 119–133, 2018.
https://doi.org/10.1007/978-3-319-93846-2_23

# 1 Introduction

Knowledge decay has been consistently reported across long breaks in education and training. In most cases, these breaks are beyond the control of educational institutions. The most familiar example is the annual summer break at virtually all levels of American formal education, which at K–12 levels is reported to result in a loss of knowledge equivalent to about one month of education, with more decay at higher grades [5, 6, 22]. Military training has even more varied challenges, which can include irregular delays between training and using skills, maintaining readiness for reserve units who may use skills only during sporadic training, and qualitative differences in job skills based on location and mission (e.g., deployed vs. stateside, on land vs. at sea). Knowledge decay has also been studied in this context, with reports of decay effect sizes of $d = -0.1$ after a day and $d = -1.4$ after a year [1].

Adaptive learning systems include many features, such as self-paced and always-available content, designed to overcome the traditional barriers to practice over time [28, 37]. However, for such systems to be effective in the long-term, learners must share ownership for maintaining and expanding their knowledge. Except for highly regimented domains, educational and employment institutions are unlikely to have sufficient oversight to anticipate the knowledge that every learner needs—particularly because these needs depend not just on the institution but also on the long-term goals that the learner is pursuing. Consequently, learners need autonomy, motivational enhancements, and tools to pursue life-long learning [15]. Self-regulating learning can be challenging [10], so autonomy in learning must be scaffolded and practiced. Also, learners can seldom accurately assess their own knowledge levels [19, 21]. Most challenging of all, self-regulated learning (particularly via digital interface) presents the "competing with the Internet" problem; every hour spent learning is one that a learner might have spent on streaming videos, playing video games, or other activities.

To address this challenge, a mobile adaptive learning system called the Personal Assistant for Life-Long Learning (PAL3) was designed specifically to support learning and prevent knowledge decay through voluntary use during unsupervised breaks [35]. The current implementation limits its pedagogical scope to electronics knowledge for a specific Navy career field (the Fire Controlman rate) that experiences a long delay (often six to twelve months) between training on electronics fundamentals and training on specific systems. To encourage voluntary use, PAL3 incorporates features to increase engagement, including an embodied pedagogical agent and game-like mechanisms (e.g., open learner models, teams, leaderboards, effort-based point rewards, unlocking customizations).

In this paper, we report the results of a quasi-randomized controlled trial that evaluates in-vivo deployment and voluntary use of PAL3 over an extended period (one month). The primary research question was whether voluntary engagement with this PAL3 learning environment is sufficient to mitigate knowledge decay, or at least reduce it compared with a control condition without PAL3. Related to this primary research question are questions about the variability of usage levels of the system (e.g., how often the learners used it, when they discontinued use) and which skills the system supported best. This paper begins with a review of background research, discussing voluntary engagement in learning systems, and design features of the PAL3 system. Next, we discuss the study design and participant sample. Finally, we present the study results and implications for future work on mitigating knowledge decay.

## 2 Background

### 2.1 Voluntary Learning

Studies have looked at the effects of motivational and game-like features in intelligent tutoring systems on both learning and the amount of use by learners [14, 24, 25, 32]. Games provide a useful structure to reinforce existing knowledge or teach superficial information (e.g., memorization and simple skills), but the use of game-like tasks to facilitate deeper learning and train complex skills is less established [8, 9]. Both research-based systems and commercial applications may have insights into this problem. Systems used in courses or professional development are confronted with a broader range of learners although they may be only externally motivated to use the system. Conversely, most mobile and online learning systems are only used by self-motivated learners who may be more likely to "shop around" and try multiple platforms, leading to a different adoption case.

Interactive Strategy Training for Active Reading and Thinking (iSTART) represents an example of a course-aligned system. iSTART was developed to teach reading strategies that improve comprehension of difficult texts [20, 23]. A subsequent effort designed to encourage self-regulated use, called iSTART-ME (for *Motivationally Enhanced*), overlaid engagement strategies focusing on feedback, incentives, and task difficulty [12]. For example, the system included points that allowed users to advance through levels and purchase rewards and customizable avatars. These additions tended to improve engagement and enjoyment but showed lower learning efficiency, with similar learning gains to the standard iSTART over a longer period of use [13]. This suggests the presence of trade-offs between efficiency and increased motivation.

Duolingo represents a successful mobile application that learners voluntarily download and use, part of a larger growth in educational applications on mobile platforms covering a wide range of topics, from teaching children to count to drilling world geography. Duolingo, the most popular learning application on both iOS and Android platforms, currently has upwards of 200 million active users learning new languages [29], demonstrating the willingness of a sizable portion of the population to dedicate personal time to learning on a mobile interface. However, these examples primarily represent shallow knowledge, approachable with simple stimulus–response pairings. Learner's voluntary engagement for more complex content is unknown.

### 2.2 PAL3 Design

The Personal Assistant for Life-Long Learning (PAL3) system attempts to reduce knowledge decay by implementing motivational features when studying is not mandatory. An overview of the core design principles and features of an earlier prototype of PAL3 has been presented in Swartout et al. [35], so this section will only review the features that are most salient to this evaluation study. The core concept of PAL3 is that a learner can use it throughout their career, including across transitions where their learning is not supervised and may compete with both full-time work and leisure time. The first principle is availability: a mobile system that learners can use in many locations, and a persistent online learning record to facilitate use across time and devices. These are intuitive choices for a life-long learning technology, with persistent mobile learning reported as early as 2000 [32] and persistent virtual learning companions proposed during a similar period [4]. However, despite over a decade using mobile technology and intelligent assistants to support self-directed informal learning, there remain unanswered questions about how to engage a broad cross-section of learners, rather than the self-selected learners commonly studied in MOOC's and mobile apps.

To address this issue, PAL3 anchors content in terms of real-life goals, using a nested approach which assumes that learners make decisions at different time horizons that align to different time scales of cognition [26]. The premise of PAL3's design is that learners revise their longer-term goals on the order of months (called Milestones, such as career advances), that they shift their learning goals on the order of days or weeks (called Topics), and that they shift between specific learning resources on the order of minutes (called Resources). Milestones and Topics are represented internally as a directed prerequisite graph, with Topic mastery framed as preparing for a real-life goal outside of the system (e.g., a promotion, passing a high-stakes test). The final Topic before a Milestone will typically be a Capstone topic, which requires integrating skills from all Topics leading up to the milestone. Topics are presented to the learner in a User Roadmap (see Fig. 1), where a tree of Topics leads up to a career Milestone.

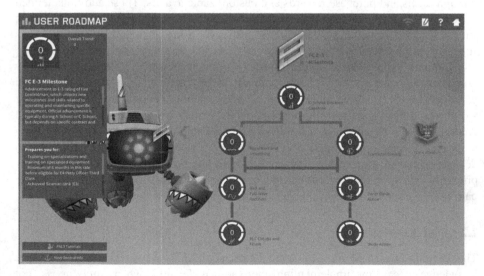

**Fig. 1.** PAL3 User Roadmap, which presents an open learner model on topics needed for a career Milestone

Topics contain a collection of resources and a set of knowledge components (KCs) [17] that the topic aggregates to present the mastery level of that topic (currently an average of KCs). Each resource is associated with a set of knowledge components (KCs) [17] and a learner model estimates understanding of the KCs based on learner performance, where each KC represents a skill or knowledge that is practiced. Each KC is estimated individually, as described in prior work [35]. Because KCs might be tracked by multiple topics, improvement on one topic can also improve another. One unique feature of KC modeling in PAL3 is that forgetting is explicitly modeled, using a variation of Averell and Heathcote's [2] forgetting toward an asymptote of stable knowledge. As discussed later, our model attempts to estimate both the asymptote and the current mastery simultaneously, where each observation is weighted based on the expected amount of forgetting (i.e., three high scores, each a month apart, raise the asymptote greatly, but three high scores a minute apart will raise current mastery with little change to the asymptote).

Resources in PAL3 include both active material that informs the learner model, and passive content, such as external links and embedded videos. One goal for PAL3 was to blend custom intelligent tutoring system (ITS) content with existing web-based resources (e.g., links to online tutorials and how-to videos) to decrease cost and increase coverage over a custom ITS-only approach. Two ITS types were integrated as active resources: AutoTutor dialogs [7], and Dragoon model-building exercises [36]. AutoTutor simulates the dialogue moves of human tutors as well as ideal pedagogical strategies. Dragoon tutors by staged progressions through deconstructed systems-dynamics models. Formative studies on PAL3 resources indicated that Dragoon activities were appreciated by some users, but universally considered to be challenging. This feedback was incorporated into the design of the PAL3 recommender system, which attempts to present increasingly challenging learning activities in a topic as learners increase their mastery.

### 2.3    PAL3 Mechanisms for Motivation and Engagement

A primary mechanism to foster engagement and motivation is a pervasive open learner model and feedback loop for presenting and rewarding mastery [30]. In principle, the open learner model helps learners monitor their knowledge and provide a sense of progress, which is known to facilitate learning [3]. The User Roadmap is the central open learner model for the system (see Fig. 1). However, topic mastery levels are referenced throughout the system, such as when learners complete resources (shown as "mastery points"), on resource menus, on leaderboards and social activity feeds, and by the Pal character who will celebrate reaching new levels of mastery. Mastery level also determines what topics are recommended on the PAL3 home screen. Based on formative studies with small groups of learners, mastery level was broken down into "tiers" so that learners could feel greater accomplishment while working on a single topic and to facilitate spaced practice (i.e., after learners reach a certain mastery level, topics would not be recommended until other topics have been practiced).

Social mechanisms such as leaderboards, teams, an activity feed, and the Pal animated pedagogical agent were also implemented in PAL3 to increase motivation. Social ties are a key element for long-term learning habits and are evident in professional communities of practice, online gaming communities, and some cohorts of massive online courses [16, 31]. Leaderboards present rankings based on mastery levels, with a distinct leaderboard for each Topic. The leaderboard only shows the top tier of students and the rank of the current student. While leaderboards are not necessarily appropriate for all groups, formative studies indicated that social competition was a popular feature. Learners are also grouped into teams. Team membership supports team leaderboards and also affects the notifications in the activity feed. The activity feed shows a digest of notable events by the learner, his team, and members of competing teams. Based on feedback from formative studies, the Pal animated agent acts as a supporter and motivator for the student, with dialog and animations coordinated by the Virtual Human toolkit [34]. Pal's personality was designed to engage learners and to keep the student using PAL3 longer and more often through a combination of humor, useful knowledge, and support when using the system.

Finally, effort-based gamification was implemented in PAL3, with experience points aligned to completion of resources and achievements. Point systems aligned to certain types of effort have been reported to have positive effects on persistence in learning [11, 27]. These rewards increase the user's level and enable them to unlock customizations for the Pal character, which a subset of learners in formative studies found motivating. While an in-depth analysis of the value of each feature to engagement is beyond the scope of this study, the design strategy for engagement was to implement multiple qualitatively different mechanisms as learners might be motivated by different aspects of the PAL3 system.

## 3  Method

### 3.1  Participant Sample

This study was conducted at Naval Station Great Lakes, the Navy's only boot camp and where Navy enlisted sailors train on skills specific to their rates (specialties). This research focused on the Fire Controlman (FC) rate, which is responsible for operating and maintaining weapons systems on board a ship. The FC rate completes approximately nine weeks of Apprentice Technical Training (ATT), which covers circuit fundamentals, and then follows with approximately 20 weeks of more advanced electronics training in "class A-School" training (see Fig. 2). Sailors then await their assignment to "C-School", where they train to operate and maintain a specific weapon system. The FC rate is notable for skill decay for two reasons. First, it is a technically challenging rate which requires learning electronics content analogous to multiple college electrical engineering courses (e.g., linear circuits, semiconductors). Second, due to high demand for FCs and limited training berths for their specialized systems, this rate has experienced notable delays awaiting assignment between A-School and C-School (often more than six months). During this interim, sailors have duties equivalent to a full-time job, but are not under the command of the training center and in general cannot be ordered to review their knowledge to prevent decay. A small set of additional sailors ($N = 3$) were included from the Electronics Technician (ET) rate, which receives similar training until branching off to learn different systems.

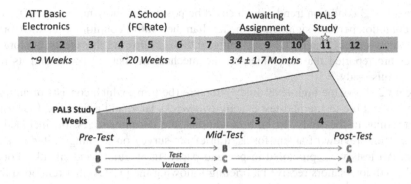

**Fig. 2.** Navy FC rate schoolhouse progression (top) and PAL3 study schedule (bottom)

A total of 107 sailors participated in the study; this includes 70 in the PAL3 intervention condition and 37 sailors in the control condition. Recruitment of sailors was conducted by arranging a series of three briefing sessions where sailors were briefed on the project goals using a slide deck presentation. Two of the briefing sessions offered the ability to participate in the PAL3 condition, while the last constituted the control condition. Participation was voluntary, and two sailors in each condition declined to participate. The in-person study activities excused sailors from their normal duties, which likely helped with attendance for enrollment and test sessions. There were 17 sailors who received the briefing but were unable to participate due to scheduling conflicts (e.g., scheduled to start C-school during the study period, scheduled personal leave during the study). The majority of subjects who missed test sessions were reported to have similar conflicts that geographically removed them from the study pool. The average age of participants was 22.0 years old ($SD = 2.9$) with a positive skew (ranged from 19 to 30). The sample was approximately 84% male. The average amount of time that sailors were awaiting assignment before enrolling in the study was 3.4 months, with a standard deviation of 1.7 months.

## 3.2   Experiment Design

The study design was a quasi-randomized controlled trial, based on sailors' availability to participate in a briefing session at a given time. Participants were not informed about which condition they would be able to enroll into in advance and were not able to switch briefings after attending a session. While we did not have the ability to randomly assign groups, the constraints that determined participant assignment to experimental or control conditions were administrative and practical with no reason to expect the resulting groups would have had different ability levels. The study design was unbalanced, with 70 sailors in the PAL3 condition and 37 in the control condition. The rationale for an unbalanced sample was that we wanted to explore variations in the use of the PAL3 system, and that a larger sample would offer more insight into mitigating decay. This sample size was intended to test the primary hypothesis, namely: "can using PAL3 as an adaptive learning system successfully mitigate knowledge decay, even if the level of use is voluntary?" This hypothesis can be subdivided conceptually.

Is there a PAL3 condition trend, which could be positive or show no change? Does the PAL3 condition perform significantly better than the control condition (i.e., the Control condition does decay, but PAL3 helps mitigate this)? Following these tests, exploratory analyses are reported that help interpret the mechanisms behind decay and its mitigation in this study.

Figure 2 shows the high-level study structure (bottom), which consists of an initial orientation and pre-test, a mid-test exactly two weeks later, and a final test four weeks after enrolling in the study. In both conditions, the enrollment session included the initial briefing, review of assent forms, a brief pre-survey on learning attitudes, and a pre-test. All tests were proctored in pen-and-paper, individually and silently. For the control condition, sailors received a briefing following the pre-test that reminded them to study as they normally would, as well as a reminder about the upcoming tests. For the PAL3 condition, before being dismissed, sailors were set up with the system, assigned teams, and given approximately 20–30 min to familiarize themselves with the system and to help troubleshoot any problems. The mid-test session was much shorter, consisting only of a test and (for the PAL3 condition) an offer to troubleshoot any problems, while welcoming any informal verbal feedback (which was limited). During the final test session, learners completed a post-test and a post-survey, as well as a final opportunity to provide verbal feedback and to troubleshoot problems.

For each briefing group, three equivalent tests (A, B, and C) were administered with partial counterbalancing as indicated in Fig. 2. A third of each group began with a different test number and took the subsequent tests. The test was comprehensive with respect to PAL3, in that at least one skill from each topic in PAL3 was covered. The content registered in PAL3 was tailored to a subset of fundamental topics that Navy instructors reported were challenging for learners during their ATT training. These topics were: Resistor-Inductor-Capacitor (RLC) Circuits and Filters, Diode Action, Zener Diodes (as voltage regulators), Rectifiers, Voltage Regulators, and Transistors. Each test was 18 items, with two items on each of 9 different knowledge components: Diodes, Full Wave Rectifiers, Half-Wave Rectifiers, Inductors, Kirchhoff's Current Laws, Ohm's Law: Voltage, RC Filters, Transistors, and Zener Diodes. Analysis of test results showed no significant differences in difficulty between the test versions.

After the initial timed exam session was complete, the PAL3 condition was introduced to the *Surface 3* tablets. Participants in the PAL3 condition were also instructed to self-select into teams based on the tables at which they sat. The choice of *Surface 3* platforms in this study was to align with a hardware platform being considered for a Navy initiative called e-Sailor, which was evaluating the feasibility of issuing sailors tablets that they carry for their entire career [18]. We informed the participants that, while the tablets were officially the property of the U.S. military and their primary use was for studying, the participants would be free to use them in any way compliant with military conduct standards. Further, we reserved the right to re-issue the tablets to new sailors in the event that they chose to discontinue the study. This caveat was necessary to cover the case where PAL3 use was so low that a supplemental cohort might need to be recruited to study usage patterns. Sailors were likewise informed that at the discretion of the Navy, that sailors might be able to continue studying on the tablets after the conclusion of the study (which ultimately occurred for interested sailors). These statements could have constituted an exogenous incentive to use the system, though overall interest in the tablets as devices was relatively low. The FC rate tended to include sailors who are tech savvy (e.g., many had multiple devices and computers already), and the most common negative feedback was that they would prefer to have PAL3 on their own device(s). This may also be affected by the fact that *Surface 3* tablets were low-cost machines (about $300), which limited their performance on many tasks beyond web-based or streaming content.

This study relies on data from three sources: the pen-and-paper multiple-choice tests, PAL3 database learning records, and a limited set of Navy background student record data. Database session and resource times needed to be adjusted to accurately quantify effort. As part of PAL3's design, each resource was assigned a minimum expected duration that is used to help the Pal character react effectively to users' time on a resource (e.g., "Wow, back so fast? Did you even read it?"). The duration for a learner's time in each resource was capped at that maximum duration, to truncate outliers into a reasonable range.

## 4  Results and Discussion

During the study, PAL3 captured a large amount of data, but this analysis focuses on knowledge decay as its primary outcome of interest. Since sailors had already completed their electronics coursework an average of three months previously, decay had already occurred. Despite not knowing the initial knowledge of the sailors, a statistically significant correlation was identified between sailors' pretest scores and the number of days since they graduated ($r = 0.20$, df $= 77$, $t = 1.75$, $p = 0.042$). To explore if the PAL3 intervention mitigates further decay, we compare test results for the control versus experimental groups to determine initial overall effectiveness of the PAL3 system. Additional analyses were conducted as well. We examined which topics benefited most from the intervention, as evident from the frequency of use and change in test outcomes. We analyzed voluntary usage patterns regarding when learners used the system and how much. We analyzed a model of the impact of learner effort in PAL3 on test outcomes.

### 4.1  Simple Main Effect

A mixed model that compares the PAL3 and control condition shows significant improvements for the treatment condition, treating the test session number (Assessment Progression) as a numerical variable (the subject ID and test types were included as random effects. Table 1 shows the significant effect of access to PAL3 on increasing performance ($p = .040$, one-tailed t-test). It also shows a reduction in performance loss due to forgetting ($p = .007$, one-tailed t-test). The progression of test scores for each condition and the model are shown in Fig. 3. Due to the structure of the analysis, participants with partial data could still be included. This model included 94 participants who completed the pre-test and either the mid-test only ($N = 20$), post-test only ($N = 12$), or both tests ($N = 62$). There were no statistically significant differences noted in attrition or test participation between the conditions. Students in the control condition effectively lost one piece of knowledge per month out of nine (roughly in line

**Table 1.** Pre-test versus post-test (simple). General linear mixed model in the form: Test Score ~ Assessment Progression + Assessment Progression: Condition + (1|Name) + (1|Test)

| | *Dependent variable:* Response (total posttest score) |
|---|---|
| Assessment progression | –0.031 (–0.056, –0.006), t = –2.461, p = 0.014** |
| Assessment progression x condition | 0.025 (–0.003, 0.053), t = 1.753, p = 0.080* |
| Constant | 0.451 (0.423, 0.478), t = 31.773, p = 0.000*** |
| Fixed factor $R^2$ | 0.022 |
| Random factor $R^2$ | 0.244 |
| Participant RE *SD* | 0.064 |
| Test form RE *SD* | 0.011 |

*Note:* All tests two-tailed. *$p < 0.1$; **$p < 0.05$; ***$p < 0.01$.

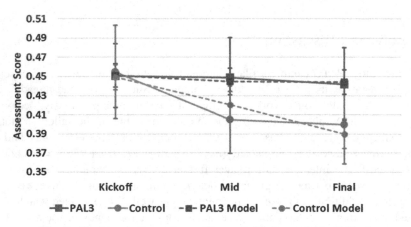

**Fig. 3.** Test scores for each condition and for the model in Table 1.

with established literature [1]). On the converse, the performance of those with access to PAL3 on the final assessment did not significantly differ from the pre-test.

## 4.2   Effect by Topic Use

We were interested in which knowledge was particularly affected by the PAL3 intervention. We conducted a mixed model that estimated test scores based on performance on items associated with specific knowledge components (KCs). Of the KCs, RC Input Filters showed a significant difference between conditions based on the test session number (t = 2.334; p = 0.02). While we only found significant correlation on this topic, that may have been due to the non-uniform user engagement across topics: this particular KC was prominent in the RLC Circuits and Filters topic, which was among the first two Topics recommended by PAL3 to learners (the other being Diode Action). The majority of resources completed were split between these topics, with 682 resources attempted in Diode Action and 319 resources in RLC Circuits and Filters.

By comparison, the next most frequent topic was Half and Full-Wave Rectifiers (86 resource visits). RC Input Filters was also knowledge that re-occurred in resources for later topics (e.g., Regulators and Smoothing). This suggests that learners mostly accepted the system recommendations (i.e., earlier topics).

## 4.3   Patterns in Usage Over Time

As expected, the PAL3 system demonstrated significant effectiveness for those who engaged with it regularly, but the voluntary nature of our study (and many comparable settings) requires consideration of those who chose not to engage. We found that among our initial population of 70 learners in the treatment condition, many dropped off after the initial introduction and registration. Total usage in terms of number of resources completed each day appears in Fig. 4, showing the steady decline. There was a small spike close to each test, but otherwise a pronounced decline following the first week until usage in the final week was minimal. Three metrics for effort were considered as predictors for the final test score for the study: adjusted resource time ($r = 0.39$), the total resource time ($r = 0.24$), and total number of resources completed ($r = 0.22$). While all were reasonable predictors, adjusted resource time was notably stronger and was selected for an additional mixed model which considered the test session scores as a function of the adjusted resource time. This model was structured similarly to the simple model, except using the adjusted resource time as the predictor rather than Condition. This model was statistically significant ($p < 0.01$) and offered a better model fit than the simple condition-based model earlier (Fixed $R^2 = 0.05$ in this model vs. $R^2 = 0.02$ for the simple main effect in Table 1).

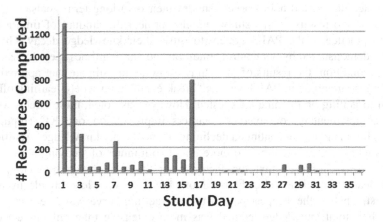

**Fig. 4.** Number of resources completed on each study day

## 5 Conclusions

The main finding from this study was that the PAL3 system showed gains over the control condition and also mitigated knowledge decay over the course of a month, despite the majority of practice occurring in the first two weeks. This effect on knowledge was best predicted by the adjusted resource time spent studying in the system, which suggests that these gains were the result of the system's effectiveness rather than due to greater motivation during test-taking or other possible explanations. The main finding is particularly encouraging given the larger context in which the evaluation was conducted. PAL3 presented the subject population with challenging review material at a point in their career when they were on break from studying and would not be required to use or practice these skills until months later. As such, motivation to learn this particular content at that time was quite low. Despite this, the sailors as a group remained sufficiently engaged to mitigate their knowledge decay.

It is important to acknowledge that the sailors' use of the system was fairly low. The average usage was on the order of 1–3 h across four weeks, depending on the metric of usage (e.g., less than 5 min/day, even with 20 min up-front during the orientation). Even though there were many motivational features in PAL3, there is substantial room to improve usage levels. Ongoing research looking at such motivational features. That said, even among sailors with low levels of use, verbal feedback indicated that they would find a system like PAL3 useful and engaging if it covered different content. In particular, some sailors were interested in PAL3 for preparing for their advancement test that influences promotions. This indicates the importance building life-long learning systems that demonstrate how they contribute to learners' authentic goals. While PAL3 is approaching this challenge, the version used in the current study only contained a subset of content aligned to one milestone, rather than a broader space that would help learners choose their own long-term goals.

Based on the results of this study, we also project the amount of time a learner needed to practice in the PAL3 system to offset their knowledge decay. Given the decay rate demonstrated by our control condition and varying times spent by learners in the PAL3 condition, the results of this study allow us to estimate that approximately 43 min of resource time in PAL3 was the "break-even" point where learning offset the effects of forgetting on the nine KCs tested. However, as noted, these effects were not entirely complementary: on average, learners improved on one KC (Input Filter Behavior) but in aggregate continued declining on most other knowledge. Additionally, while it might be interpreted that no more than two minutes of studying per day offset knowledge decay in this context, two factors make this relationship more complicated. First, this learner population already had a long break between learning electronics and the pre-test. That is, the steepest part of their forgetting curve was likely in the past. Second, their total knowledge learned was more extensive than only nine KCs. As such, we speculate that their total decline in knowledge should be greater if measured through a comprehensive test with a larger number of topics. This reinforces the position that mitigating knowledge decay requires a well-defined knowledge space, along with an estimate of losses already incurred relative to an eventual point of stability (i.e., knowledge decay asymptote [4]). By representing forgetting and defining knowledge priorities explicitly, learning technologies can help build knowledge that is ready and relevant to the future.

Finally, this initial step forward for PAL3 opens up a large number of challenging research problems. Critical research questions include how to motivate additional voluntary learning and what mechanisms or life-events can be leveraged to motivate learners? It would be particularly valuable to begin an ontology of teachable moments and impasses across the life span. For example, initiatives on women's health have found that pregnancy creates a desire to learn to the extent that illiterate expectant mothers may work to develop their reading skills, so they can find out what to expect [22, 25]. While gamification can likely be useful to encourage learning, the core mechanism that must drive life-long learning is life: authentically anchoring learning toward real goals. Social mechanisms are also a critical area that require further study. The current study does not allow us to disentangle the role of different motivations (e.g., mastery, social, gamification rewards), but social ties are presumably influential for building habits and communities (including for learning). This raises the question of how a life-long learning system might contribute to a culture of learning. These problems are not likely to be resolved in the immediate future but conducting studies under challenging conditions such as unsupervised breaks in instruction offer valuable testbeds to build effective learning technology. To pursue these gals, research on PAL3 is currently developing a smartphone version of the system to enable broader use and also to investigate advantages and disadvantages for this technology on other learning populations (e.g., K–12, University, community centers).

**Acknowledgements.** PAL3 was supported by the Office of Naval Research (ONR) through Army Research Lab W911NF-04-D-0005 and ONR N00014-12-C-0643. However, the contents of this paper are the responsibility of the authors alone.

# References

1. Arthur Jr., W., Bennett Jr., W., Day, E.A., McNelly, T.L.: Skill decay: a comparative assessment of training protocols and individual differences in the loss and reacquisition of complex skills. Air Force Research Lab Mesa AZ Human Effectiveness Directorate (2002)
2. Averell, L., Heathcote, A.: The form of the forgetting curve and the fate of memories. J. Math. Psychol. **55**, 25–35 (2011)
3. Bull, S., Kay, J.: Open learner models. In: Nkambou, R., Bourdeau, J., Mizoguchi, R. (eds.) Advances in Intelligent Tutoring Systems. Studies in Computational Intelligence, vol. 308, pp. 301–322. Springer, Heidelberg (2010). https://doi.org/10.1007/978-3-642-14363-2_15
4. Chou, C.-Y., Chan, T.-W., Lin, C.-J.: Redefining the learning companion: the past, present, and future of educational agents. Comput. Educ. **40**, 255–269 (2003)
5. Cooper, H., Nye, B., Charlton, K., Lindsay, J., Greathouse, S.: The effects of summer vacation on achievement test scores: a narrative and meta-analytic review. Rev. Educ. Res. **66**, 227–268 (1996)
6. Custers, E.J.: Long-term retention of basic science knowledge: a review study. Adv. Health Sci. Educ. **15**, 109–128 (2010)
7. Graesser, A.C.: Conversations with AutoTutor help students learn. Int. J. Artif. Intell. Educ. **26**, 124–132 (2016)

8. Graesser, A.C.: Reflections on serious games. In: Wouters, P., van Oostendorp, H. (eds.) Instructional Techniques to Facilitate Learning and Motivation of Serious Games. AGL, pp. 199–212. Springer, Cham (2017). https://doi.org/10.1007/978-3-319-39298-1_11

9. Graesser, A.C., Hu, X., Nye, B., Sottilare, R.: Intelligent tutoring systems, serious games, and the Generalized Intelligent Framework for Tutoring (GIFT). In: O'Neil, H.F., Baker, E. L., Perez, R.S. (eds.) Using games and simulation for teaching and assessment, pp. 58–79. Routledge, Abingdon (2016)

10. Hacker, D.J., Dunlosky, J., Graesser, A.C.: Metacognition in Educational Theory and Practice. Routledge, New York (1998)

11. Hamari, J., Koivisto, J., Sarsa, H.: Does gamification work?–A literature review of empirical studies on gamification. In: 47th Hawaii International Conference on System Sciences (HICSS), pp. 3025–3034. IEEE (2014)

12. Jackson, G.T., Boonthum, C., McNamara, D.S.: iSTART-ME: situating extended learning within a game-based environment. In: Proceedings of the Workshop on Intelligent Educational Games at the 14th Annual Conference on Artificial Intelligence in Education, AIED, Brighton, pp. 59–68 (2009)

13. Jackson, G.T., Dempsey, K.B., McNamara, D.S.: Short and long term benefits of enjoyment and learning within a serious game. In: Biswas, G., Bull, S., Kay, J., Mitrovic, A. (eds.) AIED 2011. LNCS (LNAI), vol. 6738, pp. 139–146. Springer, Heidelberg (2011). https://doi.org/10.1007/978-3-642-21869-9_20

14. Jackson, G.T., McNamara, D.S.: Motivational impacts of a game-based intelligent tutoring system. In: FLAIRS Conference, pp. 1–6 (2011)

15. Jarvis, P.: Adult Education and Lifelong Learning: Theory and Practice. Routledge, New York (2004)

16. Klamma, R., Chatti, M.A., Duval, E., Hummel, H., Hvannberg, E.T., Kravcik, M., Law, E., Naeve, A., Scott, P.: Social software for life-long learning. J. Educ. Technol. Soc. 10, 72–83 (2007)

17. Koedinger, K.R., Corbett, A.T., Perfetti, C.: The knowledge-learning-instruction framework: bridging the science-practice chasm to enhance robust student learning. Cognit. Sci. 36, 757–798 (2012)

18. Krawczyk, S.: MCPON Launches eSailor Initiative at RTC (2015). Navy.mil/submit/display. asp?story_id=86458

19. Kruger, J., Dunning, D.: Unskilled and unaware of it: how difficulties in recognizing one's own incompetence lead to inflated self-assessments. J. Pers. Soc. Psychol. 77, 1121 (1999)

20. Levinstein, I.B., Boonthum, C., Pillarisetti, S.P., Bell, C., McNamara, D.S.: iSTART 2: improvements for efficiency and effectiveness. Behav. Res. Methods 39, 224–232 (2007)

21. Lüftenegger, M., Schober, B., Van de Schoot, R., Wagner, P., Finsterwald, M., Spiel, C.: Lifelong learning as a goal–do autonomy and self-regulation in school result in well prepared pupils? Learn. Instruct. 22, 27–36 (2012)

22. McCombs, J.S., Augustine, C.H., Schwartz, H.L.: Making summer count: how summer programs can boost children's learning. Rand Corporation (2011)

23. McNamara, D.S., Levinstein, I.B., Boonthum, C.: iSTART: Interactive strategy training for active reading and thinking. Behav. Res. Methods Instrum. Comput. 36, 222–233 (2004)

24. McQuiggan, S.W., Robison, J.L., Lester, J.C.: Affective transitions in narrative-centered learning environments. Educ. Technol. Soc. 13, 40–53 (2010)

25. Millis, K., Forsyth, C., Wallace, P., Graesser, A.C., Timmins, G.: The impact of game-like features on learning from an intelligent tutoring system. Technol. Knowl. Learn. 22, 1–22 (2017)

26. Newell, A.: Unified theories of Cognition. Harvard University Press (1994)

27. O'Rourke, E., Peach, E., Dweck, C.S., Popovic, Z.: Brain points: a deeper look at a growth mindset incentive structure for an educational game. In: Proceedings of the Third (2016) ACM Conference on Learning@ Scale, pp. 41–50. ACM (2016)
28. Pavlik, P.I., Kelly, C., Maass, J.K.: The mobile fact and concept training system (MoFaCTS). In: Micarelli, A., Stamper, J., Panourgia, K. (eds.) ITS 2016. LNCS, vol. 9684, pp. 247–253. Springer, Cham (2016). https://doi.org/10.1007/978-3-319-39583-8_25
29. Pearson: Pearson, Duolingo Partner to Enhance Mobile Learning in College and University Language Courses. https://www.pearson.com/corporate/news/media/news-announcements/2017/08/pearson–duolingo-partner-to-enhance-mobile-learning–in-college.html
30. Pintrich, P.R.: Multiple goals, multiple pathways: the role of goal orientation in learning and achievement. J. Educ. Psychol. **92**, 544 (2000)
31. Rosé, C.P., Carlson, R., Yang, D., Wen, M., Resnick, L., Goldman, P., Sherer, J.: Social factors that contribute to attrition in MOOCs. In: Proceedings of the First ACM Conference on Learning@ Scale Conference, pp. 197–198. ACM (2014)
32. Sabourin, J.L., Rowe, J.P., Mott, B.W., Lester, J.C.: Considering alternate futures to classify off-task behavior as emotion self-regulation: a supervised learning approach. JEDM. J. Educ. Data Min. **5**, 9–38 (2013)
33. Sharples, M.: The design of personal mobile technologies for lifelong learning. Comput. Educ. **34**, 177–193 (2000)
34. Swartout, W.R., Gratch, J., Hill Jr., R.W., Hovy, E., Marsella, S., Rickel, J., Traum, D.: Toward virtual humans. AI Mag. **27**, 96 (2006)
35. Swartout, W.R., Nye, B.D., Hartholt, A., Reilly, A., Graesser, A.C., VanLehn, K., Wetzel, J., Liewer, M., Morbini, F., Morgan, B.: Designing a personal assistant for life-long learning (PAL3). In: FLAIRS Conference, pp. 491–496 (2016)
36. VanLehn, K., Wetzel, J., Grover, S., Van De Sande, B.: Learning how to construct models of dynamic systems: an initial evaluation of the Dragoon intelligent tutoring system. IEEE Trans. Learn. Technol. **10**, 154–167 (2017)
37. Xiong, X., Wang, Y., Beck, J.B.: Improving students' long-term retention performance: a study on personalized retention schedules. In: Proceedings of the Fifth International Conference on Learning Analytics and Knowledge, pp. 325–329. ACM (2015)

# Computational Thinking Through Game Creation in STEM Classrooms

Avery Harrison[✉], Taylyn Hulse, Daniel Manzo, Matthew Micciolo,
Erin Ottmar, and Ivon Arroyo

Worcester Polytechnic Institute, Worcester, MA 01609, USA
aeharrison@wpi.edu

**Abstract.** Our research uses game creation and play to explore methods for computational thinking assessment and practice in mathematics classrooms. We present the first iteration of this research that aims to evaluate the feasibility of using game creation with high school students. Students designed math-related games, modified the game to incorporate technology, then visually depicted the technological behavior in a finite state machine diagram (FSMD). We found that students were able to create math-related games, meet the constraints given for game creation, and design logical FSMDs. These findings preliminarily suggest that game creation can be used as a method for students to practice CT.

**Keywords:** Computational thinking · Collaborative learning · STEM

## 1 Introduction

Computational thinking (CT) has been used as a term to define algorithmic thinking within computer science contexts, but this type of thinking can map onto problem solving within almost any STEM domain [5]. Students in STEM classrooms are expected to engage in CT skills such as decomposing problems, testing solutions, and critically evaluating decision-making processes just as a computer scientist would when developing software. Given the necessity of analytical skills for success in STEM fields [2] but focus on CT at the undergraduate level in computer science education [1], attention should be directed to the development, practice, and scientific study of CT in K-12 education prior to post-secondary studies.

We aim to develop students' CT for advancement in STEM-related disciplines through game creation and game play in the classroom. We present the first iteration of this research that analyzes the game design processes and products of students as they create math games. To expand on literature exploring the development and assessment of CT, we intend to use the game representations as measures of CT that do not require programming. We designed this study to answer the following questions. RQ1: *What type of multiplayer games did students create?* RQ2: *How successful were students in meeting the given criteria for games?* RQ3: *How feasible was it for students to modify their games to incorporate and represent technology and how can we interpret the complexity of this process as evidence of CT?*

C. Penstein Rosé et al. (Eds.): AIED 2018, LNAI 10948, pp. 134–138, 2018.
https://doi.org/10.1007/978-3-319-93846-2_24

## 2  Methods

This study was conducted in the spring of 2017 at a public high school over three days. In teams of three, 54 students received a different task each day: design a math game that incorporates movement, play an established game that utilizes wearable technologies [4] as an example, and modify the designed game to incorporate technology. Additionally, students were given a brief lecture on finite state machine diagrams (FSMDs). On the final day, students were tasked with representing the behavior of technology in their game within a FSMD. For homework each day, teams were asked to summarize their games in a "Day Summary" with any supplemental pictures.

Students were instructed to design multiplayer games that fit within constraints. The games must be designed for at least six players, focus on math content designed for 4th–6th grade students, and incorporate movement or action among players. On the last day, students were also asked to modify their games to incorporate technology and represent the behavior of that technology within a FSMD.

We collected Day Summaries from teams on both days of game creation (Day 1/2: N = 18; Day 3: N = 16). The summaries for 16 games and any included pictures and diagrams are the measures for analysis. We developed a coding guide to assess student-created games with a training protocol and 92 possible items to code using each Day Summary. Two researchers each coded the 34 Day Summaries, maintaining an average of 79% chance agreement across 5 randomly chosen summaries.

## 3  Results

Table 1 describes the variety in games that students created through general game elements, team characteristics, and the competitive nature of games. These results show that students can create a variety of games that vary in structure and novelty.

**Table 1.**  General game and team characteristics of student multiplayer games.

| Game Elements | N | Percent | Team Characteristics | N | Percent | Collaboration/ Competition | N | Percent |
|---|---|---|---|---|---|---|---|---|
| Established Game | 10 | 63 | Team-Based Games | 9 | 56 | Player: | | |
| | | | | | | *Competitive* | 4 | 25 |
| | | | | | | *Collaborative* | 1 | 6 |
| Progressive Levels | 3 | 19 | Team-Optional Games | 2 | 13 | Team: | | |
| | | | | | | *Competitive* | 9 | 56 |
| | | | | | | *Collaborative* | 0 | 0 |
| Content Adaptability | 9 | 56 | Between Teams: | | | Facilitator: | | |
| | | | *Parallel* | 9 | 56 | *Competitive* | 0 | 0 |
| | | | *Turn-based* | 0 | 0 | *Collaborative* | 0 | 0 |
| Game Facilitator | 14 | 88 | Within Teams | | | | | |
| | | | *Parallel* | 6 | 38 | | | |
| | | | *Turn-based* | 3 | 19 | | | |
| End Goal | 15 | 94 | No Teams: | | | | | |
| | | | *Parallel* | 1 | 6 | | | |
| | | | *Turn-based* | 3 | 19 | | | |

Next, we assessed the incorporation of mathematics (Table 2). Student games spanned across 7 content areas that are appropriate for 4th–6th grade students. To assess how well students incorporated mathematics as content, games were also coded in regard to mathematical importance and utilization.

**Table 2.** Incorporation of mathematics across student multiplayer games.

| Mathematical Content | N | Percent | Importance | N | Percent |
|---|---|---|---|---|---|
| Operations and Algebraic Thinking | 12 | 75 | No | 0 | 0 |
| Number and Operations in Base Ten | 11 | 67 | Low | 3 | 23 |
| Counting and Cardinality | 10 | 63 | High | 13 | 81 |
| Fractions | 5 | 31 | **Utilization** | **N** | **Percent** |
| Geometry | 2 | 13 | Never | 0 | 0 |
| The Number System | 1 | 6 | Sometimes | 3 | 23 |
| Expressions and Equations | 1 | 6 | Mostly | 13 | 81 |

Then, we assessed the incorporation of motion (Table 3). Physicality describes the amount of movement required by players. Most games required occasional movement but most of that movement did not require cardiac intensive activities, as defined by sweat factor. Math motion relationship is defined as how closely the movement in the game represents the math concepts. Teams were able to incorporate math and action into games, showing that they were able to create games that met given constraints.

**Table 3.** Incorporation of action and motion components in student games.

| Physicality Level | | | Sweat Factor | | | Math Motion Relationship | | |
|---|---|---|---|---|---|---|---|---|
| Measure | N | Percent | Measure | N | Percent | Measure | N | Percent |
| Low | 3 | 19 | None | 9 | 56 | None | 12 | 75 |
| Medium | 10 | 62 | Low | 4 | 25 | Weak | 3 | 19 |
| High | 3 | 19 | High | 3 | 19 | Strong | 1 | 6 |

Lastly, we assessed the feasibility of game modification and using game products to assess CT. Table 4 describes how students represented game facets through three representations on the first day (Day 1 or 2) and second (Day 3) of game design. Next, we assessed whether students incorporated technology on Day 3. By Day 3, 15 of the 16 games incorporated technology (i.e. cell phones and tablets) with 7 of those games coded as technologically dependent, suggesting more rigorous modification.

We analyzed the feasibility of creating FSMDs by aggregating data from Day 3 (Table 5). FSMD Elements marked the presence of input types, the domain level of the FSMD, and features such as If-Then Statements that would suggest Evidence of Programming Language Knowledge (EPLK). The FSMD Criteria regarding representation, consistency, and completion were coded on a Likert scale (0 = Never, or mostly never meeting criteria; 3 = Always, or Almost Always meeting criteria) while

**Table 4.** Game elements addressed across game representations and days of game design.

| Game Elements by Representation | Written | | | | Pictorial | | | | FSMD | | | |
|---|---|---|---|---|---|---|---|---|---|---|---|---|
| | Day 1 or 2 | | Day 3 | | Day 1 or 2 | | Day 3 | | Day 1 or 2 | | Day 3 | |
| | N | % | N | % | N | % | N | % | N | % | N | % |
| Rules | 16 | 100 | 16 | 100 | 6 | 38 | 4 | 25 | 2 | 13 | 9 | 56 |
| Physical Objects | 16 | 100 | 16 | 100 | 13 | 81 | 8 | 50 | 2 | 13 | 12 | 75 |
| Physical Space | 15 | 94 | 15 | 94 | 15 | 94 | 10 | 63 | 1 | 6 | 3 | 19 |
| Timing | 15 | 94 | 15 | 94 | 4 | 25 | 3 | 19 | 0 | 0 | 10 | 63 |
| Physicality | 16 | 100 | 15 | 94 | 5 | 39 | 3 | 19 | 1 | 6 | 7 | 44 |

**Table 5.** Aggregated coding data from Day 3 finite state machine diagrams.

| FSMD Elements | N | Percent | FSMD Criteria | Mean | SD | Mode |
|---|---|---|---|---|---|---|
| Input Types: RFID | 2 | 15 | Output State Representation | 2.85 | 0.55 | 3 |
| Input Types: Buttons | 10 | 77 | Transition State Representation | 2.69 | 0.63 | 3 |
| Input Types: GPS | 1 | 8 | Consistency with Rules | 2.92 | 0.28 | 3 |
| Input Types: Keyboard | 4 | 31 | State Consistency | 2.77 | 0.44 | 3 |
| Input Types: Touch Interface | 4 | 31 | Transition Consistency | 2.38 | 0.77 | 3 |
| Input Types: Timer | 7 | 54 | Completion | 2.46 | 0.52 | 2 |
| Input Types: Another Player | 3 | 23 | **FSMD Quantitative Analysis** | **Mean** | **SD** | **Mode** |
| Input Types: Other (please write) | 0 | 0 | States/Boxes | 8.15 | 4.00 | 7 |
| Domain Level: Management-Level | 4 | 31 | Transitions/Arrows | 10.69 | 7.05 | 7 |
| Domain Level: Team-Level | 3 | 23 | Labeled Arrows | 8.15 | 5.49 | 7 |
| Domain Level: Player-Level | 11 | 85 | Numbered States | 2.92 | 4.82 | 0 |
| EPLK: If-then Statements | 2 | 15 | | | | |
| EPLK: Programmatic Loops | 0 | 0 | | | | |
| EPLK: Loop to Prior State Arrows | 12 | 92 | | | | |

Quantitative Analysis items were coded on a continuous scale. Teams represented games through different mediums, incorporated technology, and created FSMDs, suggesting that meeting constraints for modification is feasible for high school students.

## 4 Discussion

We conclude that it is feasible for high school students to create multiplayer games under constraints such as incorporating math content, motion, and technology. Over the two days of game design, teams generated games with a variety of structure, math application, and technology. Broadly, this creative thinking, iterative design, and execution of design ideas, as well as measurable components of the FSMD, demonstrate skills that map onto CT. These results suggest that game design with constraints is appropriate for high school students with the potential to measure the development of CT in the future based on current measures and a novel programming platform [3].

As CT is beneficial across STEM subjects and fields, we believe that these components of higher level thinking should be developed in students from an early age. Our first study in this line of research suggests that CT can be practiced and measured through methods such as game-design activities that do not require computer science skills or tools. This enables teachers in other subjects, such as mathematics and science, to provide students with activities to develop CT skills such as problem decomposition, abstract design thinking, and execution that can lead students to success not only in higher-level STEM courses, but also within STEM careers.

**Acknowledgements.** This material is based upon work supported by the National Science Foundation under grants #1647023 and #1652579. Any opinions, findings, and conclusions or recommendations expressed in this material are those of the author(s) and do not necessarily reflect the views of the National Science Foundation.

# References

1. Grover, S., Pea, R.: Computational thinking in K-12: a review of the state of the field. Educ. Res. **42**(1), 38–43 (2013)
2. Henderson, P., Cortina, T., Hazzan, O., Wing, J.: Computational thinking. ACM SIGSCE Bullet. **39**(1), 195–196 (2007)
3. Micciolo, M.: Physical Games for Learning II. Major Qualifying Project. Worcester Polytechnic Institute (2017)
4. Rountree, W.: Redesigning traditional children's games to teach number sense and reinforce measurement estimation skills using wearable technology (Master's thesis). Worcester Polytechnic Institute, Massachusetts (2015)
5. Wing, J.: Computational thinking. Commun. ACM **49**(3), 33–35 (2006)

# Behavioral Explanation versus Structural Explanation in Learning by Model-Building

Tomoya Horiguchi[1(✉)], Tetsuhiro Masuda[1], Takahito Tomoto[2], and Tsukasa Hirashima[3]

[1] Graduate School of Maritime Sciences, Kobe University, Kobe, Japan
horiguti@maritime.kobe-u.ac.jp, tetsu9988@gmail.com
[2] Faculty of Engineering, Tokyo Polytechnic University, Tokyo, Japan
t.tomoto@cs.t-kougei.ac.jp
[3] Department of Information Engineering, Hiroshima University,
Higashihiroshima, Japan
tsukasa@isl.hiroshima-u.ac.jp

**Abstract.** How students learn modeling skills and concepts of system dynamics through building models was investigated, focusing on how students' behavior and understanding are influenced by the type of assistance and their prior knowledge. We implemented a function in a model-building learning environment that detects the difference between a model by students and the correct model and gives one of the two types of feedback: *structural explanation* which indicates structurally erroneous parts of a model by students to promote model completion, while *behavioral explanation* which suggests erroneous behavior of a model by students to promote reflection on the cause of error. Our experiment revealed: (1) Students assigned to structural explanation showed high model completion, but their understanding depended on whether they used feedback appropriately or not. (2) Students assigned to behavioral explanation showed less model completion, but once they completed models, they acquired a deeper understanding.

**Keywords:** Learning by modeling · Model building learning environment
System dynamics · Adaptive feedback
Behavioral explanation and structural explanation

## 1 Introduction

For promoting students' understanding of dynamical systems and modeling skills, several model building learning environments (MBEs) have been developed in which students are given a set of model components and build models by combining them [3–6, 10, 11]. They can also simulate their model to see whether it behaves as they expected. If it doesn't, they modify the model and try simulation again.

It is, however, a difficult task for most students to build correct models in MBEs. Therefore, several methods for assisting students have been implemented. Some MBEs have a help system that explains mathematical/physical concepts components stand for [6, 7], a syntax checker of models [6]. Others have a function that detects the difference

© Springer International Publishing AG, part of Springer Nature 2018
C. Penstein Rosé et al. (Eds.): AIED 2018, LNAI 10948, pp. 139–144, 2018.
https://doi.org/10.1007/978-3-319-93846-2_25

between the model by students and the correct model [4, 7], and a function that gives causal explanation for models' unexpected behavior [1, 2].

However, the verification of these methods' usefulness has been limited so far [4, 6, 7, 11]. Most studies evaluated their effectiveness by measuring the degree of model completion by students [4, 7] or the total learning effect that consists of several types of assistance [11]. Few studies investigated the relation among the type of assistance, students' understanding, their behavior, and prior knowledge in detail. Especially, it is unclear what kind of knowledge was acquired through the learning by modeling. In this study, we examined this issue. The detail is described in the next section.

## 2   Functions for Assistance and Their Effects

In order for learning in MBE to be beneficial, students need to build at least syntactically correct (i.e., calculable) models. In addition, in order for simulation to provide useful information for testing models, students need to build models with a certain degree of completion that include a certain number of constraints on models' behavior. It is, however, reported students often build syntactically incorrect or very 'sparse' initial models that include few constraints [7]. This is one of the reasons why not a few MBEs provide functions that directly guide students in model building (and are evaluated by the degree of model completion). Even if students initially build a model without understanding, it is expected they improve their understanding through repeated simulation and modification. There is, however, still a possibility such functions are overused by students whose concern is completion of models [11].

On the other hand, some MBEs provide functions that less directly assist students (e.g., by suggesting the cause of unexpected behavior of models). Such functions promote students' reflection that would deepen their understanding. However, it doesn't necessarily lead to correction of errors, that is, there is a possibility students can't receive useful feedback because of the low degree of model completion. There is a tradeoff between these two types of assistance. However, few studies have compared these two types of assistance considering the relation with students' behavior, model completion, understanding and prior knowledge.

In this study, therefore, we made an experiment to compare these two types of assistance. We used a model-building learning environment called *Evans* we have been developing [8, 9], in which students can build qualitative models of dynamical systems and observe its behavior by qualitative simulation [12]. In Evans, we implemented a function called *difference-list* that compares a model by students and the correct model and enumerates their differences (i.e., erroneous parts of the former). Difference-list provides one of the two types of explanation about the differences: (1) *Structural explanation* aims at the increase of model completion that simply indicates structural differences (e.g., lacking/unnecessary amounts, reverse direction of a relation between amounts). Students can easily (without understanding) correct their models. (2) *Behavioral explanation* aims at the reflection on semantic errors in models that indicates the unnaturalness of erroneous models' behavior (e.g., when students' model lacks a 'promotional' relation between two amounts, it indicates one of them doesn't necessarily increase even if another increases). In order to correct models, students need to understand the relation between structure and behavior of models, which would promote their reflection on the cause of semantic errors.

# 3   Experiment

## 3.1   Design

**Purpose.** We compared students who received structural explanation and students who received behavioral explanation from the viewpoints of their behavior, degree of model completion, understanding of dynamical systems, and prior knowledge.

**Hypothesis-1.** Students in behavioral explanation group (who are encouraged to reflect on the cause of errors) improve their understanding better than students in structural explanation group (who are directly taught how to correct their models).

**Subjects.** Seventeen graduate and undergraduate students whose major is engineering.

**Instruments.** We used a set of teaching/testing materials in addition to Evans.

Modeling Task: We made students build the model of 'bathtub system' by using Evans, that dealt with the change of the amount of water in a bathtub (in which constant amount enters from a inlet and the amount proportional to the water level exits from an outlet). In order to avoid models by students being 'sparse,' we gave students all the necessary components with appropriate parameters that were made by disassembling the correct model by the experimenter.

Test on System Dynamics: It consists of problem-1 (10 questions) and problem-2 (9 questions) that deal with the bathtub system and a simple RC electric circuit respectively. Full marks are 37.

**Procedure.** First, students worked on the test on system dynamics (pre-test). Then, after a practice of building basic models, they worked on the modeling task with Evans (modeling session). Eight of them were assigned to structural explanation group, while nine of them were assigned to behavioral explanation group. During the session, they could use difference-list freely. Finally, they worked on the same test (post-test). About a month later, they worked on the same test (delayed post-test).

**Measure.** The improvement of students' understanding of system dynamics was measured by the increase of scores between tests. The degree of model completion was calculated by comparing the 'final model' by students with the correct model (full marks are 3). The frequency of using assistance was calculated by using log files.

## 3.2   Results and Discussion

The average scores of tests and the result of statistical analysis are shown in Table 1. In two-factor ANOVA of 2 (explanation: structural/behavioral) $\times$ 3 (test: pre/post/ delayed post), because the interaction of the factors was significant ($p < .10$), we tested the simple main effect of each factor. As a result, the factor 'explanation' wasn't significant while the factor 'test' was significant (test(structural): F = 23.783; p < .01, test(behavioral): F = 7.039; p < .01). Multiple comparison revealed the following facts: In structural explanation group, there were significant differences between pre- and post-test (p < .01) and between pre- and delayed post-test (p < .01). In behavioral explanation group, there were significant differences between post- and delayed post-test (p < .05) and between pre- and delayed post-test (p < .01).

**Understanding Immediately After Learning by Modeling.** According to Table 1, only the score of students in behavioral explanation group significantly increased between post- and delayed post-test, while only the score of students in structural explanation group significantly increased between pre- and post-test. In addition, there was no significant difference between groups. Because these results are contrary to *Hypothesis-1*, we need an explanation about why the understanding of students in structural explanation group improved better than those in behavioral explanation group immediately after learning. For this purpose, we made correlation analysis between several factors, which revealed there was a medium positive correlation between the increase of (all) students' score from pre- to post-test and the degree of their model completion (R = 0.476). Therefore, we built up the following hypothesis.

**Hypothesis-2.** The completion of models is important for students in receiving useful feedback and improving understanding. The experience (or memory) works well especially in post-test.

**Table 1.** Result of tests

|  | Pre-test Mean (SD) | Post-test Mean (SD) | Delayed post- test Mean (SD) | Simple main effect of test (df = 2) | Increase between pre- and post-test | Increase between post- and delayed post-test | Increase between pre- and delayed post-test |
|---|---|---|---|---|---|---|---|
| Structural explanation (n = 8) | 15.500 (4.416) | 20.750 (4.969) | 22.625 (3.773) | F = 23.783 p = 0.0000**** | t = 4.764 p = 0.0000**** | t = 1.701 p = 0.0992 † | t = 6.465 p = 0.0000**** |
| Behavioral explanation (n = 9) | 17.667 (5.312) | 19.333 (4.738) | 21.667 (6.733) | F = 7.039 p = 0.0031*** | t = 1.604 p = 0.1192 | t = 2.246 p = 0.0322* | t = 3.850 p = 0.0006**** |

According to *Hypothesis-2*, if the degree of model completion of students in structural explanation group is significantly greater, we can explain why only their score significantly increased between pre- and post-test. Though there was no signif-icant difference in the degree of model completion between two groups (U-test, p > .10), the result of correlation analysis gave some interesting suggestions: In behavioral explanation group, there was a medium positive correlation between the degree of model completion and the increase of score from pre- to post-test (R = 0.412), while there wasn't in structural explanation group (R = 0.183). That is, in behavioral explanation group, model completion contributed to the improvement of students' understanding, while it didn't in structural explanation group. In addition, in behavioral explanation group, there was no correlation between the frequency of assistance (by difference-list) and the increase of score from pre- to post-test ($R = 0.190$), while there was a medium negative correlation in structural explanation group ($R = -0.550$). This fact suggests a certain number of students in structural explanation group overused assistance to complete models without understanding why their models were erroneous.

Based on the above discussion, we modify *Hypothesis-2* as follows.

*Findings (derived by modifying Hypothesis-2):*

As for students who were assisted by behavioral explanation, completing models contributed to improving their understanding. However, because behavioral explanation's promotion of model completion was relatively weak, their scores between pre- and post-test didn't significantly increase. As for students who were assisted by structural explanation, the improvement of their understanding through model completion depends on how they utilized the assistance. Because structural explanation's promotion of model completion was strong, there were a certain number of students who overused assistance to complete models without understanding.

**Understanding After a Certain Period of Time.** In this experiment, the score of 82% of (all) students increased between post- and delayed post-test, and the increase was significant as to students in behavioral explanation group. Though the reproducibility of this result should be carefully verified, we can suggest the following: Learning by modeling in Evans contributed to the acquisition of not only the knowledge of a specific model, but also the generalized knowledge of system dynamics.

Our important future work is to verify the reproducibility of these results, and to clarify the process of acquisition of modeling skills and concepts of system dynamics.

# References

1. Beek, W., Bredeweg, B.: Context-dependent help for novices acquiring conceptual systems knowledge in DynaLearn. In: Cerri, S.A., Clancey, W.J., Papadourakis, G., Panourgia, K. (eds.) ITS 2012. LNCS, vol. 7315, pp. 292–297. Springer, Heidelberg (2012). https://doi.org/10.1007/978-3-642-30950-2_38
2. Beek, W., Bredeweg, B.: Providing feedback for common problems in learning by conceptual modeling using expectation-driven consistency maintenance. In: Proceedings of QR12 (2012)
3. Biswas, G., Leelawong, K., Schwartz, D., Vye, N.: Learning by teaching: a new agent paradigm for educational software. Appl. Artif. Intell. **19**, 363–392 (2005)
4. Bravo, C., van Joolingen, W.R., de Jong, T.: Modeling and simulation in inquiry learning: checking solutions and giving intelligent advice. Simulation **82**(11), 769–784 (2006)
5. Bredeweg, B., Linnebank, F., Bouwer, A., Liem, J.: Garp3 - workbench for qualitative modelling and simulation. Ecol. Inform. **4**(5–6), 263–281 (2009)
6. Forbus, K.D., Carney, K., Sherin, B.L., Ureel II, L.C.: VModel: a visual qualitative modeling environment for middle-school students. AI Mag. **26**, 63–72 (2005)
7. Gracia, J., Liem, J., Lozano, E., Corcho, O., Trna, M., Gómez-Pérez, A., Bredeweg, B.: Semantic techniques for enabling knowledge reuse in conceptual modelling. In: Patel-Schneider, P.F., Pan, Y., Hitzler, P., Mika, P., Zhang, L., Pan, Jeff Z., Horrocks, I., Glimm, B. (eds.) ISWC 2010. LNCS, vol. 6497, pp. 82–97. Springer, Heidelberg (2010). https://doi.org/10.1007/978-3-642-17749-1_6

8. Horiguchi, T., Hirashima, T., Forbus, K.D.: A Model-Building Learning Environment with Explanatory Feedback to Erroneous Models. In: Cerri, S.A., Clancey, W.J., Papadourakis, G., Panourgia, K. (eds.) ITS 2012. LNCS, vol. 7315, pp. 620–621. Springer, Heidelberg (2012). https://doi.org/10.1007/978-3-642-30950-2_90

9. Horiguchi, T., Masuda, T.: Evaluation of the function that detects the difference of learner's model from the correct model in a model-building learning environment. In: Yamamoto, S. (ed.) HIMI 2017. LNCS, vol. 10274, pp. 40–49. Springer, Cham (2017). https://doi.org/10.1007/978-3-319-58524-6_4

10. isee systems STELLA (1985). http://www.iseesystems.com/

11. Vanlehn, K., Wetzel, J., Grover, S., Van De Sande, B.: Learning how to construct models of dynamic systems: an initial evaluation of the dragoon intelligent tutoring system. IEEE Trans. Learn. Technol. **10**(2), 154–167 (2016)

12. Weld, D.S., deKleer, J.: Readings in Qualitative Reasoning About Physical Systems. Morgan Kaufmann, Burlington (1990)

# Temporal Changes in Affiliation and Emotion in MOOC Discussion Forum Discourse

Jing Hu[✉], Nia Dowell[✉], Christopher Brooks[✉], and Wenfei Yan[✉]

University of Michigan, Ann Arbor, MI 48104, USA
{jihu, ndowell, brooksch, wenfeiy}@umich.edu

**Abstract.** Studies have shown discourse constructs of affiliation and emotion to be critical factors influencing learning performance and outcomes in both traditional environments and Massive Open Online Courses (MOOCs). However, there is limited research investigating the affiliation and emotions of MOOC learners and how these factors develop over time. To gain a deeper understanding of the MOOC population and to facilitate MOOC environment design, we addressed this gap by conducting a longitudinal analysis of change of affiliation and emotions presented in discussion forums of five Coursera courses. They have been offered numerous times from 2012 to 2015. We demonstrate that discussion forums have reflected decreasing affiliation and increasing negative emotions over the four years for most courses, with no significant overall change in positive emotions.

**Keywords:** MOOC · Discourse · Affiliation · Emotion · Longitudinal

## 1 Introduction

In traditional learning environments, school affiliation and connectedness, or the extent to which students feel included, accepted, or supported by others [1, 2], have been shown to play an important role, associated with learning processes including test grades [3], dropout [4], academic [5], and educational attainment [3]. In the scaled learning environments (i.e., MOOCs), a recent case study also found that learners who are more connected to the networks on the course discussion forum tend to exhibit better performance and higher test scores [6].

In traditional learning settings, research suggests that higher levels of connectedness are associated with fewer negative emotions [7]. Similarly, communication also results in more positive emotions and fewer negative emotions in distance learning, mediated by the sense of support and encouragement from tutors and peers [8]. Some studies suggest that positive emotions can facilitate academic achievement, mediated by the levels of self-motivation and satisfaction with the learning process [9]. In scaled learning environments, studies have also suggested that positive emotions such as optimism and hope can improve performance, mediated by the meaningful use of learning strategies [10]. Surprisingly, studies also demonstrate particular negative emotions to be beneficial to learning performance, including mild stress [11] and confusion [12], which can serve to increase attention to learning material.

© Springer International Publishing AG, part of Springer Nature 2018
C. Penstein Rosé et al. (Eds.): AIED 2018, LNAI 10948, pp. 145–149, 2018.
https://doi.org/10.1007/978-3-319-93846-2_26

Given the critical relationship of affiliation and emotion on learning and the maturation of MOOCs as a phenomenon, it is useful to understand how these two factors have changed over subsequent offerings of courses. To date, research exploring affiliation or emotion processes in MOOCs have focused on smaller samples, typically a single MOOC over a short period (e.g. one semester). By providing an analysis here which spans the first four years of the MOOC phenomenon and up to ten iterations of course sessions, we are providing evidence that the discourse of participants in MOOCs has changed, and that analyses done in the early days of the phenomenon (circa 2012) may no longer be reflective of the state of the practice.

## 2    Methods

For this analysis, we chose five MOOCs on the Coursera platform ($N = 59,017$ participants) which ran for several sessions from 2012 to 2015. There was a total of 41 course offerings as each course ran between six to ten times ($M = 8.2$, $sd = 2.05$). The courses covered a breadth of disciplines, and varied in number of learners: "Fantasy and Science Fiction" ($M = 780.50$ students per class/iteration, $sd = 643.19$), "Instructional Methods in Health Professions Education" ($M = 303.3$, $sd = 183.768$), "Introduction to Finance" ($M = 3693$, $sd = 3351.92$), "Introduction to Thermodynamics" ($M = 346.50$, $sd = 143.59$), and "Model Thinking" ($M = 1390.20$, $sd = 1172.62$). We worked with instructional designers to ensure that each of the courses chosen experienced minimal changes between course offerings, limited to corrections and minor additions of content. The automated text analysis program LIWC 2015 was used to code the discourse features [13], which counts words into meaningful psychological categories. For example, words such as "nice" and "hope" are captured as reflections of positive emotions, while "nasty", "hate" exhibit negative emotions. Furthermore, affiliation was captured by words such as "friend" and "social". Once such target words were found, the related word category scale for that word will be incremented. Pearson correlational analyses have revealed the external validity of LIWC in successfully measuring cognitive states including positive and negative emotions [13].

## 3    Results

The relationships between time (i.e. course iteration number) and the level of affiliation, positive emotions and negative emotions reflected in learners' discourse, respectively, were analyzed using mixed effects models. Akaike Information Criterion (AIC), Log Likelihood (LL) and a likelihood ratio test were used to determine the best fitting and most parsimonious model. The tests indicate that, for the three models, the full models that include an interaction between course categories and time fit significantly better than the null models with only Participant ID as a random effect, with $\chi^2(9) = 1767.9$, $p \leq .0001$ for the affiliation model, $\chi^2(9) = 118.12$, $p \leq .0001$ for the positive emotion model, and $\chi^2(9) = 1012$, $p \leq .0001$ for the negative emotion model, respectively. Therefore, adding the interaction between course and time explains significantly better the changes in learners' discourse features above and beyond individual participant characteristics.

Subsequent paragraphs, however, are indented. In addition, we also estimate effect sizes for each model, using a pseudo $R^2$ method, as suggested by Nakagawa and Schielzeth [14]. For mixed-effects models, $R^2$ can be characterized into two varieties: marginal $R^2$ and conditional $R^2$. Marginal $R^2$ is associated with variance explained by fixed factors, and conditional $R^2$ is can be interpreted as the variance explained by the entire model, namely both random and fixed factors. For the affiliation model $(R^2_m = .296, R^2_c = .405)$, the time, course and individual participant features together accounted for 40.47% of the predictable variance, with 2.96% of the variance explained only by the interaction between course and time. Moreover, the interaction effects and main effects are both significant, demonstrating that while different courses have different affiliation trends, the overall level of affiliation reflected in the discussion forums of the five chosen courses has been declining over time (see Fig. 1a). In terms of each course, "Instructional Methods in Health Professions Education" and "Introduction to Thermodynamics", with smaller class size over time and fewer iterations, experienced no significant change in the level of affiliation, while the other three courses with larger class sizes and more terms of iteration witnessed significant decrease in the level of affiliation.

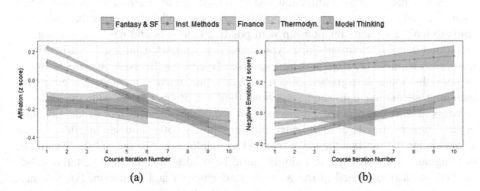

**Fig. 1.** Affiliation (a) and Negative emotion (b) over course iterations. All values are in standard z-scores.

With regard to the positive emotion model $(R^2_m = .002, R^2_c = .239)$, and negative emotion model $(R^2_m = .171, R^2_c = .145)$, despite the fact that different courses demonstrate different trends, in slope and direction, there is an overall increasing trend in negative emotions (see Fig. 1b) but no significant overall change in positive emotions (not figured). Interestingly, while most courses experienced increasing negative emotions, the two courses experiencing no significant decrease in affiliation had significant decreases in negative emotions, suggesting a potential relationship between affiliation and negative emotion in scaled learning environments.

## 4 Discussion

Our findings show that learners in most courses exhibited a clear trend of less affiliation and higher negative emotion in subsequent iterations of the course from 2012 to 2015, while there was no clear tendency in positive emotions. We would not necessarily expect to see the same level of affiliation in two different modalities (e.g. face to face and online courses) due to instructional design differences [6]. However, we held instructional design constant in this study, and thus the decrease was attributable to other exogenous factors and not course design per se. An existing limitation is the fact that while the current scaled learning environment offers text and video communication that imitate voice and facial expressions that directly convey feelings, some peripheral physiological connections were inevitably missing, which are important components of affiliation [15]. On the other hand, MOOC discussion forums tend to be overloaded with a large amount of course-irrelevant posts that greatly disrupt navigation and participation. A potential method to address this issue is to help learners navigate through discussion forums easier by developing tools to automatically identify course-related threads [16], thus facilitating forum involvement.

With regard to emotions, which are generally associated with affiliation [7], it is intriguing that the overall affiliation level dropped and negative emotions increased, whereas positive emotions incurred no significant changes. It is also interesting that courses that had decreased affiliation had increased negative emotions as well, while such connection was not seen in the positive emotion model. It appears that affiliation tends to have a separate relationship with positive emotions and negative emotions in the scaled learning environment. Beyond this, it is somewhat unclear what is driving learners to be more negative in their discourse. To address this issue, we would like to explore the more fine-grained affective states that make up "negative emotion", including stress and confusion, and how they might be related with the different contents in different courses. Furthermore, it would also be valuable to identify individual learners' trends as they enter different phases of a course. In addition, we acknowledge the fact that the LIWC method we deployed in the present study could be limiting and that more NLP techniques could be used to further validate the results.

We are also interested in the within-thread emotion and affiliation. For instance, repeated negative emotion in a thread's posts may be indicative of a severe learning issue (e.g. a system failure for interactive exercises) which needs immediate attention. However, a thread which alternates positive and negative emotions, and is highly aligned with content, may represent peer help. To understand these trends we would not only want to look at the content of the posts, but also the roles of the actors, using a more complex linguistic analysis such as Group Communication Analysis [17].

Moving forward, we will be exploring the practical implications of the current findings for MOOC learners and instructional designers. Should the general online learner population continue to feel less connected over a long period of time, the phenomenon could eventually lead to adverse learning experience and outcomes. This line of research is becoming more pressing, as the MOOC learner population continues to expand, and more universities are transitioning to hybrid teaching environments by adding distanced learning to their traditional way of teaching [10].

# References

1. Libbey, H.P.: Measuring student relationships to school: attachment, bonding, connected-ness, and engagement. J. Sch. Health **74**(7), 274–283 (2004)
2. Weiss, C.L.A., Cunningham, D.L., Lewis, C.P., Clark, M.G.: Enhancing student connect-edness to schools. Center for School Mental Health Analysis and Action. Department of Psychiatry, University of Maryland School of Medicine, Baltimore (2005)
3. Centers for Disease Control and Prevention.: School connectedness: Strategies for increasing protective factors among youth. Department of Health and Human Services, Atlanta (2009)
4. Goodenow, C.: Classroom belonging among early adolescent students: relationships to motivation and achievement. J. Early Adolesc. **13**(1), 21–43 (1993)
5. Danielsen, A.G., Wiium, N., Wilhelmsen, B.U., Wold, B.: Perceived support provided by teachers and classmates and students' self-reported academic initiative. J. Sch. Psychol. **48**(3), 247–267 (2010)
6. Zhu, M., Bergner, Y., Zhang, Y., Baker, R., Wang, Y., Paquette, L.: Longitudinal engagement, performance, and social connectivity: a MOOC case study using exponential random graph models. In: Proceedings of the Sixth International Conference on Learning Analytics and Knowledge, pp. 223–230. ACM, New York (2016)
7. Anderman, E.M.: School effects on psychological outcomes during adolescence. J. Educ. Psychol. **94**(4), 795–809 (2002)
8. Angelaki, C., Mavroidis, I.: Communication and social presence: the impact on adult learners' emotions in distance learning. Eur. J. Open Distance E-learn. **16**(1), 78–93 (2013)
9. Um, E.R., Plass, J.L., Hayward, E.O., Homer, B.D.: Emotional design in multimedia learning. J. Educ. Psychol. **104**(2), 485–498 (2012)
10. Marchand, G.C., Gutierrez, A.P.: The role of emotion in the learning process: comparisons between online and face-to-face learning settings. Internet High. Educ. **15**(3), 150–160 (2012)
11. Vogel, S., Schwabe, L.: Learning and memory under stress: implications for the classroom. Npj Sci. Learn. **1**, 16011 (2016)
12. D'Mello, S., Lehman, B., Pekrun, R., Graesser: A confusion can be beneficial for learning. Learn. Instr. **29**, 153–170 (2014). (Supplement C)
13. Pennebaker, J.W., Boyd, R.L., Jordan, K., Blackburn, K.: The development and psychometric properties of LIWC2015. University of Texas at Austin, Austin (2015)
14. Nakagawa, S., Schielzeth, H.: A general and simple method for obtaining R2 from generalized linear mixed-effects models. Methods Ecol. Evol. **4**(2), 133–142 (2013). https://doi.org/10.1111/j.2041-210x.2012.00261.x
15. Cheng, J.C.: An exploratory study of emotional affordance of a massive open online course. Eur. J. Open Distance E-learn. **17**(1), 43–55 (2014)
16. Wise, A.F., Cui, Y., Vytasek, J.: Bringing order to chaos in MOOC discussion forums with content-related thread identification. In: Proceedings of the Sixth International Conference on Learning Analytics and Knowledge, pp. 188–197. ACM, New York (2016)
17. Dowell, N.M., Nixon, T., Graesser, A.C.: Group communication analysis: a computational linguistics approach for detecting sociocognitive roles in multi-party interactions. Behavior Research Methods (2018). https://arxiv.org/abs/1801.03563

# Investigating Influence of Demographic Factors on Study Recommenders

Michal Huptych[1,2], Martin Hlosta[1(✉)], Zdenek Zdrahal[1,2], and Jakub Kocvara[1]

[1] Knowledge Media Institute, The Open University, Milton Keynes, UK
{michal.huptych,martin.hlosta,zdenek.zdrahal,jakub.kocvara}@open.ac.uk
[2] CIIRC, Czech Technical University in Prague, Prague, Czech Republic

**Abstract.** Recommender systems in e-learning platforms, can utilise various data about learners in order to provide them with the next best material to study. We build on our previous work, which defines the recommendations in terms of two measures (i.e. *relevance* and *effort*) calculated from data of successful students in the previous runs of the courses. In this paper we investigate the impact of students' socio-demographic factors and analyse how these factors improved the recommendation. It has been shown that education and age were found to have a significant impact on engagement with materials.

**Keywords:** Personalised learning · Educational recommender systems

## 1 Introduction

In distance education, most of the learning takes place in Virtual Learning Environments (VLE) allowing learners flexible way of studying. E-learning systems minimise the costs of education and enable to scale up the number of students, which would be impossible or very difficult to achieve in a traditional face to face learning environment. On the other hand, the students lose frequent contact with teachers, their supervision and possible valuable feedback, which can help them with guidance and organisation of their study. As a result, many students drop out before completing the course.

Due to the digital nature of students' interaction with study resources, their actions can be recorded and analysed to explore how different types of students learn. The available data motivated the research and development of recommender systems (RS). Recommenders in education introduce domain-specific challenges. For example, if the goal is to improve students performance, following the activities of those with a similar learning behaviour is unlikely to deliver the desired result. Moreover, educational domains usually specify the time learners have to reserve to achieve a task, dependencies and prerequisites among study materials and others.

According to review [2], most of the educational recommenders used Collaborative Filtering (CF), with growing interest of incorporating characteristics of

C. Penstein Rosé et al. (Eds.): AIED 2018, LNAI 10948, pp. 150–154, 2018.
https://doi.org/10.1007/978-3-319-93846-2_27

the educational domain. For example, prioritising features and ratings of good performing students was used in [3]. Personalised recommender systems take into account the past activities of each individual learner. CF achieves this by behavioural or rating pattern. However, it suffers from a cold-start problem, needing initial information about the users, which is not available at the start of the course [6]. The cold-start problem hinders also content-based methods, which operates on the similarity of the items that users liked in the past rather than similarity to users.

Demographic data can be used to tackle the cold-start, yet the existing research in educational domain is very limited. In [5] the student educational background plays only a marginal role; [7] aims at recommending courses rather than study materials. In [1] socio-demographic features serve to improve the student engagement with MOOCs by recommending students to connect with peers of similar demographic factors.

## 2   Personalisation by Socio-Demographic Factors

The goal of this paper is to investigate methods of personalisation as described in our previous work in [4]. We design the personalised study recommender by constructing a click-based behavioural pattern from the activities of successful students. We define two new measures: *relevance* and *effort*. The *relevance* measures the average activity spent by the selected cohort (the excellent group) on each educational material in the previous presentation, while the *effort* indicates the engagement of each individual student with the educational material in the current presentation. *Relevance* is the 'content to be learned' while the *effort* shows what has the individual 'already learned'. The recommendation strategy says that for each educational resource and each current student his/her *effort* should balance the resource *relevance*.

At the start of the course no student has engaged with any study material. *Relevance* calculated from activities of the excellent group in the previous presentation is the same for all students.

However, demographic and other static data about each student are available. Could we enrich the VLE activity data by this additional information to further refine and personalise the recommendations for groups of students with similar VLE characteristics? In another word, do students with different demographic data and equal VLE behaviour manifest different responses in the educational process? The available features included (1) **Highest education**; from 'No formal' to 'Postgrad', (2) flag if student **is new** to the university, (3) **Motivation**, (4) **Occupation**, (5) **Age**, (6) **Gender**, (7) **IMD** – Index of Multiple Deprivation.

## 3   Experiments and Impact of Socio-Demographic Factors

The experiments were performed on 4 presentations of a technology-related course. The goal was to evaluate the impact of each individual socio-demographic factor on students' effort. The values of investigated factors were split into two groups. For categorical-valued factors, the groups were defined by the selection of categories, for ordinal-valued factors the groups were defined by selecting the threshold. The contingency table was constructed for each analysed factor and the groups of excellent students ($\geq 75\%$) and others. The dependency was evaluated by Mann-Whitney test at the significance level $p < 0.1$. The following results have been achieved:

The comparison of students with A level or higher education and the rest of the cohort revealed differences in activities depending on their **educational backgrounds**. For excellent students group, the mean cumulative *effort* was 11% higher for students with lower than A level education. These students were more active on relevant materials, although these differences were less noticeable among students with scores lower than 75%. These findings proved to be consistent across all presentations that were tested.

The most influential factor affecting students' behaviour was their **age**. The biggest gap in activities was found for the split at the age of 30 years. Therefore two groups were created: up to 29 years and 30+ years. Although the mean cumulative *effort* of these groups has similar values at the end of the presentation, important differences have been found at individual blocks and materials, e.g. 18 % higher activity for students 30+ in Block 3 Part 2 (see Fig. 1). Older students systematically showed higher engagement with materials and also started interacting with these materials earlier, often even before they were assigned by the tutor. This was the case for both performance groups and all presentations.

Influence of factors new/continuing, occupation, motivation and IMD did not prove to be statistically significant.

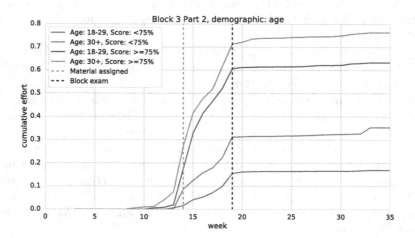

**Fig. 1.** Change of cumulative *effort* over time on Block 3 Part 2 in 2015. After a block exam in week 19, *effort* becomes saturated.

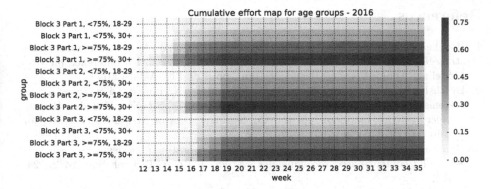

**Fig. 2.** Heat-map of cumulative *effort* over time for age and performance groups in 2016. Darker squares indicate higher engagement.

The cumulative *effort* has a similar pattern for the corresponding performance and age groups across study materials. The 30+ groups have always been more active and started with each Block/Part earlier than the 18–29 group, see Figs. 1 and 2.

## 4   Discussion and Conclusions

We presented the analysis of demographic factors with the aim of investigation their impact on recommendations. Recommendation are defined using two measures: *relevance* and *effort*, which reflect the importance of the study material and engagement of the individual student with this material. We selected 4 presentations of one technology-related course and performed the examination of the impact of 5 factors' categories on the *effort* of students.

As expected, there are significant and consistent differences in *effort* between groups of students divided according to their performance. This fact is prevalent among all demographic factors and it confirms our presumption that correlation between *effort* and performance is always evident.

Furthermore, we analysed the *effort* within the excellent group and its relationship with students' demographic factors. We found two factors that contribute to the differences in *effort*: education and age. Based on our investigation, the students from the 30+ group had considerably higher engagement with the study materials. They started to interact with them earlier and reached higher values of *effort* at the moment of the Block exam, especially in the Parts of the Block 3. One of the reasons might be that younger students are more familiar with learning from online materials in general. But a closer investigation revealed that the Block 3 is focused on modern technologies such as Cloud computing and GPS.

The results also show that older students need more time to study such topics. This applies both to excellent students and their lower performing colleagues.

# References

1. Bouchet, F., Labarthe, H., Yacef, K., Bachelet, R.: Comparing peer recommendation strategies in a MOOC. In: Adjunct Publication of the 25th Conference on User Modeling, Adaptation and Personalization, pp. 129–134. ACM (2017)
2. Drachsler, H., Verbert, K., Santos, O.C., Manouselis, N.: Panorama of recommender systems to support learning. In: Ricci, F., Rokach, L., Shapira, B. (eds.) Recommender Systems Handbook, pp. 421–451. Springer, Boston, MA (2015). https://doi.org/10.1007/978-1-4899-7637-6_12
3. Ghauth, K.I., Abdullah, N.A.: The effect of incorporating good learners' ratings in e-learning content-based recommender system. J. Educ. Technol. Soc. **14**(2), 248 (2011)
4. Huptych, M., Bohuslavek, M., Hlosta, M., Zdrahal, Z.: Measures for recommendations based on past students' activity. In: LAK 2017 Proceedings of the 7th International Learning Analytics & Knowledge Conference on - LAK 2017, pp. 404–408 (2017)
5. Kerkiri, T., Manitsaris, A., Mavridis, I.: How e-learning systems may benefit from ontologies and recommendation methods to efficiently personalise resources. Int. J. Knowl. Learn. **5**(3–4), 347–370 (2009)
6. Nabizadeh, A.H., Mário Jorge, A., Paulo Leal, J.: Rutico: Recommending successful learning paths under time constraints. In: Adjunct Publication of the 25th Conference on User Modeling, Adaptation and Personalization, pp. 153–158. UMAP 2017. ACM, New York (2017)
7. Wen-Shung Tai, D., Wu, H.J., Li, P.H.: Effective e-learning recommendation system based on self-organizing maps and association mining. Electron. Libr. **26**(3), 329–344 (2008)

# A Design-Based Approach to a Classroom-Centered OELE

Nicole Hutchins[(⊠)], Gautam Biswas, Miklos Maroti, Akos Ledezci,
and Brian Broll

Vanderbilt University, Nashville, TN 37212, USA
nicole.m.hutchins@vanderbilt.edu

**Abstract.** The sustainable, synergistic integration of computational thinking (CT) and STEM learning environments into K12 classrooms requires consideration of learner-centered and classroom-centered design. In other words, not only do we have to take into account the learning goals and capabilities of students, but also the technological capabilities of the classroom environment and the combined impact of the teacher and technology on the classroom dynamics, curriculum, and progress. This paper discusses the design and development of an open ended learning environment aimed at high school physics curriculum taught within a CT-based framework. We conclude with preliminary results from a semester-long implementation study in a high school physics classroom.

**Keywords:** Computational thinking · STEM · Blended learning environments

## 1 Introduction

The sustainable integration of innovative, open ended learning environments (OELEs) in K12 classrooms requires the aggregation of learner-centered [8] and classroom-centered design approaches. This approach takes into consideration the prior knowledge and capabilities of the student and scaffolds their individual learning processes. It also takes into account the logistics and environment of the classroom, and how to achieve a cohesive balance between the role of the teacher and the technology. OELEs provide students meaningful learning opportunities by adopting a pedagogy that enables students to acquire domain information, construct, test, and revise solutions to authentic, problem solving tasks [3, 4, 7, 9]. However, in previous work, OELE frameworks have primarily focused on learner-centered design, with little consideration of the role of the teacher in helping to orchestrate classroom dynamics, progression through the curriculum, and student engagement to support learning. While technological advancements have introduced adaptive tools in K-12 classrooms that provide personalized learning opportunities, assimilation as part of a standard classroom environment has remained elusive.

This paper outlines the design and development of a classroom-centered OELE aimed at integrating computational modeling into a high school physics classroom. To do so, we will describe the classroom and student-learning components relevant to our architecture, provide an overview of our system design, and conclude with results,

© Springer International Publishing AG, part of Springer Nature 2018
C. Penstein Rosé et al. (Eds.): AIED 2018, LNAI 10948, pp. 155–159, 2018.
https://doi.org/10.1007/978-3-319-93846-2_28

analysis, and necessary system modifications derived from lessons learned in our semester-long classroom study.

## 2   C2STEM

The Collaborative, Computational STEM (C2STEM) environment utilizes a novel paradigm that combines visual programming [6] with domain specific modeling languages (DSMLs) [2] to promote learning of physics and CT concepts and practices.

### 2.1   Classroom Structure

Like a typical classroom curriculum, C2STEM tasks are made up of easily identifiable Instructional, Model Building, Assessment, and Challenge tasks. *Instructional tasks* help students focus on learning and applying primary physics concepts, often one at a time, to prepare students for building computational models. This helps address students' lack of knowledge in physics and programming. Instructional tasks build on previous content to make it easier for students to learn in small chunks.

Following instructional tasks, students work on *model building tasks* that require them to combine the information gained from *instructional tasks* along with CT practices to build a correct computational model of a Physics phenomena. A third component, *formative assessments* or *assessment tasks*, assess student learning in Physics and CT with multiple choice and short answer questions and small model building exercises. Finally, *challenge tasks* require students to solve more difficult problems that test their abilities to put together concepts and practices emphasized in the module. For instance, in the one-dimensional kinematics motion challenge, students are required to program a medical delivery truck that completes a straight path trip whilst adhering to various speed limits on the path and then safely stops at a STOP sign, before continuing on to its final destination.

### 2.2   Modeling

Modeling tasks are broken down into conceptual and computational modeling tasks. These two connected activities "support modeling at different levels of abstraction and operationalize the important CT concepts of abstraction and decomposition" [1].

**Conceptual Modeling.** Conceptual modeling allows for systematic planning of the objects and their associated properties and behaviors needed to build a correct computational model for the assigned problem. This model building activity is completed in the "Plan" tool of the C2STEM environment. When conceptual model elements are selected, their relevant block(s) appear in the "Build" component of the learning environment. Similarly, if objects or behaviors are removed from the conceptual model, the associated blocks are removed in the Build component. Students are allowed to move between the two model-building representations as they build their simulations.

**Computational.** Computational modeling is implemented by embedding the SNAP! programming environment in C2STEM. As mentioned in our primary research objective, we utilize a physics-based DSML. A DSML is "a programming language or executable specification language that offers, through appropriate notations and abstractions, expressive power focused on, and usually restricted to, a particular problem domain" [10]. It allows students to express solutions in the physics domain, and it provides students with precise, self-documenting code [5] supporting the application of relevant CT practices and constructs.

Our computational modeling environment also has a graphing module and a table generator that generates a spreadsheet of data values for selected variables. These tools help students interpret their simulation behaviors and debug their models.

## 2.3 Architecture

The C2STEM system uses a modular architecture that allows for seamless integration of its components for classroom instruction. A simple infrastructure was essential to accomplish sustainability in the classroom, and to minimize common logistical issues regarding installation and software updates on a large number of school-owned computers. The system is web-based and runs off a cloud server thereby allowing student access at school and at home. Figure 1 illustrates the overall architecture of our environment, including the ability to handle multiple clients simultaneously. This architecture provides researchers with the ability to grade student work in real-time through a logging functionality not described in this paper, as well as collaboration opportunities (e.g. students sharing computational workspaces).

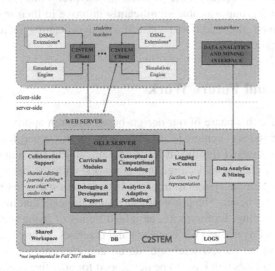

**Fig. 1.** System architecture

While our architecture supports our goal of a sustainable learning environment, the components of our system allow for scalability and adaptability by the teacher, instructional scaffolding, and quick grading of student assignments. Users have continuous access to all instructional tasks (Sect. 2.1) and resources, supporting the open-ended nature required of OELEs [5]. All tasks are composed of HTML components (task descriptions, multiple choice and short answer questions, etc.), the conceptual modeling component, and the computational modeling component.

## 3 Classroom Implementation

Following a preliminary usability study, our team conducted a semester-long study in a Physics high school classroom in Nashville, Tennessee. The study included 174 students taking an Honors Physics course; 84 students participated in the experimental group and used our C2STEM environment, and 90 students were in the control group – they did not use the system. Students completed four physics modules: three in Kinematics: 1D motion (with acceleration), 2D motion with constant velocity, and 2D motion with gravitational forces, and an introductory unit on 1D Force.

Our experimental group utilized the C2STEM environment an average of three out of four classroom sessions a week, with non-system days dedicated to content lectures by the physics teacher (delivered to both control and experimental groups). Participants completed pre- and post- tests in Kinematics, Mechanics, and CT.

For our preliminary results for the pre-posttests we randomly selected 30 experimental group participants. In the Kinematics pre-posttests, the experimental group's average score on the pre-test was a 22.4(5.4) and increased to an average score of 34.2 (3.4) in the post-test. For CT, the average score on the pre-test was a 22.4(4.7) on the pre-test, improving to 30.7(4.2) on the post-test. These preliminary results demonstrate that the experimental group was able significantly improve in their learning of physics content and received the additional benefit of significantly increasing their CT knowledge in the process.

## 4 Conclusion and Future Work

Our research goal for this phase of our design-based research approach was to develop and implement a classroom-centered OELE focused on the synergistic learning of CT and STEM. Results showed significant learning gains in Physics and CT. The Physics instructor combined classroom lectures and lab work with the use of C2STEM, and used the assessments on the system to improve his instruction and to help students learn their Physics concepts better. The pre-post test results indicate that the additional effort also led to better learning. Furthermore, an added bonus of using the system is that it taught students both Physics and CT concepts and practices. However, it is clear that to build this system up to its full learner-centered and classroom-centered potential, a number of additional tools will have to be developed for adaptive scaffolding of student learning, and also to aid the teacher in assessing students and keeping track of students' progress.

**Acknowledgments.** We thank Luke Conlin, Kevin McElhaney, Shuchi Grover, Satabdi Basu, Kristen P. Blair, Doris Chin, and our other collaborators from Vanderbilt University and Stanford University for their numerous contributions. This research is supported by NSF grant #1640199.

# References

1. Basu, S., Biswas, G., Kinnebrew, J.S.: Learner modeling for adaptive scaffolding in a computational thinking-based science learning environment. User Model. User-Adap. Inter. **27**(1), 5–53 (2017)
2. Basu, S., Biswas, G., Kinnebrew, J.S.: Using multiple representations to simultaneously learn computational thinking and middle school science. In: Thirtieth AAAI Conference on Artificial Intelligence, pp. 3705–3711. MIT Press, Boston (2016)
3. Biswas, G., Segedy, J.R., Bunchongchit, K.: From design to implementation to practice - a learning by teaching system: Betty's brain. Int. J. Artif. Intell. Educ. **26**(1), 350–364 (2016)
4. Hannafin, M.J., Hill, J.R., Land, S.M., Lee, E.: Student-centered, open learning environments: research, theory, and practice. In: Spector, J., Merrill, M., Elen, J., Bishop, M. (eds.) Handbook of Research on Educational Communications and Technology. Springer, New York (2014). https://doi.org/10.1007/978-1-4614-3185-5_51
5. Hasan, A., Biswas, G.: Domain specific modeling language design to support synergistic learning of STEM and computational thinking. In: Proceedings of the International Conference on Computational Thinking Education (2017)
6. Kelleher, C., Pausch, R.: Lowering the barriers to programming: a taxonomy of programming environments and languages for novice programmers. ACM Comput. Surv. **37**(2), 83–137 (2005)
7. Land, S.: Cognitive requirements for learning with open-ended learning environments. Educ. Tech. Res. Dev. **48**(3), 61–78 (2000)
8. Quintana, C., Krajcik, J., Soloway, E.: Exploring a structured definition for learner-centered design. In: 4th International Conference of the Learning Sciences, Erlbaum, Mahwah, NJ, pp. 264–265 (2000)
9. Sengupta, P., Kinnebrew, J.S., Basu, S., Biswas, G., Clark, D.: Integrating computational thinking with K-12 science education using agent-based computation: a theoretical framework. Educ. Inf. Technol. **18**(2), 351–380 (2013)
10. Van Deursen, A., Klint, P., Visser, J.: Domain-specific languages: an annotated bibliography. SIGPLAN Not. **35**(6), 26–36 (2000)

# On the Value of Answerers in Early Detection of Response Time to Questions for Peer Recommender Systems

Oluwabukola Mayowa (Ishola) Idowu$^{(\boxtimes)}$ and Gordon McCalla$^{(\boxtimes)}$

ARIES Laboratory, Department of Computer Science,
University of Saskatchewan, Saskatoon, Canada
bukola.idowu@usask.ca, mccalla@cs.usask.ca

**Abstract.** Most research in peer recommender systems in online learning communities (OLCs) is focused on the problem of identifying the *answerers* who can provide the best answers to a question soon after the question has been asked. In fact, we have explored exactly this issue in another research project [5]. In contrast, in the research reported in this paper we devised methods of predicting in Stack Overflow (a very large online community of programmers) at the time a question is asked, whether the question will receive an answer at all, and, if so, whether the answer will come early or late (i.e. after the median response time). Overall, in a study that used 5 months of Stack Overflow data our methods worked well enough that we feel they could usefully inform support systems such as peer recommender systems about questions that might prove to be unanswered or answered late.

**Keywords:** Lifelong learning · Online help · Predictive models
Learner modelling · Peer recommender systems

## 1 Introduction

Peer help recommender systems are a common tool used in online learning communities (OLCs) to suggest prospective answerers to questions. In studies [2, 6] the quality of the recommender system is often measured by its ability to predict answerers who will provide both high quality and on time answers. In a real-world system, such peer recommenders would be deemed to be especially useful if a learner would otherwise receive no answer or a late answer. We have developed methodologies for predicting at the time a question is asked whether it will be unanswered or answered late. We explored how well these methodologies make predictions of unanswered or late question in the Stack Overflow OLC that supports millions of programmers [1, 2].

## 2 Methodology

In predicting whether a question will receive an answer and how soon such an answer will be provided (early or late), we employed three general approaches: using the features of the question asked (*question content-based* approach), using features of the

C. Penstein Rosé et al. (Eds.): AIED 2018, LNAI 10948, pp. 160–165, 2018.
https://doi.org/10.1007/978-3-319-93846-2_29

active answerers (*answerer-based* approach) and using features that examine the popularity of the tags used in the question (*tag-popularity* approach). Among the three approaches a total of 13 features were employed which are largely based on those from past studies in SO [5–7].

## 2.1 Question Content-Based Approach

In the question content-based approach, we look at aspects of the question and question asker to make our predictions. There are 5 features we compute, drawn from features defined in a previous study [7] as described below :

### 2.1.1 *Title Length* (TitleLength)
The title of a question provides a summarized description of the question. This feature measures the string length of the title of the question using the length function in SQL.

### 2.1.2 *Body Length* (BodyLength)
The body of a question contains the text of the question asked. This feature measures the string length of the body of the question.

### 2.1.3 *Code Present* (CodePresent)
This feature checks if the question contains code or not by searching for the presence of the <code> and </code> html tags in the body of the question. Also, as code could be posted as an image, we also searched for the presence of the <img tag in the body of the question. The possible state of this feature is *yes* or *no*.

### 2.1.4 *Tag Count* (TagCount)
Tag(s) used in a question indicate the knowledge required to answer the question. A maximum of 5 tags can be used in a question. This feature counts the number of tag(s) included in the question asked.

### 2.1.5 *Question Asked Count* (QuestionAskedCount)
This feature is the total number of questions the user has asked in the past in SO.

## 2.2 Answerer-Based Approach

In the answerer-based approach we look at features of potential answerers to questions. The tags used in a question serve as a guide to the knowledge required to answer the question. Therefore, for the answerer-based approach, we consider only answerers who have earned a tag-based badge for at least one of the tags in the question, (that is answerers who have provided at least 20 quality answers to questions relating to a question tag). As in a previous study [5] we also consider only active answerers, i.e. those who have recently (a month prior to when the question is asked) provided answers to questions containing any of the tags used in the question under consideration. The features about the answerers extracted are as defined in [5]:

### 2.2.1   Number of Active Answerers

For each of the tags employed in the question, we count the total number of distinct active answerers who have provided answers to any of the tag(s) used in the question a month before the question was asked.

### 2.2.2   Regularity

Regularity represents how often the active answerers provide an answer to a topic.

### 2.2.3   Knowledgeability

Knowledgeability represents the know-how of the answerers about a given topic. This is the aggregate score earned by all active answerers for providing answers to questions relating to the tags used in the question.

### 2.2.4   Eagerness

Eagerness represents the keenness of the active answerers to deal with a topic when compared to other topics.

### 2.2.5   Willingness

Willingness represents how vigorous the active answerers are in providing answers to questions on a topic as compared to other users.

As the eagerness and willingness values computed in Sects. 2.2.4 and 2.2.5 above resulted in very small numbers, we took the log of the respective values obtained. Also based on the results from our previous study [5], in predicting the answer and the RTFA classes, we multiplied the values computed for the features in Sects. 2.2.2–2.2.5 with the probability of an early answer (the proportion of questions answered within the median response time of 38 min as compared to the total number of questions asked a month prior to when the question is asked).

## 2.3   Tag-Popularity Approach

In the tag-popularity approach the goal is to see if the popularity of the tags used in the question will allow us to predict whether a question will be answered, and if so, if it will be answered early or late. Tags have been usefully employed in previous studies [1, 6, 7] of users in SO, so we thought this to be a promising approach. The 3 features extracted are described below:

### 2.3.1   Tag Popularity Count

With this feature, we compute how many popular tags are used in the question, that is the total number of tags used that are among the top 10% of all tags used (the top 5,000 of the approximately 50,000 tags used in SO).

### 2.3.2   Minimum Tag Usage

This feature is the count of the number of times the least popular tag employed in the question have been used in SO.

### 2.3.3 Average Tag Usage

This feature is the average number of times all the tags employed in a question have been used in SO.

## 3 Our Study

Our initial goals were to make two different binary predictions. First, we wished to predict whether a question in SO would be answered or not. Second, we wished to predict for an answered question whether it would be answered early or late, i.e. before the median response time to first answer (RTFA) or after this median RTFA. For our dataset we used the 1,079,947 questions asked in SO from January to May 2017. Before making our first "answered or not" prediction we noted that our dataset had 751,819 questions that were classified as answered and 328,128 that were classified as unanswered. Noting the class size imbalance, to avoid biased results we applied the undersampling technique described in [3] by randomly selecting 328,128 questions from the answered question class so that the two classes are the same size. For our second "early or late" prediction we used the median RTFA of 38 min as the dividing line between the two classes, which left us with class sizes of 389,935 questions answered early and 361,884 answered late.

The performance of the 3 general approaches in predicting whether a question will be answered or not and predicting whether a question will be answered early or late were compared using 4 classification models using the features defined for each of the approaches. We employed two decision tree models (*J48* and *Random Forest*), a Bayesian classifier (*Bayes Net*), and a logistic model (*Logistic Regression*), all as defined in Weka [4]. The performance of each of the predictive models was evaluated using 10-fold cross validation. The prediction accuracy and F-measure obtained for both goals are shown in Tables 1 and 2 respectively.

**Table 1.** Prediction accuracy and F-Measure values in predicting whether a question will be answered or not

| | Prediction Accuracy | | | | F-Measure | | | |
|---|---|---|---|---|---|---|---|---|
| Approach Used | J48 | Random Forest | Bayes Net | Logistic Regression | J48 | Random Forest | Bayes Net | Logistic Regression |
| Question Content-based | 56.339% | 56.426% | 56.103% | 55.763% | 0.559 | 0.561 | 0.557 | 0.542 |
| Answerer-based | 59.368% | 60.293% | 58.866% | 58.910% | 0.592 | 0.602 | 0.588 | 0.586 |
| Tag-Popularity | 56.146% | 56.738% | 56.064% | 53.776% | 0.561 | 0.567 | 0.560 | 0.537 |

Tables 1 and 2 show that the question content-based approach had the least accuracy. The decision tree models (J48 and Random Forest) performed better than the other classifiers with Random Forest achieving the highest prediction accuracy and F-measure using the answerer-based approach. Overall, in predicting questions that will be unanswered or answered late, the answerer-based approach ranked higher.

**Table 2.** Prediction accuracy and F-Measure values in predicting whether an answered question will be answered early or late

| | Prediction Accuracy | | | | F-Measure | | | |
|---|---|---|---|---|---|---|---|---|
| Approach Used | J48 | Random Forest | Bayes Net | Logistic Regression | J48 | Random Forest | Bayes Net | Logistic Regression |
| Question Content-based | 58.182% | 58.400% | 57.988% | 57.798% | 0.579 | 0.582 | 0.577 | 0.569 |
| Answerer-based | 67.638% | 68.400% | 66.700% | 65.100% | 0.676 | 0.684 | 0.665 | 0.651 |
| Tag-Popularity | 63.890% | 64.315% | 63.580% | 61.616% | 0.638 | 0.642 | 0.636 | 0.615 |

## 4  Discussion

The long term goal of our research is to investigate how to support lifelong professional learners in an online learning community to meet their learning needs on time. This is especially a serious problem with the growth in the proportion of unanswered and late answered questions in SO [5]. This enhances the importance of being able to identify such problematic questions at the time they are asked and immediately recommending a peer helper in such cases. Previous studies have used a tag-popularity approach [6] and a question-content approach [7] in determining the response time to a question, but the latter approach had very low precision and recall values of 0.35 and 0.403 respectively. We, too, had lower levels of accuracy using the question content-based approach, suggesting that, perhaps, modelling the answerers will be a key requirement when building tools to support learners in an online learning community. We believe these results can provide insight to future researchers and educational system builders in both knowing the reasons why some questions are answered late (or not at all) and in designing peer recommender systems and other help tools that can intervene to improve the response time to first answer for questions asked in an online learning community. We believe these results can provide insight to future researchers and educational system builders in both knowing the reasons why some questions are answered late (or not at all) and in designing peer recommender systems and other help tools such as a virtual teaching assistant [8] that can intervene to improve the response time to first answer for questions asked in an online learning community.

**Acknowledgements.** We would like to thank the Natural Sciences and Engineering Research Council of Canada and the University of Saskatchewan for their financial support for this research.

## References

1. Ishola (Idowu), O.M., McCalla, G.: Personalized tag-based knowledge diagnosis to predict the quality of answers in a community of learners. In: André, E., Baker, R., Hu, X., Rodrigo, M.M.T., du Boulay, B. (eds.) AIED 2017. LNCS (LNAI), vol. 10331, pp. 113–124. Springer, Cham (2017). https://doi.org/10.1007/978-3-319-61425-0_10
2. Ishola (Idowu), O.M., McCalla, G.: Predicting prospective peer helpers to provide just-in-time help to users in question and answer forums. In: 10th International Conference on Educational Data Mining, EDM 2017, Wuhan, China, pp. 238–243, June 2017

3. Chawla, N.V.: Data mining for imbalanced datasets: an overview. In: Maimon, O., Rokach, L. (eds.) Data Mining and Knowledge Discovery Handbook, pp. 875–886. Springer, Boston (2009). https://doi.org/10.1007/978-0-387-09823-4_45

4. Dekker, G., Pechenizkiy, M., Vleeshouwers, J.: Predicting students' drop out: a case study. In: 2nd International Conference on Educational Data Mining, EDM 2009, Cordoba, Spain, pp. 41–50, July 2009

5. Idowu (Ishola), O.M., McCalla, G.: Better late than never but never late is better: towards reducing the answer response time to questions in an online learning community. In: Penstein Rosé, C., Martínez-Maldonado, R., Hoppe, U., Luckin, M., Mavrikis, M., Porayska-Pomsta, K., McLaren, B., du Boulay, B. (eds.) AIED 2018, LNAI, vol. 10947, pp. 184–197. Springer, Cham (2018)

6. Bhat, V., Gokhale, A., Jadhav, R., Pudipeddi, J., Akoglu, L.: Min(e) d your tags: analysis of question response time in StackOverflow. In: IEEE/ACM International Conference on Social Networks Analysis and Mining, ASONAM 2014, pp. 328–335. IEEE, August 2014

7. Asaduzzaman, M., Mashiyat, A.S., Roy, C.K., Schneider, K.A.: Answering questions about unanswered questions of Stack Overflow. In: 10th IEEE Working Conference on Mining Software Repositories, MSR 2013, pp. 97–100. IEEE, May 2013

8. Eicher, B., Polepeddi, L., Goel, A.: Jill Watson doesn't care if you're pregnant: grounding AI ethics in empirical studies. In: AAAI/ACM Conference on Artificial Intelligence, Ethics, and Society, New Orleans, LA, 7 p, February 2018

# Intelligent Evaluation and Feedback in Support of a Credit-Bearing MOOC

David Joyner[⊠] [iD]

Georgia Institute of Technology, Atlanta, GA 30332, USA
david.joyner@gatech.edu

**Abstract.** Massive Open Online Courses (MOOCs) may reach a massive number of people, but few MOOCs count for credit. Scaling rigorous assessment, feedback, and integrity checks presents difficulties. We implemented an AI system for a CS1 MOOC-for-credit to address both scale and endorsement. In this analysis, we present the design of the system and an evaluation of the course. We observe that students in the online course achieve comparable learning outcomes, report a more positive student experience, and identify AI-equipped programming problems as the primary contributor to their experiences.

**Keywords:** Automated evaluation · MOOCs · CS1

## 1 Introduction

In this work, we present an online version of a CS1 class at a large state university. The course aims to be a MOOC-for-credit: it is offered to on-campus students for degree credit, but is also available to MOOC students from all over the world for free. In order to accomplish this, mechanisms must be found for scaling up the human grading found in a traditional campus while preserving (or improving) the learning outcomes and student experience. Toward this end, the CS1 course we present here is built with a strong emphasis on applying AI to the evaluation and feedback process. At time of writing, 440 students have enrolled in the course for credit, while 12,000 students have participated in the free massive open online course (MOOC) on edX.

## 2 Related Work

Work has been done on applying AI to computer science evaluations. There are many historical (Web-CAT [4], OKPy [14], and Autolab [17]) and modern (Vocareum [9], Zybooks, Coursera [1], Udacity [7]) platforms and frameworks targeting this space. Wilcox [16] gives an overview of the automated evaluation space. These tools mostly focus on evaluation, but it is also important to provide feedback. Wiese et al. [15], for example, automatically generate style feedback for students, and Glassman et al. categorize submissions into patterns for tailored feedback [5]. There also exist several intelligent tutoring systems for computer programming [2, 3, 12, 13].

© Springer International Publishing AG, part of Springer Nature 2018
C. Penstein Rosé et al. (Eds.): AIED 2018, LNAI 10948, pp. 166–170, 2018.
https://doi.org/10.1007/978-3-319-93846-2_30

# 3   Intelligent Evaluation and Feedback

The online CS1 class described herein can be taken by any student to fulfill their state CS requirement and routinely draws more than 1000 students per year. To scale, assignments generally need to be automatically evaluated, but to maintain credit worthiness, the evaluations must be rigorous, authentic, and comparable to traditional on-campus offerings of the course. To support this, we constructed an infrastructure for intelligent evaluation and feedback. We then populated it with 300 programming problems, including 30 proctored exam problems, leveraging this framework. Additional details of the course design can be found in [8–10]; this analysis emphasizes the design of the course's intelligent feedback.

## 3.1   Global and Local Infrastructure

The infrastructure for intelligent evaluation and feedback has two parts: a global, general framework for initializing automated evaluation, gathering results, and presenting results to the user; and a set of local, specific parameters targeted at individual problems. We dub the global framework "Phineas" and the local parameters "Ferb".

When a student submits a coding problem, Phineas gathers together the student's code and bundles it into an inspectable object, allowing for deep code inspection and unit testing. Phineas sends these arguments to Ferb, a set of problem-specific parameters, such as a routine for intelligently generating new unit tests, a set of forbidden or required code, and explicit requirements such as method signatures.

Local evaluation of a student's submission against Ferb's parameters runs through three stages: pre-processing, unit testing, and post-processing. This **pre-processing** covers those checks necessary for the unit tests to be inspected. This stage focuses on the presence of specific functions, objects, methods, and variables.

If those preprocessing checks fail, the student is informed of that failure immediately, and subsequent checks are not run. If the preprocessing checks pass, the code is executed for **unit tests** generated by Ferb. This generates a list of the results, with each result including the input arguments, the expected output, the actual output, and whether the result is considered a pass, fail, or warning.

After running unit tests, the code is finally checked against the **post-processing** checks. These checks are typically against data generated during runtime, such as a count of the number of loop iterations or recursive calls, and thus may only run after execution. The results from these checks are appended to the corresponding lists of passed and failed results.

These results are then returned to Phineas in the form of three lists: a list of successes, a list of failures, and a list of warnings. Phineas then performs a follow-up check on the list of failures and searches for corresponding global feedback. For example, if one of the failures references an unsupported operand TypeError, Phineas may inject general feedback on the likely causes of this error.

Then, Phineas uses these lists to write a file named full_results.txt; this file lists the failed requirements, then the warnings, and then the successes. Phineas then writes a brief result summary to provide in the console window. If there are any failures, Phineas selects the first failure to provide, closing with a pointer to the full results file.

If there are no failures, Phineas first informs students that their code passed the problem; if there are warnings, it then lets the student know that there may nonetheless be room for improvement. Once the student passes the problem, Phineas adds to their workspace one or more sample solutions written by the problem author. These sample solutions demonstrate optimal or alternate solutions for implicit feedback [6].

## 3.2  Problem Content

The course has over 300 coding problems, each with its a version of Ferb with parameters suited to the problem's requirements. Four problem templates are available:

- **Variable Inspection:** Direct inspection of variables and their values.
- **Console Output:** Inspection of content printed when executing student code after injecting intelligently-generated alternate values for existing variables.
- **Function Output:** Comparison of output of function calls from students' code with correct code based on intelligently-generated test cases.
- **Object Inspection:** Experimenting with the success of certain object instantiations and follow-up method calls or attribute checks.

All four problem templates come equipped with additional intelligent tolerance, such as the option to ignore minor differences in whitespace in output, to automatically perform type conversions, and to ignore rounding errors as deemed necessary.

# 4  Course Evaluation

In checking the credit-worthiness of the online course, we are concerned with learning outcomes and student experience. Students should learn as much in the online course as in the traditional, and the student experience should be at least comparably positive. To check this, we performed a pseudo-experiment comparing students in two semesters of this online for-credit course to the equivalent on-campus course.

## 4.1  Learning Outcomes

To evaluate learning outcomes, students in both the online and the traditional version of the course were given the SCS1 computer science assessment as a pre-test and post-test [11]. In this analysis, we investigated the effect that the AI-supported course may have on students of different levels of prior experience. We compared students within four specific subgroups: those who have previously completed a CS course ("Prior Expertise"), those who have previously started by failed or withdrawn from a CS course ("Prior Experience"), those who are self-taught or otherwise have some informal experience ("Informal Experience"), and those with no prior experience ("No Experience"). Table 1 shows these results.

We performed t-tests on each of these eight pairs. "Prior Experience" was statistically significant at $\alpha = 0.05$ (t = 2.14, $p = 0.0445$). "Prior Expertise" was statistically significant at $\alpha = 0.10$ (t = 1.84, $p = 0.0699$). No other differences were significant. However, these subdivisions mean that the sample sizes are small and this data has

**Table 1.** Pre-test and post-test scores of both course versions by prior experience. Mean test scores are bolded; sample sizes are italicized; standard deviations are unstylized.

| | Prior expertise | | | | | | Prior experience | | | | | |
|---|---|---|---|---|---|---|---|---|---|---|---|---|
| | Traditional | | | Online | | | Traditional | | | Online | | |
| Pre-test | **8.49** | *75* | 7.65 | **10.31** | *39* | 5.43 | **6.33** | *18* | 4.01 | **6.73** | *15* | 2.46 |
| Post-test | **10.00** | *37* | 5.92 | **12.26** | *39* | 4.74 | **7.11** | *9* | 5.90 | **11.43** | *14* | 3.84 |
| | Informal experience | | | | | | No experience | | | | | |
| | Traditional | | | Online | | | Traditional | | | Online | | |
| Pre-test | **9.41** | *41* | 5.46 | **7.95** | *22* | 4.16 | **5.40** | *103* | 2.14 | **5.22** | *46* | 2.27 |
| Post-test | **10.30** | *20* | 7.15 | **13.00** | *20* | 6.56 | **8.79** | *53* | 5.08 | **9.33** | *46* | 4.04 |

been re-tested, and so replication in future semesters is needed. Additionally, this analysis only evaluates starting points and outcomes, not learning gains: difference in pre-test scores suggests students with prior expertise did not learn significantly more in the online section than the traditional (+2.34 vs. +1.51), but students with informal experience may have learned far more (+5.05 in the online version, +0.89 in the traditional version). The sample sizes are too small, however, to include only students who took both tests, and so this difference may be due to a response bias.

### 4.2 Student Experience

We asked students in both sections to evaluate their version of the course on a 7-point Likert scale. We performed a two-tailed Mann-Whitney $U$ Test on the distributions to test for differences and summarized responses with interpolated medians. Online students rated their version higher than traditional students (6.35 to 5.58) with statistical significance ($Z = -5.09$, $p < 0.01$). When asking students to compare the class to other courses, students rated the online course as comparing more favorably (6.07) than the traditional course (5.37) with statistical significance ($Z = -4.61$, $p < 0.01$).

## 5 Conclusions

These evaluations support this AI-based MOOC-for-credit. Compared to a traditional section, students in the online section learned as much (as assessed by pre-test and post-test scores) while also reporting a higher student satisfaction. These empirical advantages come alongside procedural and economic advantages as well. Due to the heavy emphasis on AI-based grading and feedback, no teaching assistants are required to administer the course (although support for office hours, recitations, and forums are helpful). This, in turn, allows the course to be released in a self-paced MOOC because there is no manual evaluation to mandate a human grading workflow. Finally, the persistent nature of the MOOC mean that improvements carry over automatically to future semesters: all work is an investment into all future semesters instead of only into the current semester.

# References

1. Alber, S., Debiasi, L.: Automated assessment in massive open online courses. Seminar aus Informatik, University of Salzburg, July 2013
2. Brusilovsky, P., Schwarz, E., Weber, G.: ELM-ART: an intelligent tutoring system on world wide web. In: Frasson, C., Gauthier, G., Lesgold, A. (eds.) ITS 1996. LNCS, vol. 1086, pp. 261–269. Springer, Heidelberg (1996). https://doi.org/10.1007/3-540-61327-7_123
3. Butz, C.J., Hua, S., Maguire, R.B.: A web-based intelligent tutoring system for computer programming. In: Web Intelligence 2004, pp. 159–165. IEEE, September 2004
4. Edwards, S.H., Perez-Quinones, M.A.: Web-CAT: automatically grading programming assignments. In: ACM SIGCSE Bulletin, vol. 40, no. 3, pp. 328–328. ACM, June 2008
5. Glassman, E.L., Scott, J., Singh, R., Guo, P.J., Miller, R.C.: OverCode: visualizing variation in student solutions to programming problems at scale. ACM Trans. Comput. Hum. Interact. (TOCHI) 22(2), 7 (2015)
6. Goel, A., Joyner, D.A.: Formative assessment and implicit feedback in online learning. In: Proceedings of Learning with MOOCs III, Philadelphia, PA (2016)
7. Goel, A., Joyner, D.A.: Using AI to teach AI: lessons from an online AI class. AI Mag. 38 (2), 48–58 (2017)
8. Joyner, D.A.: Congruency, adaptivity, modularity, and personalization: four experiments in teaching introduction to computing. In: Proceedings of the Fourth (2017) ACM Conference on Learning @ Scale, pp. 307–310. ACM, April 2017
9. Joyner, D.: Building purposeful online learning: outcomes from blending CS1. In: Margulieux, L., Goel, A. (eds.) Blended Learning in Practice: A Guide for Researchers and Practitioners. MIT Press (in press)
10. Joyner, D.: Towards CS1 at scale: building and testing a MOOC-for-credit candidate. In: Proceedings of the Fifth (2018) ACM Conference on Learning @ Scale. ACM, June 2018
11. Parker, M.C., Guzdial, M., Engleman, S.: Replication, validation, and use of a language independent CS1 knowledge assessment. In: Proceedings of the 2016 ACM Conference on International Computing Education Research, pp. 93–101. ACM, August 2016
12. Reiser, B.J., Anderson, J.R., Farrell, R.G.: Dynamic Student Modelling in an Intelligent tutor for LISP programming. In: IJCAI 1985, pp. 8–14, August 1985
13. Soloway, E.M., Woolf, B., Rubin, E., Barth, P.: MENO-II: an intelligent tutoring system for novice programmers. In: Proceedings of the 7th International Joint Conference on Artificial Intelligence Volume 2, pp. 975–977. Morgan Kaufmann Publishers Inc., August 1981
14. Sridhara, S., Hou, B., Lu, J., DeNero, J.: Fuzz testing projects in massive courses. In: Proceedings of the Third (2016) ACM Conference on Learning @ Scale, pp. 361–367. ACM, April 2016
15. Wiese, E.S., Yen, M., Chen, A., Santos, L.A., Fox, A.: Teaching students to recognize and implement good coding style. In: Proceedings of the Fourth (2017) ACM Conference on Learning @ Scale, pp. 41–50. ACM, April 2017
16. Wilcox, C.: Testing strategies for the automated grading of student programs. In: Proceedings of the 47th ACM Technical Symposium on Computing Science Education, pp. 437–442. ACM, February 2016
17. Zimmerman, J. Autolab: Autograding for All. Accessed http://autolab.github.io/2015/03/autolab-autograding-for-all/

# Boosting Engagement with Educational Software Using Near Wins

Mohammad M. Khajah[1,2(✉)], Michael C. Mozer[2], Sean Kelly[3], and Brent Milne[3]

[1] Kuwait Institute for Scientific Research, Kuwait, Kuwait
mmkhajah@kisr.edu.kw
[2] University of Colorado, Boulder, USA
[3] Woot Math Inc., Boulder, CO, USA

**Abstract.** Boosting engagement with educational software has been promoted as a means of improving student performance. We examine two promising and relatively understudied manipulations from the realm of gambling: the *near-win effect* and *anticipation*. The near-win effect occurs when an individual comes close to achieving a goal, while anticipation refers to the build-up of suspense as an outcome is revealed (e.g., losing early vs. late). Gambling psychologists have long studied how near-wins affect engagement in pure-chance games but it is difficult to do the same in an educational context where outcomes are based on skill. We manipulate the display of outcomes such that artificial near-wins are introduced largely independent of a student's performance. In a study involving thousands of students using an online math tutor, we examine how this manipulation affects a behavioral measure of engagement. We find a near-win effect on engagement when the 'win' indicates to the student that they may continue to the next lesson. Nonetheless, when we experimentally induce near wins in a randomized controlled trial, we do not obtain a reliable effect of the near win. We conclude by describing manipulations that might increase the effect of near wins on engagement.

**Keywords:** Near-win · Educational applications · Anticipation

## 1 Introduction

The *near-win effect* is a manipulation that has been studied extensively in the gambling addiction literature. This effect occurs when a player almost wins a game, e.g., getting two cherries and a lemon in slot machine. Reid [1] argues that near-win events are useful in skill-based games, such as darts, because they provide feedback that winning is close. Even though such feedback is useless in games of pure chance, Reid notes that gamblers still think they can influence the outcome with behaviors such as whispering to the dice, choosing lottery numbers carefully, or consulting books of lucky numbers. Differences in engagement are often found between losing early (also known as a *clear loss*) and nearly winning.

© Springer International Publishing AG, part of Springer Nature 2018
C. Penstein Rosé et al. (Eds.): AIED 2018, LNAI 10948, pp. 171–175, 2018.
https://doi.org/10.1007/978-3-319-93846-2_31

For example, Reid cites a study in which subjects preferred a near-win over a clear-loss. Reid's own study also showed a trend in that direction. A complementary manipulation that often gets studied alongside the near-win effect is *anticipation*, which refers to the build-up of suspense as an outcome is revealed. For example, revealing cherry-cherry-lemon in that order drives expectations of winning more than revealing lemon-cherry-cherry.

We explore whether the benefits of near-wins and anticipation transfer to an educational context. We designed a novel manipulation of the near-win effect that independently induces near-wins in a skill-based context, and we continuously manipulate anticipation using Bezier-curve-based animations. Finally, we analyze the impact of those two manipulations on a behavioral measure of engagement in a large-scale math-tutoring software used by thousands of students.

## 1.1  Related Research

In an educational setting, one wishes to maximize learning or performance on a test. However, conducting experiments to evaluate learning is difficult; it requires pre- and post-testing of students in a controlled setting. We use *engagement* as a proxy for learning, with the assumption that greater engagement leads to greater learning gains. Engagement has no precise definition and researchers have operationalized it via surveys, such as the Game Engagement Questionnaire (GEQ) [2], physiological measures, such as galvanic skin response, and behavioral measures, such as voluntary duration of play, also known as *persistence* [3].

Researchers have explored the impact of various *overt* task-irrelevant gamelike manipulations on engagement in educational contexts. Cordova and Lepper [4] looked at contextualization, personalization, and choice, Denny [5] studied virtual achievements, and Katz et al. [6] investigated the removal of gamification features. Less-salient or *covert* manipulations have been explored in video games. Denisova and Cairns [7] manipulated players' prior information about adaptive AI in the game, and Khajah et al. [3] covertly assisted players in simple two-dimensional casual games.

The near-win effect is also a subtle manipulation but it has not received much attention outside of the gambling psychology literature. In gambling, near-wins can be induced by rigging a slot machine to deliver a certain frequency of almost-winning sequences. Kassinove and Schare [8] found that subjects voluntarily play a slot machine for longer when the proportion of near-wins is medium, not too small nor too large. In education, Lomas [9] studied the effect of close/far losses/wins on engagement in an fraction learning game used by thousands of students. Lomas found that the number of additional exercises attempted increased as the absolute difference between the target criterion and the actual score decreased. However, Lomas' work is observational, and without randomized controlled trials we cannot determine whether near wins have a causal effect.

## 2    Experimental Manipulation

In this paper, we manipulate near-wins independently of actual performance in a skill-based context. This enables assessment of the effect of near-wins on engagement. We also vary anticipation by manipulating the temporal dynamics of the animation that reveals a student's performance score.

Woot Math® [10], an interactive web-based fraction learning software used by thousands of students, served as our platform to implement the near-win and anticipation manipulations. In Woot Math, students engage in a series of lessons where each lesson consists of a set of exercises that are chosen dynamically depending on the student's performance. After every lesson, a scorecard is shown with a *performance bar* indicating the score and three *goal posts* corresponding to thresholds for earning an additional *star* (Fig. 1). Between zero and three stars can be awarded on any lesson, and the performance bar range is continuous in [0, 3]. Through animation, the performance bar (the yellow coloring in the figure) is filled from left to right, and then stars appear based on the goal posts and the student's score. Replay and continue buttons on the scorecard allow students to retry the current lesson or return to a main lesson-selection screen.

The awarding of one star is of critical importance to students because they cannot advance to the next lesson unless they score at least one star. The additional stars may be intrinsically rewarding to a student, but over the population of students, the common goal is passing the threshold to obtain one star.

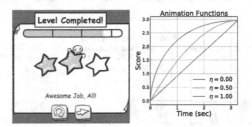

**Fig. 1.** (left) Post-lesson scorecard in Wootmath. (right) Examples of manipulating anticipation for a given score. (Color figure online)

Near-wins are artificially induced at random. Artificially induced near-win events boost the score to within 0.1 of the next goal post The score is not manipulated if the student's true score is already within 0.1 of the next goal post—a *natural* near win—or is just over the goal post. The time course of animating the performance bar is determined by a parameter $\eta \in [0, 1]$, which we refer to as the *ease-out magnitude*; $\eta$ controls the deceleration of the animation as it approaches the target score. Figure 1 graphs the proportion of the performance bar that is colored as a function of time for various ease-out magnitudes and for various target scores. Animation duration depends on the score because otherwise the mean speed would change, enabling prediction of the target score early on. We hypothesized that $\eta = 1$ produces more anticipation than $\eta = 0$ because in the case of near-wins, the first creates more anticipation as the animation slows down while the latter distributes anticipation evenly over multiple goal posts.

Engagement is assessed by whether students replay the lesson.Students were randomly assigned to a an ease-out magnitude $\eta$. Although students typically practice over multiple sessions, we simply concatenate lessons from multiple sessions to form one sequence per student for analysis.

## 3    Results

After excluding perfect and zero scores and instances where the student moved on before the progress bar animation had completed, the dataset has 29,470 completed lessons from 5,953 students. The median number of lessons per student is 3 (std. 6.54, range 1–124), over 2 sessions (std. 3.20, range 1–39).

Figure 2 shows the mean replay probability as a function of score (the graph abscissa), type of near-win event—*natural* (first row) or *induced* (second row)— and anticipation level—low, medium, high (left, middle, and right columns, respectively). In each graph, as the score increases, there is a clear downward trend in mean replay probability for both near-win and non-near-win lessons (orange and blue bars, respectively). Students are most likely to replay following lessons in which their displayed score is lower than 1.0—which makes sense given that 1.0 is the criterion for advancing to the next lesson. These lessons

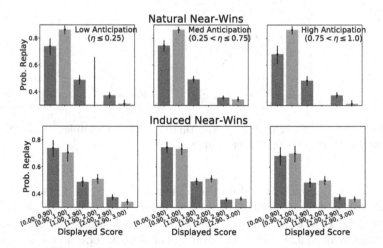

**Fig. 2.** Analysis of replay rates as a function of the displayed score. Each bar corresponds to a score range $(a, b)$, with $a$ included and $b$ excluded. Bar heights indicate the mean replay probability of observations in the corresponding score range. Blue and orange bars correspond to no-near-win and near-win events, respectively. Error bars correspond to the 95% confidence interval for a binomial proportion, using Wilson's score interval. (Color figure online)

also show a reliable near-win effect in case of natural near-wins but the effect is not reliable for induced near-wins. One explanation is that students who achieve natural near-wins may be more skilled than those who get induced near-wins because the manipulation only induces near-wins when the score is not within 0.1 of a goalpost. It may also be that effective near-wins require high anticipation to build suspense; the figure does show an unreliable trend that direction.

That students typically completed only 3 lessons (the median) was problematic for the study of engagement. Also, the anticipation manipulation may not have been effective in building suspense due to a duration limit of 3 s. For future studies, we suggest completely de-coupling near-wins from performance (e.g., by showing the student a fake class rank), and increasing the maximum animation duration. If a near-win effect can be made to reliably influence behavior, lesson replay can be encouraged or discouraged based on an adaptive controller's expectation of benefit to the student.

**Acknowledgments.** The authors would like to thank Krista Marks, Bill Troxel, and Adam Holt from Woot Math for their help and cooperation in conducting this study. The research was supported by NSF Grants SES-1461535 and DRL-1631428.

# References

1. Reid, R.: The psychology of the near miss. J. Gambl. Stud. **2**(1), 32–39 (1986)
2. Brockmyer, J.H., Fox, C.M., Curtiss, K.A., McBroom, E., Burkhart, K.M., Pidruzny, J.N.: The development of the game engagement questionnaire: a measure of engagement in video game-playing. J. Exp. Soc. Psychol. **45**(4), 624–634 (2009)
3. Khajah, M.M., Roads, B.D., Lindsey, R.V., Liu, Y.-E., Mozer, M.C.: Designing engaging games using bayesian optimization. In: Proceedings of the 2016 CHI Conference on Human Factors in Computing Systems, pp. 5571–5582. ACM (2016)
4. Cordova, D.I., Lepper, M.R.: Intrinsic motivation and the process of learning: beneficial effects of contextualization, personalization, and choice. J. Educ. Psychol. **88**(4), 715 (1996)
5. Denny, P.: The effect of virtual achievements on student engagement. In: Proceedings of the SIGCHI Conference on Human Factors in Computing Systems, ser. CHI 2013. New York, pp. 763–772. ACM (2013). https://doi.org/10.1145/2470654.2470763
6. Katz, B., Jaeggi, S., Buschkuehl, M., Stegman, A., Shah, P.: Differential effect of motivational features on training improvements in school-based cognitive training. Front. Hum. Neurosci. **8**, 1–10 (2014)
7. Denisova, A., Cairns, P.: The placebo effect in digital games: phantom perception of adaptive artificial intelligence. In: Proceedings of the 2015 Annual Symposium on Computer-Human Interaction in Play, pp. 23–33. ACM (2015)
8. Kassinove, J.I., Schare, M.L.: Effects of the "near miss" and the "big win" on persistence at slot machine gambling. Psychol. Addict. Behav. **15**(2), 155 (2001)
9. Lomas, J.D.: Optimizing motivation and learning with large-scale game design experiments. Unpublished Doctoral Dissertation, HCI Institute, Carnegie Mellon University, November 2014
10. Wootmath: Woot math - engaging, research-based tools for the math classroom, August 2017. https://www.wootmath.com/

# "Mind" TS: Testing a Brief Mindfulness Intervention with an Intelligent Tutoring System

Kristina Krasich[1(✉)], Stephen Hutt[2], Caitlin Mills[3],
Catherine A. Spann[4], James R. Brockmole[1],
and Sidney K. D'Mello[2,4]

[1] Department of Psychology, University of Notre Dame, Notre Dame, IN, USA
{kkrasich, jbrockml}@nd.edu
[2] Department of Computer Science, University of Colorado Boulder,
Boulder, CO, USA
{sthu0966, sidney.dmello}@colorado.edu
[3] University of British Columbia, Vancouver, BC, Canada
caitlin.s.mills@psych.ubc.ca
[4] Institute of Cognitive Science, University of Colorado, Boulder, CO, USA
{catherine.spann, sidney.dmello}@colorado.edu

**Abstract.** Attention is critical for learning, but difficult to sustain. Here, we investigated the possibility of integrating a short mindfulness exercise into an ITS to reduce mind wandering (MW)—an attentional shift from task-relevant to task-irrelevant thoughts—and improve learning. Participants were randomly assigned to engage with a 5-min auditory mindfulness exercise (experimental group), a relaxation exercise (active control group), or nothing (control group) before completing a 20-min ($SD = 5.77$) learning session from GuruTutor, a conversational biology ITS. Participants self-reported MW in response to pseudo-random thought probes during learning and completed pre- and posttest assessments that measured learning. On average, participants reported MW on 25% ($SD = 20\%$) of probes, but there was no evidence that MW rates or learning varied across conditions. Our findings suggest that integrating this mindfulness exercise did not improve attention or learning within the ITS.

**Keywords:** Intelligent tutoring systems · Mindfulness · Mind wandering
Learning

## 1 Introduction

Attention is a critical part of learning. It facilitates cognitive processes that are important for comprehension, such as prior knowledge activation and inference generation [1]. Without maintaining avid attentional focus, learners are more likely to engage in self-distracting behaviors that lead to superficial understanding of learning content [2]. Here, we integrated a short mindfulness exercise—designed to enhance attentional control—into an intelligent tutoring system (ITS) with aims to preemptively reduce attentional lapses and improve learning.

**Related Work.** Attention lapses frequently. People spend at least 20–30% of their time *mind wandering* (MW)—defined here as an attentional shift away from task-relevant to task-irrelevant thoughts [3]—which is negatively associated with learning [4]. As one illustrative example, participants learning from GuruTutor—a dialogue-based ITS that is effective at promoting learning in biology [5]—reported MW on average once every two minutes, and MW was negatively correlated with learning [6]. Importantly, MW occurred even during the most interactive learning phase, a scaffolded dialogue between GuruTutor and the learner. Further work with GuruTutor confirms the prevalence and influence of MW in both lab [7] and classroom [8] contexts. Collectively, findings demonstrate the need to develop strategies that combat MW to promote learning within ITS.

One promising strategy includes training in *mindfulness*—a mental state of intentional focus on the present moment, such as on thoughts of kindness or breathing [9]. Mindfulness training, which typically involves long-range longitudinal practice, can increase attentional control [10], reduce stress [9], lower emotional reactivity [11], and improve learning [12]. Shorter mindfulness exercises may likewise improve vigilance and reduce MW [13], although it is unclear whether findings are generalizable to learning contexts. For instance, although novices can learn mindfulness practices [14], the short- and long-term benefits of mindfulness training in students have yet to be conclusively established [12].

**Current Study.** We asked whether integrating a short mindful exercise into an ITS could enhance ITS effectiveness by promoting attention and learning. If successful, mindfulness could be a quick, low-cost, and low-tech strategy to prospectively improve attentional focus to a learning task. Accordingly, we integrated a short mindfulness exercise into GuruTutor (described below) and tested its effectiveness on reducing MW and improving learning.

## 2 Methods

**Participants.** Ninety-four undergraduate students from a Midwestern private university were randomly assigned to three groups: *mindfulness* ($n = 30$), *relaxation* (active control; $n = 33$), or *no intervention* (control; $n = 31$). Six participants from the mindfulness group, four participants from the relaxation group, and one participant from the no intervention group were excluded due to technical errors that prevented data collection. Thus, analyses were based on 83 participants ($M_{age} = 19$ yr, $SD = 1.1$).

**GuruTutor.** GuruTutor [5] is an ITS designed to teach biology topics through collaborative conversations in natural language (Fig. 1). The tutor communicates via synthesized speech and gestures, and students communicate by typing responses, which are analyzed using natural language processing techniques. GuruTutor maintains a student model throughout the session to provide tailored instruction.

GuruTutor began with a collaborative lecture covering basic information and terminology relevant to the topic. Students then constructed a natural language summary of the material, which was automatically analyzed to determine which concepts required further instruction in the remainder of the session. For these target concepts,

**Fig. 1.** Screenshot of GuruTutor in the collaborative lecture phase

students completed skeleton concept maps—node-link structures that are automatically generated from text—and a scaffolded natural language dialogue in which GuruTutor used a Prompt → Feedback → Verification Question → Feedback → Elaboration cycle. The session concluded with a cloze task requiring students to read and complete an ideal summary of the topic by filling in missing information within the summary.

**Experimental Manipulation and Procedures.** Participants completed a multiple-choice pretest to gauge prior knowledge on their randomly assigned biology topic. Next, participants in the mindfulness group listened to a one-minute guided relaxation exercise and a four-minute guided mindfulness exercise from a web-based application (http://stopbreathethink.org). Participants in the relaxation group also completed the guided relaxation exercise but then sat in silence for the remaining four minutes. Those in the no intervention group received no intervention. Participants then interacted with GuruTutor ($M_{time}$ = 20.0 min, $SD$ = 5.77) on one of six randomly selected biology topics (biochemical catalysts, protein function, carbohydrate function, osmosis, facilitated diffusion, and interphase), which were counterbalanced across conditions. Participants concluded the session with a multiple choice posttest to assess learning gains.

Intentional (deliberate) and unintentional (spontaneous) MW [15] was measured during the GuruTutor session using pseudo-random thought probes. The probes were triggered every 90–120s, upon which GuruTutor paused until participants reported MW with a key press. The entire experimental session was video recorded and lasted about 1-h.

## 3  Results

**Intervention Compliance.** To assess fidelity of the intervention, three judges rated the video recordings during the intervention phase (Cohen Kappa > .80) using a 1–3 scale with 1 denoting proper intervention compliance and 3 denoting no compliance. One participant in the nothing group and three participants in the mindfulness group did not have video recordings, so their intervention compliance variable was treated as missing. This procedure resulted in average video rankings of 1.23 ($SD$ = .612) for the mindfulness group and 1.72 ($SD$ = .882) for the relaxation group.

**Learning.** Performance on the pre- and posttests were computed as the proportion of items answered correctly. A paired-samples $t$-test showed that pretest ($M$ = .717, $SD$ = .176) and posttest scores ($M$ = .809, $SD$ = .141) were significantly different, $t$ (79) = 5.29, $p$ < .001, $d$ = .592, indicating that participants learned from GuruTutor. A one-way ANOVA showed that, while pretest scores were consistent across biology topics, $F$ (5,77) = 1.03, $p$ = .409, $n_p^2$ = .062, posttest scores did vary across topics, $F$ (5,74) = 3.96, $p$ = .003, $n_p^2$ = .211. Next, we conducted a linear regression analysis that modeled *posttest performance* with *condition* (3 levels: mindfulness, relaxation, and no intervention [reference group]) as an independent variable and biology *topic*, *pretest scores*, and *time* spent in GuruTutor as covariates. *Intervention compliance* ratings were included as a categorical covariate (4 levels: 1 [reference group], 2, 3 and 0 [no video recording] to account for fidelity of treatment implementation. Important to our main research question, the regression showed that posttest scores did not significantly vary across the mindfulness ($M$ = .810, $SD$ = .117; $B$ = −.009; 95% $CI$ = −.075, .057; $p$ = .789), relaxation ($M$ = .817, $SD$ = .134; $B$ = .007; 95% $CI$ = −.057, .071; $p$ = .820), and no intervention ($M$ = .799, $SD$ = .165) conditions.

**MW Rates.** On average, participants reported MW for 25% ($SD$ = 20%) of the thought probes, with 14% ($SD$ = 13%) of responses reported as intentional MW and 11% ($SD$ = 12%) as unintentional MW. We conducted the same linear regression analysis as before with overall MW rate as the dependent variable, finding that it did not significantly vary across the mindfulness ($M$ = .275, $SD$ = .193; $B$ = .077; 95% $CI$ = −039, .194; $p$ = .187), relaxation ($M$ = .258, $SD$ = .228; $B$ = .021; 95% $CI$ = −.095, .136; $p$ = .724), and nothing ($M$ = .215, $SD$ = .190) conditions. Repeating the same analyses for MW type showed that intentional MW was similar across the mindfulness ($M$ = .050, $SD$ = .135; $B$ = .050; 95% $CI$ = −.027–.128, $p$ = .198), relaxation ($M$ = .006, $SD$ = .146, $B$ = .006, 95% $CI$ = −.071, .083; $p$ = .877), and no intervention ($M$ = .116, $SD$ = .118) conditions. Likewise, unintentional MW was similar across the mindfulness ($M$ = .110, $SD$ = .094; $B$ = .027; 95% $CI$ = −.045, .099; $p$ = .458), relaxation ($M$ = .106, $SD$ = .128; $B$ = .014; 95% $CI$ = −.057, .086; $p$ = .690), and no intervention ($M$ = .099, $SD$ = .136) conditions. Considered collectively, findings indicate that the interventions did not affect MW rates.

## 4    General Discussion

We integrated a short mindfulness exercise into an ITS to assess as a possible strategy to improve attention and learning. Our findings showed that learning gains and MW rates were consistent across conditions, suggesting null effects. Still, mindfulness training may be an effective strategy if several key challenges were addressed. First, conceptualizing the effects of mindfulness within education is still unclear, and the effects observed from long-term training may not easily generalize to short-term approaches. Furthermore, the current work focused effects on self-reported MW and learning, but mindfulness training can also reduce stress [9] and lower emotional reactivity [11]. Therefore, measuring other factors related to mindfulness training, could provide a more comprehensive understanding of how integrating mindfulness training could enhance ITS effectiveness.

**Limitations.** Thought probes are a validated approach to measuring MW [15], but they require individuals to be mindful of their MW and respond honestly. It is possible that incorporating a mindfulness exercise—which is designed to increase awareness to the present moment [9]—confounded the reliability of self-reported MW across conditions. Future investigations could measure behavioral markers to identify MW without relying on self-reports [7, 8]. This approach could form the foundation for integrating both preemptive as well as real-time intervention strategies to combat MW.

**Conclusion.** Given that attention is critical for learning, ITS should incorporate strategies that facilitate attentional focus. Although our approach of integrating a short mindfulness exercise did not significantly reduce MW or promote learning, our work does suggest several critical challenges that should be addressed to optimize the use of mindfulness training as a preemptive approach to enhance ITS effectiveness.

**Acknowledgments.** This research was supported by the National Science Foundation (NSF) (DRL 1235958 and IIS 1523091). Any opinions, findings and conclusions, or recommendations expressed in this paper are those of the authors and do not necessarily reflect the views of the NSF.

# References

1. Graesser, A.C., Louwerse, M.M., McNamara, D.S., Olney, A., Cai, Z., Mitchell, H.H.: Inference generation and cohesion in the construction of situation models: some connections with computational linguistics. In: Schmalhofer, F., Perfetti, C. (eds.) Higher Level Language Processes in Brain Inference Comprehension Process, pp. 289–310. Erlbaum, Mahwah (2007)
2. Forbes-Riley, K., Litman, D.: When does disengagement correlate with learning in spoken dialog computer tutoring? In: Biswas, G., Bull, S., Kay, J., Mitrovic, A. (eds.) AIED 2011. LNCS (LNAI), vol. 6738, pp. 81–89. Springer, Heidelberg (2011). https://doi.org/10.1007/978-3-642-21869-9_13
3. Smallwood, J., Schooler, J.W.: The restless mind. Psychol. Bull. **132**, 946–958 (2006)
4. D'Mello, S.K.: What do we think about when we learn? In: Millis, K., Magliano, J., Long, D.L., Weimer, K. (eds.) Understanding Deep Learning, Educational Technologies and Deep Learning, and Assessing Deep Learning. Routledge/Taylor and Francis (in press)
5. Olney, Andrew M., D'Mello, S., Person, N., Cade, W., Hays, P., Williams, C., Lehman, B., Graesser, A.: Guru: a computer tutor that models expert human tutors. In: Cerri, Stefano A., Clancey, William J., Papadourakis, G., Panourgia, K. (eds.) ITS 2012. LNCS, vol. 7315, pp. 256–261. Springer, Heidelberg (2012). https://doi.org/10.1007/978-3-642-30950-2_32
6. Mills, C., D'Mello, S., Bosch, N., Olney, Andrew M.: Mind Wandering During Learning with an Intelligent Tutoring System. In: Conati, C., Heffernan, N., Mitrovic, A., Verdejo, M. Felisa (eds.) AIED 2015. LNCS (LNAI), vol. 9112, pp. 267–276. Springer, Cham (2015). https://doi.org/10.1007/978-3-319-19773-9_27

7. Hutt, S., Mills, C., White, S., Donnelly, P.J., D'Mello, S.K.: The eyes have it: gaze-based detection of mind wandering during learning with an intelligent tutoring system. In: Barnes, T., Chi, M., Feng, M. (eds.) The 9th International Conference on Educational Data Mining, Raleigh, NC, USA, pp. 86–93 (2016)

8. Hutt, S., Mills, C., Bosch, N., Krasich, K., Brockmole, J., D'Mello, S.: "Out of the Fr-Eye-ing Pan": towards gaze-based models of attention during learning with technology in the classroom. In: Proceedings of the 25th Conference on User Modeling, Adaptation and Personalization, pp. 94–103. ACM, New York (2017)

9. Brown, K.W., Ryan, R.M.: The benefits of being present: mindfulness and its role in psychological well-being. J. Pers. Soc. Psychol. **84**, 822–848 (2003)

10. Tang, Y.Y., Ma, Y., Wang, J., Fan, Y., Feng, S., Lu, Q., Yu, Q., Sui, D., Rothbart, M.K., Fan, M.: Short-term meditation training improves attention and self-regulation. PNAS **104**, 17152–17156 (2007)

11. Davidson, R.J.: Empirical explorations of mindfulness: conceptual and methodological conundrums (2010)

12. Meiklejohn, J., Phillips, C., Freedman, M.L., Griffin, M.L., Biegel, G., Roach, A., Frank, J., Burke, C., Pinger, L., Soloway, G., Isberg, R., Sibinga, E., Grossman, L., Saltzman, A.: Integrating mindfulness training into K-12 education: fostering the resilience of teachers and students. Mindfulness **3**, 291–307 (2012)

13. Mrazek, M.D., Smallwood, J., Schooler, J.W.: Mindfulness and mind-wandering: finding convergence through opposing constructs. Emotion **12**, 442–448 (2012)

14. Dickenson, J., Berkman, E.T., Arch, J., Lieberman, M.D.: Neural correlates of focused attention during a brief mindfulness induction. Soc. Cogn. Affect. Neurosci. **8**, 40–47 (2012)

15. Seli, P., Risko, E.F., Smilek, D.: On the necessity of distinguishing between unintentional and intentional mind wandering. Psychol. Sci. **27**, 685–691 (2016)

# A Question Generation Framework for Teachers

Nguyen-Thinh Le[✉], Alejex Shabas, and Niels Pinkwart

Department of Computer Science,
Humboldt-Universität Zu Berlin, Berlin, Germany
nguyen-thinh.le@hu-berlin.de

**Abstract.** We report on the results of a study with 105 teachers about the practice of question asking in German schools. Most teachers deploy questions as an important teaching method, however, just a small number of them possess systematic question asking techniques and prepare questions systematically for their lessons. This is a motivation for us to propose a framework for question generation, which is intended to help teachers prepare questions for their lessons.

**Keywords:** Question generation · Questioning techniques
Question taxonomies

## 1 Introduction

For school teachers, question asking is an indispensable teaching technique. Dillon [5] investigated questions that were asked by teachers in 27 classes in six secondary schools in the USA and reported that asking question accounts for about 60% of a teaching session. The benefits of question asking in teaching are multifaceted and were investigated in many research studies [8, 9, 13]. How do teachers ask questions in their class? Which question asking methods are applied by school teachers? Indeed, teachers could at-tend a training workshop or self-study some guidelines for effective question asking [9, 10]. Some effective question asking strategies and techniques were proposed and validated empirically. For example, Stahl [12] suggested that teachers should give three seconds wait-time for each question to help students think about the question and verbalize a good answer. With respect to adapting questions to students, researchers reported controversial results. While Chafi and Elkhozai [3] suggested asking more questions of higher cognitive levels, Chin [4] argued that questions of higher order would not necessarily motivate students to give answers at the required level. Instead, Chin proposed a cognitive ladder for question asking, where teachers should first ask low order questions before starting with higher order questions. Unfortunately, this cognitive ladder has not been validated yet. In this paper, we investigate the practice of question asking in German schools. The collected best practice of question asking is intended to serve to build a framework of automatic question generation, which may help teachers prepare questions for their lessons systematically.

© Springer International Publishing AG, part of Springer Nature 2018
C. Penstein Rosé et al. (Eds.): AIED 2018, LNAI 10948, pp. 182–186, 2018.
https://doi.org/10.1007/978-3-319-93846-2_33

## 2  Pilot Study

We conducted an online questionnaire study. The participation in the study was anonymous and voluntary. Therefore, we can expect that teachers who participated in this study were not under time pressure and gave their answers honestly. In order to collect answers of teachers from different federal states of Germany, we announced our survey using the "Education Servers"[1] in Germany). 143 teachers participated in this survey. Some of them did not complete the questionnaire, and thus their data had to be eliminated. After eliminating incomplete questionnaire data, 105 complete data entries remained. The questionnaire was divided into three sections. The first section was intended to collect general data about the teacher. The second section concerned the aims of asking questions and the frequently used specific question types. The third section focused on the question strategies, i.e., when a question of which type should be asked (e.g., sequence of questions of different types), the questioning techniques, i.e., how a question should be asked (e.g., verbalization), the wait-time for students, and the used question taxonomics (e.g., Bloom's [1], Wilen's [14]).

Table 1 summarizes results of the study. The participants reported that they had long teaching experience (on average 19 years), and thus, their experience with question asking is of high reliability. Teachers reported that they ask about 16 questions and prepare about six questions for each teaching session. (Note, answers were given based on the memory of participants. Thus, these numbers should be considered rather an estimation of teachers than statistics.)

Regarding the aims of question asking, the result of this study is partly in accordance with several reported research studies. A recent study conducted in Moroccan schools reported that most questions are aimed to check the understanding of students [3]. In addition, another aim of question asking found by this study is to recall factual knowledge and to diagnose the difficulties of students. Another study [6] was conducted to investigate the cognitive support of question asking practice in secondary schools in Pakistan. 267 questions were collected and classified. Khan and Inamullah [6] reported that 67% of questions serve to test the knowledge level as well as to recall student's memory, and 23% of questions are used to support the understanding of students. Another study showed that about 10% of questions used by teachers are intended to stimulate students' thinking [2]. Our study also shows similar results in that the participants use 10.66% of question for reflecting and critical thinking. We also learn from the results of our study that in German schools, teachers deploy a large part of questions to enhance motivation (19.29%) and to support student-teacher interaction and maybe also student-student interaction (19.80%). To our best knowledge, these results have not been reported in previous research studies regarding question asking.

Regarding special question types used by study participants, in addition to the most frequently used question types (W-questions, open questions, questions using learning subject specific operators), six teachers could only give examples instead of question types. Four teachers stated that suitable question types depend on the learning/teaching

---

[1] "Education Server" ("Bildungsserver" in German) is a platform in Germany, where information about education in each federal state is published.

**Table 1.** Study results.

| No. | Question | Results |
|-----|----------|---------|
| 1 | Teaching subject | 42.01% Nature Science; 31.6% Language; 21.18% Social Science; 5.21% Sport |
| 2 | School level/type | 42.86% Secondary level 1 (grade 5–10); 41.55% Secondary level 2 (grade 11–12/13); 2.6% Vocational schools; 3.25% special needs schools |
| 3 | Teaching experience | Between 1 and 42 years, on average 19 years |
| 4 | No. questions/ teaching session | 16 asked questions (6 prepared questions) |
| 5 | Aims of question asking | 22.83% Enhance understanding; 19.80% Support interaction; 19.29% Motivate/stimulate students; 6.6% Support analysis; 3.05% Examine/test; 5.08% Evaluate learning performance |
| 6 | Frequently used question types | 60%: No question types; 39.2%: Yes: W-questions[a] (13 times), open questions (10 times), questions using subject specific operators[b] (3 times) |
| 7 | Question strategies | 74.7%: No strategy; 25.3%: Yes, with strategies |
| 8 | Questioning techniques | 62%: No technique; 38%: Yes, with techniques |
| 9 | Question taxonomy | 64.4%: No question taxonomy; 31.6% Bloom's; 4% Wilen's |
| 10 | Wait-time | On average, 1 min |

[a] Not all W-questions in the German language are identical with W-questions in English.
[b] Question operators are verbs for defining tasks on each competency level of each subject.

subject, the age of students, and on a specific situation, for example, "questions vary according to the grades,.., for younger students questions are verbalized in form of request and rather sound friendly than imperative."

Regarding the strategies of question asking (e.g., sequence of questions of different types), 25.3% of participants (Table 1, Question 7) described their individual strategies of question asking, which are very diverse. For example, one teacher described her strategy that "questions should be asked from the simplest to the most complex" and "involve the students with weak performance first, then students with the strong performance". Another teacher suggested asking questions "from most difficult to easiest" and "from general to detail". In the context of techniques of question asking (e.g., verbalization), similar to results of questioning strategies, 38% of participants have questioning techniques (Table 1, Question 8), e.g., "raise motivation through discrepancy", "if possible, no decision question", "expression should be diversified". 64.4% of participants do not know any question taxonomy. These results indicate that teachers lack a systematic approach for question asking. A reason for explaining this phenomenon might be that question asking has not been integrated in the curriculum for teacher training. Aiming at balancing this deficit, we intend to develop a framework for automatic question generation in order to help teachers (especially pre-service teachers and teachers with least teaching experience) prepare questions for their lessons systematically and (in long term) internalize question taxonomies and some question types.

# 3   An Adaptable Framework for Question Generation

Since the strategies and techniques of question asking recommended by teachers participated in the study are diverse and do not have features in common, it would not be easy to integrate them into the framework for automatic question generation. Since 31.6% of the participating teachers know the Bloom's question taxonomy, integrating it into the framework for automatic question generation could make sense. To help teachers apply question taxonomies and special question types systematically, our proposed framework for question generation uses a set of question templates based on a specific question taxonomy. To integrate frequently used question types in the framework, a list of templates for W-questions may be specified. Open questions could be deployed using the question classes "application" and "evaluation" of the Bloom's taxonomy or applying the six classes of Socratic questions [11]. Similarly, question templates using operators for a specific subject could also be specified. Questions can be generated using the specified tem-plates. The detailed description of the question generation process is referred to [7].

The initialized question templates can be modified by teachers to adapt to their students (e.g., according to students' age). The question generation algorithm uses a lesson topic as input and generates questions using the templates. The question gen-eration process also considers relevant concepts related to a lesson topic by querying a semantic/lexical database (e.g. ConceptNet, WordNet). Since many relevant concepts may be retrieved from a semantic/lexical database, and thus many questions may be generated by integrating the retrieved concepts into the pre-specified question tem-plates, approaches for ranking the relevance of generated questions need to be researched. In this paper, we investigate the applicability of the vector space model approach, because it suites to the questions generated by our framework. A detailed description of this ranking algorithm is available in [7]. To research whether the vector space model based ranking algorithm contributes to more relevant questions, we integrated that algorithm into the framework for question generation. We used the German version of the semantic database ConceptNet to retrieve relevant concepts related to a lesson topic. We acquired participants (computer science teachers) for this study by contacting 25 schools in Berlin and via the "Education server" platform of each federal state in Germany. There were ten participants: nine computer science school teachers and one university professor. Since the professor taught computer science, this participant was also included in the analysis. The participants had an average of 11.7 years of teaching experience. One participant had problems to access the system, hence, nine subjects remained in this study. We collected sixteen lesson topics that participants input into the framework for question generation: HTML, Encryption, Java, Algorithm, Automaton, Object, Parser, Grammar, Recursion, Net-work, Database, Compiler, Object-oriented programming, Turing machine, Byte, Programming. Out of all the generated questions, 171 questions were selected as useful by the participants. Then, we compared the number of selections made by participants against the ranking position calculated by the ranking algorithm. The ranking algorithm demonstrated mixed results. For example, for the lesson topic "HTML", the related concept "Xhtml" was ranked on the first place, followed by the concepts "Tag" and

"Element". The questions generated using the concept "Xhtml" were marked as useful 23 times by participants, followed by the concepts "Tag" with eight times, and "Element" with six times. This might indicate that the ranking algorithm resulted in good accuracy for the lesson topic "HTML". For the lesson topic "network", the related concepts of the first two places "Net" and "Internet" yielded questions with most selections as useful questions. However, questions, which were generated using concepts on the 3rd and 4th ranking places ("System" and "Computer network") were not totally in agreement with the selection by participants. Concepts ("Al Qaida", "Terror network", "Client", "Link" "Backbone", "Terror cell") on the ranking place from 5 to 10 were least marked as useful by participants. Thus, for the topic "network", the ranking algorithm achieved relative good performance. However, the concepts "Al Qaida", "Terror network", "Backbone", "Terror cell" should have been eliminated by the ranking algorithm, because they do not belong to the context of Computer Science. The problem is that the concept "network" is related with different contexts in the ConceptNet database. Thus, we plan to improve the ranking algorithm by distinguishing the context of related concepts.

# References

1. Bloom, S.: Taxonomy of Educational Objectives: Cognitive Domain. Addison Wesley, New York (1956)
2. Brown, G., Wragg, E.C.: Questioning. Routledge, London (1993)
3. Chafi, M.E., Elkhouzai, E.: Classroom interaction: investigating the forms and functions of teacher questions in moroccan primary school. J. Innov. Appl. Stud. 6(3), 352–361 (2014)
4. Chin, C.: Classroom interaction in science: teacher questioning and feedback to students' responses. Int. J. Sci. Educ. 28(11), 1315–1346 (2007)
5. Dillon, J.T.: Questioning and Teaching: A Manual of Practice. Croom Helm, London (1988)
6. Khan, W.B., Inamullah, H.M.: A study of lower-order and higher-order questions at secondary level. Asian Soc. Sci. 7(9), 149–157 (2011)
7. Le, N.T., Shabas, A., McLaren, P.: QUESGEN: A Framework for automatic question generation using semantic web and lexical databases. In: Frontiers of Cyberlearning, Chap. 4 (2018). ISBN for Paper version: 978-981-13-0649-5, ISBN for Electrical version: 978-981-13-0650-1
8. Lin, L., Atkinson, R.K., Savenye, W.C., Nelson, B.C.: Effects of visual cues and self-explanation prompts: empirical evidence in a multimedia environment. Interact. Learn. Environ. J. 24, 799–813 (2014)
9. Morgan, N., Saxton, J.: Asking Better Questions. Pembroke Publishers, Makhma (2006)
10. Ontario Ministry of Education: Asking effective questions. Capacity Building Series (2011)
11. Paul, R., Elder, L.: Critical thinking: the art of socratic questioning, Part I. J. Dev. Educ. ProQuest Educ. J. 31(1), 36–37 (2007)
12. Stahl, R.J.: Using "Think-Time" and "Wait-Time" Skillfully in the Classroom. ERIC Clearinghouse for Social Studies/Social Science Education, ED370885 (1994)
13. Tenenberg, J., Murphy, L.: Knowing what i know: an investigation of undergraduate knowledge and self-knowledge of data structures. Comput. Sci. Educ. 15(4), 297–315 (2005)
14. Wilen, W.W.: Questioning Skills for Teachers. National Education Asso, Washington, DC (1991)

# Data-Driven Job Capability Profiling

Rong Liu[1], Bhavna Agrawal[2(✉)], Aditya Vempaty[2], Wanita Sherchan[3],
Sherry Sin[4], and Michael Tan[4]

[1] Stevens Institute of Technology, Hoboken, NJ, USA
rong.liu@stevens.edu
[2] IBM Research, Yorktown Heights, NY, USA
{bhavna,avempat}@us.ibm.com
[3] IBM Research, Melbourne, Australia
wanita.sherchan@au1.ibm.com
[4] DeakinCo., Melbourne, Australia
{michael.tan,sherry.sin}@deakinco.com

**Abstract.** Automated identification of soft skills requirements in the marketplace has been sparse at best despite the recognition of the importance of soft-skills in a successful career. We propose a data-driven approach based on deep learning to identify the soft skills requirements from job descriptions with almost 80% accuracy. We show that the capabilities requirements change as employees transition from one position to the next, and also as organizations transform from one focus area to another.

## 1 Introduction

There is an increased recognition of the importance of soft-skills in the workplace because these skills are hard to automate, and are the only portable skills in an environment of rapidly changing technical job requirements. Identification and matching of professional capabilities (soft skills) to those of job requirements has remained a significant challenge. This work presents an AI-based data-driven approach along with natural language processing to automatically identify the professional capabilities (or soft skills) from given job requirements. We start with an introduction to the capability framework used in identifying soft-skills.

## 2 Capability Framework

We use the capability framework by DeakinCo which extends the result of the 2015 The Economist Intelligence unit research program [1] to include a number of critical capability standards expected in professional practice. This framework is also aligned with the Australian Qualifications Framework [9].

---

R. Liu—The work was done while the author was at IBM.

© Springer International Publishing AG, part of Springer Nature 2018
C. Penstein Rosé et al. (Eds.): AIED 2018, LNAI 10948, pp. 187–192, 2018.
https://doi.org/10.1007/978-3-319-93846-2_34

This framework includes ten core professional capabilities: (1) Self Management, (2) Digital Literacy, (3) Teamwork, (4) Communication, (5) Emotional Judgement, (6) Problem Solving, (7) Innovation, (8) Critical Thinking, (9) Global Citizenship and (10) Professional Ethics), and four leadership capabilities: (1) Lead and Develop People , (2) Empower Others, (3) Adapt and Change, (4) Drive Strategic Results. The details of these can be found in [1].

In the following sections, we describe an innovative data-driven approach to profiling jobs for these capabilities.

## 3    Data-Driven Approach

Our dataset consists of 100,000 job postings downloaded from an online jobs site (www.applyq.com). These job postings are distributed unevenly across 185 professions, 4,050 companies, 52,548 job titles, and 118 countries.

We randomly selected 1000 job postings for classification model training, segmented each job description into meaningful sentences (total of 19,701). Each sentence could have zero, one or more capabilities associated with it. Zero capabilities indicates that the sentence describes the organization or perks/benefits of the position. Such sentences were given a specific class label.

We asked two domain experts to annotate all sentences with appropriate capabilities class labels. Clearly, the two experts did not always agree on all the labels, given the subjective nature of capabilities definition. To train our model, we use only the annotations that both annotators agreed on (17,502 sentences).

Capability extraction was done using the following MLC approaches. The first method implemented is the typical CNN, similar to the one described in [5]. The network is configured with ReLUs in the hidden layer, filter windows of 1, 2, 3, 4, 5 with 64 feature maps each, a dropout rate [8] of 0.5, $\ell_2$ regularization of 0.01, a mini-batch size of 64, and softmax function as the activation function. Each word in input sentences is converted to a pre-trained word vector using the publicly available word2vec vectors of 300 dimensions [7].

The second method implemented was the ADIOS architecture with CNN features [2]. The features extracted from the CNN experiment described above, are used as input features. Next, the capabilities were split into two partitions: (1) the bottom-level consisting of a hidden layer of 1024 ReLU nodes and sigmoidal output layer for the four labels with more than 1000 samples (i.e., C,D,T, and CT), (2) hidden layer for the remaining six capabilities consisted of 2048 ReLU nodes followed by a sigmoidal output layer. Note that unlike [2], no Markov Blanket Chain was used to determine the partition as we know the structure of our labels. A dropout rate of 0.5 was used to avoid overfitting.

The third approach, as shown Fig. 1, is a hierarchical system that builds on IBM Watson Natural Language Classifier (NLC) [4], a tool integrates CNN with a number of advanced techniques to capture the interdependencies between labels [6]. With a sentence as an input, the first step is a binary classifier, which identifies whether a sentence has a capability or not. If a sentence is found to indicate capabilities, we further exclude sentences that describe the employer (by determining if the subject of the sentence is the hiring company or the position). We implemented this rule using Alchemy API [3].

If a sentence is relevant and it indicates the capability requirements for the candidate/position, then it is sent to the next step to detect specific capabilities. Due to skewness of the dataset, we split capabilities into two groups, one for high volume capabilities and the other for low volume capabilities. Accordingly, we train two NLC models. Sentences are sent to Classifier L2 to determine capabilities C, D, T, CT or "Others". If "Others", then the sentence will continue to Classifier L3 to detect the remaining capabilities. The capability at the job posting level is defined as the union of all the capabilities at the sentence level.

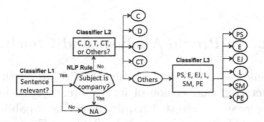

**Fig. 1.** Capability extraction architecture

**Performance Evaluation.** For evaluating the classification performance, we applied 4-fold cross validation: 75% of the job postings data for training and the rest 25% for testing. As shown in Table 1, the job-level classification performance of the three classifiers is almost equivalent. In our experiments, we set a minimal recall rate for each capability, then decide the confidence threshold for each capability, and finally pick capabilities that are above their respective confidence thresholds. Without taking into account error propagation from the classification pipeline, each individual NLC model can achieve in general good recall rates. Thus, the minimum recall rate is set to 70% to tune the confidence thresholds[1].

The performance of high-volume capabilities (C, D, T, CT), is very good (both precision & recall above 80%) because these capabilities may be mentioned many times in a job posting. However, the low-volume capabilities, are usually mentioned just once in a job posting and thus the end-to-end performance is more prone to the errors propagated through the classification pipeline. In general, the end-to-end performance is still reasonably good considering all the noisy job posting descriptions as our input. NLC achieved slightly better performance and hence is used in the remainder of the paper.

The following analysis is agnostic to the specific classifier used as long as performance is comparable.

---

[1] In the experiments with CNN and ADIOS, the minimum recall rate is set to 60% since their recall rates are a little lower.

**Table 1.** Classification performance comparison at job level, with best scores highlighted

| Capability | Name | Size | NLC | | | ADIOS | | | CNN | | |
|---|---|---|---|---|---|---|---|---|---|---|---|
| | | | Prec | Recall | F1 | Prec | Recall | F1 | Prec | Recall | F1 |
| C | Communication | 2027 | **0.94** | 0.93 | **0.93** | 0.93 | 0.91 | 0.92 | 0.93 | **0.94** | 0.93 |
| D | Drive strategic results | 1335 | 0.80 | **0.90** | **0.85** | 0.80 | 0.88 | 0.84 | **0.83** | 0.87 | **0.85** |
| T | Teamwork | 1029 | **0.84** | 0.88 | **0.86** | **0.84** | 0.86 | 0.85 | 0.83 | **0.90** | **0.86** |
| CT | Critical thinking | 1005 | **0.86** | **0.83** | **0.84** | 0.81 | 0.82 | 0.81 | 0.84 | 0.81 | 0.82 |
| PS | Problem solving | 534 | 0.84 | **0.88** | **0.86** | 0.84 | 0.79 | 0.81 | 0.84 | 0.83 | 0.83 |
| E | Empower others | 280 | **0.67** | 0.71 | **0.69** | 0.57 | 0.68 | 0.62 | 0.62 | **0.74** | 0.67 |
| EJ | Emotional judgement | 402 | **0.82** | 0.74 | 0.78 | 0.79 | **0.81** | **0.80** | 0.77 | 0.78 | 0.77 |
| L | Lead & Develop people | 606 | **0.68** | 0.71 | 0.69 | 0.64 | **0.83** | **0.72** | 0.61 | **0.83** | 0.70 |
| SM | Self management | 213 | 0.65 | 0.66 | 0.65 | 0.85 | 0.59 | 0.70 | **0.92** | **0.71** | **0.80** |
| PE | Professional ethics | 386 | **0.78** | **0.80** | **0.79** | 0.64 | 0.76 | 0.69 | 0.75 | 0.77 | 0.76 |

# 4 Job Capability Profile Analysis and Conclusion

Job capability profiles are created from the 100,000 job postings, by grouping the jobs by the meta data dimension of interest (e.g. job title, industry), and calculating the percentage of jobs that require a specific capability. Figures 2 and 3 show the profiles for IT Project Manager vs. Software Engineer and IT Project Managers vs. Sales Managers. As explained in the captions, these profile differences are what we would expect given the job requirements, thus demonstrating the validity of our approach. Next, we compare profiles by profession in Fig. 4 for IT and Healthcare. Both professions highly demand C (Communication) capability, and differences are explained in the caption. However, if we consider the subset of IT jobs within the healthcare profession (Fig. 5), professional capability requirements show a significant jump in all capability requirements.

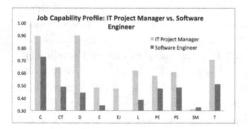

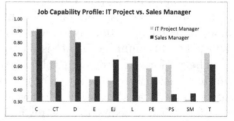

**Fig. 2.** Project Managers are more often required to have D (*Drive Strategic Results*), EJ (*Emotional Judgement*), L (*Leadership*) and T (*Teamwork*) Capabilities, while software engineers will need higher technical expertise.

**Fig. 3.** IT project managers more often require CT (*Critical Thinking*), PS (*Problem Solving*) and T(*Teamwork*), whereas Sales managers require EJ (*Emotional Judgement*) capability, while all others are similar.

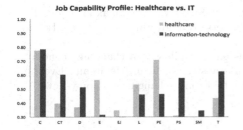

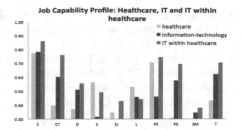

**Fig. 4.** Heathcare more often requires higher PE (*Professional Ethics*), E (*Empower Others*), whereas IT professionals more often require PS (*Problem Solving*), CT (*Critical Thinking*), T (*Teamwork*) and D (*Drive Strategic Results*).

**Fig. 5.** Professional Capabilities profile of IT, Heathcare, and IT professional in Healthcare - almost all the capabilities requirements for IT in Healthcare are greater than those required by either IT or Healthcare individually.

Our new approach to profile professional capabilities (soft-skills) across job descriptions using natural language processing (with an accuracy of almost 80%), shows that the capabilities requirements change as organizations transform from one focus area to another. This work could be extended to identifying capabilities of people (instead of jobs), matching the capabilities to suggest best matches for jobs and/or candidates, and for identifying the skill gaps.

# References

1. Bowles, M., Lanyon, S.: Demystifying credentials: Growing capabilities for the future (2014). https://www.deakindigital.com/articles/demystifying-credentials-growing-capabilities-for-the-future-a-white-paper. Accessed 17 Oct 2016
2. Cissé, M., Al-Shedivat, M., Bengio, S.: ADIOS: architectures deep in output space. In: Proceedings of The 33rd International Conference on Machine Learning, pp. 2770–2779 (2016)
3. IBM: Alchemy API (2016). http://www.alchemyapi.com/products/alchemylanguage
4. IBM Watson Natural Language Classifier (2016). https://www.ibm.com/watson/developercloud/nl-classifier.html. Accessed 17 Oct 2016
5. Kim, Y.: Convolutional neural networks for sentence classification. In: Proceedings of the 2014 Conference on Empirical Methods in Natural Language Processing (EMNLP), pp. 1746–1751 (2014)
6. Kurata, G., Xiang, B., Zhou, B.: Improved neural network-based multi-label classification with better initialization leveraging label co-occurrence. In: Proceedings of the 2016 Conference of the North American Chapter of the Association for Computational Linguistics: Human Language Technologies, pp. 521–526 (2016)
7. Mikolov, T., Sutskever, I., Chen, K., Corrado, G., Dean, J.: Distributed representations of words and phrases and their compositionality. In: Proceedings of the 26th International Conference on Neural Information Processing Systems, NIPS 2013, pp. 3111–3119 (2013)

8. Srivastava, N., Hinton, G.E., Krizhevsky, A., Sutskever, I., Salakhutdinov, R.: Dropout: a simple way to prevent neural networks from overfitting. J. Mach. Learn. Res. **15**(1), 1929–1958 (2014)
9. Universities Australia, Education enhances employability in a changing economy: new report (2016). https://www.universitiesaustralia.edu.au/Media-and-Events/ media-releases/Education-enhances-employability-in-a-changing-economy-new-report. Accessed 17 Oct 2016

# Assessing Free Student Answers in Tutorial Dialogues Using LSTM Models

Nabin Maharjan[✉], Dipesh Gautam, and Vasile Rus

Department of Computer Science and Institute for Intelligent Systems,
The University of Memphis, Memphis, TN 38152, USA
{nmharjan,dgautam,vrus}@memphis.edu

**Abstract.** In this paper, we present an LSTM approach to assess free
short answers in tutorial dialogue contexts. A major advantage of the
proposed method is that it does not require any sort of feature engineering. The method performs on par and even slightly better than existing
state-of-the-art methods that rely on expert-engineered features.

**Keywords:** Intelligent tutoring system · Student answer assessment
Deep learning models · LSTM

## 1 Introduction

A major limitation of previous semantic similarity approaches [1,2,6,9,10] to
assessing such student answers is the assumption that student answers are
explicit, self-contained statements that can be used in as-they-are when compared to the benchmark, expert-generated responses. That is definitely not the
case as student answers vary a lot in their level of explicit information they
contain due to differences in knowledge levels and verbal and cognitive abilities
among students as well as the very nature of human conversation in which utterances are heavily contextualized by the previous dialogue history. Indeed, the
variation in explicitly information is even more extreme in conversational tutoring environments where students make frequent use of pronouns and ellipsis. For
instance, Niraula and colleagues [13] analyzed tutorial conversational logs and
showed that 68% of the pronouns used by students were referring to entities in
the previous dialogue turn or in the problem description.

Table 1 illustrates the diversity of student answers in terms of explicit information. The table shows four different correct student answers to the same question asked by the state-of-the-art intelligent tutoring system (ITS) DeepTutor
[14,15]. Evaluating these student answers (A1–A4) using a standard semantic
similarity approach [5,16] would yield similarity scores of 0.37, 0.44, 0.5 and 0.83,
respectively, which are quite different considering that student answers A1–A4
are all correct responses. As expected, traditional methods are biased towards
complete student answers such as A4. The other student responses (A1–A3)

© Springer International Publishing AG, part of Springer Nature 2018
C. Penstein Rosé et al. (Eds.): AIED 2018, LNAI 10948, pp. 193–198, 2018.
https://doi.org/10.1007/978-3-319-93846-2_35

require more than the student answer to be properly assessed; that is, context must be considered because these student answers imply information available in the previous context. For instance, the noun "forces" in the student answer *A1* refers to the forces that the truck and the car apply on each other. However, the truck and car need to be inferred from the context as they are not explicitly mentioned in the student response *A1*. Similarly, the pronoun *"they"* in answer *A2* refers to the amounts of forces exerted by the car and truck on each other. Answer *A3* is elliptical - it is an incomplete statement whose missing parts are implied by the context. Context is required in this case as well in order to properly assess it. Our approach presented here aims at handling such heavily contextualized student responses.

Bailey and colleagues [3] used the previous question text as context for implicit pronoun resolution and distinguished between new and given concepts. Banjade and colleagues [4] developed a dataset called DT-Grade for assessing student answers in context. They also presented a simple logistic regression model where they computed the similarity score by weighing words in the student answers based on context. Maharjan and colleagues [11] presented a Gaussian Mixture Model (GMMs; [12]) method that used a number of context aware features based on counts and word weighted lexical and alignment similarity scores. We present here an LSTM-based network approach for handling student answers in context. Specifically, we handle context inherently by utilizing LSTM layers ([7]) to capture long-term dependencies between a target student answer to be assessed and the previous context in which that answer was generated by the student.

**Table 1.** An example of a problem and student answers to a tutor question.

| Description |
| --- |
| **Problem description (PD):** While speeding up, a large truck pushes a small compact car. |
| **Tutor question (TQ):** How do the magnitudes of forces they exert on each other compare? |
| **Reference answer (RA):** The forces from the truck and car are equal and opposite. |
| **Student answers (SA):** |
| *A1*. The magnitudes of the forces are equal and opposite to each other due to *Newtons third law of motion.* |
| *A2. they are equal and opposite in direction* |
| *A3. equal and opposite* |
| *A4. the truck applies an equal and opposite force to the car.* |

## 2  Approach

Figure 1 illustrates our approach based on an LSTM network architecture. We generate a tri-letter vocabulary (size 1,147) from all the words in the DT-Grade dataset (see Sect. 3) and use the vocabulary to encode the words as vectors [8].

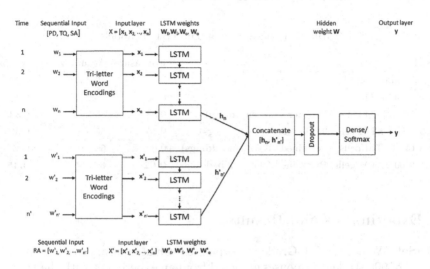

**Fig. 1.** LSTM model architecture with tri-letter word encodings.

The input consists of the extended student answer which is the result of concatenating the previous context, i.e., the related problem description and the previous tutor question, to the student answer. For example, an extended answer based on the student answer A1 in Table 1 will be [PD,TQ,A1]: "*While speeding up, a large truck pushes a small compact car. How do the magnitudes of forces they exert on each other compare? They are equal and opposite in direction*". The second input is the expert provided reference answer RA: "*The forces from the truck and car are equal and opposite.*". The input is a sequence of words which are represented as word vectors. In both figures, $X = [\mathbf{x}_1, \mathbf{x}_2, ..., \mathbf{x}_n]$ and $X' = [\mathbf{x'}_1, \mathbf{x'}_2, ..., \mathbf{x'}_{n'}]$ represent the sequential inputs [PD,TQ,SA] and RA, respectively, where $\mathbf{x}_i$ and $\mathbf{x}'_i$ indicate the word vector representations for words $w_i$ and $w'_i$, respectively. $n$ and $n'$ refer to the length of the sequence $X$ and $X'$. It should be noted that not extending the expert provided reference answers with contextual information was a conscious design decision - these answers are typically self-contained, i.e. they do not require an expansion to recover implied information. Further, the network consists of two LSTM components corresponding to the two sequential inputs. The first LSTM component generates an embedded representation output $\mathbf{h}_n$ at time step n (end of sequence X) while the other LSTM component generates an embedded representation $\mathbf{h'}_{n'}$ at time step $n'$ (end of sequence X'). We generated an embedded representation of both the extended student answer and the expert provided reference answer $[\mathbf{h}_n, \mathbf{h'}_{n'}]$ by concatenating both LSTM outputs. This embedding is then fed to a dense softmax layer via a dropout layer to produce an output classification vector $\mathbf{y}$ which represents the correctness class for the given student answer instance. The student answers in our case can fall into one of the following correctness classes: *correct, partially correct, incorrect* or *contradictory*.

**Table 2.** Performance of The LSTM Models.

| Model | F-measure | Accuracy (%) | Kappa |
|---|---|---|---|
| Logistic Model [4] | - | 49.33 | 0.22 |
| GMM Model [11] | 0.58 | 58.2 | 0.40 |
| NN_1 (50 LSTM cells, Tri-letter word encodings) | 0.53 | 53.3 | 0.33 |
| NN_2 (100 LSTM cells, Tri-letter word encodings) | 0.55 | 55.4 | 0.36 |
| NN_3 (50 LSTM cells, Pretrained GloVe embeddings) | 0.6 | 60.11 | 0.42 |
| NN_4 (100 LSTM cells, Pretrained GloVe embeddings) | **0.62** | **62.22** | **0.45** |

## 3    Experiments and Results

**DataSet:** We use the DT-Grade [4] corpus to evaluate our approach. DT-Grade consists of 900 student responses gathered from an experiment with the DeepTutor intelligent tutoring system [14,15]. The student answers were annotated with one of the four correctness labels, namely, (i) *Correct*, (ii) *Correct-but-incomplete*, (iii) *Contradictory* and (iv) *Incorrect*.

We experimented with four different types of neural networks by varying the number of LSTM cell units and type of word vector representation (see Table 2). We used a batch of size 30 and a dropout rate 0.5 empirically. We used a 10-fold cross validation methodology for evaluating trained networks.

The results shown in Table 2 indicate that increasing the number of LSTM cell units while keeping other factors constant improved the performance of the underlying model, in general (NN_1 vs NN_2, NN_3 vs NN_4). Next, we found that using pre-trained GloVe embeddings over tri-letter encodings improved the network performance (NN_1 vs NN_3, NN_2 vs NN_4). This result suggests that using pre-trained word embeddings such as GloVe to represent words is useful. Such word embeddings are typically developed from a large corpus of text and therefore can better represent word semantics than simple word-based or tri-letter based one-hot encodings.

We also note that all our neural networks performed better than a logistic model based on a single sentence similarity computed using a word alignment method which weights words based on context [5]. None of our networks using tri-letter word encodings outperformed the GMM based method [11]. On the other hand, NN_3 and NN_4 with pre-trained GloVe word embeddings did outperform the state-of-the-art methods on the DTGrade dataset. The best model NN_4 yielded an average F1-score of 0.62 and average accuracy of 62.2% and a kappa of 0.45. A larger training dataset may lead to better results for both the tri-letter models and the GloVe models.

## 4  Conclusion

We presented in this paper a novel deep learning approach using LSTM to assess free student answers in tutorial dialogues by taking context into account. The approach outperforms state-of-the-art methods evaluated on the DTGrade dataset.

Our approach is particularly useful because student answers can vary significantly in the level of explicit information they contain. Additionally, it does not require the tedious task of manually crafting features. We plan to further our investigation of using deep neural networks for assessing students' freely generated responses. In particular, we plan to combine the proposed solution with an alignment based solution such that besides a holistic outcome such as *Incorrect* or *Contradictory* we also generate an explanation for the decision which would enable dynamic and automatic generation of personalized hints.

**Acknowledgments.** This research was partially sponsored by the University of Memphis and the Institute for Education Sciences under award R305A100875 to Dr. Vasile Rus.

## References

1. Agirre, E., Banea, C., Cer, D.M., Diab, M.T., Gonzalez-Agirre, A., Mihalcea, R., Rigau, G., Wiebe, J.: Semeval-2016 task 1: semantic textual similarity, monolingual and cross-lingual evaluation. In: SemEval@ NAACL-HLT, pp. 497–511 (2016)
2. Bachman, L.F., Carr, N., Kamei, G., Kim, M., Pan, M.J., Salvador, C., Sawaki, Y.: A reliable approach to automatic assessment of short answer free responses. In: Proceedings of the 19th International Conference on Computational Linguistics, vol. 2, pp. 1–4. Association for Computational Linguistics (2002)
3. Bailey, S., Meurers, D.: Diagnosing meaning errors in short answers to reading comprehension questions. In: Proceedings of the Third Workshop on Innovative Use of NLP for Building Educational Applications, pp. 107–115. Association for Computational Linguistics (2008)
4. Banjade, R., Maharjan, N., Niraula, N.B., Gautam, D., Samei, B., Rus, V.: Evaluation dataset (DT-Grade) and word weighting approach towards constructed short answers assessment in tutorial dialogue context. In: BEA@ NAACL-HLT, pp. 182–187 (2016)
5. Banjade, R., Niraula, N.B., Maharjan, N., Rus, V., Stefanescu, D., Lintean, M.C., Gautam, D.: Nerosim: A system for measuring and interpreting semantic textual similarity. In: SemEval@ NAACL-HLT, pp. 164–171 (2015)
6. Cer, D., Diab, M., Agirre, E., Lopez-Gazpio, I., Specia, L.: Semeval-2017 task 1: semantic textual similarity-multilingual and cross-lingual focused evaluation (2017). arXiv preprint arXiv:1708.00055
7. Hochreiter, S., Schmidhuber, J.: Long short-term memory. Neural Comput. **9**(8), 1735–1780 (1997)

8. Huang, P.S., He, X., Gao, J., Deng, L., Acero, A., Heck, L.: Learning deep structured semantic models for web search using clickthrough data. In: Proceedings of the 22nd ACM International Conference on Conference on Information & Knowledge Management, pp. 2333–2338. ACM (2013)

9. Landauer, T.K., Foltz, P.W., Laham, D.: An introduction to latent semantic analysis. Discourse Process. **25**(2–3), 259–284 (1998)

10. Leacock, C., Chodorow, M.: C-rater: automated scoring of short-answer questions. Comput. Humanit. **37**(4), 389–405 (2003)

11. Maharjan, N., Banjade, R., Rus, V.: Automated assessment of open-ended student answers in tutorial dialogues using Gaussian mixture models. In: Proceedings of the Thirtieth International Florida Artificial Intelligence Research Society Conference, pp. 98–103 (2017)

12. McLachlan, G., Peel, D.: Finite mixture models. Wiley, New York (2004)

13. Niraula, N.B., Rus, V., Banjade, R., Stefanescu, D., Baggett, W., Morgan, B.: The dare corpus: a resource for anaphora resolution in dialogue based intelligent tutoring systems. In: LREC, pp. 3199–3203 (2014)

14. Rus, V., D'Mello, S., Hu, X., Graesser, A.: Recent advances in conversational intelligent tutoring systems. AI Mag. **34**(3), 42–54 (2013)

15. Rus, V., Niraula, N.B., Banjade, R.: DeepTutor: an effective, online intelligent tutoring system that promotes deep learning. In: AAAI, pp. 4294–4295 (2015)

16. Sultan, M.A., Bethard, S., Sumner, T.: Back to basics for monolingual alignment: exploiting word similarity and contextual evidence. Trans. Assoc. Comput. Linguist. **2**, 219–230 (2014)

# Towards Better Affect Detectors: Detecting Changes Rather Than States

Varun Mandalapu and Jiaqi Gong[(✉)]

University of Maryland, Baltimore County, Baltimore, MD 21050, USA
{varunml, jgong}@umbc.edu

**Abstract.** Affect detection in educational systems has a promising future to help develop intervention strategies for improving student engagement. To improve the scalability, sensor-free affect detection that assesses students' affective states solely based on the interaction data between students and computer-based learning platforms has gained more and more attention. In this paper, we present our efforts to build our affect detectors to assess the affect changes instead of affect states. First, we developed an affect-change model to represent the transitions between the four affect states; boredom, frustration, confusion and engagement concentration with ASSISTments dataset. We then reorganized and relabeled the dataset to develop the affect-change detector. The data science platform (e.g., RapidMiner) was adopted to train and evaluate the detectors. The result showed significant improvements over previously reported models.

**Keywords:** Affect change · Affect states · Sensor-Free
Educational data mining

## 1 Introduction

The intelligent tutoring systems have come to force in recent years, especially with the rise of affective computing that deals with the possibility of making computers to recognize human affective states in diverse ways [1, 2]. The relationship between the students' emotions and affective states and their academic performance, the college enrollment rate, and their choices of whether majored in STEM field has been revealed through learning data captured by these tutoring systems [3–6].

In this paper, we attempt to enhance sensor-free affect detection derived from the existing psychological studies. Previous affect detectors have focused on single affective states and used a clip slice of learning data captured by the learning system as a data sample for model training and testing. We focus on the changes of affective states, reorganize the dataset to emphasize the transitions among the affective states and verify whether the models of affect changes can produce a better predictive accuracy than those prior algorithms.

© Springer International Publishing AG, part of Springer Nature 2018
C. Penstein Rosé et al. (Eds.): AIED 2018, LNAI 10948, pp. 199–203, 2018.
https://doi.org/10.1007/978-3-319-93846-2_36

## 2  Dataset

This work adopts the dataset drawn from the ASSISTments learning platform to evaluate our proposed approach to detecting affective states. Most of the previous papers have mentioned the concern of the imbalance issue of the dataset and developed resampling methods to solve this problem [7, 8]. However, none of them illustrated the imbalance issue explicitly and did not provide much detail regarding the resampling methods. However, the resampling methods have a significant influence on the performance of machine learning algorithms adopted by previous affect detectors. Therefore, transparent detail regarding resampling methods is needed to increase the confidence of the affect detectors.

Since this paper focuses on the transitions among the four types of affective states, we also conducted statistical analysis of these transitions. Figure 1(a) represents the transition between affective states of students. Table 1 illustrates the statistical analysis of the students who did/not experienced affect changes. We examined the students who were always confused or bored, none of their number of the clips are longer than 3.

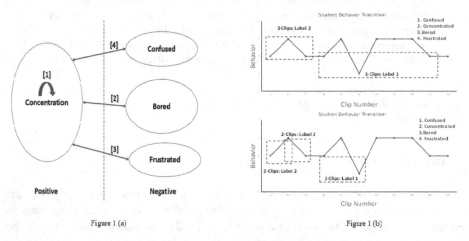

Figure 1 (a)                    Figure 1 (b)

**Fig. 1.** (a) The affect-change model. (b) Illustration of the organizing and labeling process of 3-clip (up) and 2-clip (down) dataset. (student number: 4)

The analysis in Table 1 has two implications. First, we can simplify the models to four types of transitions; (Always Concentrated), (Concentration <> Confusion), (Concentration <> Bored), and (Concentration <> Frustration), which is equivalent to the trained models in previous work [7]. Second, down sampling the clips of the students who were always concentrated should be an excellent solution to solve the imbalance issue, because the clips without affect change should have reliable feature distribution that is not influenced significantly by the down sampling process. Based on these implications, we developed our method to build the affect detectors for detecting affect changes rather than states.

**Table 1.** The students who did/not experienced affect changes.

| Affect change | Number of students | Percentage of students |
|---|---|---|
| Always concentrated | 511 | 67.60% |
| Always bored | 7 | 0.93% |
| Always confusion | 1 | 0.13% |
| Always frustration | 0 | 0% |
| Concentration <> Confusion | 58 | 7.67% |
| Concentration <> Bored | 126 | 16.66% |
| Concentration <> Frustration | 53 | 7.01% |
| Bored <> Confusion | 15 | 1.98% |
| Confusion <> Frustration | 7 | 0.93% |

## 3   Methodology

According to our affect-change model, we reorganize and relabel the dataset, and then generate two types of the dataset with new format and labels. We adopt the RapidMiner [9] as the model training and testing platform, and test six training models; Logistic Regression, Decision Tree, Random Forest, SVM, Neural Nets, and AutoMLP. To conduct a fair comparison with previous work, we keep the settings for trained models as the same as previous work [7].

Based on the affect-change model, we developed two types of organizational strategies for the dataset, called "3-clips" and "2-clips" data format as shown in Fig. 1(b). It is noteworthy that we conduct a down sampling process on the clips that are always concentrated. The data organization with down sampling process solved the imbalance issue of the original dataset.

To facilitate the comparable experiments with previous work, we adopted the same data science platform, RapidMiner, as the tool for model training and testing. The selected models include Logistic Regression, Decision Tree, Random Forest, SVM, Neural Nets, and AutoMLP. All models are evaluated using 5-fold cross-validation, split at the student level to determine how the models perform for unseen students. These training and testing strategies were set up as the same as previous work [7].

## 4   Results

The evaluation measures for the results of each of our models include two statistics, AUC ROC/A' and Cohen's Kappa. Each Kappa uses a 0.5 rounding threshold. The best detector of each kind of affect change is identified through a trade-off between AUC and Kappa. The performance of efficient model is compared in Tables 2 and 3. In all the detectors, the models trained by SVM performed better than others both AUC and Kappa wise. There is no much difference between the raw data and average data. Most of the evaluation measures are close to each other. The only difference is that for 3-clip data, AutoMLP performs slightly better than neural nets. To save the computation complexity, we prefer to choose the average data to reduce the data dimension.

**Table 2.** Model performance for each individual affect label using the 2-clip dataset.

| Affect change | Raw data | | | Average data | | |
|---|---|---|---|---|---|---|
| | Models | AUC | Kappa | Models | AUC | Kappa |
| Always concentration | SVM | 0.818 | 0.470 | SVM | 0.839 | 0.530 |
| Concentration ◇ Confusion | Neural Nets | 0.674 | 0.162 | Neural Nets | 0.727 | 0.308 |
| Concentration ◇ Bored | SVM | 0.826 | 0.482 | SVM | 0.836 | 0.498 |
| Concentration ◇ Frustration | Neural Nets | 0.678 | 0.179 | Neural Nets | 0.687 | 0.137 |
| Average | | 0.749 | 0.323 | | 0.772 | 0.368 |
| Wang et al. [7] | | 0.659 | 0.247 | | | |
| Botelho et al. [8] | | 0.77 | 0.21 | | | |

**Table 3.** Model performance for each individual affect label using the 3-clip dataset.

| Affect change | Raw data | | | Average data | | |
|---|---|---|---|---|---|---|
| | Models | AUC | Kappa | Models | AUC | Kappa |
| Always concentration | SVM | 0.817 | 0.435 | AutoMLP | 0.828 | 0.457 |
| Concentration ◇ Confusion | Neural Nets | 0.651 | 0.100 | Neural Nets | 0.668 | 0.123 |
| Concentration ◇ Bored | SVM | 0.789 | 0.402 | SVM | 0.761 | 0.409 |
| Concentration ◇ Frustration | Neural Nets | 0.757 | 0.344 | AutoMLP | 0.708 | 0.258 |
| Average | | 0.753 | 0.320 | | 0.741 | 0.311 |
| Wang et al. [7] | | 0.659 | 0.247 | | | |
| Botelho et al. [8] | | 0.77 | 0.21 | | | |

## 5 Conclusion and Future Work

In this paper, we attempt to develop an affect-change model to build the relationship between the domain knowledge and the learning dataset previously studied using traditional feature engineering and machine learning algorithms. Our future work will include (1) developing models integrating semantic context to identify the affect states, (2) verifying and validating the trained models in population studies, such as Blackboard System that has collected plenty of interaction data at University of Maryland, Baltimore County, (3) combining sensor-free models and sensor-based models to develop more robust and flexible systems.

## References

1. Ma, W., Adesope, O.O., Nesbit, J.C., Liu, Q.: Intelligent tutoring systems and learning outcomes: a meta-analysis. J. Educ. Psychol. **106**(4), 901 (2014)
2. Steenbergen-Hu, S., Cooper, H.: A meta-analysis of the effectiveness of intelligent tutoring systems on college students' academic learning. J. Educ. Psychol. **106**(2), 331 (2014)

3. San Pedro, M.O.Z., Baker, R.S.J.d., Gowda, S.M., Heffernan, N.T.: Towards an understanding of affect and knowledge from student interaction with an intelligent tutoring system. In: Lane, H.C., Yacef, K., Mostow, J., Pavlik, P. (eds.) AIED 2013. LNCS (LNAI), vol. 7926, pp. 41–50. Springer, Heidelberg (2013). https://doi.org/10.1007/978-3-642-39112-5_5
4. Pardos, Z.A., Baker, R.S.J.d., San Pedro, M.O.C.Z, Gowda, S.M., Gowda, S.M.: Affective states and state tests: investigating how affect throughout the school year predicts end of year learning outcomes. In: Proceedings of the Third International Conference on Learning Analytics and Knowledge, pp. 117–124. ACM (2013)
5. Pedro, M.O., Baker, R., Bowers, A., Heffernan, N.: Predicting college enrollment from student interaction with an intelligent tutoring system in middle school. In: Educational Data Mining 2013 (2013)
6. Pedro, S., Ofelia, M., Ocumpaugh, J., Baker, R.S., Heffernan, N.T.: Predicting STEM and Non-STEM college major enrollment from middle school interaction with mathematics educational software. In: EDM, pp. 276–279 (2014)
7. Wang, Y., Heffernan, N.T., Heffernan, C.: Towards better affect detectors: effect of missing skills, class features and common wrong answers. In: Proceedings of the Fifth International Conference on Learning Analytics and Knowledge, pp. 31–35. ACM (2015)
8. Botelho, A.F., Baker, R.S., Heffernan, N.T.: Improving sensor-free affect detection using deep learning. In: André, E., Baker, R., Hu, X., Rodrigo, Ma.Mercedes T., du Boulay, B. (eds.) AIED 2017. LNCS (LNAI), vol. 10331, pp. 40–51. Springer, Cham (2017). https://doi.org/10.1007/978-3-319-61425-0_4
9. Mierswa, I., Wurst, M., Klinkenberg, R., Scholz, M., Euler, T.: Yale: rapid prototyping for complex data mining tasks. In: Proceedings of the 12th ACM SIGKDD International Conference on Knowledge Discovery and Data Mining, pp. 935–940. ACM (2006)

# Identifying Implicit Links in CSCL Chats Using String Kernels and Neural Networks

Mihai Masala[1,3]([✉]), Stefan Ruseti[1,3], Gabriel Gutu-Robu[1], Traian Rebedea[1,3], Mihai Dascalu[1,2], and Stefan Trausan-Matu[1,2]

[1] University Politehnica of Bucharest,
313 Splaiul Independentei, Bucharest, Romania
mihai.masala@gmail.com,
{stefan.ruseti,gabriel.gutu,traian.rebedea,mihai.dascalu,
stefan.trausan}@cs.pub.ro
[2] Academy of Romanian Scientists, 54 Splaiul Independentei, Bucharest, Romania
[3] Autonomous Systems, 22 Tudor Vladimirescu, Bucharest, Romania

**Abstract.** Chat conversations between more than two participants are often used in Computer Supported Collaborative Learning (CSCL) scenarios because they enhance collaborative knowledge sharing and sustain creativity. However, multi-participant chats are more difficult to follow and analyze due to the complex ways in which different discussion threads and topics can interact. This paper introduces a novel method based on neural networks for detecting implicit links that uses features computed with string kernels and word embeddings. In contrast to previous experiments with an accuracy of 33%, we obtained a considerable increase to 44% for the same dataset. Our method represents an alternative to more complex deep neural networks that cannot be properly used due to overfitting on limited training data.

**Keywords:** Computer Supported Collaborative Learning
Natural Language Processing · String kernels · Neural networks
Implicit links

## 1 Introduction

With the latest technological advancements occurring at an increased pace, communication between individuals has slowly moved to social networking platforms or standalone chat environments. In education, chat technologies provide an alternative means of communication for distant learners and they are quite frequently employed as a supplement to traditional, in class, learning activities. However, the existence of multiple discussion threads make chat conversations difficult to understand and follow, especially for larger groups of participants. Some of the applications designed to support multi-participant chats provide functionalities to manually annotate a set of referred contributions whenever

© Springer International Publishing AG, part of Springer Nature 2018
C. Penstein Rosé et al. (Eds.): AIED 2018, LNAI 10948, pp. 204–208, 2018.
https://doi.org/10.1007/978-3-319-93846-2_37

the speaker creates a new utterance [1]. These annotations are called *explicit links* between chat utterances and are added by participants in real-time during the conversation.

Although explicit links are an useful facility for CSCL chats, they are not always enough for structuring complex conversations with several discussion threads evolving in parallel. Despite the annotation facility offered by some environments, sometimes participants prefer not to annotate every utterance as this process reduces the speed of writing new contributions, or they consider it is not necessary, because the implicit link is obvious. Thus, an automated mechanism to discover implicit links between utterances is necessary to improve the readability of a multi-participant chat. This can be done with the help of Natural Language Processing (NLP) techniques, which support the automated parsing and partial understanding of texts, as well as the estimation of semantic similarity scores between different units of texts [2].

This paper introduces a supervised approach to identify implicit links using string kernels and neural networks, previously used for answer selection [3]. This method improves performance compared to previous studies employing both semantic models and semantic distances computed using the WordNet ontology [4,5].

## 2   Related Work

The process of manually annotating conversations with explicit links has two main limitations: (a) it is time consuming and it may disturb the participant to focus on the conversation; and (b) it may be subjective to users' preferences. Mechanisms for automated annotation of links have been designed to replace or to supplement the manual labour performed by chat participants. As the links discovered by such algorithms and techniques are not explicitly added by users, the process is called implicit links detection [6] or chat disentanglement [7]. Previous experiments performed by Gutu et al. [4] used semantic distances based on the **WordNet ontology**, together with **semantic models** in order to determine the optimal window (in terms of distance or time) to identify implicit references in CSCL chats. The utterance belonging to the current window that had the highest semantic similarity score with the referred utterance was chosen as its implicit reference.

Recent advancements in NLP have been obtained by employing **neural networks** architectures for various tasks. Their main advantage is the ability to automatically extract complex combinations of features from simpler inputs, such as word embeddings or syntactic dependencies. By using Recurrent Neural Networks, Mehri and Carenini [8] managed to surpass all previous results on a chat disentanglement dataset. **String kernels** [9] represent an efficient method for comparing documents by working at character level on different sized character n-grams. The most frequently used kernel functions are the spectrum, presence, and intersection kernels [10], all of which are based on the number of occurrences of shared character n-grams. Combining multiple kernels in a supervised manner has been studied at large and results show that multiple kernel methods are capable of surpassing single kernel methods for various tasks, including protein fold prediction and digit recognition [11]. Adding non-linearities to string kernels was hinted in the work of Beck et al. [12] and Masala et al. [3]. The latter proposed a simple network architecture that combines string kernels with non-linear functions that was successfully used for question answering.

## 3  Method

The corpus used for this experiment consists of 55 chat conversations among undergraduate Computer Science students enrolled at University Politehnica of Bucharest [4]. Students had to debate about web technologies supporting collaborative work and how theie benefits can be efficiently used by a software company.

Two methods were considered for the matching process between the automatically detected implicit links and the manually annotated explicit links. The first one is the *exact match* in which the two referenced utterances are identical. The second one is the *in-turn matching* - i.e., the detected implicit link belongs to a uninterrupted block of subsequent utterances written by the same participant as the manually annotated explicit link [5].

One of our main insights is that links between utterances in chats perpetuate the topic under discussion in a similar manner to how an answer connects to a question. Exploiting this resemblance, we propose a neural model adapted from the similar task of answer selection. Given a question and a set of possible answers, usually a document or a set of documents, answer selection involves detecting the correct answer (either the most suitable sentence from a single candidate document or the most suitable document from a set of candidate items). Inspired from the architecture initially proposed by Masala et al. [3], we aim to find a combination of different string kernels to embody the notion of implicit links between utterances. The neural network is trained to compute a score for each candidate utterance and the previous utterance with the highest score is marked as the implicit link to the current one.

We use a total of 15 string kernel functions by combining three types of string kernels (spectrum, intersection and presence) with five n-gram ranges: 1–2, 3–4, 5–6, 7–8, and 9–10. We concatenate all the obtained values into a feature vector for each pair of utterances. Over these feature vectors we train a classifier based on a feed-forward neural network with one hidden layer. The network is used to compute a score for each utterance that is a candidate for an implicit link, candidates being samples from previous utterances. The utterance with the highest score is selected as implicit link. For these experiments, the hidden size of the network was set to 8 neurons and we used a batch size of 100, in combination with Adam optimizer for training. The objective function is the hinge loss as defined by Hu and Lu [13], with the margin $M$ set to 0.1.

# 4   Results and Conclusions

We evaluate our method on the dataset described in the previous section by comparing our supervised neural model with state-of-the-art methods used for detecting implicit links and answer selection. For all supervised models in this section, we have employed a 10-fold cross-validation. In addition to string kernel features, we have also added semantic features computed using word embeddings (i.e. word2vec [14] pretrained on the Google News Dataset and GloVe [15] trained on Wikipedia 2014 dump) and chat specific features such as the distance in time and in-between utterances between the current turn and each implicit link candidate. For computing string kernels we employed an open-source library[1].

**Table 1.** Performance of the proposed method for implicit link detection (Exact matching - first row & In-turn matching - second row).

| Window (utterances) | 5 | | | 10 | | |
|---|---|---|---|---|---|---|
| Time (mins) | 1 | 2 | 3 | 1 | 2 | 3 |
| Path Length Similarity [4] | 32.44 | 32.44 | N/A | 31.88 | 31.88 | N/A |
| | 41.49 | 41.49 | | 40.78 | 40.78 | |
| NN using sk + sem | 36.45 | 36.90 | 36.00 | 36.68 | 35.10 | 31.26 |
| | 38.14 | 40.47 | 40.29 | 38.14 | 38.26 | 34.76 |
| NN using sk + window + time | 33.40 | 40.40 | 41.87 | 33.74 | 41.30 | 42.66 |
| | 35.21 | 44.01 | 45.25 | 35.44 | 45.25 | 47.29 |
| NN using sk + sem + window + time | 34.98 | 41.64 | 44.24 | 35.32 | 42.21 | **44.48** |
| | 36.68 | 45.03 | 48.53 | 36.90 | 45.93 | **49.32** |

Note: sk - string kernel features; sem - semantic similarity features; window - # of in-between utterances; time - elapsed time between contributions

The results of the experiments are presented in Table 1. While there were no significant differences in performance between the tested word embeddings, word2vec obtained the best performance for the first experiment (second row in Table 1), while GloVe (of size 100) obtained the highest accuracy on the second experiment (last row in Table 1). Adding semantic information to our classifier improved the performance of the system, albeit not as much as chat specific features. We believe this is due to the simplistic method used for extracting semantic information (i.e., averaging word embeddings in each utterance).

This paper proposed the usage of state-of-the-art answer selection techniques for implicit links detection in chats. We explored a supervised neural model using string kernels, as well as additional domain-specific and semantic features. While string kernels alone performed similarly to semantic similarity methods used in previous studies, the neural network model learned how to combine lexical, semantic and chat related features efficiently, and significantly increased the accuracy for the detection of implicit links.

---

[1] http://string-kernels.herokuapp.com/.

**Acknowledgements.** This research was partially supported by the following projects: FP7-212578 LTfLL, EC H2020-644187 Realising an Applied Gaming Eco-system (RAGE), and POC-2015 P39-287 IAVPLN.

# References

1. Holmer, T., Kienle, A., Wessner, M.: Explicit referencing in learning chats: needs and acceptance. In: Nejdl, W., Tochtermann, K. (eds.) EC-TEL 2006. LNCS, vol. 4227, pp. 170–184. Springer, Heidelberg (2006). https://doi.org/10.1007/11876663_15
2. Manning, C.D., Schtze, H.: Foundations of statistical Natural Language Processing. MIT Press, Cambridge (1999)
3. Masala, M., Ruseti, S., Rebedea, T.: Sentence selection with neural networks using string kernels. Procedia Comput. Sci. **112**, 1774–1782 (2017)
4. Gutu, G., Dascalu, M., Rebedea, T., Trausan-Matu, S.: Time and semantic similarity what is the best alternative to capture implicit links in cscl conversations? In: 12th International Conference on Computer-Supported Collaborative Learning (CSCL 2017), p. 223230. ISLS (2017)
5. Gutu, G., Dascalu, M., Ruseti, S., Rebedea, T., Trausan-Matu, S.: Unlocking the power of word2vec for identifying implicit links. In: 17th IEEE International Conference on Advanced Learning Technologies (ICALT2017), p. 199200. IEEE (2017)
6. Trausan-Matu, S., Rebedea, T.: A polyphonic model and system for inter-animation analysis in chat conversations with multiple participants. In: Gelbukh, A. (ed.) CICLing 2010. LNCS, vol. 6008, pp. 354–363. Springer, Heidelberg (2010). https://doi.org/10.1007/978-3-642-12116-6_29
7. Elsner, M., Charniak, E.: Disentangling chat. Comput. Linguist. **36**(3), 389–409 (2010)
8. Mehri, S., Carenini, G.: Chat disentanglement: identifying semantic reply relationships with random forests and recurrent neural networks. In: Proceedings of the Eighth International Joint Conference on Natural Language Processing (Volume 1: Long Papers), vol. 1, pp. 615–623 (2017)
9. Lodhi, H., Saunders, C., Shawe-Taylor, J., Cristianini, N., Watkins, C.: Text classification using string kernels. J. Mach. Learn. Res. **2**, 419–444 (2002)
10. Ionescu, R.T., Popescu, M., Cahill, A.: Can characters reveal your native language? a language-independent approach to native language identification. In: EMNLP, pp. 1363–1373 (2014)
11. Gönen, M., Alpaydın, E.: Multiple kernel learning algorithms. J. Mach. Learn. Res. **12**, 2211–2268 (2011)
12. Beck, D., Cohn, T.: Learning kernels over strings using gaussian processes. In: Proceedings of the Eighth International Joint Conference on Natural Language Processing (Volume 2: Short Papers), vol. 2, pp. 67–73 (2017)
13. Hu, B., Lu, Z., Li, H., Chen, Q.: Convolutional neural network architectures for matching natural language sentences. In: Advances in Neural Information Processing Systems, pp. 2042–2050 (2014)
14. Mikolov, T., Sutskever, I., Chen, K., Corrado, G.S., Dean, J.: Distributed representations of words and phrases and their compositionality. In: Advances in Neural Information Processing Systems, pp. 3111–3119 (2013)
15. Pennington, J., Socher, R., Manning, C.D.: Glove: global vectors for word representation. In: Empirical Methods in Natural Language Processing (EMNLP), pp. 1532–1543 (2014). http://www.aclweb.org/anthology/D14-1162

# Fractions Lab Goes East: Learning and Interaction with an Exploratory Learning Environment in China

Manolis Mavrikis[1]([⊠]), Wayne Holmes[2], Jingjing Zhang[4], and Ning Ma[3]

[1] UCL Knowledge Lab, University College London, London, UK
m.mavrikis@ucl.ac.uk
[2] Institute of Educational Technology, The Open University, Milton Keynes, UK
[3] Advanced Innovation Center for Future Education, Faculty of Education, Beijing Normal University, Beijing, China
[4] Big Data Centre for Technology-mediated Education, Faculty of Education, Beijing Normal University, Beijing, China
jingjing.zhang@bnu.edu.cn

**Abstract.** In a bid to better understand cultural differences and feed into the design of an exploratory learning environment for learning fractions in China, we conducted a study in three schools in Beijing. A mixed methods protocol was followed involving 186 children. In this paper, we report several results, including a paired t-test suggesting a statistically significant difference between pre- and post-tests and effect sizes warranting further research. Beyond learning gains, we also report preliminary results from analysis of student interaction data that points to similarities as well as differences between the UK and China. This is important because it helps us determine next steps in terms of the design, implementation and integration of the technology in the two contexts, and raises future hypotheses.

**Keywords:** Exploratory learning environments · Cultural differences
Gaming

## 1 Introduction

While educational technologies can promote both learning and interconnectivity between people in widely different contexts, issues arise when differences between cultural identities are ignored. In particular, especially given the increasing globalisation of technology in learning, much of it driven by western corporations, research is needed to investigate the impacts of specific technologies in different contexts. This is important in the AIED field as limited research so far has looked into cultural differences and commonalities (e.g., [1]) yet the role of affect and feedback in different cultures is critical for the design that underpins AIED systems.

Our focus is on the UK and China, two educational systems that are literally a world apart [2]. Despite the emphasis on 'mastery learning' in both countries, the implementations differ widely [3], as do the results (the most recent PISA reports put

© Springer International Publishing AG, part of Springer Nature 2018
C. Penstein Rosé et al. (Eds.): AIED 2018, LNAI 10948, pp. 209–214, 2018.
https://doi.org/10.1007/978-3-319-93846-2_38

the UK at 26 out of 40 countries in mathematics education, while Shanghai China tops the list (see http://www.oecd.org/pisa/). Nonetheless, given the importance placed on mathematics in both cultures, our case study is fractions, a core mathematics topic that can prove difficult for young students to master, with important implications later on. We are particularly interested in the role of digital multiple representations and intelligent feedback on the conceptual and procedural knowledge of fractions.

Accordingly, this paper presents work aimed at improving our understanding of the role of a particular digital environment on learning, known as Fractions Lab, which is a virtual manipulative with exploratory tasks and intelligent feedback. Our overarching aim was to investigate how Fractions Lab worked in China and what kind of differences and commonalities one can observe in its use. The current study builds upon earlier research in the UK and Germany [4], by investigating the use of Fractions Lab in three schools in Beijing involving 186 children (Fig. 1). In particular, beyond learning gains, we look at key issues such as the use of feedback, student perceived difficulty of the activities and gaming behaviours, comparing findings from the UK and China.

**Fig. 1.** Fractions Lab being used by students in a Beijing school.

## 2    Fractions Lab

Fractions Lab is an exploratory learning environment that enables interaction via direct manipulation [5]. It was developed as a component of the EU-funded iTalk2Learn project's intelligent tutoring platform (for details see [6, 7]). While we have evidence from the UK and Germany about the overall efficacy of the platform [4, 7], the impact of cultural identity (even between two West European countries) is not well understood. This is especially true for exploratory learning environments and student interaction.

Fractions Lab, which is now a stand-alone programme (Fig. 2), aims to foster conceptual knowledge, which we define as implicit or explicit understanding about underlying principles and structures of a domain [8]. The focus of this type of knowledge lies in understanding why, for example, different mathematical principles refer to each other and on making sense of these connections. Conceptual understanding of equivalent fractions, for example, includes being able to make connections between fraction representations by understanding what is the same and what is different and by showing that a fraction represents a number [9].

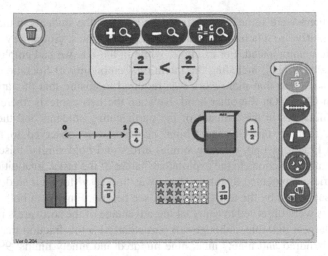

**Fig. 2.** Screenshot of Fractions Lab with various representations.

A detailed description of the design decisions behind Fractions Lab can be found in [5]. Here it suffices to say that various tools enable a student to change a fraction representation's numerator and denominator, to partition a representation, or to copy it.

The addition, subtraction and comparison tools (at the top of the screen shown in Fig. 2) allow students to check their hypotheses and adopt a constructivist stance to learning. Corresponding tasks support students' conceptual development [4, 5].

## 3  Research Objectives and Methodology

The aim of our research was to explore both (i) how to support students' conceptual knowledge of fractions in China, and (ii) the cultural similarities and differences between UK and Chinese students concerning their acceptance of and interaction with digital technology for learning, exploratory learning environments and Fractions Lab.

Most of the design of Fractions Lab and its tasks were unchanged from previous studies in the UK and Germany [4], mainly to be able to see its impact on student learning. However, the interface and feedback were translated into Simplified Chinese. Our UK and China studies each involved three primary/elementary schools (in rural, inner-city and suburban contexts). The China schools were all in or around Beijing (in Changping District, Shijingshan District, and Fangshan District). 210 students participated in the UK, and 189 students (92 female and 97 male students, aged between 9 and 10 years old, from a total of six classes) participated in China. In each context, the students engaged with Fractions Lab for approximately 45 min.

## 4  Findings and Discussion

As expected, there were some **clear differences** between the students in the UK and in China, particularly in relation to institutional practicalities. Some key differences, however, were unanticipated. For example, while in the UK we had employed several 'levels' of feedback [10], including the intentional ambiguity of Socratic questioning, early trials made clear that more work was required to ensure that this approach was appropriate in China. On the other hand, between the two contexts, there were **clear observed similarities** in the attitudes of the participating students and their teachers. For example, in both the UK and China, students were observed to be similarly engaged with Fractions Lab, to make similar errors and hold similar misconceptions, and to have similar reactions to the exploratory nature of the tasks. In addition, teachers in both countries commented that the pre-test was 'too easy' for their students (a claim that was not supported by the test's outcomes, see below). Finally, in both the UK and China, students were observed to enjoy taking advantage of the software's functionality to create the largest possible, although not particularly useful, fraction that the system affords (nine hundred and ninety nine, nine hundred and ninety ninths: 999/999).

In relation to **student learning gains**, and again consistent with our findings from the UK, pre- and post-test scores were lower than anticipated by the teachers. However, also consistent with the UK, paired samples t-tests showed statistically significant differences between the pre- and post-tests (Table 1), with effect sizes (Cohen's $d$) of 0.44 (School A), 0.70 (School B) and 1.00 (School C), all of which together warrant further research.

Regarding **student perceptions,** we classified the 18 Fractions Lab exploratory tasks into three groups: *creation, comparison,* and *addition and subtraction,* and investigated the students' perception of task difficulty (by means of self-reports between each task). However, the data showed no obvious differences in the level of perceived difficulty, suggesting that the support provided by the system helps iron out the differences in what are a range of cognitively demanding tasks (c.f. [11]).

**Table 1.** Pre- and post-test scores (each out of a possible 6) of students in the China schools.

| School | n | Pre-test | Post-test | t-test |
|--------|---|----------|-----------|--------|
| A | 64 | M = 2.53, SD = 1.268 | M = 3.11, SD = 1.326 | t(65) = 3.470, p = 0.01 |
| B | 63 | M = 2.63, SD = 1.180 | M = 3.48, SD = 1.239 | t(64) = 4.308, p < 0.05 |
| C | 62 | M = 1.69, SD = 1.207 | M = 3.11, SD = 1.575 | t(63) = 7.102, p < 0.05 |

Lastly, although further analysis of interaction data is underway, as in previous research (c.f. [12]), we observe a **general tendency for help-avoidance in both countries**. Moreover, although we have not observed extensive gaming, perhaps due to novelty effects and the engaging nature of the exploratory tasks, a paired t-test shows a statistically significant difference in post-test grades for a group of students who tried to abandon the tasks without spending time interacting (M = 2.935 SD = 0.245) compared with a group who did not attempt to game the system as such (M = 3.287 SD = 0.109); t(195) = 1.292, P = 0.099.

# 5  Conclusion

In conclusion, this paper presents work towards a better understanding of cultural differences in relation to educational technology and specifically learning and interaction with exploratory tasks. While at a high-level we are satisfied by the learning performance of students, we are beginning to observe subtle differences in the interaction (more pronounced gaming) but also many similarities that help us develop hypotheses to be answered by more detailed data analysis. This is important because it will help us determine next steps in terms of the design, implementation and integration of the technology in the two contexts.

**Acknowledgements.** This research received funding from the Big Data Centre for Technology-Mediated Education and Beijing Advanced Innovation Center for Future Education. We would like to thank the students and teachers who took part in the studies.

# References

1. Ogan, A., Walker, E., Baker, R.S.J.D., et al.: Collaboration in cognitive tutor use in Latin America: field study and design recommendations. In: Conference on Human Factors in Computing Systems - Proceedings (2012)
2. Miao, Z., Reynolds, D., Harris, A., Jones, M.: Comparing performance: a cross-national investigation into the teaching of mathematics in primary classrooms in England and China. Asia Pac. J. Educ. **35**(3), 392–403 (2015)
3. Boylan, M., Wolstenholme, C., Maxwell, B., Jay, T., Stevens, A., Demack, S.: Longitudinal evaluation of the mathematics teacher exchange: China-England interim research report, Sheffield Hallam University, DEF-RR559 (2016)
4. Rummel, N., et al.: Combining exploratory learning with structured practice to foster conceptual and procedural fractions knowledge. In: ICLS, Singapore (2016)

5. Hansen, A., Mavrikis, M., Geraniou, E.: Supporting teachers' technological pedagogical content knowledge of fractions through co-designing a virtual manipulative. J. Math. Teach. Educ. **19**(2–3), 205–226 (2016)
6. Mazziotti, C., et al.: Robust student knowledge: adapting to individual student needs as they explore the concepts and practice the procedures of fractions (workshop paper), presented at AIED, Madrid (2015)
7. Grawemeyer, B., Mavrikis, M., Holmes, W., Gutiérrez-Santos, S., Wiedmann, M., Rummel, N.: Affective learning: improving engagement and enhancing learning with affect-aware feedback. User Model. User-Adapt. Interact. **27**(1), 119–158 (2017)
8. Rittle-Johnson, B., Alibali, M.W.: Conceptual and procedural knowledge of mathematics: does one lead to the other? J. Educ. Psychol. **91**, 175–189 (1999)
9. Wong, M., Evans, D.: 'Students' conceptual understanding of equivalent fractions. Math. Essent. Res. Essent. Pract. **2**, 824–833 (2007)
10. Holmes, W., Mavrikis, M., Hansen, A., Grawemeyer, B.: Purpose and level of feedback in an exploratory learning environment for fractions. In: Conati, C., Heffernan, N., Mitrovic, A., Verdejo, M.F. (eds.) AIED 2015. LNCS (LNAI), vol. 9112, pp. 620–623. Springer, Cham (2015). https://doi.org/10.1007/978-3-319-19773-9_76
11. Grawemeyer, B., Mavrikis, M., Mazziotti, C., van Leeuwen, A., Rummel, N.: The impact of affect-aware support on learning tasks that differ in their cognitive demands. In: Artificial Intelligence in Education Proceedings (to appear)
12. Roll, I., Baker, R.S.D., Aleven, V., Koedinger, K.R.: On the benefits of seeking (and avoiding) help in online problem-solving environments. J. Learn. Sci. **23**(4), 537–560 (2014)

# iSTART-E: Reading Comprehension Strategy Training for Spanish Speakers

Kathryn S. McCarthy[1(✉)], Christian Soto[2], Cecilia Malbrán[3],
Liliana Fonseca[3], Marian Simian[3], and Danielle S. McNamara[1]

[1] Arizona State University, Tempe, AZ, USA
{ksmccarl, dsmcnamal}@asu.edu
[2] University of Concepción, Concepción, Chile
christiansoto@udec.cl
[3] National University of San Martín, Buenos Aires, Argentina
ceciliamalbran@gmail.com,
{lfonseca, msimian}@unsam.edu.ar

**Abstract.** Interactive Strategy Training for Active Reading and Thinking en Español, or iSTART-E, is a new intelligent tutoring system (ITS) that provides reading comprehension strategy training for Spanish speakers. This paper reports on studies evaluating the efficacy of iSTART-E in real-world classrooms in two different Spanish-speaking countries. In Study 1, Chilean high school students (n = 22) who practiced with iSTART-E showed significant gains on a standardized comprehension assessment (LECTUM) from pretest to posttest. In Study 2 (n = 85), Argentinian middle school students who practiced with iSTART-E showed greater gains on the ECOMPLEC.Sec comprehension test compared to those in control classrooms. Together these results suggest that iSTART-E is an effective means of enhancing Spanish speakers' reading comprehension, with demonstrated transfer of training to standardized reading tests.

**Keywords:** Intelligent tutoring · Reading comprehension · Spanish

## 1 Introduction

While there has been an increase in educational technologies for reading and writing [1, 2], most have been developed for English-speaking students. Standardized assessments indicate that students from Spanish-speaking countries also struggle with reading comprehension [3]. Though a few Spanish educational technologies have emerged (e.g., [4–6]), the need remains for further development. This paper describes the development of one such technology, iSTART-E, and initial empirical evidence for the promise of iSTART-E as a reading comprehension tutor for Spanish speakers.

### 1.1 iSTART-E

The Interactive Strategy Training for Active Reading and Thinking en Español, or iSTART-E, is the Spanish translation of iSTART [7]. iSTART is founded on research showing that explaining a text to yourself as you read, or *self-explaining* enhances

C. Penstein Rosé et al. (Eds.): AIED 2018, LNAI 10948, pp. 215–219, 2018.
https://doi.org/10.1007/978-3-319-93846-2_39

comprehension [8]. iSTART increases reading comprehension for English speakers across middle, high school, and college students [9, 10].

iSTART-E provides self-explanation training and game-based practice for five comprehension strategies: comprehension monitoring, paraphrasing, prediction, bridging, and elaboration. Students first watch video lessons introducing self-explanation and the strategies and then practice using the strategies in *Práctica Dirigida* (Coached Practice), wherein students read a text and are prompted to write self-explanations for target sentences. A pedagogical agent provides a score (0–3) and actionable feedback to revise and improve the self-explanations. After one round of Práctica Dirigida, students are given access to the practice environment which includes game-based practice designed to enhance engagement and motivation [9]. For example, in the generative game *Conquista del Mapa* (Map Conquest), students try to conquer more squares on the board than their CPU opponents. Higher self-explanation scores earn more flags to place on the board. At the end of each game, students' points are converted to *iFichas*, the in-system currency. iFichas can be used to purchase plays of identification games. In identification games (*Partido de Estrategia, Constructor de Puentes, Estallido del Globo,* and *Escape del Calbozo*), students read a text and view example self-explanations. Correctly identifying the strategy earns points, advancing them in the game. Students can also rewatch the videos and to go through additional rounds of Práctica Dirigida.

Transforming iSTART into iSTART-E was a significant undertaking. First, a Spanish-speaking Psychology expert translated the videos, texts, and example self-explanations from English into Spanish [11]. Then, a new Spanish NLP algorithm was developed to evaluate self-explanations using word-based and deep features of language [12]. This genetic-based (evolutionary) algorithm yielded 69.5% exact accuracy and 94.1% adjacent accuracy with human raters.

### 1.2   The Current Project

This paper describes evaluations of iSTART-E in two classroom studies in two locations (Chile, Argentina). Two different comprehension measures (LECTUM, ECOMPLEC.Sec) were used to evaluate comprehension, reflecting varying national and international objectives.

## 2   Study 1

This study employed a small-scale, single classroom pretest/posttest design as an initial evaluation of the effects of iSTART-E comprehension strategy training.

Participants were 22 Chilean Spanish-speaking students (14 female, 8 male, age range: 13–14) enrolled in their first high school course. The comprehension test was LECTUM, a 60-min standardized reading comprehension assessment developed to evaluate students in the Chilean school system. The test evaluates shallow and deep comprehension using textual, pragmatic, and critical items and yields a percentile score [13, 14]. There are two equal forms of the assessment: LECTUM A & B.

Students completed LECTUM B (pretest), nine 45-min sessions (6.75 h) of iSTART-E, and one in-class activity that reiterated the comprehension strategies through a video and examples. In the final session, students completed the LECTUM A (posttest).

Students' comprehension scores increased from pretest ($M = 38.39$, $SD = 22.50$), to posttest ($M = 72.13$, $SD = 29.65$), $t(22) = 3.88$, $p < .01$, Cohen's $d = 1.28$.

## 3 Study 2

In Study 1, the increase in score from pretest to posttest could be a practice effect or could reflect learning that occurred outside of iSTART-E. Study 2 included a control condition to more systematically investigate the effect of iSTART-E on these reading comprehension gains.

Participants were 85 8th grade Spanish-speaking students enrolled in six classrooms in Argentina, excluding outliers. The comprehension test was ECOMPLEC.Sec [15], a 68-item, 75-min, multiple-choice test with established validity and reliability [16]. It is modeled after international assessments [3, 17]. Students read three texts (narrative, expository, discontinuous) and answered shallow and deep comprehension questions. Students received half of the items at pretest and half at posttest (counterbalanced across students). Training condition was assigned at the classroom level (iSTART-E = 53, control = 32). Students in the iSTART-E condition received 7 h of training across 7 weeks. Students in the control condition engaged in business-as-usual classroom activities.

A 2(test: pretest, posttest) × 2(training: control, iSTART) mixed analysis of variance (ANOVA)[1] indicated comprehension scores increased from pretest to posttest, $F(1, 83) = 14.38$, $p < .001$, $\eta_p^2 = .15$. Training condition was not significant, $F < 1.00$. However, there was a significant interaction, $F(1, 83) = 6.40$, $p < .02$, $\eta_p^2 = .07$, indicating that iSTART-E resulted in significant comprehension test gains, $t(52) = 5.05$, $p < .001$, whereas the control condition did not, $t(31) = .83$, $ns$ (Fig. 1).

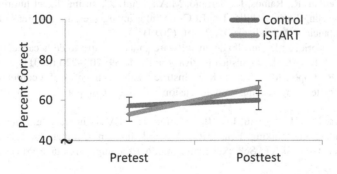

**Fig. 1.** ECOMPLEC.Sec percent score as a function of test and training condition

---

[1] Notably, a multi-level analysis yielded the same results; however, because classroom variance is not a factor, the ANOVA is presented here.

## 4 Discussion

This paper reflects the culmination of developmental work by providing empirical evidence that iSTART-E improves reading comprehension. In both studies, students who received iSTART-E training demonstrated significant gains in reading comprehension. Further research will include classroom and laboratory studies. In addition to increased ecological validity, larger classroom samples will allow us to more precisely represent potential classroom level variance. In turn, laboratory settings afford assignment to conditions at the student level as well as empirical testing of modifications of the system (e.g., new games, more texts, additional feedback).

We anticipate additional testing and modification of the iSTART-E system. We plan to investigate how the system features affect motivation, enjoyment, and comprehension gains. These initial studies are promising indicators of the impacts that iSTART-E may have for Spanish language readers.

**Acknowledgements.** This research was supported by the Institute of Education Sciences (R305A130124), Office of Naval Research (N00014140343 and N000141712300), and FONDEF, CONICYT (IT15I10036 and IT16I10044). Opinions are those of the authors and do not represent views of the IES, ONR, or CONICYT.

## References

1. Crossley, S.A., McNamara, D.S. (eds.): Adaptive educational technologies for literacy instruction. Routledge, New York (2016)
2. Passonneau, R.J., McNamara, D.S., Muresan, S., Perin, D.: Preface: special issue on multidisciplinary approaches to AI and education for reading and writing. Int. J. Artif. Intell. Educ. **27**(4), 665–670 (2017)
3. Programme for International Student Assessment (PISA): PISA 2015 Results in Focus. OEDC Publishing (2016)
4. Vidal-Abarca, E., Gilabert, R., Ferrer, A., Ávila, V., Martínez, T., Mañá, A., Llorens, A.C., Gil, L., Cerdán, R., Ramos, L., Serrano, M.A.: TuinLEC, an intelligent tutoring system to improve reading literacy skills/ TuinLEC, un tutor inteligente para mejorar la competencia lectora. Infancia y Aprendizaje **37**, 25–56 (2014)
5. Véliz, M., Osorio, J.: Desarrollo de un software para el desarrollo de la capacidad de lectura crítica. RLA Revista de lingüística teórica y aplicada **39**, 203–220 (2001)
6. Ponce, H.R., López, M.J., Mayer, R.E.: Instructional effectiveness of a computer-supported program for teaching reading comprehension strategies. Comput. Educ. **59**(4), 1170–1183 (2012)
7. McNamara, D.S., Levinstein, I.B., Boonthum, C.: iSTART: interactive strategy trainer for active reading and thinking. Behav. Res. Methods Instrum. Comput. **36**, 222–233 (2004)
8. McNamara, D.S.: SERT: Self-explanation reading training. Discourse Processes **38**, 1–30 (2004)
9. Jackson, G.T., McNamara, D.S.: Motivation and performance in a game-based intelligent tutoring system. J. Educ. Psychol. **105**, 1036–1049 (2013)
10. Magliano, J.P., Todaro, S., Millis, K., Wiemer-Hastings, K., Kim, H.J., McNamara, D.S.: Changes in reading strategies as a function of reading training: a comparison of live and computerized training. J. Educ. Comput. Res. **32**, 185–208 (2005)

11. Soto, C.M., McNamara, D.S., Jacovina, M.E., Snow, E.L., Dai, J., Allen, L.K., Perret, C.A., Johnson, A.M., Russell, D.G.: iSTART-E: Desarrollando un tutor inteligente para la comprensión lectora de estudiantes de habla hispana. In: García, M. (ed.), Proceedings of the 15th Annual Colloquium on Peninsular and Spanish American Literature, Linguistics and Culture. Orlando, FL (2015)

12. Dascalu, M., Jacovina, Matthew E., Soto, Christian M., Allen, Laura K., Dai, J., Guerrero, Tricia A., McNamara, Danielle S.: Teaching iSTART to understand Spanish. In: André, E., Baker, R., Hu, X., Rodrigo, Ma.Mercedes T., du Boulay, B. (eds.) AIED 2017. LNCS (LNAI), vol. 10331, pp. 485–489. Springer, Cham (2017). https://doi.org/10.1007/978-3-319-61425-0_46

13. Campos, D., Contreras, P., Riffo, B., Véliz, M., Reyes, F.: Lecturabilidad y rendimiento lector en una prueba de comprensión en escolares adolescentes. Universitas Psychologica **13** (3), 1135–1146 (2005)

14. Riffo, B., Véliz, M., Castro, G., Reyes, F., Figueroa, B., Salazar, O., Herrera, M.O.: LECTUM. Prueba de comprensión lectora (2011)

15. Leon, J.A., Escudero, I., Olmos, R.: Evaluación de la comprensión lectora (ECOMPLEC). TEA Ediciones, Madrid (2012)

16. Olmos Albacete, R., León Cascón, J.A., Martín Arnal, L.A., Moreno Pérez, J.D., Escudero Domínguez, I., Sánchez Sánchez, F.: Psychometric properties of the reading comprehension test ECOMPLEC. Sec. Psicothema **28**(1), 89–95 (2016)

17. Mullis, I.V.S., Martin, M.O. (eds.): PIRLS 2016 Assessment Framework, 2nd edn. Retrieved from Boston College, TIMSS PIRLS International Study Center (2015)

# The Wearable Learning Cloud Platform for the Creation of Embodied Multiplayer Math Games

Matthew Micciolo$^{(\boxtimes)}$, Ivon Arroyo, Avery Harrison,
Taylyn Hulse, and Erin Ottmar

Worcester Polytechnic Institute, Worcester, MA, USA
mmicciolo@wpi.edu

**Abstract.** Games as a means of education have been starting to become more of an everyday reality. Not only are games used in classrooms, but they are used in industry to train soldiers, medical staff, and even surgeons. This paper focuses on physically active (i.e. embodied) multiplayer games as a means of education; not only by having students play, but also by having students create games. The embodied multiplayer aspect allows for a more interactive experience between players and their environment, making the game immersive and collaborative. In order to create these games, students must exercise their computational thinking abilities. The Wearable Learning Cloud Platform has been developed to enable students to design, create, and play multiplayer games for STEM. This platform allows users to create, edit, and manage the behavior of mobile technologies that act as support to players of these games, specified as finite-state machines. The platform provides a means of testing created games, as well as executing (running) these games wirelessly by serving them to smart phones (or smart watches) so that students can play them with other students, in teams, or as individual players.

**Keywords:** Computational thinking · Learning games · Embodied
Authoring tools · Multiplayer game creation platform

## 1 Introduction

In recent years, games as a way of education have been growing in popularity, and a large amount of research has been conducted to show the effectiveness and impact of playing games as a way to learn and practice curricular content (Steinkuehler et al. 2012, Habgood and Ainsworth (2011), Lester et al. (2013)). Most of this research focuses on students playing games as a means of education, while little research seems to have focused on game creation as a means of education. There are benefits to having students "create" games as a way of engaging with STEM content.

The goal of this research project is the generation of a programming language, and a software platform, that would allow students to experiment with both creating and playing multiplayer educational math games that involve the use of mobile technologies to assist players as they practice and learn, while moving around in a highly social and physical space. By creating these games, participants should engage in a deep process of computational thinking, as well as experience, discuss, and deepen their understanding of mathematics concepts in a community of practice.

## 1.1 Background Research

Over the past few decades, technology has exploded into something that we use and interact with every day without even thinking about it. Its constantly used in schools for things such as performing research, writing papers and other stereotypical school tasks, but we forget about many of the intriguing possibilities that could be used in classrooms (Van Horn 2007). One such possibility is the integration of games into the curriculum and using them as an educational tool. This could include both playing and creating games and could help by adding fun to learning, and in response, make the subject matter much more appealing to students (Micciolo 2017). By making the games interactive, it could also get students up and moving instead of sitting in front of a whiteboard all day long. According to a 2009 High School Survey of Student Engagement, in which more than 42,000 students participated in, only 2% said they'd never been bored in school and only 41% said they went to school because of what they learn in class (Yazzie-Mintz 2010). Playing and creating educational games may be a way to fix this.

*Computational Thinking.* Playing and creating digital educational games not only has the ability to educate the creator in the topic that the game addresses, but also gets the mind thinking computationally. While playing the games, players may think or be curious about how the game works behind the scenes. More importantly, when creating games, creators must think computationally and programmatically about how they can implement the game they want to. Over the past decade, computational thinking has become a very hot topic and the push to educate students on this topic has been increasing (Shute et al. 2017). Developing digital games is a great exercise for computational thinking

*Visual Programming Languages as Educational Tools.* Over the past few years, there has been a large push to teach computational and programming skills in American schools. Computer science courses for children have proliferated and a 2016 Gallup report found that 40% of American schools now offer coding classes (Tarnoff 2017). This percent has almost doubled from a few years ago. Because of the complexity of traditional languages, programming environments intentionally designed to support novices have become increasingly popular (Price et al. 2017). These environments allow students to experiment with programming without having to worry about a complex syntax or about making errors, using a visual programming language that involves dragging and placing blocks, designing their programs graphically rather than textually. At the same time, these programming languages tend to give the user feedback and suggestions. One of the most famous visual programming languages is Scratch created by the MIT Media Lab (Maloney et al. 2010), where children program by dragging blocks that indicate a flow of behaviors, loops, conditional statements, and other programming language functions. The key to a programming environment such as this is its user-friendly nature, so that programming itself can be learned very easily.

## 2 Multiplayer Embodied Games for Mathematics Learning

One of the major goals of the research presented here was to create an infrastructure that would allow both the play and the creation of technology-based games that are: (a) physically active games; (b) social games; (c) involve a mobile device to guide players; (d) educational and blend math into them; (e) players can "input" objects found via button pushes, QR scans and keyboard inputs.

### 2.1 Game Playing Studies

One of the large feasibility questions that we had was whether school students would be able to understand these games in order to play them, or whether the complexity was too much for them. In order to do this, we conducted two studies in which elementary and high school students played and created games.

**Elementary School Study**

The result of a controlled study carried out with 53 fourth graders in two schools was an overwhelming "yes". Participants were 53 students from two math classes in two schools in the Philippines. Students from each school were randomly assigned to one of three conditions: a lecture-only condition, a lecture-plus-game condition, and a game-only condition. The lecture-only group was given a lecture. The lecture-plus-game group was given the same lecture and then played a scavenger hunt game called *EstimateIt!*, where students had to find, measure, and estimate the measurements of target geometric objects in the classroom that had been color coded (and had to be "input" in the cell phones via colored button presses). The game-only group played *EstimateIT!* but did not experience the lecture. Results suggested that the groups playing *EstimateIT!* obtained the highest means in math post-test performance scores, and that the lecture-only group obtained the lowest means in math post-test performance. Also, students really liked the active embodied math game. When asked if the game was fun, 93% of students said the game was "fun." 86% of students said they would prefer playing the *EstimateIT!* game over usual classroom instruction (Arroyo et al. 2017; Casano et al. 2016).

**High School Study**

One of the questions we had was whether middle/high school students would be able to manage to conceive and create such physically active math games. In order to answer this question, fifty-four (54) sixteen-year-old students from a high school in Massachusetts were involved in a "math game design" study. Students worked on a variety of activities during three one-hour sessions, three consecutive days in 2017. Students played *EstimateIT!*, with the purpose of having students understand the role that mobile devices could play as guides and assistants/tutors in the math game. They also worked in teams to create, draw, and specify multiplayer active math games on large paper pads. Lastly, the groups redesigned the games they had created before to include mobile devices, similar to *EstimateIT!* (guiding and supporting the players). After each day, students were given a homework assignment, writing a two-page summary of what they had produced each day. After analyzing these homeworks, the result to the feasibility of at least high school students creating these games was extremely positive (Arroyo et al. 2017, Hulse et al. submitted; Harrison et al. submitted).

# 3   The Wearable Learning Cloud Platform

The Wearable Learning Cloud Platform (WLCP) is our latest development of infrastructure for the creation and deployment of active embodied math games. This platform allows for users to play games, manage groups of players, as well as create games using a visual game editor. During gameplay, the game client is physically used by players who carry a connected mobile technology. The WLCP now uses the multi-tenant cloud platform paradigm, which means there one dedicated central server that all users access. Instead of schools downloading their own instance of the platform, they can now simply use a web browser to log in to the Wearable Learning Cloud Platform.

The platform is split up into 3 components: (1) the game manager, (2) game editor and (3) the game player device. The manager allows you manage your players as well as start and stop games. The game editor allows students to visually program (using finite state machines) games and debug them. Lastly, the game player device allows students to play these games on mobile device in their classrooms.

# 4   Discussion and Future Work

We have described the Wearable Learning Cloud Platform, a software web-based platform that allows the easy creation and play of physically active educational math games, which are aided by mobile technologies. There are a variety of potential users for the WLCP: elementary and middle school students could play the games; middle and high school students can create games for younger students to play using the game editor, exercising their computational thinking.

The WLCP was created as infrastructure for basic research on the role and relevance of Embodied Cognition, Games and ubiquitous Learning Technologies in Learning and Education. An important aspect that is relevant to the AIED community is the potential of these technologies for personalization in games that include embodied/physical elements that are harder to manipulate and vary compared to digital tasks. We do consider that personalizing the level of challenge of individual tasks is valuable and can yield benefits, specifically being able to adjust the level of difficulty for individual students depending on recent performance and ability.

In summary, we have created what we consider a novel and valuable infrastructure for embodied games for learning, computational thinking, and hands-on mathematics education supported by technology. It is only a matter of time to see what new findings and contributions to AIED and Learning Sciences this architecture would allow.

**Acknowledgement.** This material is based upon work supported by the National Science Foundation under Grants #1647023 and #1652579. Any opinions, findings, and conclusions or recommendations expressed in this material are those of the author(s) and do not necessarily reflect the views of the National Science Foundation.

# References

Arroyo, I., Micciollo, M., Casano, J., Ottmar, E., Hulse, T., Rodrigo, M.: Wearable learning: multiplayer embodied games for math. In: Proceedings of the ACM SIGCHI Annual Symposium on Computer-Human Interaction in Play (CHI PLAY), Amsterdam, Netherlands (2017)

Casano, J., Arroyo, I., Agapito, J.L., Rodrigo, M.T.: Wearable learning technologies for math on SmartWatches: a feasibility study. In: Chen, W., et al. (eds.) Proceedings of the 24th International Conference on Computers in Education. Asia-Pacific Society for Computers in Education, India (2016)

Habgood, M.J., Ainsworth, S.E.: Motivating children to learn effectively: exploring the value of intrinsic integration in educational games. J. Learn. Sci. 20(2), 169–206 (2011)

Lester, J.C., Rowe, J.P., Mott, B.W.: Narrative-centered learning environments: a story-centric approach to educational games. In: Emerging Technologies for the Classroom, pp. 223–237. Springer, New York (2013)

Maloney, J., Resnick, M., Rusk, N., Silverman, B., Eastmond, E.: The scratch programming language and environment. ACM Trans. Comput. Educ. (TOCE) 10(4), 16 (2010)

Micciolo, M.: Physical Games for Learning II, Major Qualifying Project. Worcester Polytechnic Institute (2017)

Price, T.W., Dong, Y., Lipovac, D.: iSnap: towards intelligent tutoring in novice programming environments. In: ACM Technical Symposium on Computer Science Education (2017)

Shute, V., Sun, C., Asbell-Clarke, J.: Demystifying computational thinking. Educ. Res. Rev. 22, 142–158 (2017)

Steinkuehler, C., Squire, K., Barab, S.: Games, Learning, and Society: Learning and Meaning in the Digital Age. Cambridge University Press, Cambridge (2012)

Tarnoff, B.: Tech's Push to Teach Coding Isn't About Kids' Success – It's About Cutting Wages. ACM Careers (2017)

Van Horn, R.: Educational Games. Phi Delta Kappan 89(1), 73–74 (2007)

Yazzie-Mintz, E.: Latest HSSSE results show familiar theme: bored, disconnected students want more from schools. UI News Room (2010)

# Autonomous Agent that Provides Automated Feedback Improves Negotiation Skills

Shannon Monahan[1], Emmanuel Johnson[2], Gale Lucas[2(✉)],
James Finch[3], and Jonathan Gratch[2]

[1] The American University of Paris, 75007 Paris, France
[2] University of Southern California, Los Angeles, CA 90007, USA
lucas@ict.usc.edu
[3] Michigan State University, East Lansing, MI 48824, USA

**Abstract.** Research has found that individuals can improve their negotiation abilities by practicing with virtual agents [1, 2]. For these pedagogical agents to become more "intelligent," the system should be able to give feedback on negotiation performance [3, 4]. In this study, we examined the impact of providing such individualized feedback. Participants first engaged in a negotiation with a virtual agent. After this negotiation, participants were either given automated individualized feedback or not. Feedback was based on negotiation principles [4], which were quantified using a validated approach [5]. Participants then completed a second, parallel negotiation. Our results show that, compared to the control condition, participants who received such feedback after the first negotiation showed a significantly greater improvement in the strength of their first offer, concession curve, and thus their final outcome in the negotiation.

**Keywords:** Negotiation · Individualized feedback · Automated metrics

## 1 Introduction

Emerging research suggests that learning technology holds promise for assessing and teaching a range of interpersonal skills [6–8], including negotiation [1, 2]. Skills in negotiation are essential in many careers, especially politics [9], military [10], law [11, 12], and business [13]. However, Intelligent Tutoring Systems for negotiation training are not yet common practice. Typically, during negotiation training sessions, students practice against each other while the instructor walks around the room, observing and evaluating their use of negotiation principles. The issue with this approach is that instructors' attention is limited and they cannot evaluate all students' use of the negotiation principles, especially in large classes. This is problematic as receiving constructive individualized feedback is integral to skill development [14]. Virtual agents that allow users to practice negotiation and provide individualized feedback holds great potential for addressing these limitations. Previous research has shown that individuals can improve their negotiation abilities just by practicing with these agents *even without receiving individualized feedback* [1, 2]. Importantly, however, the systems could be more intelligent if they provided individualized feedback [14]. Accordingly, in the current work, we extend one of these previous systems [1] to automatically provide such

© Springer International Publishing AG, part of Springer Nature 2018
C. Penstein Rosé et al. (Eds.): AIED 2018, LNAI 10948, pp. 225–229, 2018.
https://doi.org/10.1007/978-3-319-93846-2_41

feedback using negotiation principles established by Kelley [4]. Kelley identified a set of principles that have been correlated with good negotiation outcomes [4]. Importantly, these principles have been quantified through automated methods [5]. Here, we take the important next step: we empirically test the impact of providing students such automated feedback about their negotiation skills.

One "theme" in Kelley's principles is to avoid early commitment. Avoiding early commitment means negotiators should avoid conceding to their opponent early on. To do this Kelley suggests negotiators should (1) *make high initial offers*, (2) *use more of the available time* while (3) *maintaining strong offers* throughout. These practices may lead to more satisfactory solutions as they discourage naively accepting deals that are presented early in a negotiation. In this paper, we focus on teaching these three specific, established negotiation principles.

## 2   Current Work

**Participants and Design.** We recruited 63 participants (34 females) through Craigslist; and they were paid $30. Technical failures resulted in unusable data for 3 participants, leaving 60 participants (30 per condition). They were also incentivized to perform well in the negotiation with entries into a $100 lottery based on the items that they got in the negotiation. Participants were randomly assigned to either receive (or not) individualized feedback on their first negotiation performance prior to a second negotiation beginning. Feedback that the experimental group received is described below in the Task and Feedback section. Controls received their negotiation score following the first round and were told to just reflect on the negotiation for 5 min.

**Agent.** Participants completed two negotiations with a virtual agent (CRA [15]). CRA is a semi-automated system capable of carrying out a negotiation with a user. The virtual human toolkit [16] executed low-level dialogue functions automatically, while two wizards (WoZ) provide high-level guidance for the agent's behaviors. We tested the impact of automated individualized feedback (which would be equivalent when using WoZ) to see if this feature should be implemented in a fully-automated system.

Like the AI system's choices will be based on algorithms, wizards' selected actions were based on a script. First, the agent revealed its preferences if the participant revealed theirs. The agent waited for participants to make the first offer, and the script (see Fig. 1) used this offer as an anchor [4]. For example, if the participant's first offer gave the agent items worth 50–60 points, the agent's initial acceptance threshold would be 90 points, and the ultimate acceptance threshold would be 75 points. This means that the agent would reject the initial offer made by the participant and counter-offer with a claim of 90 points (e.g. offering the participant to take the painting and lamps while the agent keeps all the records), and the agent would never accept a deal affording it less than 75 points. If the participants' next offer was not above the current acceptance threshold, the agent would reject it. Then, the agent would attempt to make a triangulating offer (e.g. claiming both lamps and two records if the previous offer claimed all three records). If a triangulating offer had already been made or none was possible, the agent would lower its acceptance threshold by the minimum possible difference in point value (e.g. from 90 to 80 points). This process would repeat until an agreement was reached or the ultimate threshold was reached, at which point the agent would continue to make the same offer at the ultimate threshold.

| Participant initial offer strength (claimed points) | Initial acceptance threshold | Ultimate acceptance threshold |
|---|---|---|
| 0-50 | 75 | None* |
| 60-65 | 95 | 80 |
| 75-80 | 95 | 65 |
| 90-95 | 80 | 50 |
| 105-110 | 65 | 35 |
| 120-125 | 120 | None** |

*If the participant claimed 50 or less points with the initial offer, the agent accepted immediately
**If the participant claimed 120 or more points with the initial offer, the agent retaliated by counter-offering with a claim of 120 points. However, the agent would adjust the initial and ultimate acceptance thresholds based on the next offer the participant made.

**Fig. 1.** Negotiation rules for agent.

**Task and Feedback.** Figure 2 depicts the payoff matrices for the two negotiation tasks. Prior to each negotiation, participants were given the relative value of each item. In the feedback condition, we provided feedback using Johnson et al.'s [5] metrics. Participants were shown a graphical display of negotiation metrics automatically collected from the participant's first negotiation (Fig. 3), accompanied by an automatically generated script explaining the feedback (for user comprehension). Although the script will be read by the VH in future iterations, here it was read by an experimenter.

**Participant Payoff**

| Records | | Lamps | | Painting | |
|---|---|---|---|---|---|
| Level | Value (points) | Level | Value (points) | Level | Value (points) |
| 0 | 0 | 0 | 0 | 0 | 0 |
| 1 | 30 | 1 | 15 | 1 | 5 |
| 2 | 60 | 2 | 30 | | |
| 3 | 90 | | | | |

**Agent Payoff**

| Records | | Lamps | | Painting | |
|---|---|---|---|---|---|
| Level | Value (points) | Level | Value (points) | Level | Value (points) |
| 0 | 0 | 0 | 0 | 0 | 0 |
| 1 | 30 | 1 | 15 | 1 | 0 |
| 2 | 60 | 2 | 30 | | |
| 3 | 90 | | | | |

**Fig. 2.** Payoff matrix for participant and agent in negotiation task.

# 3 Results and Discussion

The metrics described above based on Johnson et al. [5] were also used to measure the extent to which participants adhered to the negotiation principles. Using 2 (feedback: feedback vs. no) x 2 (time: 1 vs. 2) mixed ANOVAs, we analyzed strength of initial offer, use of available time, and value claimed. Analysis of initial offer revealed a significant main effect of time ($F(1,47) = 9.10, p = .004$), which was qualified by feedback condition ($F(1,47) = 8.26$, $p = .006$). Participants who received feedback made stronger initial offers in the second negotiation ($M = 95.42$, $SE = 2.91$) than the first ($M = 78.96$, $SE = 2.97$; $F(1,23) = 15.07$, $p = .001$), but there was no difference in the control condition ($M = 80.60$, $SE = 2.91$ vs. $M = 80.20$, $SE = 2.91$; $F(1,24) = 0.01$, $p = .91$).

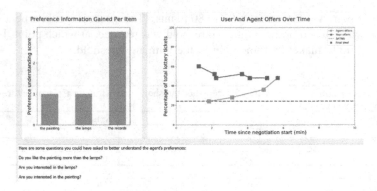

**Fig. 3.** Feedback interface.

In contrast, for use of available time, there was only a main effect of time ($F(1,47) = 4.48$, $p = .04$), and no interaction ($F(1,47) = 0.25$, $p = .62$). Participants spent longer negotiating in the first negotiation ($M = 599618.76$ ms, $SE = 36913.79$) than the second ($M = 506452.28$ ms, $SE = 28345.94$).

Analysis of average value claimed revealed a main effect of time ($F(1,47) = 24.79$, $p < .001$), which was qualified by feedback condition ($F(1,47) = 7.14$, $p = .01$). While the control group only claimed marginally more value in the second negotiation ($M = 73.37$, $SE = 2.00$) than the first ($M = 69.90$, $SE = 1.65$; $F(1,24) = 3.38$, $p = .08$), those who received feedback made higher claims in the second negotiation ($M = 82.42$, $SE = 2.05$) than the first ($M = 70.88$, $SE = 1.68$; $F(1,23) = 23.81$, $p < .001$).

Also, we measured the final outcome (score) in the negotiation (based on Fig. 2). A main effect of time ($F(1,58) = 45.28$, $p < .001$) was qualified by feedback condition ($F(1,58) = 13.47$, $p = .001$). While the control group obtained only marginally better outcomes in the second negotiation ($M = 58.50$, $SE = 1.92$) than the first ($M = 54.33$, $SE = 2.19$; $F(1,29) = 3.92$, $p = .06$), those who received feedback improved in the second negotiation ($M = 67.33$, $SE = 1.92$) compared to the first ($M = 53.17$, $SE = 2.19$; $F(1,29) = 67.05$, $p < .001$). Compared to those who did not receive feedback, providing *automated* individualized feedback about negotiation principles improved use of those principles. In addition to participants in the feedback condition showing greater improvement over time in their initial offer and value claimed, they also improved more at achieving good outcomes for themselves in the negotiation. As such, all but one of the metrics based on the principle of avoiding early commitment were impacted by feedback condition: extending negotiation time was only affected by practice (i.e. negotiation 1 vs. negotiation 2). However, these observed shorter durations in the second negotiation could simply be a consequence of the participants becoming more familiar with the virtual negotiator system. Here we establish that individualized feedback is superior to no feedback. While individualized feedback is theorized to be important in learning negotiation skills [14], it should be explicitly compared to a generic lesson about negotiation principles. Nevertheless, the current research establishes that pedagogical systems that provide *automated individualized feedback* on negotiations have potential to improve upon current approaches.

**Acknowledgments.** This research was supported by the US Army and the National Science Foundation. The content does not necessarily reflect the position or the policy of any Government, and no official endorsement should be inferred.

# References

1. Gratch, J., DeVault, D., Lucas, G.: The benefits of virtual humans for teaching negotiation. In: Traum, D., Swartout, W., Khooshabeh, P., Kopp, S., Scherer, S., Leuski, A. (eds.) IVA 2016. LNCS (LNAI), vol. 10011, pp. 283–294. Springer, Cham (2016). https://doi.org/10.1007/978-3-319-47665-0_25

2. Lin, R., Oshrat, Y., Kraus, S.: Investigating the benefits of automated negotiations in enhancing people's negotiation skills. In: Proceedings of The 8th International Conference on Autonomous Agents and Multiagent Systems-Volume 1, pp. 345–352. International Foundation for Autonomous Agents and Multiagent Systems, May 2009

3. Kolb, A.Y., Kolb, D.A.: Experiential learning theory. In: Encyclopedia of the Sciences of Learning, pp. 1215–1219. Springer US

4. Kelley, H.H.: A classroom study of the dilemmas in interpersonal negotiations. Berkeley Institute of International Studies, University of California (1966)

5. Johnson, E., Gratch, J., DeVault, D.: Towards an autonomous agent that provides automated feedback on students' negotiation skills. In: Proceedings of the 16th Conference on Autonomous Agents and MultiAgent Systems, pp. 410–418. International Foundation for Autonomous Agents and Multiagent Systems, May 2017

6. Rosen, Y.: Assessing students in human-to-agent settings to inform collaborative problem-solving learning. J. Educ. Meas. **54**(1), 36–53 (2017)

7. Graesser, A.C., Cai, Z., Hu, X., Foltz, P.W., Greiff, S., Kuo, B.C., Shaffer, D.W.: Assessment of collaborative problem solving. Des. Recomm. Intell. Tutoring Syst. **275** (2017)

8. O'Neil, H.F., Chuang, S.S., Baker, E.L.: Computer-based feedback for computer-based collaborative problem solving. In: Ifenthaler, D., Pirnay-Dummer, P., Seel, N. (eds.) Computer-Based Diagnostics and Systematic Analysis of Knowledge, pp. 261–279. Springer, Boston (2010). https://doi.org/10.1007/978-1-4419-5662-0_14

9. Hall, R.L.: Measuring legislative influence. Legis. Stud. Q. **17**(2), 205–231 (1992)

10. Wunderle, W.: How to negotiate in the middle east. Mil. Rev. **87**(2), 33 (2007)

11. Eisenberg, T., Lanvers, C.: What is the settlement rate and why should we care? J. Empir. Leg. Stud. **6**(1), 111–146 (2009)

12. Samborn, H.V.: Vanishing trial, the. ABAJ **88**, 24 (2002)

13. Movius, H.: The effectiveness of negotiation training. Negotaiation J. **24**(4), 509–531 (2008)

14. Hattie, J., Timperley, H.: The power of feedback. Review of educational research **77**(1), 81–112 (2007)

15. DeVault, D., Mell, J., Gratch, J.: Toward natural turn-taking in a virtual human negotiation agent. In: AAAI Spring Symposium on Turn-taking and Coordination in Human-Machine Interaction. AAAI Press, Stanford, March 2015

16. Hartholt, A., Traum, D., Marsella, Stacy C., Shapiro, A., Stratou, G., Leuski, A., Morency, L.-P., Gratch, J.: All together now. In: Aylett, R., Krenn, B., Pelachaud, C., Shimodaira, H. (eds.) IVA 2013. LNCS (LNAI), vol. 8108, pp. 368–381. Springer, Heidelberg (2013). https://doi.org/10.1007/978-3-642-40415-3_33

# Efficient Navigation in Learning Materials: An Empirical Study on the Linking Process

Pedro Mota[1,2]($\boxtimes$), Luisa Coheur[1], and Maxine Eskenazi[2]

[1] IST/INESC-ID, Rua Alves Redol 9, 1000-029 Lisbon, Portugal
{pedro.mota,luisa.coheur}@inesc-id.pt
[2] Carnegie Mellon University, 5000 Forbes Ave, Pittsburgh, PA 15213, USA
max@cs.cmu.edu

**Abstract.** We focus on the task of linking topically related segments in a collection of documents. In this scope, an existing corpus of learning materials was annotated with links between its segments. Using this corpus, we evaluate clustering, topic models, and graph-community detection algorithms in an unsupervised approach to the linking task. We propose several schemes to weight the word co-occurrence graph in order to discovery word communities, as well as a method for assigning segments to the discovered communities. Our experimental results indicate that the graph-community approach might BE more suitable for this task.

## 1 Introduction

Nowadays, it is easy to obtain documents collections with information about a target subject. For instance, learning materials about Neural Nets, World War II or Picasso. However, if search engines are effective in retrieving these collections, the task of putting them in a coherent picture remains a challenge [12]. As suggested in [8], linking topically related segments from different documents could help building friendlier user interfaces. In this paper, we study this linking task in learning materials.

The task of linking text pieces is not new. Several works aim at establishing connections at the document level (e.g. [5,12,13]); others relate keywords with documents (e.g. [7]) or set up relations between sentences (e.g. [6,10]). However, we target the linking process at a different level of granularity: we want to link segments which describe closely related information. To the best of our knowledge, the Similar Segments in Social Speech (4S) task, in the MediaEval campaign [15], provides the only corpus in which segments are linked (although the task, itself, had a different goal). However, in the (4S) corpus segments are linked based on a very high level topic label (for example, Math, Research, Family, Games, Movies, *etc.*). This is because the documents themselves are comprised of a mixture of such topics. This contrasts with our scenario where documents follow a single overarching subject and linked segments describe a specific topic. As a consequence, a substantial part of the main vocabulary is shared among segments and abrupt vocabulary changes are not prominent. The lack of readily available resources to study discourse structure in the previous conditions has been identified before in a document segmentation study [9]. In this context, the authors proposed a corpus containing learning materials about Adelson-Velsky and Landis' (AVL)s, from different media sources (presentation, video lectures, and Wikipedia articles), fitting perfectly in the navigation scenario of related documents. However, only the documents segments labels are provided, as the this research focused on the segmentation process.

In this paper, we extend the AVL corpus by linking the topically related segments, and study how clustering techniques and a topic model (LDA [2]) behave in this scenario[1]. We also propose a graph-community detection algorithm [11,16] for this task. Moreover, we test the impact of weighting the word co-occurrence graph according to the relevance of a word, rather than relying on raw word counts. Our research target is, thus, to assess the viability of state of the art approaches in the task of linking related segments, contributing to the emergent problem of navigating document collections.

## 2    The Graph-Community Approach

We propose the use of graph-community detection techniques, in which the analysis of a weighted co-occurrence graph (built from document segments) leads to word communities, representing the different topics. As in [12], the input is a weighted co-occurrence graph $G_{co} = (W, E)$, where $W$ is the set of nodes and $E$ the set of edges. $W$ corresponds to the set of words from a given set $S$ of segments. An edge $(w_i, w_j)$ exists if words $w_i$ and $w_j$ occur in some segment $S_k \in S$; the output is a mapping from words $w_k \in W$ to communities $c \in 1, ..., C$. In addition, we propose the following edge weighting schemes: (a) Count: the number of times the words co-occurred in different segments (as in [12]); (b) Best *tf-idf*: the sum of the highest segment wise *tf-idf* of each individual word; (c) Count + Best *tf-idf*: the sum of the previous weights; (d) Count + Avg *tf-idf*: the sum of the *count* weight and the sum of the average *tf-idf* word scores.

After discovering communities, we assign segments to them using a scoring function, that is, segment $s$ belongs to the highest scoring community $c$. Segments with the same community are considered linked. We tested the following scoring functions:

$$sc_c(s,c) = \frac{|s \cap c|}{|c|}, \quad sc_s(s,c) = \frac{|s \cap c|}{|s|}, \quad sc_{tf-idf}(s,c) = \frac{\sum_{w_i}^{|s \cap c|} tf - idf(w_i)}{\sum_{w_i}^{s} tf - idf(w_i)}$$

[1] Source code and annotated corpus available at: https://github.com/pjdrm/SegmentLinkingAVL.

The first two functions treat all words in the same way, as they simply count the common words between the segment and the community. The third function scores words' contribution according with their relevance.

## 3   Experimental Setup

The AVL corpus has 3181 sentences, and 86 segments [9]. A total of 15 different topics were found (and linked) in the 86 segments. From these, we considered the 5 main topics, covering 49 segments (Table 1).

**Table 1.** The extended AVL corpus in which segments are linked.

| Topics | Segments | #Words | #Vocab |
|---|---|---|---|
| BST | 7 | 1822 | 284 |
| Tree Height | 5 | 1800 | 338 |
| Tree Rotation | 13 | 3762 | 538 |
| Tree Balance | 13 | 3670 | 483 |
| AVL Rebalance | 11 | 8142 | 700 |

In the clustering setting, we tested the following algorithms [1], using bag-of-words features: (a) k-means; (b) Agglomerative clustering; (c) DBSCAN; (d) Mean Shift; (e) Spectral Clustering; (f) NMF clustering. We set the parameters of the algorithms as follows: (a) k-means: the number $k$ of clusters was set to 5 (the number of subtopics in the corpus); (b) Agglomerative Clustering: cosine, Euclidean, and Gaussian metrics were considered. For the Gaussian metric, variances ranging from 1 to 500 (step size 1) were tested. Different merge functions were assessed, namely: ward, complete, and average; (c) DBSCAN: all combinations of $Eps$, ranging from 0.1 to 0.9 (step size 0.1), and $MinPts$, ranging from 1 to 14 (step size 1), were tested. All the previously mentioned similarity metrics were tested; (d) Mean Shift: the Radial Basis Function (RBF) kernel was tested with bandwidth values from 1 to 1000 (step size 1); (e) Spectral Clustering: the number of clusters was set to 5. The previous similarity metrics were used to test different similarity graphs; (f) NMF Clustering: the number of clusters was set to 5.

For LDA, the top-$n$ most probable words from each topic were used as word communities. A range between the top-1 and top-200 words was assessed. The LDA model was run 10 times and the results averaged. The previously described scoring functions were applied to assign segments to communities.

Finally, considering the graph-community detection approach, we surveyed the following techniques [4]: (a) Label Propagation (LP); (b) CNM; (c) Louvain [3]; (d) Walktraps; (e) Leading Eigenvector; (f) Bigclam [16]. These techniques were tested using all the proposed weighting schemes and scoring functions. As in [12], we used *tf-idf* to filter stopwords. A top-100 word cutoff was used in each segment.

As evaluation measures, we considered the Adjusted Rand Index (ARI) [14], $F_1$, and Acc(uracy), which are standard metrics in this scenario.

# 4   Results

Table 2 shows the best results obtained, using the previous experimental setup. It should be noted that we observed significant variance in performance when testing different parameter configurations. LDA results (0.10, 0.31 and 0.44) were obtained with $score_c$ and top-19 words from each topic distribution. Considering the weighting schemes, Best *tf-idf* led Louvain to its best results, Count + Best *tf-idf* was the best weighting scheme to the Leading Eigenvector and Count + Avg *tf-idf* to the Walktraps algorithm. With respect to the score functions, LP, Louvain and Walktraps obtained the best results with $sc_c$, CNM and Leading Eigenvector with $sc_{tf-idf}$, and Bigclam with $sc_{seg}$.

**Table 2.** Best results for Clustering and Graph-Community algorithms.

| Clustering | *ARI* | $F_1$ | *Acc* | Graph-Community | *ARI* | $F_1$ | *Acc* |
|---|---|---|---|---|---|---|---|
| k-means | 0.011 | 0.34 | 0.31 | LP | 0.0 | 0.35 | 0.27 |
| Agglomerative | 0.11 | 0.32 | **0.52** | CNM | 0.05 | 0.31 | 0.42 |
| DBSCAN | 0.03 | 0.26 | 0.27 | Louvain | 0.12 | 0.31 | 0.42 |
| Mean Shift | 0.009 | 0.35 | 0.29 | Walktraps | **0.19** | **0.39** | **0.48** |
| Spectral | **0.15** | **0.36** | 0.41 | Leading Eigenvector | 0.05 | 0.35 | 0.38 |
| NMF | 0.046 | 0.22 | 0.45 | Bigclam | 0.06 | 0.1 | 0.25 |

Walktraps has the best performance, considering *ARI* and $F_1$. A clustering technique, Agglomerative, has the best results for *Acc*. This also indicates that there is no strict correlation between the different evaluation metrics (e.g. Mean Shift obtained the lowest *ARI*, but is one of the best performing techniques if we consider $F_1$).

Considering word co-occurrence weights, results indicate that it is important to distinguish relevant words in the document collection, rather than just relying on word counting. As for the score function, $sc_c$ worked better for Walktraps, but also for other techniques. This demonstrates that after discovering the communities, words should be treated equally when performing segment linking, as higher *tf-idf* words can induce unwanted bias. If words are assigned to the same community they represent the topic as a whole and, thus, any subset should not be expressive enough to represent that topic.

# 5  Conclusion and Future Work

Given the importance of navigating in learning materials, we establish a benchmark for the task of linking topically related segments. An inherent property of this scenario is that vocabulary is shared across topics, making the task more challenging. We extended the AVL corpus by linking its segments, and tested different state of the art techniques in this scenario, including graph-community detection algorithms. Given the observed performance variance, the results obtained should be interpreted with caution. Nonetheless, they indicate that a graph-community-based approach is more suitable.

As future work, instead of *tf-idf*, other measures should be tested. Another possibility that can lead to the improvement of the results is the use of edge pruning. Tests in other datasets should also be carried out in order to determine if the best performing parameter configuration can be generalized to other domains.

**Acknowledgements.** This work was supported by national funds through Fundação para a Ciência e a Tecnologia (FCT) with reference UID/CEC/50021/2013; also under projects LAW-TRAIN (H2020-EU.3.7, contract 653587), and INSIDE (CMUP-ERI/HCI/0051/2013), and also through the Carnegie Mellon Portugal Program under Grant SFRH/BD/51917/2012.

# References

1. Aggarwal, C.C., Reddy, C.K.: Data Clustering. Algorithms and Applications. Chapman & Hall/CRC, Boca Raton (2013)
2. Blei, D.M.: Probabilistic topic models. Commun. ACM **55**(4), 77–84 (2012)
3. Blondel, V., Guillaume, J., Lambiotte, R., Mech, E.: Fast unfolding of communities in large networks. J. Stat. Mech. Theory Exp. **2008**(10), P10008 (2008)
4. Fortunato, S.: Community detection in graphs. Physics Reports (2010)
5. Malioutov, I., Barzilay, R.: Minimum cut model for spoken lecture segmentation. In: Proceedings of the 21st International Conference on Computational Linguistics and the 44th annual meeting of the Association for Computational Linguistics, pp. 25–32. Association for Computational Linguistics (2006)
6. Maziero, E., Jorge, M., Pardo, T.: Identifying multi-document relations. In: Proceedings of the International Workshop on NLP and Cognitive Science (2010)
7. Mihalcea, R., Csomai, A.: Wikify!: Linking documents to encyclopedic knowledge. In: Proceedings of the sixteenth ACM Conference on Conference on Information and Knowledge Management, pp. 233–242. ACM (2007)
8. Minwoo, J., Ivan, T.: Multi-document topic segmentation. In: Proceedings of the 19th ACM international conference on Information and knowledge management. ACM (2010)
9. Mota, P., Eskenazi, M., Coheur, L.: Multi-document topic segmentation. In: Proceedings of the 2016 International Workshop on Semantic Multimedia (2016)
10. Radev, D.R., Jing, H., Styś, M., Tam, D.: Centroid-based summarization of multiple documents. In: Information Processing Management (2004)
11. Reichardt, J., Bornholdt, S.: Statistical mechanics of community detection. Phys. Rev. E **74**(1), 016110 (2006)

12. Shahaf, D., Guestrin, C., Horvitz, E.: Trains of thought: generating information maps. In: Proceedings of the 21st International Conference on World Wide Web. ACM (2012)
13. Sil, D.K., Sengamedu, S.H., Bhattacharyya, C.: Supervised matching of comments with news article segments. In: Proceedings of the 20th ACM International Conference on Information and Knowledge Management. ACM (2011)
14. Vinh, N.X., Epps, J., Bailey, J.: Information theoretic measures for clusterings comparison: is a correction for chance necessary? In: Proceedings of ICML (2009)
15. Ward, N.G., Werner, S.D., Novick, D.G., Shriberg, E.E., Oertel, C., Kawahara, T.: The similar segments in social speech task (2013)
16. Yang, J., Leskovec, J.: Overlapping community detection at scale: a nonnegative matrix factorization approach. In: Proceedings of the Sixth ACM International Conference on Web Search and Data Mining. ACM (2013)

# Syntax-Based Analysis of Programming Concepts in Python

Martin Možina[(✉)] and Timotej Lazar

Faculty of Computer and Information Science,
University of Ljubljana, Ljubljana, Slovenia
`martin.mozina@fri.uni-lj.si`

**Abstract.** Writing programs is essential to learning programming. Most programming courses encourage students to practice with lab and homework assignments. By analyzing solutions to these exercises teachers can discover mistakes and concepts students are struggling with, and use that knowledge to improve the course. Students however tend to submit many different programs even for simple exercises, making such analysis difficult. We propose using tree regular expressions to encode common patterns in programs. Based on these patterns we induce rules describing common approaches and mistakes for a given assignment. In this paper we present a case study of rule-based analysis for an introductory Python exercise. We show that our rules are easy to interpret, and can be learned from a relatively small set of programs.

**Keywords:** Learning programming · Educational data analysis
Error diagnosis · Abstract syntax tree · Tree regular expressions

## 1 Introduction

Providing feedback to students is among the most time-consuming tasks when teaching programming. In large courses with hundreds of students, feedback is therefore often limited to automated program testing. While test cases can reliably determine whether a program is correct or not, they cannot easily be associated with specific errors in the code.

Several attempts have been made to automatically discover common errors in student programs [1–4]. This would allow a teacher to annotate a representative subset of submissions with feedback messages, which could then be automatically propagated to similar programs. These techniques are used for instance by the OverCode tool to visualize variations in student programs [5].

We use *tree regular expressions* to specify important patterns in a program's abstract syntax tree (AST) while disregarding irrelevant parts. We have previously demonstrated this approach with Prolog programs [6]. Here we refine the AST patterns and show that they can be applied to Python – a different programming paradigm – with only a few modifications.

© Springer International Publishing AG, part of Springer Nature 2018
C. Penstein Rosé et al. (Eds.): AIED 2018, LNAI 10948, pp. 236–240, 2018.
https://doi.org/10.1007/978-3-319-93846-2_43

## 2  AST Patterns

We encode structural patterns in ASTs using tree regular expressions (TREs). In this work we consider (only) patterns describing child and sibling relations in an AST. We write them as S-expressions, such as (a (b ^ d . e $) c). This expression matches any tree satisfying the following constraints:

- the root a has at least two children, b and c, adjacent and in that order; and
- the node b has three children: d, followed by any node, followed by e.

As in ordinary regular expressions, caret (^) and dollar sign ($) anchor a node to be respectively the first or last sibling, and a period (.) matches any node.

Using TREs we can encode interesting patterns in a program while disregarding irrelevant parts. Take for example the following, nearly correct Python function that prints the divisors of its argument $n$:

```
def divisors(n):
    for d in range(1, n):
        if n % d == 0:
            print(d)
```

The highlighted fragments correspond to the following patterns:

1. (Function (body (For (body If)))) and
2. (Function (name divisors) (args ^ Var $)
      (body (For (iter (Call (func range) (args ^ . Var $)))))).

The first TRE encodes a single path in the AST and describes the program's control-flow structure: Function–For–If [4]. The second TRE relates the argument in the definition of divisors to the last argument to range. This pattern shows a common mistake for this problem: range(1,n) will only generate values up to n-1, so n will not be printed as its own divisor. A correct pattern would include the operator + on the AST path to n, indicating a call to range(1,n+1).

Patterns are extracted automatically from student programs. We first canonicalize [2] each program using code from ITAP[1]. For each pattern we select a subset of nodes in the AST, then construct the TRE by walking the tree from each selected node to the root.

While pattern extraction is completely automated, we have manually defined the kinds of node subsets that are selected. After analyzing solutions to several programming problems, we decided to use the following kinds of patterns:

1. We select each pair of leaf nodes $\{a, b\}$ that refer to the same variable.
2. For each control-flow node $n$ we construct a pattern from the set $\{n\}$; we do the same for each Call node representing a function call.
3. For each expression – such as (F-32)*5/9 – we select the different combinations of literal and variable nodes in the expression. In these patterns we include at most one node referring to a variable.

---

[1] Available at https://github.com/krivers/ITAP-django.

We found that patterns constructed from such node subsets are useful for discriminating between programs. Note that every constructed pattern refers to at most one variable. We used patterns to induce classification rules for predicting program correctness. The next section demonstrates that these rules are easy to interpret in terms of bugs and strategies for a given problem.

## 3   Rules: A Case Study

The goal of learning rules in this paper is to discover and explain common approaches and mistakes in student programs. We use a similar rule learner to the one described in [6], implemented within the Orange data mining library [7]. Each program is represented in the feature space of AST patterns described in the previous section. Based on test results each program is classified either as *correct* or *incorrect*. Rules are then learned to explain why a program is correct or incorrect. Rules for incorrect programs are called *n-rules* and rules for correct programs are called *p-rules*. Patterns mentioned within the condition part of a rule can be used to analyze student programming. For example, patterns from a rule for incorrect programs are more often present in incorrect than in correct programs, therefore they likely correspond to errors.

This section describes several rules induced for the Fahrenheit to Celsius Python exercise, which reads a value from standard input and calculates the result. To solve this exercise, a student must ask the user to input a temperature, and print the result. A sample correct program is:

```
F = float(input("Fahrenheit: "))
C = 5 / 9 * (F - 32)
print("Celsius: ", C)
```

Students have submitted 1177 programs for this problem, with 495 correct and 682 incorrect programs. Our system extracted 891 relevant AST patterns, which were used as attributes in rule learning. The rule learner induced 24 n-rules and 16 p-rules.

Two examples of highly accurate n-rules were:

P20 ⇒ incorrect [208, 1]
P5 ∧ P35 ⇒ incorrect [72, 0]

The first rule covers programs where the pattern P20 is present. The rule implies an incorrect program, and covers 208 incorrect and one correct program. P20 is the AST pattern describing a call to the **int** function:

(Module (body (Assign (value (Call (func (Name (id int) (ctx Load))))))))

The pattern P5 in the second rule matches programs where the result of the **input** call is not cast to **float** but stored as a string. Pattern P35 matches programs where the value 32 is subtracted from a variable on the left-hand side of a multiplication. Sample programs matching the first rule (left) and the second rule (right) are:

```
g2 = input()                    g2 = input('Temperature [F]? ')
g1 = int(g2)                    g1 = ((g2 - 32) * (5 / 9))
print(((g1-32)*(5/9)))          print(g2, 'F equals', g1, 'C')
```

These rules describe two common student errors. The left program fails when the user inputs a decimal. The right program is incorrect because the input string must be cast to a number. Not casting it (pattern P5) and then using it in an expression (pattern P35) will raise an exception.

In some cases, n-rules imply a missing pattern. For example:

$$\neg P0 \Rightarrow \text{incorrect } [106, 0]$$

Pattern P0 matches programs with a call to function `print`. A program without a `print` is always incorrect, since it will not output anything.

Let us now examine the other type of rules. A sample p-rule was:

$$P2 \wedge P8 \Rightarrow \text{correct } [1, 200]$$

Patterns in the condition of the rule, P2 and P8, correspond respectively to expressions of the form `float(input(?))` and `print((?-32)*?)`. Programs matching both patterns wrap the function `float` around `input`, and have an expression that subtracts 32 and then uses multiplication within the `print`.

This rule demonstrates an important property of p-rules: although patterns P2 and P8 are in general not sufficient for a correct program (it is trivial to implement a matching but incorrect program), only one out of 201 student submissions matching these patterns was incorrect. This suggests that the conditions of p-rules represent critical elements of the solution. Once students have figured out these patterns, they are almost certain to have a correct solution. A sample program matching this rule is:

```
g1 = float(input('Temperature [F]: '))
print(((g1 - 32) * (5 / 9)))
```

## 4   Discussion and Further Work

Our primary interest in this paper is to help manual analysis of student submissions. We proposed to first represent submitted programs with patterns extracted from abstract syntax trees and then learn classification rules that distinguish between correct and incorrect programs. We showed that both rules and patterns are easy to interpret and can be used to explain typical mistakes and approaches.

The accuracy of automatic classification plays a secondary role, but it is a good measure to estimate the expressiveness of patterns. Over 12 exercises a random forest model achieved about 17% overall higher accuracy than the majority classifier. This result indicates that a significant amount of information can be gleaned from simple syntax-oriented analysis. To further improve the quality of patterns, we intend to analyze misclassified programs in exercises and derive new formats of patterns, which should enable better learning.

We have demonstrated how AST patterns can be encoded with TREs, and how patterns can be combined to discover important concepts and errors in student programs. Currently, analyzing patterns and rules is quite cumbersome. We plan on developing a tool to allow teachers to easily construct and refine patterns based on example programs. Ideally we would integrate our approach into an existing analysis tool such as OverCode [5].

# References

1. Jin, W., Barnes, T., Stamper, J., Eagle, M.J., Johnson, M.W., Lehmann, L.: Program representation for automatic hint generation for a data-driven novice programming tutor. In: Cerri, S.A., Clancey, W.J., Papadourakis, G., Panourgia, K. (eds.) ITS 2012. LNCS, vol. 7315, pp. 304–309. Springer, Heidelberg (2012). https://doi.org/10.1007/978-3-642-30950-2_40
2. Rivers, K., Koedinger, K.R.: Data-driven hint generation in vast solution spaces: a self-improving Python programming tutor. Int. J. Artif. Intell. Educ. 1–28 (2015)
3. Nguyen, A., Piech, C., Huang, J., Guibas, L.: Codewebs: scalable homework search for massive open online programming courses. In: Proceedings of the 23rd International World Wide Web Conference (WWW 2014), pp. 491–502 (2014)
4. Hovemeyer, D., Hellas, A., Petersen, A., Spacco, J.: Control-flow-only abstract syntax trees for analyzing students' programming progress. In: Proceedings of the 2016 ACM Conference on International Computing Education Research, pp. 63–72. ACM (2016)
5. Glassman, E.L., Scott, J., Singh, R., Guo, P.J., Miller, R.C.: OverCode: visualizing variation in student solutions to programming problems at scale. ACM Trans. Comput. Hum. Interact. (TOCHI) **22**(2), 7 (2015)
6. Lazar, T., Možina, M., Bratko, I.: Automatic extraction of AST patterns for debugging student programs. In: André, E., Baker, R., Hu, X., Rodrigo, M.M.T., du Boulay, B. (eds.) AIED 2017. LNCS (LNAI), vol. 10331, pp. 162–174. Springer, Cham (2017). https://doi.org/10.1007/978-3-319-61425-0_14
7. Demšar, J., Curk, T., Erjavec, A., Gorup, Č., Hočevar, T., Milutinovič, M., Možina, M., Polajnar, M., Toplak, M., Starič, A., Štajdohar, M., Umek, L., Žagar, L., Žbontar, J., Žitnik, M., Zupan, B.: Orange: data mining toolbox in Python. J. Mach. Learn. Res. **14**, 2349–2353 (2013)

# Teaching Without Learning: Is It OK With Weak AI?

Kristian Månsson and Magnus Haake[(⊠)]

LUCS, Lund University Cognitive Science, Lund University, Lund, Sweden
{kristian.mansson,magnus.haake}@lucs.lu.se

**Abstract.** Two different learning models for a teachable agent were tested with respect to perceived intelligence, the protégé effect, and learning in Swedish grade 5 and 6 students. A strong positive correlation was found between perceived intelligence and the protégé effect, but no significant differences were found between the two different implementations of the learning algorithm. The results suggest that while the perceived intelligence of the agent relates to the induced protégé effect, this perceived intelligence did not correspond to the implemented learning model. This, in turn, suggest that a simple learning model can be sufficient for a teachable agent system, but more research is needed.

**Keywords:** Teachable agent · Learning model · Perceived intelligence
Protégé effect · Learning outcome

## 1 Introduction

Studies have shown that the 'teachable agent'-paradigm, i.e. *learning-by-teaching* using a Teachable Agent (hence TA) in educational software, benefits learning by increasing students' sense of responsibility and supporting metacognition [1, 2]. The *protégé effect* refers to how students make larger learning efforts when the goal is to teach another (social) agent than when the goal is to learn for themselves [3]. Three mechanisms are suggested to underlie this increase in learning effort: a feeling of responsibility towards the TA, an adoption of an incrementalist view of knowledge, and a protection of the ego (*ego-protective buffer*) since it is the agent who is tested for its learning and who potentially fails.

Elaborating on the TA-paradigm, there is a difference between an agent that can learn and an agent that can be taught [4], suggesting different approaches for the design of the AI in corresponding TA-software. In the learning software *Guardians of History* (GoH), the student has a teacher role and the TA appears to be learning – but is in fact only responding to pre-defined actions from the student-teacher. In this sense, the TA is taught but is not actually learning. Alternatively, an artificial neural network can be trained to make, for instance, discriminations between different breeds of dogs by processing a training set of thousands of images with dogs. In this case the system is in some sense learning, but there is not much teaching involved. This spurs the question of how much effort should be put into the development of the underlying artificial intelligence of a TA? It needs to be teachable, but to what extent does it need to learn versus seem to learn? The well-studied TA system *Betty's Brain* (BB) [5] lies

© Springer International Publishing AG, part of Springer Nature 2018
C. Penstein Rosé et al. (Eds.): AIED 2018, LNAI 10948, pp. 241–245, 2018.
https://doi.org/10.1007/978-3-319-93846-2_44

somewhere in-between the two examples above. In BB, the student-teacher is tasked with teaching Betty to make inferences by constructing concept maps representing concepts and functions. In BB, the teaching becomes akin to mapping out a visual representation of a knowledge model. This visual representation, in turn, supports the student's teaching of the agent.

If no such clear visual representation is provided, can the underlying learning model of the TA still invoke a sense of intelligence – and does such perceived intelligence affect the positive learning effects of a TA-system? This paper presents a first pilot study to explore whether the underlying artificial intelligence model of a TA can affect the suggested mechanisms of the protégé effect. In order to pursue this question, the pilot study aims to explore the relation between the protégé effect, perceived intelligence of the TA, and students' learning outcomes by comparing two different implementations of a TA in an educational software.

## 2  Method

### 2.1  The Teachable Agent Educational Software

The TA software used in the study is called *Guardians of History* (GoH) and targets middle-school history. It is developed by the Educational Technology Group at Lund University and Linköping University. In GoH, the student helps their TA (suffering from time traveling nausea) to pass a set of history tests by going on time travel missions to gather information (Fig. 1). Returning from the time travels, the student engages the TA in different so-called classroom activities (Fig. 1). The classroom activities consist of tasks such as building concept maps, sorting propositions and organizing a timeline. The student does the task while the TA observes. After being taught, the TA conducts a test consisting of filling in gaps in sentences (without the help from the student) where s/he provides answers depending on facts s/he has learned. For this study, a subset of the available time travel scenarios was selected and used for two missions.

**Fig. 1.** Example of time-travel (left) and a classroom activity (right) in the GoH software.

## 2.2    The Learning Models of the Teachable Agent

The TA was implemented with two different learning models: $TA_R$ (as in 'recency') and $TA_A$ (as in 'associative'). The recency setting ($TA_R$) corresponds to the original implementation of the TA where the agent's learning model reflects the latest facts it has been exposed to in each learning activity, i.e. for every new learning activity, the learning model overwrites all the previous facts learned in previous learning activities – whether they are correct or not. The associative agent ($TA_A$) [6] is implemented with a basic learning model modulating the agent's certainty of different facts. The certainty of the facts varies depending on the results of the learning activities. Furthermore, the $TA_A$ asks for confirmation of learned facts at random intervals.

## 2.3    Experimental Design

The study involved 94 Swedish grades 5 and 6 students from 5 classes from the same school. The students were randomly assigned to one of two conditions (GoH using the $TA_R$ model and the $TA_A$ model, respectively) of 47 students each. The students were given a short introduction to the game and the characters, whereafter they were instructed to work alone but allowed to ask for help. The whole intervention lasted for two subsequent sessions, each lasting 60 min.

A questionnaire addressing perceived intelligence of the TA and the protégé effect was distributed to the students at the end of the second session. Upon finishing the questionnaire, the students were presented with a knowledge assessment. The questionnaire as well as the knowledge test was presented using the same Google Forms format. After everyone in the class had submitted their questionnaires and knowledge assessments, a general group discussion of the experience was conducted.

Prior to the analyses, 9 students were excluded from the dataset due to: language difficulties, not completing the game, or not handing in questionnaires. The resulting data set consisted of $N = 85$ participants ($TA_R$: 41; $TA_A$: 44).

## 2.4    Measurements

The protégé effect (PE) was measured with five 5-level Likert items operationalized for studies using GoH [7]. Perceived intelligence (PI) was measured with 6 semantic difference items used for measuring perceived intelligence of a robot [8]. Learning outcome was assessed by a knowledge test consisting of 10 multiple choice questions based on the content of GoH.

# 3    Results

All statistical analyzes were performed with the statistical software R version 3.4.3 at an alpha level of 0.05; all effect sizes interpreted according to Cohen [9]. The final dataset consisted of $N = 85$ students. An analysis of grade revealed no significant effects on the measurements and the students were treated as a single population.

An independent samples $t$-test showed no significant difference in PI between the $TA_R$ ($M = 16.4$, $SD = 4.5$) and the $TA_A$ ($M = 17.8$, $SD = 4.3$) conditions ($t(83) = -1.32$, $p = .19$, Cohen's $d = .32$), i.e. there was no significant difference between the $TA_R$ group and the $TA_A$ group with regard to perceived intelligence as measured by the questionnaire items.

A strong positive correlation ($r = .64$, $p < .001$) was found between PI and PE, i.e. the students' scores for perceived intelligence and protégé effect followed each other to a high degree.

A Matt-Whitney's U test displayed no significant difference in learning outcome between the $TA_R$ (*Median* = 6; *Range* = 1–10) and $TA_A$ (*Median* = 6; *Range* = 0–9) conditions ($W = 843$, $p = .60$, Cohen's $d = 0.11$), i.e. neither the $TA_R$ group nor the $TA_A$ group performed better as measured by the knowledge assessment.

No significant correlation between PE and performance score in the knowledge test could be established.

# 4  Discussion

The students did not perceive $TA_A$ as more intelligent. The lack of any significant difference between the conditions regarding the perceived intelligence and the protégé effect might, however, point to other factors as eliciting the protégé effect, such as the narrative or the explicitly stated role for the student as the teacher.

The strong positive correlation between perceived intelligence and protégé effect may reflect that one strongly influences the other or that they strengthen each other reciprocally. The strong correlation between how the student either actively ascribe or passively perceive the TA as a thinking and learning agent and the elicited protégé effect, points to one having a strong influence on the other, or to both manifesting an underlying phenomenon. We suggest this is a correlation of interest for researchers as well as designers of TA software.

The lack of a correlation between the protégé effect and the knowledge test scores is somewhat surprising. Yet, as the protégé effect is a theoretical construct aimed at explaining the positive learning outcomes from TAs, it might be too coarse to measure it in the way done in the study, i.e. the result might be sensitive to false negatives. Another possibility is that the measurement does not actually reflect the protégé effect but instead students' general positive – or negative – attitude towards the software.

A long-term study where the students would have more time to interact with the TA might provide further insight towards how the students' perception of the TA vary over time. Validation of the measurements is also of great importance, as they were newly adapted for this study.

# References

1. Schwartz, D.L., Chase, C., Chin, D., Oppezzo, M., Kwong, H., Okita, S., Roscoe, R., Jeong, H., Wagster, J., Biswas, G.: Interactive metacognition: monitoring and regulating a teachable agent. In: Hacker, D.J., Dunlosky, J., Graesser, A.C. (eds.) Handbook of Metacognition in Education, pp. 340–358. Routledge, New York (2009)
2. Biswas, G., Leelawong, K., Schwartz, D., Vye, N.: TAG-V: learning by teaching: a new agent paradigm for educational software. Appl. Artif. Intell. **19**(3–4), 363–392 (2005)
3. Chase, C., Chin, D.B., Oppezzo, M., Schwartz, D.L.: Teachable agents and the protégé effect: increasing the effort towards learning. J. Sci. Educ. Technol. **18**(4), 334–352 (2009)
4. Brophy, S., Biswas, G., Katzlberger, T., Bransford, J., Schwartz, D.: Teachable agents: combining insights from learning theory and computer science. In: Lajoie, S.P., Vivet, M. (eds.) Artificial Intelligence in Education, pp. 21–28. IOS Press, Amsterdam (1999)
5. Chin, D., Dohmen, I., Cheng, B., Oppezzo, M., Chase, C., Schwartz, D.: Preparing students for future learning with teachable agents. Educ. Technol. Res. Dev. **58**(6), 649–669 (2010)
6. Bäckström, J., Månsson, K., Persson, M., Sakurai, E., Sundström, F.: Designing and implementing an associative learning model for a teachable agent. In: Balkenius, C., Gulz, A., Haake, M., Wallergård, M. (eds.) LUCS 168: Intelligent, Socially Oriented Technology III, pp. 5–13. Lund University, Lund (2017)
7. Kirkegaard, C.: Adding challenge to a teachable agent in a virtual learning environment. Licentiate thesis, Linköping University, Linköping (2016)
8. Bartneck, C., Kuli, D., Croft, E.: Measurement instruments for the anthropomorphism, animacy, likeability, perceived intelligence, and perceived safety of robots. Int. J. Soc. Robot. **1**(1), 71–81 (2009)
9. Cohen, J.: Statistical Power Analysis for the Behavioral Sciences. Routledge, Oxford (1988)

# Sentiment Analysis of Student Evaluations
# of Teaching

Heather Newman[(✉)] and David Joyner[(✉)]

Georgia Institute of Technology, Atlanta, GA, USA
{newman,david.joyner}@gatech.edu

**Abstract.** We used a sentiment analysis tool, VADER (Valence Aware Dictionary and sEntiment Reasoner), to analyze Student Evaluations of Teaching (SET) of a single course from three different sources: official evaluations, forum comments from another course, and an unofficial "reviews" site maintained by students. We compared the positive and negative valences of these sites; identified frequently-used key words in SET comments and determined the impact on positivity/negativity of comments that included them; and determined positive/negative values by question on the official course SET comments. Many universities use similar questions, which may make this research useful for those analyzing comments at other institutions. Previous published studies of sentiment analysis in SET settings are rare.

**Keywords:** Sentiment analysis · Student evaluation of teaching
Course evaluations · Natural language processing

## 1 Introduction

Student evaluations of teaching (SET) are an important part of universities' self-improvement programs, providing a viewpoint that may affect everything from professors' tenure case decisions to the structure of future semesters of those courses. SET typically include qualitative comments that may be difficult to present in a summary manner. Sentiment analysis, a form of natural language processing, attempts to assign a positive, negative or neutral valence or polarity to natural speech. We set out to determine whether sentiment analysis is a viable tool for analyzing evaluations.

### 1.1 Evaluation Sources

We analyzed evaluations of a single graduate-level online course of several hundred students over a period of two semesters. By limiting the evaluations to a single course, we were able to control for variability by instructor, semester, and course material. We analyzed three separate sources of SET: official course evaluations, consisting of a series of quantitative measurements followed by qualitative open-ended questions; informal peer evaluations from an unofficial online course evaluation site with quantitative and qualitative rankings and comments; and postings in another course, where students were asked to discuss specific classes they had taken.

© Springer International Publishing AG, part of Springer Nature 2018
C. Penstein Rosé et al. (Eds.): AIED 2018, LNAI 10948, pp. 246–250, 2018.
https://doi.org/10.1007/978-3-319-93846-2_45

## 1.2   VADER as a Sentiment Analysis Tool

After experiencing poor results with a standard SentiWordNet analysis [1], we turned to a more-sophisticated analytical tool for sentiment in informal postings. We found good results with VADER, the Valence Aware Dictionary for sEntiment Reasoning [2]. VADER not only analyzes individual word sentiment, but attempts to predict the normalized valence of positive or negative sentiment based on overall sentences, accounting for factors such as negation, punctuation or emoticon usage. It provided consistent analysis of SET comments, which are often written informally.

# 2   Related Work

Student evaluations may be flawed overall in how closely they track with the actual educational outcomes of a particular class; past studies have shown that positive evaluations may not correlate well with student learning, and that other factors may be in play [3–5]. Given that issue, the detailed sentiment analysis by topic discussed here may offer an option for instructors or institutions attempting to do a deeper dive into evaluations than just the summary ratings, by identifying classroom themes or components and students' positivity or negativity toward them.

Lim et al's [6] study on course evaluations did not focus on sentiment analysis per se, but a tangent: frequency analysis to determine key features of course evaluations. The applications of this work to the word groupings in our study seem very relevant. El-Halees' [7] analysis of comments to improve course evaluations comes the closest to approaching the subject of this study. The author conducted analysis identifying overall sentiment and features including teacher, exams, resources, etc., assigning sentiment to those features. He used NB, k-Nearest Neighbor and SVM methods.

# 3   Viability of Sentiment Analysis in SET

One method of determining viability for sentiment analysis in student evaluations of teaching comments using our datasets was to compare comments' sentiment polarity using a particular method with student-awarded quantitative scores. Just one set of evaluations included individually calibrated student comments and evaluation scores: the informal student website rankings. Official course evaluation survey data pre-summarized quantitative data, making it impossible to match scores with particular comments. The informal site included an overall rating for the entire class (based on a 1–5 scale) and comments on the class from the same individual.

## 3.1   Results

A clear trend can be seen between the average normalized compound sentiment scores for students awarding low quantitative scores versus those awarding high scores, suggesting that sentiment analysis does generally track with students' overall estimations of course value. A dip occurs at the "3" rating, possibly due to students' association of the mid-level "3" rating with "average," as opposed to a true progression from 1 to 5. This supports the use of sentiment as an evaluative measure, especially in these edge cases, since it can be used to tease out the true expressed negative/positive valence of comments for those awarding an "average" score (Fig. 1).

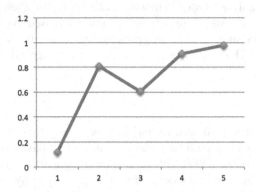

**Fig. 1.** Normalized compound VADER sentiment polarity of student comments expressed as a function of student quantitative ratings of the same course (1 low to 5 high). Normalized compound scores of sentiment range from −1 (completely negative) to +1 (completely positive.)

While evaluation comments by students overall tend to employ positive terms, the average for those who awarded 1 of 5 stars was 11.72% (.1172) in normalized VADER compound scores, while the average for those awarding 5 of 5 stars was close to universally positive, at 97.96% (.9796).

### 3.2 Differences in Evaluation Comment Sentiment Scores Based on Environment

All three sources scored roughly the same on compound ratings; however, the informal student website scores were slightly more likely to be negative (7.5%, versus 5.9% for the forum posts and 6.2% for official evaluation comments), while also being slightly more likely to include fewer positive comments (13.2%, versus 15% for forum posts and 15.5% for official evaluations.)

### 3.3 Scores for Particular Question Types

We tracked sentiment scores by question by term, since the course had changed. In general, positive questions asking about the course or instructor's strengths received the lowest negative and highest positive scores; and vice versa for questions asking about weaknesses, supporting our methodology. For instance, in Fall 2016, "course best aspect" had an average normalized positive valence of 20.2% and negative of 0.5%; "course improvements" had a positive valence of 10.7% and negative of 7.7%.

## 3.4  Scores for Comments Including Frequently-Used Keywords

One of the key findings that could be helpful for evaluating parts of a course that students resonated with more or less strongly is the list of items (nouns) that students mention most frequently. We analyzed the most frequently used terms and averaged the sentiment polarity for comments using those terms.

We iterated through the comments themselves, identifying whether they contained one of these frequently-occurring nouns, and if so, adding it to a total score for that noun. The resulting totals were averaged to produce positive, negative and compound normalized VADER sentiment scores for each noun. For samples, see Tables 1 and 2.

**Table 1.**  The top two frequently-used nouns with negative associations.

| Word | Neutral | Negative | Positive | Compound |
|------|---------|----------|----------|----------|
| Feedback | 0.812 | 0.091 | 0.097 | 0.9816 |
| Questions | 0.814 | 0.084 | 0.102 | 0.9996 |

**Table 2.**  The top two positive terms for sentiment.

| Word | Neutral | Negative | Positive | Compound |
|------|---------|----------|----------|----------|
| Interviews | 0.763 | 0.051 | 0.185 | 0.9999 |
| Idea | 0.779 | 0.064 | 0.157 | 1 |

# 4  Discussion and Limitations

Sentiment analysis cannot provide a replacement for the content and contextual analysis done manually now. It may break down in environments where student comments are too short or factually phrased to provide consistent results. This analysis focused on a single course within a single degree program, and further study is needed to determine whether the results found here carry over to other types of classes (e.g., traditional in-person instruction) and other types of evaluative measures.

# 5  Conclusion

The potential for sentiment analysis as a tool for analyzing Student Evaluations of Teaching appears to be significant. It offers an additional summarization tool for "quick looks" at positive and negative factors within a single class. Use of frequently occurring keywords might help to identify where the course instructor was strong but particular materials were weak, or vice versa. Correlation between overall sentiment analysis scores for a review and overall scores awarded to a class appear to support the validity of sentiment analysis as a measurement.

# References

1. Baccianella, S., Esuli, A., Sebastiani, F.: SENTIWORDNET 3.0: an enhanced lexical resource for sentiment analysis and opinion mining. In: Proceedings of the International Conference on Language Resources and Evaluation, LREC 2010, Valletta, Malta, 17–23 May 2010
2. Hutto, C.J., Gilbert, E.: Vader: a parsimonious rule-based model for sentiment analysis of social media text. In: Eighth International Conference on Weblogs and Social Media (ICWSM 2014)
3. Marsh, H.W., Roche, L.A.: Making students' evaluations of teaching effectiveness effective: the critical issues of validity, bias, and utility. Am. Psychol. **52**(11), 1187 (1997)
4. Uttl, B., White, C., Gonzalez, D.: Meta-analysis of faculty's teaching effectiveness: student evaluation of teaching ratings and student learning are not related. Stud. Educ. Eval. **54**, 22–42 (2017)
5. Boring, A., Ottoboni, K., Stark, P.B.: Student evaluations of teaching (mostly) do not measure teaching effectiveness. ScienceOpen Res. **10** (2016)
6. Lim, S.D., Lee, J., Park, H.S., Yu, J., Lee, K.Y., Sohn, I.S., Lee, R.: Experience and consideration on online course evaluation by medical students. Korean J. Med. Educ. **20**(4), 367–371 (2008). https://doi.org/10.3946/kjme.2008.20.4.367
7. El-Halees, A.: Mining opinions in user-generated contents to improve course evaluation. In: Zain, J.M., Wan Mohd, W.M., El-Qawasmeh, E. (eds.) ICSECS 2011. CCIS, vol. 180, pp. 107–115. Springer, Heidelberg (2011). https://doi.org/10.1007/978-3-642-22191-0_9

# Visualizing Learning Analytics and Educational Data Mining Outputs

Ranilson Paiva[(✉)], Ig Ibert Bittencourt, Wansel Lemos, André Vinicius,
and Diego Dermeval

Federal University of Alagoas (UFAL) - Computing Institute (IC), Maceió, Brazil
ranilsonpaiva@ic.ufal.br, ig.ibert@gmail.com,
wansel.lemos@arapiraca.ufal.br, andreducap@gmail.com,
diegodermeval@gmail.com

**Abstract.** The increase in supply and demand of on-line courses evidences a new educational paradigm mediated by information and communication technologies. However, an issue in this new paradigm is the high number of students who drop out (85% on average). Some of them blame the lack of instructor support. This support needs the analysis of students' data to guide teachers' decision-making. Learning Analytics (LA), Educational Data Mining (EDM) and Data Visualization (DataViz) are some tools for this analysis, but teachers do not receive appropriate technological support to use them. So, we used DataViz to help teachers understand the output from the application of LA and EDM algorithms on the students' data. We evaluated if instructors understood the information in the visualizations, and asked their opinion about the visualizations' (1) utility; (2) ease of use; (3) attitude towards use; (4) intention to use; (5) aesthetics; (6) the color scheme used; and (7) the vocabulary used. The results indicate that instructors understood the information in the visualizations and the majority of them had favorable opinions, but we noticed the vocabulary used needs improvement.

**Keywords:** Data visualization · Educational data science · e-Learning

## 1 Introduction

The increase in supply and demand of on-line courses [2,6] evidences a new educational paradigm, which relies on digital information and communication technologies (DICT) [4]. However, this new paradigm poses some issues for teachers. One issue is the high number of dropouts (85%, on average) [8,11]. Learners blame the "Lack of Instructor Support" [11], but such support demands educational data analysis to guide educational decision-making [3,7,13]. Learning Analytics (LA), pedagogical Data Mining (EDM) and Data Visualization (DataViz) are a set of tools to do that, but teachers are not, normally, trained nor receive appropriate technological support to use them [10,13]. Thus, the need to assist teachers using technology to guide pedagogical decision-making is latent. This aid should process learners' educational data is search for relevant information, showing the characteristics of the issues, guiding teachers on what they should do [3,9,12,13]. For that, we created 3 visualizations to: (1) measure the amount of interactions, from a group of students, with each educational resource (called segmented bar chart and coded as Viz1); (2) show the most impactful interactions on students' performance (ordered weights, Viz2); and (3) show the most impactful combination of interactions on students' performance (combined interactions, Viz3).

## 2    Proposal

We used data visualization to help teachers understand the output from the application of data mining and learning analytics on educational data from 196 students (an on-line high-school math course), consisting of the amount of: (1) problems solved correctly, incorrectly and in total; (2) accesses to the learning environment; (3) videos watched; (4) points earned (gamification); (5) badges/trophies achieved (gamification); and (6) level (gamification). For that, we created 3 visualizations associated with the "RAG Colors" technique [1], to analyze students as groups, based on their performance[1]. The visualizations are explained below:

**Visualization 1 - Segmented Bar Graph.** In this visualization, the interactions are counted and compared to the mean of all interactions of the same kind. Learners with scores below -1 standard deviation, were in the inadequate class; those with scores between $-1$ and $+1$ standard deviation, were in the insufficient class; and those with scores above $+1$ standard deviation, were in the adequate class. The aim was to isolate the interactions and facilitate comparison (Fig. 1 - Top).

**Visualization 2 - Ordered Weights.** In this visualization, we ran the *SimpleLogistic*[2] algorithm on the data to build a linear regression model [14]. The output is not "teacher-friendly". Thus, we transformed the textual output, considering the weights of each variable and the 3 classes of results: 0 = inadequate, 1 = insufficient and 2 = adequate. Variables with negative weights repel learners from the class. We ordered interactions that repelled students from the inadequate class (class 0) and attracted the adequate class (class 2), see (Fig. 1 - Middle).

**Visualization 3 - Combined Interactions.** In this visualization, we ran the *JRip* algorithm to infer association rules [5] based on frequent and relevant patterns in the data. The output shows some combinations of interactions leading to

---

[1] RAG stands for: red, amber, green. Red = Inadequate class: learners need urgent attention and well-planned pedagogical interventions [1]; Yellow/Amber = Insufficient class: learners need attention, monitoring and guidance [1] to progress; Green = Adequate Class: learners need incentives and/or challenges to keep them motivated and progressing well.

[2] Available at: https://www.cs.waikato.ac.nz/ml/weka/.

a particular class of results. Teachers can identify sequences of interactions that affect learning, which is potentially informative for the teachers. We calculated the "importance score", adding a point for the occurrence of a resource in the rules returned and subtracted a point for each non-occurrence. The result was the combination of the four resources with highest (green) and four resources with the lowest (red) scores (Fig. 1 - Bottom).

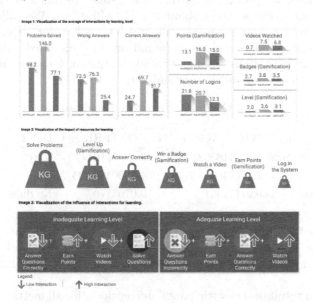

**Fig. 1.** The 3 Visualizations Created: Segmented Bar Graph (top), Ordered Weights (middle) and Combined Interactions (bottom). (Color figure onlne)

## 3   Design of the Experiment

The experiment was operationalized as an on-line questionnaire. We invited instructors (professors, teachers and tutors) to evaluate the visualizations, answering some questions to check if they understood the information displayed. We also asked them their perceptions on the visualizations, considering the: (1) perceived utility - PU[3]; (2) perceived ease of use - PEU[4]; (3) attitude towards use - ATU[5]; (4) intention to use - IU[6]; (5) perception about the aesthetics - AES[7]; (6) perception about the color scheme used (RAG Colours) - RC[8]; (7)

---

[3] If the participants considered the visualizations would be useful for helping them with their professional activities.

[4] If the participants considered the visualizations easy to use.

[5] If participants showed a positive attitude regarding the use of the visualizations.

[6] If participants would use the visualizations if they were available for them in their workplace.

[7] If the visualizations were beautiful and attractive.

[8] If the colors (red, yellow and green) helped them understand the results in the visualization.

perception about the terms used (inadequate, insufficient, adequate) to classify students' results - TU[9], all following a Likert scale from 0 to $6^{10}$.

## 4    Results and Discussion

The questionnaire was available for one month and we had 116 valid records. First, we evaluated the answers about the visualizations. We called the metric Understandability and the results showed high values for all visualizations, indicating teachers understood the information they provided. After that, we compared the visualizations among themselves, testing for statistically significant differences regarding the understandability (Table 1).

Table 1. Comparison between visualizations.

| VIZ | WILCOXON TEST | BONFERRONI | BEST |
|---|---|---|---|
| Viz1 vs. Viz2 | 0.0001185024 | 0.0007110142* | Viz1 |
| Viz1 vs. Viz3 | 7.216746e−06 | 4.330048e−05* | Viz1 |
| Viz2 vs. Viz3 | 0.01171951 | 0.07031707 | No difference |

As displayed in Table 1 Viz1 provided greater understandability to teachers. The order was: Viz1 > Viz2 = Viz3. One explanation is that Viz1 is resembles a bar graph, which is a traditional kind of graph so it was more familiar to the participants.

The median result of the participants' perceptions, for all metrics, was around 4, meaning the participants "slightly agree" that the visualizations were easy to use (ease of use), interesting (attitude towards use), they would use them if they were available (intention to use), beautiful/attractive (aesthetics) and the color scheme was appropriate (color scheme used). Regarding the perceived utility, participants "neither agree nor disagree" the visualizations would increase their productivity. Regarding the vocabulary, the participants "neither agree nor disagree" the vocabulary was appropriate (vocabulary used), signaling a need for improve these last two metrics.

## 5    Conclusion

We created 3 visualizations to help teachers understand the output from data analysis techniques, using the RAG Colors technique to group learners according to their class of results. We asked highly competent and experienced instructors to evaluate them. The participants, overall, perceived the visualizations as easy to use, interesting, attractive and that they would use it, if they were available. For the perceived utility and the vocabulary used, the results show that these metrics need improvement.

---

[9] If the terms used, helped them understand the results in the visualization.

[10] 0 = I Strongly Disagree; 3 = I Neither Agree nor Disagree; 6 = I Strongly Agree.

The visualizations were effective (about 84% of all answers were correct) in making teachers understand the information extracted from the outputs of educational data mining and analytics (understandability), suggesting the visualizations are an objective and simple way for teachers to interpret what is going on with their groups. This is important to assist teachers' daily decision-making tasks, making it evidence-based.

Some topics that need further research: (1) how can we improve the visualizations' utility? (2) what kind of vocabulary is appropriate to be used? (3) are there algorithms that are easier to visualize than others? (4) what are the other algorithms we can visualize? (5) how can we visualize different information from a single educational data mining/analytics' output?

**Acknowledgments.** We would like to acknowledge CNPQ (Brazilian National Council for Scientific and Technological Development) and PROCAD (Brazilian National Programme for Academic Cooperation) for supporting this work.

# References

1. Alexander, M., Yuk, M., Diamond, S.: Data Visualization for Dummies. Wiley, Chichester (2014)
2. Allen, I., Seaman, J., Poulin, R., Straut, T.: Online Report Card: Tracking Online Education in the United States. Babson Survey Research Group and Quahog Research Group, LLC, Babson Park, MA (2016)
3. Bienkowski, M., Feng, M., Means, B.: Enhancing teaching and learning through educational data mining and learning analytics: An issue brief, pp. 1–57. US Department of Education, Office of Educational Technology pp (2012)
4. Bittencourt, I.I., Costa, E., Silva, M., Soares, E.: A computational model for developing semantic web-based educational systems. Knowl. Based Syst. **22**(4), 302–315 (2009)
5. Cohen, W.W.: Fast effective rule induction. In: Proceedings of the Twelfth International Conference on Machine Learning, pp. 115–123 (1995)
6. de Educação à Distância, A.B.: Censo ead br (2015). Relatório Analítico da Aprendizagem a Distância no Brasil (2016)
7. Kowalski, T., Lasley, T.J.: Handbook of Data-Based Decision Making in Education. Routledge, New York (2010)
8. Liyanagunawardena, T.R., Parslow, P., Williams, S.: Dropout: Mooc participants' perspective (2014)
9. Mandinach, E.B., Honey, M., Light, D.: A theoretical framework for data-driven decision making. In: Annual Meeting of the American Educational Research Association, San Francisco, CA (2006)
10. Mandinach, E.B., Jackson, S.S.: Transforming Teaching and Learning Through Data-Driven Decision Making. Corwin Press, Thousand Oaks (2012)
11. Onah, D.F., Sinclair, J., Boyatt, R.: Dropout rates of massive open online courses: behavioural patterns. EDULEARN14 Proceedings, pp. 5825–5834 (2014)
12. Romero, C., Ventura, S.: Educational data science in massive open online courses. Data Mining and Knowledge Discovery, Wiley Interdisciplinary Reviews (2016)

13. Schildkamp, K., Lai, M.K., Earl, L.: Data-based decision making in education: Challenges and opportunities, vol. 17. Springer Science & Business Media (2012)
14. Sumner, M., Frank, E., Hall, M.: Speeding up logistic model tree induction. In: Jorge, A.M., Torgo, L., Brazdil, P., Camacho, R., Gama, J. (eds.) PKDD 2005. LNCS (LNAI), vol. 3721, pp. 675–683. Springer, Heidelberg (2005). https://doi.org/10.1007/11564126_72

# A System-General Model for the Detection of Gaming the System Behavior in CTAT and LearnSphere

Luc Paquette[1]([⊠]), Ryan S. Baker[2], and Michal Moskal[3]

[1] University of Illinois at Urbana-Champaign, Champaign, IL, USA
lpaq@illinois.edu
[2] University of Pennsylvania, Philadelphia, PA, USA
rybaker@upenn.edu
[3] University of Warsaw, Warsaw, Poland
michal.moskal@10clouds.com

**Abstract.** In this paper, we present the CTAT (Cognitive Tutor Authoring Tools) implementation of a system-general model for the detection of students who "game the system", a behavior in which students misuse intelligent tutors or other online learning environments in order to complete problems or otherwise advance without learning. We discuss how this publicly available detector can be used for both live detection of gaming behavior while students are using CTAT tutors and for retroactive application of the detector to historical data within LearnSphere. The goal of making this detector publicly available is to foster new research about how to best intervene when students game the system and to increase the large scale adoption of such detectors in the classroom.

**Keywords:** Gaming the system · System-general models
Cognitive tutor authoring tool · LearnSphere · Student model

## 1 Introduction

Research in AIED technology has sometimes been criticized for being too siloed [1]. Although high-quality research is produced by a wide variety of research teams, there has been limited effort to bridge the gap between individual projects. For example, even though multiple research teams [2–6] have contributed to the topic of building models able to detect students who "game the system" [2], a behavior in which students misuse intelligent tutors or other online learning environments in order to complete problems or otherwise advance without learning, such detectors have not been used at scale to drive pedagogical interventions or to inform teachers in the classroom. This is in part due to the difficulty of building detectors that are general enough to work in multiple tutoring contexts, requiring researchers interested in studying pedagogical interventions related to gaming to develop their own detector or validate that an existing detector is appropriate for their system, both of which require considerable resources.

In this paper, we present the Cognitive Tutor Authoring Tool (CTAT) [7] implementation of a system-general model that detects students who game the system.

© Springer International Publishing AG, part of Springer Nature 2018
C. Penstein Rosé et al. (Eds.): AIED 2018, LNAI 10948, pp. 257–260, 2018.
https://doi.org/10.1007/978-3-319-93846-2_47

By developing this general model and making it available within a widely-used tutor development framework, we aim to reduce the amount of effort required to conduct research involving gaming the system behavior and to increase adoption of gaming detectors by intelligent tutor developers, whether for driving automatic interventions or for reporting gaming behavior to teachers through dashboards.

## 2 The Model

The model we implemented was developed using data collected from Cognitive Tutor Algebra [8] where 10,397 sequences of student actions were classified as either containing or gaming behavior or not. We used a rigorous knowledge engineering process, in which we observed and interviewed the expert who classified each of those sequences, to build a model that replicated her decision process [5]. The resulting model identified 13 patterns of actions that are associated with gaming behavior, such as quick repetitions of the same answer in different text fields and sequences of incorrect answers that are similar to each other. In our CTAT implementation, every sequence of five actions (repeated help requests are counted as only one action) is compared to those 13 patterns. Students are identified as gaming the system if the actions within the sequence match any of the 13 patterns. Otherwise the student is identified as not gaming.

This model was selected due to its good generalization across different tutoring contexts. Although the model was developed for Cognitive Tutor Algebra, it was also validated in two new contexts [9]: the scatterplot lesson of Cognitive Tutor Middle School and ASSISTments [10]. This previous study showed how the model, developed using knowledge engineering approaches, outperformed a second model, developed using a combination of machine learning and knowledge engineering, in those new contexts. The knowledge-engineered model obtained a level of performance in new systems comparable with past detectors successfully used for intervention, making it a good candidate to be implemented in CTAT.

## 3 Using the Model

The detector is contained in one JavaScript file ("gaming.js") that can be downloaded from CTAT's detector library[1]. Once downloaded, the file can be integrated into a CTAT tutor to automatically detect gaming behaviors during runtime or can be loaded in the widely-used LearnSphere[2] data platform (formerly the PSLC DataShop [11]) to retroactively apply the detector to historical data from a range of learning systems.

In CTAT, the detector can be applied to any tutor created using CTAT's HTML interface. Using the detector simply requires the tutor's author to include a reference to the detector's JavaScript file in "transaction_mailer_users.js" (see CTAT's documentation for detailed instruction). Once the tutor is included in the tutor, it will

---

[1] The CTAT detector library is accessible from the CTAT detector wiki: https://github.com/d19fe8/CTAT-detector-plugins/wiki/CTAT-Detector-Library.

[2] http://learnsphere.org/.

automatically generate gaming/not gaming diagnosis every five actions (displayed in CTAT's "Variable Viewer" window).

Retroactively applying the detector to historical data using LearnSphere requires the user to create a workflow in the Tigris authoring tool. In this workflow (Fig. 1), the user can load any tab delimited text file containing data formatted according to the DataShop [11] standard as well as load the "gaming.js" file containing the gaming detector. Those two files are then used as inputs for the "Apply Detector" operator which will apply the detector to the dataset. The output of this workflow is a file containing all of the model's diagnoses. It is important to note that, although it is possible to apply the detector to any dataset stored using the DataShop standard, the detectors have not yet been validated on systems beyond Cognitive Tutors, CTAT Tutors, and ASSISTments.

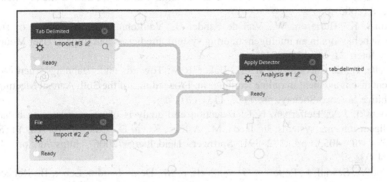

**Fig. 1.** Tigris workflow used to apply the gaming detector to historical data.

## 4 Limitations and Future Work

By making our gaming the system detector publicly available and easy to integrate into CTAT tutors, we hope to contribute to scaling up the usage of automated detectors of student behavior in research, for example by studying the impact of different pedagogical strategies, and hope to support the broader deployment of those detectors in classroom interventions.

Making our detector publicly available is only the first step, further work will need to be done to develop tools that can take advantage of the model in concrete ways. For example, we are currently evaluating the feasibility of integrating our detector to a teacher dashboard [12] that could support teachers by producing live reports of gaming behaviors in their classroom. In addition, we encourage researchers interested in the usage of models of student behaviors in adaptive learning to develop, evaluate and share their own tools and pedagogical strategies.

Finally, although our detector has been validated across multiple tutors with promising results, we intend to conduct further work to iteratively improve the detector and evaluate its applicability to additional systems. This will allow the detector to be used in an increasing number of contexts while simultaneously improving our understanding of gaming the system behaviors. We see the inclusion of this detector in CTAT as an important step towards achieving this goal.

**Acknowledgement.** We would like to thank Kenneth Holstein, Cindy Tipper, Peter Schalden-brand and Vincent Aleven for their support during the implementation of our detector in the CTAT and LearnSphere platforms.

# References

1. Luckin, R., Holmes, W., Griffiths, M., Forcier, L.B.: Intelligence Unleashed: An Argument for AI in Education (2016)
2. Baker, R.S.J., Corbett, A.T., Roll, I., Koedinger, K.R.: Developing a generalizable detector of when students game the system. User Model. User Adap. Inter. **18**, 287–314 (2008)
3. Beal, C.R., Qu, L., Lee, H.: Classifying learner engagement through integration of multiple data sources. In: Proceedings of the 21st National Conference on Artificial Intelligence, pp. 2–8 (2006)
4. Muldner, K., Burleson, W., Van de Sande, B., VanLehn, K.: An analysis of students' gaming behaviors in an intelligent tutoring system: predictors and impact. User Model. User Adap. Inter. **21**, 99–135 (2011)
5. Paquette, L., de Carvalho, A.M.J.B., Baker, R.S.: Towards understanding expert coding of student disengagement in online learning. In: Proceedings of the 36th Annual Meeting of the Cognitive Science Society, pp. 1126–1131 (2014)
6. Walonoski, J.A., Heffernan, N.T.: Detection and analysis of off-task gaming behavior in intelligent tutoring systems. In: Ikeda, M., Ashley, Kevin D., Chan, T.-W. (eds.) ITS 2006. LNCS, vol. 4053, pp. 382–391. Springer, Heidelberg (2006). https://doi.org/10.1007/11774303_38
7. Aleven, V., Sewall, J., Popescu, O., van Velsen, M., Demi, Sandra, Leber, B.: Reflecting on twelve years of its authoring tools research with CTAT. In: Design Recommendation for Adaptive Intelligent Tutoring Systems, vol. 3, pp. 263–283 (2015)
8. Koedinger, K.R., Corbett, A.T.: Cognitive tutors: technology bringing learning sciences to the classroom. In R.K. Sawyer (ed.) The Cambridge Handbook of the Learning Sciences, pp. 61–77 (2006)
9. Paquette, L., Baker, R.S., de Carvalho, A.M.J.B., Ocumpaugh, J.: Cross-system transfer of machine learned and knowledge engineered models of gaming the system. In: Proceedings of the 23rd Conference on User Modelling, Adaptation and Personalization, pp. 183–194 (2015)
10. Razzaq, L., et al.: The assistment project: blending assessment and assisting. In: Proceedings of the 12th Annual Conference on Artificial Intelligence in Education, pp. 555–562 (2005)
11. Koedinger, K.R., Baker, R.S.J., Cunningham, K., Skogsholm, A., Leber, B., Stamper, J.: A data repository for the EDM community: the PSLC dataShop. In: Romero, C., Ventura, S., Pechenizkiy, M., Baker, R.S.J. (eds.) Handbook of Educational Data Mining, pp. 43–56 (2010)
12. Holstein, K., McLaren, B.M., Aleven, V.: Intelligent tutors as teachers' aides: exploring needs for real-time analytics in blended classrooms. In: Proceedings of the 7th International Learning Analytics and Knowledge Conference, pp. 257–266 (2017)

# Automatic Generation of Multiple-Choice Fill-in-the-Blank Question Using Document Embedding

Junghyuk Park, Hyunsoo Cho[✉], and Sang-goo Lee

Seoul National University, Seoul, Korea
{jhpark123,johyunsoo,sglee}@europa.snu.ac.kr
http://ids.snu.ac.kr

**Abstract.** Automatic question generation is a challenging task [11] that aims to generate questions from plain texts, and has been widely and actively researched in various fields. Generated questions can be used for educational purposes, largely for mid-terms, final exams, and also for pop quizzes. In this paper, we propose a novel similarity-based multiple choice question generation model without any pre-knowledge or additional dataset.

## 1 Introduction

One of the main applications of artificial intelligence in education is the generation of study questions to assist students practice and study course materials. Specifically, multiple-choice fill-in-the-blank questions are used widely in educational assessments, starting from small quizzes to final exams. But manually creating such questions can be a tedious process, and often requires intense amount of human labor. There have been attempts to automize the process of question creation which use domain-specific knowledge [1,4,8], or a large corpus with additional outside knowledge [3,13], but they still involve lots of time and effort. This paper aims to build an automatic multiple-choice fill-in-the-blank question generation model that doesn't require any pre-knowledge or additional dataset, to provide a cost-effective and efficient approach to the problem.

We use a simple text embedding model to project documents, sentences, and word vectors onto the same semantic space, which we hypothesize will enable us to discover sentences and words of significance. These sentences and words are ranked based on similarity, and are turned into a question sentence and a corresponding blank space to fill, respectively.

## 2 Related Work

### 2.1 Question Generation

Traditional question generation studies largely rely on hand-engineered and domain-dependent rules. [8] generated *wh*-question via parsing to extract keywords and WordNet [7] to generate distractors. [4] used parse tree to generate

© Springer International Publishing AG, part of Springer Nature 2018
C. Penstein Rosé et al. (Eds.): AIED 2018, LNAI 10948, pp. 261–265, 2018.
https://doi.org/10.1007/978-3-319-93846-2_48

declarative sentence and hand-engineered features to rank questions. [1] defined features on what good sentences, blanks, and distractors are, and used those features to score questions, which is used as a baseline model in this paper.

Recent question generation take advantage of neural network. [3, 13] proposed encoder-decoder model with attention mechanism which is capable of generating diverse questions. However, those models are trained through SQuAD dataset which means that they need extra supervised-dataset to train.

## 3　Model

Fill-in-the-blank question generation focuses on finding *important* sentences from a document, and *important* keywords from the sentences. We measure this *importance* of a sentence or a word by their similarity in contents to the document they belong to. This is based on the intuition that these sentences and keywords will best express the topic or the essence of a given document.

In this section, we propose an embedding model, which projects documents, sentences, and words onto the same dimensional vector space. Then we are able to rank the similarities of the sentence and word embeddings to the document.

### 3.1　Document Embedding Model

Our embedding model is based on the idea of the paragraph vector model of [5].[1]

While the existing paragraph vector model learns word and paragraph embeddings simultaneously, our newly proposed model is capable of jointly learn the embeddings of the word, paragraph, as well as the entire document (Fig. 1).

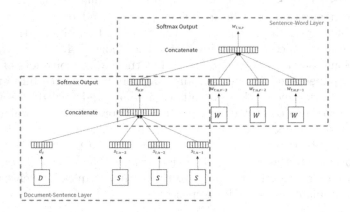

**Fig. 1.** Proposing model

Our embedding model can roughly be divided into Sentence-Word Layer and Document-Sentence Layer. To be specific, in the Sentence-Word Layer, word

---

[1] Due to page limitation, we refer readers to [5] for further detail.

embedding and sentence embedding are learned simultaneously by predicting the next coming word. Likewise, in Document-Sentence Layer, we treat the sentence as a *word* that constitutes a document so that the document embedding can be learned from the sentence embedding by predicting the next sentence. This model enables *similarity-based question generation* method described below.

## 3.2  Similarity-Based Question Generation

Using the proposed text embedding model above, we can now project words, sentences, and the document to the same $n$-dimensional vector space. Then by measuring the cosine similarities of the sentences and the words with the document vector, we can rank them in order by semantic similarity to the document. The details are as follows.

**Algorithm 1.** Similarity-Based MC GF Question Generation

```
Input:   Document List D, Embedding List E, Vocabulary V
             Constant k_ds, k_sg, k_gt
Output:  Multiple-Choice fill-in-the-blank Question List Q
    Q ←[ ]
    for d in D
        for s in sent_tokenize(d)
            Calculate dist(E[d], E[s])
        S_d  ← top-k_ds closest sentences to the document d
        for s in S_d
            for g in word_tokenize(s)
                Calculate dist(E[s], E[g])
            G_s  ← top-k_sg closest blanks to the sentence s
            for g in G_s
                for t in V
                    Calculate dist(E[g], E[t])
                T_g  ← top-k_gt closest sentences to the blank g
                q  ← (s, g, T_g)
                Q.append(q)
    return Q
```

We decided that blanks must be nouns and cardinals due to the manual analysis that important words are almost always nouns or numbers. Also to avoid the selection of synonyms of the answer, we use POS tags, lexicographer file and synset of WordNet in distractor selection step.

## 4  Result and Discussion

In the experiment, we used Database System Concepts 6th ed. [12] and Campbell Biology 9th ed [10]. We trained the data set using the embedding model presented

... For example, in the *student* and *takes* relations Figures 4.1 and 4.2, note that student Snow, with ID 70557, has not taken any courses. Snow appears in *student*, but Snow's ID number does not appear in the *ID* column of *takes*. Thus, Snow does not appear in the result of the natural join. More generally, some tuples in either or both of the relations being joined may be "lost" in this way. *The outer join operation works in a manner similar to the join operations we have already studied, but preserve those tuples that would be lost in a join, by creating tuples in the result containing null values.* For example, to ensure that the student named Snow from our earlier example appears in the result, a tuple could be added to the join result with all attributes from the *student* relation set to the corresponding values for the student Snow, and all the remaining attributes which come from the *takes* relation, namely *course_id, sec_id, semester*, and *year*, set to *null*. Thus the tuple for the student Snow is preserved in the result of the outer join. ...

The _____ join operation works in a manner similar to the join operations we have already studied, but preserve those tuples that would be lost in a join, by creating tuples in the result containing null values.

1) inner               2) outer               3) right               4) left

**Fig. 2.** Raw paragraph and generated question

in this paper, initializing word embedding previously learned through GloVe [9]. Generated sample question from our model are shown in Fig. 2.

We evaluated our model using [1] as our baseline because no external resource was used in that study. And it is a study that generates questions using textbook like our work.

To compare performance between models, 10 university students evaluated sentence and blank of each question as good(1) or bad(0) and for distractor, students are asked to answer the number of good distractors as it was done in [1]. Among massive amount of generated questions, 50 questions are randomly selected and evaluated from top-500 highest similarity questions (Table 1).

**Table 1.** Experimental result (Scores are averages of evaluators)

| Method | Sentence | Blank | Distractor |
|---|---|---|---|
| Database_baseline | 0.5 | 0.504 | 1.472 |
| Database_proposed | 0.588 | 0.62 | 1.672 |
| Biology_baseline | 0.708 | 0.764 | 1.788 |
| Biology_proposed | 0.748 | 0.8 | 2.088 |

The results show that our similarity-based method was particularly effective in selecting distractors. This is because the semantics of words play a crucial role in the selection of distractors. The questions generated by our model made more sense in general, and showed much more diversity in selection of distractors. The complete comparison results are on https://github.com/sporenet/question-generation.

# References

1. Agarwal, M., Mannem, P.: Automatic gap-fill question generation from text books. In: Proceedings of the 6th Workshop on Innovative Use of NLP for Building Educational Applications, pp. 56–64. Association for Computational Linguistics (2011)
2. Bengio, Y., Ducharme, R., Vincent, P., Jauvin, C.: A neural probabilistic language model. J. Mach. Learn. Res. **3**, 1137–1155 (2003)
3. Du, X., Cardie, C.: Identifying where to focus in reading comprehension for neural question generation. In: Proceedings of the 2017 Conference on Empirical Methods in Natural Language Processing, pp. 2067–2073 (2017)
4. Heilman, M., Smith, N.A.: Question generation via overgenerating transformations and ranking. Technical report, CARNEGIE-MELLON UNIV PITTSBURGH PA LANGUAGE TECHNOLOGIES INST (2009)
5. Le, Q., Mikolov, T.: Distributed representations of sentences and documents. In: Proceedings of the 31st International Conference on Machine Learning (ICML 2014), pp. 1188–1196 (2014)
6. Mikolov, T., Chen, K., Corrado, G., Dean, J.: Efficient estimation of word representations in vector space. arXiv preprint arXiv:1301.3781 (2013)
7. George, A.: Miller. Wordnet: a lexical database for english. Commun. ACM **38**(11), 39–41 (1995)
8. Mitkov, R., Ha, L.A.: Computer-aided generation of multiple-choice tests. In Proceedings of the HLT-NAACL 03 Workshop on Building Educational Applications Using Natural Language Processing, vol. 2, pp. 17–22. Association for Computational Linguistics (2003)
9. Pennington, J., Socher, R., Manning, C.: Glove: global vectors for word representation. In: Proceedings of the 2014 Conference on Empirical Methods in Natural Language Processing (EMNLP), pp. 1532–1543 (2014)
10. Reece, J.B., Urry, L.A., Cain, M.L., Wasserman, S.A., Minorsky, P.V., Jackson, R., et al.: Campbell Biology. Pearson, Boston (2014)
11. Rus, V., Wyse, B., Piwek, P., Lintean, M., Stoyanchev, S., Moldovan, C.: The first question generation shared task evaluation challenge. In: Proceedings of the 6th International Natural Language Generation Conference, pp. 251–257. Association for Computational Linguistics (2010)
12. Silberschatz, A., Korth, H.F., Sudarshan, S., et al.: Database system concepts, vol. 4. McGraw-Hill, New York (1997)
13. Zhou, Q., Yang, N., Wei, F., Tan, C., Bao, H., Zhou, M.: Neural question generation from text: a preliminary study. arXiv preprint arXiv:1704.01792 (2017)

# Prediction of Interpersonal Help-Seeking Behavior from Log Files in an In-Service Education Distance Course

Bruno Elias Penteado[1(✉)], Seiji Isotani[1], Paula M. Paiva[2],
Marina Morettin-Zupelari[2], and Deborah Viviane Ferrari[2]

[1] Institute of Mathematical and Computer Sciences, University of São Paulo,
São Carlos, SP 13566-900, Brazil
brunopenteado@usp.br
[2] Speech Language Pathology and Audiology Department - Bauru Dental
School, University of São Paulo, Bauru, Bauru, SP 17012-901, Brazil

**Abstract.** We propose a machine learning approach to automate the estimation of the interpersonal help-seeking level of students in an online course, based on their behavior in an LMS platform. We selected behavioral and performance features from the LMS logs, using forum and wiki variables in the context of a professional development course in audiology rehabilitation (N = 93). Then, we applied different state-of-the-art regression algorithms to predict their responses, using student-level cross-validation in the training set and evaluated the resulting models in a separate test set. As result, we had approximately an error of one point with our model, on average. We discuss some deviant cases and how this information can be used to inform tutors in online courses.

**Keywords:** Interpersonal help-seeking · Regression · Educational data mining
Learning strategies

## 1 Introduction

A manner to harness the student participation more efficiently is by exploring students' *learning strategies* (Warr and Allan 1998; Pantoja 2004), especially in professional education, where participants are more likely to be older, spend less time in learning and arguably have different motivations and anxieties in addition to the emphasis in procedural knowledge, more than in formal education. The learning strategies are mediators of learning outcomes, developed by individuals during their learning activities to control their own psychological learning processes, such as attention, acquisition, memorization, and transference (Zerbini and Abbad 2008). No specific strategy is the best, but they can be suited according to the context of the instructional activity. The adequacy of a strategy is dependent on the context of the instructional practice, such as the nature and the complexity of the activity. Warr and Allan (1998) and Warr and Downing (2000) developed the theoretical model, in three main axes: cognitive strategies, interpersonal help-seeking; self-regulatory strategies.

C. Penstein Rosé et al. (Eds.): AIED 2018, LNAI 10948, pp. 266–270, 2018.
https://doi.org/10.1007/978-3-319-93846-2_49

This work aims to infer the degree of interpersonal help-seeking (the procedures to obtain assistance from other people) of individual students in an online course based on their behavior, by building automatic detectors of this construct using machine learning techniques and studying its fitness to the task.

Help-seeking behavior in digital learning environments has been a promising area of research, particularly in the ITS field. Some of the earlier works sought to model the help-seeking behavior according the interaction of the student with the tutoring system and to develop adaptive tutorial interventions to help students improve these skills, such as suggesting the student to ask for help when he needs to, but did not make at that point (Aleven et al. 2006; Roll et al. 2007; Ogan et al. 2015). Other studies on that topic include help abuse (gaming the system) (Baker et al. 2004) and self-explanation about the help (Baker et al. 2011). However, they concentrate on how the student interacts with the ITS, modeled according to interaction within the software. In this work, we model a slightly different construct, the interpersonal aspect of help-seeking.

## 2 Methodology

The data was gathered from a specialization distance course in Audiology – "Auditory rehabilitation in children", developed by Speech-Language Pathology and Audiology Department (University of São Paulo in Bauru); Samaritano Association and Brazilian Ministry of Health, composed by professionals working across Brazilian territory. It lasted 18 months with a course load of 400 h. All communication and interactions between students and staff were asynchronous. In this work, the responses of 93 students (95,7% women, avg. age: 36.3, sd: 7.7) who successfully completed the course were considered. The dataset is composed of the log records registered by Moodle. It is important to note that one of the teaching strategies adopted by the course administrators was the incentive given by instructors so that student could share with their colleagues the experiences and doubts about the subject matter and their professional practice. The pedagogical model adopted sought to build collaborative activities so that students could share their experiences and reflect upon their practice, seeking for help to build up their ideas.

The variable to be predicted are the responses given by the students to the *Learning Strategy Scale* (LSS) (Zerbini and Abbad 2008). The instrument consists of 28 Likert items divided into 7 factors (0 to 10, ranging from 'Never' to 'Always'). In this work, we chose the 'interpersonal help-seeking' factor, measured by 6 items (Cronbach's alpha = 0.87), and it was applied by the end of the course.

*Features.* Course specialists chose variables from 3 tools inside the course: the wiki and the forum, with 2 instances – a graded forum, where the student had to construct responses on a generating question posed by the instructors, interacting with colleagues; and the 'Stand-by Support' (SbS), where the students could ask questions related to the subject matter to the instructors. The wiki consisted of a group work in which every student in the group could collaborate in a web page and the result was submitted for grading. We selected variables to triangulate from different perspectives: active (number of posts, length of the posts, time between posts) and passive (views and time spent) interactions, scores (assessing the content of the posts) and demographic (age). These were the selected variables:

- *Forum*: avg. scores, # of posts, avg. post length, avg. time on the tool, # of post visualizations;
- *Stand-by support*: median of days for posting questions, # of posts, avg. post length, avg. time on the tool, # of post visualizations;
- *Wiki*: median of days for editing the wiki page, avg. scores, avg. # of edits, avg. time in the tool, # of page visualizations, avg. # of chars in the edits;
- *Other*: age.

*Model Creation and Evaluation.* To predict the individual scores, we applied different algorithms using the features described in the previous section. We selected state-of-the-art algorithms to build the predictions, using Weka 3.8 as the tool to execute and evaluate the performance of the algorithms. The following algorithms were selected: Linear regression (*M5'* feature selection), Support vector machines with radial basis (SMOReg); Multilayer Perceptron; Random Forest; M5P and M5Rules.

The dependent variable was very imbalanced, with a high right-skewness ($-0.78$). To deal with this issue, we split the data into 67% for training (62 instances) and 33% testing (n = 31), balancing the output. Also, we used an oversampling technique (sampling with replacement), duplicating the values of the lowest quartile in the training set, resulting in 89 instances (skewness = $-0.45$).

To estimate the model parameters and performance, we applied 10-fold student-level cross-validation to the training set and applied the resulting model to the held-out test dataset. The metrics used to evaluate the performance of the algorithms were: mean absolute error (MAE), root mean square error (RMSE) and Pearson correlation.

## 3   Results

The regression analysis considered the self-reported 'interpersonal help-seeking' as the dependent variable in a 0–10 scale and the selected features as the explanatory variables. In this experiment, the SVM for Regression (SMOReg) had the best performance with MAE and RMSE metrics. It presented an average of 1.025 points of error in the instances in the test set. The linear regression presented the best value for the correlation between real and predicted values with r = 0.339. To make interpretation easier, we rely on the linear regression model, since it resulted in good values of the metrics. The resulting model: **0.0057** * ViewsSbS + **0.0019** * AvgLengthMsgSbS + **$-0.0067$** * TimeOnForum + **0.0849** * MedianDaysWikiEdits + **7.3321**

*Deviant Cases.* We analyzed the cases in terms of highest residual errors, with values above 2 points. In total, there were four cases. One of them was related to a very low value for self-report and the other three comes from the top self-report scores. Table 1 summarizes the four cases of interest in comparison with the average for all students.

**Table 1.** Model values for the most deviant cases.

| Instance # | True value | Predicted value | Abs. Diff. | Views SbS | AvgLength MsgSbS | TimeOn Forum | MedianDays WikiEdits |
|---|---|---|---|---|---|---|---|
| 1 | 4.83 | 7.43 | *2.60* | 13 | 103.0 | 50.7 | 2 |
| 24 | 9.17 | 6.71 | *2.46* | 1 | 0 | 119.4 | 2 |
| 28 | 9.67 | 7.50 | *2.17* | 42 | 136.2 | 67.8 | 1.5 |
| 31 | 10.0 | 7.42 | *2.58* | 38 | 135.5 | 82.3 | 2 |
| *Avg.* | | | | *80.6* | *244.3* | *74.8* | *3.8* |

## 4  Discussion

Recent studies have explored how to infer latent constructs, traditionally measured by self-report questionnaires, from user behavior in computer-mediated environments, what is valuable in situations where, e.g., users don't have much time or avoid social undesirable responses. As a contribution of this work, we proposed a prediction model for inferring interpersonal help-seeking using behavioral, performance and demographic data from an online learning environment and tested with machine learning algorithms with a fair accuracy. As the output score was very imbalanced, the over-sampling technique we adopted helped to alleviate the imbalance of the dependent variable. One of the drawbacks of this technique is the increase in the likelihood to overfit training data; however, in our experiment, it generalized well.

Our results indicate that our method can identify patterns that make possible to predict the scores for interpersonal help-seeking construct. The resulting model of the linear regression algorithm depicts which variables were selected to build the model. The 'Stand-by Support' (SbS) forum, where students could interact with the instructors about content-related doubts, presented two significant positive variables: the 'number of views of messages' in these forums and the 'average length of messages that the users posted' in this tool, in the presence of the other selected variables. The wiki variable of 'median days of editing before due date' also showed significance, with a positive relation to the predicted construct. On the other hand, the 'time spent on forum' variable (here, the forum was an graded activity) had a negative relation to the construct, i.e., the more the student interacted in the forum, the lower his interpersonal help-seeking score. The visualization of others' messages may not seem as important to the perception of the respondents as suggested by their self-reported scores. By analyzing the deviant cases, it suggests that some other factors may be present. As with any other online course, there is always the opportunity for students to interact with each other by means other than the learning management system. Even though the students in this work were far apart from each other, they communicated with social digital tools like Facebook and Whatsapp messenger, very popular social tools in Brazil. Another factor that may influence this score is the self-concept since most students self-reported a very high score. For instance, a student may think that his behavior is adequate when, in fact, it lags in various aspects. In a future study, we will build a software detector that, by the end of each module and with the resulting model, can inform the tutors which students present a low level of interpersonal help-seeking - closing the loop of educational technology research.

**Acknowledgments.** The 'Auditory Rehabilitation in Children' course was funded by the Brazilian Ministry of Health - Support Program for Institutional Development of the National Health System (Proadi/SUS - Grant 25000.024953/2015-89). The authors also thanks CNPq (Grant 307887/2017-0), CAPES and FAPESP (Grant15/24507-2) for the funding support.

# References

Aleven, V., McLaren, B., Roll, I., Koedinger, K.: Toward meta-cognitive tutoring: a model of help seeking with a cognitive tutor. Intl. J. Artif. Intell. Educ. **16**(2), 101–128 (2006)

Baker, R.S., Corbett, A.T., Koedinger, K.R.: Detecting student misuse of intelligent tutoring systems. In: Lester, J.C., Vicari, R.M., Paraguaçu, F. (eds.) ITS 2004. LNCS, vol. 3220, pp. 531–540. Springer, Heidelberg (2004). https://doi.org/10.1007/978-3-540-30139-4_50

Baker, R.S.J.d., Gowda, S.M., Corbett, A.T.: Automatically detecting a student's preparation for future learning: help use is key. In: International Conference on Educational Data Mining, pp. 179–188 (2011)

Ogan, A., Walker, E., Baker, R., Rodrigo, M.M.T., Soriano, J.C., Castro, M.J.: Towards understanding how to assess help-seeking behavior across cultures. Int. J. Artif. Intell. Educ. **25**(2), 229–248 (2015)

Pantoja, M.J.: Estratégias de aprendizagem no trabalho e percepções de suporte à aprendizagem contínua - Uma análise multinível. Ph.D. thesis - University of Brasília, Institute of Psychology (2004)

Roll, I., Aleven, V., McLaren, B.M., Koedinger, K.R.: Designing for metacognition—applying cognitive tutor principles to the tutoring of help seeking. Metacognit. Learn. **2**(2), 125–140 (2007)

Warr, P., Allan, C.: Learning strategies and occupational training. Int. Rev. Ind. Org. Psychol. **13**(2), 83–121 (1998)

Warr, P., Downing, J.: Learning strategies, learning anxiety and knowledge acquisition. Br. J. Psychol. **91**(3), 311–333 (2000)

Zerbini, T., Abbad, G.: Estratégias de aprendizagem em curso a distância: validação de uma escala. Psico-USF **13**(2), 177–187 (2008)

# Control of Variables Strategy Across Phases of Inquiry in Virtual Labs

Sarah Perez[✉], Jonathan Massey-Allard, Joss Ives, Deborah Butler,
Doug Bonn, Jeff Bale, and Ido Roll

University of British Columbia, Vancouver V6T1Z4, Canada
{sarah.perez,deborah.butler,ido.roll}@ubc.ca,
{jmassall,joss,bonn,jcbale}@phas.ubc.ca

**Abstract.** Control of Variables Strategy (CVS) is the process of isolating the effect of single variables when conducting scientific inquiry. We assess how CVS can help student achieve different levels of understanding when implemented in different parts of the inquiry process. 148 students worked with minimally-guided inquiry activities using virtual labs on two different physics topics. The virtual labs allowed for exploration, data collection, and graphical analysis. Using student log data, we identified how CVS manifests itself through these phases of students' inquiry process. We found that students using CVS during data collection and plotting was associated with students achieving more qualitative and quantitative models, respectively. This did not hold, however, for more complicated mathematical relationships, emphasizing the importance of mathematical and graphical interpretation skills when doing CVS.

**Keywords:** Inquiry learning · Control variable strategies · Virtual lab

## 1 Introduction

Control of Variables Strategy (CVS) is an important scientific inquiry strategy where the impact of variables is tested one at a time [2]. Using CVS is however a particularly challenging aspect of inquiry learning for students [5] and much work has gone into understanding and developing instructional methods to teach students how to conduct and interpret controlled experiments [2,11,12].

CVS is often studied in the context of data collection [1,11]. We expand on this work by investigating student actions consistent with CVS across the whole investigation phase of the inquiry process [8], which, besides data collection (CVS-collect), also includes exploration (CVS-explore) and graphical analysis (CVS-plot). We do so using virtual labs, an environment apt for studying inquiry learning [4,6,9,10] such as assessing CVS [1,11]. Specifically, we pose the following research questions: (1) what is the relationship between a student's final scientific model and the use of CVS in different parts of their inquiry process? (2) Is the relationship dependent on the mathematical relationship underlying the simulated physics concept?

© Springer International Publishing AG, part of Springer Nature 2018
C. Penstein Rosé et al. (Eds.): AIED 2018, LNAI 10948, pp. 271–275, 2018.
https://doi.org/10.1007/978-3-319-93846-2_50

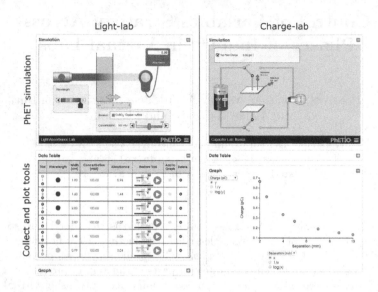

**Fig. 1.** The light-lab (left) and charge-lab (right) are embedded in an interface with two collapsible tools: a table to record data (left) and a graph to plot data (right).

## 2  Methods

148 first to second year students from a Canadian University participated in this study outside of class. There were 96 (65%) women, 50 (34%) men and two (1%) students identified as a non-conforming/binary gender or preferred not to answer. Students used two PhET simulations (https://phet.colorado.edu/) [13]. One on light absorbance of solutions (light-lab) and one on the charge of parallel plate capacitors (charge-lab; Fig. 1). Both simulations have one outcome variable (absorbance or charge), two independent sim variables (hereafter referred to as "sim variables") and similar underlying mathematical relationships: outcome variables are proportional to the sim variables with the exception of plate separation: *Absorbance* $\propto$ *concentration* $*$ *width* and *Charge* $\propto$ *area* $* \frac{1}{separation}$.

The virtual labs include lab tools that enable students to organize and analyze data. These include a data table, a graph, and a digital notepad (not studied here). Students can record observations from the simulation in the table, which they can then choose to add to the graph. The graphing tools also allow students to specify variables for the axes and a scale (linear, inverse, and log).

Students were randomly assigned to do either the light-lab (51.4%) or charge-lab (48.6%) activity first. The inquiry activities consisted of a 5 min pre-activity and a 15 min main activity with the virtual lab. For both, students were asked the following: (1) "How do different factors determine the light absorbance measured by the detector/amount of charge on the plates of the capacitor?" (2) "How can you predict light absorbance/plate charge given the factors that affect it?". The pre-worksheet serves as a measure of the student's incoming model of the phenomena; the main worksheet reflects the final model students built through their inquiry. We use the following scale to encode the highest correct level of model demonstrated by the student in both worksheets:

**(3) Quantitative description** "when width doubles, the absorbance doubles"
**(2) Qualitative description** "when width increases, absorbance increases"
**(1) Identified variable** "width of beaker affects absorbance"
**(0) No mention or all above incorrect** "width doesn't affect absorbance"

Inter-rater reliability was calculated from a random sample of 27% of worksheets coded by two raters. Moderate to strong agreement was found for all variables (Cohen's kappa between 0.75 and 0.86 [3,7]).

Using a cognitive tasks analysis and student log data, we identify key actions at various points of the inquiry process that are consistent with the use of CVS. First, students often inform their inquiry by changing the value of a sim variable and observing the outcome. Since the simulation allows interacting with one variable at a time, this form of qualitative exploration is CVS compliant. We refer to this type of action as "CVS-explore". Students can record their observations as trials in a table. Since the virtual lab allows any observations to be recorded, the recorded trials may or may not form confounded datasets. The "CVS-collect" action is thus defined as the sequential collection of three or more unconfounded trials for a certain sim variable. This strict definition captures deliberate CVS-like collection behavior with higher precision (but possibly low sensitivity). Finally, we define "CVS-plot" as adding three or more unconfounded trials to a graph (recorded sequentially or not) with the varied and outcome variables for the two axes. Since we found that students who do CVS-plot for a variable also do CVS-collect for that variable, and since CVS-collect necessarily implies doing CVS-explore, we denote $CVS\_context$ as a categorical variable with 3 levels (CVS-explore, CVS-collect and CVS-plot) that indicate how deeply in the inquiry process a student consistently used CVS.

We compare students' scientific model and CVS-context level for each variable by predicting their final model scores using a linear regression: $final\_score = \beta_1 \cdot CVS\_context + \beta_2 \cdot pre\_score + \beta_3 \cdot activity + \beta_4 \cdot sim\_variable + \beta_5 \cdot student\_id$ (EQ1), where $pre\_score$ is their pre model score, $activity$ is the order in which that virtual lab was done (first or second), $sim\_variable$ is the variable studied (area, separation, width or concentration), and $student\_id$ controls for individual students ($student\_id$) since our regression data includes scores and level of CVS-context for all variables (i.e. four student-variable pairs per student).

# 3   Results

We begin our analysis by looking at how many students performed actions consistent with CVS. All but one student varied all sim variables (we exclude this student from analysis); therefore all students perform CVS-explore for all sim variables. For a given sim variable, 53.3 to 64.9% of students do CVS-collect and 43.2 to 50% of students do CVS-plot. Overall, comparing pre score to final model scores averaged over all sim variables (pre: $1.22 \pm 0.82$; final: $2.30 \pm 0.70$) shows that students generally improve their models from simply identifying sim variables (score of 1) to gaining a qualitative (score of 2) or quantitative understanding (score of 3) of the relationship between sim variable and outcome with high effect size (Wilcoxon sum of ranks: $Z = -19.28$, $p < 0.001$, effect size $= 1.59$).

In order to evaluate scientific model improvement, we removed student-variable pairs with a pre-score of 3 from the analysis (39 out of 592 pairs removed in total). We run an analysis of variance (ANOVA) on the linear regression (EQ 1). The factor $CVS\_context$ was a significant predictor of final score ($F(2, 154) = 10.49, p < 0.001, \eta^2 = 0.02$) as was the order in which students did the activity ($F(1, 154) = 12.00, p < 0.001, \eta^2 = 0.01$). Specifically the second activity had higher final scores (pre: $1.26 \pm 0.79$; final: $2.40 \pm 0.67$) than the first (pre: $1.19 \pm 0.84$; final: $2.20 \pm 0.72$). Pre score was not a significant predictor of the final model score ($F(1, 154) = 0.11, p = 0.75$).

We conduct a post-hoc analysis to compare the different levels of $CVS\_context$ (applying Bonferroni-Holmes correction). All pair-wise comparisons were significant: CVS-collect vs. CVS-explore: $F(2, 130) = 5.90, p < 0.01, \eta^2 = 0.02$; CVS-plot vs. CVS-collect: $F(2, 93) = 6.58, p = 0.01, \eta^2 = 0.02$; and CVS-plot vs. CVS-explore: $F(2, 154) = 7.66, p < 0.001, \eta^2 = 0.02$. Specifically, final scores for a given sim variable for student doing CVS-plot (pre: $1.31 \pm 0.85$; final: $2.55 \pm 0.64$) were higher than students doing CVS-collect (pre: $1.24 \pm 0.87$; final: $2.16 \pm 0.69$) which were higher than doing CVS-explore (pre: $1.11 \pm 0.74$; final: $2.05 \pm 0.66$).

We run an ANOVA on a similar linear regression model but for each sim variable separately (c.f. EQ 1; with Bonferroni-Holmes correction). We find that CVS-plot remains a predictor of the final model score for all variables except for Separation (Width: $F = (2, 8) = 13.05, p < 0.001$; Concentration: $F = (2, 8) = 12.81, p < 0.001$; Area: $F = (2, 8) = 7.85, p < 0.001$; Separation: $F = (2, 8) = 1.88, p = 0.16$).

## 4    Conclusion

We evaluated students' use of CVS in two virtual labs. The large effect size of the pre to final scientific models demonstrate that the virtual labs allowed the majority of students to engage in a productive inquiry activity. We identified actions in the students' inquiry learning process that are consistent with the use of CVS: CVS-explore, CVS-collect, and CVS-plot. Applying CVS during data collection was indicative of achieving more qualitative scientific models while pursuing CVS all the way through graphical analysis was associated with more students achieving a quantitative model. The association between CVS_plot and model score was strong for all sim variables except one which had an inverse relationship with the outcome variable. This indicates the importance of other skills such as graphical interpretation, linearization techniques and other mathematic skills. It was also found that model scores were higher in the second activity, possibly indicating that students learned and transferred inquiry strategies. Overall, this work suggests that definitions of CVS should address its application along all phases of inquiry in relation to different sense-making opportunities it provides.

# References

1. Bumbacher, E., Salehi, S., Wierzchula, M., Blikstein, P.: Learning environments and inquiry behaviors in science inquiry learning: how their interplay affects the development of conceptual understanding in physics. In: International Educational Data Mining Society, pp. 61–68 (2015)
2. Chen, Z., Klahr, D.: All other things being equal: acquisition and transfer of the control of variables strategy. Child Dev. **70**(5), 1098–1120 (1999)
3. Cohen, J.: A coefficient of agreeement for nominal scales. Educ. Psychol. Meas. **20**(1), 37–46 (1960)
4. De Jong, T.: Technological advances in inquiry learning. Science **312**, 532–533 (2006)
5. De Jong, T., Van Joolingen, W.R.: Scientific discovery learning with computer simulations of conceptual domains. Rev. Educ. Res. **68**(2), 179–201 (1998)
6. Gobert, J.D.: Microworlds. In: Gunstone, R. (ed.) Encyclopedia of Science Education, p. 638. Springer, Dordrecht (2021)
7. McHugh, M.L.: Interrater reliability: the kappa statistic. Biochem. Med. **22**, 276–282 (2012)
8. Pedaste, M., Mäeots, M., Siiman, L.A., De Jong, T., van Riesen, S.A.N., Kamp, E.T., Manoli, C.C., Zacharia, Z.C., Tsourlidaki, E.: Phases of inquiry-based learning: definitions and the inquiry cycle. Educ. Res. Rev. **14**, 47–61 (2015)
9. Perez, S., Massey-Allard, J., Butler, D., Ives, J., Bonn, D., Yee, N., Roll, I.: Identifying productive inquiry in virtual labs using sequence mining. In: André, E., Baker, R., Hu, X., Rodrigo, M.M.T., du Boulay, B. (eds.) AIED 2017. LNCS (LNAI), vol. 10331, pp. 287–298. Springer, Cham (2017). https://doi.org/10.1007/978-3-319-61425-0_24
10. Roll, I., Butler, D., Yee, N., Welsh, A., Perez, S., Briseno, A., Perkins, K., Bonn, D.: Understanding the impact of guiding inquiry: the relationship between directive support, student attributes, and transfer of knowledge, attitudes, and behaviours in inquiry learning. Instr. Sci. **46**, 1–28 (2017)
11. Sao Pedro, M.A., Gobert, J.D., Raziuddin, J.J.: Comparing pedagogical approaches for the acquisition and long-term robustness of the control of variables strategy. J. Learn. Sci., 1024–1031 (2010)
12. Schwichow, M., Croker, S., Zimmerman, C., Höffler, T., Härtig, H.: Teaching the control-of-variables strategy: a meta-analysis. Dev. Rev. **39**, 37–63 (2016)
13. Wieman, C.E., Adams, W.K., Perkins, K.K.: PhET: simulations that enhance learning. Science **322**, 682–683 (2008)

# Female Robots as Role-Models? - The Influence of Robot Gender and Learning Materials on Learning Success

Anne Pfeifer and Birgit Lugrin[(✉)]

Human-Computer Interaction, University of Wuerzburg, Wüerzburg, Germany
birgit.lugrin@uni-wuerzburg.de

**Abstract.** Social robots are likely to become a part of everybody's future. One of their major areas of application lies in the domain of education. Especially for female learners, female teachers can act as role models in what learners might perceive as stereo-typical male learning domains. The present contribution investigates whether the gender of a social robot and learning materials that were either designed stereo-typically male or stereotypically female, influence the learning success of female learners. A user study revealed that female students gained more knowledge when learning with a female robot using stereotypical male materials. We were thus taking a first step towards the possibility that social robots could serve as a tool to counteract social believes and minimize stereotypes.

**Keywords:** Gender · Social robots · Learning · Programming
User study

## 1 Motivation

In today's society life-long learning is gaining increased importance. Adults tend to learn in a self-directed manner, which is why it is important to provide them with adequate learning material that points out the relevance of the content and how it is embedded with learners' goals and experiences [1].

Due to digitization, and with it the increased importance of the internet, the World Wide Web and interconnected devices, education in computer science and (web-)programming are becoming more and more valued skills. It is known that particularly girls are, e.g. when choosing secondary schools, more likely to deepen their education in social areas and languages while boys are more likely to concentrate on science and economical subjects [2]. The belief, that this is not actually based on inherently different interests, but can be traced back to stereotypical thinking, see for example [3], is widely shared by researchers in the field of gender in STEM (science, technology, engineering and mathematics) education. Trying to remedy this issue, it seems sensible to break with these stereotypical beliefs by using female role-models in education. Often girls have

© Springer International Publishing AG, part of Springer Nature 2018
C. Penstein Rosé et al. (Eds.): AIED 2018, LNAI 10948, pp. 276–280, 2018.
https://doi.org/10.1007/978-3-319-93846-2_51

little self-confidence in the area of computer science [4] and even seem to relate their successes to luck and their failures to their lack of ability [5], cited after [4]. In addition, for example, Cheryan et al. [6] have shown that females are less likely to look into Computer Science courses, the more stereotypically male they appear.

To fill the gap of female role-models in computer science, social robots might provide a considerable option. This idea is further supported by findings from Denner et al. [7], who investigated female learners in the domain of programming. Their results show, that particularly females benefit from learning with peers. However to date, it is unclear, whether the supporting function of role-models and peers in the domain of programming can be transferred to social robots in the role of female teaching companions.

## 2    Related Work

Social robots seem to bear great potential as a future trend in learning: They provide an entertaining interface to enhance learning and can have an advantage compared to more traditional e-learning devices, e.g. Leyzberg et al. [8]. Even in comparison to a human teacher, it has been shown that feelings of shame and anxiety can be reduced when using a social robot [9]. While the majority of studies focus on educating children, lately robots are also successfully employed in teaching adults, e.g. [10].

For our endeavour it is crucial that robots are attributed with human-like genders. It has successfully been shown that even rather simple changes in visual features of a social robot activate gender-specific stereotypes. In particular, by varying hair style and lips of a robotic head [11], or varying a robot's body shape in terms of shoulder width and waist-to-hip-ratio [12], stereo-typical male or female looking robots were associated with gender-stereotypical traits and different application areas were ascribed for them.

Regarding robots in gender-specific tasks, findings are somewhat differentiate. For example, Kuchenbrandt et al. [13] investigated user's performances while sorting in a toolbox vs. a sewing basket in cooperation with gender-specific robots (varied by name and voice). Results showed that both the simulated gender of the robot and the gender of the user influenced their task performance and perception of the robot. Partly contrary, Reich-Stiebert [14] did not find evidence that gender-stereotypes do apply to robots that interact in gender-stereotypical tasks (e.g. memorizing fictive words in the domains of cosmetics products or art history vs. architecture or maths). Although the simulated genders were correctly recognized by participants, it did not influence their task performance. Interestingly, the authors found that a mismatch of robot gender and stereotypical task positively influenced participants' perceived interaction with the robot.

## 3    Implementation of the Learning Environment

To investigate whether the gender of a social robot in the role of a learning companion impacts the learning success of female learners in the domain of computer science, we created a learning environment (see Fig. 1). A social robot[1] is connected to a user interface on a screen where the user can answer questions while the robot comments on the questions and the user's answers[2].

**Fig. 1.** Student interacting with the learning environment consisting of a social robot and learning material presented on a screen.

A set of 12 questions and answers was developed in a multiple choice format. The content of the learning material consisted of learning the basics about website development using HTML. To provide a practical relevance, the material guided students through the creation of their own blog. For each question the robot provided a short introduction, e.g. *"It is impossible to give valuable hints to your followers without providing pictures. So let's add a picture to your blog"*. After each answer the robot provided feedback, e.g. *"I'm afraid that's not how it works. In this case you don't need the backslash"*. The robot also displayed non-verbal reactions (e.g. tilting the head or nodding) and emotions (e.g. happiness or sadness) depending on the situation.

Following [13,14], we manipulated the robot's gender by varying its name (Lena vs. Leon) and voice (female and male text-to-speech). The robots' verbal and non-verbal behaviours were identical for both robot versions. In addition, two versions of our learning material were created: a prototypical female version developing a lifestyle blog using a purple colour scheme, and a prototypical male version creating a tech blog using a blue colour scheme.

## 4   User Study

We conducted a user study in a between participants design with 2 independent variables: the gender of the robot (Rf vs. Rm) and the gendered presentation of the learning material (Mf vs. Mm), resulting in four conditions. The **subjective evaluations** of the learning environment were measured with established scales on the robot's believability [16], participants' identification with the robot

---

[1] Reeti Robot: http://www.reeti.fr/index.php/en/.
[2] The robots behaviour was modelled using the Visual Scenemaker tool [15].

[17], and the abilities of the robot as a learning companion [18]. The **objective learning success** was investigated in a pre- post-test design. To measure the learning success a test was developed with 11 score-able points in an open question format, e.g. *Type the headline 'Welcome to my lifestyle blog' with the subheading 'today I want to review candles'.*

After having completed the pre-test online, participants interacted with one version of the learning environment for approximately 15 min. Then participants filled in the questionnaires and conducted the same knowledge test again.

### 4.1   Selected Results

After excluding male participants and outliers, the data of $N = 45$ female students ($M_{age} = 20.51$, $SD = 1.71$) was analysed. In this paper only results on the objective learning success are reported.

Students were able to solve more tasks correctly in the post-test, after interacting with the learning environment, compared to the pre-test, with a mean difference of $M = 2.27$ ($SD = 1.36$). A t-test revealed a significant improvement in knowledge over all conditions ($t(44) = 11.22$, $p = .00^*$, Cohen's $d = 1.02$), highlighting the suitableness of the implemented learning environment.

To test differences between the conditions, a two-way independent ANCOVA was conducted on the change scores with the between-subject factors 'robot gender' and 'material gender', and the covariate 'scores in the pre-test'. Results revealed no significant main effect of the robot's gender on the learning success ($F(1, 40) = 0.00, ns$), and also no significant main effect for presentation of the material on the learning success ($F(1, 40) = 1.07, ns$). However, there was a significant interaction effect for robot gender*material ($F(1, 40) = 6.68, p < .015, \eta^2 > .14$) indicating a difference between the conditions with a strong effect. A one-way independent ANOVA ($F(3, 41) = 4.03, p < .02$) with Bonferroni Post-hoc tests revealed differences between the Rf/Mf and the Rf/Mm conditions ($p < .02$), and between the Rf/Mm and the Rm/Mm conditions ($p < .05$). In both significant comparisons, participants that took part in the condition using a female robot explaining male learning materials gained the most learning success.

## 5   Conclusion

In this paper, we showcased the development of a motivating, interactive learning environment featuring a social robot in the domain of computer science. By varying the robot's gender and gender-specific learning material, we investigated their impact on female learners' learning success. While students in all conditions significantly improved their knowledge, females that learned with a female robot companion and prototypically male learning materials benefited the most. We thus think that gender should be considered when designing learning environments. In the future social robots in the role of teaching companions might be able to help break with societal stereotypes and potentially even pose as role-models for female learners.

# References

1. Smith, M.K.: Malcom Knowles, informal adult education, self-direction and adragogy. The Encyclopedia of Informal Education, pp. 1–8 (2002)
2. Korpershoek, H., Kuyper, H., van der Werf, M.: The role of personality in relation to gender differences in school subject choices in pre-university education. Sex Roles **67**, 630–645 (2012)
3. Gupta, U.G., Houtz, L.E.: High school students perceptions of information technology skills and careers. J. Ind. Technol. **16**(4), 2–8 (2000)
4. Funke, A., Berges, M., Muehling, A., Hubwieser, P.: Gender differences in programming: research results and teachers perception. In: 15th Koli Calling Conference on Computing Education Research. ACM (2015)
5. Margolis, J., Fisher, A.: Unlocking the Clubhouse: Women in Computing. The MIT Press, Cambridge (2002)
6. Cheryan, S., Meltzoff, A.N., Kim, S.: Classroom matter: the design of virtual classrooms influences gender disparities in computer science classes. Comput. Educ. **57**, 1825–1835 (2011)
7. Denner, J., Werner, L., Bean, S., Campe, S.: The girls creating games program: strategies for engaging middle-school girls in information technology. Front. J. Women Stud. **26**(1), 90–98 (2005)
8. Leyzberg, D., Spaulding, S., Toneva, M., Scassellati, B.: The physical presence of a robot tutor increases cognitive learning gains. In: Proceedings of the Annual Meeting of the Cognitive Science Society, vol. 34 (2012)
9. Yang, S.C., Chen, Y.J.: Technology-enhanced language learning: a case study. Comput. Hum. Behav. **23**(1), 860–879 (2007)
10. Schodde, T., Bergmann, K., Kopp, S.: Adaptive robot language tutoring based on bayesian knowledge tracing and predictive decision-making. In: Proceedings of the 2017 ACM/IEEE International Conference on Human-Robot Interaction, pp. 128–136. ACM (2017)
11. Eyssel, F., Hegel, F.: (S)he's got the look: gender stereotyping of robots. J. Appl. Soc. Psychol. **42**(9), 2213–2230 (2012)
12. Bernotat, J., Eyssell, F., Sachse, J.: Shape it - the influence of robot body shape on gender perception in robots. In: International Conference on Social Robotics (ICSR 2017) (2017)
13. Kuchenbrandt, D., Haering, M., Eichberg, J., Eyssel, F., André, E.: Keep an eye on the task! How gender typicality of tasks influence human-robot interactions. Int. J. Soc. Robot. **6**(3), 417–427 (2014)
14. Reich-Stiebert, N., Eyssel, F.: (Ir)relevance of gender? On the influence of gender stereotypes on learning with a robot. In: ACM/IEEE International Conference on Human-Robot Interaction (HRI 2017), pp. 166–176 (2017)
15. Gebhard, P., Mehlmann, G., Kipp, M.: Visual scenemaker–a tool for authoring interactive virtual characters. J. Multimodal User Interfaces **6**(1–2), 3–11 (2012)
16. McCroskey, J.C., Teven, J.J.: Goodwill: a reexamination of the construct and its measurement. Commun. Monogr. **66**, 90–103 (1999)
17. Roth, J., Mazziotta, A.: Adaptation and validation of a german multidimensional and multicomponent measure of social identification. Soc. Psychol. **46**(5), 277–290 (2015)
18. Fasola, J., Mataric, M. (eds.) Using Socially Assistive Human-Robot Interaction to Motivate Physical Exercise for Older Adults, vol. 8 (2008)

# Adolescents' Self-regulation During Job Interviews Through an AI Coaching Environment

Kaśka Porayska-Pomsta[1(⊠)] and Evi Chryssafidou[2]

[1] UCL Knowledge Lab, University College London, London, UK
K.Porayska-Pomsta@ucl.ac.uk
[2] Metanoia Institute, Faculty of Research Strategy and Innovation, London, UK

**Abstract.** The use of Artificial Intelligence in supporting social skills development is an emerging area of interest in education. This paper presents work which evaluated the impact of a situated experience coupled with open learner modelling on 16–18 years old learners' verbal and non-verbal behaviours during job interviews with AI recruiters. The results revealed significantly positive trends on certain aspects of learners' verbal and non-verbal performance and on their self-efficacy.

## 1 Introduction

Despite the importance of social interaction to human quotidian functioning, social skills require substantial training, socio-cultural conditioning and highly developed metacognitive competencies, involving ongoing, targeted self-monitoring and regulation. Emotional self-monitoring and regulation are primary in motivating people to communicate, with emotions also playing a dominant role in learning [1].

Social interaction and emotional self-regulation skills cannot be supported merely through showing or telling people how to feel or behave. Instead, they require access to (ii) repeatable embodied experiences in contexts that credibly approximate real-life scenarios, and (ii) opportunities for situated recall and guided scrutiny of the behaviours enacted first-hand by the learners. Delivering the desired learning experiences is challenged by the time-consuming nature of both the set-ups and the support required in this domain.

Currently, two approaches dominate: (i) *vicarious learning*, popular in special needs interventions, e.g. autism, where learners observe recorded or written social stories, which they then discuss with practitioners; (ii) *role-playing* in mock scenarios based on some well-defined rules, often followed by debriefing with practitioners. The vicarious approach permits detailed analysis of the scenarios studied, but not first-hand experiences. Role-playing offers first-hand experiences, but a detailed analysis may be limited by the quality of the data collected. Socially plausible interactions that are supported by AI agents and open learner modelling (OLM) provide a useful alternative to the methods available

C. Penstein Rosé et al. (Eds.): AIED 2018, LNAI 10948, pp. 281–285, 2018.
https://doi.org/10.1007/978-3-319-93846-2_52

[2]). They also enable a systematic study of social interactions and of learning support needed.

This paper presents a study which evaluated the impact of an intelligent coaching environment, called TARDIS, involving embodied conversational agents and open learner modelling, on 16–18 years old learners' job interview skills and on their self-efficacy.

## 2    TARDIS Coaching Environment

TARDIS is a coaching environment for learners who are at risk of social exclusion through unemployment. It supports learning and exploration of social interaction and self-presentation skills in job interview contexts [3]. It comprises two overarching elements: (i) *a job interview simulator*, for situated rehearsals of learners' job interview skills with AI recruiters (AIRs), (Fig. 1, left) and (ii) an OLM, used to scaffold reflection about learners' behaviours during job interviews (Fig. 1, right).

The simulator comprises an interaction scenarios model, and models of socio-affective and behavioural competencies of the recruiters [3]. All of the models are utilised in an orchestrated data-driven way by the FAtiMA [4] emotion-enhanced planning architecture, which allows to create a variety of emotionally nuanced AIRs [5]. The OLM is based on the pre-existing platform called NOVA [3], which was extended and tailored for use in TARDIS, based on knowledge elicitation with practitioners and annotated interactions of human-human mock job interviews [6]. Learners engage with AIRs verbally, through head mounted ear-/microphone, and through gestures detected by Microsoft Kinect.

**Fig. 1.** Left:TARDIS' AIR Gloria; Right: NOVA-supported OLM.

The data recorded through TARDIS tools include videos of learners interacting with the agents, their specific dialogue moves along the interview timeline, as well as learners' verbal and non-verbal behaviours, e.g. head pose and upper-body gestures, and voice quality including pitch, amplitude, energy and duration of their utterances. In the post-interview debriefing phase, these data sources are synchronised with NOVA's analyses and are displayed to the learners and practitioners through the NOVA tool (Fig. 1, right) to facilitate discussion and reflection. The pedagogical set up of TARDIS was designed through a series of studies with learners and practitioners to complement the existing real-world practices used in youth organisations and job centres, and to leverage in a blended way the strengths of both TARDIS and of human practitioners [7].

# 3    Study Design and Results

TARDIS was evaluated with adolescents aged 16–18 years old (Mean = 17.07 years; SD = 0.6), who were identified as at risk of becoming NEETs (*Not in Education, Employment or Training*) after leaving school. The study used a pre- and post-test design, with (i) human-to-human mock interviews, (ii) self-reports of *self-efficacy, anxiety* and *quality of performance* as the pre and post baseline measures, and (iii) a control intervention using a web-based programme that is representative of the type of practice currently recommended by job centres in the UK.

**Participants.** 28 adolescents were divided into intervention (**IG**) and control groups (**CG**) using a randomised matched pairs approach.

**Procedure.** Mock interview with a human practitioner and a self-report questionnaire were administered to both groups pre- and post-intervention. In both groups the participants viewed their recorded mock interviews and received feedback on three aspects of their performance requiring improvement. In the TARDIS condition, the participants then engaged in three one-hour sessions over three days involving two practice-and-reflection cycles, including (a) learner practicing with AIRs and (b) individualised feedback delivered by a practitioner using the NOVA OLM according to a prescribed procedure. An interaction with an 'understanding' AIR and a 'demanding' AIR provided two test conditions, which were delivered always in the same order. The AIRs behaved in a manner aligned with their respective styles, e.g. involving more or less face-threat.

The control intervention involved two web-based training exercises that were completed over two sessions. The first exercise required the participants to choose the correct answers to a series of video recorded interview questions. Unlike in the TARDIS condition, the participants' responses were automatically scored within the programme, followed by suggestions on possible improvements and a second attempt by the participants to improve their scores. The second exercise involved reading through 100 job interview questions, which were accompanied by examples and tips for possible answers.

**Measures.** Nine measures were used to compare the interventions: (i) *quality of response*: the degree of relevance of learners' responses to interview questions, quality of response structure and the level of content elaboration; (ii) *eye contact*, e.g. rare vs. well-maintained eye contact with the interviewer, (v) *tone of voice*, e.g. monotonous vs. modulated speech, and (vi) *facial expressions*, e.g. indifferent vs. interested. Additionally, learners self-reported on: (vii) *self-efficacy*: their belief that they can do well; (viii) *anxiety*: feelings of apprehension and tension caused by a job interview; and (ix) *quality of performance*.

**Results.** Two independent annotators coded the human-human interviews using a bespoke schema enhanced with training videos exemplifying the specific behaviours and the recommended scores, and inter-rater agreement was calculated. Respective Kappa's were: k = 0.64 for quality of response; k = 0.3 for eye contact; k = 0.3 for tone of voice; k = 0.45 for facial expressions. Note that it is not unusual for post-hoc annotations of voice to yield moderate to low kappa values, indicating that this dimension may be context and culture dependent as well as it may depend on the individual communicative preferences of the annotator. The examples from the affective computing literature (e.g. [8–10]) suggest that the results obtained are not out of line with the existing research with respect to voice-based emotion judgements. Similarly eye-gaze is very hard to judge based only on video data and the discrepancies between the two annotator's judgments may be explained by their differing levels of what is acceptable in terms of frequency of saccades, lowering of the gaze or looking up. The fair agreement points to the need for tightening of the guidelines for how to interpret youngsters' eye-gaze patterns in job interview situations and for additional moderation of the annotations – a task which is presently under way.

An analysis of variance (ANOVA) of interviewees' pre- and post- *quality of response* revealed significant improvements for both *intervention* (**IG**) and *control* (**CG**) groups, with significantly greater improvements for the IG on two of the most challenging questions (in total there were 16 questions asked): *Q1: 'Why are you applying for this post?'* $(F(1, 26) = 5.45, p < .05)$; *Q2: 'Why do you think we should hire you?'* $(F(1, 26) = 6.30, p < .05)$. Both groups also improved at post-test on non-verbal behaviours, with the IG showing significantly greater improvements than the CG on *eye contact* $(F(1, 26) = 14.07, p < .01)$, *tone of voice* $(F(1, 26) = 13.88, p < .01)$, and *facial expression* $(F(1, 26) = 7.5, p < .05)$.

ANOVA was also conducted on the three self-reported measures. The results suggest that both groups improved significantly on all of the three measures at post-test (*self-efficacy:* $F(1, 26) = 20.33, p < .0005$; *anxiety:* $F(1, 26) = 13.40, p < .01$; *quality of performance:* $F(1, 26) = 33.33, p < .0001$). However, no intervention effect was found on any of the measures, suggesting that participants in both IG and CG thought that they benefited equally well from their respective experiences.

## 4   Discussion and Conclusions

Overall, the study results are encouraging, suggesting that although social interaction skills and self-perception improvements can be gained through both types of intervention, the situated practice coupled with OLM-supported feedback from a human may be more effective than the vicarious observation and testing, or tips and advice on impression management. The study highlights the potential role of AIED technologies in supporting social skills acquisition and development of metacognitive competencies in this context, particularly in providing a situated repeatable experience to the learners and opportunities to revisit those experiences post hoc in a manner that is conducive to concrete and systematic reflection and discussion, and ultimately to learning. Future methodological improvements such as a more extensive moderation of the annotations, and an abductive approach will allow to address questions about the impact of the individual aspects of the intervention, e.g. use of TARDIS with and without OLM, on learners' performance.

# References

1. Immordino-Yang, M.H., Damasio, A.: We feel, therefore we learn: the relevance of affective and social neuroscience to education. Mind, Brain Educ. 1(1), 3–10 (2007)
2. Hoque, M.E., Courgeon, M., Martin, J.C., Mutlu, B., Picard, R.W.: Mach: my automated conversation coach. In: Proceedings of the 2013 ACM International Joint Conference on Pervasive and Ubiquitous Computing (UbiComp 2013), pp. 697–706. ACM, New York (2013)
3. Anderson, K., André, E., Baur, T., Bernardini, S., Chollet, M., Chryssafidou, E., Damian, I., Ennis, C., Egges, A., Gebhard, P., Jones, H., Ochs, M., Pelachaud, C., Porayska-Pomsta, K., Rizzo, P., Sabouret, N.: The TARDIS framework: intelligent virtual agents for social coaching in job interviews. In: Reidsma, D., Katayose, H., Nijholt, A. (eds.) ACE 2013. LNCS, vol. 8253, pp. 476–491. Springer, Cham (2013). https://doi.org/10.1007/978-3-319-03161-3_35
4. Dias, J., Paiva, A.: Feeling and reasoning: a computational model for emotional characters. In: Bento, C., Cardoso, A., Dias, G. (eds.) EPIA 2005. LNCS (LNAI), vol. 3808, pp. 127–140. Springer, Heidelberg (2005). https://doi.org/10.1007/11595014_13
5. Chollet, M., Ochs, M., Clavel, C., Pelachaud, C.: Multimodal corpus approach to the design of virtual recruiters. affective computing and intelligent interaction. In: Proceedings of the Affective Computing and Intelligent Interaction. hal-01074861, Genve, Switzerland, ACII, pp. 19–24 (2013)
6. Porayska-Pomsta, K., Rizzo, P., Damian, I., Baur, T., André, E., Sabouret, N., Jones, H., Anderson, K., Chryssafidou, E.: Who's afraid of job interviews? definitely a question for user modelling. In: Dimitrova, V., Kuflik, T., Chin, D., Ricci, F., Dolog, P., Houben, G.-J. (eds.) UMAP 2014. LNCS, vol. 8538, pp. 411–422. Springer, Cham (2014). https://doi.org/10.1007/978-3-319-08786-3_37
7. Porayska-Pomsta, K.: AI as a methodology for supporting educational praxis and teacher metacognition. Int. J. Artif. Intell. Educ. 26(2), 679–700 (2016)
8. Litman, D.J., Forbes-Riley, K.: Predicting student emotions in computer-human tutoring dialogues. In: Proceedings of the 42nd Annual Meeting of the Association For Computational Linguistics. Association for Computational Linguistics, East Stroudsburg, PA (2004)
9. Ang, J., Dhillon, R., Krupski, A., Shriberg, E., Stolcke, A.: Prosody-based automatic detection of annoyance and frustration in human-computer dialog. Paper presented at the International Conference on Spoken Language Processing, Denver, Co (2002)
10. Shafran, I., Riley, M., Mohri, M.: Voice signatures. Paper presented at the Proceedings IEEE Automatic Speech Recognition and Understanding Workshop, Genve, Switzerland (2003)

# Bandit Assignment for Educational Experiments: Benefits to Students Versus Statistical Power

Anna N. Rafferty[1(✉)], Huiji Ying[1], and Joseph Jay Williams[2]

[1] Computer Science Department, Carleton College, Northfield, MN 55057, USA
arafferty@carleton.edu
[2] School of Computing, Department of Information Systems and Analytics,
National University of Singapore, Singapore, Singapore

**Abstract.** Randomized experiments can lead to improvements in educational technologies, but often require many students to experience conditions associated with inferior learning outcomes. Multi-armed bandit (MAB) algorithms can address this by modifying experimental designs to direct more students to more helpful conditions. Using simulations and modeling data from previous educational experiments, we explore the statistical impact of using MABs for experiment design, focusing on the tradeoff between acquiring statistically reliable information and benefits to students. Results suggest that while MAB experiments can improve average benefits for students, at least twice as many participants are needed to attain power of 0.8 and false positives are twice as frequent as expected. Optimistic prior distributions in the MAB algorithm can mitigate the loss in power to some extent, without meaningfully reducing benefits or further increasing false positives.

Randomized controlled experiments are common in educational technologies. These experiments typically assign half of students to one version of technology components and half to another, investigating questions like whether video or text hints will be better. This approach is indifferent to benefits for learners: even if one condition is clearly ineffective, half of students experience it.

Using multi-armed bandit (MAB) algorithms in experimental designs could benefit learners by considering the utility of different versions of content. These algorithms learn a dynamically changing policy for choosing actions, balancing exploiting information already collected with exploring actions to collect additional information. Educational experimentation can be viewed as a MAB problem by treating condition assignments as action choices, with the dependent outcome serving as the reward. For example, in an experiment comparing hint types, the reward (outcome) might be 1 if the attempt after the hint was correct and 0 otherwise. Rather than assigning half of students to each condition, MABs sequentially assign students to conditions based on the rewards for previous students; more can thus be assigned to better conditions. MABs have been used in education to discover what version of a system to give to learners [8,9].

However, using MABs in experiment design creates a tension between benefits for students and information gained about differences between conditions [4,6]. Because MABs assign students to conditions unevenly and change assignment proportions based on previous results, some conditions can be under-sampled and systematic measurement errors occur [4], limiting the inferences that can be drawn from results. We investigate the tradeoff between benefits to students and scientific gain, focusing on a systematic exploration of how MAB assignment impacts inferential statistics, such as the effects on power.

# 1    Statistical Consequences of MAB-Assigned Conditions

We use simulations of two-condition experiments to investigate the statistical consequences of assigning conditions via Thompson sampling, a MAB algorithm with logarithmic bounds on regret growth [1] that performs well in practice [2]. We focus on Thompson sampling as a typical regret-minimizing MAB algorithm, where regret is incurred by choosing actions with lower benefit to students; we expect trends in results to hold for other regret-minimizing MAB algorithms.

## 1.1    Simulation Methods

All simulations were repeated 500 times and across simulations, we varied:

- Method of condition assignment: MAB versus uniformly at random.
- Reward type: Binary (e.g., whether a student completes an activity) versus real-valued rewards (e.g., time to finish a problem). For MAB assignment, real-valued rewards were assumed to be normally distributed, and conjugate priors were used.
- True effect size: Zero and non-zero effect sizes were included. Non-zero effect sizes used thresholds for small, moderate, and large effects (binary: Cohen's $w = 0.1, 0.3, 0.5$; normally-distributed: Cohen's $d = 0.2, 0.5, 0.8$) [3]. Binary reward simulations fixed the average reward across conditions to 0.5, and normally-distributed reward simulations used fixed means and adjusted the variances across effect sizes.
- Number of participants (sample size): Sample sizes were $0.5m$ (lowest power), $m$, $2m$, and $4m$ (highest power) simulated students, where $m$ is the sample size for 0.8 power with equally balanced conditions given false positive rate of 0.05. The same sample sizes were used when effect size was zero.
- Prior distributions (MAB): *Prior between* had a mean between the two conditions.[1] *Prior above* is optimistic about condition effectiveness, with the mean above both conditions. *Prior below* is pessimistic, placing the mean below both conditions.

---

[1] For zero effect size, the mean was equal to the mean of each condition.

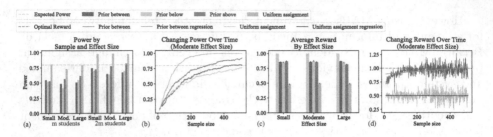

**Fig. 1.** Power and rewards by assignment type for normally-distributed rewards; binary rewards showed a similar pattern. Error bars represent one SE.

## 1.2 Results

*Conditions differ:* When conditions have different benefits for students, the goal is to detect that the difference is reliable and assign more students to the better condition. MAB assignment without an optimistic or pessimistic prior (*prior between*) decreased power from an expected 0.80 to 0.54 for binary rewards and 0.51 for normally-distributed rewards (Fig. 1a). Doubling the sample size raised power to 0.78 and 0.69, but increasing sample size is less effective over time as evidence for the superiority of one condition leads to assigning few students to the alternative (Fig. 1b). Type S errors [5] were rare ($< 0.15\%$), and no difference by assignment type was detected. An optimistic prior (*prior above*) led to higher power and more accurate effect sizes due to more equal sampling across conditions initially that provided better evidence for statistical inferences.

MAB assignment obtained greater rewards than uniform: longer experiments are offset by a larger proportion of students in the better condition. Expected reward per student approached the mean of the more effective condition (Fig. 1d), and was only modestly decreased with more optimistic priors (Fig. 1c).

*Conditions do not differ:* MAB assignment increased false positives from an expected rate of 5% to 9.7% of simulations using MAB assignment. Thus, analyzing data collected via MAB assignment and using typical statistical tests may lead to higher false positives than expected based on setting $\alpha$ (the expected Type I error rate). Type I error rate was slightly higher for normally-distributed rewards than for binary, primarily due to insufficient exploration with small variances.

## 2    MAB-assignment in Educational Experiments

To understand how effects found in simulation might translate to real educational experiments, we analyzed MAB assignment in the context of ten significant/marginal results from twenty-two randomized experiments [7]. These experiments included both binary outcomes (whether a student *completed* an assignment by solving three consecutive problems correctly) and real-valued outcomes (the *problem count* for completion and logarithm of the problem count).

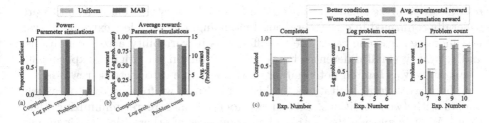

**Fig. 2.** Results based on educational experiments. (a–b) Power (a) and reward or cost per step (b) averaged across the *parameter* simulations. For rewards, higher is better for *completed*; lower is better for the other measures. (c) *Outcome* simulation rewards. "Better" and "worse" are observed experimental rewards for each condition.

*Parameter* simulations used measured means (and variances) from the experiments to generate samples, allowing unlimited students but assuming rewards are accurately modeled by a given distribution. *Outcome* simulations directly sampled a student in the chosen condition from the data set (without replacement) and using their measured outcome for the reward. *Parameter* simulations had sample sizes equal to the original experiments, while *outcome* simulations terminated when no students remained in a chosen condition.

## 2.1    Results

*Parameter* simulations: As shown in Fig. 2a, MAB assignment resulted in small improvements on average reward per student across all outcome measures ($t(9989) = 5.10$, $p < .0001$; median effect size $d = 0.70$). Figure 2b shows that MAB assignment decreased power for the *completed* measure. Counterintuitively, MAB assignment increased power for *problem count* by oversampling highly variable conditions, leading to more confident estimates of effectiveness. Average Type S error rates were small (uniform assignment: 0.3%; MAB: 0.4%). *Outcome* simulations: MAB assignment achieved small improvements on average reward for eight out of ten experiments (Fig. 2c); these rewards were almost as good as the better condition, which is the maximum possible.

For the nine experiments that had a significant effect, 65% of simulations found a significant difference between conditions, which compares favorably to the 0.55 power for uniform assignment in the *parameter* simulations.

## 3    Discussion

Experiments using uniform random assignment can identify more effective educational strategies, but there are ethical concerns about their impact on students. Our simulations demonstrate MABs can assign a greater proportion of students to the better condition, but can also lead to higher Type I error rates than expected and the need for doubled sample sizes to achieve expected power when results are analyzed using traditional inferential statistics. These results were generally confirmed in our experimental modeling, but were less extreme: power was increased in some cases due to differences in variability across conditions, and relatively small differences between conditions in the original experiments meant there was limited potential for MAB assignment to increase rewards.

There are several limitations to this work. First, we focused only on experiments with two conditions. Second, we focused on a regret-minimizing algorithm. While exploring the statistical consequences of other objectives is important future work, our goal is to illustrate how standard MAB algorithms impact conclusions for researchers who may be excited by the potential benefits to students. We hope this will lead to careful consideration of how to achieve *both* research and pedagogical aims, and that our focus on statistical significance shows that MAB assignment can lead to erroneous generalizations in addition to measurement error. MAB assignment is one way to mitigate costs to students as educational experiments become more ubiquitous, but caution must be used when interpreting results and applying standard statistical methods.

# References

1. Agrawal, S., Goyal, N.: Analysis of thompson sampling for the multi-armed bandit problem. In: Mannor, S., Srebro, N., Williamson, R.C. (eds.) Proceedings of the 25th Annual Conference on Learning Theory, vol. 23, pp. 39.1–39.26. PMLR, Edinburgh, Scotland (2012)
2. Chapelle, O., Li, L.: An empirical evaluation of thompson sampling. In: Advances in Neural Information Processing Systems, pp. 2249–2257 (2011)
3. Cohen, J.: Statistical Power Analysis for the Behavioral Sciences, 2nd edn. Routledge, New York (1988)
4. Erraqabi, A., Lazaric, A., Valko, M., Brunskill, E., Liu, Y.E.: Trading off rewards and errors in multi-armed bandits. In: International Conference on Artificial Intelligence and Statistics (2017)
5. Gelman, A., Carlin, J.: Beyond power calculations: assessing type S (sign) and type M (magnitude) errors. Perspect. Psychol. Sci. **9**(6), 641–651 (2014)
6. Liu, Y.E., Mandel, T., Brunskill, E., Popovic, Z.: Trading off scientific knowledge and user learning with multi-armed bandits. In: Educational Data Mining 2014 (2014)
7. Selent, D., Patikorn, T., Heffernan, N.: Assistments dataset from multiple randomized controlled experiments. In: Proceedings of the Third (2016) ACM Conference on Learning@ Scale, pp. 181–184. ACM (2016)
8. Whitehill, J., Seltzer, M.: A crowdsourcing approach to collecting tutorial videos-Toward personalized learning-at-scale. In: Proceedings of the Fourth (2017) ACM Conference on Learning@ Scale, pp. 157–160. ACM (2017)
9. Williams, J.J., Kim, J., Rafferty, A., Maldonado, S., Gajos, K.Z., Lasecki, W.S., Heffernan, N.: Axis: generating explanations at scale with learnersourcing and machine learning. In: Proceedings of the Third (2016) ACM Conference on Learning@ Scale. pp. 379–388. ACM (2016)

# Students' Responses to a Humanlike Approach to Elicit Emotion in an Educational Virtual World

Hedieh Ranjbartabar[1], Deborah Richards[1(✉)], Anupam Makhija[1], and Michael J. Jacobson[2]

[1] Department of Computing,
Macquarie University, Sydney, NSW 2109, Australia
{hedieh.ranjbartabar,
anupam.makhija}@students.mq.edu.au,
deborah.richards@mq.edu.au
[2] Sydney School of Education and Social Work,
The University of Sydney, Sydney, Australia
michael.jacobson@sydney.edu.au

**Abstract.** In the context of an educational virtual world to assist students to gain research inquiry skills, we are seeking to use Animated Pedagogical Agents (APAs) to capture students' emotional states and provide motivational support. We have conducted a classroom study involving an Educational Virtual World for acquiring and testing knowledge of biological concepts and science inquiry skills with a total of 30 students in Years 8–9 at a co-educational selective school. To ascertain their emotional feelings while using the VW, students encountered five APAs who greeted them by inquiring "How are you?" We found students were generally willing to disclose their emotional feeling and there were differences in emotions reported based on gender. The approach captures emotions during learning but is minimally disruptive and could aid relationship development with the APA while providing a means to validate other emotion elicitation methods.

**Keywords:** Animated pedagogical agents · Educational virtual worlds

## 1 Introduction

Awareness of the learner's emotional state plays an important role in achieving the learning goals in online digital environments [1]. Thus, recent research seeks to improve the capabilities of virtual learning environments by making them more adaptive and responsive to learners' emotional needs [2–4]. Animated pedagogical agents (APAs) with affective capabilities can assist learning by assessing the learner's emotional state and providing appropriate support in the form of encouragement and motivation by building social connections with learners [5]. APAs are lifelike virtual characters with teaching goals and strategies for achieving these goals in a learning environment [6]. APAs can provide both educational and emotional support to students [5, 7–13].

© Springer International Publishing AG, part of Springer Nature 2018
C. Penstein Rosé et al. (Eds.): AIED 2018, LNAI 10948, pp. 291–295, 2018.
https://doi.org/10.1007/978-3-319-93846-2_54

Towards this goal, we are seeking to enhance our Educational Virtual World (EVW) with empathic virtual agents. The EVW has been developed to improve students' attitudes and understanding of science, specifically targeting biology and ecology concepts that students struggle with and scientific inquiry skills. In line with the pedagogical theory underlying our Educational VW, known as productive failure [14], we do not want to provide high scaffolding or interrupt them when they are engaged in the learning task.

As a novel but humanlike and natural method to find out how the students' are feeling about the learning task, the main virtual characters in our EVW greet students by asking the familiar question "How are you?" and providing a set of possible answers, including the option to go straight to asking the character a question about the task. Our APAs seek to be friendly and cooperative, rather than disruptive. To find out the appropriateness of our strategy, we ask:

1. Is a student willing to disclose their emotions to a virtual character? If so, how often is the student willing to disclose their emotion? When do students stop disclosing their emotion?
2. How do students find the APAs' responses to their emotions? Can they suggest better responses? Do they respond differently to different APAs?

## 2   Method

We ran a classroom study in late 2016 to evaluate the learning activities we had created in alignment with the Australian National Science curriculum and assess the pedagogical value of our EVW. The study was conducted in a metropolitan co-educational (boys and girls) selective (academic achievers in the top 5–10% in the state) public high school. The studies were approved by the University's Human Research Ethics Committee and the NSW State Department of Education.

As a key design choice in this aspect of the study, we wanted to capture all the data within the context of the students using the VW and workbooks, not as a separate data collection exercise. This meant that we chose to find out about the student, their emotional feeling, their response to the characters' empathic responses through conversation with characters and within the VW. The responses to the "How are you? Question covered the main emotions associated with learning including interested/engaged, frustrated, anxious, confident, satisfied and bored [12] and were presented in random order to avoid the same emotion being selected based on its position.

## 3   Results

In total we had 30 participants, 9 females and 21 males aged between 13–15 years old. This gender split is representative of the selective school studied. Three students declined to express any feeling to any character. Results for emotions disclosed by gender are presented in Table 1. During the study, students were asked "How are you?" 182 times and students chose an emotion 109 times, rather than choosing to ask a question, thus revealing their emotion more than half the time when asked. 72.4% of the time students had positive feelings (interested 40.4%, satisfied 11.8%, confident 20.2%). In contrast 27.6% of the feelings chosen were negative (anxious 8.4%, bored 9.1%, frustrated 10.1%). "Interested" was chosen most frequently and positive feelings were selected more than negative feelings. Figure 1 illustrates chronologically the number of times students expressed emotional feelings at each meeting with the character. Students disclosed an emotion a maximum of 9 times in response to being greeted by a character.

**Table 1.** Emotion reported by gender

|  | Boys (N = 21) | | | Girls (N = 9) | | | Total | | |
|---|---|---|---|---|---|---|---|---|---|
|  | #Stud | Cnt | %Stud | #Stud | Cnt | %Stud | #Stud | Cnt | % |
| Anxious | 4 | 6 | 80% | 1 | 2 | 20% | 5 | 9 | 8.4% |
| Bored | 5 | 5 | 55.6% | 4 | 5 | 44.4% | 9 | 10 | 9.1% |
| Confident | 6 | 15 | 60% | 4 | 7 | 40% | 10 | 22 | 20.2% |
| Frustrated | 4 | 4 | 57.1% | 3 | 7 | 73.9% | 7 | 11 | 10.1% |
| Interested | 15 | 29 | 75% | 5 | 15 | 25% | 20 | 44 | 40.4% |
| Satisfied | 11 | 11 | 84.6% | 2 | 2 | 15.4% | 13 | 13 | 11.8% |
| Total |  | 71 |  |  | 38 |  |  | 109 |  |

## 3.1 Students Responses to Empathic Feedback

Each APA responded using different words to the student's reported emotional state. To minimise the number of times we asked students for feedback on the APA's empathic response, we elicited feedback for different characters in different learning modules. To elicit the feedback, after the character responded to the student's emotion, the game engine popped up a window asking "What did you think of the character's response? The combined results by character are shown in Table 2. Two of the options were positive (encouraging and helpful) whereas the other three were negative (strange, stupid and unhelpful). Overall, the feedback was more positive (49 + 12 = 61%) than negative (3 + 16 + 12 = 31%).

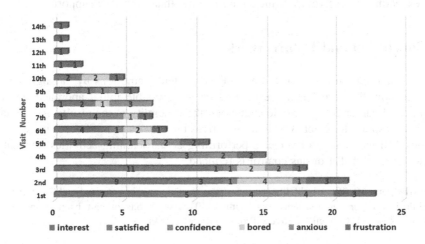

**Fig. 1.** Overall emotions weights in each time meeting characters

**Table 2.** Overall students' reactions to the characters' responses

| Character | Kim | Charlie | | Zafirah | | Lyina | | Pedro | | AVG | | Over all AVG |
|---|---|---|---|---|---|---|---|---|---|---|---|---|
| School | SC | GC | SC | GC | SC | GC | SC | GC | SC | GC | SC | |
| Encouraging | 50% | 36% | 39% | 36% | 60% | 36% | 83% | 14% | 14% | 31% | 49% | 41% |
| Helpful | 0% | 21% | 15% | 14% | 0% | 7% | 17% | 7% | 29% | 12% | 12% | 12% |
| Strange | 0% | 29% | 15% | 29% | 0% | 7% | 0% | 14% | 0% | 20% | 3% | 11% |
| Stupid | 33% | 7% | 8% | 14% | 40% | 29% | 0% | 21% | 0% | 18% | 16% | 17% |
| Unhelpful | 17% | 7% | 15% | 7% | 0% | 7% | 0% | 21% | 29% | 11% | 12% | 11% |
| Unanswered | 0% | 0% | 8% | 0% | 0% | 14% | 0% | 21% | 29% | 9% | 7% | 8% |

# 4    Discussion

In answer to the first research question, initially, nearly all students chose to disclose their emotion instead of taking the option to ask a question and carry on with their work. Whether a student chooses to ask the character a question or disclose how they are feeling, both responses were related to the task – one involves performing the learning task and the other concerns how the student feels about the task. They may have stopped answering with an emotion once they determined there was no further value to do so and they could better spend their time asking a question instead.

In answer to the second research question, more than half of the students found the APA's responses to their emotions encouraging and helpful and all character, except for one found the characters' dialogues acceptable. In general, if students expressed a positive emotion (e.g. confident, interest) they wanted to receive empathic and encouraging responses to motivate them to continue. However, when students were experiencing negative emotions (e.g. anxious, frustrated) during their school study they were expecting to receive academic support rather than empathic support.

# 5    Conclusion and Future Work

In conclusion, our strategy for finding out the students' emotions by having an APA ask them how they are feeling seemed to be a reasonable initial approach. Further research with larger cohorts would strengthen the generality of the results. As we have done in this study, for external validity we stress the importance of future studies to be conducted in the context of students performing actual learning activities relevant to their studies, even if it means control is reduced.

**Acknowledgement.** We would like to thank the participants in our study. Also, we thank Meredith Taylor for her assistance with Omosa. This work has in part been supported by Australian Research Council Discovery Project DP150102144.

# References

1. Shen, L., Wang, M., Shen, R.: Affective e-learning: Using "emotional" data to improve learning in pervasive learning environment. J. Educ. Technol. Soc. **12**(2), 176 (2009)
2. Arguel, A., Lane, R.: Fostering deep understanding in geography by inducing and managing confusion: an online learning approach (2015)
3. Ranjbartabar, H., Richards, D.: Student designed virtual teacher feedback. In: Proceedings of the 9th International Conference on Computer and Automation Engineering. ACM (2017)
4. Arguel, A., et al.: Inside out: detecting learners' confusion to improve interactive digital learning environments. J. Educ. Comput. Res. **55**(4), 526–551 (2017)
5. Sabourin, J., Mott, B., Lester, J.: Computational models of affect and empathy for pedagogical virtual agents. In: Standards in Emotion Modeling, Lorentz Center International Center for Workshops in the Sciences (2011)
6. Johnson, W.L., Rickel, J.W., Lester, J.C.: Animated pedagogical agents: Face-to-face interaction in interactive learning environments. Int. J. Artif. Intell. Educ. **11**(1), 47–78 (2000)
7. Burleson, W.: Affective learning companions: strategies for empathetic agents with real-time multimodal affective sensing to foster meta-cognitive and meta-affective approaches to learning, motivation, and perseverance. Massachusetts Institute of Technology (2006)
8. D'Mello, S., Calvo, R.A.: Beyond the basic emotions: what should affective computing compute?. In: CHI 2013 Extended Abstracts on Human Factors in Computing Systems. ACM (2013)
9. Gwo-Dong, C., et al.: An empathic avatar in a computer-aided learning program to encourage and persuade learners. J. Educ. Technol. Soc. **15**(2), 62 (2012)
10. Robison, J.L., Mcquiggan, S.W., Lester, J.C.: Modeling task-based vs. Affect-based feedback behavior in pedagogical agents: an inductive approach. In: AIED (2009)
11. Schertz, M.: Empathic pedagogy: community of inquiry and the development of empathy. Anal. Teach. **26**(1), 8–14 (2006)
12. Kort, B., Reilly, R., Picard, R.W.: An affective model of interplay between emotions and learning: reengineering educational pedagogy-building a learning companion. In: 2001 Proceedings of the IEEE International Conference on Advanced Learning Technologies. IEEE (2001)
13. Paiva, A., et al.: Learning by feeling: evoking empathy with synthetic characters. Appl. Artif. Intell. **19**(3–4), 235–266 (2005)
14. Kapur, M.: Productive failure. Cogn. Instr. **26**(3), 379–424 (2008)

# Active Learning for Efficient Testing of Student Programs

Ishan Rastogi[✉], Aditya Kanade, and Shirish Shevade

Department of Computer Science and Automation,
Indian Institute of Science, Bangalore, India
{ishanr,kanade,shirish}@iisc.ac.in

**Abstract.** In this work, we propose an automated method to identify semantic bugs in student programs, called ATAS, which builds upon the recent advances in both symbolic execution and active learning. Symbolic execution is a program analysis technique which can generate test cases through symbolic constraint solving. Our method makes use of a reference implementation of the task as its sole input. We compare our method with a symbolic execution-based baseline on 6 programming tasks retrieved from CodeForces comprising a total of 23 K student submissions. We show an average improvement of over 2.5x over the baseline in terms of runtime (thus making it more suitable for online evaluation), without a significant degradation in evaluation accuracy.

**Keywords:** Student programs · Automated testing
Active learning for classification · Symbolic execution

## 1 Introduction

Recent times have seen a rise in the popularity of massive open online courses (MOOCs), which are attended by hundreds of students. This necessitates the development of automatic feedback generation techniques since human-based feedback may be prohibitively expensive, if not impossible. Owing to this, a number of automated feedback generation techniques for computer programming have been proposed in the recent literature. These include the automated generation of syntactic [1] and semantic repairs or hints [2–4], the automated generation of test cases [5] for judging program correctness, etc.

In this work we focus on test case based feedback in an online education setting, such as on CodeForces [6], CodeChef [7], LeetCode [8], TopCoder [9], etc. These popular platforms are usually geared towards students who are proficient in programming but want to hone their algorithm design skills. Thus, the problem of interest in these scenarios is to check whether an incoming submission has a semantic/logical bug, which is typically accomplished by running the submission against a set of test cases. Most often, these test cases are manually designed and require a significant amount of human effort and expertise as it is difficult to anticipate all the errors which may be made by students. Additionally,

© Springer International Publishing AG, part of Springer Nature 2018
C. Penstein Rosé et al. (Eds.): AIED 2018, LNAI 10948, pp. 296–300, 2018.
https://doi.org/10.1007/978-3-319-93846-2_55

the online nature of these environments makes temporal efficiency a necessary concern for any automated solution.

We tackle the problem of efficiently and automatically generating a set of quality test cases. We dub our solution, which is inspired by recent advances in symbolic execution-based [10] test case generation (specifically klee [11]) and active learning [12] (for classification), Automated Testing using Active learning and Symbolic execution (ATAS).

ATAS uses symbolic execution to check the semantic equivalence of a submission with a reference implementation and generates a failing test case if the submission has a logical bug. This method is more accurate than using a hand-designed test suite since it can handle all possible distributions of logical bugs that may be present in the submission. However, as this process can be computationally intensive, ATAS makes novel use of active learning to dramatically reduce the number of submissions for which equivalence checking is performed. In our experiments, ATAS achieves an average speedup of over 2.5x (in terms of runtime) over a baseline (that exclusively performs the aforementioned expensive analysis) without a significant degradation in evaluation accuracy. ATAS reduced the number of expensive program analysis calls by over an order of magnitude, thus yielding a near-optimal speedup in practice over the baseline[1].

## 2   Automated Evaluation of Student Programs

The input to our task is a queue of program submissions $Q$ corresponding to a particular algorithmic task and a reference implementation $R$ solving the task. Our output is a two-partition of $Q$ into $A$, the *correct* submissions (i.e. those that solve the algorithmic task correctly) and $W$, the *incorrect* submissions (i.e. which have some logical error). Since our work focuses on only logical errors, we restrict ourselves to those programs which produce an incorrect answer but otherwise compiles and executes successfully.

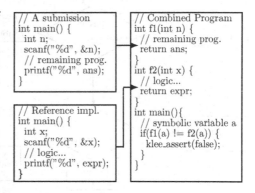

**Fig. 1.** Generating the *combined* program

Figure 1 demonstrate how klee can be used to check semantic equivalence of a program submission given $R$. We wrote a simple abstract syntax tree (AST) rewrite phase (using pycparser [13]) which generates a *combined* program, having the property that a failing test case (which executes klee_assert(false)) is generated only if there exists a test case on which the submission's output differs from that of $R$. We store all such generated test cases for later use. We now explain the two methods which use this process to solve the task.

---

[1] An extended version of this work will be made available on the arxiv soon.

Figure 2 show the workflow of symbolic execution based baseline. For every submission, it first runs all stored test cases to check for failure. If all these test cases are successfully passed, it sends the submission to `klee` which checks for semantic equivalence using the aforementioned process. By first running the stored test cases, we avoid having to run the expensive `klee`-based analysis for re-encountered bugs. However, this algorithm is unable to exploit any redundancy present in the *correct* submissions.

ATAS is designed to address this drawback. It employs a classifier to eliminate the `klee` based expensive analysis for already encountered *correct* submissions, a step inspired by uncertainty sampling (active learning). It runs in two phases. In the first phase, ATAS labels the first $i$ submissions using `klee`. It then trains a classifier and proceeds with the second phase shown in Fig. 3. The classifier is subsequently retrained after every $r$ submissions. The classifier's threshold for labeling a submission as correct is set to be the least value which results in a false positive rate of less than $F$ (algorithm's parameter) on a held-out dataset (20% of the already labeled submissions). The programs are encoded as a bag of trigram features, using only the trigrams present in the first $i$ submissions (after anonymizing the identifiers).

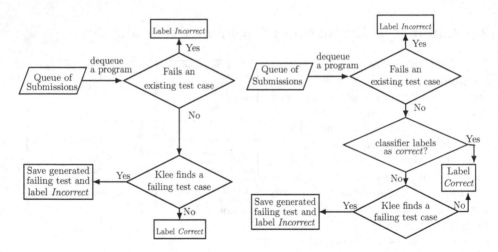

**Fig. 2.** The baseline algorithm          **Fig. 3.** ATAS's Phase 2

## 3    Experiments

To analyze the speedup achieved by ATAS over the baseline, we choose two parameters, the number of submissions which are analyzed using `klee` (henceforth `klee` *calls*) and the runtime. All our experiments are performed on an Intel(R) Xeon(R) E5-1620 4-core 8-thread machine with 24 GB of RAM. The algorithms are implemented to make use of all 8 threads. Also, we run `klee` based analysis for a maximum of 15 s. If no failing test cases are generated at the end of klee's analysis, we assume the submission to be correct. Our datasets consist of C submissions corresponding to six algorithmic tasks downloaded from CodeForces (only from the Accepted and Wrong Answer categories) consisting of a total of 23460 submissions. We set aside 10% of the data as test data and use the remaining 90% (henceforth, *comparison data*) for comparison with baseline. Test data is used to gauge the generalization ability of the classifier. We tried three different classifier families, namely, k-nn, decision trees and XGBoost [14]. Using XGBoost, we got an average precision and recall of 0.86 and 0.85 respectively on the test data. All the remaining stated results are for the *comparison data*. For hyperparameters, we found that $r = i = 10\%$ of all the submissions and $F = 0.3$ works well in practice. Our implementation is written in python, and makes use of scikit-learn [15].

Since CodeForces uses hand designed test cases, it can only be compared for labeling inaccuracies and not for temporal efficiency. The baseline, found 124 bugs missed by CodeForces while it missed 104 bugs detected by CodeForces. Tables 1 and 2 summarize the performance of ATAS (against the baseline). Based on this, we recommend XGBoost [14] as the classifier of choice due to its consis-

**Table 1.** Comparison of XGBoost, k-nn classifier and decision tree for speedup and Error(*incorrect* submissions marked as *correct*)

| Dataset | k-nn | | XGBoost | | Decision tree | |
|---|---|---|---|---|---|---|
| | Speedup | Error | Speedup | Error | Speedup | Error |
| Buy a Shovel (D1) | 1.42 | 4/182 | **1.88** | 2/182 | 1.73 | 1/182 |
| Buttons (D2) | 1.81 | 0/375 | **2.61** | 1/375 | 1.88 | 0/375 |
| Insomnia Cure (D3) | 1.45 | 4/235 | **3.23** | 5/235 | 2.59 | 5/235 |
| Game Sticks (D4) | 1.69 | 3/834 | **2.71** | 1/834 | 1.76 | 3/834 |
| Soldiers and Banana (D5) | 1.87 | 2/908 | **3.25** | 2/908 | 2.13 | 2/908 |
| Watermelon (D6) | 0.81 | 5/8333 | **2.38** | 13/8333 | 0.97 | 2/8333 |

**Table 2.** Comparison of XGBoost, k-nn and decision tree classifier for the number of klee calls made. Last 90% denotes the number of klee calls made by the ATAS with corresponding classifier against those made by the baseline during ATAS's Phase 2.

| Dataset | Baseline | k-nn | | XGBoost | | Decision tree | |
|---|---|---|---|---|---|---|---|
| | Total | Total | Last 90% | Total | Last 90% | Total | Last 90% |
| D1 | 407 | 158 | 101/351 | **150** | **93/351** | 154 | 97/351 |
| D2 | 530 | 158 | 68/458 | **145** | **55/458** | 216 | 126/458 |
| D3 | 719 | 327 | 233/639 | **140** | **46/639** | 192 | 98/639 |
| D4 | 804 | 290 | 128/692 | **205** | **43/692** | 354 | 192/692 |
| D5 | 1319 | 496 | 274/1175 | **313** | **91/1175** | 514 | 292/1175 |
| D6 | 6496 | 2170 | 688/5752 | **1530** | **48/5752** | 2265 | 783/5752 |

tent speedup without significant error and an order of magnitude smaller number of `klee` calls than the baseline.

In future, we intend to evaluate ATAS's pedagogical limitations by performing a user study in educational environments.

# References

1. Gupta, R., Pal, S., Kanade, A., Shevade, S.: Deepfix: fixing common C language errors by deep learning. In: Proceedings of the 31st AAAI Conference on Artificial Intelligence, pp. 1345–1351 (2017)
2. Singh, R., Gulwani, S., Solar-Lezama, A.: Automated feedback generation for introductory programming assignments. In: Proceedings of the 34th ACM SIGPLAN Conference on Programming Language Design and Implementation, pp. 15–26 (2013)
3. Kaleeswaran, S., Santhiar, A., Kanade, A., Gulwani, S.: Semi-supervised verified feedback generation. In: Proceedings of the 2016 24th ACM SIGSOFT International Symposium on Foundations of Software Engineering, pp. 739–750 (2016)
4. Rivers, K., Koedinger, K.R.: Data-driven hint generation in vast solution spaces: a self-improving python programming tutor. Int. J. Artif. Intell. Educ. **27**(1), 37–64 (2017)
5. Tang, T., Smith, R., Rixner, S., Warren, J.: Data-driven test case generation for automated programming assessment. In: Proceedings of the 2016 ACM Conference on Innovation and Technology in Computer Science Education, pp. 260–265 (2016)
6. http://codeforces.com
7. https://www.codechef.com
8. https://leetcode.com
9. https://www.topcoder.com
10. Baldoni, R., Coppa, E., D'Elia, D.C., Demetrescu, C., Finocchi, I.: A survey of symbolic execution techniques. CoRR abs/1610.00502 (2016)
11. Cadar, C., Dunbar, D., Engler, D.: Klee: Unassisted and automatic generation of high-coverage tests for complex systems programs. In: Proceedings of the 8th USENIX Conference on Operating Systems Design and Implementation, pp. 209–224 (2008)
12. Settles, B.: Active learning literature survey. Technical report (2010)
13. https://github.com/eliben/pycparser
14. Chen, T., Guestrin, C.: Xgboost: A scalable tree boosting system. In: Proceedings of the 22nd ACM SIGKDD International Conference on Knowledge Discovery and Data Mining, pp. 785–794 (2016)
15. Pedregosa, F., Varoquaux, G., Gramfort, A., Michel, V., Thirion, B., Grisel, O., Blondel, M., Prettenhofer, P., Weiss, R., Dubourg, V., Vanderplas, J., Passos, A., Cournapeau, D., Brucher, M., Perrot, M., Duchesnay, E.: Scikit-learn: machine learning in python. J. Mach. Learn. Res. **12**, 2825–2830 (2011)

# Improving Question Generation with the Teacher's Implicit Feedback

Hugo Rodrigues[1,2,3(✉)], Luísa Coheur[1,2], and Eric Nyberg[3]

[1] Tecnico Lisboa, Lisboa, Portugal
[2] INESC-ID, Lisboa, Portugal
{hpr,lcoheur}@l2f.inesc-id.pt
[3] Language Technologies Institute, Carnegie Mellon University, Pittsburgh, PA, USA
ehn@cs.cmu.edu

**Abstract.** Although current Question Generation systems can be used to automatically generate questions for students' assessments, these need validation and, often, manual corrections. However, this information is never used to improve the performance of QG systems, where it can play an important role. In this work, we present a system, GEN, that learns from such (implicit) feedback in a online learning setting. Following an example-based approach, it takes as input a small set of sentence/question pairs and creates patterns which are then applied to learning materials. Each generated question, after being corrected by the teacher, is used as a new seed in the next iteration, so more patterns are created each time. We also take advantage of the corrections made by the teacher to score the patterns and therefore rank the generated questions. We measure the teacher's effort in post-editing required and show that GEN improves over time, reducing from 70% to 30% in average corrections needed per question.

## 1 Introduction

Many applications for educational purposes have been built in the last decades (e.g. [1–3]), from tutoring systems to online courses. However, one aspect that all of these applications share is the need to have an expert manually validating or even correcting the obtained results. Following in the challenging research area of Question Generation (QG), we look at the problem of automatically generating questions from text, which can be later used by a teacher to evaluate the students. Considering that the teacher needs to validate/correct the generated questions, we propose a system (from now on GEN) that takes advantage of the teacher's implicit feedback to improve its performance.

Even without the explicit goal of generating questions for educational purposes, QG systems can contribute to it [4]. QG has been studied for some time now [5], and several works study the generation of questions from unstructured text [6–9]. However, in none of the current systems the user feedback resulting from the corrections can be easily used to improve the system's performance, and we believe these can be essential to make QG useful in real world applications.

© Springer International Publishing AG, part of Springer Nature 2018
C. Penstein Rosé et al. (Eds.): AIED 2018, LNAI 10948, pp. 301–306, 2018.
https://doi.org/10.1007/978-3-319-93846-2_56

Most systems rely on hand-crafted rules that establish how to transform input sentences into questions, either by using a set of designed rules to manipulate the sentences' parse trees and transform them into questions [6], or resorting to lexico-syntactic patterns to create questions, based on constituent [10] and dependency parsers [7], or taking advantage of Semantic Role Labelers (SRLs) instead [11,12]. A different approach is followed by THE-MENTOR [13], which automatically learns patterns from a set of sentence/question/answer triples, forming patterns from the chunks shared among them. More recently, some systems have successfully applied deep neural networks to create questions, from ontology triples [14] or by using large datasets like SQuAD [15] with sequence-to-sequence models [8,9]. However, to the best of our knowledge, none of the above systems (expect for THE-MENTOR) could be easily adapted to gain from the teacher's feedback. Therefore, we propose an example-based QG system, which takes the basic idea from THE-MENTOR, no longer available. GEN generates questions from patterns automatically learned from a set of sentence/question seeds. As a consequence, every pair constituted by a generated question plus its source sentence in the learning material can be used by GEN, after the teacher's corrections, as a new seed. However, if a teacher needs to parse dozens of questions to find a good one, then the system's usefulness is diminished. Here, we take advantage of the teacher's effort to score the patterns and, therefore, rank the generated questions. We perform online learning in small batches and use the Weighted Majority Algorithm [16] to update the score of each pattern. We show that GEN improves its performance over time, measured with Levenshtein, as a proxy for editing effort, and coverage and precision, compared with a reference corpus.

## 2    Generating Questions with GEN

GEN first step consists in creating the semantic patterns from a given set of seeds, constituted by 'question/support sentence' pairs. Then, it applies the created patterns to new sentences. Questions are generated every time there is a semantic match. The details on the generation process are out of the scope of this paper.

GEN takes advantage of the teacher's corrections to increase the number of seeds (used to create new patterns) and also rank the previously applied patterns. The first enlarges the pool of patterns. However, simply generating more questions is not a reasonable approach if they are of poor quality, as only the best questions should be listed. GEN takes advantage of the teacher's intervention by scoring patterns according to that (implicit) feedback; that score is used to rank the generated questions.

GEN works by applying the patterns to batches of sentences, resulting in new questions at each step. Each question is presented to the teacher to be corrected or discarded. After being corrected, questions form with the source sentence a new seed, allowing the creation of new patterns; at the same time, this implicit feedback is used to score the source pattern. The process repeats for all batches, each time with a larger pool of patterns. We apply the Weighted Majority Algorithm [16] to score a pattern $p$, which is updated at each step $t$ based on its success in generating questions, starting at 1.0:

$$w_t(p) = \begin{cases} w_{t-1} & \text{if successful,} \\ w_{t-1}(1-l) & \text{otherwise,} \end{cases} \tag{1}$$

where $l$ is the loss penalty for a non successful generation. The successfulness of a generation is determined by the similarity between the question and its corrections: $successful(q, q') = sim(q, q') > th$, being $q$ a question generated by $p$, $q'$ its corrected version, $th$ a threshold and $sim$ a function of similarity.

## 3    Experimental Setup

The generated questions were evaluated against a corpus, representing the questions that should be asked about the learning materials. We took as learning materials two online texts (73 sentences), in English, about a specific palace. Seven non-native English speakers were asked to create all the questions they considered to be relevant, resulting in a reference with 415 questions[1]. The corpus was split in batches of 10 sentences[2].

Multiple configurations were tested for Weighted Majority Algorithm, but no significant differences were found between configurations, so we report just one, Lev, with penalty set to 0.1, and threshold value $th$ for function $successful$ set to 0.8. The function used was a normalized version of Levenshtein [17], as it gives an intuitive way to evaluate the effort of the teacher in correcting a question. One of the authors, playing the teacher's role, corrected the generated questions, or discarded them if no reasonable fix could be found. As a guideline, the corrected question had to respect the original type of the question.

To evaluate the generated questions against the reference $(ref)$, we considered precision and recall: $P@N = \frac{\sum_i^N match(q_i, ref)}{|N|}$, $R@N = \frac{\sum_i^N match(q_i, ref)}{|ref|}$, where $N$ is a cut to the top questions in the list returned. To allow a certain degree of flexibility on the $match$, we used a threshold that needs to be surpassed, instead of requiring an exact match. We use ROUGE_L, a measure often employed in such tasks, as it accounts for the longest common subsequences between the questions being compared. In these experiments we set the threshold to 0.8 and we take $N = 20$, as if the teacher would be only presented those top 20 questions. The editing effort was calculated with normalized Levenshtein as well. Finally, we set the baseline as GEN without weighting strategy, which means the generated questions for each batch are not ordered[3].

---

[1] https://www.l2f.inesc-id.pt/~hpr/corpora/.
[2] The results for the final batch of 3 sentences are not reported.
[3] All the reported results correspond to the average of three different random orderings.

# 4 Results

Table 1 shows, for each one of the batches, the statistics of the experiment, along with the results obtained. We can see that, despite batches 2 and 3 not providing questions belonging to the reference, for the remaining batches the precision goes up. In fact, the baseline is on par with the lowest precision that can be obtained, and the weighting allows to improve on that axis. A similar trend is observed for recall, with the baseline far from best achievable, while the weighting strategy is closer to it.

**Table 1.** Overall statistics of the experiment, per batch, including number of seeds, questions generated and percentage of questions discarded. Ref Size is the number of possible questions in the reference. Results show Precision, Recall and Editing Effort, measured with normalized Levenshtein $(L_n)$, when considering the top 20 ranked questions.

| | | $b_0$ | $b_1$ | $b_2$ | $b_3$ | $b_4$ | $b_5$ | $b_6$ |
|---|---|---|---|---|---|---|---|---|
| Seeds | | 8 | 15 | 27 | 22 | 31 | 33 | 36 |
| Questions | | 24 | 86 | 134 | 127 | 142 | 226 | 442 |
| Discarded | | 0.25 | 0.34 | 0.82 | 0.69 | 0.62 | 0.53 | 0.53 |
| Ref Size | | 68 | 68 | 43 | 52 | 35 | 70 | 46 |
| P@all | | 0.08 | 0.08 | 0 | 0.01 | 0.01 | 0.02 | 0.03 |
| P@20 | Bsl | 0.08 | 0.05 | 0 | 0 | 0.02 | 0.02 | 0.02 |
| | Lev | - | **0.15** | 0 | 0 | 0.05 | 0.10 | **0.15** |
| R@all | | 0.03 | 0.06 | 0 | 0.02 | 0.03 | 0.03 | 0.20 |
| R@20 | Bsl | 0.02 | 0.02 | 0 | 0 | 0.01 | 0 | 0.02 |
| | Lev | - | **0.06** | 0 | 0 | 0.03 | 0.01 | **0.11** |
| $L_n$@20 | Bsl | - | 0.60± 0.25 | 0.89± 0.23 | 0.79± 0.24 | 0.74± 0.22 | 0.66± 0.24 | 0.71± 0.25 |
| | Lev | - | 0.41± 0.20 | 0.59± 0.32 | 0.56± 0.27 | 0.55± 0.25 | 0.44± 0.31 | **0.27± 0.31** |

The normalized Levenshtein $(L_n)$ between the generated questions and their corrected version after the teacher's corrections was also computed. This experiment clearly shows the improvement gained when using the weights on the patterns. The editing effort is considerably lesser, specially in later batches, going as low as needing to make corrections to only 30% of a given question, on average.

# 5 Conclusions and Future Work

In this work we present GEN, a semi-supervised QG system that uses automatically learned semantic patterns to generate questions from new text and takes advantage of the teacher's corrections as implicit feedback regarding the quality of the generated questions. We employ a Weighted Majority Algorithm to weigh the patterns, based on their success in generating questions. Results have shown that this strategy is able to push better questions towards the top of each batch, reaching an improvement of down to 30% in the editing effort required. These experiments showed the effectiveness of our approach, without needing large datasets or feature engineering, just by using the teacher's implicit feedback given by the corrections.

As future work, we would like to exhaustively address different similarity measures and values for the penalty and thresholds. On a different axis, the impact of the number of batches – and their dimension – should be measured, as we believe GEN might need more iterations to show stronger results. Finally, experiments with more teachers will also an important step in the future.

**Acknowledgements.** This work was supported by national funds through Fundação para a Ciência e a Tecnologia (FCT) with reference UID/CEC/50021/2013. Hugo Rodrigues was supported by the Carnegie Mellon-Portugal program (SFRH/BD/51916/2012) and LAW-TRAIN project (H2020-EU.3.7, contract 653587).

# References

1. Mitkov, R., An Ha, L., Karamanis, N.: A computer-aided environment for generating multiple-choice test items. Nat. Lang. Eng. **12**(2), 177–194 (2006)
2. Vinu, E.V., SreenivasaKumar, P.: A novel approach to generate MCQS from domain ontology: considering Dl semantics and open-world assumption. Web Semant. Sci. Serv. Agents World Wide Web **34**, 40–54 (2015)
3. Chen, W., Mostow, J.: Generating questions automatically from informational text. In: AIED 2009 Workshop on Question Generation, pp. 17–24 (2009)
4. Le, N.T., Kojiri, T., Pinkwart, N.: Automatic question generation for educational applications - the state of art. In: van Do, T., Thi, H.A.L., Nguyen, N.T. (eds.) Advanced Computational Methods for Knowledge Engineering, pp. 325–338. Springer International Publishing, Cham (2014)
5. Rus, V., Wyse, B., Piwek, P., Lintean, M., Stoyanchev, S., Moldovan, C.: Overview of the first question generation shared task evaluation challenge. In: Proceedings of the Sixth International Natural Language Generation Conference (INLG 2010), July 2010
6. Heilman, M.: Automatic factual question generation from text. Ph.D. thesis. School of Computer Science, Carnegie Mellon University, Pittsburgh, PA (2011)
7. Mazidi, K., Nielsen, R.D.: Leveraging multiple views of text for automatic question generation. In: Conati, C., Heffernan, N., Mitrovic, A., Verdejo, M.F. (eds.) AIED 2015. LNCS (LNAI), vol. 9112, pp. 257–266. Springer, Cham (2015). https://doi.org/10.1007/978-3-319-19773-9_26
8. Du, X., Shao, J., Cardie, C.: Learning to ask: Neural question generation for reading comprehension. CoRR abs/1705.00106 (2017)
9. Yuan, X., Wang, T., Gülçehre, Ç., Sordoni, A., Bachman, P., Subramanian, S., Zhang, S., Trischler, A.: Machine comprehension by text-to-text neural question generation. CoRR abs/1705.02012 (2017)
10. Ali, H., Chali, Y., Hasan, S.A.: Automation of question generation from sentences. In: Proceedings of the Third Workshop on Question Generation, QG 2010, June 2010

11. Mannem, P., Prasad, R., Joshi, A.: Question generation from paragraphs at UPENN: QGSTEC system description. In: Proceedings of the Third Workshop on Question Generation, QG 2010, pp. 84–91 (2010)
12. Pal, S., Mondal, T., Pakray, P., Das, D., Bandyopadhyay, S.: Qgstec system description-juqgg: a rule based approach. Boyer Piwek **2010**, 76–79 (2010)
13. Curto, S., Mendes, A.C., Coheur, L.: Question generation based on lexico-syntactic patterns learned from the web. Dialogue Discourse **3**(2), 147–175 (2012)
14. Serban, I.V., García-Durán, A., Gülçehre, Ç., Ahn, S., Chandar, S., Courville, A.C., Bengio, Y.: Generating factoid questions with recurrent neural networks: The 30m factoid question-answer corpus. CoRR abs/1603.06807 (2016)
15. Rajpurkar, P., Zhang, J., Lopyrev, K., Liang, P.: Squad: 100,000+ questions for machine comprehension of text. CoRR abs/1606.05250 (2016)
16. Littlestone, N., Warmuth, M.K.: The weighted majority algorithm. Inf. Comput. **108**(2), 212–261 (1994)
17. Levenshtein, V.I.: Binary codes capable of correcting deletions, insertions and reversals. Soviet Physics Doklady **10**, 707–710 (1966)

# Adaptive Learning Open Source Initiative for MOOC Experimentation

Yigal Rosen[1]([⊠]), Ilia Rushkin[1], Rob Rubin[2], Liberty Munson[3],
Andrew Ang[1], Gregory Weber[3], Glenn Lopez[1], and Dustin Tingley[1]

[1] Harvard University, Cambridge, USA
yigal_rosen@harvard.edu
[2] Cambridge, USA
[3] Microsoft, Redmond, USA

**Abstract.** In personalized adaptive systems, the learner's progress toward clearly defined goals is continually assessed, the assessment occurs when a student is ready to demonstrate competency, and supporting materials are tailored to the needs of each learner. Despite the promise of adaptive personalized learning, there is a lack of evidence-based instructional design, transparency in many of the models and algorithms used to provide adaptive technology or a framework for rapid experimentation with different models. ALOSI (Adaptive Learning Open Source Initiative) provides open source adaptive learning technology and a common framework to measure learning gains and learner behavior. This paper provides an overview of adaptive learning functionality developed by Harvard and Microsoft in collaboration with edX and other partners, and shared results the recent deployment in Microsoft MOOC on edX. The study explored the effects of two different strategies for adaptive problems (i.e., assessment items) on knowledge and skills development. We found that the implemented adaptivity in assessment, with emphasis on remediation is associated with a substantial increase in learning gains, while producing no big effect on the drop-out. Further research is needed to confirm these findings and explore additional possible effects and implications to course design.

**Keywords:** Adaptivity · Personalization · Assessment

## 1 Adaptive Learning Architecture

Adaptive technologies build on decades of research in intelligent tutoring systems, psychometrics, cognitive learning theory and data science [1, 2, 6]. Pioneer studies on adaptive technologies in MOOCs indicated both technical feasibility and the educational promise [3–5]. Despite the promise of adaptive learning, there is a lack of evidence-based instructional design, transparency in many of the models and algorithms used to provide adaptive technology or a framework for rapid experimentation with different models. Harvard University partnered with Microsoft to develop ALOSI

R. Rubin—Independent.

(Adaptive Learning Open Source Initiative) provides open source adaptive learning technology and a common framework to measure learning gains and learner behavior. The key insights gained from the modeling and analysis work enables us to address the development of evidence-based guidelines for instructional design of future courses, and provides insights into our understanding of how people learn effectively. ALOSI uses Bayesian Knowledge tracing to both develop a predictive model of skills mastery for the learner, and improve the predictive attributes associated with the content. The key features in ALOSI's current adaptive framework include knowledge tracing and recommendation engine, while user modeling, feedback and recommendation of targeted learning materials are in development. The engine improves over time from the use of additional learner data and provides direct insights into the optimization processes (by contrast with commonly used commercial "black box" adaptive engines). Additionally, the architecture of the adaptive engine enables rapid experimentation with different recommendation strategies.

First, in order to operationalize ALOSI framework we developed the Bridge for Adaptivity and the adaptive engine, two open source applications supporting a modular framework for implementing adaptive learning and experimentation that integrates several components: the Bridge for Adaptivity, an Adaptive Engine (such as the ALOSI adaptive engine), a Learning Management System (an LTI consumer such as Canvas or edX), and a Content Source (for example, an LTI provider like Open edX). The Bridge for Adaptivity handles the integration of all system components to provide the adaptive learning experience, while the Adaptive Engine provides the adaptive strategy and is

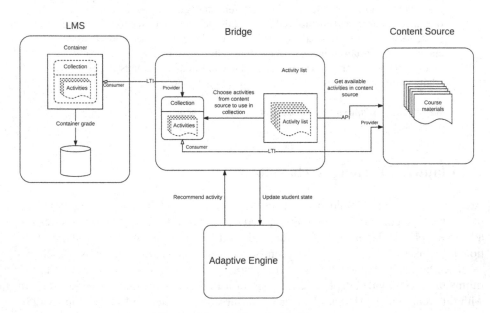

**Fig. 1.** Adaptive learning architecture

designed to be swapped in and out with compatible engines for experimentation and comparison. The diagram in Fig. 1 describes the data passing in the system.

In this study, the Bridge for Adaptivity was used with the ALOSI adaptive engine to adaptively serve assessments from an Open edX platform instance in the Microsoft MOOC on edX. Every problem-checking event by the user sends the data to the adaptive engine, to update the mastery information real-time. Every "Next Question" event in an adaptive assessment sends to the engine a request for the next content item to be served to the user (this could a learning or an assessment content). The engine sends back the recommendation, which is accessed as an edX XBlock and loaded.

Next, we developed Adaptive Engine that consists of two blocks: Bayesian Knowledge Tracing (BKT) and the recommendation engine, which uses the output of knowledge tracing as an input. The strategy we use for recommending the next item is a weighted combination of a number of sub-strategies (remediation, continuity, appropriate difficulty and readiness of pre-requisites). Each sub-strategy comes in with an importance weight (the vector of these weights is a governing parameter of the adaptive engine).

## 2  Pilot Study in Microsoft MOOC on EdX

Adaptive functionality has been deployed in Microsoft MOOC on edX "Essential Statistics for Data Analysis Using Excel". The instructional design team significantly enhanced the assessment scope, and included over 35 knowledge components and 400 assessment items tagged to those knowledge components. Our experimental design randomly assigned learners in the course to three independent groups: in the first adaptive group ALOSI prioritized a strategy of remediation – serving learners items on topics with the least evidence of mastery (Group A); in the second adaptive group ALOSI prioritized a strategy of continuity – that is learners would be more likely served items on similar topic in a sequence until mastery is demonstrated (group B); the control group followed the pathways of the course as set out by the instructional designer, with no adaptive algorithms (Group C). Thus, groups A and B of the students experienced two varieties of the adaptive engine. The difference was in the recommendation sub-strategy weights. For group A, the weight of remediation was set to 2, and that of continuity to 1. For group B these values were reversed. The weights of the remaining two sub-strategies were the same for both groups: 1 for pre-requisite readiness and 0.5 for difficulty matching. The mastery threshold L* was set to 2.2 (corresponding to p* about 0.9. The pre-requisite forgiveness r* was set to 0. The serving policy "stop on mastery" was not used: as long as a user requested more adaptive questions, they were served until the available pool was exhausted.

We observe no substantial differences across the groups in the average problem score in the pre-test, confirming the assumption that initially the composition of the three groups is comparable[1]. If anything, group A was at a slight disadvantage initially.

---

[1] Everywhere in this paper, by p value we mean the p-value from the two-tailed t-test, and by the effect size (ES) we mean Cohen's d.

The learning gains are observed as the difference between the average problem score in the post-test and in the pre-test. It appears that group A experienced the greatest learning gain (ES = 0.641). Group B, whose version of adaptivity was weaker (continuity was emphasized rather than remediation), has lesser learning gains (ES = 0.542), and the control Group C had still less (0.535). We estimate standard error of the post-test participation rates with the help of binomial distribution as slightly over 1% in all three groups, which means that the differences between the post-test participation are insignificant.

We further investigate the effect of the experimental groups on learning gains: how much of it was due to the simple fact that experimental users had access to many more questions in the learning modules than the control users, and therefore had more chances to practice their knowledge? The number of questions in the fixed sequences in the pre-test and post-test for the experimental groups was 34 and 35, respectively. The number of questions in the pre-test and the post-test for the Control group was 29 and 30 respectively. We have 793 (Remediation/Continuity/Control = 238/263/292) users who submitted at least one question in the pre-test and at least one question in the post-test, but restricting the analysis to those who submitted the minimum of 29 pre-test and 30 post-test questions (the numbers of questions from the Control group). As a result, the number of users left is 448 (Remediation/Continuity/Control = 127/154/167). Defining the learning gain as the difference between a user's post-test mean score and pre-test mean score, we train on these users a linear model where the outcome is the learning gain and the explanatory variables are the pre-test mean score, the experimental group, and the number of questions submitted in the modules 1–5 of the course. The adjusted R-squared of the model is 0.24. As a result, belonging to group A ("remediation") increases the gain by 0.057 (p = 0.03) compared to the control group C; belonging to group B ("continuity") has no significant effect (p = 0.54). Furthermore, the number of problems turns out to have no statistically significant effect on the learning gain (p = 0.65), suggesting that the benefit of remediation adaptivity is not explained as simply the benefit of practicing with more questions.

Additionally, we found that in many assessment modules the learning curves of adaptive groups were smoother, i.e. adaptivity produced a smoother learning experience.

Our experimentation with adaptive assessments provided initial evidence on the effects of adaptivity in MOOCs on learning gains and dropout rates. Furthermore, the architecture of the Bridge for Adaptivity and the Adaptive Engine developed in this project enables rapid experimentation with different recommendation strategies in the future. Our future work will include more integrated learning and assessment adaptive experiences, further experimentation with recommendation strategies and adaptive engines, as well as expanding our studies to other online learning offerings and LTI-compliant Learning Management Systems on a large scale.

# References

1. Hawkins, W.J., Heffernan, N.T., Baker, R.S.J.D.: Learning Bayesian knowledge tracing parameters with a knowledge heuristic and empirical probabilities. In: Trausan-Matu, S., Boyer, K.E., Crosby, M., Panourgia, K. (eds.) ITS 2014. LNCS, vol. 8474, pp. 150–155. Springer, Cham (2014). https://doi.org/10.1007/978-3-319-07221-0_18
2. Koedinger, K., Stamper, J.: A data driven approach to the discovery of better cognitive models. In: Baker, R.S.J.d., Merceron, A., Pavlik Jr., P.I. (eds.) Proceedings of the 3rd International Conference on Educational Data Mining (EDM 2010), Pittsburgh, pp. 325–326 (2010)
3. Pardos, Z., Tang, S., Davis, D., Vu Le, C.: Enabling real-time adaptivity in MOOCs with a personalized next-step recommendation framework. In: Proceedings of the Fourth ACM Conference on Learning @ Scale (2017)
4. Rosen, Y., Rushkin, I., Ang, A., Federicks, C., Tingley, D., Blink, M.-J.: Designing adaptive assessments in MOOCs. In: Proceedings of the Fourth ACM Conference on Learning @ Scale (2017)
5. Rushkin, I., Rosen, Y., Ang, A., Fredericks, C., Tingley, D., Blink, M.J., Lopez, G.: Adaptive assessment experiment in a HarvardX MOOC. In: Proceedings of the 10th International Conference on Educational Data Mining (2017)
6. Stamper, J.C., Eagle, M., Barnes, T., Croy, M.: Experimental evaluation of automatic hint generation for a logic tutor. In: Biswas, G., Bull, S., Kay, J., Mitrovic, A. (eds.) AIED 2011. LNCS (LNAI), vol. 6738, pp. 345–352. Springer, Heidelberg (2011). https://doi.org/10.1007/978-3-642-21869-9_45

# Impact of Learner-Centered Affective Dynamics on Metacognitive Judgements and Performance in Advanced Learning Technologies

Robert Sawyer[✉], Nicholas V. Mudrick, Roger Azevedo,
and James Lester

North Carolina State University, Raleigh, NC 27603, USA
{rssawyer, nvmudric, razeved, lester}@ncsu.edu

**Abstract.** Affect and metacognition play a central role in learning. We examine
the relationships between students' affective state dynamics, metacognitive
judgments, and performance during learning with MetaTutorIVH, an advanced
learning technology for human biology education. Student emotions were tracked
using facial expression recognition embedded within MetaTutorIVH and transitions between emotions theorized to be important to learning (e.g., confusion,
frustration, and joy) are analyzed with respect to likelihood of occurrence. Transitions from confusion to frustration were observed at a significantly high likelihood, although no differences in performance were observed in the presence of
these affective states and transitions. Results suggest that the occurrence of
emotions have a significant impact on students' retrospective confidence judgments, which they made after submitting their answers to multiple-choice questions. Specifically, the presence of confusion and joy during learning had a positive
impact on student confidence in their performance while the presence of frustration
and transition from confusion to frustration had a negative impact on confidence,
even after accounting for individual differences in multiple-choice confidence.

**Keywords:** Affect · Learner-centered emotions · Metacognition
Affect dynamics · Affect detection

## 1 Introduction

Research has shown that affect and metacognition play a significant role in learning. When
students accomplish learning goals, they are likely to experience joy [1], while negative
emotions during learning, such as frustration and confusion, can lead to disengagement
with the learning material and prevent effective learning [2, 3]. To enable advanced
learning technologies (ALTs) to effectively interact with students, it is important to allow
ALTs to take actions to address students' affective states, and understand the relationship
between these affective states and students' metacognitive monitoring processes [4, 5].
Developing an understanding of the relationship between students' affect and their cognitive and metacognitive self-regulated learning (SRL) processes can contribute to the
design of practical, scalable ALTs [6, 8]. This work moves toward affect-aware ALTs by

© Springer International Publishing AG, part of Springer Nature 2018
C. Penstein Rosé et al. (Eds.): AIED 2018, LNAI 10948, pp. 312–316, 2018.
https://doi.org/10.1007/978-3-319-93846-2_58

using automated affect detection through facial expression recognition of emotion. Automatic affect detection has been an area of active research and builds on theoretical frameworks such as the Facial Action Coding Scheme [7] and machine learning-based affect detectors [e.g. 3, 5, 9]. While automatic affect detection has been used to accurately predict learning outcomes using lower-level action units [e.g., 10], previous research using automatically detected affect has not considered the metacognitive processes that are also influenced by student affect and integral to the self-regulated learning processes that can influence students' performance during learning with ALTs.

## 2  MetaTutorIVH Study

A total of 66 students enrolled in a mid-Atlantic North American University participated in this study. Data from 12 students were removed due to calibration issues, resulting in 54 students (72% female). Students' ages ranged from 18 to 29 ($M = 20.5$, $SD = 2.34$). An 18-item, multiple-choice question pre-test assessing prior knowledge of the biology concepts covered during learning with MetaTutorIVH indicated students had low to moderate (questions correct ranging from 6 to 14) prior knowledge ($M = 11.0$ [61.1%], $SD = 1.46$ [8.1%]).

### 2.1  MetaTutorIVH

MetaTutorIVH is an ALT with which students learn human biology concepts through text and diagrams while making metacognitive judgments, answering multiple-choice questions, and observing a virtual human. Students interacted with MetaTutorIVH over the course of 18 counter-balanced, randomized, self-paced trials that consisted of a complex biology question, metacognitive judgment prompts, a virtual human, and science content presented in text and diagrams. For each trial, a student was first presented with a science question and then performed an ease of learning metacognitive judgment. Then students were presented with the content page (Fig. 1) containing the science text and diagram, as well as the virtual human. Students decided when to progress from the content page to the 4-foil multiple-choice question, which was then followed by a retrospective confidence judgment (RCJ), where students evaluated their multiple-choice answer confidence. Each trial concluded with the students providing a justification and RCJ for their justification.

Facial expression features were extracted automatically from a facial expression recognition system, FACET [13]. FACET extracts facial measurements from video streams that correspond to the Facial Action Coding System [11]. A discretization process filtered out subject and measurement variance to provide conservative estimates of emotion events that are stable across students. Once the evidence scores were converted to discrete events, sequences of emotion were created for each student. Students engaged in complex learning processes on the content page (Fig. 1), thus only emotion events that occur during the content page were considered. We examined page-level sequences each of which are a sequence of emotions produced by a student on a single content page, which have short sequence lengths ($M = 5.97$, $SD = 6.47$) due to the brief time students spent per content page ($M = 100.5$ s, $SD = 47.3$).

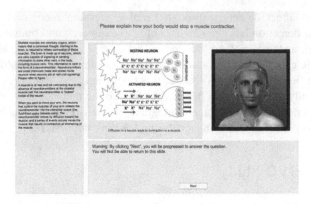

**Fig. 1.** Screenshot of MetaTutorIVH content page, the main interface containing the science question, text, diagram, and intelligent virtual human (IVH).

## 3 Results

The observed rates of occurrence for each emotion during student interaction with the content page indicate that joy ($M = 0.67$, $SD = 0.61$) and frustration ($M = 0.66$, $SD = 0.60$) were the most frequently occurring emotions, while contempt ($M = 0.36$, $SD = 0.42$) was the least frequently occurring emotion.

We calculate the likelihood metric for transitions, calculated similarly to Cohen's Kappa (see [6] for additional details), of key learner-centric transitions averaged over page-level sequences. The likelihood of transitions between confusion and frustration were both significantly above 0 (Confusion to Frustration *Average Likelihood* = 0.40, $SD = 0.30$; Frustration to Confusion *Average Likelihood* = 0.19, $SD = 0.20$), which is not surprising considering the strong correlation between these emotions ($r(54) = 0.70$, $p < 0.001$). However, the transitions from confusion to frustration have a significantly higher likelihood measured across the 54 students than transitions from frustration to confusion ($t(53) = 5.89$, $p < 0.001$), indicating that while correlated, confusion was seen more often to precede frustration than frustration preceding confusion during learning.

Proportional to the frequencies observed on the student level, joy was observed in 51.4% of trials, frustration in 45.3%, confusion in 35.4% and a transition from confusion to frustration in 21.2% of trials. A mixed effects logistic regression model performed in R with the lme4 package [12] predicting multiple choice correctness using the presence of confusion, frustration, joy, and transition from confusion to frustration as fixed effects and random intercepts for students found no significant predictors among the fixed effects from a likelihood test against a null model using only the random intercepts for students ($\chi^2(4) = 3.73$, $p = 0.44$). This mixed effect model indicates there was no effect of the presence of these emotions and transition from confusion to frustration on multiple-choice performance after accounting for individual differences.

The relationship between presence of learner-centric emotions and RCJs was examined through a linear mixed effect model using fixed effects for the presence of confusion, frustration, joy, and transition between confusion to frustration and random intercepts for each test subject. A significant impact of the fixed effects of emotions was found through a nested F-test using the full model as the linear mixed effects model and reduced model being a random effects model with intercepts for students ($F(4, 915) = 2.45$, $p = 0.045$, $R^2 = 0.36$). The fixed effects are reported in Table 1 and indicate that the presence of confusion and joy have a positive impact on student RCJs, specifically multiple-choice confidence, while the presence of frustration and a transition from confusion to frustration have a negative impact.

**Table 1.** Linear mixed effect model for predicting multiple-choice confidence

|  | Linear mixed effect model | | |
|---|---|---|---|
|  | Estimate | Std error | t value |
| Confusion | 2.36 | 1.45 | 1.63 |
| Frustration | -2.12 | 1.29 | -1.64 |
| Joy | 1.40 | 1.11 | 1.26 |
| Confusion to frustration | -2.49 | 1.73 | -1.44 |
|  |  | $R^2 = 0.355$ | |

Additionally, to assess the relationship between multiple choice performance (a binary measure of correctness) with multiple choice confidence (i.e., an RCJ) a Welch's two sample t-test accounting for unequal variance among groups indicated the confidence levels of students was significantly greater ($t(842) = 9.1$, $p < 0.001$, Cohen's $d = 0.60$) in trials where the multiple-choice question was answered correctly ($M = 84.0$, $SD = 15.5$) than when students answered incorrectly ($M = 74.5$, $SD = 16.2$).

# 4   Conclusion

Using an automatic affect detection system embedded in MetaTutorIVH, we conducted an analysis of learner-centered emotions and their influence on students' learning and RCJs. Joy and frustration were found to be the most frequently occurring emotions when examining the absolute frequency of discrete emotions. Analysis of the affective dynamics revealed transitions between confusion and frustration to be significantly more likely than chance, with transitions specifically from confusion to frustration being especially prominent. The presence of learner-centered emotions (joy, confusion, frustration), and transitions from confusion to frustration during complex learning did not reveal any effect of learner-centered emotions on learning. Additional analyses revealed positive effects of confusion and joy on RCJs and negative effects of frustration and transitions from confusion to frustration. These results can inform the design of ALTs that assist learners in both cognitive and metacognitive processes through monitoring and intervening based on their affective expressions.

**Acknowledgements.** This research was supported by funding from the National Science Foundation (DRL #1431552). The authors would also like to thank members of the SMART Lab and IntelliMedia Group for their contributions to this project.

# References

1. D'Mello, S., Graesser, A.: Dynamics of affective states during complex learning. Learn. Instruct. **22**(2), 145–157 (2012)
2. Baker, R., D'Mello, S., Rodrigo, M.M.T., Graesser, A.: Better to be frustrated than bored: the incidence, persistence, and impact of learners' cognitive affective states during interactions with three different computer-based learning environments. Int. J. Hum. Comput. Stud. **68**(4), 223–241 (2010)
3. Lallé, S., Conati, C., Carenini, G.: Predicting confusion in information visualization from eye tracking and interaction data. In: International Joint Conference on Artificial Intelligence, pp. 2529–2535 (2016)
4. Boulay, B., Centred, H.: Towards systems that care: a conceptual framework based on motivation, metacognition and sffect. Int. J. Artif. Intell. Educ. **20**(3), 197–229 (2010)
5. D'Mello, S., Graesser, A.: Feeling, thinking, and computing with affect aware learning. In: Calvo, R., D'Mello, S., Gratch, J., Kappas, A. (eds.) The Oxford Handbook on Affective Computing, pp. 419–434. Oxford Library of Psychology (2014)
6. Azevedo, R., Mudrick, N., Taub, M., Wortha, F.: Coupling between metacognition and emotions during STEM learning with advanced learning technologies: a critical analysis, implications for future research, and design of learning systems. In: Michalsky, T., Schechter, C. (eds.) Self-regulated Learning: Conceptualization, Contribution, and Empirically Based Models for Teaching and Learning. Teachers College Press, New York (2017)
7. Ekman, P., Friesen, W.V.: Measuring facial movement. Environ. Psychol. Nonverbal Behav. **1**(1), 56–75 (1976)
8. Calvo, R., Mello, S.: Affect detection: an interdisciplinary review of model, methods, and their applications. IEEE Trans. Affect. Comput. **1**(1), 18–37 (2010)
9. Botelho, A.F., Baker, R.S., Heffernan, N.T.: Improving sensor-free affect detection using deep learning. In: André, E., Baker, R., Hu, X., Rodrigo, M.M.T., du Boulay, B. (eds.) AIED 2017. LNCS (LNAI), vol. 10331, pp. 40–51. Springer, Cham (2017). https://doi.org/10.1007/978-3-319-61425-0_4
10. Sawyer, R., Smith, A., Rowe, J., Azevedo, R., Lester, J.: Enhancing student models in game-based learning with facial expression recognition. In: Proceedings of the Twenty-Fifth Conference on User Modeling, Adaptation, and Personalization, pp. 192–201. ACM, Bratislava, Slovakia (2017)
11. Ekman, P., Friesen, W.: Facial action coding system (1977)
12. Bates, D., Mächler, M., Bolker, B.M., Walker, S.C.: Fitting linear mixed-effects models using lme4. J. Stat. Softw. **67**, 1–48 (2015)
13. iMotions Biometric Research Platform 6.0, iMotions A/S, Copenhagen, Denmark (2016)

# Combining Difficulty Ranking
# with Multi-Armed Bandits to Sequence
# Educational Content

Avi Segal[1(✉)], Yossi Ben David[2], Joseph Jay Williams[3], Kobi Gal[1],
and Yaar Shalom[1]

[1] Ben-Gurion University of the Negev, Beersheba, Israel
avisegal@gmail.com
[2] Microsoft, Herzliya, Israel
[3] National University of Singapore, Singapore, Singapore

**Abstract.** We address the problem of how to personalize educational
content to students in order to maximize their learning gains over
time. We present a new computational approach to this problem called
MAPLE (Multi-Armed Bandits based Personalization for Learning Environments) that combines difficulty ranking with multi-armed bandits.
Given a set of target questions MAPLE estimates the expected learning
gains for each question and uses an exploration-exploitation strategy to
choose the next question to pose to the student. It maintains a personalized ranking over the difficulties of question in the target set and updates
it in real-time according to students' progress. We show in simulations
that MAPLE was able to improve students' learning gains compared to
approaches that sequence questions in increasing level of difficulty, or
rely on content experts. When implemented in a live e-learning system
in the wild, MAPLE showed promising initial results.

## 1 Introduction

As e-learning systems become more prevalent they are accessed by students of
varied backgrounds, learning styles and needs. There is thus a growing need for
them to accommodate individual difference between students and adapt to their
changing pedagogical needs over time.

We provide a novel algorithm for sequencing content in e-learning systems
that combines offline learning from students' past interactions with an online
exploration-exploitation approach in order to maximize students' learning gains.
Our algorithm, called MAPLE (Multi-Armed Bandits based Personalization for
Learning Environments), extends prior multi-armed bandit approaches in education [2], by explicitly considering question difficulty when initializing the online
behavior of the algorithm, and when updating its behavior over time.

We first evaluated MAPLE in a simulation environment comparing its performance to a variety of sequencing algorithms. MAPLE outperformed all other
approaches for average and strong students while showing the need for further

© Springer International Publishing AG, part of Springer Nature 2018
C. Penstein Rosé et al. (Eds.): AIED 2018, LNAI 10948, pp. 317–321, 2018.
https://doi.org/10.1007/978-3-319-93846-2_59

tuning for weak students. We then implemented MAPLE in the wild in an existing e-learning system in a school with 7th grade students. MAPLE showed promising results when compared to an existing educational expert approach, and a state of the art approach based on Bayesian Knowledge Tracing [3]. Further experiments with larger student groups are needed.

## 2    Related Work

Our work relates to past research on using historical data to sequence content to students, and to work on multi-armed bandits for online adaptation of educational content.

Several approaches within the educational artificial intelligence community have used computational methods for sequencing content to students. Ben David et al. [3] developed a BKT based sequencing algorithm. Their algorithm (which we refer to in this paper as YBKT) uses knowledge tracing to model students' skill acquisition over time and sequence questions to students based on their mastery level and predicted performance. It was shown to enhance student learning beyond sequencing designed by pedagogical experts. Segal et al. [6] developed EduRank, a sequencing algorithm that combines collaborative filtering with social choice theory to produce personalized learning sequences for students. The algorithm constructs a "difficulty" ranking over questions for a target student by aggregating the ranking of similar students when sequencing educational content.

Multi-armed bandits provide a fundamental model for tackling the "exploration-exploitation" trade-off [1, 7]. Williams et al. [8] used Thompson Sampling to identify highly rated explanations for how to solve Math problems, and chose uniform priors on the quality of these explanations. Clement et al. [2] used human experts' knowledge to initialize a multi-armed bandit algorithm called EXP4, that discovered which activities were at the right level to push students' learning forward. In our work we do not rely on human experts, but rather use personalized difficulty rankings to guide the initial exploitation and update steps of our algorithm.

## 3    Problem Formulation and Approach

We consider an e-learning setting with a group of students $S$ and a set of practice questions $Q$. The sequencing problem requires choosing at each time step a question to present to the student that will maximize her learning gains over the length of the practice session. The goal is to present students with challenging problems, while ensuring a high likelihood that they will be able to solve these problems.

Our approach to solve the problem, called MAPLE, maintains a belief distribution over expected learning gains to the student for solving each of the questions in $Q$. This distribution is initialized with a personalized difficulty ranking over the questions in $Q$. MAPLE samples the next question to the student from this distribution and updates it at each step given the student's performance on the question and its inferred difficulty to the student. When a student successfully solves a question, the distribution is adjusted to make harder questions more likely to be presented, and explore a broader range of questions. When a student fails to solve a question, it is adjusted to make easier questions more likely to be presented, and explore a narrower set of questions.

## 4 Simulations with Synthesized Data

We compared four different sequencing algorithms in a set of simulations: (1) The *MAPLE* approach which used the EduRank [6] algorithm for difficulty ranking. (2) The *Ascending* approach sequenced questions according to an absolute difficulty ranking that was determined by pedagogical experts. (3) The *EduRank* approach sequenced questions from the easiest estimated question to the hardest estimated question per student. (4) The *Naive Maple* approach sequenced questions using the multi-armed bandit algorithm with random initialization.

We model questions in the simulation using a ⟨skill, difficulty⟩ pair; students are modeled as a vector of skill values for each question type. The probability that a student successfully solves a question is based on Item Response Theory [4] and on the difference between her skill level and the level of the question. Estimates of student's skill levels are increased and decreased based on successes and failures in question solving (respectively), proportional to the question difficulty.

Each algorithm was run with 1000 simulated students, and sequenced 200 questions for each student. Each question belonged to one of 10 skills (uniformly distributed) and to one of 5 difficulty levels (uniformly distributed). Students' initial competency levels in each skill were uniformly distributed between 0 (no skill knowledge) and 1 (full knowledge of skill). All algorithms had access to "historical" data generated by the simulation engine in a pre-simulation step, to build their internal models.

In simulations (Fig. 1), MAPLE outperformed all other algorithms for strong and average students. For weak students the Ascending and Naive Maple approaches failed altogether. Both MAPLE and EduRank presented initial good progress but then experienced a decline in average skill level. This implies that MAPLE's adaptation scheme needs to be improved for this segment of students.

## 5 Deployment and Evaluation in the Classroom

We then conducted a field study in the wild where students used different sequencing approaches in class. MAPLE was implemented in an e-learning system used for Math education. The study compared MAPLE in a school with 7th grade students to two existing sequencing algorithms. The experiment was conducted between May 9th 2017 and June 19th 2017 (end of school year). The students were randomly divided into 3 cohorts: (1) MAPLE Sequencing (2) YBKT Sequencing (3) Ascending Sequencing.

All students in the experiment were initially exposed to a pretest session. In this session they solved 10 questions hand picked by a pedagogical expert.

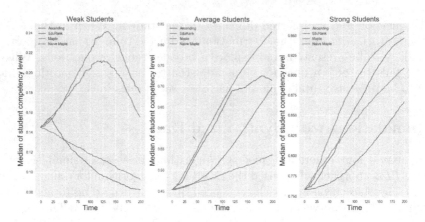

**Fig. 1.** Skill level progression per algorithm and student type.

Ninety two students solved the questions and there was no statistically significant difference between the three groups in the average score on this preliminary test. We thus concluded that each group exhibited similar baseline knowledge.

The students then engaged in multiple practice sessions in the e-learning system for the next 35 days, solving 10 assignment questions in each practice session. For each cohort, assignment questions were sequenced by the cohort's respective algorithm (i.e. MAPLE, YBKT or Ascending). At the end of this period, students were asked to complete a post test session, solving the same questions (in the same order) as in the pretest session. Twenty eight students completed the post test session. We attribute the decrease in students' response from pretest to post test to the pending end of the academic year (there was no difference in the dropout rates across the 3 cohorts).

**Table 1.** Post test results per cohort: time per question and average grade.

| Cohort | Time per question (s) | Average grade |
|--------|-----------------------|---------------|
| Ascending | 6.49 | 43.76 |
| MAPLE | 10.69 | 71.28 |
| YBKT | 12.86 | 67.08 |

Table 1 shows the students' average grade and the time spent on post-test questions. As can be seen, students assigned to the MAPLE condition achieved higher post test results than students assigned to the Ascending condition or to the YBKT condition. Further experiments with larger student groups are needed to evaluate statistical significance.

# 6     Conclusion

We presented a new method called MAPLE for sequencing questions to students in on-line educational systems. MAPLE combines difficulty ranking based on past student experiences with a multi-armed bandit approach using these difficulty rankings in on-line settings. We tested our approach in simulations and compared it to other algorithms. We then performed an initial experiment running MAPLE in a classroom in parallel to two baseline algorithms. MAPLE showed promising results in simulations and in the wild. Further simulations and experiments are needed to adapt and verify MAPLE's performance in more complex settings. For more information on the MAPLE algorithm and the simulation and field results please see [5].

# References

1. Bubeck, S., Cesa-Bianchi, N., et al.: Regret analysis of stochastic and nonstochastic multi-armed bandit problems. Found. Trends® Mach. Learn. **5**(1), 1–122 (2012)
2. Clement, B., Roy, D., Oudeyer, P.-Y., Lopes, M.: Multi-armed bandits for intelligent tutoring systems. J. Educ. Data Min. (JEDM) **7**(2), 20–48 (2015)
3. Ben David, Y., Segal, A., Gal, Y.K.: Sequencing educational content in classrooms using Bayesian knowledge tracing. In: Proceedings of the Sixth International Conference on Learning Analytics and Knowledge, pp. 354–363. ACM (2016)
4. Hambleton, R.K., Swaminathan, H., Rogers, H.J.: Fundamentals of Item Response Theory, vol. 2. Sage, Newbury Park (1991)
5. Segal, A., David, Y.B., Williams, J.J., Gal, K., Shalom, Y.: Combining difficulty ranking with multi-armed bandits to sequence educational content. arXiv (2018)
6. Segal, A., Katzir, Z., Gal, K., Shani, G., Shapira, B.: EduRank: a collaborative filtering approach to personalization in e-learning. In: Educational Data Mining (2014)
7. Thompson, W.R.: On the likelihood that one unknown probability exceeds another in view of the evidence of two samples. Biometrika **25**(3/4), 285–294 (1933)
8. Williams, J.J., Kim, J., Rafferty, A., Maldonado, S., Gajos, K.Z., Lasecki, W.S., Heffernan, N.: Axis: generating explanations at scale with learnersourcing and machine learning. In: Proceedings of the Third (2016) ACM Conference on Learning@ Scale, pp. 379–388. ACM (2016)

# TipsC: Tips and Corrections
# for programming MOOCs

Saksham Sharma, Pallav Agarwal, Parv Mor, and Amey Karkare[✉]

Indian Institute of Technology, Kanpur, India
{sakshams,pallavag,parv,karkare}@cse.iitk.ac.in

**Abstract.** With MOOC sizes increasing every day, improving scalability and practicality of grading and tutoring of such courses is a worthwhile pursuit. To this end, we introduce `TipsC`. By analyzing a large number of correct submissions, `TipsC` can search for correct codes resembling a given incorrect solution. `TipsC` then suggests changes in the incorrect code to help the student fix logical errors.

We evaluate the effectiveness of `TipsC`'s clustering algorithm on data collected from past offerings of an introductory programming course conducted at IIT Kanpur. The results show the weighted average variance of marks for clusters when similar submissions are grouped together is 47% less compared to the case when all programs are grouped together.

**Keywords:** Intelligent tutoring system
Automated program analysis · MOOC · Clustering
Program correction

## 1   Introduction

With Massively Open Online Courses (MOOCs) being widely adopted among academic institutions and online platforms alike, the number of students studying programming through such courses has sky-rocketed. In contrast, the availability of personalized help through Teaching Assistants (TAs) can not scale accordingly due to human limitations.

The challenge here is two-fold. Firstly, human TAs grading a large number of submissions may introduce bias and variance as shown in [9]. Secondly, manually helping students stuck at a problem (by providing relevant tips and suggestions) is simply not tractable for MOOCs due to the scale involved. This problem is receiving lots of attention recently [1,2,4–7,9,10,12]. These works differ mainly in the approach used. We have seen use of rule based rewrites [9], neural networks [1,2,10], deep learning [1,6] to generate feedbacks/hints.

We introduce `TipsC`, a tool to parse, analyze, and cluster programming MOOC submissions. It can be plugged into a MOOC in order to tackle the above challenges. It allows instructors and TAs to obtain a bird's eye view of the spectrum of solutions received from the students. In addition, it generates fixes

© Springer International Publishing AG, part of Springer Nature 2018
C. Penstein Rosé et al. (Eds.): AIED 2018, LNAI 10948, pp. 322–326, 2018.
https://doi.org/10.1007/978-3-319-93846-2_60

```
int main() {                          int main() {
  int n; float f;                       float y; int x;
  scanf("%d %f", &n, &f);               scanf("%d %f", &x, &y);
  if (n%5==0 && (n+.5)<=f && f<=2000)   if ((x%5==0) && (x+0.5)<=y)
    printf("%0.2f", f-n-.5);             printf("%0.2f", y-x-.50);
  else printf("%0.2f", f);              else printf("%0.2f", y);
}                                     }
```

**Fig. 1.** Two programs with a small logical difference. **Source:** codechef.com/problems/ HS08TEST.

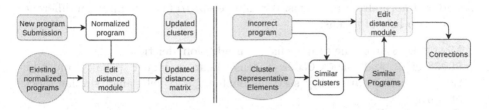

**Fig. 2.** Workflow of `TipsC`

for logical mistakes done by students. `TipsC` is an open source software, released under the Apache 2.0 License, on GitHub.[1]

The primary idea behind `TipsC` is that most introductory programming assignments have a finite number of solution variants at abstract syntax tree (AST) level, with minor variations in between them (see Fig. 1). Thus a student's solution would often resemble some previously existing solution(s). `TipsC` finds *correct* programs which are similar to a user's *incorrect* attempt. It can then suggest relatively small changes to fix the user's program. This is done by parsing submissions, converting them to a normalized representation, and then clustering them by their pair-wise distances. The edit distance metric and normalized form are tailored for this specific problem through the use of domain-specific heuristics [11].

## 2   Method

`TipsC` uses syntactically and semantically correct C language programs to create clusters. These clusters are used to offer corrections on syntactically correct but semantically incorrect programs, as shown in Fig. 2. A more detailed description of the algorithm can be found in [11].

### 2.1   Program Normalization

The program is first converted to a linear representation, rather than one with nested constructs (AST). For example, an if-else construct gets converted to:

---

[1] The source code is available at https://github.com/HexFlow/tipsy. The web playground for `TipsC` is deployed at http://tipsy.hexflow.in.

IF(condition) BLOCK_START...BLOCK_END ELSE BLOCK_START...BLOCK_END.

All expressions are converted into postfix notation to account for different bracketing. This is followed by renaming variables within expressions to generic names, based on their order of use *within that expression*. For instance, the expression $(a + b/a)$ after normalization would become: $(var_1\ var_2\ var_1\ /\ +)$

## 2.2  Edit Distance

We use a variant of the Levenshtein edit distance algorithm to compare two linearized and normalized programs. It will attempt to find the minimal difference between two lists of tokens.

- Most tokens incur the same penalty on addition/deletion.
- BLOCK_OPEN and BLOCK_CLOSE tokens incur a higher penalty on addition/deletion because they serve as anchors, and help align similar blocks of code.
- Expressions distances are calculated with a similar algorithm, incurring a granular cost. This cost is normalized by expression size and later scaled.

## 2.3  Comparing Programs

We choose to consider the edit-distance between different function bodies of the program separately, to capture function reordering and code redistribution properly. To pair up functions, we do Depth-First-Traversal on expressions in the 'main' function, to reorder functions in the order of invocation. This also removes any unused functions. We also look at out-of-order function matching, albeit with a higher penalty for increasing mismatch in terms of use-order.

## 2.4  Clustering Programs

Owing to lack of triangle inequality, we cannot map the programs onto a vector space that accurately captures their distance matrix. We use hierarchical clustering [8] which does not require an assertion of the inequality. We precompute $\mathcal{O}(1)$ representative elements in each cluster, to speed up searching for similar programs. Representative elements of a cluster are those with the least root mean square distance from all elements of the cluster. We create $\Omega(\sqrt{n})$ clusters, each having $\mathcal{O}(\sqrt{n})$ programs. This allows an initial search over just the cluster's representative elements, to prune the program search space.

# 3  Experimental Results

## 3.1  Scalability

TipsC's scalability depends on the time required to update the distance matrix and the clusters. The former is run only for correct submissions and takes up to

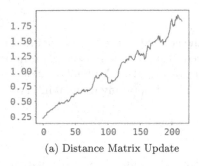
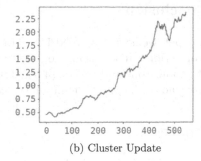

(a) Distance Matrix Update          (b) Cluster Update

**Fig. 3.** Performance tests for `TipsC` (50 LOC per program). X axis: No. of existing programs. Y axis: time (sec) taken for update.

$\mathcal{O}(n)$ per submission. The step is amenable to parallelization, and its performance is sufficient for most MOOCs (Fig. 3a). The latter scales as $\mathcal{O}(n^2)$, but is run infrequently. According to our tests, this is not a major overhead (Fig. 3b). These metrics were collected on a Linux desktop with 16 GB RAM, and an Intel(R) Core(TM) i7 CPU @ 3.40 GHz with 4 cores.

Fetching corrections has a worst case time complexity of $\mathcal{O}(n)$ in the rare case when there are $\mathcal{O}(n)$ clusters. On real data, collected from Prutor [3] system used in ESC101 (The *Introduction to Programming* course at IIT Kanpur), we see 30–40 clusters among 100 submissions for each problem, with 20–30 of them being singleton clusters of outliers. It takes around 0.6–0.8 s to fetch corrections for one program.

## 3.2 Variance Before and After Clustering

`TipsC` was run on data from previous iterations of ESC101. To compare the effectiveness of the clustering by `TipsC`, we computed the variance of marks in each cluster for several problems as shown in Table 1. The results show that variance within a cluster is (on an average) 47% less than when all the submissions are considered together. This suggests that `TipsC` is indeed able to group similar programs together, a fact that can help in effective grading by assigning similar programs to the same TA.

**Table 1.** Comparison of variance of marks with and without clustering

| Assignment ID | # submissions | Variance (overall) | Average cluster variance |
|---|---|---|---|
| Lab3-1633 | 84 | 1.54 | 0.78 |
| Lab4-1822 | 68 | 2.15 | 0.70 |
| Lab6-2012 | 64 | 3.33 | 1.97 |
| Lab8-2289 | 68 | 1.92 | 1.30 |
| Exam1-1938 | 69 | 6.93 | 3.74 |

# 4    Conclusion

In this paper, we have described `TipsC` in the context of programming and logical error corrections. It is a scalable system requiring a very reasonable number of correct submissions and can be plugged into any existing MOOC to allow aiding students who are having difficulty in the course without any manual intervention.

# References

1. Ahmed, U.Z., Kumar, P., Karkare, A., Kar, P., Gulwani, S.: Compilation error repair: for the student programs, from the student programs. In: ICSE-SEET 2018, pp. 13–22 (2018)
2. Bhatia, S., Singh, R.: Automated correction for syntax errors in programming assignments using recurrent neural networks. arXiv:1603.06129 (2016)
3. Das, R., Ahmed, U.Z., Karkare, A., Gulwani, S.: Prutor: a system for tutoring CS1 and collecting student programs for analysis. arXiv:1608.03828 (2016)
4. Gulwani, S., Radicek, I., Zuleger, F.: Feedback generation for performance problems in introductory programming assignments. In: FSE 2014, pp. 41–51 (2014)
5. Gulwani, S., Radicek, I., Zuleger, F.: Automated clustering and program repair for introductory programming assignments. arXiv:1603.03165 (2016)
6. Gupta, R., Pal, S., Kanade, A., Shevade, S.: DeepFix: fixing common C Language errors by deep learning. In: AAAI 2017 (2017)
7. Head, A., Glassman, E., Soares, G., Suzuki, R., Figueredo, L., D'Antoni, L., Hartmann, B.: Writing reusable code feedback at scale with mixed-initiative program synthesis. In: L@S 2017 (2017)
8. Murtagh, F.: A survey of recent advances in hierarchical clustering algorithms. Comput. J. **26**(4), 354–359 (1983)
9. Parihar, S., Dadachanji, Z., Singh, P.K., Das, R., Karkare, A., Bhattacharya, A.: Automatic grading and feedback using program repair for introductory programming courses. In: ITiCSE 2017 (2017)
10. Pu, Y., Narasimhan, K., Solar-Lezama, A., Barzilay, R.: Sk_P: a neural program corrector for MOOCs. In: SPLASH Companion 2016 (2016)
11. Sharma, S., Agarwal, P., Mor, P., Karkare, A.: TipsC: tips and corrections for programming MOOCs. arXiv:1804.00373 (2018)
12. Yi, J., Ahmed, U.Z., Karkare, A., Tan, S.H., Roychoudhury, A.: A feasibility study of using automated program repair for introductory programming assignments. In: ESEC/FSE 2017 (2017)

# Empirically Evaluating the Effectiveness of POMDP vs. MDP Towards the Pedagogical Strategies Induction

Shitian Shen[✉], Behrooz Mostafavi[✉], Collin Lynch[✉], Tiffany Barnes[✉], and Min Chi[✉]

Department of Computer Science, North Carolina State University,
Raleigh, NC 27695, USA
{sshen,bzmostaf,cflynch,tmbarnes,mchi}@ncsu.edu

**Abstract.** The effectiveness of Intelligent Tutoring Systems (ITSs) often depends upon their *pedagogical strategies*, the policies used to decide what action to take next in the face of alternatives. We induce policies based on two general Reinforcement Learning (RL) frameworks: POMDP &. MDP, given the limited feature space. We conduct an empirical study where the RL-induced policies are compared against a random yet reasonable policy. Results show that when the contents are controlled to be equal, the MDP-based policy can improve students' learning significantly more than the random baseline while the POMDP-based policy cannot outperform the later. The possible reason is that the features selected for the MDP framework may not be the optimal feature space for POMDP.

**Keywords:** Reinforcement Learning · POMDP · MDP · ITS

## 1 Introduction

Reinforcement Learning (RL) offers one of the most promising approaches to applying data-driven decision-making to improve student learning in Intelligent Tutoring Systems (ITSs), which facilitates learning by providing step-by-step support and contextualized feedback to individual students [4,12]. These step-by-step behaviors can be viewed as a sequential decision process where at each step the system chooses an action (e.g. give a hint, show an example) from a set of options. *Pedagogical strategies* are policies that are used to decide what action to take next in the face of alternatives.

A number of researchers have applied RL to induce pedagogical policies for ITSs [2,3,5,8]: some apply Markov Decision Processes (MDPs) thus treating the user-system interactions as fully observable processes [6,11] while others utilize partially-observable MDPs (POMDPs) [9,13,14] to account for hidden states. In this work, we focus on comparing POMDPs vs. MDPs directly and induce the policies based upon these two frameworks given a small feature set. Besides, we

© Springer International Publishing AG, part of Springer Nature 2018
C. Penstein Rosé et al. (Eds.): AIED 2018, LNAI 10948, pp. 327–331, 2018.
https://doi.org/10.1007/978-3-319-93846-2_61

employ a simple baseline pedagogical policy where the system *randomly* decides whether to present the next problem as Worked Example (WE) or as Problem Solving (PS). Because both PS and WE are always considered to be *reasonable* educational intervention in our learning context, we refer to such policy as *random yet reasonable* policy or *random* in the following. The empirical result indicates that the RL-induced policies can improve students' learning significantly more than the random baseline for a particular type of students.

## 2   Methods

**MDP** is defined as a 4-tuple $\langle S, A, T, R \rangle$, where $S$ denotes the observable state space, defined by a set of features that represent the interactive learning environment; $A$ denotes the space of possible actions for the agent to execute; $T$ represents the transition probability, and $R$ represents expected reward of transiting from a state to another one by taking an action. In our work, the optimal policy $\pi^*$ of an MDP is generated by Value Iteration algorithm.

**POMDP** is an extension of MDP, defined by a 7-tuple $\langle S, A, R, P_h, P_o, B, prior \rangle$, where $A$ and $R$ have the same definitions as in MDPs. $S$ represents the *hidden* state space. $P_h$ denotes the transition probability among the hidden state by taking the action, and $P_o$ is the conditional observation probability. *Prior* denotes the prior probability distribution of hidden states. $B$ denotes the belief state space, which is constructed through Input-Output Hidden Markov Model (IOHMM) [1] in our work.

The POMDP policy induction procedure can be divided into three steps. First, we transform the training corpus into the hidden state space through the Viterbi algorithm. Second, we implement Q-learning to estimate the Q-values for each hidden state and action pair: $(s, a)$. Third, we estimate the Q value of belief state $b$ and action $a$ at time step $t$ as:

$$Q_t(b, a) = \sum_s B_t(s) \cdot Q(s, a) \tag{1}$$

Thus, $Q_t(b, a)$ is a linear combination of the $Q(s, a)$ for each hidden state with its corresponding belief $B_t(s)$. When the process converges, $\pi^*$ is induced by taking the optimal action $a$ at time $t$ associated with the highest $Q_t(b, a)$.

## 3   Experiment

**Participates and Conditions.** 124 undergraduate students who enrolled in Fall 2016 were randomly assigned to one of three conditions: MDP ($N = 45$), POMDP ($N = 40$), Random ($N = 39$). We subdivided the conditions into Fast ($n = 61$) and Slow ($n = 63$) groups based upon their average response time on Level 1. Combining conditions with Fast and Slow, we had a total of 6 groups: MDP-Fast ($N = 22$), MDP-Slow ($N = 23$), POMDP-Fast ($N = 18$), POMDP-Slow ($N = 22$), Random-Fast ($N = 21$), Random-Slow ($N = 18$).

The Chi-square test demonstrated that there was no significant difference on distribution of Fast vs. Slow among three conditions: $\chi^2 = 0.03, p = 0.86$.

**Procedure.** Deep Thought (DT) was a data-driven ITS that teaches logic proofs and it was used as part of an assignment in an undergraduate discrete mathematics course. DT consists of 6 strictly ordered levels of proof problems [7]. Students were required to complete 3–4 problems per level and a total of 18–24 problems overall. Students could skip problem if they encountered an issue to solve this problem. We treat level 1 as the pre-test phase to measure student's incoming confidence since students received the same problems in level 1 where all of the problems were PS. From level 2 to level 6, students were assigned a PS at the end of each level for evaluating student's performance fairly. Implemented policies made other decisions during the training process. ITS made total 10–15 decisions during a complete training process for each student.

**Performance Evaluation.** To fully evaluate student performance, we modified our in-class exam, referred as Post-test. Students' answers were graded to the scale of 1–100 by the Teaching Assistants of the class (who are not part of the research group). We mainly treated the Post-test score as Students' learning outcome measure in the following.

**Training Data** was collected in the Fall 2014 and Spring 2015 semesters. All of the students used the same ITS, followed the same general procedure, studied the same training materials, and worked through the same set of training problems. The only substantive difference was the presentation of the materials, WE or PS, randomly decided. The training dataset contained the interaction logs of 306 students and the average number of problems solved by students was 23.7 and the average time that students spent in the tutor was 5.29 h. There are a total of 133 features to represent students' behaviors. We generate the same feature space for both MDP and POMDP through a MDP-based feature selection approach [10], which selects a total of six features, shown as follows:

1. **totalPSTime**: total time that students spend on PS.
2. **easyProbCount**: easy problem that students solved so far.
3. **newLevel**: whether students jump into a new level.
4. **avgStepTime**: average step time so far.
5. **hintRatio**: the ratio between hint count and number of applying rules.
6. **numProbRule**: number of rules in the current problem's solution.

## 4   Results

**Pre-test Score.** A two-way ANOVA using condition {MDP, POMDP, Random} and type {Fast, Slow} as factors, shows that there is no significant interaction effect with the students' pre-test scores. Additionally, a one-way ANOVA indicates that there is no significant difference in the pre-test scores among the three conditions, or between the Fast and Slow groups. Therefore, we can conclude that all of the six groups have a similar incoming competence. Table 1 presents the mean and (SD) of pre- and post-test score for each group.

**Post-test Score.** A two-way ANCOVA, using condition and type as factors and pre-test as the covariate, shows a significant interaction effect on the post-test score: $F(2, 117) = 4.06, p = .019$. Additionally, one-way ANCOVA tests show that there is no significant difference either among conditions or between Fast and Slow. Furthermore, one-way ANCOVA tests on policy using pre-test as the covariate shows no significant difference among the three Fast groups on the post-test score: $F(2, 57) = 0.74, p = 0.48$, but the significant difference among the three Slow groups: $F(2, 59) = 5.03, p = .009$. Specifically, pairwise t-tests indicate that *MDP-Slow* scored significantly higher post-test than both *POMDP-Slow* and *Random-Slow*: $p = .004$ and $p = .015$ respectively, and no significant difference is found between the latter two groups. Therefore, our results exhibited an Aptitude-Treatment Interaction effect: all of three Fast groups learned equally well after training on ITS regardless of the policies employed while the Slow groups were indeed more sensitive to induced policies. For Slow groups, the MDP policy significantly outperformed the POMDP and Random policies while no significant difference existed between the latter two policies.

**Table 1.** Pre- and Post-test scores for each group

| Policy | Pre-test score | | | Post-test score | | |
|---|---|---|---|---|---|---|
| | Total | Fast | Slow | Total | Fast | Slow |
| MDP | 74.90 (26.3) | 75.34 (27.6) | 74.48 (25.5) | 88.26 (15.2) | 84.23 (17.7) | **92.12 (11.3)** |
| POMDP | 75.18 (25.9) | 74.01 (29.1) | 76.15 (23.2) | 79.53 (24.4) | 86.47 (23.6) | 73.86 (24.1) |
| Random | 65.99 (28.1) | 67.69 (28.8) | 64.02 (27.8) | 82.85 (22.3) | 88.98 (17.9) | 75.69 (25.3) |

Furthermore, we compared the Fast and Slow groups within each condition. Two-sample t-tests shows no significant difference between Fast and Slow under the POMDP condition: $t(38) = 1.67$, $p = 0.11$, but the marginal significant difference between Fast and Slow under either MDP or Random condition: $t(43) = -1.78, p = .081$ and $t(37) = 1.91, p = .063$ respectively.

## 5   Conclusions and Future Work

In this study, we induced two types of RL policies using MDP and POMDP framework respectively and compared their effectiveness against the random baseline in the context of ITS. Besides, we split students into Fast and Slow groups based on their average step time in the initial tutorial level. The empirical results exhibited an Aptitude-Treatment interaction effect: Fast groups were less sensitive to the policies in that they learned equally well regardless of the policies while the Slow groups were more sensitive in that the MDP policy could help slow groups score significantly higher post-test than the POMDP and Random policies. This suggested that the MDP policy is more effective than either POMDP or Random policy for Slow groups. One of the possible reasons for the ineffectiveness of the POMDP policy is that the feature selection and discretization limit the full power of the POMDP framework. In future work, we plan to maintain the continuous features and design effective feature extraction method for POMDP in order to show the full power of POMDP.

**Acknowledgements.** This research was supported by the NSF Grants #1726550, #1651909, and #1432156.

# References

1. Bengio, Y., Frasconi, P.: An input output HMM architecture. In: Advances in Neural Information Processing Systems, pp. 427–434 (1995)
2. Chi, M., VanLehn, K., Litman, D., Jordan, P.: Empirically evaluating the application of reinforcement learning to the induction of effective and adaptive pedagogical strategies. User Model. User Adap. Inter. **21**(1–2), 137–180 (2011)
3. Doroudi, S., Holstein, K., Aleven, V., Brunskill, E.: Towards understanding how to leverage sense-making, induction and refinement, and fluency to improve robust learning. In: International Educational Data Mining Society (2015)
4. Koedinger, K.R., Anderson, J.R., Hadley, W.H., Mark, M.A.: Intelligent tutoring goes to school in the big city (1997)
5. Koedinger, K.R., Brunskill, E., Baker, R.S., McLaughlin, E.A., Stamper, J.: New potentials for data-driven intelligent tutoring system development and optimization. AI Mag. **34**(3), 27–41 (2013)
6. Levin, E., Pieraccini, R., Eckert, W.: A stochastic model of human-machine interaction for learning dialog strategies. IEEE Trans. Speech Audio Process. **8**(1), 11–23 (2000)
7. Mostafavi Behrooz, Z.L., Barnes, T.: Data-driven proficiency profiling. In: Proceedings of the 8th International Conference on Educational Data Mining (2015)
8. Rowe, J.P., Lester, J.C.: Improving student problem solving in narrative-centered learning environments: a modular reinforcement learning framework. In: Conati, C., Heffernan, N., Mitrovic, A., Verdejo, M.F. (eds.) AIED 2015. LNCS (LNAI), vol. 9112, pp. 419–428. Springer, Cham (2015). https://doi.org/10.1007/978-3-319-19773-9_42
9. Roy, N., Pineau, J., Thrun, S.: Spoken dialogue management using probabilistic reasoning. In: Proceedings of the 38th Annual Meeting on Association for Computational Linguistics, pp. 93–100. Association for Computational Linguistics (2000)
10. Shen, S., Chi, M.: Aim low: correlation-based feature selection for model-based reinforcement learning. In: EDM, pp. 507–512 (2016)
11. Singh, S., Litman, D., Kearns, M., Walker, M.: Optimizing dialogue management with reinforcement learning: experiments with the NJFun system. J. Artif. Intell. Res. **16**, 105–133 (2002)
12. Vanlehn, K.: The behavior of tutoring systems. Int. J. Artif. Intell. Educ. **16**(3), 227–265 (2006)
13. Williams, J.D., Young, S.: Partially observable Markov decision processes for spoken dialog systems. Comput. Speech Lang. **21**(2), 393–422 (2007)
14. Zhang, B., Cai, Q., Mao, J., Chang, E., Guo, B.: Spoken dialogue management as planning and acting under uncertainty. In: INTERSPEECH, pp. 2169–2172 (2001)

# Understanding Revisions in Student Writing Through Revision Graphs

Antonette Shibani[(✉)], Simon Knight, and Simon Buckingham Shum

University of Technology Sydney, PO Box 123 Broadway,
Ultimo, NSW 2007, Australia
antonette.aileenshibani@student.uts.edu.au

**Abstract.** Text revision is regarded as an important process in improving written products. To study the process of revision activity from authentic classroom contexts, this paper introduces a novel visualization method called *Revision Graph* to aid detailed analysis of the writing process. This opens up the possibility of exploring the stages in students' revision of drafts, which can lead to further automation of revision analysis for researchers, and formative feedback to students on their writing. The Revision Graph could also be applied to study the direct impact of automated feedback on students' revisions and written outputs in stages of their revision, thus evaluating its effectiveness in pedagogic contexts.

**Keywords:** Learning Analytics · Writing Analytics · Revision analysis
Writing · Revision process · Visualizations · Revision Graph

## 1 Introduction

Text revision is considered an important process in writing to support the reworking of writer's thoughts and ideas, playing a major role in the outcome of the writing [1]. The cognitive process theory of writing defines revision as a recursive process that can be called any time during writing [2]. Writers engage in task definition, evaluation, goal-setting and strategy selection to make revisions, thus leading to improvements in a text. To teach students revision skills to improve their writing, it is essential for researchers and educators to understand what contributes to good revision and how it occurs. This can be supported by Writing Analytics, which could be thought of as a sub field of Learning Analytics that involves "the measurement and analysis of written texts for the purpose of *understanding writing processes and products*, in their educational contexts" [3]. Such analytics might be deployed both to provide feedback to students on their revisions, and in research to understand the revision process using textual features.

The focus of this article is on studying the *process* of revision, which can help researchers and educators gain insights into the processes involved in the creation of a written document and the use of feedback in various stages of revision (an extended version can be found at [4]). In earlier work, such processes in revision have been studied using personal testimonies of participants regarding their cognitive process in

---

An extended version of this paper can be found at Technical Report [4].

© Springer International Publishing AG, part of Springer Nature 2018
C. Penstein Rosé et al. (Eds.): AIED 2018, LNAI 10948, pp. 332–336, 2018.
https://doi.org/10.1007/978-3-319-93846-2_62

revising, or by process tracing and participant-observer methods that observe the behaviors involved in revision [1]. Resource intensive manual observation and coding can be improved with advanced online trace data collection and analysis techniques to develop visualizations that represent the process of drafting and revision. To visualize modification patterns in an online document, Caporossi and Leblay [5] developed a graph theory approach to represent the movement of text through a document using log data of keystrokes and cursor movements from the document editing process. However, there is no evidence that educators would find keystroke-level data insightful for understanding revision patterns, nor that students would find this meaningful feedback to improve their writing. More recent work introduced the use of Sequence Homology Analysis (SHA) to study the evolution of public speech drafts by comparing the changes in characters, and proposing a draft network based on the strength of revisions made [6]. In this paper, we introduce a 'Revision Graph' to visualize the evolution of writing in terms of the actions that led to the final product, and explain its potential for studying writing revisions in various contexts.

## 2   Research Context

The research context for this paper is a pedagogic intervention that made use of a web-based tool integrated with multiple tasks to help students write better essays for their subject in authentic classroom settings [7]. In the main revision task, students worked on revising a short essay that was provided to them, to produce an improved version (rationale in [8]), in study conditions with and without using automated writing feedback. To study the features of revision, the revised essays were marked by tutors on a scale of 0–3 (0- degraded, 1-no change, 2- minor improvement, 3-major improvements), based on which the essays are characterized as improved or degraded. Drafts from students' revisions were captured every one minute (unobtrusively) for collecting revision data using the AWA-Tutor tool which scaffolds the tasks in the intervention, and students' usage of automated feedback was also recorded [9].

## 3   A Novel Approach to Revision Analysis

We provide a novel analysis of revisions over multiple drafts created through the text-revision exercise using a 'Revision Graph', exemplified by a sample improved essay and a sample degraded essay written by the students in our context. This draft level analysis can aid to uncover the previously unknown processes involved in the editing of the final revised essay. This new manual analysis focuses on the ordering of sentences and revision actions, which could be potentially automated. In this revision graph (Fig. 1), the nodes represent sentences from the drafts and the edges represent changes in the organization of sentences across multiple drafts. The sentences are represented in the sequence of occurrence across the paragraphs. The colors of the nodes indicate the type of revision action made at the sentence level: (i) minor revisions are when students predominantly use the given text, but add or substitute few words, (ii) major revisions are when students add a substantial number of words and explanations to the given text with the inclusion of their own writing, (iii) no changes made and (iv) no change in the current stage, but deleted in the next stage. Red triangles represent that automated feedback was requested during the revision process. Dotted edges are used to represent the repetition of similar concepts across multiple sentences inside a draft. This could be a good indicator of word repetition/overlap leading to high cohesion in the document.

Figure 1 (left) shows the revision graph constructed from the sample improved essay's drafts to show the evolution of a high-scoring revised essay. The drafts were selected from certain intervals (every 6 min in this analysis) using the time spent on revision. The graph shows the stages in the revision of the given text containing four paragraphs and 15 sentences to the final product containing two paragraphs and 10 sentences. In the first draft stage, the student has deleted some broad introductory sentences from the original essay. The first paragraph of the draft has been shaped up by making minor and major revisions to the given sentences and reordering them, while the other paragraphs remain untouched. In the second stage of drafting, the student has deleted the previous second paragraph and mainly worked on the revision of this paragraph from the other paragraph sentences. Here the text has been reduced to three paragraphs.

From the third draft, the first paragraph remains stable. The student has made some extensive changes to the sentences by revising and consolidating them to produce a final text consisting of only two paragraphs. The number of references to the previously written words increases in each stage of the draft as shown by the dotted edges. The final text has many such cross references made to the previous sentences, which has improved the cohesion of the text. This student requested automated feedback (red triangle) after completing the final text and made no more changes after that. This information is made visible by matching the timestamp of feedback request with those of the drafts. It informs that the changes made to the text by the student were *not an effect of the feedback received*. In cases where we do not have such process information to study writing, it is feasible that the revision effect is attributed to feedback, but they are in fact not related. This revision graph is thus serving its purpose of making visible, at an appropriate granularity, the nature of the revisions, and whether the automated feedback component impacted subsequent revisions.

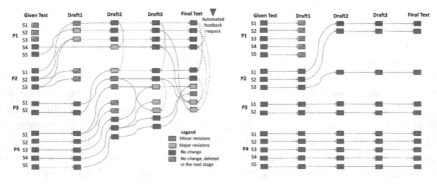

**Fig. 1.** Revision graph of sample improved essay (left) and sample degraded essay (right)

In the revision graph of a sample degraded essay shown in Fig. 1 (right), there are no edits made by the student to the given sentences. The introductory sentences have been removed in the first draft, and sentences have been reorganized in the second draft. No further changes have been made from the second draft to create the final revised essay, leading to a degraded version of the given text. The last three drafts have remained stable, meaning the student has stopped working in the last few minutes of the revision task. The above manually constructed revision graphs could potentially be automated for a large scale analysis of revision process.

## 4 Conclusion and Future Work

This paper introduced a process centric method to study revision with the construction of a 'Revision Graph' to study the evolution of writing. This novel visualization revealed a pattern of actions that led to the final product like addition, deletion and re-organization of sentences in the generation of the text, showing the importance of understanding textual restructuring and the revision process in writing. It demonstrated the opportunity to study the diverse ways in which good or poor writing may evolve in its revision stages. One could also imagine the visualization being applied to other specific changes we would like to study, like the types of revisions (e.g. content, concepts, rhetorical moves, surface errors, etc.) instead of the revision actions.

An application of this revision graph, as mentioned previously in the revision process analysis of a good revised essay, is to study the effect of automated writing feedback using actual revisions made by students at multiple stages, thus helping to find effective forms of feedback leading to revisions. This way of evaluating the effectiveness of Learning Analytics applications (automated writing feedback in this case) is thus made possible using Learning Analytics itself (tracking the revision process in student drafts for detailed study). This could be the first step towards studying the contexts in which automated feedback can work better, and other contexts in which other forms of feedback like human feedback are well suited. Further cognitive processes can be studied using think aloud techniques to capture the mental models while adopting/rejecting the feedback. We do not yet know if these techniques can be used to differentiate texts that are not extreme cases of performance; thus, having demonstrated the utility of the revision graph in principle, to test its performance on text corpora at scale requires software implementation. Finally, to extend their usage in educational contexts, further work has to be done to characterize essays based on the discussed features to provide meaningful feedback to educators and students. The feedback might be based on writing patterns that emerge or revision types, e.g. to draw attention to the fact that there have been no substantive changes in graphs after 2 drafts or within a defined time interval, or changes that only involve surface level error corrections. Validation of the Revision Graph in terms of usability and usefulness should also be conducted as to supports its application in future writing research.

# References

1. Fitzgerald, J.: Research on revision in writing. Rev. Educ. Res. **57**(4), 481–506 (1987)
2. Flower, L., Hayes, J.R.: A cognitive process theory of writing. Coll. Compos. Commun. **32**(4), 365–387 (1981)
3. Buckingham Shum, S., Knight, S., McNamara, D., Allen, L., Bektik, D., Crossley, S: Critical perspectives on writing analytics. In: Proceedings of the Sixth International Conference on Learning Analytics and Knowledge, pp. 481–483. ACM, NewYork (2016)
4. Shibani, A., Knight, S., Buckingham Shum, S.: Understanding Students' Revisions in Writing: From Word Counts to the Revision Graph. Technical report CIC-TR-2018-01, Connected Intelligence Centre, University of Technology Sydney, Australia (2018). https://utscic.edu.au/research/publications/
5. Caporossi, G., Leblay, C.: Online writing data representation: a graph theory approach. In: Gama, J., Bradley, E., Hollmén, J. (eds.) IDA 2011. LNCS, vol. 7014, pp. 80–89. Springer, Heidelberg (2011). https://doi.org/10.1007/978-3-642-24800-9_10
6. Wininger, M.: Measuring the evolution of a revised document. J. Writ. Res. **6**(1), 1–28 (2014)
7. Shibani, A., Knight, S., Buckingham Shum, S., Ryan, P.: Design and implementation of a pedagogic intervention using writing analytics. In: 25th International Conference on Computers in Education. Asia-Pacific Society for Computers in Education, New Zealand (2017)
8. Rijlaarsdam, G., Couzijn, M., Van Den Bergh, H.: The study of revision as a writing process and as a learning-to-write process. In: Allal, L., Chanquoy, L., Largy, P. (eds.) Revision Cognitive and Instructional Processes. Studies in Writing, vol. 13. Springer, Dordrecht (2004). https://doi.org/10.1007/978-94-007-1048-1_12
9. Shibani, A.: AWA-Tutor: a platform to ground automated writing feedback in robust learning design. In: 8th International Conference on Learning Analytics and Knowledge (LAK 2018), Sydney (2018)

# Exploring Online Course Sociograms Using Cohesion Network Analysis

Maria-Dorinela Sirbu[1], Mihai Dascalu[1,2(✉)], Scott A. Crossley[3],
Danielle S. McNamara[4], Tiffany Barnes[5], Collin F. Lynch[5],
and Stefan Trausan-Matu[1,2]

[1] University Politehnica of Bucharest, Splaiul Independenței 313,
60042 Bucharest, Romania
maria.sirbu@cti.pub.ro,
{mihai.dascalu, stefan.trausan}@cs.pub.ro
[2] Academy of Romanian Scientists, 54 Splaiul Independenței,
050094 Bucharest, Romania
[3] Department of Applied Linguistics/ESL,
Georgia State University, Atlanta, GA 30303, USA
scrossley@gsu.edu
[4] Institute for the Science of Teaching and Learning,
Arizona State University, Tempe, AZ, USA
dsmcnama@asu.edu
[5] North Carolina State University, Raleigh, NC 27607, USA
tiffany.barnes@gmail.com, cflynch@ncsu.edu

**Abstract.** Massive Open Online Courses (MOOCs) have become an important platform for teaching and learning because of their ability to deliver educational accessibility across time and distance. Online learning environments have also provided new research opportunities to examine learning success at a large scale. One data tool that has been proven effective in exploring student success in online courses has been Cohesion Network Analysis (CNA), which offers the ability to analyze discourse structure in collaborative learning environments and facilitate the identification of learner interaction patterns. These patterns can be used to predict students' behaviors such as dropout rates and performance. The focus of the current paper is to identify sociograms (i.e., interaction graphs among participants) generated through CNA on course forum discussions and to identify temporal trends among students. Here, we introduce extended CNA visualizations available in the *ReaderBench* framework. These visualizations can be used to convey information about interactions between participants in online forums, as well as corresponding student clusters within specific timeframes.

**Keywords:** Cohesion Network Analysis · Online courses · Sociograms
Participants clustering · Interaction patterns

© Springer International Publishing AG, part of Springer Nature 2018
C. Penstein Rosé et al. (Eds.): AIED 2018, LNAI 10948, pp. 337–342, 2018.
https://doi.org/10.1007/978-3-319-93846-2_63

# 1   Introduction

Instructors have a limited amount of time to manually assess and grade learning materials produced by students. Assessment is even more difficult and time-consuming for instructors who want to monitor and score students' participation or collaboration with peers in a learning environment. Hence, there is a need for automated analyses of student production and interaction; however, there are few automated analyses of participation and collaboration. In this paper, we rely on Cohesion Network Analysis (CNA) [1] that can automatically assess participation and collaboration by examining cohesive links spanning throughout student discourse. CNA is grounded in text cohesion and theories of dialogism and polyphony [2] because it considers both the content of the discourse, as well as participants' interactions [1]. CNA is tightly coupled with Social Network Analysis (SNA) because it relies on equivalent indices to quantify participation using network graphs that reflect the interactions among participants (i.e., sociograms) [1, 3]. However, CNA enhances SNA by taking into account semantic cohesion while modeling participants' interactions. Thus, different CNA indices derived from the sociograms are used to evaluate participants' involvement. For instance, outdegree (i.e., the sum of contribution scores uttered by each participant or out-edges from the sociograms) reflects higher participation or active involvement, whereas indegree (i.e., the sum of in-edges) is indicative of collaboration.

The CNA approach is fully integrated within the *ReaderBench* framework [1, 3], which is a fully functional open-source framework centered on discourse analysis that consists of various Natural Language Processing (NLP) techniques designed to support students and teachers in their educational activities. The quality of the underlying dialogue is reflected in our cohesion graph based on the semantic relatedness between posts which relies on semantic distances in WordNet and multiple semantic models, namely Latent Semantic Analysis, Latent Dirichlet Allocation and word2vec [1].

In this paper we introduce CNA visualizations using data from a large blended online course, where lectures are face-to-face but most other course interactions between the 250 students occur in an online Piazza forum. Personalized instructor assessments in terms of collaboration and participation are difficult due to the size of classes. Nevertheless, student motivation, engagement, and success should be closely monitored because attrition rates in online courses are notoriously high [4], and students in large blended courses may face similar challenges in making the connections needed to take advantage of collaborative learning. This paper presents extensions of a previous analysis [5] based on visualizations introduced by Sirbu, Panaite, Secui, Dascalu, Nistor and Trausan-Matu [6] to a new dataset. The visualizations presented here can be used to convey information about interaction patterns between participants in large online course forums, as well as corresponding student clusters within specific timeframes that are dynamically generated using student contributions.

## 2   Method

### 2.1   Course Data

We use the data from a discrete math course for undergraduate students in a computer science department [7], which consisted of face-to-face lectures and support from online tools including a standard online question-answer Piazza forum. Data were collected from 250 students, out of which 169 made 2548 posts on the course forum. More than half of participants ($N = 87$) had less than or equal to 5 posts, while only 5 participants made more than 50 contributions.

### 2.2   CNA Online Course Modeling

Similar to the method proposed by Nistor, Panaite, Dascalu and Trausan-Matu [8], the clustering of members was performed using CNA *indegree* and *outdegree* indices. We applied a hierarchical clustering algorithm based on the Ward Criterion in order to minimize the variance after merging the clusters. The process stops when three clusters are detected corresponding to the central, active, and peripheral layers in descending order of the average indegree scores [9]. These layers can be identified within any community of practice [10].

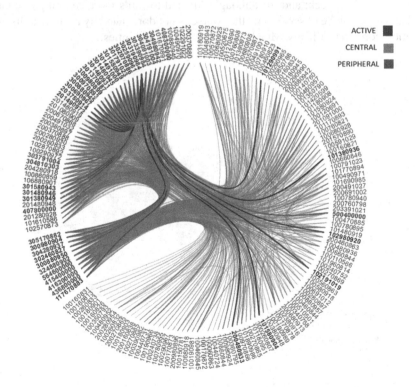

**Fig. 1.** Global sociogram for the entire course period (Aug 23rd – Dec 24th, 2013). (Color figure online)

Two interactive sociograms were introduced to display the interactions between participants. The hierarchical edge bundling perspective in Fig. 1 shows the interaction in a radial manner where dependencies are grouped into spline bundles and participants are grouped into their corresponding cluster/layer. Central participants are colored in blue, active members are displayed in green, and peripheral members in orange. On mouseover, the user can see the incoming and outcoming edges. Incoming edges and corresponding nodes (dependents) are displayed in dark blue, while outgoing links and outbound nodes (dependencies) are colored in red (see Fig. 1 for participant ID 303190984). Figure 2 shows a *force-directed graph* that considers the strength of the communication between nodes (i.e., students). The width of the edges is proportional to the text quality from CNA (i.e., cumulative contribution scores of exchange messages), whereas the length of each edge is automatically rendered by the visualization library. In addition, each node's size is proportional to the average indegree and outdegree scores of each participant.

Specific traits of the behavioral interaction patterns can be observed from the two types of visualizations, namely: (a) a dominance of peripheral members having the lowest number of interactions; (b) a growing degree of collaboration from the peripheral layer to the active members, and more importantly, to the central participants (including the course instructors and teaching assistants); (c) a rather slow start of the community (week 1), followed by an increase in participation (week 9) and a drastic decrease in the last week; and (d) although directed towards more central participants, free discussions can be observed and the course is not dominated by a single individual, a situation common in many MOOCs and online communities.

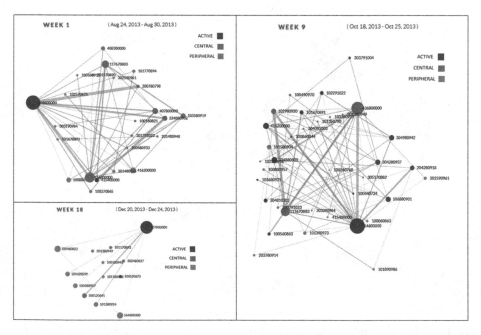

**Fig. 2.** Weekly snapshots of course sociograms.

# 3   Conclusions

Cohesion Network Analysis is a powerful analytics technique that connects natural language processing and network analysis, while transcending traditional SNA measurements. The CNA visualizations presented in the paper are particularly relevant for the study of online discussions found in education settings by presenting the interactions between participants based on the quality and cohesion of the underlying dialogue. The community structure is subsequently clustered into three layers that denote different degrees of participation. The series of graphs generated at different timeframes depict the trends in student participation and represents a solid ground for further exploration in terms of course structure dynamics. These visualizations can be used by instructors and researchers to better understand participation and collaboration within large-scale learning environments.

**Acknowledgments.** This research was partially supported by the 644187 EC H2020 RAGE project and the FP7 2008-212578 LTfLL project. In addition, this research was supported in part by the National Science Foundation (DRL- 1418378). Ideas expressed in this material are those of the authors and do not necessarily reflect the views of the National Science Foundation.

# References

1. Dascalu, M., McNamara, D.S., Trausan-Matu, S., Allen, L.K.: Cohesion network analysis of CSCL participation. Behavior Research Methods, 1–16 (2017)
2. Trausan-Matu, S.: The polyphonic model of hybrid and collaborative learning. In: Wang, F. L., Fong, J., Kwan, R.C. (eds.) Handbook of Research on Hybrid Learning Models: Advanced Tools, Technologies, and Applications, pp. 466–486. Information Science Publishing, Hershey (2010)
3. Dascalu, M., Trausan-Matu, S., McNamara, D.S., Dessus, P.: ReaderBench – automated evaluation of collaboration based on cohesion and dialogism. Int. J. Comput. Support. Collaborative Learn. **10**(4), 395–423 (2015)
4. Ramesh, A., Goldwasser, D., Huang, B., Daume, H., Getoor, L.: Understanding MOOC discussion forums using seeded LDA. In: 9th Workshop on Innovative Use of NLP for Building Educational Applications, pp. 28–33. ACL, Baltimore (2014)
5. Crossley, S.A., Dascalu, M., Baker, M., McNamara, D.S., Trausan-Matu, S.: Predicting success in massive open online courses (MOOC) using cohesion network analysis. In: 12th International Conference on Computer-Supported Collaborative Learning (CSCL 2017), pp. 103–110. ISLS, Philadelphia (2017)
6. Sirbu, M.D., Panaite, M., Secui, A., Dascalu, M., Nistor, N., Trausan-Matu, S.: ReaderBench: building comprehensive sociograms of online communities. In: 9th International Symposium on Symbolic and Numeric Algorithms for Scientific Computing (SYNASC 2017). IEEE, Timisoara (2017)
7. Crossley, S.A., Barnes, T., Lynch, C., McNamara, D.S.: Linking language to math success in a blended course. In: 10th International Conference on Educational Data Mining (EDM), pp. 180–185, Wuhan, China (2017)

8. Nistor, N., Panaite, M., Dascalu, M., Trausan-Matu, S.: Identifying socio-cognitive structures in online knowledge communities (OKCs) using cohesion network analysis. In: 9th International Symposium on Symbolic and Numeric Algorithms for Scientific Computing (SYNASC 2017). IEEE, Timisoara (2017)
9. Lave, J., Wenger, E.: Situated Learning: Legitimate Peripheral Participation. Cambridge University Press, Cambridge (1991)
10. Wenger, E.: Communities of Practice, Learning, Meaning, and Identity (Learning in doing: Social, Cognitive and Computational Perspectives). Cambridge University Press, Cambridge (1999)

# Gamified Assessment of Collaborative Skills with Chatbots

Kristin Stoeffler[1](✉), Yigal Rosen[2], Maria Bolsinova[2],
and Alina A. von Davier[2]

[1] ACT, Inc., Iowa City, IA 52240, USA
kristin.stoeffler@act.org
[2] ACTNext, by ACT, Inc., Iowa City, IA 52240, USA
{yigal.rosen,maria.bolsinova,alina.vondavier}@act.org

**Abstract.** Game-based assessments and learning environments create unique opportunities to provide learners with the ability to demonstrate their proficiency with cognitive skills and behaviors in increasingly authentic environments. Effective task designs, and the effective alignment of tasks with constructs, are also improving our ability to provide learners with insights about their proficiency with these skills. Sharing these insights within the industry with those working toward the same goal contributes to the rising tide that lifts all boats. In this paper we present insights from our work to develop and measure collaborative problem solving skills using a game-based assessment "Circuit Runner." Our innovative educational game design allows us to incorporate item response data, telemetry data, and stealth- telemetry data to provide a more authentic measure of collaborative problem solving skills. Our study design included 379 study participants on Amazon Mechanical Turk (MTurk), who completed the "Circuit Runner" CPS assessment. The paper provides details on the design of educational games and scoring techniques and discusses findings from the pilot study.

**Keywords:** Game · Assessment · Stealth

## 1 Background

In our efforts to measure 21st century skill sets such as Collaborative Problem Solving (CPS) we have created an educational game, "Circuit Runner." The online game-based environment uses task elements designed to explore specific cognitive skills and behaviors using interactive game elements, a human-agent interface, chatbot functionality, and dialog trees. CPS is generally considered to be one of the critical components of a 21st century skill set [1–3]. Innovation in this area continues to expand our understanding of this space and our ability to measure it [1, 4]. Our operational definition of CPS refers to *the knowledge, skills, and behaviors required to effectively participate in a joint activity to transform a current state to a goal state.* Our CPS framework is divided into two major categories: Team Effectiveness and Task Effectiveness, which are supported by 'functional categories.' The skills required to fulfill the functions outlined by these subcategories are drawn from the Thinking Skills and Behavior domains of the

© Springer International Publishing AG, part of Springer Nature 2018
C. Penstein Rosé et al. (Eds.): AIED 2018, LNAI 10948, pp. 343–347, 2018.
https://doi.org/10.1007/978-3-319-93846-2_64

ACT Holistic Framework [5]. Skills are organized to the subcomponent and Performance Level Descriptor (PLD) levels. Skills are also captured with sensitivity to the appropriate developmental levels and organized by levels of effectiveness. We chose 5 primary subskills supporting a range of CPS functional categories: Persistence (P), Perspective Taking (PT), Reaching the Goal (G), Strategy (S), and Problem Feature Awareness (PFA).

## 1.1    Game Design

In the collaborative game, Circuit Runner, a participant navigates a 3-D maze in a first-person perspective. The participant must collaborate with a participant "bot," or computer agent, via a dialog panel to share the information required to complete challenges presented at locked gates. The challenges are content agnostic and require information and resources that have been distributed asymmetrically between the 'bot' and the participant. The goal of the game is to collaborate with the bot via the chat panel to solve a number of challenges presented at locked gates, and then solve the final challenge of repairing the circuit. The chat bot functionality is built on a series of complex dialog trees (see Fig. 1).

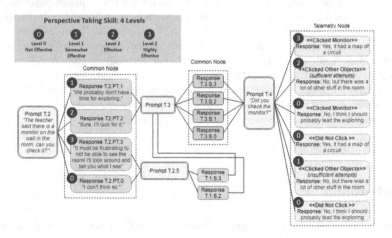

**Fig. 1.**  Circuit runner dialog tree design

The dialog trees contain a series of prompts from the bot followed by dialog choices (response options) for the participant. The response options are designed as ordered multiple choice items [6] to align with the four levels of that skill and are scored accordingly. The response options are designed to reflect authentic and appropriate responses for each of the four levels of the skill being measured. Each prompt and response instance explores only one of the five subskills included in the game.

The dialog tree also presents 'stealth-telemetry' nodes. These nodes are prompt and response sets that were not scored solely from the participant response choice, but incorporated a telemetry cross-check which informed the node's scoring.

## 2  Validation of Gamified Assessment

The current study was focused on exploring feasibility and validity of measuring CPS skills via CPS Gamified Assessment – Circuit Runner. More specifically, the following research questions were examined empirically: (RQ1) To what extent CPS Gamified Assessment provides valid and reliable data on a broad range of CPS sub-skills, including: Reaching the goal, persistence, problem feature analysis, perspective taking, and strategy? (RQ2) How does the quality of measurement change with the inclusion of the supplemental and telemetry nodes? (RQ3) What are the relationships (i.e., correlations) between CPS sub-skills, as measured by the CPS Gamified Assessment? (RQ4) What are the relationships (i.e., correlations) between CPS sub-skills as measured by CPS Gamified Assessment and more traditional CPS assessment instruments: CPS Situational Judgment Test and CPS self-report questionnaire?

A total of 500 unique users participated in the study through the Amazon MTurk platform. Of the 500 study participants, 379 provided a complete dataset (mean age = 33.76, SD = 9.14; 45% female,). Participants ranged in age from 18–68 with the majority of participants (63.32%) falling between the ages of 25 and 40.

### 2.1  CPS Assessment Instruments

Participants were directed that the study should take less than three hours to complete their interaction with CPS Gamified Assessment, CPS Situational Judgment Test and CPS self-report questionnaire. In addition to the "Circuit Runner" game, a CPS Situational Judgement Test (SJT) was designed to measure three sub-skills from the CPS construct. The CPS-SJT includes three videos that provide situational context for a workplace scenario involving CPS, each followed by ten questions. The questions reflect three of the five sub-skills being measured across the game and the CPS-SJT and are followed by four response options designed to align with the four levels of that skill as defined in the CPS framework. Factor and reliability analyses for CPS-SJT revealed three conceptually supported factors: Strategy (6 items, Cronbach's Alpha = .589), Problem Feature Analysis (8 items, Cronbach's Alpha = .622) and Perspective Taking (4 items, Cronbach's Alpha = .590). Overall reliability (internal consistency) of CPS-SJT is Cronbach's Alpha = .782.

A CPS Self-report Questionnaire was also included in the study. Participants reported on a 1–5 Likert scale (1-Not at all; 5-To a Great Extent) their competence level in CPS. Sample items adopted from prior studies included [2, 4]: Identify strengths of my teammates; Detect gaps in shared understanding in a group; Delegate tasks to others to accomplish goals; Have the ability to competently lead a group of people. Factor and reliability analyses for CPS Questionnaire provided further validation for two CPS sub-skills: Strategy (7 items, Cronbach's Alpha = .890) and Perspective Taking (6 items, Cronbach's Alpha = .854). Overall reliability (internal consistency) of CPS Questionnaire is Cronbach's Alpha = .907.

# 3  Results

IRT analysis was performed for the data from the gamified assessment. For each of the CPS skills the graded response model was fitted to the set of common nodes selected based on factor analysis and reliability analysis. As illustrated below, IRT and correlation analyses provided preliminary support for the use of the game for assessment of the intended CPS skills and possible pathways for improvement (Fig. 2).

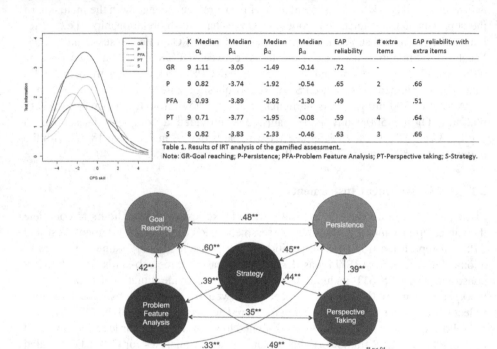

| | K | Median $\alpha_i$ | Median $\beta_{i1}$ | Median $\beta_{i2}$ | Median $\beta_{i3}$ | EAP reliability | # extra items | EAP reliability with extra items |
|---|---|---|---|---|---|---|---|---|
| GR | 9 | 1.11 | -3.05 | -1.49 | -0.14 | .72 | - | - |
| P | 9 | 0.82 | -3.74 | -1.92 | -0.54 | .65 | 2 | .66 |
| PFA | 8 | 0.93 | -3.89 | -2.82 | -1.30 | .49 | 2 | .51 |
| PT | 9 | 0.71 | -3.77 | -1.95 | -0.08 | .59 | 4 | .64 |
| S | 8 | 0.82 | -3.83 | -2.33 | -0.46 | .63 | 3 | .66 |

Table 1. Results of IRT analysis of the gamified assessment.
Note: GR-Goal reaching; P-Persistence; PFA-Problem Feature Analysis; PT-Perspective taking; S-Strategy.

**Fig. 2.**  IRT and correlation analysis of CPS Gamified Assessment

In addition to the correlations based on the sum scores on the subskills, we also performed correlation analysis on the IRT-scores of the CPS skills from the gamified assessment, the Situational Judgement Test and the Questionnaire. Our current research effort focused on expanding the range of CPS skills measured to include additional problem solving and behavioral components in the context of workplace (adults) and also the exploration of new scalable technologies for chatbot-powered learning and assessment solutions [7].

# References

1. von Davier, A.A., Zhu, M., Kyllonen, P.C. (eds.): Innovative Assessment of Collaboration. Springer, Cham (2017). https://doi.org/10.1007/978-3-319-33261-1
2. OECD: PISA 2015 Results: Collaborative Problem Solving. PISA, OECD Publishing, Paris (2017)
3. Griffin, P., Care, E., McGaw, B.: The changing role of education and schools. In: Griffin, P., McGaw, B., Care, E. (eds.) Assessment and Teaching 21st Century Skills, pp. 1–15. Springer, Heidelberg (2012). https://doi.org/10.1007/978-94-007-2324-5_1
4. Rosen, Y.: Computer-based assessment of collaborative problem solving: exploring the feasibility of human-to-agent approach. Int. J. Artif. Intell. Educ. **25**(3), 380–406 (2015)
5. Camara, W., O'Connor, R., Mattern, K., Hanson, M.A.: Beyond Academics: A Holistic Framework for Enhancing Education and Workplace Success. ACT Research Report Series. ACT, Inc. (2015)
6. Briggs, D.C., Alonzo, A.C., Schwab, C., Wilson, M.: Diagnostic assessment with ordered multiple-choice items. Educ. Assess. **11**(1), 33–63 (2006)
7. Rosen, Y.: Chatbot Authoring Tool for Innovative Learning and Assessment Tasks: Microsoft-Harvard-TalkCoaches Collaboration. Microsoft Symposium on Advancements in Assessments, Stanford (2018)

# Deep Knowledge Tracing for Free-Form Student Code Progression

Vinitra Swamy[(✉)], Allen Guo, Samuel Lau, Wilton Wu, Madeline Wu,
Zachary Pardos, and David Culler

UC Berkeley, Berkeley, CA, USA
{vinitra,allenguo,samlau95,wiltonwu,
wumadeline,pardos,culler}@berkeley.edu

**Abstract.** Knowledge Tracing, and its recent deep learning variants, have made substantial progress in modeling student knowledge acquisition through interactions with coursework. In this paper, we present a modification to Deep Knowledge Tracing to model student progress on coding assignments in large-scale computer science courses. The model takes advantage of the computer science education context by encoding students' iterative attempts on the same problem and allowing free-form code input. We implement a workflow for collecting data from Jupyter Notebooks and suggest future research possibilities for real-time intervention.

**Keywords:** Knowledge tracing · Deep learning · Student Modeling
Recurrent Neural Networks (RNN) · Computing Education

## 1 Introduction

With students far outnumbering teachers in online learning platforms, there is increased demand for tools to maintain and improve learning. Since 1-on-1 instructor support is not feasible at this scale, educational technology seeks to use artificial intelligence to provide similar guidance and model students' knowledge.

A popular approach called Knowledge Tracing models students' knowledge as they correctly or incorrectly answer exercises. Accurate modeling allows students to spend more time working on questions that are suited for their level of understanding.

Recent work uses recurrent neural networks to more effectively encode representations in an approach called Deep Knowledge Tracing (DKT). DKT models use the accuracy of prior attempts to predict students' future performance on questions, as well as automatically learn question clusterings [1].

As instructors for large scale computer science courses at UC Berkeley, we are particularly interested in modifying DKT for the computing education context. Traditional knowledge tracing techniques succeed in intelligent tutoring contexts, where students attempt each exercise once. In computing education, however,

© Springer International Publishing AG, part of Springer Nature 2018
C. Penstein Rosé et al. (Eds.): AIED 2018, LNAI 10948, pp. 348–352, 2018.
https://doi.org/10.1007/978-3-319-93846-2_65

students often attempt a single exercise multiple times until it is solved. We modify DKT to take this into account and make the following contributions:

1. We modify the model to take vectorized free-form student code as input.
2. We map questions to multiple skills and train one model per skill.
3. We implement a workflow for collecting data from Jupyter Notebooks and OkPy autograding.
4. We suggest possible applications of this model for determining a point of intervention in real-time.

## 2 Related Work

Knowledge Tracing traditionally uses Hidden Markov Models to track student knowledge as they solve exercises [2]. Deep Knowledge Tracing (DKT), introduced by Piech et al. [3], is an approach to knowledge tracing that utilizes recurrent neural networks, specifically Long-Short Term Memory (LSTM) cells, to produce improvements in model capabilities over previous methods. Piech et al. [1] also use DKT to automatically cluster math exercises into skill groups.

Blikstein and Piech [4,5] show that a student's trajectory of attempts while solving programming exercises is predictive of their success. Wang et al. [6,7] expand on this work by using DKT to model student trajectories as they solve programming exercises in the block-based programming language Scratch. We replicate the Wang et al. work in our setting, making a modification of input to the model in order to formulate the problem in terms of free-form code.

## 3 Context

We examine data from student code submissions from UC Berkeley's introductory data science course, Data 8. This course hosts over a thousand students a semester and introduces programming fundamentals, statistical inference, and prediction techniques.

Students complete assignments using Jupyter notebooks, a cell-based Python execution environment, with problem descriptions and starter code [8]. Through a combination of technologies including Kubernetes, Docker, and JupyterHub, students are only required to install a web browser to access their Jupyter environment. Instructors manually create assignment skeletons and autograder tests for each assignment. Every time the autograder is run, students' code and accompanying notebook metadata are backed up to the OkPy server [9]. This creates time series data recording a student's progression through a given assignment. The Jupyter environment enables rapid, iterative learning—students can write, run, and check their programs' correctness in near real-time.

The OkPy API allows us to retrieve one student backup for each autograder run, final submissions, and OkPy-specific assignment metadata. The raw submission data contains question numbers, student code responses, and accompanying autograder test results.

All student code is written in Python 3. Students use both *NumPy* and UC Berkeley's in-house *datascience* package, a tabular data manipulation library that is inspired by the *pandas* library.

# 4    Methodology

We make a number of data modifications to make raw student code amenable for DKT techniques. We also modify the baseline DKT approach to model student knowledge using code submissions from failed attempts.

## 4.1    Data Featurization and Sanity Check

To featurize code submissions, we use the default tokenization scheme in *scikit-learn* [10], which splits on non-alphanumeric characters. For example, consider the following code submission:

```
murder_rates.join('State',death_penalty,'State')
    .pivot('Death Penalty','Year','Murder Rate', np.average)
    .select(0,2,1)
```

The first 10 extracted tokens are:

```
['murder_rates','join','state','death_penalty',
 'state','pivot','death','penalty','year','murder']
```

For each distinct word, we compute the term frequency-inverse document frequency (tf-idf) score across all submissions. Each code submission is represented as a vector of length $K$, where $K$ is the vocabulary size: the total number of distinct words across all code submissions.

## 4.2    Model

We train a LSTM network on sequences of student code submissions. Instead of a single network as in DKT, we train a separate neural network for each skill (as shown in Fig. 1) using the vectorized code representation described in the previous section.

The inputs to the LSTM network are a vector containing the one-hot encoded anonymized student identifier, the one-hot encoded question number, the one-hot encoded attempt number, and the vectorized representation of the code. The output of the model at each time-step is a vector of predictions for the number of attempts remaining for each question of the same skill.

Each of these arrays have taken the students' progression (question each student attempted at each attempt number) and one-hot-encoded the inputs to create these arrays. We deal with the problem of each student having a different number of attempts on a skill by padding our data to the max number of attempts a student has for a skill, but we can also truncate data to an arbitrary "pad number" as well (e.g. 100 attempts).

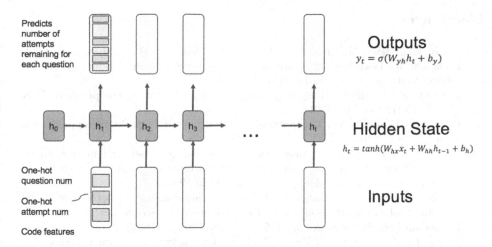

**Fig. 1.** Architecture of Our DKT-Inspired LSTM network

# 5 Conclusion and Future Work

Our modifications to DKT motivate several lines of future research in intervention and hint generation. For each student, our model predicts the number of attempts remaining to complete the questions for each skill. This suggests a simple way to provide live feedback by subject or question for instructors in a lab setting. For example, an instructor can identify a potentially useful time to intervene when a student's total predicted number of attempts remaining is consistently higher than those of other students (i.e., falling in the top $k$-th percentile for some manually tuned $k$).

The learned representation of student knowledge suggests a method to automatically provide hints to students. By simulating modifications to student code and checking the predicted attempts remaining, we can use the trained networks to find the keywords that most quickly help the student complete the exercise.

# 6 Note on Results

We have run preliminary models on mock data, and have found that DKT with free-form code reduces error significantly in comparison to baseline DKT. Future work will involve writing up the analysis and insights gained from student code attempts as well as the specifics of our trial results.

**Acknowledgements.** Thank you to UC Berkeley Data 8 course staff, the UC Berkeley Division of Data Sciences, the Machine Learning in Education course, the Jupyter team, and the OkPy team for their support throughout this process.

# References

1. Piech, C., Bassen, J., Huang, J., Ganguli, S., Sahami, M., Guibas, L.J., Sohl-Dickstein, J.: Deep knowledge tracing. In: Advances in Neural Information Processing Systems, pp. 505–513 (2015)
2. Corbett, A.: Cognitive computer tutors: solving the two-sigma problem. User Model. **2001**, 137–147 (2001)
3. Gers, F.A., Schmidhuber, J., Cummins, F.: Learning to forget: Continual prediction with LSTM (1999)
4. Blikstein, P.: Using learning analytics to assess students' behavior in open-ended programming tasks. In: Proceedings of the 1st International Conference on Learning Analytics and Knowledge, pp. 110–116. ACM (2011)
5. Piech, C., Sahami, M., Huang, J., Guibas, L.: Autonomously generating hints by inferring problem solving policies. In: Proceedings of the Second (2015) ACM Conference on Learning @ Scale, pp. 195–204, New York, ACM (2015)
6. Wang, L., Sy, A., Liu, L., Piech, C.: Deep knowledge tracing on programming exercises. In: Proceedings of the Fourth (2017) ACM Conference on Learning @ Scale, L@S 2017, New York, pp. 201–204. ACM (2017)
7. Wang, L., Sy, A., Liu, L., Piech, C.: Learning to represent student knowledge on programming exercises using deep learning. In: Proceedings of the 10th International Conference on Educational Data Mining; Wuhan, China, pp. 324–329 (2017)
8. Kluyver, T., Ragan-Kelley, B., Pérez, F., Granger, B.E., Bussonnier, M., Frederic, J., Kelley, K., Hamrick, J.B., Grout, J., Corlay, S., et al.: Jupyter notebooks-a publishing format for reproducible computational workflows. In: ELPUB, pp. 87–90 (2016)
9. DeNero, J., Sridhara, S., Pérez-Quiñones, M., Nayak, A., Leong, B.: Beyond auto-grading: advances in student feedback platforms. In: Proceedings of the 2017 ACM SIGCSE Technical Symposium on Computer Science Education, pp. 651–652. ACM (2017)
10. Pedregosa, F., Varoquaux, G., Gramfort, A., Michel, V., Thirion, B., Grisel, O., Blondel, M., Prettenhofer, P., Weiss, R., Dubourg, V., Vanderplas, J., Passos, A., Cournapeau, D., Brucher, M., Perrot, M., Duchesnay, E.: Scikit-learn: machine learning in Python. J. Mach. Learn. Res. **12**, 2825–2830 (2011)

# Time Series Model for Predicting Dropout in Massive Open Online Courses

Cui Tang, Yuanxin Ouyang[(✉)], Wenge Rong, Jingshuai Zhang,
and Zhang Xiong

School of Computer Science and Engineering,
Beihang University, Beijing 100191, China
{tangcui.c,oyyx,w.rong,zhangjs,xiongz}@buaa.edu.cn

**Abstract.** MOOCs are playing an increasing important role in modern education, but the problem of high dropout rate is quite serious. Predicting users' dropout behavior is an important research direction of MOOCs. In this paper, we extract some raw features from MOOCs uses' logs and apply the MOOCs users' daily activities into a recurrent neural network (RNN) with long short-term memory (LSTM) cells, viewing this problem as a time series problem. We collect rich MOOCs users' log information from XuetangX to test the time series model predicting course drop out. The experiments results indicate that the time series model perform better than other contrast models.

**Keywords:** MOOCs · Dropout prediction
Long short-term memory · User behavior

## 1 Introduction

With the development of internet and communication technology, many industries have changed the mode of operation. In the most closely related area of teaching, there is Massive Open Online Courses (MOOCs) [1,2]. Due to their open and mostly free, they have attracted millions of users' enrollment all over the world [3,4]. However, the high dropout rate is widespread in MOOCs platforms. As is reported, only twenty percent of MOOCs users can complete the courses [5–7].

In reality, the results of dropout prediction can be fed back to the teacher to improve teaching contents and avoid the occurrence of dropout behavior. From the view of finding a more reasonable description of the problem, the dropout prediction can be considered as a time series problem. Imagine that if a student never accesses the course, it is impossible that he/she would complete the course suddenly. On the consequence, we can predict the students' behaviors in the future according to his/her previous behaviors. So we can easily get to apply an recurrent neural network (RNN) [11] with long short-term memory (LSTM) [9] to deal with the problem [9].

C. Penstein Rosé et al. (Eds.): AIED 2018, LNAI 10948, pp. 353–357, 2018.
https://doi.org/10.1007/978-3-319-93846-2_66

The rest of the paper is organized as follows. In Sect. 2 we will describe the related work about MOOCs users' behavior prediction. Section 3 shows time series problem and our model to this problem. The dataset we used and the experiments will be presented in Sect. 4. Section 5 will show the conclusion and future work of this research.

## 2    Related Work

In this section, we will review some related researches on analysing the big data of MOOCs to get a brief look at the field of research content and status.

**Engagement Analysis:** Increasing researchers have begun to analyze students' engagement in MOOCs courses. Ramesh [14] put forward a potential representation model, which can be applied to abstract student participation types and prediction of dropouts. Most of the existing studies estimated the time spent on different resources and examine the correlation between time and student performance.

**Forum Analysis:** Forum is an important part of a MOOCs platform. Some interesting work reviews MOOCs forum, like research [6] investigated the factors associated with the decline of the forum. These studies may isolate and exaggerate the importance of the forum's performance.

**Attribute Analysis:** These studies pay attention to the relationship between the user's demographic properties and their behavior patterns in MOOCs. According to the demographic results, there was no correlation between the skills and the completion rate of the curriculum, which is found in research [15].

To the best of our knowledge, there are little work pay attention to the time series problem of the MOOCs dropout prediction, and time information is essential factor in analysing MOOC users' behavior. So we apply RNN and LSTM, the commonly used tool for the time series model to solve the problem.

## 3    Time Series Model

### 3.1    Time Series Problem

We suppose one lesson will span for $t$ days. For a student, we collect his/her day-by-day activities expressed with $(x_1, ..., x_t)$, and the result that whether the student drop the course is denoted by $y_t$. Our goal is to predict the label at day $t$. The result of day $t$ is determined by not only the current input $x_t$ but also the previous input $(x_1, ..., x_{t-1})$.

Naturally, we apply this problem to the LSTM network, and the input is the students' daily activities. The final output is whether the student will drop out the class. Figure 1 shows our time series model framework. From next section, we will give the details of the framework.

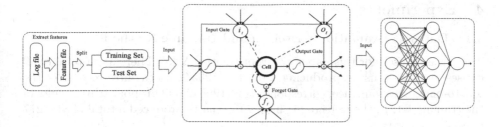

**Fig. 1.** Time series model framework

## 3.2 Time Series Features

We choose 7 features that can represent the user's behavior in the day. These 7 features are in two categories. One is related to forum, and another category is about the learning behavior. These 7 features are the number of asking problems on forum, discussing on forums, operating navigate, operating access, closing a page, watching video and accessing wiki by a student in one day.

## 3.3 LSTM Network

We explore $Z_t$ as the input of our LSTM network, so we can get the input gate $i_t$. It means when we get the new user's behaviors, we update our input for better predicting.

Similarly, we compute the forget gate $f_t$, which represent we drop some information about user's behaviors generating a few days ago or insignificant.

Then, the memory cell $c_t$ can be received. The cell state is very easy for information to just flow along it unchanged. And we achieve the output gate $o_t$. Apparently, we decide what parts of the cell state we are going to output.

At last, we put the cell state through tanh and multiply it by the output of the sigmoid gate.

## 3.4 Full Connected Network

We use the output of LSTM network $h_T$ as the input of the following full connected work $d^{(1)}$. We compute the next layer of full connected network which each node of it connect all the nodes of this layer. It can be described as,

$$d^{(2)} = \sigma_1(W_1 d^{(1)} + b_1) \tag{1}$$

where $W_1$ is weight matrix, $b_1$ is the bias and the $\sigma_1(.)$ is the activation function. Then we will connect all the nodes in this layer to one node which represent predict of our model,

$$y = \sigma_2(W_2 d^{(1)} + b_2) \tag{2}$$

where $W_2$ and $b_1$ is the weight matrix and bias. Similarly, $\sigma_2(.)$ is also the activation function. $y$ is the final output, and we regard $y$ as the possibility that the student will drop out the course.

## 4    Experiments

### 4.1    Dataset, Evaluation Criterion and Baseline Methods

The datasets used for this paper are from XuetangX [8]. There are a total of 39 classes and 79186 users, producing a total of 120542 user course records of the one-to-one correspondence, corresponding to 120542 real dropout truth results in the training set. In the website log files, 79186 users produced a total of 8157277 operating records.

We evaluate the performance of experiments by Area Under Curve (AUC) score [13], which is the area under the Receiver Operating Characteristic (ROC) curve [12]. AUC is a model evaluation criterion, which can only be used for the evaluation of two classification model.

In order to verify the validity of the model, we compare the LSTM network with several common predictive models: Logistic regression [16], Random forest [10] and Gradient Boosting Decision Trees(GBDT) [8].

### 4.2    Model Performance

In terms of AUC scores, the time series model performs better than Logistic Regression, Random Forest and GBDT (Table 1). It proves the time series model can describe MOOCs users' behavior better, and will predict the users' behavior more accurate. But for the running time, LSTM network requires a long time training [9], which is determined by its own network structure, and in our experiment, the running time is acceptable.

**Table 1.** Performance of four models

| Models | AUC scores |
|---|---|
| Logistic regression | 0.674 |
| Random forest | 0.864 |
| GBDT | 0.871 |
| Time series model | 0.881 |

## 5    Conclusion

In this paper, we present a more reasonable and natural method, viewing as a time series problem and apply LSTM network to solve it. The datasets we used in experiments are also showed in this paper. The final experimental results show that time series model performs better than Logistic Regression, Random Forest and GBDT. From the dropout result, the MOOCs' instructors can easily acquire that which student is easily dropout and make a quick adjustment for the course to prevent the appearance of dropout immediately. In hence, the problem of drop out rate will get improved, that is also the destination of this paper.

**Acknowledgments.** This work was partially supported by the National Natural Science Foundation of China (No. L1724045), and the Education Research Projects of Beihang University.

# References

1. Ouyang, Y., Tang, C., Rong, W., Zhang, L., Yin, C., Xiong, Z.: Task-technology fit aware expectation-confirmation model towards understanding of MOOCs continued usage intention. In: Hawaii International Conference on System Sciences (2017)
2. Alraimi, K.M., Zo, H., Ciganek, A.P.: Understanding the MOOCs continuance: the role of openness and reputation. J. Comput. Educ. **80**, 28–38 (2015)
3. Ho, A.D., Reich, J., Nesterko, S.O., Seaton, D.T., Mullaney, T., Waldo, J., Chuang, I.: HarvardX and MITx: The first year of open online courses, fall 2012-summer 2013 (2014)
4. Rehfeldt, R.A., Jung, H.L., Aguirre, A., Nichols, J.L., Root, W.B.: Beginning the dialogue on the e-transformation: behavior analysis first massive open online course (MOOC). J. Behav. Anal. Pract. **9**(1), 3–13 (2016)
5. Breslow, L., Pritchard, D.E., DeBoer, J., Stump, G.S., Ho, A.D., Seaton, D.T.: Studying learning in the worldwide classroom: research into edX's first MOOC. J. Res. Pract. Assess. **8**, 13–25 (2013)
6. Jordan, K.: Initial trends in enrolment and completion of massive open online courses. Int. Rev. Res. Open Distrib. Learn. **15**(1), 133–160 (2014)
7. Kolowich, S.: The professors who make the MOOCs. Chronicle High. Educ. **18**, A20–A23 (2013)
8. He, X., Pan, J., Jin, O., Xu, T., Liu, B., Xu, T., Candela, J. Q.: Practical lessons from predicting clicks on ads at facebook. In: Proceedings of the Eighth International Workshop on Data Mining for Online Advertising, pp. 1–9. ACM (2014)
9. Hochreiter, S., Schmidhuber, J.: Long short-term memory. Neural Comput. **9**(8), 1735–1780 (1997)
10. Breiman, L.: Random forests. J. Mach. Learn. **45**(1), 5–32 (2001)
11. Medsker, L., Jain, L.C.: Recurrent Neural Networks: Design and Applications. CRC Press, USA (1999)
12. Brzezinski, D., Stefanowski, J.: Prequential AUC: properties of the area under the ROC curve for data streams with concept drift. J. Knowl. Inf. Syst. **52**(2), 531–562 (2017)
13. Fawcett, T.: An introduction to ROC analysis. J. Pattern Recogn. Lett. **27**(8), 861–874 (2006)
14. Goldsborough, P.: A tour of tensorflow. arXiv preprint arXiv:1610.01178 (2016)
15. Kloft, M., Stiehler, F., Zheng, Z., Pinkwart, N.: Predicting MOOC dropout over weeks using machine learning methods. In: Proceedings of the EMNLP 2014 Workshop on Analysis of Large Scale Social Interaction in MOOCs, pp. 60–65 (2014)
16. Mansournia, M.A., Geroldinger, A., Greenland, S.: Heinze, G: Separation in logistic regressionCcauses, consequences, and control. J. Am. J. Epidemiol. **187**, 864–870 (2017)

# Machine Learning and Fuzzy Logic Techniques for Personalized Tutoring of Foreign Languages

Christos Troussas[(⊠)], Konstantina Chrysafiadi, and Maria Virvou

Software Engineering Laboratory, Department of Informatics,
University of Piraeus, Piraeus, Greece
{ctrouss,kchrysafiadi,mvirvou}@unipi.gr

**Abstract.** Intelligent computer-assisted language learning employs artificial intelligence techniques to create a more personalized and adaptive environment for language learning. Towards this direction, this paper presents an intelligent tutoring system for learning English and French concepts. The system incorporates a novel model for error diagnosis using machine learning. This model employs two algorithmic techniques and specifically Approximate String Matching and String Meaning Similarity in order to diagnose spelling mistakes, mistakes in the use of tenses, mistakes in the use of auxiliary verbs and mistakes originating from confusion in the simultaneous tutoring of languages. The model for error diagnosis is used by the fuzzy logic model which takes as input the results of the first or the knowledge dependencies existing among the different domain concepts of the learning material and decides dynamically about the learning content that is suitable to be delivered to the learner each time.

**Keywords:** Adaptivity · Fuzzy logic · Intelligent Tutoring Systems
Language learning · Machine learning · Personalization

## 1 Introduction

Towards the last decade, Intelligent Tutoring Systems (ITSs) have been used for teaching a variety of knowledge domains [1]. One important area of ITSs involves Intelligent Computer-Assisted Language Learning (ICALL), in which students are taught a language (e.g. English, French etc.) using artificial intelligence techniques [2]. It has to be emphasized that foreign language learning is widely promoted by many countries and clusters of countries [3]. For example, the European Union promotes such guidance for its country members. Due to the currents global promotion of language learning, countries, such as Greece, have adopted foreign language teaching in the education curriculum of schools. Even though the English and French languages have common characteristics so that their learning can be joined, there is the risk of students being confused in multiple language learning.

The main goal of the research, described in this paper, is to present an adaptive tutoring system for foreign languages, which includes a novel way for error diagnosis using machine learning, in combination with a fuzzy logic model for adaptive instruction.

© Springer International Publishing AG, part of Springer Nature 2018
C. Penstein Rosé et al. (Eds.): AIED 2018, LNAI 10948, pp. 358–362, 2018.
https://doi.org/10.1007/978-3-319-93846-2_67

In particular, our prototype application uses techniques of machine learning and fuzzy logic in order to offer optimized English and French learning. Machine learning techniques are used for performing error diagnosis. More specifically, they are used when a student makes a mistake so that the system can detect it and reason about it. Then, the student is offered a more personalized instruction using the fuzzy logic techniques which take as input the results of error diagnosis or the knowledge dependencies that exist among the different domain concepts of the learning material and automatically models the learning or forgetting process of a student.

## 2  Error Categories, Diagnosis and Response

The presented tutoring system is able to detect three categories of students' errors, namely: spelling mistakes, mistakes in the use of tenses and mistakes in the use of auxiliary verbs. Apart from these mistakes, the system can diagnose mistakes that come from the confusion of a student when s/he learns multiple foreign languages (English and French) by transferring his/her knowledge from one language to the other. The aforementioned three categories were reported to be the most common when students learn the English and French languages at the same time. These reports are the result of a small-scale experiment which was conducted in public and private schools of Athens (Greece); according to this experiment, the tutors of English and French languages attested in a large percentage that these three error categories need to be confronted when students learn the two languages simultaneously.

For the diagnosis of students' errors and misconceptions, a novel error diagnosis mechanism is introduced. This mechanism is composed by two machine learning algorithms which are able to diagnose the reason of each mistake and act collaboratively. The first algorithm of the error diagnosis mechanism is the Approximate String Matching. This algorithm is activated to diagnose a spelling mistake happening because of students' negligence or lack of knowledge. More specifically, Approximate String Matching is used for errors happening in the context of the same language. It tries to discover string similitude by collating a student's precise wrong answer with the correct answers which are stored in the database of the application. This method is in charge of discovering strings that match a specific pattern in an approximate way. The issue of collating string approximately is normally partitioned into two sub-issues: finding surmised substring matches inside a given string and discovering lexicon strings that match the pattern approximately. In the event that a string collation happens in a high rate, the application chooses whether the misconception is a spelling mistake coming from negligence or lack of knowledge.

The second algorithm is the String Meaning Similarity which is activated to diagnose all the other error categories. This algorithm can reason about a mistake lying between the spelling mistakes due to language confusion causes, the tenses mistakes and the auxiliary verbs mistakes. Additionally, the application discovers meaning similitude between the given and the right answer by making an interpretation of these two responses to the application's languages, in particular the English and French languages. Also, the application takes after a similar method of reasoning, as previously, customized to the meaning similarities. Through this technique, the mistakes coming from language learning confusion can be distinguished and analyzed.

When the system diagnoses a mistake derived provides advice to students in order to render them careful when answering to exams or make revisions and improve their knowledge performance. Furthermore, in case of a spelling mistake derived from confusion in multiple language learning or a mistakes in the use of tenses and auxiliary verbs, the system employs the fuzzy logic technique in order to further support the students and place them in the center of education by providing a more personalized instruction tailored to the learning needs and pace of each one.

## 3   The Fuzzy Logic Model and Rules

For the efficient teaching of English and French, we use fuzzy sets to represent the student's knowledge level of each domain concept, either of English language or French language and a mechanism of rules over the particular fuzzy sets. Furthermore, a set of knowledge dependencies among the domain concepts of the two foreign languages have been defined. These dependencies concern how the knowledge of concepts about grammatical issues in English affects the learning of corresponding concepts about grammatical issues in French and vice versa. Dependencies of the presented system are restricted to tenses and auxiliary verbs, which are considered adequate for the research scope of this work. The particular dependencies have been defined by 15 foreign languages teachers, whose experience either in teaching English and French, or in the educational process and instruction, ensured an accurate assessment of concept inter-dependency. They are symbolized as $d(C_i, C_j)$, which is a function that represents the degree that the knowledge of concept $C_i$ affects the knowledge level of concept $C_j$ and takes a value among 0 to 1. Some examples of the defined dependencies are: d('Simple present', 'Le présent') = 0..6, d('Simple future', 'Le futur simple') = 0..55, d('Le passé composé', 'Simple past') = 0.4, d('Plus-que-parfait', 'Past perfect') = 0.65.

The following four fuzzy sets (Fig. 1) for representing students' knowledge level of a domain concept are defined (x indicates the student's degree of success in a domain concept): (a) Unknown (Un): $0 \leq x < 45$, (b) Unsatisfactory Known (UnK): $30 < x < 75$, (c) Known (K): $60 < x < 90$, (d) Learned (L): $80 < x \leq 100$.

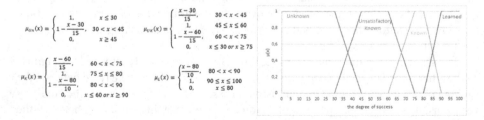

**Fig. 1.** The membership functions of the fuzzy sets

Therefore, a quadruplet ($\mu_{Un}$, $\mu_{UK}$, $\mu_K$, $\mu_L$) for each concept is used to determine the knowledge level [4]. Bellow, the rules representing how a change to the knowledge level (KL) of a concept of English ($C_E$) affects the KL of a corresponding concept of French ($C_F$) and vice versa (replacing $C_E$ with $C_F$, $C_F$ with $C_E$ and $d(C_E, C_F)$ with $d(C_F, C_E)$), are presented. L1 and L2 (L1 < L2) represent fuzzy sets and L1', L2' represent the 'neighbor' fuzzy set of L1 and L2 that are active, correspondingly. Given that in a quadruplet only two active values exist and they are complementary (to 1), only one of them, that of the lower level, is used to represent the KL of the corresponding concept.

**R1:** If $KL(C_F) = L1$ and $KL(C_E) = L1$, then $KL(C_F) = L1$ with $\mu_{L1}(C_F) = \max [\mu_{L1}(C_F), \mu_{L1}(C_E) * d(C_E, C_F)]$

**R2:** If two 'neighbor' fuzzy sets are active and $KL(C_F) = L1$, $KL(C_E) = L2$, then $KL(C_F) = L2$ with $\mu_{L2}(C_F) = 1 - \mu_{L2'}(C_E) * d(C_E, C_F)$

**R3:** If only one fuzzy set is active: $KL(C_F) = L1$ and $KL(C_E) = L2$, then $KL(C_F) = L2'$ (L2' is the lower 'neighbor' fuzzy set of L2) with $\mu_{L2'}(C_F) = 1 - \mu_{L2}(C_E) * d(C_E, C_F)$

**R3.1:** If L2 = 'Unknown', then $KL(C_F) = $ 'Unknown' with $\mu_{L2}(C_F) = 1$

**R4:** If $KL(C_F) = $ Learned, with $\mu_L(C_F) = 1$ (100%), then it does not change

**R5:** If $KL(C_F) = L2$ and $KL(C_E) = L1$, then $KL(C_F) = L1'$ (L1' is the upper 'neighbor' fuzzy set of L1) with $\mu_{L1'}(C_F) = 1 - \mu_{L1}(C_E) * d(C_E, C_F)$

Next, the system decides dynamically the number of exercises (n) of each concept that the learner has to solve each time regarding her/his current state of knowledge level of each concept of the foreign language that s/he is taught. The decisions about the exercises are taken applying the following rules:

- If KL = 'Un', then n = 20.
- If KL = 'UK' with $\mu UK(x) \geq 0.5$, then n = 15.
- If KL = 'UK' with $\mu UK(x) < 0.5$ or KL = 'K' with $\mu K(x) \geq 0.5$, then n = 10.
- If KL = 'K' with $\mu K(x) < 0.5$ or KL = 'L' and the learner is interacting with the corresponding domain for the first time, then n = 5.
- If KL = 'L' and the learner has studied the corresponding concept already, the system considers that the learner has learnt the particular concept and does not provide her/him with exercises (n = 0).

## 4  Conclusions and Future Work

In this paper, a novel approach for error diagnosis using machine learning techniques and a learning content delivery module using fuzzy logic have been presented and evaluated. More specifically, an adaptive tutoring system for learning English and French has been implemented incorporating the aforementioned models. The model for effective error diagnosis uses the Approximate String Matching and the String Meaning Similarity techniques for diagnosing spelling mistakes and mistakes in the use of tenses auxiliary verbs. The model of fuzzy logic is used towards the determination of the learner's knowledge level in French according to her/his knowledge level in English, and vice versa, allowing the system to make decisions about the adaptation of the instructional content.

It is in our future plans to add the tutoring of more foreign languages and extend the system's functionalities by incorporating an authoring module.

# References

1. Nkambou, R., Mizoguchi, R., Bourdeau, J.: Advances in Intelligent Tutoring Systems, 1st edn. Springer, Heidelberg (2010). https://doi.org/10.1007/978-3-642-14363-2
2. Troussas, C., Virvou, M., Espinosa, K.J.: Using Visualization algorithms for discovering patterns in groups of users for tutoring multiple languages through social networking. J. Netw. **10**(12), 668–674 (2015). https://doi.org/10.4304/jnw.10.12.668-674
3. Dooly, M.: "I do which the question": students' innovative use of technology resources in the language classroom. Lang. Learn. Technol. **2**(1), 184–217 (2018). https://dx.doi.org/0125/44587
4. Chrysafiadi, K., Virvou, M.: Modeling student's knowledge on programming using fuzzy techniques. In: Tsihrintzis, G.A., Damiani, E., Virvou, M., Howlett, R.J., Jain, L.C. (eds.) Intelligent Interactive Multimedia Systems and Services. Smart Innovation, Systems and Technologies, vol. 6, pp. 23–32. Springer, Heidelberg (2010). https://doi.org/10.1007/978-3-642-14619-0_3

# Item Response Theory Without Restriction of Equal Interval Scale for Rater's Score

Masaki Uto[✉] and Maomi Ueno

University of Electro-Communications, Tokyo, Japan
uto@ai.lab.uec.ac.jp, ueno@ai.is.uec.ac.jp

**Abstract.** With the spread of large-scale e-learning environments such as MOOCs, peer assessment has been used recently to measure learner ability. Nevertheless, peer assessment presents the important difficulty that the ability assessment accuracy depends strongly on rater characteristics. To resolve that difficulty, item response theory (IRT) models that incorporate rater characteristic parameters have been proposed. However, those models rely upon the assumption of an equal interval scale for raters' scores although the scales are known to vary across raters. To resolve the difficulty, this study proposes a new IRT model without the restriction of an equal interval scale for raters. The proposed model is expected to improve model fitting to peer assessment data. Furthermore, the proposed model can realize more robust ability assessment than conventional models can. This study demonstrates the effectiveness of the proposed model through experimentation with actual data.

**Keywords:** Educational measurement · E-learning
Item response theory · Peer assessment · Rating scale

## 1 Introduction

Peer assessment, which is mutual assessment among learners, has become popular with the widespread use of large-scale e-learning environments such as massive open online courses (MOOCs) [1–3]. Peer assessment has been adopted in various learning and assessment situations because it provides many benefits (e.g., [2,3]). One important use of peer assessment is for summative assessment, which provides a measure of learner ability [4,5]. Peer assessment is justified as an appropriate summative assessment method because the learner ability is definable naturally in the learning community as a social agreement [3,6]. Furthermore, even when learners are numerous, as in MOOCs, peer assessment can be conducted by assigning a few peer-raters to each learner, although assessment by instructors becomes difficult [2,4,7,8].

Peer assessment, however, presents the difficulty that the assessment accuracy of learner ability depends strongly on rater characteristics such as rating

© Springer International Publishing AG, part of Springer Nature 2018
C. Penstein Rosé et al. (Eds.): AIED 2018, LNAI 10948, pp. 363–368, 2018.
https://doi.org/10.1007/978-3-319-93846-2_68

severity and consistency [2,3,9,10]. Item response theory (IRT) models incorporating rater characteristic parameters have been proposed to resolve that difficulty, (e.g., [3,9,11,12]). A traditional model is the many facet Rasch model (MFRM) [12], which is defined as a partial credit model [13] incorporating a rater severity parameter. Additionally, an extension of this model using the generalized partial credit model [14] has been proposed [11]. Furthermore, to resolve the difficulty that raters are not always consistent, a graded response model [15] incorporating rater consistency and severity parameters has been proposed recently [3]. Those IRT models are known to provide more accurate ability assessment than average or total scores do because they can estimate the ability considering some rater characteristics [3].

However, when the diversity of raters' assessment skills increases as in peer assessment, the rating scales are known to vary across raters [10,16,17]. For example, some raters presumably overuse a few restricted categories, avoid some specific categories, and use all categories uniformly. However, earlier IRT models have been incapable of representing such rater characteristics because they assume an equal interval scale for raters' scores. Consequently, the models will not fit peer assessment data well. Low model fit generally reduces the ability assessment accuracy [3].

To resolve that difficulty, this study proposes a new IRT model without the restriction of the equal interval scale for raters. Specifically, the proposed model is defined as a generalized partial credit model that incorporates a rater severity parameter for each rating category. The proposed model is expected to improve the model fitting to peer assessment data because differences in the scale among raters can be represented. Furthermore, the proposed model can realize more robust ability assessment than conventional models because the introduction of the unequal interval scales for raters enables more precise representation of the characteristics of aberrant raters, who use extremely different rating scales from those used by others. This study demonstrates the effectiveness of the proposed model through the use of actual data experiments.

## 2    Proposed Model

The rating data $U$ obtained from peer assessment consist of rating category $k \in \mathcal{K} = \{1, \cdots, K\}$ given by peer-rater $r \in \mathcal{J} = \{1, \cdots, J\}$ to the outcome of learner $j \in \mathcal{J}$ for task $t \in \mathcal{T} = \{1, \cdots, T\}$. Letting $u_{tjr}$ be a response of rater $r$ to learner $j$'s outcome for task $t$, the data $U$ are described as $U = \{u_{tjr} \mid u_{tjr} \in \mathcal{K} \cup \{-1\}, t \in \mathcal{T}, j \in \mathcal{J}, r \in \mathcal{J}\}$, where $u_{tjr} = -1$ denotes missing data. This study was conducted to estimate the learner ability accurately from the peer assessment data $U$ using item response theory (IRT) [18].

The proposed model is defined as a generalized partial credit model that incorporates the rater severity parameter for each rating category and the rater consistency parameter. The model provides the response probability $P_{ijrk}$ as

$$P_{ijrk} = \frac{\exp \sum_{m=1}^{k} [\alpha_r \alpha_i (\theta_j - \beta_i - \beta_r - d_{rm})]}{\sum_{l=1}^{K} \exp \sum_{m=1}^{l} [\alpha_r \alpha_i (\theta_j - \beta_i - \beta_r - d_{rm})]}. \tag{1}$$

where $\theta_j$ represents the latent ability of learner $j$, $\alpha_i$ denotes the discrimination parameter for task $i$, $\beta_i$ denotes the difficulty of task $i$, $\alpha_r$ signifies the consistency of rater $r$, $\beta_r$ denotes the severity of rater $r$, and $d_{rk}$ represents the severity of rater $r$ to give category $k$. Here, $\alpha_{r=1} = 1$, $\beta_{r=1} = 0$, $d_{r1} = 0$, and $\sum_{k=2}^{K} d_{rk} = 0$ are assumed for model identification.

In the proposed model, $d_{rk}$ controls the intervals between adjacent categories for each rater. Furthermore, the intervals determine the rater's response probability for each category. Specifically, as interval $d_{rk+1} - d_{rk}$ becomes larger, the response probability for category $k$ increases. As interval $d_{rk+1} - d_{rk}$ becomes smaller, the probability of responding with category $k$ decreases.

The proposed model can represent such differences in the rating scale among raters although earlier IRT models with rater parameters (e.g., [3,11,12]) incorporate the assumption of an equal interval scale for raters' scores. The scales generally vary among raters in peer assessment, as described in Sect. 1. Therefore, the proposed model is expected to provide higher model fitting to peer assessment data than the conventional models. Because better model fitting generally improves the ability assessment accuracy [3], the proposed model is expected to provide higher accuracy than the conventional models provide.

## 3    Actual Data Experiment

This section presents a description of evaluation of the effectiveness of the proposed model using actual peer assessment data. Actual data were gathered using the following procedures. (1) 30 university students were enrolled in this study as participants. (2) They were asked to complete four essay-writing tasks that were set in the national assessment of educational progress (NAEP) 2002 [19] and 2007 [20]. (3) After the participants completed all tasks, they were asked to evaluate the essays of all other participants for all four tasks. The assessments were conducted using a rubric that includes five rating categories.

Using the peer assessment data, we conducted the following experiment. (1) The parameters of the proposed model, MFRM [12], the model proposed by Patz and Junker [11] (designated as *Patz1999*), and that proposed by Uto and Ueno [3] (designated as *Uto2016*) were estimated using the MCMC algorithm. The widely applicable information criteria (WAIC) and log marginal likelihood (ML) were also calculated for each model. (2) Given the estimated task and rater parameters, the learner ability was re-estimated from each rater's data. Then, we calculated the RMSE between the ability values estimated from each rater's data and those estimated using complete data in Procedure 1. The average value of the RMSE over all raters was calculated for each model. In addition, this index was calculated for a method by which the ability is given as the averaged value of the raw ratings (designated as *Averaged*).

Table 1 presents results. As shown in Table 1, the proposed model was selected as the best model by both information criteria. Results show that the proposed model presented the lowest RMSE value. Here, we conducted multiple comparisons using the Dunnet method to ascertain whether the RMSE value of the

**Table 1.** Information criteria and ability assessment accuracies

|          | Information criteria | | RMSE | | |
|----------|----------|----------|----------|----------|----------------|
|          | WAIC     | ML       | Mean     | SD       | Test statistic |
| Proposed | **−4396.07** | **−4324.23** | **0.313** | 0.053 | – |
| MFRM     | −4646.46 | −4615.25 | 0.379 | 0.075 | 2.745 ($p = 0.024$) |
| Patz1999 | −4646.08 | −4575.41 | 0.464 | 0.067 | 6.348 ($p < 0.001$) |
| Uto2016  | −4434.82 | −4385.57 | 0.382 | 0.065 | 2.897 ($p = 0.016$) |
| Averaged | –        | –        | 0.499 | 0.157 | 6.997 ($p < 0.001$) |

**Table 2.** Rater parameters estimated from actual data

| Rater | $\alpha_r$ | $\beta_r$ | $d_{r2}$ | $d_{r3}$ | $d_{r4}$ | $d_{r5}$ | Rater | $\alpha_r$ | $\beta_r$ | $d_{r2}$ | $d_{r3}$ | $d_{r4}$ | $d_{r5}$ |
|----|----|----|----|----|----|----|----|----|----|----|----|----|----|
| 1 | 1.000 | 0.000 | −1.169 | −0.154 | 0.152 | 1.171 | 16 | 1.249 | 0.148 | −0.111 | −1.637 | −0.295 | 2.043 |
| 2 | 0.638 | 0.132 | −0.383 | −0.460 | −0.163 | 1.007 | 17 | 1.261 | −0.413 | −1.231 | −0.846 | 0.567 | 1.509 |
| 3 | 1.267 | 0.393 | −0.991 | −0.308 | 0.477 | 0.822 | 18 | 1.670 | 0.206 | −1.307 | −0.299 | 0.393 | 1.213 |
| 4 | 1.115 | 0.025 | −1.695 | −0.416 | 0.051 | 2.059 | 19 | 1.770 | 0.455 | −2.278 | −0.459 | 1.829 | 0.908 |
| 5 | 0.963 | −0.334 | −1.740 | −0.372 | 0.740 | 1.372 | 20 | 1.261 | 0.698 | −1.506 | −0.599 | 0.340 | 1.764 |
| 6 | 0.928 | −0.078 | −1.774 | −0.145 | 0.386 | 1.532 | 21 | 0.745 | 0.004 | −1.137 | 0.083 | 0.623 | 0.431 |
| 7 | 0.746 | 0.856 | −0.357 | −0.546 | 0.882 | 0.022 | 22 | 1.354 | 0.249 | −2.051 | −0.308 | 0.755 | 1.604 |
| 8 | 1.809 | 0.301 | −1.511 | −0.680 | 0.701 | 1.489 | 23 | 1.153 | 0.188 | −1.493 | −1.501 | 0.927 | 2.068 |
| 9 | 1.091 | 0.793 | −1.857 | −0.034 | 0.414 | 1.477 | 24 | 0.568 | 0.231 | −1.376 | −0.458 | 0.792 | 1.042 |
| 10 | 0.797 | −0.111 | −0.445 | −0.089 | 0.133 | 0.401 | 25 | 0.829 | −0.126 | −0.536 | 0.030 | 0.236 | 0.270 |
| 11 | 1.137 | −0.262 | −1.645 | −0.584 | 0.626 | 1.602 | 26 | 0.571 | 0.773 | −1.027 | 0.106 | 0.268 | 0.653 |
| 12 | 1.029 | −0.182 | −1.780 | −0.651 | 0.603 | 1.828 | 27 | 0.920 | −0.079 | −0.941 | 0.130 | −0.374 | 1.185 |
| 13 | 0.858 | 0.648 | −1.171 | −0.129 | 0.694 | 0.606 | 28 | 0.855 | −0.397 | −0.589 | −0.943 | −0.441 | 1.973 |
| 14 | 0.881 | 0.235 | −1.935 | −0.017 | 0.595 | 1.358 | 29 | 1.338 | 0.118 | −1.423 | −0.253 | 0.494 | 1.182 |
| 15 | 1.374 | −0.128 | −1.480 | −0.897 | 0.618 | 1.759 | 30 | 0.834 | −0.285 | −1.741 | 0.715 | −0.067 | 1.092 |

proposed model is significantly lower than that of the other models, or not. The results, which are shown in *Test statistic* column of Table 1, demonstrate that the RMSE of the proposed model was significantly lower than those of the conventional models.

The proposed model outperformed the conventional model when assessing raters with various rating scales. To emphasize this point, Table 2 presents rater parameters estimated using the proposed model. From the table, we can confirm the large variety of rating scales among the raters. The proposed model can represent those rater characteristics appropriately, although the conventional models cannot represent them. Therefore, in this experiment, the proposed model presented the highest model fitting and ability assessment accuracy.

## 4    Conclusion

This study proposed a new IRT model without the restriction of the equal interval scale for raters' scores. Experiments conducted with actual data demonstrated that the proposed model can improve the model fitting and ability assessment accuracy when raters have different rating scales. Although this study specifically addressed only peer assessment accuracy, the proposed model is useful for various purposes such as evaluating assessment skills, creating peer assessment groups, and selecting optimal peer-raters for each learner. Such applications are left as subjects for future work.

# References

1. Moccozet, L., Tardy, C.: An assessment for learning framework with peer assessment of group works. In: Proceedings of International Conference on Information Technology Based Higher Education and Training, pp. 1–5 (2015)
2. Shah, N.B., Bradley, J., Balakrishnan, S., Parekh, A., Ramchandran, K., Wainwright, M.J.: Some scaling laws for MOOC assessments. In: ACM KDD Workshop on Data Mining for Educational Assessment and Feedback (2014)
3. Uto, M., Ueno, M.: Item response theory for peer assessment. IEEE Trans. Learn. Technol. 9(2), 157–170 (2016)
4. Staubitz, T., Petrick, D., Bauer, M., Renz, J., Meinel, C.: Improving the peer assessment experience on MOOC platforms. In: Proceedings of Third ACM Conference on Learning at Scale, New York, NY, USA, pp. 389–398 (2016)
5. Terr, R., Hing, W., Orr, R., Milne, N.: Do coursework summative assessments predict clinical performance? a systematic review. BMC Med. Educ. 17(1), 40 (2017)
6. Lave, J., Wenger, E.: Situated Learning - Legitimate Peripheral Participation. Cambridge University Press, New York (1991)
7. Uto, M., Thien, N.D., Ueno, M.: Group optimization to maximize peer assessment accuracy using item response theory. In: André, E., Baker, R., Hu, X., Rodrigo, M.M.T., du Boulay, B. (eds.) AIED 2017. LNCS (LNAI), vol. 10331, pp. 393–405. Springer, Cham (2017). https://doi.org/10.1007/978-3-319-61425-0_33
8. Nguyen, T., Uto, M., Abe, Y., Ueno, M.: Reliable peer assessment for team project based learning using item response theory. In: Proceedings of International Conference on Computers in Education, pp. 144–153 (2015)
9. Eckes, T.: Introduction to Many-Facet Rasch Measurement: Analyzing and Evaluating Rater-Mediated Assessments. Peter Lang Publishing Inc., Frankfurt (2015)
10. Myford, C.M., Wolfe, E.W.: Detecting and measuring rater effects using many-facet Rasch measurement: Part I. J. Appl. Measur. 4, 386–422 (2003)
11. Patz, R.J., Junker, B.: Applications and extensions of MCMC in IRT: multiple item types, missing data, and rated responses. J. Educ. Behav. Stat. 24, 342–366 (1999)
12. Linacre, J.: Many-Faceted Rasch Measurement. MESA Press, Chicago (1989)
13. Masters, G.: A Rasch model for partial credit scoring. Psychometrika 47(2), 149–174 (1982)
14. Muraki, E.: A generalized partial credit model: application of an EM algorithm. Appl. Psychol. Measur. 16(2), 159–176 (1992)
15. Samejima, F.: Estimation of latent ability using a response pattern of graded scores. Psychometrika Monography 17, 1–100 (1969)
16. Kassim, N.L.A.: Judging behaviour and rater errors: an application of the many-facet Rasch model. GEMA Online J. Lang. Stud. 11(3), 179–197 (2011)
17. Rahman, A.A., Ahmad, J., Yasin, R.M., Hanafi, N.M.: Investigating central tendency in competency assessment of design electronic circuit: analysis using many facet Rasch measurement (MFRM). Int. J. Inf. Educ. Technol. 7(7), 525–528 (2017)

18. Lord, F.: Applications of Item Response Theory to Practical Testing Problems. Erlbaum Associates, Hillsdale (1980)
19. Persky, H., Daane, M., Jin, Y.: The nation's report card: Writing 2002. Technical report, National Center for Education Statistics (2003)
20. Salahu-Din, D., Persky, H., Miller, J.: The nation's report card: Writing 2007. Technical report, National Center for Education Statistics (2008)

# The Effect of Digital Versus Traditional Orchestration on Collaboration in Small Groups

Kurt VanLehn[1]([⊠]), Hugh Burkhardt[2], Salman Cheema[1],
Seokmin Kang[1], Daniel Pead[2], Alan Schoenfeld[3], and Jon Wetzel[1]

[1] Arizona State University, Tempe, AZ 85287, USA
kurt.vanlehn@asu.edu
[2] University of Nottingham, Nottingham, UK
[3] University of California, Berkeley, Berkeley, CA, USA

**Abstract.** We are developing an intelligent orchestration system named FACT (Formative Assessment using Computational Technology). Orchestration refers to the teacher's management of a face-to-face classroom workflow that mixes small group, individual and whole class activities. FACT is composed of an unintelligent Media system and an intelligent Analysis system. Although the Analysis system, which is still being refined, is designed to increase collaboration, prior work suggests that the Media system could possibly harm collaboration. Thus, we conducted an evaluation of the FACT Media system in classrooms, comparing it against traditional classrooms. We coded videos of small groups in order to measure their collaboration. The FACT Media system did no harm: the distribution of collaboration codes in FACT classrooms is statistically similar to the distribution in traditional classrooms. This null result is welcome news and sets the stage for testing the benefits of the Analysis system.

**Keywords:** Orchestration · Collaboration · Digital media

## 1 Introduction

The FACT Media system [1–5] is a general purpose orchestration system similar to Group Scribbles [6]. It is unintelligent in that it does not know about the task the students are doing, so it cannot give feedback and advice. Such feedback and advice will eventually be given by the overall FACT system, which combines the FACT Analysis system and the FACT Media system.

For the FACT Media system, the biggest risk is probably its impact on collaboration. When students work face-to-face in small groups on digital media, then either (a) all the members of the group work on a shared display, or (b) each member of the group works on their own display of a shared document. Let us consider first case (a).

When a whole group is trying to edit the same display, it is easy for one person to dominate the interaction, thus harming collaboration [7]. This can occur even when everyone in the group has their own mouse [7–9] or when the display is a large horizontally mounted multi-touch screen [10, 11].

© Springer International Publishing AG, part of Springer Nature 2018
C. Penstein Rosé et al. (Eds.): AIED 2018, LNAI 10948, pp. 369–373, 2018.
https://doi.org/10.1007/978-3-319-93846-2_69

Now for case (b). When each person has their own view on a shared document, students often try to refer to an object by pointing at their own screen, which fails because the other group members cannot see what the finger is pointing at [7]. This can harm grounding (i.e., group members arriving at a common understanding of noun phrases and other referential phrases). Grounding is an essential component of collaboration [12].

## 2    Evaluation

This study compared the amount of collaboration in classrooms that were using either traditional paper-and-pencil media or the FACT Media system. The classes enacted one of 8 Classroom Challenges, which are formative assessment lessons developed by the Mathematics Assessment Project (MAP, see http://map.mathshell.org). The traditional classes used the original paper-based versions of the Classroom Challenges. Pairs worked on a large paper poster. Their problem solving usually involved taking turns arranging paper cards on the poster or writing explanations on cards or on the poster. When they were finished, they glued the cards down.

In the FACT classes, pairs of students worked on the same Classroom Challenges but used electronic versions of posters and cards. They wrote, typed or drew on the cards or the posters, and they arranged cards on the poster. In both FACT and traditional classes, the teacher walked around the classroom visiting groups.

The participating classrooms were in schools near Nottingham, England or the South San Francisco bay area. Teachers were recruited by the MAP researchers in England and by the Silicon Valley Mathematics Initiative in the San Francisco bay area. All teachers were experts at enacting the Classroom Challenges.

The students were in $6^{th}$ grade math classes, but some schools mixed grade levels in the same classroom. We asked teachers to choose Classroom Challenges that were at the right level of difficulty for their particular classes.

Every lesson was recorded by three cameras. One shoulder-mounted camera followed and recorded the teacher. Two other cameras, which were mounted on tall tripods, focused downward on the students' desk. Each recorded a single group (pair). Students' conversation was recorded by a boundary microphone on the table.

For each class, the 3 video streams were synched in Elan (https://tla.mpi.nl/tools/tla-tools/elan/), a video annotation system, and then divided into 30-second segments. We first used the teacher videos to locate segments of small group activity. Only lessons with at least 30 segments of small group activity were included. Then, using the videos of pairs, we assigned to each segment a code indicating the pair's behavior during that segment.

Our coding scheme was based on Michelene Chi's ICAP framework [13] which is perhaps the only coding scheme for collaboration that has associated its categories with learning gains. Our codes are shown in Table 1, along with their corresponding ICAP categories. The table rows are ordered from most desirable to least.

Most videos were coded by two coders. Interrater agreements (Kappa) averaged 0.74. Disagreements were resolved in a meeting of the two coders and one of this paper's authors.

**Table 1.** Average percentage of number of segments per code

|    | Description (ICAP categories in parentheses) | FACT | Paper |
|----|----------------------------------------------|------|-------|
| 1  | *Co-construction.* Both students shared their thinking. Their contributions built upon each other. (Interactive) | 2.8% | 4.0% |
| 2  | *Cooperation.* The students worked simultaneously and independently on different parts of the poster. (Constructive + Constructive) | 10.6% | 7.1% |
| 3  | *Unclear.* One or both the students explained their thinking, but the audio was not clear enough to determine whether it was one or two. (Constructive + Passive, or Interactive) | 0.4% | 0.9% |
| 4  | *One explaining.* One student explained his or her thinking (talking constructively) but the other student was either silent or merely agreeing. (Constructive + Passive) | 4.0% | 4.2% |
| 5  | *None explaining.* Students made edits, but neither explained their thinking. If they talked at all, their speech merely repeated their edits. For example, one student might say "Let's put card B here," and the other student agrees. (Constructive + Passive) | 53.8% | 67.7% |
| 6  | One student was off-task; the other worked without much talk. (Constructive + Disengaged) | 4.5% | 0.9% |
| 7  | The teacher was visiting the pair. (Passive + Passive) | 3.3% | 6.6% |
| 8  | The teacher was making a brief comment to the whole class, and these students were listening. (Passive + Passive) | 1.1% | 5.0% |
| 9  | The students were stuck and waiting for help from the teacher. (Disengaged + Disengaged) | 0.6% | 0% |
| 10 | The students were done with the task and waiting for the teacher to give them something else to do. (Disengaged + Disengaged) | 11.8% | 2.8% |
| 11 | Both students were off-task. (Disengaged + Disengaged) | 7.1% | 0.8% |

## 2.1 Results

We coded 15 traditional pairs and 59 FACT pairs. For each pair, we counted the number of segments per code. Because the total number of segments was different for different pairs, we converted the counts into percentages. Table 1 presents the averages.

To understand these results, it helps to first consider the first 5 codes, which represent students doing problem solving together. Figure 1 shows the distribution of just these 5 codes. They are not reliably different (Chi-square, $p = 0.3$, $N = 59$, traditional distribution treated as expected probabilities). Thus it appears that FACT did not make a difference in how students worked together.

There were differences in the distribution of codes 6 through 11, where students were not working together. FACT seems to have reduced the amount of teacher intervention (codes 7 and 8), increased off-task behavior (codes 6 and 11), and increased the time students spend waiting for the teacher (codes 9 and 10).

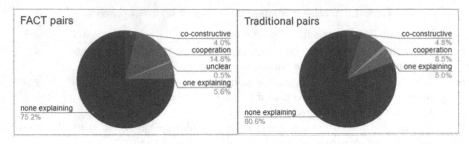

**Fig. 1.** Distribution of working-together codes (codes 1 through 5)

## 2.2   Discussion

Because this was a field study, we had no control over many important factors, including the participants, activities, time of year and time of day. Also, we compared the treatments with a single level of analysis (pairs) rather than the customary multi-level analyses (e.g., pairs nested in classroom nested in teacher nested in school). Thus, our results should be viewed with as preliminary.

Despite its limitations, the study suggests that the FACT Media system does not harm collaboration compared to the traditional, paper-based enactments of the Classroom Challenges. The proportion of the 5 working-together codes is the same for both FACT pairs and traditional pairs.

The amount of good collaboration (code 1, co-construction) in both venues is surprisingly small, under 5%. Gweon et al. [14], Hausmann et al. [15] and Viswanathan et al. [1] coded 14%, 20% and 25% of their segments as co-construction, respectively. However, all three studies involved undergraduates working in labs, whereas our data came from middle school students working in classrooms. Although the amount of co-construction was low, this finding sets the stage for the next phase of the FACT research agenda, which is to use AI technology to increase the amount of Interaction.

**Acknowledgements.** This research was supported by the Bill and Melinda Gates Foundation under OPP1061281. We gratefully acknowledge the contributions of all the members of the FACT project, past and present.

## References

1. Viswanathan, S.A., VanLehn, K.: Using the tablet gestures and speech of pairs of students to classify their collaboration. IEEE Transactions on Learning Technologies (2017). in press
2. VanLehn, K., et al.: Some less obvious features of classroom orchestration systems. In: Lin, L., Atkinson, R.K. (eds.) Educational Technologies: Challenges. Applications and Learning Outcomes. Nova Science Publishers, Incorporated, Hauppauge (2016). in Press
3. VanLehn, K., et al.: How can FACT encourage collaboration and self-correction? In: Millis, K., et al., (Eds.) Multi-Disciplinary Approaches to Deep Learning. Routledge, New York (in press)

4. Wetzel, J., et al.: A preliminary evaluation of the usability of an AI-infused orchestration system. Artificial Intelligence in Education. Springer, London (2018)
5. Cheema, S., et al.: Electronic posters to support formative assessment. In: CHI EA Proceedings of the 2016 CHI Conference Extended Abstracts on Human Factors in Computing Systems, pp. 1159–1164. ACM (2016)
6. Looi, C.-K., Lin, C.-P., Liu, K.-P.: Group scribbles to support knowledge building in a jigsaw method. IEEE Trans. on Learn. Technol. 1(3), 157–164 (2008)
7. Scott, S.D., Mandryk, R.L., Inkpen, K.M.: Understanding children's collaborative interactions in shared environments. J. of Comput. Assist. Learn. 19, 220–228 (2003)
8. Alcoholado, C., et al.: Comparing the use of the interpersonal computer, personal computer and pen-and-paper when solving arithmetic exercises. Br. J. Edu. Technol. 47(1), 91–105 (2016)
9. Nussbaum, M., Alcoholado, C., Buchi, T.: A comparative analysis of interactive arithmetic learning in the classroom and computer lab. Comput. Hum. Behav. 43, 183–188 (2015)
10. Mercier, E., Vourloumi, G., Higgens, S.: Student interactions and the development of ideas in multi-touch and paper-based collaborative mathematics problem solving. Br. J. Educ. Technol. 48(1), 162–175 (2015)
11. Higgins, S.E., et al.: Multi-touch tables and collaborative learning. Br. J. Educ. Technol. 43(6), 1041–1054 (2012)
12. Roschelle, J., Teasley, S.D.: The construction of shared knowledge in collaborative problem solving. In: O'Malley, C. (ed.) Computer-Supported Collaborative Learning. Springer, Heidelberg (1995)
13. Chi, M.T.H., Wylie, R.: ICAP: A hypothesis of differentiated learning effectiveness for four modes of engagement activities. Ed. Psychol. 49(4), 219–243 (2014)
14. Gweon, G., et al.: Measuring prevalence of other-oriented transactive contributions using an automated measure of speech style accommodation. Int. J. Comput.-Support. Collab. Learn. 8(2), 245–265 (2013)
15. Hausmann, R.G.M., Chi, M.T.H., Roy, M.: Learning from collaborative problem solving: An analysis of three hypothesized mechanisms. In: Cognitive Science Conference (2004)

# Modeling Student Learning Behaviors in ALEKS: A Two-Layer Hidden Markov Modeling Approach

Guoyi Wang[1], Yun Tang[1(✉)] ⓘ, Junyi Li[1], and Xiangen Hu[1,2]

[1] Central China Normal University, Wuhan 430079, Hubei, China
tangyun@mail.ccnu.edu.cn
[2] University of Memphis, Memphis, TN 38152, USA

**Abstract.** This study analyzed 25,783 log data entries of student learning activities on a self-paced online intelligent tutoring system. The behavior patterns between the high- and low-achievement students and of different mathematical topics were compared using two-layer hidden Markov model. The results showed that high-achievement students exhibited more effective learning behaviors, such as asking for explanation and practicing after making an error. In contrast, low-achievement students tended to make consecutive errors without seeking help. Moreover, students' learning behaviors tended to be more effective when learning simple topics. Our findings implied that intelligent tutoring systems could track the behavior patterns of students and detect ineffective learning states, so as to provide learning support accordingly.

**Keywords:** Intelligent tutoring system · Two-layer hidden Markov model Behavior pattern

## 1 Introduction

It is commonly believed that human tutors are more effective than computer tutors when teaching the same content. Human tutors were found to be better at scaffolding learners, as well as giving feedback that encourages learners to engage in interactive and constructive behaviors [1]. Another key property of effective tutoring was the granularity of the interaction [1]. For example, Intelligence tutoring systems (ITS) can be classified into answer based, sub step-based, and step-based tutor according to the grain size. The step-based ITSs—which have the finest granularity—were nearly as effective as human tutoring [1–3]. To determine the granularity of interaction and deliver necessary support in ITSs, it is critical to unveil the behavior patterns through student modeling. Because ITSs automatically record student activities in the log data, educational data mining techniques can be applied for understanding the behavior patterns and further facilitate the improvement of learning process [4].

In the present study, we propose to use two-layer hidden Markov model (TL-HMM) to model the sequential patterns in ITS log data. TL-HMM is a method developed on the basis of Hidden Markov Models (HMM) [5]. It decomposes the process into two nested layers of models. The first layer is treated using a non-hidden Markov model. Each micro

© Springer International Publishing AG, part of Springer Nature 2018
C. Penstein Rosé et al. (Eds.): AIED 2018, LNAI 10948, pp. 374–378, 2018.
https://doi.org/10.1007/978-3-319-93846-2_70

activity is treated as an observable symbol and the state is produced from the transition between each activity upon the distribution condition. The second layer treats the state from the first layer as a latent state in a hidden Markov model. The transitions between latent states are constructed by the relations and dependencies of these micro activities. TL-HMM can be used to decode the latent state sequences of students. Instructors may use the representation of student behavior patterns and behavior transitions to identify the hidden knowledge and understand the dynamic change of the latent behaviors in massive interaction datasets [5].

The present study attempted to discover specific behavior patterns from ITS log data using TL-HMM. The investigation into behavioral patterns may help us to understand how students learn in the system and predict their performance level.

## 2  Methods

The data in the present study were obtained from Assessment and Learning in Knowledge Spaces (ALEKS) [6], a web-based intelligent tutoring system. In ALEKS, practice problems are organized into topics, while each problem is attached with an explanation of concepts and procedures in the form of worked examples. Students may request for explanations at any time, or ALEKS would prompt students with explanations after two consecutive errors. After a certain number of practice, students would be graded as mastering or failing the topic according to the scoring rules, of which the artificial intelligence is based in the Knowledge Space Theory [7].

The data we used consisted of 25,783 entries from six high schools in the United States from 2010 to 2014. Table 1 lists the four topics. The unique ID of schools and students were omitted for anonymity. Each entry represents a completed sequence of actions (M = 5.81, SD = 4.32) for practicing a specific topic. There were four kinds of actions: L (receiving an explanation prompted by ALEKS), E (requesting an explanation), C (answering correct) and W (answering wrong). The duration of each action was also contained in the data. Due to the lack of individual information, we treated each entry as from an independent student and categorized the students who mastered the topic as high-achievement, while those who failed as low-achievement.

**Table 1.** Contents of the four mathematical topics in the data set.

| Topic | Content |
| --- | --- |
| Algebra 208 | Solving a two-step equation with signed fractions |
| Algebra 209 | Solving a linear equation with several occurrences of the variable |
| Algebra 703 | Solving a word problem using a quadratic equation with rational roots |
| Algebra 224 | Solving a word problem using a system of linear equations |

The sequences of actions were analyzed using TL-HMM implemented in the MeTA toolkit [8]. Two patterns were derived to characterize student behaviors: the latent state representations and the latent state transitions. We then used python-igraph [9] to visualize these behavior patterns.

## 3 Results and Discussion

In this section, we compared the behavior patterns of high- and low-achievement students. All data entries were classified into failure and mastery according to the end results and were respectively fitted. TL-HMM uses latent states to model these behavior patterns, while the transitions between latent states captured the progress of learning over time. [5] suggested that the number of states should be empirically determined and based on the goal of analysis. Accordingly, we fit models of 2-10 states and plotted the corresponding latent state representations. We then examined these representations and picked the ones with meaningful patterns. Likelihood-based or predictive accuracy-based methods, such as BIC or cross validation, may also be used to assist the model selection process.

Figure 1 shows the latent state representations of a 3-state TL-HMM that best fits the sequence of actions of low-achievement students (i.e., those who failed an item). Figure 2 shows the latent states of a 4-state TL-HMM that best fits the actions of high-achievement students (i.e., those who mastered an item). In each representation, the nodes stand for different behaviors. The size of every node is set to be proportional to its probability of being visited during a random walk. The arrows indicate the direction of transfer between two nodes. The thickness of the curves reflects the probability of the nodes transfer.

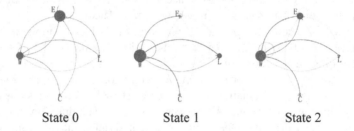

State 0            State 1            State 2

**Fig. 1.** A 3-state TL-HMM fit to actions preceding failure. The thickness of the paths indicate the relative size of transition probability.

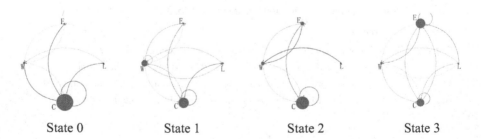

State 0            State 1            State 2            State 3

**Fig. 2.** A 4-state TL-HMM fit to actions preceding mastery.

Figure 3 presents the latent state transition diagrams. The nodes in the transition diagram stand for different behavior patterns reflected by the latent states in Figs. 1 and 2. For low-achievement students, there is a very high probability of staying in State 1 (constantly answer wrong without calling for explanation) while State 0 (help-seeking) has the lowest probability. On the other hand, for high-achievement students, there is a relatively high probability of State 0 (always answer correct) while State 3(ineffectively overusing help) has the lowest probability. In either category, the probabilities of transferring between latent states are very small. It is reasonable because each learning sequence has an average length of about 12.5 min. Hence we did not expect a frequent transfer between latent states.

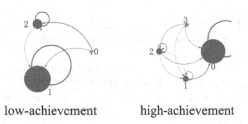

low-achievement          high-achievement

**Fig. 3.** The latent state transition diagrams for the 3-state TL-IIMM fit to the low-achievement students (left panel) and the 4-state TL-HMM fit to the high-achievement students (right panel).

We further classified the data entries of failure and mastery into the four topics (see Table 1). The 3-states model learned on the "failure" students was retrofitted to train the data set of "failure" students on each topic. The model parameters associated with their Markov model representations were forced to be fixed, so the latent state meanings would not drift. Similar analysis was also performed to the mastery data set of four topics. The general patterns of latent state transitions were held in each topic, although there are some topic-specific differences of interest. On one hand, when solving complex topics (i.e., Algebra 224 and Algebra 703), the high-achievement students mastered the item without much help from explanations (State 0), while the low-achievement students requested more explanations (State 2) along with practice. It may be inferred that explanation alone was not as effective as the system may expect. On the other hand, when solving simpler topics (i.e., Algebra 208 and Algebra 209), the high-achievement students benefitted more from repeated practice (State 1) or help-seeking (State 2), while the low-achievement students were trapped in ineffective practice (State 1) but fail to learn from explanations.

## 4   Conclusion

The present study explored the patterns of learning behaviors in ALEKS using a TL-HMM approach. The results demonstrated that this approach could facilitate the interpretation of learning process in ALEKS or similar ITSs. Specifically, low-achievement students rarely asked for explanation. Upon detecting ineffective learning states, ITSs may consider providing additional assistance or even bringing outside support (e.g., a human tutor) to help the students learn.

**Acknowledgement.** This study was partially supported by Self-determined Research Funds of CCNU from the Colleges' Basic Research and Operation of Ministry of Education, China (No. CCNU15A05049; No. CCNU16JYKX38).

# References

1. VanLehn, K.: The relative effectiveness of human tutoring, intelligent tutoring systems, and other tutoring systems. Educ. Psychol. **46**(4), 197–221 (2011). https://doi.org/10.1080/00461520.2011.611369
2. Hu, X., Craig, S.D., Bargagliotti, A.E., et al.: The effects of a traditional and technology-based after-school program on 6th grade student's mathematics skills. J. Comput. Math. Sci. Teach. **31**(1), 17–38 (2012)
3. Ma, W., Adesope, O.O., Nesbit, J.C., et al.: Intelligent tutoring systems and learning outcomes: a meta-analysis. J. Educ. Psychol. **106**(4), 901–918 (2014)
4. Koedinger, K.R., Brunskill, E., Baker, R.S.J.D., et al.: New potentials for data-driven intelligent tutoring system development and optimization. AI Mag. **34**(3), 27–41 (2013)
5. Geigle, C., Zhai, C.: Modeling student behavior with two-layer hidden Markov models. J. Educ. Data Min. **9**(1), 1–24 (2017)
6. Craig, S.D., Hu, X., Graesser, A.C., et al.: The impact of a technology-based mathematics after-school program using ALEKS on student's knowledge and behaviors. Comput. Educ. **68**, 495–504 (2013)
7. Huang, X., Craig, S.D., Xie, J., et al.: Intelligent tutoring systems work as a math gap reducer in 6th grade after-school program. Learn. Individ. Differ. **47**, 258–265 (2016)
8. Massung, S., Geigle, C., Zhai, C.: MeTA: a unified toolkit for text retrieval and analysis. In: Proceedings of the 54th Annual Meeting of the Association for Computational Linguistics—System Demonstrations, pp. 91–96. Association for Computational Linguistics, Berlin (2016). https://doi.org/10.18653/v1/p16-4016
9. Csardi, G., Nepusz, T.: The igraph software package for complex network research. InterJ. Complex Syst. **1695**(5), 1–9 (2006)

# A Preliminary Evaluation of the Usability of an AI-Infused Orchestration System

Jon Wetzel[1]([⊠]), Hugh Burkhardt[2], Salman Cheema[1], Seokmin Kang[1], Daniel Pead[2], Alan Schoenfeld[3], and Kurt VanLehn[1]

[1] Arizona State University, Tempe, AZ 85287, USA
jwetzel4@asu.edu
[2] University of Nottingham, Nottingham, UK
[3] University of California, Berkeley, Berkeley, CA, USA

**Abstract.** Artificial intelligence (AI) holds great promise for improving classroom orchestration—the teacher's management of a classroom workflow that mixes small group, individual, and whole class activities. Although we have developed an orchestration system, named FACT, that uses AI, we were concerned that usability issues might decrease its effectiveness. We conducted an analysis of classroom video recordings that classified and compared the time FACT students spent to the time spent by students using paper versions of the same lessons. FACT wasted half the time that paper did. However FACT students spent slightly more time off task and had difficulties referring to objects on shared documents.

**Keywords:** Orchestration · Usability · Digital media

## 1 Introduction

Classroom orchestration refers to a teacher's management of classroom workflows that involve small group, individual, and whole-class activities [1, 2]. An orchestration system helps by increasing teacher awareness and facilitating management of the workflow [3]. Combining orchestration features with an intelligent tutoring system (ITS) should both facilitate orchestration and enhance adoption of the ITS [4]. We have iteratively developed, over 50 classroom trials, an AI-infused orchestration system, FACT (Formative Assessment Computing Technologies) [5–8]. Although FACT employs traditional ITS technology, its primary function is to help the teacher orchestrate a lesson. It is similar to Lumilo [9], MT Classroom [10] and Group Scribbles [11].

However, before the benefits of AI can be evaluated in any such system, the usability of the system vs. paper baseline classes must be assessed, just as Hao [12] did for Group Scribbles. Otherwise, the AI might be blamed when it is the usability of the media that is flawed. This paper presents a preliminary evaluation of the usability of FACT compared to paper.

**The FACT User's Experience.** Students may use a desktop, laptop, or tablet with a web browser. Teachers should carry a tablet so that they can access FACTs dashboard as they circulate. When the class begins, everyone logs in, and the teacher can select a lesson and step through a series of activities. Whenever the teacher selects an activity,

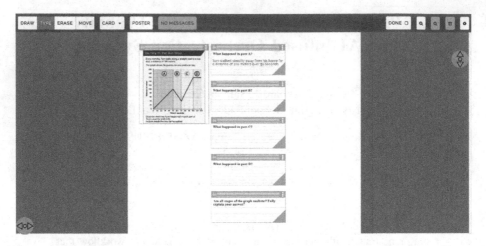

**Fig. 1.** A digital poster as displayed by a student's editor in FACT

FACT gives the appropriate digital poster to the students. Figure 1 shows a poster with 6 cards on it. Students can edit both cards and the poster itself. They can draw, type, move, or erase. FACT supports group work as well as individual work. Once students have joined a group, they can edit the group's poster simultaneously in real time using conventions similar to other online collaborative editors like Google Docs.

**FACT's Intelligence.** FACT monitors the students' edits and updates the teachers' dashboard in real time to show progress and alerts. The alerts are driven by a variety of technology including AI, image analysis, sketch recognition, handwriting recognition, and collaboration detection. Until recently, FACT used a human-in-the-loop policy, so all actions were taken by the teacher. However, teachers in our trials still had too many students to visit, so we have begun to experiment with human-ON-the-loop policies, where FACT sometimes takes actions by itself given the teachers' prior or concurrent approval.

## 2   An Evaluation of FACT's Usability

Our evaluation aims to answer two questions. First, how does the amount of wasted time in lessons done with FACT compare to those done on paper? Second, what are the specific usability defects of FACT, and how frequently do they occur?

We analyzed video data from 13 lessons: six done on paper and seven done with FACT. The videos were taken in classrooms in middle/high schools in Nottingham, England and the South San Francisco bay area. The grade level varied, but primarily consisted of 6th grade students. Each class we observed was working on one of eight lessons selected from the Mathematics Assessment Project (MAP, http://map. mathshell.org) Classroom Challenges.

Although the classes typically had 25 students, our data source for this study was videos taken by fixed cameras positioned over two pairs of students per class. We coded the behavior of just one student per pair, typically the student whose workspace was most clearly visible.

The coders watched for and coded the following events: **Disconnected** – Student lost their connection to FACT or the internet; **JoiningGroups** – Student was at the Join Groups screen; **LearnToResizeCard** – Student was figuring out how to resize a card for the first time; **LostCardSearch** – Student was looking for a specific card; **OtherGlitch** – Student's time was wasted by some glitch in FACT; **OtherStruggleWithMedia** – Student was having trouble using FACT but not due to a glitch.

If the medium was paper, the following codes were used: **PaperNoMath** – Student was either (a) manipulating traditional media without discussing math, (b) discussing traditional media, (c) waiting for their partner to manipulate traditional media without engaging in math, or (d) waiting for media to distributed; **LostCardSearch** – Student was looking for a specific card. Here, "traditional media" refers to the tools: paper, cards, glue, pencils/pen, etc.

When coders found one of these situations, they entered the code, start time, end time, and an optional brief description of the event in a spreadsheet. To calculate the amount of wasted time due to the medium for a student in a given lesson, we summed the durations as shown in Table 1.

**Table 1.** Average time spent on key event for students in lessons (m:ss format)

| Code | Avg time used (FACT) | Avg time used (paper) |
|---|---|---|
| LoggingIn | 1:22 | N/A |
| Disconnected | 0 | N/A |
| JoiningGroups | 0:51 | N/A |
| LearnToResizeCard | 0:07 | N/A |
| OtherGlitch | 1:18 | N/A |
| OtherStruggleWithMedia | 0:18 | N/A |
| LostCardSearch | 0:01 | 1:07 |
| PaperNoMath (distributing paper) | N/A | 1:23 |
| PaperNoMath (other) | N/A | 5:39 |
| Avg. wasted time (% lesson time) | 3:57 (6.30%) | 8:09 (12.45%) |

Our analysis found that using FACT resulted in less time wasted due to the medium. On average 12.45% (8 m 09 s) of the student's time was wasted manipulating or waiting for paper, while only 6.30% (3 m 56 s) was wasted when using FACT. That is, the FACT wasted half the time that paper wasted.

Table 1 summarizes the sources of wasted time. Time at the login screen was between 10 s and 4 m 49 s, because some teachers had students wait there while introducing the lesson. Glitches were a close second on wasted time for FACT. All but one instance of JoiningGroups were finished within 45 s. During the outlier event, which took 2 m 20 s, most students joined their group within a few seconds, but then had to wait for the rest of the class. The most notable case of OtherStruggleWithMedia occurred when a student tried for 30+ s to move a card with their cursor in erase mode.

We also coded both the FACT and paper videos for off-task behavior. Students using FACT spent slightly more time off task than those on paper: average time 2 m 34 s (3.9% of class time) for paper vs 3 m 20 s (5.3% of class time) for FACT.

Hao [12] and others have noticed that when students want to refer to an object in a shared document, they often try to point to their own screen and their partners cannot see what they are pointing at. This could impede collaboration. To evaluate this issue, we coded: **ReferPoint** – The student being coded pointed at the other student's tablet; **ReferShow** – The student showed their own tablet to the partner and pointed to it; **ReferID** – The student orally mentioned the number or letter label on the card; **ReferOther** – The student used some other method. Our analysis, summarized in Table 2, found that pointing at the other person's tablet was the most frequent method. References using the ID on the card were less frequent (and all cards had IDs except in Lesson 7). On average, students spent 61 s per lesson getting their partners to understand what they were referring to. Presumably, referring would take much less time if students were using a paper poster instead of a shared electronic poster.

**Table 2.** Counts of instances of co-referring by students in FACT lesson

| Student | ReferPoint | ReferID | ReferOther | ReferShow |
|---|---|---|---|---|
| 1 | 11 | 3 | 1 | 1 |
| 2 | 3 | 0 | 1 | 0 |
| 3 | 3 | 0 | 6 | 0 |
| 4 | 8 | 0 | 0 | 2 |
| 5 | 3 | 0 | 0 | 1 |
| 6 | 0 | 17 | 0 | 0 |
| 7 | 7 | 0 | 0 | 1 |
| % of instances | 51.47% | 29.41% | 11.76% | 7.35% |

## 3   Conclusion

While our sample size is small, our analysis leaves us optimistic about FACT's usability. From our observations so far, we see FACT wastes less time than paper, and we identified several ways to lower its wasted time. We are addressing the largest time-waster, glitches, by continuing to fix bugs in FACT.

FACT students tend to go off-task more than paper students. It is not clear why and could be just a sampling artifact.

Referring to objects in a shared document seems to occupy a relatively short time per lesson, so we hypothesize that collaboration is unhindered. However, confirmation requires a closer study of this issue which also coded students' references to objects on paper posters.

**Acknowledgements.** The FACT project is sponsored by the Bill and Melinda Gates Foundation under grant OPP10612881. We also thank all the students at ASU who have worked on FACT and the video analyses. Finally, we thank the Silicon Valley Mathematics Initiative and the Shell Center for conducting the classroom testing.

# References

1. Dillenbourg, P.: Design for classroom orchestration. Comput. Educ. **69**, 485–492 (2013)
2. Roschelle, J., Dimitriadis, Y., Hoppe, U.: Classroom orchestration: Synthesis. Comput. Educ. **69**, 523–526 (2013)
3. Prieto, L.P., Dlab, M.H., Abdulwahed, M., Balid, W.: Orchestrating technology enhanced learning: a literature review and conceptual framework. Int. J. Technol. Enhanc. Learn. **3**(6), 583–598 (2011)
4. Holstein, K., McLaren, B., Aleven, V.: Intelligent tutors as teachers' aids: exploring teacher needs for real-time analytics in blended classrooms. In: Proceedings of the. Learning Analytics and Knowledge: LAK 2017, Vancouver, BC, Canada (2017)
5. Cheema, S., VanLehn, K., Burkhart, H., Pead, D., Schoenfeld, A.H.: Electronic posters to support formative assessment. In: Proceedings of the CHI 2016: Extended Abstracts (2016)
6. VanLehn, K., Cheema, S., Wetzel, J., Pead, D.: Some less obvious features of classroom orchestration systems. In: Lin, L., Atkinson, R.K. (eds.) Educational Technologies: Challenges, Applications and Learning Outcomes (2016)
7. Viswanathan, S.A., VanLehn, K.: Using the tablet gestures and speech of pairs of students to classify their collaboration. IEEE Trans. Learn. Technol. (2017)
8. VanLehn, K., Burkhardt, H., Cheema, S., Pead, D., Schoenfeld, A.H., Wetzel, J.: How can FACT encourage collaboration and self-correction?. In: Millis, K., Long, D., Magliano, J., Wiemer, K. (eds.) Multi-Disciplinary Approaches to Deep Learning, Routledge (in press)
9. Holstein, K., Hong, G., Tegene, M., McLaren, B., Aleven, V.: The classroom as a dashboard: co-designing wearable cognitive augmentation for K-12 teachers. In: Proceedings of the International Conference on Learning Analytics and Knowledge, Sydney, Australia (2018)
10. Martinez-Maldonado, R., Yacef, K., Kay, J.: TSCL: a conceptual model to inform understanding of collaborative learning processes at interactive tabletops. Int. J. Hum. Comput. Stud. **83**, 62–82 (2015)
11. Looi, C.-K., Lin, C.-P., Liu, K.-P.: Group Scribbles to support knowledge building in a jigsaw method. IEEE Trans. Learn. Technol. **1**(3), 157–164 (2008)
12. Hao, C.F.: A comparative study of collaborative learning in Paper Scribbles and Group Scribbles. Australas. J. Educ. Technol. **26**(5), 659–674 (2010)

# Microscope or Telescope: Whether to Dissect Epistemic Emotions

Naomi Wixon[1(✉)], Beverly Woolf[2], Sarah Schultz[3],
Danielle Allessio[2], and Ivon Arroyo[1]

[1] Worcester Polytechnic University, Worcester, MA, USA
{nbwixon,iarroyo}@wpi.edu
[2] University of Massachusetts, Amherst, MA, USA
bev@cs.umass.edu, danielle.allessio@gmail.com
[3] Carnegie Mellon School of Computer Science, Pittsburgh, USA
sschultl@andrew.cmu.edu

**Abstract.** We empirically investigate two methods for eliciting student emotion within an online instructional environment. Students may not fully express their emotions when asked to report on a single emotion. Furthermore, students' usage of emotional terms may differ from that of researchers. To address these issues, we tested two alternative emotion self-report mechanisms: the first *closed response* where students report on a single emotion via Likert scale, the second *open response* where students describe their emotions via open text.

**Keywords:** Student emotion · Learning · Behavior · Intelligent tutor
Log data · Emotion self-report

## 1 Introduction

No clear gold-standard exists for identifying affective states, which drives research to examine the intersection of theory and measurement methodology [7]. Many affective states in learning environments, such as boredom, confusion, frustration, and engaged concentration, are characterized as having an epistemic nature [6, 9]. Epistemic states may be described as emotional [11], or cognitive [4], because they are often operationalized as partly dependent on particular events or cognition [3]. In addition to the ambiguous cognitive/emotional nature of many of these epistemic emotions, there is also uncertainty regarding which constructs to consider. BROMP [8] focuses on boredom, confusion, engaged concentration, and frustration as typically being more prevalent.

Factors that are neither purely affective nor purely cognitive moderate and explain the relationship between student affect and observable events (e.g., log data). These factors include students' beliefs, narratives, expectations, motivations, and perceptions of ability and control. We propose self-report data as an assessment mechanic as a relatively direct and simple means to collect information about students' causal attributions for their feelings and chosen strategy to interact with a tutor environment.

**Research Questions.** This research serves to illustrate how tracking students' appraisals of a situation may help explain students' emotions and behaviors within a tutor

© Springer International Publishing AG, part of Springer Nature 2018
C. Penstein Rosé et al. (Eds.): AIED 2018, LNAI 10948, pp. 384–388, 2018.
https://doi.org/10.1007/978-3-319-93846-2_72

learning environment. Attribution and appraisal data including students' motivation and volition may allow the tutor to predict students' future behavior more accurately than a combination of pure affective observations and behavior alone. The following research questions are addressed: **Research Question #1:** How do students express their emotions in an online tutor and how are these emotions associated with students' actions? **Research Question #2:** Why do students believe they feel a particular way? We investigate the causal attributions students assign to their emotional states.

## 2   Student Emotion and Attribution Elicitation Methods

We now present two methods for eliciting emotion data from students working in an intelligent tutoring system. We proposed and investigated two different methods. In the *closed-response* emotion inventory questions, the tutor presents a constrained statement about emotion (e.g., "Tell us about your level of Confidence"). We survey students on four distinct emotions: confidence, excitement, frustration, and interest [1, 2, 10, 12]. Even in this closed-response condition students were asked an open-response attribution question "Why is that?" to elicit students' perceived causes of their emotional states. In the *open-response assessment,* students are provided with an open response window and asked to describe their emotions and write their responses in natural language, see Fig. 1, right. The prompts are similar to the *closed-response* prompts. Initially, students are asked how they feel, and then asked why they feel that way.

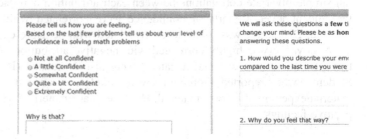

**Fig. 1.** Two self-report prompts in an online tutoring system. (Left) The closed-response emotion inventory question (top) which asks students to rate on a Likert scale. (Right) Students use an open response window and write in natural language.

Students' learning gains were assessed via pretest and posttest with items extracted from MCAS practice exams. Learning, Performance, and Work Avoidance goals were measured through the 18 item GOALS-S survey [5].

**RQ1:** Work avoidance goals were found to be negatively correlated with confidence. It is notable that a feeling of confidence in one's abilities appears to be unrelated to mastery or performance goals, but negatively related to academic motivation in the form of work avoidance [5]. Mastery goals were negatively correlated with reports of feeling neutral or positive, which may indicate that students with high mastery goals didn't feel they were meeting those goals (Tables 1 and 2).

**Table 1. Emotions vs Pre/Posttest Measures:** Bivariate correlations

| | Correlation coefficients | | | | |
|---|---|---|---|---|---|
| | Math Pre/Post gain | Mastery goals | Performance goals | Work avoid goals | N (students) |
| Closed-Response measures | | | | | |
| Confidence | 0.16 | 0.19 | 0.17 | $-0.47^{**}$ | 40 |
| Excitement | −0.06 | 0.11 | −0.18 | −0.13 | 37 |
| Frustration | 0 | −0.11 | 0.06 | $0.27^{\dagger}$ | 39 |
| Interest | 0.04 | −0.01 | −0.11 | −0.11 | 38 |
| Open-Response measures | | | | | |
| Annoyed | 0.04 | −0.18 | 0.07 | 0.19 | 39 |
| Bored | −0.22 | −0.12 | -0.04 | 0 | 39 |
| Confused | 0.03 | −0.11 | 0.04 | 0.15 | 39 |
| Negative | 0.18 | 0.09 | −0.1 | −0.1 | 39 |
| Neutral | 0.13 | $-0.33^*$ | −0.08 | 0.09 | 39 |
| Positive | −0.2 | $-0.40^*$ | −0.1 | −0.09 | 39 |

$\dagger = p \leq 0.1$, $* = p \leq 0.05$, $** = p \leq 0.01$

**RQ2:** To examine how students' causal attributions related to their emotional states we ran simple bivariate correlations between each attribution and each emotional state at the student level. Reports of confidence were correlated with attributions of easy material. Disinterest was found to be correlated with negative causal attributions.

Annoyance was highly correlated with negative attributions to the website; these two attributions (website and negative) were also correlated ($R = 0.626$, $p < 0.001$). Students who reported boredom, were likely to attribute feelings to boring material/experiences or easy material. However, easy material was also associated with positive feelings.

## 3 Discussion

**RQ1:** Confident students performed well, as expected, and surprisingly used many hints: perhaps hint use led to confidence. The negative valence emotions being negatively correlated with problem time suggests students may rush through their work due to discomfort. Boredom follows this trend with more incorrect attempts, it seems consistent that cognitively engaged negative emotions (annoyed and confused) are less error prone [3]. Yet closed response frustration shows the opposite trend.

**RQ2:** Exploring the relationship between attributions and emotions (Table 3) revealed that students identify multiple distinct causes for the same emotional state (e.g. boredom), and that the same cause can lead to different emotional states (e.g. an easy task).

**Table 2. Emotions vs Behaviors:** Bivariate correlations

| | Correlation coefficients | | | | |
|---|---|---|---|---|---|
| | SOF per prob | Time per prob | Wrong per prob | Hint per prob | N (students) |
| Closed-Response measures | | | | | |
| Confidence | **0.41**[**] | 0.07 | **−0.54**[**] | **0.33**[*] | 40 |
| Excitement | 0.13 | 0.16 | −0.22 | 0.31[†] | 37 |
| Frustration | −0.04 | −0.14 | 0.15 | −0.01 | 39 |
| Interest | 0.31[†] | 0.06 | −0.14 | 0.01 | 38 |
| Open-Response measures | | | | | |
| Annoyed | −0.07 | 0.17 | −0.11 | 0.21 | 39 |
| Bored | 0.00 | −0.26 | 0.27[†] | −0.18 | 39 |
| Confused | −0.02 | 0.25 | −0.14 | 0.15 | 39 |
| Negative | −0.18 | **−0.35**[*] | 0.07 | −0.09 | 39 |
| Neutral | 0.00 | 0.1 | −0.12 | 0.12 | 39 |
| Positive | −0.09 | 0.12 | 0.18 | −0.11 | 39 |

† = $p \leq 0.1$, * = $p \leq 0.05$, ** = $p \leq 0.01$, note: N varies for closed-response: while most students received at least 1 of each of the 4 emotions, some may not have gotten them all.

**Table 3. Emotions vs Attributions:** Bivariate Correlations

| | Attributions | | | | | |
|---|---|---|---|---|---|---|
| | Boring | Easy | Material | Negative | Success | Website |
| Closed-Response emotions | | | | | | |
| Confidence | −0.21 | **0.43**[*] | 0.19 | 0.18 | 0 | −0.18 |
| Excitement | −0.29 | 0.02 | −0.1 | −0.18 | −0.03 | −0.20 |
| Frustration | −0.16 | −0.34 | −0.29 | 0.05 | −0.15 | 0.12 |
| Interest | −0.13 | 0.09 | −0.06 | **0.38**[*] | 0.13 | −0.26 |
| Open-Response emotions | | | | | | |
| Annoyed | −0.20 | −0.11 | −0.01 | **0.70**[**] | −0.08 | **0.50**[**] |
| Bored | **0.67**[**] | **0.43**[**] | 0.08 | 0.19 | −0.09 | 0.07 |
| Confused | −0.08 | −0.03 | −0.21 | 0.16 | −0.02 | 0.25 |
| Negative | 0 | −0.15 | 0.2 | 0.11 | 0.22 | −0.05 |
| Neutral | −0.15 | −0.13 | −0.1 | −0.16 | −0.15 | −0.18 |
| Positive | 0.05 | **0.39**[*] | −0.16 | −0.24 | 0.18 | −0.22 |

N = 39, * = $p \leq 0.05$, ** = $p \leq 0.01$

**Acknowledgement.** This research is supported by the National Science Foundation (NSF) # 1324385 IIS/Cyberlearning DIP: Impact of Adaptive Interventions on Student Affect, Performance, and NSF # 1551589 IIS/Cyberlearning INT: Detecting, Predicting and Remediating Student Affect and Grit Using Computer Vision. Any opinions, findings, and conclusions, or recommendations expressed in this paper are those of the authors and do not necessarily reflect the views of NSF.

# References

1. Arroyo, I., Woolf, B.P., Cooper, D.G., Burleson, W., Muldner, K.: The impact of animated pedagogical agents on girls' and boys' emotions, attitudes, behaviors, and learning. In: Proceedings of the 11th IEEE Conference on Advanced Learning Technologies. Institute of Electrical and Electronics Engineers, Piscataway, NJ (2011)
2. Arroyo, I., Wixon, N., Allessio, D., Woolf, B., Muldner, K., Burleson, W.: Collaboration improves student interest in online tutoring. In: André, E., Baker, R., Hu, X., Rodrigo, Ma. Mercedes T., du Boulay, B. (eds.) AIED 2017. LNCS (LNAI), vol. 10331, pp. 28–39. Springer, Cham (2017). https://doi.org/10.1007/978-3-319-61425-0_3
3. Baker, R.S.J., D'Mello, S.K., Rodrigo, M.M.T., Graesser, A.C.: Better to be frustrated than bored: the incidence, persistence, and impact of learners' cognitive-affective states during interactions with three different computer-based learning environments. Int. J. Hum.-Comput. Stud. 68(4), 223–241 (2010)
4. Clore, G.L., Huntsinger, J.R.: How emotions inform judgment and regulate thought. Trends in Cogn. Sci. 11(9), 393–399 (2007)
5. Dowson, M., McInerney, D.M.: Psychological parameters of students' social and work avoidance goals: a qualitative investigation. J. Educ. Psychol. 93(1), 35–42 (2001)
6. D'Mello, S., Graesser, A.: Dynamics of affective states during complex learning. Learn. Instr. 22(2), 145–157 (2012)
7. Graesser, A., D'Mello, S.K.: Theoretical perspectives on affect and deep learning. In: Calvo, R., New perspectives on affect and learning technologies, pp. 11–21. Springer, New York (2011)
8. Ocumpaugh, J., Baker, R.S., Rodrigo, M.M.T.: Baker Rodrigo Ocumpaugh Monitoring Protocol (BROMP) 2.0 Technical and Training Manual. Technical Report. New York, NY: Teachers College, Columbia University. Manila, Philippines: Ateneo Laboratory for the Learning Sciences (2015)
9. Pekrun, R., Goetz, T., Daniels, L.M., Stupnisky, R.H., Perry, R.P.: Boredom in achievement settings: control-value antecedents and performance outcomes of a neglected emotion. J. Educ. Psychol. 102, 531–549 (2010)
10. Schultz, Sarah E., Wixon, N., Allessio, D., Muldner, K., Burleson, W., Woolf, B., Arroyo, I.: Blinded by science?: exploring affective meaning in students' own words. In: Micarelli, A., Stamper, J., Panourgia, K. (eds.) ITS 2016. LNCS, vol. 9684, pp. 314–319. Springer, Cham (2016). https://doi.org/10.1007/978-3-319-39583-8_35
11. Silvia, P.J.: Looking past pleasure: anger, confusion, disgust, pride, surprise, and other unusual aesthetic emotions. Psychol. Aesthet. Creat. 3(1), 48–51 (2009)
12. Wixon, M., Arroyo, I., Muldner, K., Burleson, W., Lozano, C., Woolf, B.: The opportunities and limitations of scaling up sensor-free affect detection. In: Proceedings of the 7th International Conference on Educational Data Mining (EDM 2014), pp. 145–152 (2014)

# Multimodal Interfaces for Inclusive Learning

Marcelo Worsley[(✉)], David Barel, Lydia Davison, Thomas Large,
and Timothy Mwiti

Northwestern University, 60208 Evanston, IL, USA
marcelo.worsley@northwestern.edu,
{davidbarel2021,lydiadavison2018,thomaslarge2019,
timothymwiti2019}@u.northwestern.edu

**Abstract.** In this paper, we propose that the artificial intelligence in education (AIED) community lead the charge in leveraging multimodal interfaces, in conjunction with artificial intelligence, to advance learning interfaces and experiences that are more inclusive. Recent years has seen the development of various multimodal technologies for capturing voice, gesture and gaze-based input modalities, as well as various forms of auditory and haptic feedback. These modalities could be powerful tools for developing inclusive learning interfaces. To ground this idea, we present a set of examples for how this work can be transformative in democratizing access to technology, while also democratizing designing and building technology. Additionally, our examples reinforce how designing for inclusive learning can result in improved learning interfaces for the general population.

**Keywords:** Accessibility · Constructionism · Speech · Tangibles
Computer vision · Haptics

## 1 Introduction

Technological growth in the areas of artificial intelligence, machine learning and multimodal sensing are beginning to blur the line between human and machine. These technologies are front and center when we consider self-driving cars and in home assistants like Google Home and Amazon's Alexa. Undergirding these systems are a complex integration of artificial intelligence, multimodal sensors and machine learning. While not perfect, these devices are poised to change the ways that communities work, play and learn. In this paper, we consider how these types of devices (i.e. one's that leverage the affordances of multimodal sensors and artificial intelligence), could help in creating more equitable learning, working and playing experiences for people with disabilities.

While the AIED community has successfully advanced a number of technological developments that could have potential benefits for people with disabilities, this is an area of study that has received little explicit mention. Put differently, AIED research has contributed to building robust models of human learning, advancing personalization through intelligent tutoring systems and MOOCs, predicting learning based on gaze and studying gesturing while learning. All of these approaches could positively contribute to

© Springer International Publishing AG, part of Springer Nature 2018
C. Penstein Rosé et al. (Eds.): AIED 2018, LNAI 10948, pp. 389–393, 2018.
https://doi.org/10.1007/978-3-319-93846-2_73

the learning experiences of people with disabilities. However, few of these systems were explicitly designed with people with disabilities as the primary user (see Alcorn, 2013; Salles, Pereira, Feltrini, Pires, & Lima-Salles, 2011 for exceptions). In this paper, we explore prototypes that utilize artificial intelligence and multimodal interfaces to advance more equitable participation among people with disabilities. This work builds on Constructionism [3, 6, 8, 9] and Multimodal Learning Analytics [13, 14], and is also motivated by AIEDSIC [1].

## 2   Intelligent Multimodal Interfaces

### 2.1   Multi-CAD

Multi-CAD is a multimodal interface for doing 2-D and 3-D design. A core of this interface is the integration of speech, gaze, and gesture recognition, computer-aided design software, and natural language understanding. By bringing together these interfaces, we aim to enable people with tremors (or other fine-motor impairments) to participate in digital 2-D and 3-D design.

In terms of technological components, the current platform uses an EyeTribe desktop eye tracker and a microphone for input. These input modalities interface with the Blender design environment. C++ is used to capture data from the eye tracker, while Python is used for all other capabilities. Namely, the Python code features the speech recognizer (PocketSphinx [12]) and a rudimentary natural language understanding engine using Spacy and Wordnet. It also integrates with Blender (the computer-aided design tool). Communication between these different code bases uses sockets.

At a high level, the platform provides tightly coupled multimodal integration (i.e., synchronous processing of speech and gaze data) to resolve terms like: 'here' and 'there.' Furthermore, the platform supports word sense disambiguation, named-entity extraction, synonym detection and includes syntactic parsing. The combination of this information allows the system to interpret instructions, and identify the appropriate modifiers, numbers, shapes, etc. MultiCAD also leverages contextual information about the current items on the user's 2-D/3-D design canvas and user gaze data to predict which objects are being referred to. Hence, this platform goes well beyond simply replacing the keyboard and mouse with alternative input modalities. Instead, it aims to offer an intelligent multimodal means for participating in 2-D and 3-D design. Such an interface would not be possible without multimodal sensing and artificial intelligence.

### 2.2   Tangicraft

Tangicraft is a platform that aims to enable people with low/no vision to play Minecraft. Beyond simply participating however, the interface has the goal of advancing equitable and collaborative participation in the game. It does this through two main components: tangible blocks and haptic feedback. First, the user can move and position physical blocks as they see fit, and then using computer vision, have their design immediately added at their current location in the Minecraft game. Second, Tangicraft, using haptic feedback to represent what is on the screen. More specifically, it includes a haptic representation of the block configuration at the users currently location. This configuration is based on the $3\times3$ grid of blocks that a sighted player would see on the screen. We represent that $3\times3$ grid by using a $3\times3$ set of vibration motors.

At a high-level, Tangicraft includes Minecraft environment manipulation, tangible block input, a haptic wearable and speech recognition, which we briefly describe below.

**Minecraft Raspberry Jam Mod.** Manipulation of the Minecraft environment is achieved through the Raspberry Jam Mod. This mod provides a Python interface for completing basic actions within the Minecraft environment. The mod also provides a programmatic interface for determining the placement of blocks within the Minecraft environment. Hence, this component is responsible for two-way communication between Minecraft and our Python code.

**Haptic Wearable.** The haptic wearable component is facilitated through data received from Minecraft and is subsequently pushed to an Arduino using a serial port. The Arduino then uses that input to activate the appropriate vibration motors using digital write commands.

**Tangible Block Input.** Within a parallel thread, the Python module communicates with a Javascript and HTML-based web application that processes Topcodes [4] and speech recognition. The current implementation utilizes Flask to orchestrate a Restful webservice. The web application reads the Topcodes, in the form of JSON and posts that information to a custom-defined Flask resource. The resource, subsequently, writes the JSON to a socket for the Python script to retrieve and process. The process of recording the TopCodes is activated via speech.

**Speech Recognition.** Speech recognition utilizes the Webkit Speech API, with a grammar that has been constrained based on words that might be used within the context of Minecraft for assigning box type. Additionally, a special keyword has been reserved for requesting that the current Topcode state be transferred into the Minecraft interface.

To reiterate then, Tangicraft allows users to build their Minecraft designs using physical blocks, and to sense the $3\times3$ structure in front of them using haptic feedback. Thus Tangicraft builds on the ability to convert images and audio information, into something that can be interpreted and used within the Minecraft interface. From this perspective, it should be apparent the extent to which this process relies on multimodal sensing and artificial intelligence.

## 3   Discussion

In this paper, we presented two prototypes of technological solutions aimed at enabling people with disabilities to participate in learning activities that are currently inaccessible to them. MultiCAD was designed to allow people with tremors (or other fine motor impairments) to do basic 2-D and 3-D design. Tangicraft endeavors to promote equitable patterns of play in Minecraft by allowing people with low/no-vision to participate in the gaming experience through tangibles and haptic feedback. These examples are still works-in-progress. They have gone through some user testing, and will continue to undergo development. Notwithstanding, these examples are not presented as the primary contribution of this paper. Instead, this paper serves as a starting point for deeply considering ways for using multimodal sensing and artificial intelligence to promote accessibility and inclusivity in contexts of teaching and learning. Furthermore, the goal of this paper is to highlight both the need and the opportunity for the AIED community to integrate multimodal sensing and artificial intelligence in the service of accessibility. Developing intelligent solutions for people with disabilities does not inhibit creating solutions for the general public. On the contrary, despite explicitly being designed for one or more populations of users with disabilities, each of the prototypes mentioned could also be of significant utility more generally [5]. For example, Tangicraft's tactile, block-based input could easily be utilized as a way for two fully sighted individuals to more easily collaborate in the building process. Furthermore, children already utilize physical blocks to prototype and/or seed different ideas when playing Minecraft [11]. Providing a means to streamline the transition from physical blocks to digital blocks using computer vision could streamline that process and help them more easily learn how to transition between 2-D and 3-D representations. In the case of MultiCAD, one could imagine young children who may not have much familiarity or understanding of the computer aided design interface being much more at ease designing using verbal commands as opposed to using traditional keyboard and mouse input. At the same time, engaging in the process of verbalizing their ideas could help them develop spatial reasoning in context [7].

## 4   Conclusion

Multimodal technology and artificial intelligence are having profound impacts on many facets of our day-to-day interactions and experiences. In this paper, we aimed to motivate ways that the AIED community might consider leveraging these technological developments in the service of designing technology and/or learning experiences for people with disabilities. Furthermore, we provided three examples of multimodal interfaces that are chiefly aimed at enabling people with different disabilities to participate in design, inventing and *making* both as an opportunity to learn, and as an opportunity for creative expression. These examples, however, were not limited to being beneficial for people with disabilities. Instead, the interfaces are ones that could be of significant benefit to the general population and could begin to drive new paradigms for collaborative working, playing and learning.

## References

1. Akhras, F.N., Brna, P.: First workshop on artificial intelligence in education to support the social inclusion of communities (AIEDSIC). In: AIED, p. 632 (2011)
2. Alcorn, A.M.: Discrepancy-Detection in virtual learning environments for young children with ASC. In: Lane, H.C., Yacef, K., Mostow, J., Pavlik, P. (eds.) AIED 2013. LNCS (LNAI), vol. 7926, pp. 884–887. Springer, Heidelberg (2013). https://doi.org/10.1007/978-3-642-39112-5_137

3. Buechley, L., Eisenberg, M., Catchen, J., Crockett, A.: The LilyPad Arduino: using computational textiles to investigate engagement, aesthetics, and diversity in computer science education. In: Proceedings of the SIGCHI conference on Human factors in computing systems, pp. 423–432 (2008)
4. Horn, M.S.: Top Code: Tangible Object Placement Codes. Accessed. http://users.eecs. northwestern.edu/~mhorn/topcodes/
5. Ladner, R.: Design for user empowerment. In: Proceedings of the Extended Abstracts of the 32nd Annual ACM Conference on Human Factors in Computing Systems - CHI EA 2014, pp. 5–6. (2014). https://doi.org/10.1145/2559206.2580090
6. Papert, S.: Mindstorms: Children, computers, and powerful ideas. Basic Books, Inc., New York (1980)
7. Ramey, K.E., Uttal, D.: Making sense of space: distributed spatial sensemaking in a middle school summer engineering camp. J. Learn. Sci. 26(2), 277–319 (2017). https://doi.org/10. 1080/10508406.2016.1277226
8. Resnick, M., Maloney, J., Monroy-Hernández, A., Rusk, N., Eastmond, E., Brennan, K., Millner, A., Rosenbaum, E., Silver, J., Silverman, B., Kafai, Y.: Scratch: programming for all. Commun. ACM 52(11), 60–67 (2009). https://doi.org/10.1145/1592761.1592779
9. Resnick, M., Myers, B., Nakakoji, K., Shneiderman, B., Pausch, R., Selker, T., Eisenberg, M.: Design principles for tools to support creative thinking. Science 20(2), 25–35 (2005)
10. Salles, P., Pereira, Mônica M.R., Feltrini, Gisele M., Pires, L., Lima-Salles, H.: Evaluating the use of qualitative reasoning models in scientific education of deaf students. In: Biswas, G., Bull, S., Kay, J., Mitrovic, A. (eds.) AIED 2011. LNCS (LNAI), vol. 6738, pp. 537–540. Springer, Heidelberg (2011). https://doi.org/10.1007/978-3-642-21869-9_94
11. Toprani, D., Yan, S., Borge, M.: A comparative analysis of the collaboration process across different technologies. In: Proceedings of the 6th annual conference on creativity and fabrication in education - FabLearn 2016, pp. 66–69 (2016). https://doi.org/10.1145/ 3003397.3003407
12. Walker, W., Lamere, P., Kwok, P., Raj, B., Singh, R., Gouvea, E., Wolf, P., Woelfel, J.: Sphinx-4 : a flexible open source framework for speech recognition. Smli, TR-2004-139: pp. 1–9 (2004). https://doi.org/10.1.1.91.4704
13. Worsley, M.: Multimodal learning analytics - enabling the future of learning through multimodal data analysis and interfaces. In: ICMI 2012 - Proceedings of the ACM International Conference on Multimodal Interaction (2012). https://doi.org/10.1145/ 2388676.2388755
14. Worsley, M., Blikstein, P.: A multimodal analysis of making. Int. J. Artif. Intell. Educ, 1–35 (2017)

# Supporting Learning Activities with Wearable Devices to Develop Life-Long Skills in a Health Education App

Kalina Yacef[1]([⊠]), Corinne Caillaud[1], and Olivier Galy[2]

[1] The University of Sydney, Sydney, Australia
{kalina.yacef,corinne.caillaud}@sydney.edu.au
[2] The University of New Caledonia, Nouméa, New Caledonia, France
olivier.galy@unc.nc

**Abstract.** 80% of Australian children do not engage in recommended minima of physical activity levels, contributing to an alarming trend in obesity levels and associated diseases in adult life. We created iEngage, an innovative health education program for 10–12 year old school children that blends a learning app, wearable technology, feedback, goal setting and gamification with practical activities to promote knowledge and behavioural changes with regards to physical activity and to guide children at their own pace towards World Health Organisation's recommended minima of daily moderate to vigorous physical activity. We present how the activity trackers are used to provide objective feedback and support the learning activities and the individual goal setting. We conducted a controlled pilot study in two Australian schools. Post-tests using research-grade accelerometer devices reveal a significant increase in moderate and vigorous activities in the experimental group, compared to none in the control group.

## 1 Introduction

The sharp increase and affordability of human-centred technologies are extending the range and transforming the way education programs can be delivered. In particular, domains where the learning does not only occur through a computing interface but also through physical activity can now be supported with wearable technology [1] and it becomes feasible to build smart educational systems that also build on wearable sensors collecting physical student data to drive instruction.

One of these areas is children's education with regards to Physical Activity (PA) and health literacy. Engaging in healthy levels of daily PA, especially at Moderate to Vigorous Physical Activity (MVPA) levels, is an important factor for health and wellbeing [2]. Sadly, studies show that children often do not meet World Health Organisation's recommended minima of PA levels, especially for MVPA, creating a significant health risk for them later in life [3]. Whilst eHealth intervention programs exist (e.g. [4]), these trends persist. An obvious reason for this is that children may be unable to associate these recommended levels with what they actually do and feel, nor know how to achieve these recommended levels, which are expressed in terms of number of steps (12,000 daily) and intensity (60 min per day of MVPA). It is therefore important to design learning systems that enable children to understand and experience what these minima mean for them.

Our multi-disciplinary team created iEngage, an innovative health education program for 10–12 year old school children that blends a learning app, wearable technology, feedback, goal setting and gamification with practical activities to increase health literacy and encourage behavioural changes with regards to physical activity at an individual pace. In iEngage, the activity trackers are only connected to the learning app and provide objective feedback to support the learning activities and the goal setting. In this paper, we describe how the technology was used and report on our pilot experiment in an Australian urban primary school.

## 2   Overview of iEngage

iEngage comprises ten learning modules of 45 min, each on a specific topic, delivered at school over several weeks. The learning contents are research-informed, with real physical activities, immediate feedback, goal setting and gamification.

**The Technology: Learning App and Activity Trackers.** The iEngage app, built on the BePatient platform [5], is accessible on android tablets. It connects seamlessly to a background app that synchronises (via Bluetooth) the learner's activity tracker and uploads the data immediately onto the iEngage server (via wifi or 3/4 G), hence allowing real-time data to be used in the learning activities. A commercial wrist-worn activity tracker (Misfit Ray [6]) is worn continuously during the whole duration of the program. It is waterproof, runs on 6 month-life batteries and is fairly secure around the wrist to prevent losses or breakages. The step count is extracted per minute.

**A Child-Friendly Learning Interface Design.** Each functional part of the program is guided by the same animal mascot so that children quickly recognise what is expected of them: a giraffe presents learning content, a bison gives quizzes, a kangaroo (Fig. 1(c)) guides the activity tracker synchronisation and data readings, a tiger is in charge of actual physical activity, a penguin supports goal setting and a bird rewards success with cues for a secret message hunt. The visualisation interfaces of PA are designed specifically to support the child's reflection and self-monitoring during the learning activities. They strictly contain the information that the child needs, without additional information that commercial interfaces of the tracker would typically have.

## 3   Personalised Learning Supported by Wearable Tracker

Learning about physically-related knowledge and skills cannot remain theoretical and abstract. The role of the activity tracker is to provide objective PA data input into the learner model, and support the child's personalised learning.

**Association Between Perceived Exertion and PA Intensities.** There are different intensity levels of physical activity, broadly called light, moderate and vigorous. Health recommendations are expressed in amount of time (minimum or maximum), that people should spend in each. Figure 1(a) shows a scale of perceived exertion. An important skill that children need to learn is what each intensity level means for them and recognise them as they engage in each.

iEngage offers experiential learning activities where children are instructed to do various physical exercises or games, and then explore their data in a simple, child-accessible way. Figure 1(b) shows one interface, where children can explore their PA in the last 15 min. The intensity for each of these minutes is color-coded: grey for sedentary times, orange for light activities and green for moderate and vigorous.

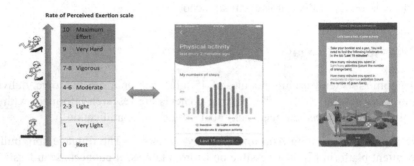

**Fig. 1.** (a) Scale of perceived exertion and (b) Interface in the app showing last 15 min activity (c) screenshot of an activity by the kangaroo mascot. (Color figure online)

A typical learning task is to (i) leave the tablet and carry out specific exercises of specific intensity for 10 min, (ii) come back to the app and answer some questions about how they feel and how they perceived their effort (iii) synchronise their tracker and explore their own data in the last 15 min (iv) compare their perceived effort with the objective data.

**Association of Perceived Activity with Step Counts.** Similarly, children can learn and associate what step counts mean for them and evaluate for themselves how many they achieve in their regular daily schedule, and what reaching the 12,000 minimum step count mean in their own context. Here, daily summaries are shown per day, week, month. Students reflect on how many steps they accumulate in their typical days, and how many more they could achieve by doing PA learned during the iEngage sessions.

**Setting Achievable Goals.** At the end of each module, students set individual goals for their daily physical activity. They can choose from lightly increasing their current PA and intensity level to more challenging goals. The aim is to guide them to reach recommended levels, gradually increase goals throughout the program, and then maintain them. At the beginning of the next module, the system guides students to synchronise their tracker, reflect on their activity and check whether they have achieved their goals. If they have, they receive a reward or just receive encouragements.

# 4 Pilot Study

**Experiment.** We conducted a pilot study in 2 urban primary schools in Sydney with 59 children aged 10–12 (27 girls and 33 boys). In both groups, girls had a distribution of aerobic fitness equivalent to the international normative values, and boys had an over-representation in the 'poor' aerobic fitness category. Both schools were similar in terms of socio-economic background, academic achievements and area. We used a pre- and post-test design to evaluate the efficacy of iEngage. In both schools, children's physical activity was measured on 5 consecutive days before and after the program with a research-grade accelerometer (Geneactiv [7]) measuring activity at 60 Hz unobtrusively, i.e. without showing any feedback to the child. In the experimental school (EXP), children (N = 33) were given access to the iEngage program during school time and followed 10 learning modules over 30 days. In the control school (CTL), children (N = 26) did not follow any particular health education program.

**Data.** The four raw Geneactiv datasets contained 60 Hz three-dimensional accelerometer data. The raw data was processed into 1 s epoch SVMg data points, before being categorised into intensity for each second. Specific cutoffs for identifying activity levels in children were used [8]. As we were interested in comparing daily behaviours, we sliced the data into 24 h periods and counted the number of seconds spent in each intensity level for each child, each day. We filtered out any day where the tracker was not worn all day.

**Results.** The average daily times spent in vigorous (V), moderate (M), light (L), sedentary (S) and sleep (Z) by each group, before and after the program, are shown in Table 1. Both Pre-test groups had similar distribution. In the EXP group, the percentage of time per day spent in MVPA increased significantly, whereas the CTL group did not (and even had a small decrease in vigorous activities). No significant effect was found in other activities. Furthermore we found that EXP students spent a lot more time (1079 s vs 682 s), in long bouts of continuous MVPA (longer than 30 s) after the program ended, which suggests that they intentionally engaged in more MVPA and that the increase is not solely due to very short bursts of activity.

**Table 1.** Percentages of time spent in specific intensities.

|           | Pre (EXP) | Post (EXP) | p value | Pre (CTL) | Post (CTL) | p value |
|-----------|-----------|------------|---------|-----------|------------|---------|
| Sleep     | 54.8      | 53         | 0.2345  | 54.9      | 55.1       | 0.8873  |
| Sedentary | 25.7      | 25.5       | 0.7829  | 25.3      | 25.9       | 0.515   |
| Light     | 13.9      | 14.8       | 0.1295  | 14.2      | 13.8       | 0.5611  |
| Moderate  | **4.4**   | **5.4**    | **0.0035** | 4.3    | 4.2        | 0.6233  |
| Vigorous  | **1.1**   | **1.4**    | **0.0175** | **1.2** | **0.9**   | **0.0185** |

## 5  Discussion and Conclusion

We have presented a case of smart educational tool that harnesses wearable devices to provide experiential and personalised learning. Results of our pilot study suggest that iEngage program can create positive behavioural changes in the targeted area of MVPA, and this through educating children rather than prescribing activity. More analysis is needed to better understand how these changes occur, and whether they are sustained in the long-term.

**Acknowledgements.** This work was funded by Diabetes Australia Research Trust. We thank colleagues and Bepatient for their various contributions in this experiment.

## References

1. Santos, O.C.: Training the body: the potential of AIED to support personalized motor skills learning. Int. J. Artif. Intell. Educ. **26**, 730–755 (2016)
2. Hardy, L.L., Okely, A.D., Dobbins, T.A., Booth, M.L.: Physical activity among adolescents in New South Wales (Australia). Med. Sci. Sports Exerc. **40**(5), 835–841 (2008). https://doi.org/10.1249/MSS.0b013e318163f286
3. Ekelund, U., Luan, J., Sherar, L.B., Esliger, D.W., Griew, P., Cooper, A., Collaborators, I.: Moderate to vigorous physical activity and sedentary time and cardiometabolic risk factors in children and adolescents. J. Am. Med. Assoc. **307**(7), 704–712 (2012). https://doi.org/10.1001/jama.2012.156
4. Kerner, C., Goodyear, V.: The motivational impact of wearable healthy lifestyle technologies: a self-determination perspective on fitbits with adolescents. Am. J. Health Educ. **48**(5), 287–297 (2017). https://doi.org/10.1080/19325037.2017.1343161
5. BePatient. https://www.bepatient.com/. Accessed 14 Apr 2018
6. Misfit. https://misfit.com/fitness-trackers/misfit-ray. Accessed 14 Apr 2018
7. Geneactiv. https://www.activinsights.com/. Accessed 14 Apr 2018
8. Phillips, L., Parfitt, G., Rowlands, A.: Calibration of the GENEA accelerometer for assessment of physical activity intensity in children. J. Sci. Med. Sport **16**, 124–128 (2013)

# Automatic Chinese Short Answer Grading with Deep Autoencoder

Xi Yang[1], Yuwei Huang[2,3], Fuzhen Zhuang[4,5(✉)], Lishan Zhang[1], and Shengquan Yu[1]

[1] Beijing Advanced Innovation Center for Future Education, Beijing Normal University, Beijing 100875, China
{xiyang85,lishan,yusq}@bnu.edu.cn
[2] Sunny Education Inc., Beijing 100102, China
huangyw95@foxmail.com
[3] Beijing University of Chemical Technology, Beijing 100029, China
[4] Key Lab of Intelligent Information Processing of Chinese Academy of Sciences (CAS), Institute of Computing Technology, CAS, Beijing 100190, China
zhuangfuzhen@ict.ac.cn
[5] University of Chinese Academy of Sciences, Beijing 100049, China

**Abstract.** Short answer question is a common assessment type of teaching and learning. Automatic short answer grading is the task of automatically scoring short natural language responses. Most previous autograders mainly rely on target answers given by teachers. However, target answers are not always available. In this paper, a deep autoencoder based algorithm for automatic short answer grading is presented. The proposed algorithm can be built without expressly defining target answers, and learn the lower-dimensional representation of student responses. For the sake of reducing the influence of data imbalance, we introduce the expectation regularization term of label ratio into the model. The experimental results demonstrate the effectiveness of our proposed method.

**Keywords:** Automatic grading · Short Answer · Deep autoencoder
Text classification

## 1 Introduction

Grading short-answer questions with a natural language response automatically has been extensively studied for a long time, due to the fact that Automatic Short Answer Grading (ASAG) systems can overcome some limitations of human scoring [1,2]. C-rater [3] is probably the most well-known system. With the development of machine learning techniques, various machine learning algorithms have been applied to ASAG task, such as Logistic Regression (LR) [4], Decision Tree [5,6], k-Nearest Neighbor [7], Naive Bayes [8], Support Vector Machine (SVM) [3,9], Deep Belief Network [10] and so on.

The traditional ASAG methods based on machine learning have the following limitations. Firstly, much of the prior researches grade the student responses

© Springer International Publishing AG, part of Springer Nature 2018
C. Penstein Rosé et al. (Eds.): AIED 2018, LNAI 10948, pp. 399–404, 2018.
https://doi.org/10.1007/978-3-319-93846-2_75

based on target answers provided by teachers. However, the target answers are not always available. Secondly, the representations of student responses extracted from natural language processing techniques are always high-dimensional and high-sparse. Finally, for most traditional machine learning models, one of the basic assumptions is that the distribution of class ratio on data should be balanced. But this assumption is not satisfied in most cases.

Based on the analysis above, this paper is aiming at presenting an algorithm for Chinese ASAG by only using graded student responses and without any target answers. The algorithm needs to be able to get the lower-dimensional representation of student responses, and overcome the imbalance of data distribution. Prompted by recent advances in learning more robust and higher-level representations in deep learning, especially deep autoencoder [11], we proposed the use of deep autoencoder for ASAG, named Deep Autoencoder Grader (DAGrader). Both accuracy and Quadratic weighted Kappa (QWKappa) are used to measure the grading model.

## 2    Grading Model with Deep Autoencoder

In this paper, we consider ASAG task as a text classification problem. The classification algorithm based on deep autoencoder [11] is employed, which is shown in Fig. 1. The deep autoencoder consists of two encoding and decoding layers. The first and second hidden layer are the encoding layers. The first encoding layer is the embedding layer, where the lower-dimensional representations of student responses are learnt. The lower-dimensional representations of student responses can retain the most salient information of the input data. The second encoding layer is the label encoding layer, where the label information (i.e., the score of the student response) is encoded using a softmax regression [12]. In addition, the

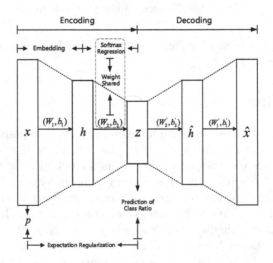

**Fig. 1.** Framework of the proposed model.

encoding weights in the second hidden layer are also used for the final prediction model. The third and fourth layer are the decoding layers, where the outputs of the first and second hidden layers are reconstructed respectively.

In order to train the deep autoencoder model, there are four factors to be considered in the loss function, i.e., the reconstruction error, the loss function of softmax regression, the expectation regularization of class ratio and the model parameter regularization. Specifically, the loss function of softmax regression can incorporate the label information of student responses into the embedding space; the expectation regularization of class ratio is introduced for reducing the influence of data imbalance.

After the parameters of deep autoencoder are learnt, we can obtain the lower-dimensional representation of student responses from the first encoding layer. Two methods can be utilized to construct the text classifiers for automatic grading task, which are named as $DAGrader_1$ and $DAGrader_2$. The first method $DAGrader_1$ is to use the second hidden layer's output $z$. The corresponding label of the maximum element of $z$ is the predicted label of the input instance. The second method $DAGrader_2$ is to use the lower-dimensional representation of student responses to train a classifier by applying standard classification algorithms. We use random forest with 100 trees in this paper.

## 3    Data Description and Preprocessing

Our corpus consists of five data sets. Each of the data sets was generated from a reading comprehension question. All responses were written by students in Grade 8. In order to ensure the reliability of the label, all responses were hand graded by two experienced human raters. The details of all data sets are showed in Table 1.

Table 1. Overview of all datasets

| Item ID | #Samples | Grading scheme | #Avg-words | #Unigram features | #QWKappa |
|---|---|---|---|---|---|
| 1 | 2579 | 5-point | 39 | 1071 | 0.9847 |
| 2 | 2571 | 3-point | 33 | 1644 | 0.9723 |
| 3 | 2382 | 4-point | 26 | 618 | 0.9427 |
| 4 | 2458 | 5-point | 27 | 655 | 0.9733 |
| 5 | 2538 | 4-point | 31 | 768 | 0.8319 |

To obtain the input of the proposed algorithm, a series of standard natural language preprocessing methods are conducted on data sets, including punctuation removal, stop word removal and tokenization. The student responses are preprocessed by using a parser called "jieba"[1], which is a Python Chinese word

---

[1] https://github.com/fxsjy/jieba.

segmentation module. Then, we utilize a Python module named scikit-learn[2] to extract the n-gram features of the student responses.

## 4    Results and Discussion

We compare our model, denoted as DAGrader$_1$ and DAGrader$_2$, with several automatic scoring models. LR (Logistic Regression) and SVM (Support Vector Machine) are two efficient and well-known ASAG models. Yang et al. proposed an ASAG model based on LSTM without grading rubrics in [13]. We utilize continuous bag-of-words model(CBOW) [14] to expand Yang's model. CBOW$_a$ and CBOW$_w$ are trained on our corpus and Chinese wikipedia corpus, respectively.

All the results of these five data sets are shown in Table 2, and we have the following observations,

(1) DAGrader is significantly better than LR on every data set, which indicates the efficiency of our proposed ASAG framework.
(2) SVM performs better than LR, which demonstrates the grading results can be improved by applying a better text classifier. Yang's expanded model CBOW$_w$ has higher performance than the corresponding figures of LR and SVM, indicating the importance of extracting deep semantic feature of student answers.
(3) DAGrader$_1$ and DAGrader$_2$ outperforms all the baselines in term of accuracy, which shows that our proposed model can combine the merits of conventional bag-of-words models and deep learning models.

**Table 2.** Accuracy and QWKappa on all data sets

| Item ID | LR | SVM | CBOW$_a$ | CBOW$_w$ | DAGrader$_1$ | DAGrader$_2$ |
|---|---|---|---|---|---|---|
| *Accuracy (%)* | | | | | | |
| 1 | 55.86 | 54.82 | 57.17 | 62.33 | **64.65** | 62.23 |
| 2 | 66.47 | 65.85 | 71.06 | 71.84 | 71.60 | **71.84** |
| 3 | 81.82 | 88.62 | 84.84 | 88.92 | **89.50** | 88.19 |
| 4 | 57.53 | 58.67 | 62.21 | 61.87 | 63.21 | **66.67** |
| 5 | 76.40 | 76.60 | 74.31 | 80.77 | **81.50** | 80.54 |
| Avg. | 67.62 | 68.91 | 69.92 | 73.15 | **74.09** | 73.89 |
| *QWKappa* | | | | | | |
| 1 | 0.3697 | 0.4015 | 0.2213 | 0.4431 | 0.5185 | **0.5221** |
| 2 | 0.3915 | 0.4254 | 0.3752 | 0.4825 | 0.4915 | **0.4940** |
| 3 | 0.7913 | **0.8680** | 0.7276 | 0.8364 | 0.8539 | 0.8407 |
| 4 | 0.5142 | 0.5789 | 0.5693 | 0.5612 | 0.6257 | **0.6599** |
| 5 | 0.6270 | 0.6522 | 0.4214 | 0.6754 | **0.7360** | 0.7056 |
| Avg. | 0.5387 | 0.5852 | 0.4630 | 0.5997 | **0.6451** | 0.6445 |

---

[2] http://scikit-learn.org/stable/index.html.

# 5  Conclusions

In this paper, we tackle the ASAG task by using a deep autoencoder. Our method does not rely on any target answer due to the fact that target answers are not always available. Specifically, there are two layers for encoding in the deep model, one is for embedding and the other is for label encoding. In the embedding layer, we can get the lower-dimensional representations of student responses, which can be used for text classifier construction. In the label encoding layer, we can easily incorporate the label information into the text representation. Additionally, to reduce the impact of data imbalance, we introduce an expectation regularization of class ratio term into the loss function of the deep autoencoder. Experiments on five Chinese data sets demonstrate the effectiveness of the proposed method.

**Acknowledgements.** This work is supported by the National Natural Science Foundation of China (No. 61773361, 61473273), the Youth Innovation Promotion Association CAS 2017146, the China Postdoctoral Science Foundation (No. 2017M610054).

# References

1. Burrows, S., Gurevych, I., Stein, B.: The eras and trends of automatic short answer grading. Int. J. Artif. Intell. Educ. **25**(1), 60–117 (2015)
2. Sung, K.H., Noh, E.H., Chon, K.H.: Multivariate generalizability analysis of automated scoring for short answer items of social studies in large-scale assessment. Asia Pac. Educ. Rev. **18**(3), 425–437 (2017)
3. Liu, O.L., Rios, J.A., Heilman, M., Gerard, L., Linn, M.C.: Validation of automated scoring of science assessments. J. Res. Sci. Teach. **53**(2), 215–233 (2016)
4. Madnani, N., Burstein, J., Sabatini, J., O'Reilly, T.: Automated scoring of a summary-writing task designed to measure reading comprehension. In: BEA@ NAACL-HLT, pp. 163–168 (2013)
5. Jimenez, S., Becerra, C.J., Gelbukh, A.F., Bátiz, A.J.D., Mendizábal, A.: Soft-cardinality: hierarchical text overlap for student response analysis. In: SemEval@ NAACL-HLT, pp. 280–284 (2013)
6. Dzikovska, M.O., Nielsen, R.D., Brew, C.: Towards effective tutorial feedback for explanation questions: a dataset and baselines. In: Proceedings of the 2012 Conference of the North American Chapter of the Association for Computational Linguistics: Human Language Technologies, pp. 200–210. Association for Computational Linguistics (2012)
7. Bailey, S., Meurers, D.: Diagnosing meaning errors in short answers to reading comprehension questions. In: Proceedings of the Third Workshop on Innovative Use of NLP for Building Educational Applications, pp. 107–115. Association for Computational Linguistics (2008)
8. Zesch, T., Levy, O., Gurevych, I., Dagan, I.: UKP-BIU: similarity and entailment metrics for student response analysis, Atlanta, Georgia, USA, p. 285 (2013)
9. Hou, W.-J., Tsao, J.-H., Li, S.-Y., Chen, L.: Automatic assessment of students' free-text answers with support vector machines. In: García-Pedrajas, N., Herrera, F., Fyfe, C., Benítez, J.M., Ali, M. (eds.) IEA/AIE 2010. LNCS (LNAI), vol. 6096, pp. 235–243. Springer, Heidelberg (2010). https://doi.org/10.1007/978-3-642-13022-9_24

10. Zhang, Y., Shah, R., Chi, M.: Deep learning + student modeling + clustering: a recipe for effective automatic short answer grading. In: EDM, pp. 562–567 (2016)
11. Zhuang, F., Cheng, X., Luo, P., Pan, S.J., He, Q.: Supervised representation learning: transfer learning with deep autoencoders. In: International Conference on Artificial Intelligence, pp. 4119–4125 (2015)
12. Friedman, J., Hastie, T., Tibshirani, R.: Regularization paths for generalized linear models via coordinate descent. J. Stat. Softw. **33**(1), 1–22 (2010)
13. Yang, X., Zhang, L., Yu, S.: Can short answers to open response questions be auto-graded without a grading rubric? In: André, E., Baker, R., Hu, X., Rodrigo, M.M.T., du Boulay, B. (eds.) AIED 2017. LNCS (LNAI), vol. 10331, pp. 594–597. Springer, Cham (2017). https://doi.org/10.1007/978-3-319-61425-0_72
14. Mikolov, T., Chen, K., Corrado, G., Dean, J.: Efficient estimation of word representations in vector space. Comput. Sci. (2013)

# Understanding Students' Problem-Solving Strategies in a Synergistic Learning-by-Modeling Environment

Ningyu Zhang[✉] and Gautam Biswas

Institute of Software Integrated Systems, Department of EECS, Vanderbilt University, 1025 16th Avenue South, Nashville, TN 37212, USA
{ningyu.zhang,gautam.biswas}@vanderbilt.edu

**Abstract.** We present a systems thinking approach to help middle school students learn about diffusion processes in liquids using CTSiM, an open-ended learning environment. Students model and analyze the collision of individual particles, and then scale up the process to understand diffusion as an emergent behavior of particles. A classroom study shows that the intervention helped students achieve significant learning gains. We also observed synergistic learning of domain knowledge and computational thinking skills. To understand students' problem-solving processes, we used a sequence mining algorithm to discover frequent activity patterns and link them to learning.

**Keywords:** Computational Thinking · Learning by modeling
Open-ended learning environment · Data-driven analysis
Pattern mining

## 1 Introduction

Computational modeling and Computational Thinking (CT) concepts and practices are important in promoting systems thinking [1,10,14]. However, students can develop misunderstandings when they attempt system-level analyses [4,5,13]. Some misunderstandings can be attributed to the confusion in the relationships between system components at different levels of abstraction and aggregation. Others may be caused by commonsense conceptions: e.g., novice learners are prone to assigning false intentionality to individuals in a system [5] or to assuming the existence of centralized control [3].

Students can gain a deep understanding of scientific phenomena if they are able to represent and reason about the phenomena with corresponding physical models [6,12]. *Open-ended learning environments* (OELEs) can provide students with an authentic and personally meaningful learning experience by engaging them in problem-solving activities [8]. In this paper, we present our work to help middle school students' learning of the diffusion processes using an agent-based modeling approach and a domain-specific block-structured modeling language

© Springer International Publishing AG, part of Springer Nature 2018
C. Penstein Rosé et al. (Eds.): AIED 2018, LNAI 10948, pp. 405–410, 2018.
https://doi.org/10.1007/978-3-319-93846-2_76

[9], students investigate and model collision of individual particles and then use a systems thinking approach to develop an understanding of diffusion as an emergent behavior.

## 2   The CTSiM Learning Environment and Methods

CTSiM is an OELE that fosters students' synergistic learning of science knowledge and CT skills and practices using a *learning by modeling* approach [9]. In CTSiM, students perform five primary learning tasks: (1) read to acquire domain and CT concepts; (2) build conceptual models of the system; (3) construct block-based computational models that define the agents' interactions; (4) execute the computational models as NetLogo [11] simulations to analyze and debug the models; and (5) compare the behaviors of student-generated computational models to the behaviors of an expert model. Detailed descriptions of the learning activities and the learning task model of CTSiM appear in our previous publications, e.g. [2,9,15,16].

In this work, students' understanding of the domain knowledge and CT skills is assessed by (1) pre-post tests, (2) model building performance, and (3) formative evaluation of their learning behaviors. The domain pre-post questions specifically targeted common false intuitions of diffusion that students may have [4,5], and the CT tests assess students' understanding of key CT practices and skills [15]. The distance between a student-created model and an expert model evaluates the students' model-building performance. To determine whether students' action sequences and problem-solving strategies result in different model building performance and learning gains, we used differential sequential pattern mining [7] to investigate the link between their action patterns and learning.

We conducted a classroom study to evaluate students' understanding of diffusion processes through model-building tasks in CTSiM. We also tracked their model-building strategies. Fifty-two $6^{th}$-grade students participated in the study over 14 school days during their 45-minute science block in spring 2017. The students worked on the five units on CTSiM: two training units, the acceleration unit, the collision unit, and the diffusion unit. In this paper, we focus on student learning in the diffusion unit. On day 1, the students took the domain and CT pre-test. On days 8–10, the students modeled the inelastic collision of spheres as preparation for the diffusion unit. On days 11–13, student modeled the diffusion of dye particles in water in the diffusion unit. The post-tests were taken on day 14.

## 3   Results and Discussion

We use the results from the classroom study to discuss three interrelated research questions: (1) Does CTSiM help students improve their understanding of diffusion-related science knowledge as well as CT skills and practices? (2) How are students' model building performance, CT, and science learning gains are correlated? (3) How did students' use of effective strategies reflect on their performance and learning gains?

To answer RQ1, we used the paired Mann-Whitney $U$-Test to evaluate the statistical significance of the *pre-to-post* learning gains. Table 1 summarizes all students' learning gains on the diffusion and CT pre-post tests. The max scores for the diffusion and CT tests are 12 and 34 points, respectively. These results indicate that students' learning gains in domain knowledge (diffusion) and fundamental CT skills were significant. Students' understanding of both the domain and CT skills and practices improved significantly.

**Table 1.** Pre-post learning gains

| Measure | Pre-test Mean (std) | Post-test Mean (std) | $p$-value | Effect size |
|---------|---------------------|----------------------|-----------|-------------|
| Diffusion | 3.65 (2.36) | 5.88 (2.40) | <0.0001 | 0.41 |
| CT | 13.34 (6.26) | 16.88 (6.29) | 0.009 | 0.23 |

We answered RQ2 using correlation analyses among four performance metrics. Table 2 lists the correlation coefficients (Spearman's $\rho$) between these performance metrics. Students' learning gains in CT were correlated with their domain learning gains. The correlation, combined with the pre-post learning gains, indicates that students synergistically learned domain and CT knowledge and skills. Secondly, both learning gains were negatively correlated with the computational model distances in the collision unit and the diffusion unit, indicating that the students who performed well in the model building activities benefited more and had higher learning gains. In addition, students' computational model building performances were consistent in the two units.

**Table 2.** Correlation between learning gains and performances (*: $p < 0.05$)

| | CT gain | Diffusion gain | Collision distance | Diffusion distance |
|---|---------|----------------|--------------------|--------------------|
| CT gain | - | | | |
| Diffusion gain | 0.28* | - | | |
| Collision distance | −0.35* | −0.13 | - | |
| Diffusion distance | −0.28* | −0.31* | 0.32* | - |

However, the large variance in the learning gains indicated an achievement gap, which led us to conduct exploratory analyses to answer RQ3 on what types of behaviors contribute to good or suboptimal learning performances. We grouped all students by their learning gains in the diffusion unit. Students who achieved learning gains greater than or less than the median were categorized into the higher performing group (HG, $n = 29$) and lower performing group (LG,

$n = 23$), respectively. HG and LG students' action patterns were then mined differentially [7]. Table 3 presents the high lift patterns in which HG and LG differed by at least 10% in support or at least 0.05 in confidence. Conceptual model edits and computational model edits are coded as **concep.** and **comp.**, meanwhile, **-EFF** and **-INEFF** indicate correct or incorrect SC actions. **-R** represents consecutive SC actions.

**Table 3.** Patterns with different support and confidence among HG and LG students

| Index | Pattern | Lift | HG Sup. | LG Sup. | HG Conf. | LG Conf. |
|-------|---------|------|---------|---------|----------|----------|
| 1 | compare→comp.-R-INEFF | 1.09 | 31.0% | 43.5% | 0.07 | 0.13 |
| 2 | compare→comp.-INEFF | 1.16 | 44.8% | 56.5% | 0.10 | 0.15 |
| 3 | compare→comp.-R-EFF | 1.10 | 57.7% | 60.9% | 0.16 | 0.13 |
| 4 | concep.-R-INEFF→comp.-EFF | 1.45 | 69.0% | 91.3% | 0.12 | 0.19 |
| 5 | concep.-R-INEFF→comp.-INEFF | 1.14 | 55.2% | 73.9% | 0.11 | 0.15 |
| 6 | comp.-EFF→concep.-R-INEFF | 1.26 | 58.6% | 91.3% | 0.09 | 0.17 |
| 7 | comp.-R-EFF→comp.-R-INEFF | 2.60 | 96.7% | 100% | 0.21 | 0.32 |
| 8 | comp.-INEFF→comp.-R-EFF | 2.41 | 96.7% | 100% | 0.35 | 0.31 |

The mined patterns indicate that HG students were better at using the information observed from solution assessment (SA) to commit correct follow-up edits. If a student consistently committed incorrect edits (i.e., making errors in model building) after SA, we concluded that the student's use of the SA→SC strategy was suboptimal. Patterns 1 and 2 illustrate this situation: after making comparisons, LG students' likelihood of making ineffective edits was much greater than that of the HG student. Conversely, pattern 3 shows that HG students were more likely to make a series of correct edits after making comparisons. HG students also had a better understanding of model building task strategies. Patterns 7, 6, and 5 indicate that after performing effective solution construction (SC) actions, LG students made more consecutive incorrect edits to both their conceptual and computational models. In addition, pattern 4 shows after making a series of incorrect edits to the conceptual model, LG students were likely to make a single correct edit in the computational model. This discrepancy indicates that LG students' model building actions were less consistent. On the other hand, pattern 8 shows that after making an incorrect computational model edit, HG students are more likely to perform consecutive correct edits afterward. This indicates that they had a better understanding of the model building task strategies.

## 4   Conclusions

In this paper, we introduced an OELE to foster students' understanding of diffusion and systems thinking as a primary CT practice. Students' learning performances not only indicate their improved understanding of diffusion through systems thinking but also shows evidence of the synergistic learning of domain content and CT practices. The data-driven analyses show that action patterns that indicate the good use of strategies appeared more in HG as indicated by the higher support; meanwhile, HG students showed a higher likelihood of using good learning strategies. These results explained the achievement gap among students.

**Acknowledgment.** This work has been supported by NSF Cyberlearning Grant #1441542.

# References

1. Barr, V., Stephenson, C.: Bringing computational thinking to k-12: what is involved and what is the role of the computer science education community? ACM Inroads **2**(1), 48–54 (2011)
2. Basu, S., Biswas, G., Kinnebrew, J.S.: Learner modeling for adaptive scaffolding in a computational thinking-based science learning environment. User Model. User Adap. Inter. **27**(1), 5–53 (2017)
3. Cheng, B.H., Ructtinger, L., Fujii, R., Mislevy, R.: Assessing systems thinking and complexity in science (large-scale assessment technical report 7). SRI International, Menlo Park (2010)
4. Chi, M.T.H.: Commonsense conceptions of emergent processes: why some misconceptions are robust. J. Learn. Sci. **14**(2), 161–199 (2005)
5. Chi, M.T.H., Roscoe, R.D., Slotta, J.D., Roy, M., Chase, C.C.: Misconceived causal explanations for emergent processes. Cogn. Sci. **36**(1), 1–61 (2012). https://doi.org/10.1111/j.1551-6709.2011.01207.x
6. Bransford, J.D., Brown, A.L., Cocking, R.R.: How People Learn: Brain, Mind, Experience, and School: Expanded Edition. The National Academies Press, Washington (2000)
7. Kinnebrew, J.S., Loretz, K.M., Biswas, G.: A contextualized, differential sequence mining method to derive students' learning behavior patterns. J. Educ. Data Min. **5**, 190–219 (2013)
8. Land, S.: Cognitive requirements for learning with open-ended learning environments. Educ. Tech. Res. Dev. **48**(3), 61–78 (2000)
9. Sengupta, P., Kinnebrew, J.S., Basu, S., Biswas, G., Clark, D.: Integrating computational thinking with k-12 science education using agent-based computation: a theoretical framework. Educ. Inf. Technol. **18**(2), 351–380 (2013). https://doi.org/10.1007/s10639-012-9240-x
10. Weintrop, D., Beheshti, E., Horn, M., Orton, K., Jona, K., Trouille, L., Wilensky, U.: Defining computational thinking for mathematics and science classrooms. J. Sci. Educ. Technol. **25**(1), 127–147 (2016). https://doi.org/10.1007/s10956-015-9581-5
11. Wilensky, U.: NetLogo: Center for Connected Learning and Computer-Based Modeling. Northwestern University, Evanston, IL (1999)
12. Wilensky, U., Reisman, K.: Thinking like a wolf, a sheep, or a firefly: learning biology through constructing and testing computational theories an embodied modeling approach. Cogn. Instr. **24**(2), 171–209 (2006)

13. Wilensky, U., Resnick, M.: Thinking in levels: a dynamic systems approach to making sense of the world. J. Sci. Educ. Technol. **8**(1), 3–19 (1999). https://doi.org/10.1023/A:1009421303064
14. Wing, J.M.: Computational thinking. Commun. ACM **49**(3), 33–35 (2006). https://doi.org/10.1145/1118178.1118215
15. Zhang, N., Biswas, G.: Assessing students computational thinking in a learning by modeling environment. In: Conference Proceedings of International Conference on Computational Thinking Education 2017, pp. 11–16 (2017)
16. Zhang, N., Biswas, G., Dong, Y.: Characterizing students' learning behaviors using unsupervised learning methods. In: André, E., Baker, R., Hu, X., Rodrigo, M.M.T., du Boulay, B. (eds.) AIED 2017. LNCS (LNAI), vol. 10331, pp. 430–441. Springer, Cham (2017). https://doi.org/10.1007/978-3-319-61425-0_36

# Industry Papers

# Adaptive Visual Dialog for Intelligent Tutoring Systems

Jae-wook Ahn(✉), Maria Chang, Patrick Watson, Ravi Tejwani,
Sharad Sundararajan, Tamer Abuelsaad, and Srijith Prabhu

IBM T.J. Watson Research Center, 1101 Kitchawan Rd,
Yorktown Heights, NY 10598, USA
{jaewook.ahn,pwatson,rtejwan,sharads,tamera,snprabhu}@us.ibm.com,
Maria.Chang@ibm.com

**Abstract.** Conversational dialog systems are well known to be an effective tool for learning. Modern approaches to natural language processing and machine learning have enabled various enhancements to conversational systems but they mostly rely on text- or speech-only interactions, which puts limits on how learners can express and explore their knowledge. We introduce a novel method that addresses such limitations by adopting a visualization that is coordinated with a text-based conversational interface. This allows learners to seamlessly perceive and express knowledge through language and visual representations.

**Keywords:** Intelligent tutoring system
Conversational dialog systems · Adaptive visualization · Visual dialog

## 1   Introduction

Conversational dialog systems allow people to communicate with intelligent software in a natural way. Natural user interfaces equipped with conversation abilities, voice recognition, and speech generation have been recognized as a future user interface in various domains [12] and are already being commercialized. Such conversational interfaces are useful in intelligent tutoring systems (ITS) [4], where mixed-initiative dialogues are commonly used to teach conceptual information [10,21]. They leverage the flexibility and expressiveness of the natural language, allowing learners to convey partial knowledge and ask questions. However, we still need to investigate what the best method is to implement effective conversational interfaces for intelligent tutoring [8], particularly considering the limitations of natural language interfaces (NLI) [19]. Some information is better conveyed via visual representations and concept maps are widely used for learners to visualize relationships and hierarchical organization of ideas.

The interface presented here is a hybrid of two approaches: textual conversation and visualization. It provides learners with a wide degree of flexibility in reporting knowledge and receiving feedback, but it also scaffolds learner behavior through automated assessment and feedback. The visualization part of the

C. Penstein Rosé et al. (Eds.): AIED 2018, LNAI 10948, pp. 413–418, 2018.
https://doi.org/10.1007/978-3-319-93846-2_77

interface adapts its topological structure and interaction mechanisms based on the changes in the text-based tutoring conversation flow. This *Adaptive Visual Dialog* provides learners with opportunities to interact with tutoring systems in novel ways that combine NLI and visualizations.

Previous related attempts are categorized into two groups: ITS and adaptive visualization. There are several studies that visualize conversations such as [20] but they do not support dynamic visual interactions between users or intelligent agents. Many ITS have been developed that use conversational dialog [18]. Concept map building has been explored in ITS as a method for modeling complex systems [6] and for learning via teachable agents [14]. Adaptive visualization adapts its visual representations depending on various user features that are explicitly provided or inferred from the trace of user actions [2], using one or more adaptation strategies: (a) visualization method adaptation [11], (b) visual structure adaptation [15], (c) adaptive annotation [16], or (d) open user (learner) models [3,5]. The current work belongs to categories (b), (c), and (d). The visual concept map adapts its structure according to the progress of text-based tutoring conversation and users' direct manipulation of the visualization. Specific concepts are visually annotated and dialog states and learner model metrics are dynamically updated. The changes in learner models cause changes in the visualization and the user is provided with greater transparency of their estimated learning state.

## 2    Adaptive Visual Dialog System

Figure 1 shows a prototype implementation of Adaptive Visual Dialog. It was designed to improve traditional text-based tutoring systems by blending an NLI with a visualization. It guides students through conversations by asking questions, evaluating student answers, eliciting concepts via hints, telling assertions, answering questions raised by the student, etc. We used IBM's Watson Conversation API [1] to implement the mixed initiative dialog. The conversation is made not just through the textual chatting box (Fig. 1(a)) but in a tight connection with an interactive visualization (b). Watson Conversation provides RESTful APIs that bridges the conversations between a learner and Watson, so the front-end could easily watch or intervene them through the visualization. The visualization uses a force-directed network layout [13]. The circular nodes represent key concepts appearing in the learning material. For example, in the visualization based on a chapter about "Earth, the Moon, and the Sun" in an Earth Science textbook, nodes represent sub-concepts (e.g., gravity) and links between nodes represent latent relationships between those concepts. The visualization allows users to freely explore and comprehend the knowledge structure. On top of the force-directed network, convex-hulls (colored areas) are drawn to indicate the corresponding group of concepts are interconnected to each other. The infomap community detection algorithm [17] was used for fast and reliable online clustering. By visually examining the communities and the included concepts, users instantly understand how they are co-related and achieve a specific learning objective (e.g., answering a question). Along with the adaptation following the interactive dialogue, an open learner model [3,5] based adaptation is supported. The prototype is equipped with a learner model that tracks students' mastery and consistency on concepts. The scores are overlaid on concepts using two black and white "arcs" that transparently show the user's mastery and consistency of the concepts.

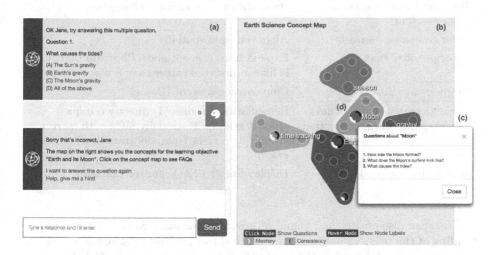

**Fig. 1.** Adaptive Visual Dialog prototype shows a textual dialog (a) and a visualization that presents concepts and clusters (b) synced with the conversation context. Student directly asks a question from visualization (c). Mastery and consistency scores loaded from an open learner model are overlaid on concepts as black and white arcs (d). (Color figure online)

**Interaction Use Case Scenario.** When a session begins, a student is asked a question about a topic. The concept visualization is activated and shows key concepts and clusters. She responds with an answer and the dialog engine assesses it and activates a visual remediation step if it is incorrect. Figure 1 depicts that the student gave a wrong answer to a question. In order to guide them to the correct answer, the system highlights the most relevant concept node (red) and its cluster (light blue border) (b). The learner may visually examine the concept and the other neighboring concepts within the cluster, and attempt the tutor-initiated question again. If they are still unsure about it, they may click on a concept to reveal a list of candidate questions about the concept (c). Clicking on a question causes it to be passed to the text-based dialog. The learner can ask the tutor the question as is, or modify it in the text entry field. This helps to the fact that sometimes the learner might not know the right set of questions to ask on a particular topic during the conversation. The system answers them by retrieving information from the textbook on which it has been trained. This enables a type of textual-visual coordination where a user expresses their intent to the system. We have devised a preliminary set of strategies for how concept graphs and text-based dialog interactions should be coordinated (Table 1).

**Table 1.** Textual-visual coordination: dialog-visualization events

| Conversational event (Cause) | Graph event (Effect) |
| --- | --- |
| Tutor initiated question or suggested topic | Highlight or glow relevant concepts |
| Tutor compares contrasts | Align concepts spatially |
| Tutor provides examples | Expand from concept node; illustrate that this is like an instance rather than a new concept |
| Graph event (Effect) | Conversational event (Cause) |
| Student creates incorrect links and/or graphical misconception | Remediation options: (1) directly critique student graph, (2) spatially align with correct graph, (3) correct (spatially transform) student graph |
| Student browses nodes | Display links to FAQs and/or examples |

Users can also create their visual representations attuned to their own understanding of the text. Visual nodes are derived from the annotations made by the users within the text using the user interface – to select text and drag it to the visual dialog interface where it is rendered as a new node. Users can then interact with this node and define relationships in the same manner as they would with the other nodes in the visual dialog (i.e., it may be assigned to clusters, explored, or linked via edges to other nodes). The very process of creating and manipulating such visual representations can be thought of as a form of self-explanation which can be learning activity [7]. These visual representations can be compared to the standard (i.e. automatically extracted) visualization via partial graph-matching algorithms [9], enabling concrete feedback on user-generated visualization. These annotated visual dialogs can also be shared by the users (students) with their peers and instructors and receive feedback.

## 3   Conclusions and Future Work

This paper describes our approach for building an adaptive visual dialog for intelligent tutoring systems, supporting adaptivity with respect (1) to the state of the conversation and the topic and (2) to learner models. Our prototype opens the door for learning experiences that take advantage of the benefits of mixed-initiative dialogues and concept mapping. It also enables learners to have a more varied experience that recruits spatial reasoning. We hypothesize that learning experiences can be further improved by selecting topics, visual, and textual events that our models predict will result in the greatest learning gains. We plan to test the prototype with real students and we are interested in using an iterative design approach so that we can discover what textual-visual coordination strategies lead to greater learning gains and if some strategies are more effective for some students than others.

# References

1. Watson Conversation (2018). https://www.ibm.com/watson/services/conversation
2. Ahn, J., Brusilovsky, P.: Adaptive visualization for exploratory information retrieval. Inf. Process. Manag. **49**(5), 1139–1164 (2013)
3. Ahn, J., Brusilovsky, P., Grady, J., He, D., Syn, S.Y.: Open user profiles for adaptive news systems: help or harm? In: WWW 2007: Proceedings of the 16th International Conference on World Wide Web, pp. 11–20. ACM Press, New York (2007). https://doi.org/10.1145/1242572.1242575
4. Anderson, J.R., Boyle, C.F., Reiser, B.J.: Intelligent tutoring systems. Science (Washington) **228**(4698), 456–462 (1985)
5. Bakalov, F., Meurs, M.J., König-Ries, B., Sateli, B., Witte, R., Butler, G., Tsang, A.: An approach to controlling user models and personalization effects in recommender systems. In: Proceedings of the 2013 International Conference on Intelligent User Interfaces, IUI 2013, pp. 49–56. ACM, New York (2013)
6. Bredeweg, B., Forbus, K.D.: Qualitative modeling in education. AI Mag. **24**(4), 35 (2003)
7. Chi, M.T., De Leeuw, N., Chiu, M.H., LaVancher, C.: Eliciting self-explanations improves understanding. Cognit. Sci. **18**(3), 439–477 (1994)
8. Coetzee, D., Fox, A., Hearst, M.A., Hartmann, B.: Chatrooms in moocs: all talk and no action. In: Proceedings of the First ACM Conference on Learning @ Scale Conference, L@S 2014, pp. 127–136. ACM, New York (2014)
9. Gold, S., Rangarajan, A.: A graduated assignment algorithm for graph matching. IEEE Trans. Pattern Anal. Mach. Intell. **18**(4), 377–388 (1996)
10. Graesser, A.C., Chipman, P., Haynes, B.C., Olney, A.: Autotutor: an intelligent tutoring system with mixed-initiative dialogue. IEEE Trans. Educ. **48**(4), 612–618 (2005)
11. Grawemeyer, B., Cox, R.: A bayesian approach to modelling users'information display preferences. User Model. **2005**, 225–230 (2005)
12. Hearst, M.A.: 'Natural' search user interfaces. Commun. ACM **54**, 60–67 (2011)
13. Jacomy, M., Heymann, S., Venturini, T., Bastian, M.: Forceatlas2, a continuous graph layout algorithm for handy network visualization. Medialab center of research 560 (2011)
14. Leelawong, K., Biswas, G.: Designing learning by teaching agents: the betty's brain system. Int. J. Artif. Intell. Educ. **18**(3), 181–208 (2008)
15. Lehmann, S., Schwanecke, U., Dörner, R.: Interactive visualization for opportunistic exploration of large document collections. Inf. Syst. **35**(2), 260–269 (2010)
16. Leuski, A., Allan, J.: Interactive information retrieval using clustering and spatial proximity. User Model. User Adapt. Interact. **14**(2), 259–288 (2004)
17. Rosvall, M., Bergstrom, C.T.: Maps of random walks on complex networks reveal community structure. Proc. Natl. Acad. Sci. **105**(4), 1118–1123 (2008)
18. Rus, V., DMello, S., Hu, X., Graesser, A.: Recent advances in conversational intelligent tutoring systems. AI Mag. **34**(3), 42–54 (2013)
19. Shneiderman, B.: A taxonomy and rule base for the selection of interaction styles. In: Shackle, B., Richardson, S.J. (eds.) Human Factors for Informatics Usability, pp. 325–342. Cambridge University Press, Cambridge (1991)

20. Viegas, F., Smith, M.: Newsgroup crowds and authorlines: visualizing the activity of individuals in conversational cyberspaces. In: Proceedings of the 37th Annual Hawaii International Conference on System Sciences, 2004, 10 pp., January 2004
21. Woolf, B.P.: Building Intelligent Interactive Tutors: Student-Centered Strategies for Revolutionizing e-learning. Morgan Kaufmann, Boston (2010)

# College Course Name Classification at Scale

Irina Borisova[(⊠)]

Chegg, Santa Clara, CA 95054, USA
irina@chegg.com

**Abstract.** Accessing college course content data at scale is often challenging due to a variety of legal and technical reasons. In this study, we classify college courses into course categories using only a college course name as an input. We describe our training data design, training process and report performance and evaluation metrics on two deep learning models– an LSTM and a word sequence-to-sequence models – trained on a three-level hierarchical course taxonomy with a number of course categories ranging from 58 to 2322. Despite scarce input data, the best performing models reach 0.91 accuracy and 88% relevance in quantitative and qualitative evaluations respectively.

**Keywords:** College course classification · Deep learning · seq2seq

## 1 Introduction

College course classification is essential for large scale educational data analysis with applications ranging from comparative research of educational programs to student outcomes research across several colleges to a course recommendation system. Traditional course classification models, such as those used for secondary school course classification (e.g. SCED [1]) or college associations (e.g. Association of American Medical Colleges [2]) rely on expert knowledge; few automated classification models (e.g. [3, 4]) are built on course content data, such as course description and syllabi. Such data and expertise dependencies determine the scope of such classifications: they mostly cover courses within an institution or just a department.

We build robust and highly accurate college course name classification models that rely only on a college course name as an input through creating a broad training data set and through applying deep learning methods. The rest of the paper further describes our data, training and evaluation.

## 2 Data

### 2.1 Overview

Our research is based on two proprietary data sources. The first one is NPD PubTrack Digital [5], a proprietary textbook-to-course classification that includes over a hundred thousand ISBNs assigned to one of 2600 courses. The course classification is hierarchical and includes 56 top-level course groups (e.g. *English, Mathematics, Engineering*) that further divide into more granular categories up to three levels deep (e.g.

*Engineering* has categories like *Mechanical* and *Electrical,* and *Mechanical Engineering* might have several specific courses covering various topics in this domain). For example, a book *A Christmas Carol* is assigned a category *English: Literature: 19$^{th}$ Century* in such classification. Here, we refer to *English* as a Level 1 category, *English Literature* as a Level 2 category, and *English Literature 19$^{th}$ Century* as a Level 3 category. As this example shows, the classification is not limited to textbooks but includes a variety of books used in courses.

A small subset of the book-course dataset has information about the course codes and the college IDs representing specific U.S. institutions that include a textbook in their coursework. This information is collected through campus bookstores. The subset covers 4000 book titles and 837 course classes: a course class has an average of 150 examples with course codes across various institutions.

Our second dataset is Market Data Retrieval dataset (MDR) [6] composed of 3.1 M records of college courses taught in the U.S. institutions from 2005 to 2016. It includes a course code, course name, very short description, department ID, year, term, and institution ID.

## 2.2    Training Data

We use the course codes and college IDs from the NPD PubTrack Digital and the MDR datasets to join the two and thus obtain 186000 training examples of course name (from the MDR data) – course category (from the NPD PubTrack Digital data) pairs, with 10% set aside for a test set. However, the coverage of course categories in this subset of data is limited to 718 – less than a third of all course categories in the taxonomy – restricting model's ability to generalize well. To address this concern, we make the following assumption about the data: some college course names might be somewhat similar to the textbook titles used in the course. We search for the book title-course category pairs in the NPD PubTrack Digital dataset that have at least one word in common, such as *American politics in the gilded age – History: U. S.: Gilded Age*. This approach helps us to extend our training data by 72,700 training examples and cover all of the course classes (Dataset A). Finally, we experiment with adding the full NPD PubTrack Digital dataset to the core dataset for training treating all book titles as course name examples (Dataset B). This allows us to get a higher word coverage for input course names.

## 3    Model Training

Two models are tested in our study. First, we use a word-level LSTM [7] model – a long-short term memory type of a recurrent neural network. We apply a fairly standard choice of hyperparameters in Keras implementation training with a dropout of 0.5, a sigmoid activation function, SGD optimization with 0.01 learning rate, and categorical crossentropy loss. We train three different LSTM models on each dataset to support three sets of course labels from the three levels of course class hierarchy.

Second, we interpret the course classification problem as a sequence-to-sequence (seq2seq) translation: indeed, we are decoding college course name into a domain of course categories. seq2seq models usually include a bidirectional recurrent neural network with an attention layer and a decoder. We use tf-seq2seq encoder-decoder framework [8] for implementation training one model that conveniently covers all course class levels.

## 4   Evaluation

First, we measure our models' accuracy: Table 1 shows accuracy of the LSTM and seq2seq models trained on Datasets A and B on different course taxonomy levels, from the highest one (Level 1) to a more granular (Level 3). While the LSTM model trained on Dataset A reaches the highest accuracy scores across all levels, its performance decreases as we add more book title data in Dataset B. While seq2seq accuracy is overall lower than LSTM and decreases with adding more data, the performance does not drop that drastically for Level 2 and 3 classification.

**Table 1.** LSTM and seq2seq models' accuracy on three levels of college course hierarchy in the test set given two training datasets.

| Level of classification | LSTM, Accuracy | | seq2seq, Accuracy | |
|---|---|---|---|---|
| | Dataset A | Dataset B | Dataset A | Dataset B |
| Level 1 | 0.91 | 0.87 | 0.89 | 0.86 |
| Level 2 | 0.78 | 0.61 | 0.76 | 0.7 |
| Level 3 | 0.68 | 0.48 | 0.66 | 0.58 |

Second, we look at models ability to predict diverse classes. For that, we look at the number of different course classes that models are able to predict in the test set: we expect this number to be very close to the actual number of classes in the test set for the best performing model. seq2seq trained on Dataset B captures 90% of the Level 2 classes in the test, 9% more compared to the best performing version of LSTM on Level 2.

Finally, we run a human evaluation on a test set of 200 college course names randomly selected from the Ohio State University 2015–2016 course catalogue [5]. A human judge was asked to review a course name and course category prediction from four models – two LSTMs trained to predict Level 2 classes and two seq2seq models – and decide whether the predicted course classes were relevant for the course name. As results in Table 2 show, the highest number of relevant predictions – 88% – belongs to seq-2-seq model trained on Dataset B.

Table 3 shows a few examples of the college course names and predictions made by our trained models. As we can see from these examples, it might be difficult to decide on the best category for a college course due to linguistic or conceptual ambiguity. A course like 'Individual Studies' might not have a good prediction in a content-based college course system, such as the one that we use. In such cases, a decision on the course class attribution should be made based on a program, department or a course of studies – the context that is not available in our approach. On the other hand, courses like 'Statistics for health pro' might have several good course class matches in the course class system. A more robust course taxonomy could alleviate such issues.

**Table 2.** Overall model relevance on a human evaluated test set. 'A' and 'B' refer to the datasets used for model training.

| Model | Relevance, % |
| --- | --- |
| LSTM-A-Lev2 | 70% |
| LSTM-B-Lev2 | 68% |
| seq2seq-A | 65% |
| seq2seq-B | 88% |

**Table 3.** Classification examples for college course names from four models.

| College course name | Statistics for health pro | Modern Arab-Muslim thought | Folklore of contemporary Greece |
| --- | --- | --- | --- |
| LSTM-A-Lev2 | Medical Sciences: Basic | English: Literature | English: Literature |
| LSTM-B-Lev2 | Mathematics: Probability and Statistics | Religion: Comparative Religion | English: Comparative Literature |
| seq2seq-A | Mathematics: Probability and Statistics | English: Literature: American: Non-fiction | English: Literature |
| seq2seq-B | Medical Sciences: Basic: Biostatistics | Political Science: Comparative Gov't: Gov't and Politics: Middle East | Classics: Greek Language and Literature |

## 5   Conclusions

We tackle a rarely approached problem of automated college course classification with an innovative use of data and an application of deep learning techniques. The resulting models reach very high accuracy using just a college course name as an input and provide a foundation for building a variety of analytical and recommendation tools; our sequence-to-sequence model performs best in human evaluation and class coverage. While our results are encouraging, a further analysis of course classes and addition of course relationship data along with associated course content might help create a more powerful and flexible college course classification model.

# References

1. Bradby, D., Pedroso, R., Rogers, A., Hoffman, L.: Secondary School Course Classification System: School Codes for the Exchange of Data (SCED). U.S. Department of Education, NCES 2007-341 (2007)
2. AMCAS Course Classification Guide. https://students-residents.aamc.org/applying-medical-school/article/course-classification-guide. Accessed 06 Feb 2018
3. Dimitrovski, A., Gjorgjevikj, A., Trajanov, D.: Courses content classification based on Wikipedia and CIP taxonomy. In: Trajanov, D., Bakeva, V. (eds.) ICT Innovations 2017. CCIS, vol. 778, pp. 140–153. Springer, Cham (2017). https://doi.org/10.1007/978-3-319-67597-8_14
4. Lee, S.-Y., Yu, H.-Y., Ahn, J.-A., Park, G.-E., Choi, W.-S.: The development of a trial curriculum classification and coding system using group technology. J. Eng. Educ. Res. **17**(2), 43–47 (2014)
5. NPD Group: http://www.npd.com. Accessed 06 Feb 2018
6. Market Data Retrieval: https://mdreducation.com. Accessed 06 Feb 2018
7. Schmidhuber, S.H.: Long short-term memory. Neural Comput. **9**, 1735–1780 (1997)
8. Britz, D., Goldie, A., Luong, T., Le, Q.: Massive Exploration of Neural Machine Translation Architectures. arXiv:1703.03906 (2017)
9. Ohio State University 2015–2016 course catalogue. http://registrar.osu.edu/scheduling/old_book3_info/course_catalog_2015_2016.pdf. Accessed 06 Feb 2018

# AUI Story Maker: Animation Generation from Natural Language

Nacir Bouali$^{(\boxtimes)}$ and Violetta Cavalli-Sforza$^{(\boxtimes)}$

School of Science and Engineering,
Al Akhawayn University, 53000 Ifrane, Morocco
{n.bouali,v.cavallisforza}@aui.ma

**Abstract.** Various research works have tried to connect Natural Language Processing NLP to computer graphics, as this connection would lay the ground for an automatic generation of computer animations. In this research we aim to provide a novel approach for connecting graphics to NLP by using OpenNLP and the Unity 3D game engine. We rely on two linguistic approaches—Vendler's verb classification and Jackendoff's Lexical Conceptual Structure LCS—and present how the technology enablers and the linguistic approaches chosen collaborate to provide the animation generation capability. We describe the overall architecture of AUI Story Maker, a system built to illustrate the feasibility of our approach, and discuss the future work required to make it a reliable tool in a modern classroom setting. We also present some writing samples gathered during field work with 1st graders at Al Akhawayn School in Ifrane (ASI), and provide sample outputs of AUI Story Maker.

**Keywords:** Natural Language Processing · Computer graphics
Animation · Vendler verb classes · Unity 3D · OpenNLP
Lexical Conceptual Structure

## 1 Introduction

Students nowadays are "Digital Natives": they grew up with technology, and they expect to use it in school [1]. Researchers and practitioners agree that animation can facilitate learning [2], but creating graphical resources is a complex task that requires expertise in both computer graphics and programming. Research efforts have aimed at overcoming this complexity by creating a paradigm wherein the users can create scenes or animations using Natural Language NL descriptions.

As an example, the Carsim system [3] is able to convert NL descriptions of car accidents into computer animations, in order to help insurance companies decide whose fault it is when an accident occurs. However, it enforces a template on its users, limiting their freedom in describing events. Confucius [4] and NLP Story Maker [5] are two similar systems offering text-to-animation capability.

With our system, AUI Story Maker, we aim to provide first graders with a tool that can convert their stories, written in English, into computer animations. We hypothesize that the tool will incite them to write by making it fun to do so as their story comes to life through animation.

© Springer International Publishing AG, part of Springer Nature 2018
C. Penstein Rosé et al. (Eds.): AIED 2018, LNAI 10948, pp. 424–428, 2018.
https://doi.org/10.1007/978-3-319-93846-2_79

For a system to be able to generate animations from NL text, it must rely on NLP component technologies. For the architecture of AUI Story Maker, we rely on two modules, NLP and graphics, to support the task of animation generation.

The rest of the paper is organized as follows. Section 2 discusses in detail how key elements of the Story Maker work, while Sect. 3 explains how the linguistic approaches take part in solving the animation generation challenge. In Sect. 4, we shed light on the field work conducted in support of this research project, and present samples of system output. We draw conclusions in Sect. 5 and discuss the future work required to make the Story Maker a tool that can be relied on in a classroom setting.

## 2 AUI Story Maker

To provide a system that successfully generates animations from natural language we need to rely on two main components. First, an NLP component must be able to understand natural language text input by the user and extract the visual elements necessary to build the animation. These are then fed to a graphics component able to render the animation to the user. All the systems providing the capability of generating graphics from natural language text share this generic architecture and our system is not different in this regard. Figure 1 illustrates the overall architecture of our story maker.

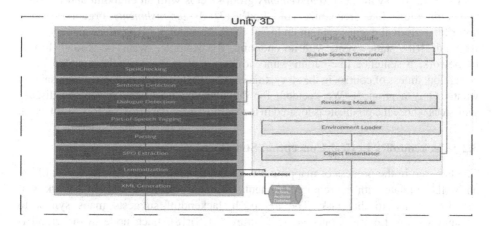

**Fig. 1.** AUI story maker generic architecture

The NLP module is made of eight components that help it achieve the NL understanding required to extract the visual components from the sentences. A critical module of the AUI Story Maker is the Subject-Predicate-Object (SPO) extraction module, which reduces sentences to include only subject-verb-object. If SPO is conducted successfully, the conversion of children's input to the formal representation of the animation will be easier. Rusu et al. presented an algorithm that allows the extraction of SPO from sentences and relies on parsing output by OpenNLP [6]. The algorithm suggested consists of three main steps, each allowing extraction of one entity at a time.

- **Extracting the Subject.** A sentence S is represented by a tree with 3 children: NP, VP and a period ('.'). S is the root of the sentence. To extract the subject, we perform a breadth first search and select the first descendant of NP that is a noun.
- **Extracting the Predicate.** To extract the predicate, the deepest verb descendant of the VP is selected.
- **Extracting the Object.** The object, which can be either a PP (Prepositional Phrase), an NP or an ADJP (Adjective Phrase), can be found in one of the three sub-trees of a VP. In NPs and PPs, the object will be in the first noun found. In ADJPs, the object will be in the first adjective found (e.g., 'happy' in "John is happy").

## 3 Linguistic Approaches

### 3.1 Vendler's Verb Classification

Vendler provided a classification of verbs based on their aspectual properties, rather than their syntactic or semantic properties [7], and more specifically based on their inherent temporal semantic features. The classes help decide which sentences can be mapped to animations and which sentences should be discarded. Vendler distinguishes 4 verb classes: (1) *Activities* contains verbs describing dynamic events without an end point like 'run', 'walk' or 'swim'; (2) *Achievements* groups verbs with an endpoint and instantaneous duration, like 'recognize' or 'find'; (3) *Accomplishments* organizes verbs describing gradual events with an endpoint (e.g., 'to paint'); (4) *Statives* gathers verbs which describe static events with no endpoint, for example, 'want' or 'know'. In this framework, a sentence like "John wants to buy a phone" cannot be mapped to an animation, unless of course, in the story, this is expressed through dialogue (John said: "I want to buy a phone"). We decided, for the first version of the system, to discard sentences whose the predicate is located in the stative verbs class (love, know, want, etc.).

### 3.2 Jackendoff's Lexical Conceptual Structure

The last step in the process of mapping NL descriptions to formal description is filling an XML template with the required elements of an animation. Jackendoff's work is of key importance to this task. The approach Jackendoff suggests maps syntax to semantics using Lexical Conceptual Structure (LCS) [8]. Each node in the graph is associated with an item of information that fills a blank in meaning space of the sentence. An LCS node type can be either an event, a state, an object (thing), a path, a place or a property.

Consider the sentence "John goes to the market". The conceptual structure is:

$$[_{event}Go([_{thing}John],]_{path}TO([_{place}IN([_{thing}Market])])])]$$

With the structure provided by LCS, we fill a template with the required elements of an animation. E.g., if the predicate extracted by SPO module is "go", the NLP module must fill the following elements before forwarding them to the graphics module:

Actor:          is taken from slot 'thing' in the LCS template
Place:          the location where the animation takes place, taken from slot 'in'
Path:           the direction to which the actor is headed, taken from slot 'path'
Predicate:      taken from slot 'event'

## 4 Working with ASI 1st Graders

To ensure AUI Story Maker fits into the curriculum of 1st graders at ASI, we conducted meetings and discussions with a 1st grade instructor and her pupils in March–July 2016. This interaction provided us with a clear idea about the nature of the input to expect and helped us design AUI Story Maker so it could be easily used by children. Figure 2 shows a sample output of AUI Story Maker. It supports human and animal characters and gives dialogue support to both. We have published a story with the corresponding animation on YouTube to show how the system works.

Link: https://www.youtube.com/watch?v=mzVbiSNqA6E

**Fig. 2.** Output for sentences "The wolf and the fox are in the forest" and "Bob is in the street, Bob said, 'Hello'"

## 5 Conclusions and Future Work

We believe that our AUI Story Maker presents a new approach to a topic that has been recently attracting more research. The novelty in our work is the reliance on game engines that provide various graphical features thereby reducing the burden of developing a graphics module from scratch. This allows research to be fully-focused on the NL understanding, which is considered the heart of the problem domain in text-to-animation systems.

One of the open problems in this area of work is the inability to create scenes for locations, actors and actions that do not exist in the system's database. This limitation restricts the freedom children have when inputting their stories to the system. Future work required to improve AUI Story Maker will involve allowing users to textually describe their own environments, characters and props and add them to the database. We also plan to improve the performance of the Story Maker in terms of speed and add VR capability to allow users to see and interact with their stories in virtual environments.

# References

1. Prensky, M.: Digital natives, digital immigrants. Horizon 9(5), 1–6 (2001)
2. Kim, S., Yoon, M., Whang, S.-M., Tversky, B., Morrison, J.B.: The effect of animation on comprehension and interest. J. Comput. Assist. Learn. **23**, 260–270 (2007)
3. Dupuy, S., Egges, A., Legendre, V., Nugues, P.: Generating a 3D simulation of a car accident from a written description in natural language: the CarSim system. In: ACL2001: Workshop on Temporal and Spatial Information Processing, Toulouse, pp. 1–8, 7 July 2001
4. Ma, M.: Automatic Conversion of Natural Language to 3D Animation. Ph.D. thesis, University of Ulster (2006)
5. Pahud, M., Lee S., Takako A.: NLP Story Maker (2006)
6. Rusu, D., Dali, L., Fortuna, B., Grobelnik, M., Mladenić, D.: Triplet extraction from sentences, Ljubljana. In: Proceedings of the 10th International Multiconference Information Society (2007)
7. Vendler, Z.: Verbs and times. Philos. Rev. **56**(1), 43–160 (1957)
8. Jackendoff, R.: Semantic Structures. The MIT Press, Cambridge (1990)

# Inferring Course Enrollment
# from Partial Data

José P. González-Brenes[(✉)] and Ralph Edezhath

Chegg, Santa Clara, CA 95054, USA
{jgonzalez,redezhath}@chegg.com

**Abstract.** We study how to infer students' course enrollment information from incomplete data. We use data collected from a leading technology company and use a novel extension of Factorization Machines that we call Weighted Feat2Vec. Our empirical evaluation suggests that we improve on popular methods, while training time is reduced by half (when using the same implementation language, and hardware).

## 1 Introduction

In this paper we study how to infer student course enrollment of undergraduate students from partial information. For example, consider that for a student we know that she's enrolled in five courses (e.g, "Fundamentals of Computer Science", "Algorithms Data Structures", etc.); our goal is to predict the entire set of courses that she will take during her degree program.

We use data from a leading educational technology company that provides services to undergraduate students including textbook rental, online tutoring, access to a forum of experts, explanations of textbook questions, and textbook rental. This company often collects only incomplete course enrollment information; and it would be an unnecessary friction to ask students to upload their entire course enrollment. Here, we study how to use the partial course enrollment information collected to infer a complete list of courses for every student. Predicting the complete list of courses enables the personalized recommendation of content and services that may be helpful to the student.

## 2 Model

We extend the popular Factorization Machine Rendle (2010) model to allow structured and weighted interactions. We call our approach Weighted Feat2Vec, and in this short paper we only explain it briefly:

$$\hat{y}(\mathbf{x}; \mathbf{b}, \boldsymbol{\beta}) = \omega\left(b_0 + \sum_{i=1}^{n} b_i x_i + \psi\left(\sum_{i=1}^{|\kappa|} \sum_{j=i}^{|\kappa|} w_{i,j}\, \lambda^s(\mathbf{x}, \boldsymbol{\beta}, \kappa_i, \kappa_j)\right)\right) \tag{1}$$

Here, $y$ is the binary output of the model (1 iff the student is enrolled in a course, 0 if not), $x$ the input features, $b_0$ a bias term, $b$ linear coefficients, the

C. Penstein Rosé et al. (Eds.): AIED 2018, LNAI 10948, pp. 429–432, 2018.
https://doi.org/10.1007/978-3-319-93846-2_80

function $\psi$ is any activation function, and $\boldsymbol{\beta}$ are factorized embeddings that are shared across the pairwise interactions. The interactions occur from features in different groups:

$$\lambda^s(\mathbf{x}, \boldsymbol{\beta}, \mathbf{I}, \mathbf{J}) \triangleq \sum_{i \in I} \sum_{j \in J} x_i \boldsymbol{\beta}_i x_j \boldsymbol{\beta}_j \tag{2}$$

For example, consider a model with four features ($n = 4$). If we define $\kappa = \{\{1, 2\}, \{3, 4\}\}$, feature $x_1$ would only interact with $x_3$ and $x_4$. Without loss of generality, we could define a model that is equivalent to a shallow Factorization Machine by allowing each feature to be in a singleton group: $\kappa = \{\{1\}, \{2\}, \{3\}, \{4\}\}$.

A challenge we face is that we only observe positive examples (i.e., whether a student is enrolled in a course), and we do not observe negative examples (i.e., if a student is *not* associated with a course). For training the model, we sample negative examples randomly using Negative Sampling Mikolov et al. (2013), Dyer (2014), where each course has an equal probability of being sampled. The number of negatives examples sampled for each student is equal to the number of observed course enrollments.

## 3   Dataset

Course names across institutions may vary widely. For example, two universities may have the same curricula, but one may name the course *Single Variable Calculus*, while the other one may choose *Calculus I*. Thus, we preprocess our dataset with an algorithm that inputs the evidence of student enrollment, and outputs normalized course names. Our normalized course names can be represented with a hierarchical ontology. The details of how this algorithm works are out of scope, so for brevity we just report that our ontology has a total of 2,930 normalized courses. For this paper, we only use a subset of the data collected from 2013 to 2016.

Table 1 summarizes the feature types we used. Because all of our features are discrete, we report the possible number of values (dimensions) that they can take. We encode these features with one-hot encoding.

## 4   Experimental Results

We build a development set to tune hyper-parameters, and a test set (that we only queried once) by selecting students with 10 or more course enrollments. For these students, we select a random enrollment for the development set, and at least one random enrollment in the testing set. Our development set has 1.2 million positive examples, and the test set has 1.46 million.

We compare Weighted Feat2Vec with the following - Factorization Machine (using the same features as our method), Matrix Factorization (only user and course dimensions); and course popularity baseline with only course biases. We

**Table 1.** Feature types used for inferring study plans

| Type | Identifiers for (feature types) | Example | Dimensions |
|---|---|---|---|
| Course | Course name | Mathematics/ Single Variable Calculus | 2,931 |
| Course | Level 1 of course name | Mathematics | 58 |
| Course | Level 2 of course name | Single Variable Calculus | 1135 |
| Course | Level 3 of course name | – | 1082 |
| User | User | 1920 | 4,659,571 |
| User | # of years between last transaction and sign up | 2 | 7 |
| User | Institution | Carnegie Mellon University | 5,407 |
| User | Data source # 1? | No | 2 |
| User | Data source # 2? | Yes | 2 |

use an evaluation metric known as Area Under the Curve (AUC) of the Receiver Operating Characteristic. For negative labels in the test set we sample courses according to the courses frequency. This ensures that if a model merely predicts course enrollments according to their popularity, it would have an AUC of 0.5.

On the test set, Weighted Feat2Vec has the highest AUC (0.80) over all the other methods, as shown in Table 2. At the same time, Weighted Feat2Vec is almost twice as fast as Factorization Machine. All the models are implemented using a popular deep learning framework known as Keras Chollet et al. (2015) and trained on an Nvidia K80 GPU.

**Table 2.** Test set results of predicting study plans

| Model | AUC | Training time (in mins) |
|---|---|---|
| Weighted Feat2Vec | **0.80** | **54.9** |
| Factorization Machine | 0.79 | 98.0 |
| Matrix Factorization | 0.72 | 103.4 |
| Item popularity baseline | 0.50 | – |

# 5  Conclusion

We present results that suggest Weighted Feat2Vec is more accurate than other general purpose factorization models, and yet it trains in roughly half the time. We are very optimistic about this results, and will report further results in the future. Additionally, Weighted Feat2Vec is general-purpose and it is not specific to course enrollment prediction. Future work may apply our model to different educational tasks.

# References

Chollet, F., et al.: Keras (2015). https://github.com/fchollet/keras

Dyer, C.: Notes on noise contrastive estimation and negative sampling. arXiv preprint arXiv:1410.8251 (2014)

Mikolov, T., Sutskever, I., Chen, K., Corrado, G.S., Dean, J.: Distributed representations of words and phrases and their compositionality. In: Advances in Neural Information Processing Systems, pp. 3111–3119 (2013)

Rendle, S.: Factorization machines. In: IEEE 10th International Conference on Data Mining (ICDM), pp. 995–1000. IEEE (2010)

# Validating Mastery Learning: Assessing the Impact of Adaptive Learning Objective Mastery in Knewton Alta

Andrew Jones[✉] and Illya Bomash

Knewton, New York, NY 10010, USA
andrew.jones@knewton.com

**Abstract.** Adaptive courseware products implementing mastery learning pedagogy must determine when each student reaches mastery. Such determinations are often made in real time, in order to inform student progress, but the validity of algorithmically determined mastery typically can only be assessed by examination of later student performance. This paper examines the impact of platform-determined mastery on future quiz and assignment preparedness in the context of Knewton alta. With simple controls for overall student initial ability, platform-wide results indicate that students achieving mastery (as calculated by Knewton's Proficiency Model) outperform students who do not, with largest future performance gains seen by students with lowest initial ability levels.

**Keywords:** Mastery learning · Adaptive learning · Efficacy

## 1 Introduction

Mastery learning, of interest to education researchers since at least the 1960s [1, 2], is implicated in a variety of current coursework redesign efforts [3, 4]. One of its assumptions is that all or most students can reach mastery – that "mastery" is not some innate, initial proficiency advanced students have with the material, but can be achieved through formative assessment, correctives, and growth [1]. This presents a challenge to adaptive learning platforms: if students take varying amounts of time, effort, and help to reach mastery, how does an algorithmic model know when a student has achieved it, and how can adaptive courseware quantify the results of that mastery independently of initial student ability levels?[1]

Knewton's adaptive platform is designed to handle this problem at scale [5]. Students work on personalized, adaptive assignments featuring curated Open Educational Resources (OER) content and complete them when Knewton's Proficiency Model indicates they have reached mastery. Most students who start a Knewton adaptive assignment go on to reach mastery (87% of student assignments across 2017) [5], but the significance and effects of that platform-defined mastery can only be validated through examination of future performance. Knewton defines this mastery and its "downstream"

---

[1] Properly setting mastery thresholds through examination performance has been a topic of considerable research [6]. Real-time mastery thresholds present a more significant validation challenge.

© Springer International Publishing AG, part of Springer Nature 2018
C. Penstein Rosé et al. (Eds.): AIED 2018, LNAI 10948, pp. 433–437, 2018.
https://doi.org/10.1007/978-3-319-93846-2_81

impacts jointly: mastery is the level of proficiency that results in good performance on summative assessments and good preparation for post-requisite learning.

As a step toward validating Knewton's mastery calculations, this paper describes a simple metric to control for initial student ability levels and assesses the impact of achieving Knewton-defined learning objective mastery on future quiz scores, assignment completion rates, and work necessary to reach assignment completion for students of comparable initial ability levels.

## 2  Analysis

In 2017, some higher-education institutions began to pilot Knewton's integrated adaptive learning courseware, alta. Instructors using alta create mastery-based adaptive assignments and static (non-adaptive) quizzes by selecting learning objectives. Students interact with the resulting personalized experience served during adaptive assignments and fixed quiz questions, and Knewton reports the results to instructors with a variety of analytics.

Instead of hand-selecting case studies for analysis, the plots below describe a random subset of student alta piloters working across four subject domains (mathematics, chemistry, economics, and statistics). The data includes approximately 10,000 students, 130,000 adaptive assignments, and 17,000 quizzes. These students were not part of a randomized, controlled trial, but they do provide an unfiltered portrait of student performance in alta.

Each student in this sample is assigned an initial ability label derived from the first two questions answered across each of the (typically several dozen) learning objectives the student encountered across their course. The percentage of those questions answered correctly provides a naive but reasonable estimate of how well the student knew the material entering the course. Students are grouped into three initial ability levels such that: "struggling" students have initial ability percent correct scores in the bottom quartile of all users in the data set, "advanced" students score in the top quartile, and "average" students fall in between. Knewton's Proficiency Model neither uses this measure nor tags students with any kind of overall ability label.

At the start of each quiz or assignment, the student's level of mastery was assessed via Knewton's Proficiency Model. Since most quizzes, tests, and assignments cover material from more than one learning objective, the analysis below treats as the variable of interest what percentage of the learning objectives relevant for a given student-assignment or student-quiz pair were mastered through work prior to the start of the assignment or quiz.

The first portion of this analysis compares the mean score of all student-quiz pairs for high-mastery (75% or more of the quiz learning objectives mastered) and low-mastery (25% or fewer of the quiz learning objectives mastered) students at each level of overall initial ability (struggling, average, or advanced).

To assess the impact of Knewton-determined mastery on preparedness for future learning, the remainder of the analysis uses the learning objective prerequisite-postrequisite relations encoded in the Knewton Knowledge Graph to identify the set of immediate prerequisites for any given adaptive assignment. For students taking an assignment, comparisons of assignment completion rate and work required to reach assignment completion are made between high-mastery (75% or more of the assignment's prerequisite learning objectives mastered) and low-mastery (25% or fewer of the assignment's prerequisite learning objectives mastered) students at each level of overall initial ability (struggling, average, advanced).

Student work is thus not grouped by topic, but rather by the student's overall initial ability (a single value for each student, independent of assignments) and level of relevant learning objective mastery at the start of the quiz or assignment (one value for each student-assignment or student-quiz pair). This process does not control for variance in student performance due to factors specific to institutions, instructors, or topic.[2]

# 3    Results and Discussion

Figure 1 plots mean quiz score for students of each overall initial ability level as a function of their level of learning objective mastery at the start of the quiz. Quiz takers who mastered at least 75% of the quiz learning objectives through previous adaptive work went on to achieve substantially higher quiz scores than similarly-skilled peers mastering 25% or fewer of the learning objectives. This was true across ability levels, but the largest gains went to students of lowest overall initial ability: mastering quiz learning objectives increased initially struggling students' average quiz scores by 38% points, raising scores for these students above the scores of otherwise advanced students who skipped the adaptive work or failed to reach mastery.

Students who mastered the learning objectives on an assignment also tended to perform better on later, more advanced assignments. As Fig. 2 shows, students who mastered 75% or more of the learning objectives prerequisite to any given assignment were more likely to complete the assignment than students who did not. This illustrates a positive feedback cycle: mastery of prerequisites increases the likelihood that students will master postrequisites, especially for students of generally low overall course preparedness. Notably, students who initially struggled overall but mastered most of the prerequisites to a particular assignment tended to outscore students of generally higher overall abilities who did not master the prerequisites.

Mastery of an assignment's learning objectives is also associated with shorter postrequisite adaptive assignments. When students began an assignment after having mastered at least 75% of its prerequisites, they tended to require fewer questions to complete it – 30–45% fewer than peers mastering fewer than 25% of the prerequisites (see Fig. 3). Again, students with low initial overall abilities saw the biggest gains: an average postrequisite assignment shortening of more than 40%.

---

[2] When students are compared only to class intra-assignment or intra-quiz peers, the outcome distributions over the resulting (much smaller) data set match the general trends shown here. The results below provide a less-controlled but wider-ranging composite picture of student performance across a variety of classroom implementations.

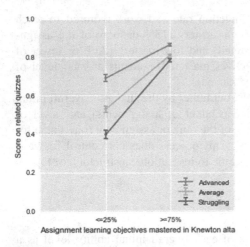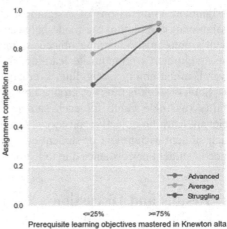

**Fig. 1.** Quiz score as a function of learning objective mastery. Error bars indicate 95% confidence interval; colors indicate student overall initial ability level.

**Fig. 2.** Percentage of students starting an assignment who ultimately complete it as a function of prerequisite learning objective mastery. Colors: student overall initial ability level. (Color figure online)

Since overall initial ability (as naively indexed here) does not appear to determine whether or not a student can reach mastery, future work will attempt to determine what factors differentiate students who reach mastery from students who do not. These differentiators may include non-cognitive factors like engagement, growth mindset, and persistence.

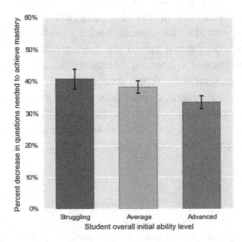

**Fig. 3.** Percentage decrease in questions necessary to reach mastery (and assignment completion) due to prerequisite learning objective mastery. Error bars: 95% confidence interval.

# References

1. Bloom, B.S.: Learning for Mastery. Instruction and Curriculum. Regional Education Laboratory for the Carolinas and Virginia, Topical Papers and Reprints, Number 1. Evaluation comment, vol. 1(2) (1968)
2. Block, J.H., Burns, R.B.: Mastery learning. Rev. Res. Educ. **4**(1), 3–49 (1976)
3. Twigg, C.A.: Models for online learning. Educause Rev. **38**, 28–38 (2003)
4. Ariovich, L., Walker, S.A.: Assessing course redesign: the case of developmental math. Res. Pract. Assess. **9**, 45–57 (2014)
5. Knewton alta homepage. www.knewtonalta.com. Accessed 28 Jan 2018
6. Gentile, J.R., Lalley, J.P.: Standards and Mastery Learning: Aligning Teaching and Assessment so all Children can Learn. Corwin Press, Thousand Oaks (2003)

# The Rise of Immersive Cognitive Assessments: Towards Simulation-Based Assessment for Evaluating Applicants

Rebecca Kantar[1], Keith McNulty[2], Erica L. Snow[1(✉)],
Richard Wainess[1], Sonia D. Doshi[1], Devon B. Walker[1],
and Matthew A. Emery[1]

[1] Imbellus, Los Angeles, CA, USA
esnow@imbellus.com
[2] McKinsey & Company, London, UK

**Abstract.** Imbellus is an assessment company that aims to test cognitive processes within the context of immersive simulation-based assessments. This paper explores our work with McKinsey & Company, a best-in-class management consulting firm, to build a simulation-based assessment that gauges applicants' cognitive skills and abilities. Leveraging a cognitive task analysis grounded in theoretical work and practical observations of on the job activities, we defined key work activities and skills needed to complete them. We then developed scenarios that abstracted and generalized the most crucial skills. To make sense of significant telemetry data from users' interactions with the assessment, we applied theoretically grounded expert models to guide our scoring algorithms. Our assessment draws inferences across seven major problem-solving constructs. We will present our initial findings and describe implications of our current work for the fields of artificial intelligence and assessment.

**Keywords:** Simulation-based assessment · Cognitive skills
Artificial Intelligence

## 1 Introduction

Imbellus is an assessment company that aims to evaluate cognitive processes within the context of simulation-based assessments. We will deploy these assessments across a variety of industries, domains, and organizations. We have partnered with McKinsey & Company, a best-in-class management consulting firm, to gauge incoming applicants' cognitive skills and abilities.

The Imbellus assessment focuses explicitly on incoming applicants' problem-solving skills and abilities. We define problem solving as a cognitive process directed at achieving a goal when no solution is obvious to the user (Mayer 2014). In partnership with McKinsey & Company, we conducted a cognitive task analysis (Schraagen et al. 2000) to conceptualize how successful problem-solving abilities manifest in the workplace. We developed our understanding of problem-solving skills from on-site interviews, case study analyses, and a review of related literature and created a problem-solving ontology representing seven major constructs (e.g. situational awareness, metacognition, decision-making). We examined the structural alignment between our problem-solving ontology and the nature of employees' work by comparing job activities at McKinsey & Company. We mapped job activities to constructs to lay the blueprint for developing scenarios within our simulation-based assessment.

Our scenarios are tasks embedded within our assessment that abstract the context of a given work environment while maintaining opportunities for users to portray problem-solving capabilities required by the job. Transposing skills and applications to a different but comparable context allows us to assess far transfer (Perkins and Salomon 1992). Each scenario in our assessment is designed based on a set of problem-solving constructs and workplace activities. The assessment requires users to interact with a series of challenges involving terrain, plants, and wildlife within a natural world setting. This setting limits bias and offers an accessible context regardless of background and prior knowledge. For example, in one scenario a user may be identifying impending environmental threats in an ecosystem, given evidence. As a user interacts with our assessment, we collect a wealth of information about *how* they approach the task. Analyzing users' telemetry data (e.g. mouse movements, clicks, choices, timestamps), we can examine their cognitive processes and overall performance.

## 2    Overview of Score Development

From our research-driven, theoretical framework, we devised Imbellus scores to quantify *how* users' actions, timestamps, and performance within each scenario related to various cognitive constructs. Cognitive science, educational psychology, and learning science theories guided the mapping of each score to relevant constructs. Our scores focus both on the product (i.e., right or wrong) and on the process (i.e., how did they get there, what choices did they make, how many mistakes did they correct), which is more nuanced than traditional cognitive assessments.

We built, tested, and iterated upon Imbellus scores using both our theoretical framework and user data. We began our score design process by outlining an expert model, informed by our literature review of problem-solving skills, for each scenario. Our expert models outlined an expert's expected telemetry stream and corresponding evidence (e.g. efficiency, systematicity) for each assessment scenario. Expert models drove our evidence statements, outlining what information we would need to see from the user in the environment to infer strong problem-solving skills. For instance, if we wanted to measure informed decision making in our tasks, we would create an evidence statement that would define what informed decision making is and how it would manifest in our assessment. All scores were programmed using these evidence statements as the scoring parameters. After scores were built, we conducted think aloud testing and internal playtests to evaluate and iterate upon our initial expert models and scoring parameters. These initial scoring parameters served as the basis for our pilot study in November 2017.

## 3  Preliminary Pilot Overview

Using the preliminary Imbellus scores, we conducted a large-scale pilot study with McKinsey & Company. The goal of this pilot was to test our assessment platform and three scenarios and to examine the predictive power of our initial Imbellus scores. Information from this pilot study is being used to iterate and design future Imbellus scores and simulations.

### 3.1  Method

The pilot test was conducted in London, United Kingdom from November 13th to 17th, 2017. The test assessed 527 McKinsey candidates, of whom 40% were female, 59% were male, and 1% did not provide gender details. Of the pilot population, 56% of the participants were native English speakers, 43% were non-native, but fluent English speakers, and 1% had a business-level proficiency in English. The ethnic breakdown of the sample based on the Equal Employment Opportunity Commission (EEOC) guidelines was 52.6% White, 29.7% Asian, 3.9% Hispanic, 4.1% Mixed, 3.3% Black, 2.8% Other, and 3.5% who did not specify ("Code of Federal Regulations Title 29 - Labor" 1980).

The pilot test was an opt-in, proctored assessment following the participants' completion of the McKinsey & Company paper-based Problem-Solving Test (PST). The PST was validated using industry standard validation procedures for relevance to job specifications, scaling, and reliability. The Imbellus assessment was administered for 1 h. Over the 5 days of testing, a total of 29 testing sessions took place on McKinsey-owned laptops in an enclosed, proctored conference room setting. Following completion of the assessment, participants completed an online survey. The survey collected demographic information and feedback on each scenario's design and usability through 4-point Likert scales supplemented by open-ended questions.

### 3.2  Initial Results

Our scoring pipeline transformed each users' telemetry data into the Imbellus scores. To examine how well our assessment performed, we validated it against the PST. If the Imbellus scores are valid, we would expect a positive correlation between our scores and the PST. A PST score above a certain threshold is used as an early screen for cognitive ability in the McKinsey hiring process. The PST is one aspect of the McKinsey and Company selection process and is combined with other inputs. As a cognitive, work sample test the PST is likely to be a reasonable predictor of job performance. When the first cohort of applicants reaches their first performance review, they will be reassessed using job performance as the target. We built an elastic net logistic regression model trained on Imbellus scores to predict whether a user reached the PST threshold. We chose to use elastic net regularization because it tends to set the weights of uninformative scores to 0 while grouping predictive but near collinear scores (Hastie et al. 2009). We withheld 25% of the data for a test set.

The PST is a challenging test and fewer people reached the threshold than did not. This class imbalance means that models that predict mostly negative outcomes for everyone could have high accuracy. We assessed the model using the $F_1$-score, which is robust to class imbalances. The $F_1$-score is the harmonic average of precision (true positives divided by predicted positives) and recall (true positives divided by all positives). An $F_1$-score of 1 means the model is a perfect classifier; a model with an $F_1$-score of 0 is always wrong. The micro-averaged $F_1$-score for the test fraction was 0.621. This suggests that the Imbellus scores do have some predictive capability of users' cognitive skills but do not duplicate PST results.

Survey results indicated that 67% of users preferred the Imbellus assessment to the PST, and 91% of users found the Imbellus assessment engaging. Similarly, 64% reported the Imbellus assessment leveraged the same type of cognitive skills required for success in the McKinsey & Company selection process. These results suggest our assessment offers a more immersive alternative to existing assessment methods while maintaining context and construct validity.

# 4 Next Steps

Our forthcoming assessments are being designed for remote deployment via timed releases where users participate across any number of locations. To ensure no two assessments are the same, we are employing artificial intelligence (AI) approaches to scenario generation. We vary data-driven properties referenced across scenarios that, in turn, build unique versions of those scenarios. Our AI and data-driven architecture will protect against cheating and gaming of the test - a significant challenge facing many existing cognitive tests.

We are currently conducting playtests with McKinsey & Company employees and candidates globally while refining our assessment in preparation for operationalization next year. We are also developing additional ontologies and assessments for hard-to-measure skills and abilities. Our goal is to provide more specific, useful data on incoming applicants and employees that can inform the structuring of teams, assigning work, and managing talent.

# References

Code of Federal Regulations Title 29 – Labor (1980). https://www.gpo.gov/fdsys/pkg/CFR-2016-title29-vol4/xml/CFR-2016-title29-vol4-part1606.xml

Mayer, R.E.: What problem solvers know cognitive readiness for adaptive problem solving. In: O'Neil, H.F., Perez, R.S., Baker, E.L. (eds.) Teaching and Measuring Cognitive Readiness, pp. 149–160. Springer, Boston (2014). https://doi.org/10.1007/978-1-4614-7579-8_8

Mayer, R.E., Wittrock, M.C.: Problem solving transfer. In: Berliner, D.C., Calfee, R.C. (eds.) Handbook of Educational Psychology, pp. 47–62. Simon & Schuster Macmillan, New York (1996)

Hastie, T., Tibshirani, R., Friedman, J.: The Elements of Statistical Learning: Data Mining, Inference, and Prediction, 2nd edn. Springer, New York (2009). https://doi.org/10.1007/978-0-387-84858-7

Schraagen, J.M., Chipman, S.F., Shalin, V.L. (eds.): Cognitive Task Analysis. Psychology Press, New York (2000)

Perkins, D.N., Salomon, G.: Transfer of learning. Int. Encycl. Educ. **2**, 6452–6457 (1992)

# Towards Competence Development
# for Industry 4.0

Milos Kravcik$^{(\boxtimes)}$, Xia Wang, Carsten Ullrich, and Christoph Igel

Educational Technology Laboratory, DFKI GmbH,
Alt-Moabit 91c, 10559 Berlin, Germany
Milos.Kravcik@dfki.de

**Abstract.** Technological changes always bring new opportunities and risks that can modify the existing marketplace. This is also valid for the Industry 4.0 trend, which raises hopes on one side and fears on the other. Especially small and medium-sized enterprises (SMEs) cannot ignore this challenge, if they want to prosper in the future. They certainly need technological support that can assist them in planning, steering, and monitoring the transition process as well as in up-skilling their employees. Design and development of such a system is the aim of the ADAPTION project. In this article we report on this ongoing work, especially on the tool using the newly created progress and maturity models, but also on the related competence development approach. These efforts should enhance the palette of novel methodologies and facilities that are needed to efficiently support workplace learning and training under new circumstances.

**Keywords:** Competence development · Workplace learning · Industry 4.0

## 1 Introduction

Intelligent tools (exploiting big data) transform work processes and it is difficult to predict related changes and their consequences [1]. The trend opens new opportunities and business executives should consider complementarities of humans and computers, to be successful in the marketplace. Another challenge is to establish organizational strategies for upskilling employees, focusing on competences that cannot be replaced by machines. The technological developments reform manufacturing and supply chains, where the competitive advantage in small and medium-sized enterprises (SMEs) depends on skilled labour and specialization. The *Industry 4.0* paradigm shift from resource-oriented planning to product-oriented planning is based on networking of intelligent machines and products, called *Cyber Physical Production Systems* (CPPS). With changing customer demands, the product will be able to request the necessary production resources autonomously. Consequently, the industrial workforce has to develop new competences in an efficient way, which requires novel education paradigms. The challenge is to develop new learning settings and measures for this purpose. To manage the related change process, it is crucial to win the support of employees. However, it is not quite clear how to successfully implement the organisational change, as the available theories and approaches are often lacking empirical evidence [2]. Critical success factors as well as methods for measuring the success of organisational change management are needed.

© Springer International Publishing AG, part of Springer Nature 2018
C. Penstein Rosé et al. (Eds.): AIED 2018, LNAI 10948, pp. 442–446, 2018.
https://doi.org/10.1007/978-3-319-93846-2_83

## 2   Related Work

In the past, there were various efforts to support professional learning. Building a technical and organizational infrastructure for lifelong competence development was already the aim of the TENCompetence project 10 years ago. Their demand-driven approach [3] was based on the qualification matrix, mapping the relevant tasks on the required competence profiles. Such a competence map was used by the staff for self-assessment. The resulting competence gap was analysed, in order to prioritise competence development needs. For the required competences, expert facilitators were identified, and competence networks were established. To support this methodology, the *Personal Competence Manager* was implemented [4], which at the individual level enabled goal setting (specification of the target competence profiles), self-assessment (to identify the knowledge gap), activity advise (selection of personal development plans), and progress monitoring (to support awareness and reflection).

As a major requirement is to develop new competences in the industrial workforce quickly and efficiently, breakthrough paradigms for continuous training of employees are needed. Previously, different approaches have been investigated. The ROLE project developed a flexible one based on the responsive and open learning environments [5], which was later customized for SMEs in the BOOST project [6]. The APPsist project implemented an advanced architecture with intelligent assistance and knowledge services at the shop floor [7]. The Learning Layers project aimed at the scalability issue, using mobile devices with collaboratively created and shared multimedia artefacts, e.g. adaptive video based on semantic annotations [8]. Affordances of augmented reality and wearable technology for capturing the expert's performance in order to support its re-enactment and expertise development are investigated in the WEKIT project [9].

A study on competence requirements in the digitized world of work [10] identifies the insufficient qualifications of employees as a major problem for the transition to Industry 4.0. Four main competence types were distinguished: Professional, Data and IT, Social, and Personal competences. The last two of them represent the soft skills, which are crucial and should be continuously developed. There is a big challenge to realize new forms of individualized and informal learning integrated in various settings (including workplace) and cultivating meta-cognitive skills (e.g. motivation and self-regulation). Key for Industry 4.0 are combinations of professional (especially production process and systemic knowledge) and IT competences (mainly data analysis, IT security and protection) with social (including cooperation, communication abilities) and personal (like lifelong and self-regulated learning, analytical ability, interdisciplinary thinking, problem solving) skills. Moreover, several dozens of other important competences were identified in this study, which need to be cultivated.

Business intelligence and analytics became an important area of study, which reflects the impact of data-related problems to be solved in contemporary business organizations [14]. In the age of big data, the emphasis in industry has shifted to data analysis and rapid business decision making based on huge amounts of information. Development of such competences requires trial-and-error and experimentation.

# 3    ADAPTION System

The ADAPTION project [11] aims at the individual support of SMEs in their transition towards Industry 4.0. Its approach is based on the progress and maturity models [12], taking into account the technical, organizational and personal aspects. The consortium put a lot of effort into the development of these models, when production system and workplace learning experts used their aggregated knowledge to formalize requirements for transition of companies to Industry 4.0. Moreover, the outcomes were intensively consulted with real SMEs regarding their appropriateness and usability. Currently, a software system is being developed, which facilitates the description of the current and target states of the company (Fig. 1), as well as the specification of actions that should be taken to overcome the identified gap (Fig. 2) and their evaluation. In larger companies it may not be easy to describe the current status consistently, as there can be differences between its various departments. Nevertheless, in all cases it is reasonable to focus on a suitable part of the company, which can be presented and assessed consistently. For similar reasons it is recommended to also consider a suitable time frame for the target status achievement (e.g. 6 months). The idea is to stay focused as well as to plan and monitor the progress properly.

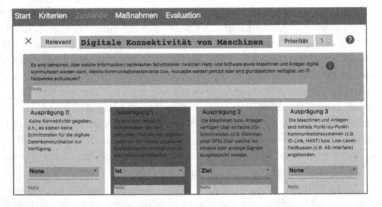

**Fig. 1.** Identification of the current and target status for one of 42 categories.

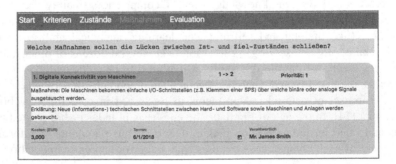

**Fig. 2.** Specification of operations that have to be performed to fill the existing gap between the current and target status for relevant categories.

# 4   ADAPTION Competence Development Concept

The operations specified to fill in the identified gap may include qualification and upskilling of employees. This should be concretely assigned to individual persons. In these cases, target competence profiles will be specified, suitable candidates, who can set up their goals and assess their current status of the required competences, in order to identify their personal competence gap, will be selected. They will then create their personal development plans (as a collection of learning resources) with the assistance of the system. Following the plan, they record their achievements and reflect on the progress, in comparison with the selected learning and training objectives.

As mentioned earlier, the related research includes an overview of the relevant competences for the Industry 4.0 area [10]. Based on the individual qualification goal the system will *advise resources* to acquire the relevant competences and *monitor progress*, supporting awareness and reflection of individual users. This means that the system will include both recommenders as well as learning analytics facilities. A good source of relevant learning resources is the MOOC *Hands on Industrie 4.0* (in German) presented by renowned experts from science and industry [15].

Following [13], we consider a service architecture with 4 layers: 1. *Data* – multimodal sensory fusion (e.g. physical environment, attention, affect), 2. *Basic Services* – data analysis (e.g. domain, user, context, pedagogical, adaptation model), 3. *Smart Services* intelligent multimodal assistance (in work) and knowledge (in training) services (e.g. guidance and recommendations, awareness and reflection). 4. *User Interface* – personalized and adaptive learning and training (e.g. with wearables and augmented reality), including soft and motor skill training as well as immersive procedural training (like capturing and re-enactment of expert performance). In order to gain the trust of the user, it is necessary to keep clear privacy rules as well as to provide explainable machine decisions. Later on, the system will be evaluated, using the Technology Acceptance Model.

# 5   Conclusion

Industry 4.0 changes the manufacturing world dramatically and especially SMEs need and deserve special support in order to be able to benefit from the new conditions. Such a transition includes change management at the technical, organizational as well as personal level. The ADAPTION project deals with design and development of a software system that can help identify the current and target status of the company, plan the necessary operations to overcome the existing gap as well as monitor and evaluate the progress. A crucial part of these changes represents the human factor with upskilling of the workforce and development of required competences. This work is in progress and in this paper we report on the current status of the software tool and the principles of the competence development approach.

**Acknowledgement.** The project underlying this report is funded by the German Federal Ministry of Education and Research under the funding code 02P14B023. Responsibility for the content of this publication lies with the authors.

# References

1. Zysman, J., Kenney, M.: The next phase in the digital revolution: intelligent tools, platforms, growth, employment. Commun. ACM **61**(2), 54–63 (2018)
2. Todnem By, R.: Organisational change management: a critical review. J. Change Manag. **5**(4), 369–380 (2005)
3. Kravcik, M., Koper, R., Kluijfhout, E.: TENCompetence training approach. In: Proceedings of EDEN 2007 Annual Conference, pp. 105–110 (2007)
4. Kluijfhout, E., Koper, R.: Building the technical and organisational infrastructure for lifelong competence development (2010)
5. Nussbaumer, A., Kravčík, M., Renzel, D., Klamma, R., Berthold, M., Albert, D.: A Framework for Facilitating Self-Regulation in Responsive Open Learning Environments. arXiv preprint arXiv:1407.5891 (2014)
6. Kravčík, M., Neulinger, K., Klamma, R.: Boosting vocational education and training in small enterprises. In: Verbert, K., Sharples, M., Klobučar, T. (eds.) EC-TEL 2016. LNCS, vol. 9891, pp. 600–604. Springer, Cham (2016). https://doi.org/10.1007/978-3-319-45153-4_72
7. Ullrich, C., Aust, M., Blach, R., Dietrich, M., Igel, C., Kreggenfeld, N., Kahl, D., Prinz, C., Schwantzer, S.: Assistance- and knowledge-services for smart production. In: Proceedings of the 15th International Conference on Knowledge Technologies and Data-Driven Business. ACM (2015)
8. Kravčík, M., Nicolaescu, P., Siddiqui, A., Klamma, R.: Adaptive video techniques for informal learning support in workplace environments. In: Wu, T.-T., Gennari, R., Huang, Y.-M., Xie, H., Cao, Y. (eds.) SETE 2016. LNCS, vol. 10108, pp. 533–543. Springer, Cham (2017). https://doi.org/10.1007/978-3-319-52836-6_57
9. Limbu, B., Fominykh, M., Klemke, R., Specht, M., Wild, F.: Supporting training of expertise with wearable technologies: the WEKIT reference framework. In: Yu, S., Ally, M., Tsinakos, A. (eds.) Mobile and Ubiquitous Learning. PRRE, pp. 157–175. Springer, Singapore (2018). https://doi.org/10.1007/978-981-10-6144-8_10
10. Schmid, U.: Kompetenzanforderungen für Industrie 4.0. mmb Institute (2017)
11. ADAPTION Homepage: http://www.adaption-projekt.de. Accessed 30 Jan 2018
12. Kravčík, M., Ullrich, C., Igel, C.: Supporting awareness and reflection in companies to move towards industry 4.0. In: Proceedings of the 7th Workshop on Awareness and Reflection in Technology Enhanced Learning (ARTEL). CEUR (2017)
13. Kravčík, M., Ullrich, C., Igel, C.: Towards industry 4.0: leveraging the internet of things for workplace learning and training. In: Proceedings of the Workshop on European TEL for Workplace Learning and Professional Development (2017)
14. Chen, H., Chiang, R.H., Storey, V.C.: Business intelligence and analytics: from big data to big impact. MIS Q. **36**, 1165–1188 (2012)
15. Kagermann, H., Meinel, C.: Hands on Industrie 4.0. mooc.house, Hasso Plattner Institute for Digital Engineering gGmbH (2016)

# Smart Learning Partner: An Interactive Robot for Education

Yu Lu[✉], Chen Chen, Penghe Chen, Xiyang Chen, and Zijun Zhuang

Advanced Innovation Center for Future Education, School of Educational Technology,
Beijing Normal University, Beijing 100875, China
{luyu,cchen,chenpenghe,chenxiyang,zhuangzijun}@bnu.edu.cn

**Abstract.** Driven by the latest technologies in artificial intelligence
(e.g., natural language processing and emotion recognition), we design
a novel robot system, called smart learning partner, to provide a more
pleasurable learning experience and better motivate learners. The self-
determination theory is used as the guideline to design its human-robot
interaction. The large-scale deployment of SLP in local schools and families would bring both research and commercial opportunities.

## 1 Introduction

Different from the formal education and massive open online course (MOOC)
platforms that mainly provide standard courses and learning resources, today's
education more emphasizes on providing intelligent and personalized learning
services for individual learners. Driven by the fast advancements in AI techniques, typically including natural language processing and emotion recognition,
the robot industry for education, especially for K-12 education, significantly
grows to satisfy the increasing demands for both schools and families in recent
years.

The existing educational robots, in general, can be divided into two categories. The first one, providing teachers' manipulative tools for students' learning
of scientific knowledge and skills, has been widely used in STEM (Science, Technology, Engineering and Mathematics) courses [1]. The second category mainly
belongs to socially assistive robotics [2], which assists learners through their
social interactions and daily activities.

In this paper, we introduce a novel robot, called smart learning partner
(SLP), which adopts the self-determination theory(SDT) [3] as the design principle to provide a more pleasurable learning experience and better motivate
learners during their interaction with the robot. Specifically, it provides the
personalized learner-robot interaction services by leveraging on the latest techniques, typically including the conversational agent, question-answering system
and emotion recognition. Different from most socially assistive robots targeting on pre-school or primary school students, the SLP robot mainly works as a
learning assistant for secondary school students.

© Springer International Publishing AG, part of Springer Nature 2018
C. Penstein Rosé et al. (Eds.): AIED 2018, LNAI 10948, pp. 447–451, 2018.
https://doi.org/10.1007/978-3-319-93846-2_84

## 2     System Description

From the perspective of system design, the SLP system can be simply divided into two modules, namely *learner interactive module* and *data aggregation module*, as illustrated in Fig. 1. We will elaborate the two modules respectively.

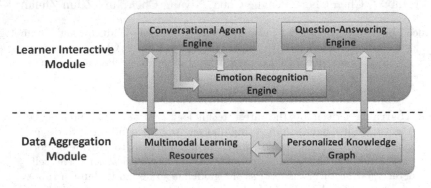

**Fig. 1.** The block diagram of SLP system

### 2.1     Learner-Robot Interactive Module

This module is the core of the SLP system, as it is mainly in charge of the learner-robot interaction. As mentioned earlier, SDT theory is used as the key design principles. Briefly speaking, SDT is a theory of human motivation and personality that highlights the importance of human inherent growth tendencies and innate psychological needs, typically including *autonomy*, *competence* and *relatedness*. The satisfaction of such psychological needs may effectively motivate learning process, incentivize learners, and eventually enhance their learning performance and achievement. In accordance with SDT, a number of strategies can be implemented and have been successfully applied in designing e-learning tools [4,5]. Similarly, we utilize such three psychological needs to design the module as below:

– *Autonomy*: it refers to the sense of volition or willingness when doing a task. Normally, choice, acknowledgment of feelings and opportunities for self-direction allow people a great feeling of autonomy. To satisfy a learner's autonomy, a dedicated question-answering (QA) engine is designed based on individual learner's personalized knowledge graph to generate questions and answers. Meanwhile, it provides multi-modal learning resources (e.g., videos and slides) for learners to choose. Figure 2(a) shows the SLP playing a micro-lecture video on the topic of factorization, and Fig. 2(b) demonstrates part of the corresponding learner's personal knowledge graph for mathematics subject. Moreover, by leveraging on the foreground camera on SLP, an emotion recognition engine is implemented to recognize learner's real-time emotion status from his or her facial expression(e.g., happiness, surprise and disgust), where the image-based multiple deep network learning is used [6]. Using such emotion detection results, we further enhance the interactive module to provide a more appropriate real-time feedback for learners. For example, when a learner keeps showing negative emotions (e.g., disgust) during the learning process, SLP may query about his or her current feelings or directly suggest the learner have a rest to alleviate the pressure.

- **Competence**: it refers to the need for a challenge and the feeling of effectance. To fulfill a learner's competence, SLP periodically provides positive feedback and incentives when the learner makes a significant progress on the current learning topic. Meanwhile, it tentatively encourages the learner to try a learning topic with a higher difficulty level.
- **Relatedness**: it refers to the feeling connected with others. To enhance a learner's relatedness to the robot, a dedicated conversational agent (CA) engine is designed to support casual chatting with learners. The designed CA is essentially a computer program which tries to generate human like responses during a conversation. Similar to other end-to-end non-goal-driven dialogue system [7], our CA system is mainly based on the generative probabilistic model. Moreover, we adopt face recognition techniques to automatically identify learner's identity, and accordingly use his or her name and favorite greetings at the beginning of different learning activities.

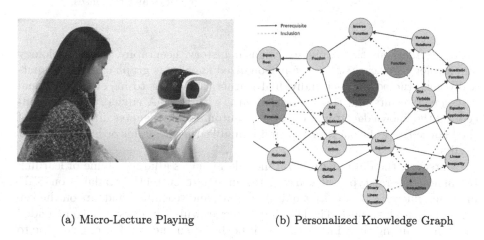

(a) Micro-Lecture Playing            (b) Personalized Knowledge Graph

**Fig. 2.** Personalized knowledge graph supporting question-answering and multi-modal learning resources

Table 1 summarizes the three psychological needs in SDT, design principles and our current implementations for this module.

## 2.2   Data Aggregation Module

As mentioned earlier, our SLP robot targets on the education for primary and secondary school students, and thus it currently supports a number of subjects,

**Table 1.** Design principle and implementation

| Psychological needs | Design principle | Current implementation |
|---|---|---|
| **Autonomy** (The sense of volition or willingness when doing a task) | • Providing choice and meaningful rationales for learning activities<br>• Acknowledge learner's feelings about the current study topics<br>• Minimizing pressure and control | • Question-answering engine with personalized knowledge graphs<br>• Emotion recognition engine with real-time feedback<br>• Multi-modal learning resources |
| **Competence** (The need for a challenge and the feeling of effectance) | • Providing positive comments and reinforcement during the learning process | • Periodically incentivizing learner's significant progress<br>• Properly encouraging learning topics at a higher difficulty level |
| **Relatedness** (Feeling connected with others) | • Conveying a personal, relevant and respectful messages and information | • Conversational agent for casual chatting with learners<br>• Learner identity recognition with personalized greetings and responses |

including mathematics, Chinese, English, history, geography, physics, biology and ideology. For each subject, a personalized knowledge graph can be automatically constructed for each individual learner, according to his or her personal assessment results and the interaction data with the QA engine. For each concept on the knowledge graph, the system automatically denotes different level of the knowledge proficiency for that individual learner using his or her assessment results.

Moreover, the data aggregation module manages a large volume of learning resources. Several types of learning resources are currently available on SLP, including micro-lecture videos, quiz questions, and teaching handouts on the key concepts of each subject. The learning resources will be selectively recommended to learners during their interaction with both QA engine and CA engine. Due to the limited space, we will not elaborate the recommendation algorithm design in this paper.

## 3    Conclusion and Deployment

We introduce our SLP robot system, which emphasizes on the interaction with individual learner and satisfying learners' innate psychological needs. We adopt the SDT as the design guideline, and the latest techniques in emotion recognition, CA and QA systems. We are currently working with the local government agencies to deploy SLP to more than 60 local schools and their students.

**Acknowledgment.** This research is partially supported by the National Natural Science Foundation of China (No. 61702039), and the Humanities and Social Sciences Foundation of the Ministry of Education of China (No. 17YJCZH116).

# References

1. Alimisis, D.: Educational robotics: open questions and new challenges. Themes Sci. Technol. Educ. **6**(1), 63–71 (2013)
2. Feil-Seifer, D., Matarić, M.J.: Socially assistive robotics. IEEE Robot. Autom. Mag. **18**(1), 24–31 (2011)
3. Ryan, R.M., Deci, E.L.: Self-determination theory and the facilitation of intrinsic motivation, social development, and well-being. Am. Psychol. **55**(1), 68 (2000)
4. Henkemans, O., et al.: Design and evaluation of a personal robot playing a self-management education game with children with diabetes type 1. Int. J. Hum. Comput. Stud. **106**, 63–76 (2017)
5. Jeno, L.M., Grytnes, J.A., Vandvik, V.: The effect of a mobile-application tool on biology students' motivation and achievement in species identification: a self-determination theory perspective. Comput. Educ. **107**, 1–12 (2017)
6. Yu, Z., Zhang, C.: Image based static facial expression recognition with multiple deep network learning. In: Proceedings of the 2015 ACM on International Conference on Multimodal Interaction, pp. 435–442. ACM (2015)
7. Serban, I.V., Sordoni, A., Bengio, Y., Courville, A.C., Pineau, J.: Building end-to-end dialogue systems using generative hierarchical neural network models. In: AAAI, vol. 16, pp. 3776–3784 (2016)

# Short-Term Efficacy and Usage Recommendations for a Large-Scale Implementation of the Math-Whizz Tutor

Manolis Mavrikis[1]($\boxtimes$), David Sebastian Schlepps[1], and Junaid Mubeen[2]

[1] UCL Knowledge Lab, University College London, London, UK
m.mavrikis@ucl.ac.uk
[2] Whizz Education, London, UK
junaid.mubeen@whizzeducation.com

**Abstract.** This paper adds to the evidence of the efficacy of intelligent tutoring systems (ITS) in mathematics learning by evaluating a large-scale intervention at the state of Aguascalientes, Mexico. We report the results of a quasi-experimental study, addressing at the same a particular request of the decision-makers responsible for the rollout to provide, from early stages of the intervention, independent evidence of the efficacy of Math-Whizz Tutor beyond its internal metrics, and recommendations in terms of the expected weekly usage levels to guide the blended learning approach.

**Keywords:** Intelligent tutoring systems · Evaluation · Large-scale

## 1 Introduction

Although there is mounting evidence that intelligent tutoring systems, under the right conditions, can offer a significant advantage in supporting students' learning [1, 8], understandably educators or other stakeholders responsible for their adoption require evidence of large-scale evaluations and specific recommendations about classroom integration in their context.

Our case study involves the rollout of the intelligent tutoring system, Math-Whizz, in the state of Aguascalientes, Mexico. While previous studies have demonstrated positive results (e.g. [6, 9]) and Whizz Education has developed global usage guidelines for implementations based on historical data, the decision-makers in charge of the state-wide adoption required (i) guidance on how much time students should spend on the Math-Whizz tutor each week, and (ii) independent evidence, at early stages of the roll-out, that demonstrates the intervention's potential in their context.

This paper presents our approach to providing weekly usage recommendations for Math-Whizz in Aguascalientes based on internal system metrics, and reports the results of a quasi-experimental study evaluating the efficacy of the overall approach using a mixture of standardized exams and locally appropriate tests. The late addressing the common concern in the field that the type of test affects evaluation results [4]. As such, beyond the

© Springer International Publishing AG, part of Springer Nature 2018
C. Penstein Rosé et al. (Eds.): AIED 2018, LNAI 10948, pp. 452–457, 2018.
https://doi.org/10.1007/978-3-319-93846-2_85

results of interest to the specific study, the paper makes a methodological contribution and aims to add to the debate of efficacy of intelligent tutoring systems in general.

## 2  Math-Whizz

Math-Whizz is an intelligent online tutor for 5 to 13-year-olds. It comprises 1200 learning objectives which have been organised into 22 topics and sequenced within each topic based on a curriculum map developed by educationalists. Maths-Whizz is being used by hundreds of schools in eight international territories and currently serves over 150,000 students worldwide (Fig. 1).

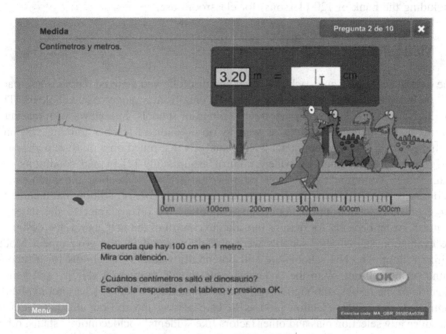

**Fig. 1.** An example of a Maths-Whizz exercise

The student experience begins with an adaptive assessment that measures the student's knowledge across several maths topics. The tutor then guides students through an individualised learning pathway, privileging topics in which the student is behind with the goal of helping each student achieve a rounded learning profile.

Each lesson begins with a Teaching Page, which uses direct instruction to introduce the concept or method. This is followed by an interactive exercise, which use rich visual representations and scaffolded prompts to guide learners. During the exercise, a student receives hints (including the solution). If a student passes a certain threshold of correct answers, they are given a test where they can demonstrate what they learnt in a different context than the initial activity.

The tutor uses real-time learner data to offer remedial support when students are stuck and advancing them when they have demonstrated a good understanding of each learning objective. The topic sequencing policy thus relies on the assumption that a student will be able to solve the exercises of the selected difficulty level and only advances students when they have acquired the relevant prior knowledge. As such it implements a type of mastery learning approach, guided by its internal metric, 'Maths Age'™, which has a natural interpretation: a Maths Age of nine corresponds to the knowledge expected of a nine-year old according the curriculum map. Maths Age is calculated for each topic, and an arithmetic mean is then assigned as an overall Maths Age for each student. Maths Age is aimed at informing teachers and parents about students' mathematics ability [9]. In addition, the overall platform offers live reports as a monitoring tool for teachers, as well as a collection of instructional resources (including the bank of 1200 lessons) for classroom use.

## 3  Methodology

The overall evaluation approach in Aguascalientes followed a mixed methods approach that included both qualitative and quantitative data from a range of stakeholders. The qualitative part relies on observations in a range of schools, interviews with teachers, parents and students themselves as well as observation of teacher training sessions. In this paper, we focus on the quantitative analysis that relied on a quasi-experimental design, particularly a non-equivalent control group study [2] in two conditions: the Math-Whizz condition (MW) with schools that are implementing the intervention (and take part in the teacher training), and the non-users (NU) condition that included a range of state schools throughout Aguascalientes. We do not refer to the latter as 'control' group because, for reasons outside the control of the first author, the design of the evaluation started after schools were already selected for the government Math-Whizz rollout. The NU schools are still potentially future MW schools for a second round of the roll-out. With the understandable threats to internal validity and gener-alisation of the results, although the group assignment (MW vs NU) was not explicitly controlled, the initial selection process to take part in the roll-out did not seem to introduce any selection bias and other factors like students' socioeconomic status, other government metrics were the same. All schools were also following the same cur-riculum and the main difference between the MW and NU schools were that the MW schools took time out of the normal class for the students to interact with Math-Whizz.

The focus of the work reported here are the primary school students aged between 8 and 9 years old. This is because of the availability of state-wide data from the Mexican PLANEA test (see http://www.planea.sep.gob.mx/), which we used as an achievement 'snapshot'. The need to provide an independent evaluation of the intervention at early stages meant that we could not rely on a state-administered test to measure students' levels of achievement as these are run at the start and end of the year. Due to other factors, including holidays and other school priorities we also had a limited time window (7 weeks) in which to apply a test. We used the corresponding PLANEA that runs every September as a pre-test (with relevant permissions granted). For the post-test (end of October) we selected 10 questions from the 'numbers and counting' and 'addition' problems, as these were among the topics covered by Maths-Whizz at this period. We will refer to these tests as Sep and Oct respectively from now on. Internal consistency for the Sep test was $\alpha = 0.85$ and for Oct $\alpha = .76$. Note that Whizz Education did not make any changes to their adaptive algorithm, nor were they aware of the exact contents of the test, which was the responsibility of the first author.

# 4 Results

Due to the short duration of the implementation, we were pragmatic and did not expect large effect size in learning gains between the two conditions, particularly given the difficulty of isolating the effects of a complex socio-technical intervention to just the introduction of an ITS system. Nevertheless, despite the limitations (discussed in Sect. 5), the results are promising and warrant further research.

For a sample of 3407 4th grade students ($N_{MW} = 2188$, $N_{NU} = 1219$), results were obtained using a linear regression model that resembles the ANCOVA method for measuring change in time and using cluster robust and heteroscedasticity-consistent standard errors [3, 7]. Accounting for the differences in students' test achievement in September, the predicted achievement score for Maths-Whizz users in the sample is 0.659 points on a scale 0 to 10 higher than non-Whizz users ($\beta = 0.659$, $p < 0.05$).

If the change is not due to unobserved variables, this significant difference in progress seems associated with the Whizz intervention. Accounting for previous achievement and for whether students belong to the Whizz user group explains around 18.6% of the differences in students' scores in October. A corresponding multilevel model suggests very similar values with an effect size of about $d = 0.22$, commensurate with others in the area (e.g. [5]). Analysing the interaction effect of students' condition and their initial achievement in September, we found no significant relationship ($\beta = -0.086$ $\beta = 0.659$, $p > 0.05$), suggesting that the relationship between students' improvement and their membership in the Whizz user group did not depend on their previous achievement.

To derive both a recommendation for teachers and parents in relation to usage levels and a way to group students for analysis, we conducted a linear regression of time in the system again the internal Math Age metric of the system for the Mexico cohort.

This showed that a student needs to use the system approximately 33 min per week to achieve a progress rate of one (which corresponds to an expected increase of Maths Age of 1.00 over one year) and 45 min for a Progress Rate of 1.50. These findings are consistent with Whizz's global recommendations, suggesting that the effort required by Aguascalientes students to achieve learning gains on Maths-Whizz is comparable to the rest of the world. Accordingly, we create groups of high usage (45 min or more), minimum recommended usage (34–44 min), low usage (5–33 min) and very low (less than five mins) and conducted an additional cluster-robust and heteroscedasticity-consistent regression analysis [7] of the September and October test scores (Fig. 2).

Among other interesting results, we observe, first no significant difference between non-users and those who used the software less than five minutes ($\beta = 0.081$, $p > 0.05$). The high usage group is associated with an additional 1.26 point progress

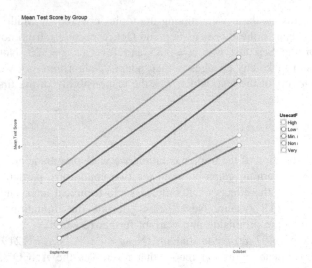

**Fig. 2.** Mean score in Sep. and Oct. by usage group

compared to the non-user group ($\beta = 1.255$, p < .001). Similarly, a significant difference to the progress of the non-user group was found for minimum usage ($\beta = 0.969$,
p < 0.01) and low usage ($\beta = 0.831$, p < .01). We briefly discuss these below.

## 5  Discussion

The results from the evaluation described in this paper add to the evidence of the
efficacy of intelligent tutoring systems (ITS) in mathematics learning in a large-scale
implementation at the state of Aguascalientes in Mexico. Of course, the disentanglement of causal relationships between the use of any technology and learning outcomes
and other factors that may distort the view on such relationships, is a well-known
problem in the field[1]. As the data are from a real live context, some factors were outside
the scope of this study and of course, this raises some limitations here. For example,
there could be systematic differences between schools or homes that, unknown to us,
led implicitly to initial intervention selection or self-selection in usage groups. The lack
of any significant difference in the learning gains of non-users and those Whizz users
with minimal usage, speaks against a selection bias that arises from prior differences
between the groups. However, further studies should investigate the relationship of
previous achievement and usage.

Lastly, qualitative and teacher survey data (not discussed here), paint a positive
picture for the overall implementation attributing to its success other factors such as the
intense professional development offered to the teachers and strong parental involvement at home. Taking also into account the novelty of the intervention and findings

---

[1] c.f. OECD http://www.oecd.org/education/students-computers-and-learning-97892642
39555-en.htm.

from meta-analysis such as [8] that short-term interventions appear generally more successful than more lengthy ones, future work should look at large-scale and long-term experimental evaluation that takes into account government initiatives on pupil testing, a robust sampling procedure and testing instruments and a systematic way to include student and teacher opinions and their role in the intervention.

**Acknowledgements.** This evaluation was possible with co-funding and support from the State of Aguascalientes. We would like to thank the teachers and students who took part in the studies and colleagues at UCL and Whizz Education for the support with the data analysis.

# References

1. du Boulay, B.: Artificial intelligence as an effective classroom assistant. IEEE Intell. Syst. **31**(6), 76–81 (2016)
2. Fife-Schaw, C.: Quasi-experimental designs. In: Breakwell, G.M., Hammond, S., Fife-Schaw, C., Smith, J.A. (eds.) Research Methods in Psychology. SAGE (2006)
3. Graham, N., Arai, M., Hagströmer, B.: multiwayvcov: Multi-Way Standard Error Clustering. R version 1.2.3 (2016). https://CRAN.R-project.org/package=multiwayvcov
4. Kulik, J.A., Fletcher, J.D.: Effectiveness of intelligent tutoring systems: a meta-analytic review. Rev. Educ. Res. **86**, 42–78 (2016)
5. Roschelle, J., Feng, M., Murphy, R.F., Mason, C.A.: Online mathematics homework increases student achievement. AERA Open **2**(4) (2016)
6. Schlepps, D.S.: Intelligent Tutoring Systems in K-12 Education – An Evaluative Study of Maths- Whizz and Maths Age. Unpublished MA dissertation. UCL (2015)
7. Snijders, T., Bosker, R.: Multilevel Analysis: An Introduction to Basic and Advanced Multilevel Modeling, 2nd edn. Sage Publishers, London (2012)
8. Steenbergen-Hu, S., Cooper, H.: A meta-analysis of the effectiveness of intelligent tutoring systems on K–12 students' mathematical learning. J. Educ. Psychol. **105**(4), 970–987 (2013)
9. Whizz Education Ltd.: FAQs. Parents Help (2015). http://www.whizz.com/help/parents-help/. Accessed 2 Feb 2017
10. Yearly, S.: Report by Simon Yearley. In: Pedagogical Foundations and Evidence of Impact for Maths-Whizz (2014)

# Leveraging Non-cognitive Student Self-reports to Predict Learning Outcomes

Kaśka Porayska-Pomsta[1]([✉]), Manolis Mavrikis[1], Mutlu Cukurova[1], Maria Margeti[2], and Tej Samani[2]

[1] UCL Knowledge Lab, University College London, London, UK
K.Porayska-Pomsta@ucl.ac.uk
[2] Performance Learning Education Ltd., London, UK

**Abstract.** Metacognitive competencies related to cognitive tasks have been shown to be a powerful predictor of learning. However, considerably less is known about the relationship between student's metacognition related to non-cognitive dimensions, such as their affect or lifestyles, and academic performance. This paper presents a preliminary analysis of data gathered by Performance Learning Education (*PL*), with respect to students' self-reports on non-cognitive dimensions as possible predictors of their academic outcomes. The results point to the predictive potential of such self-reports, to the importance of students exercising their self-understanding during learning, and to the potentially critical role of incorporating such student's self-reports in learner modelling.

## 1 Introduction

Academic performance is typically measured through assessments on standardised tests, which are often used formatively together with teachers' assessments of students' attitudes and motivation to predict final grades on high-stake exams. However, there is no standardised way in which the predicted grades do actually reflect students' attitudinal and motivational traits. Although the importance of students' emotions, motivation and lifestyles to learning is confirmed by substantial research [1], the lack of teacher training with respect to 'diagnosing' students motivation and attitudes, coupled with the known challenges related to accessing reliably other people's mental states (e.g. [2], leads to a whole variety of subjective judgements which are hard to validate and operationalise in everyday educational practices.

Owing to a prevalent emphasis on subject-specific education together with a predominantly didactic, *'teacher in charge of the assessments'* approaches that are adopted in mainstream education, one aspect which is often overlooked in school contexts is the value of engaging students in their own assessments, for example through self-reporting on how they feel, what motivates them and what they consider the possible barriers to their learning. Such self-assessments, involving the metacognitive competencies of self-monitoring, play a crucial role

© Springer International Publishing AG, part of Springer Nature 2018
C. Penstein Rosé et al. (Eds.): AIED 2018, LNAI 10948, pp. 458–462, 2018.
https://doi.org/10.1007/978-3-319-93846-2_86

in allowing students to reflect on their experiences, motivation and attitudes and in helping them first, to understand their own behaviours, and second, to plan actions, set goals and aspirations, and ultimately – to make informed decisions [3].

Although metacognitive competencies have been established as a powerful predictor of learning [4], they have been mainly examined in literature and applied in educational practice in relation to subject specific tasks, e.g. in explaining away problem solving [5]. Self-explanations by students in relation to socio-emotional, attitudinal and life-style choices do not figure explicitly on the mainstream curriculum agenda, despite the observed benefits, because: (1) it is not clear to what extent students' self-explanations in relation to such non-cognitive dimensions are actually reflected in their academic performance; (2) asking students to self-explain in terms of such dimensions may be considered intrusive, especially in whole classroom situations. AIED approaches, especially those concerned with learner modelling and open learner models, can potentially address both those concerns and provide a powerful means for supporting students in engaging in self-monitoring and in self-regulation.

In this paper we present a preliminary analysis of data generated by Performance Learning Education (PL) in live high-stakes intervention contexts in two schools (A and B), involving a total of 48 students aged 16–17 preparing for pre-university examinations. We describe the self-reporting instrument (PLOA) used to elicit responses from the students on key aspects of their socio-emotional states and lifestyle habits related to a potential risk of their underachieving in their exams.

## 2  Performance Learning Online Assessment: PLOA

PL supports schools in raising students' academic achievement as measured through high-stakes exams, which are required for entry to university, further educational, or professional development. The company works at all levels of education from primary and secondary, through further education to the university level. Its main user base are state-funded schools catering for pupil cohorts from low socio-economic backgrounds. The attainment in those schools tends to be poor and often below national average, with many pupils leading hectic lives and not prioritising or valuing academic achievement.

PL's approach emphasises the importance of students developing a good understanding of their own strengths and weaknesses along with the possible causes for both. Its approach is structured around four overlapping trait categories known to be of critical importance to students' learning and development: (i) *motivation*, linked to student's goal orientation; (ii) *organisation* related to the executive functions of planning and attentional control; (iii) *memory* broadly related to attentional control and cognitive flexibility; (iv) *lifestyle* related to sleep and physical and emotional wellbeing of the students. There are two elements to PL: (1) self-assessment by students aimed to ascertain their strengths and weaknesses along the four trait categories described; (2) curriculum, which coaches students in how to attend to specific aspects of their lifestyles, attitudes, emotions and goal management.

The students' self-assessments (henceforth referred to as PLOA) are conducted online at the start and end of pupils' PL's curriculum, to establish any changes in their self-assessments over time. Twenty eight questions are used to elicit self-assessment from individual students in relation to the four categories assessed. Student's responses are scaffolded through multiple choice questions that are associated with each trait category, each question linked to a risk level (1: low risk, to 5: high risk), with each level representing the relative degree to which a particular trait may be a barrier to a given student's academic achievement. For example, if under the motivation category a student declares that they cannot cope with and tend to panic under pressure, this is linked to a relatively high PLOA risk level. PLOA scores associated with each student answer choice are aggregated at the end of the assessment and an overall PLOA is calculated using a PL's proprietary weighted means function which is further associated with percentage ranges; the lower the percentage, the higher the PLOA risk level. For further details about PL's approach and the development thereof see [6].

## 3   Data Analysis and Results

Two UK schools which use PL as an approach to raise student attainment have been included in the analysis presented. Both are co-educational secondary schools, catering for between 400 (School A) and 1300 (School B) pupils aged 11–18 years old. In both schools there is an equal boy-girl ratio and both schools have a medium to high free school meals percentage which is used as a key socio-economic school indicator in the UK. Additionally, school A has a special educational needs provision for pupils with moderate learning difficulties.

Initial and final PLOA, gathered before and after PL intervention, were used in the analysis, along with the estimated exam grades (EEGs) and final exam grades. Both sets of grades were provided by the schools and were based on subject-specific tests and, in case of EEGs, on test results and assessments of individual students' attitude and overall effort in each subject. For both schools Pearson correlations coefficient analysis revealed significant correlations between students' PLOA and their final overall grades (School A $N = 35$, $r = .583$, $p < .001$); (School B $N = 13$, $r = .878, p < .001$). Partial correlations analysis for each subject for which PL intervention was given, revealed a similar pattern. In addition, a paired-samples t-test was conducted to test the change in the initial and final PLOA. As expected, this significant increase was also apparent in each school. School A: Initial PLOA ($M = 48.522$, $SD = 10.293$) vs. final PLOA ($M = 53.456$, $SD = 11.617$) $t(34) = 12.646, p < 0.00$; School B: Initial PLOA ($M = 56.269$, $SD = 10.934$) vs. the final PLOA ($M = 56.654$, $SD = 11.998$), $t(12) = 7.028, p < 0.00$.

As part of a regression analysis, we explored the respective potential of (i) the EEGs and (ii) EEGs together with PLOA in predicting the final exam grades. The results show that EEGs alone explain 26.1% of the variance of the average final score, whereas EEGs with PLOA explain 29.7% of the variance. This statistically significant increase in variance suggests that using both predictors as part of a regression model is more accurate when EEGs and PLOA are used together. The results are summarised in Table 1.

**Table 1.** Regression coefficients and statistics

| Predictors | School A (N = 36) | | | School B (N = 13) | | |
|---|---|---|---|---|---|---|
| | Coefficients | t | Sig. | Coefficients | t | Sig. |
| Constant | −1.97 | −1.96 | .058 | −1.614 | −1.661 | .128 |
| Overall initial score | .504 | 4.341 | .000 | .181 | 1.147 | .278 |
| Final PLOA score | .489 | 4.217 | .000 | .800 | 5.069 | .000 |
| Overall model | $r = .764$, $r^2 = .584$, $p<.00$ | | | $r = .893$, $r^2 = .798$, $p<.00$ | | |

To help interpret these results, and given that the long term goal of this research is to automate the process of predicting student learning outcomes (here as measured by exam grades) in order to offer personalised support to different students, we also aggregated the data across schools and subjects. As expected, there is a significant increase in the PLOA for the aggregated data set $t(47) = 7.028, p = p < .00$. The corresponding regression analysis also resulted in a significant model, $F(2, 45) = 19.383$, $p < .001$, $r = .680$, $R^2 = .463$ with both EEGs and PLOA being significant predictors ($score_f = -1.166 + .617 * score_i + .053 * ploa_f$, standardized Beta $score_i = .416$, $ploa_f = .459$, $p < .000$).

## 4 Discussion and Conclusions

Whilst the main limitation of the analysis presented is that it is based on small number of students, the fact that the PLOA increases significantly suggests that the PL's curriculum, which coaches students in how to attend to specific aspects of their lifestyles, attitudes, emotions and goal management is effective. The regression analysis suggests that final PLOA together with EEGs predict the final scores better than either one alone. To contextualise this, the regression function together with the corresponding coefficients indicate that as the average initial score increases the average final score will increase by around 62% (if the final PLOA is held constant). Similarly, as the final PLOA increases by one unit (one percentage), the average final score will increase by 5% (if the initial score is held constant). Considering that these results were generated in low-achieving schools in which the students taking part in the PL intervention are the lowest of the achievers, together with the fact that the intervention was of a relatively short duration (a total of eight hours per school), provides a particularly powerful motivation for investing further in understanding and modelling the relationship between students' self-explanations and metacognitive competencies, especially as relates to students' attitudes, motivation and lifestyles, and their academic achievement in high-stakes exams. The results also suggest that providing a systematic and consistent way in which student's can self-report on those 'non-cognitive' aspects of their learning may be an important learning and assessment tool.

In summary, the results of the analysis presented in this paper are promising with respect to supporting the long-term goal of this research to develop and automate further the student self-reporting functionality of the PL approach.

# References

1. Immordino-Yang, M.H., Damasio, A.: We feel, therefore we learn: the relevance of affective and social neuroscience to education. Mind Brain Educ. 1(1), 3–10 (2007)
2. Porayska-Pomsta, K., Mavrikis, M., D'Mello, S., Conati, C., Baker, R.S.J.: Knowledge elicitation methods for affect modelling in education. Int. J. Artif. Intell. Educ. 22(3), 107–140 (2013)
3. Terricone, P.: The taxonomy of metacognition (2011)
4. Richardson, M., Abraham, C., Bond, R.: Psychological correlates of university students' academic performance: a systematic review and meta-analysis. Psychol. Bull. 138(2), 353 (2012)
5. Aleven, V.A., Koedinger, K.R.: An effective metacognitive strategy: learning by doing and explaining with a computer-based cognitive tutor. Cognit. Sci. 26(2), 147–179 (2002)
6. Samani, T., Porayska-Pomsta, K., Luckin, R.: Bridging the gap between high and low performing pupils through performance learning online analysis and curricula. In: André, E., Baker, R., Hu, X., Rodrigo, M.M.T., du Boulay, B. (eds.) AIED 2017. LNCS (LNAI), vol. 10331, pp. 650–655. Springer, Cham (2017). https://doi.org/10. 1007/978-3-319-61425-0_82

# ITADS: A Real-World Intelligent Tutor
# to Train Troubleshooting Skills

Sowmya Ramachandran[1(✉)], Randy Jensen[1], Jeremy Ludwig[1],
Eric Domeshek[1], and Thomas Haines[2]

[1] Stottler Henke Associates Inc., San Mateo, CA 94402, USA
Sowmya@stottlerhenke.com
[2] Comtech TCS, Pensacola 32502, USA

**Abstract.** Real-world intelligent tutoring systems are important ambassadors for promoting wide adoption of the technology. Questions about affordability, quality control, operational readiness, training effectiveness, and user acceptance are significant in this context. This paper describes ITADS, an intelligent tutor developed to provide a problem-based, experiential learning tool to complement schoolhouse training. The goal was to train US Navy Information Systems Technology support staff in troubleshooting skills through the use of realistic simulations and automated assessment and feedback. This paper describes the tutoring system and a preliminary validation study of its training effectiveness. The results demonstrate that the system is effective in improving troubleshooting knowledge and skills. The ITADS system was successfully developed in twenty-six months from requirements to validation, following strict systems engineering procedures. The results of the training effectiveness study indicate that the ITS also leads to significantly improved performance among Navy IT recruits in troubleshooting tasks.

**Keywords:** Intelligent tutoring system · Automated performance assessment
Troubleshooting skills · IT skill training

## 1 Introduction

While research and development of intelligent tutoring systems (ITS) has been ongoing for decades and many significant advances have been made, tutoring systems for training real-world, professional skills have been emerging [2]. These systems are developed under the constraints of operational-level software development with its attendant emphasis on cost-effectiveness, ambitious development schedules, and rigorous software engineering processes. Proof of effectiveness is also an important consideration when developing such systems. This paper describes a highly immersive, situated intelligent tutoring system called ITADS, that targets professional training and was developed under real-world budgetary and schedule constraints. The focus of this paper in on the results of a study of its training effectiveness. We will first describe the ITS and then present the study.

© Springer International Publishing AG, part of Springer Nature 2018
C. Penstein Rosé et al. (Eds.): AIED 2018, LNAI 10948, pp. 463–468, 2018.
https://doi.org/10.1007/978-3-319-93846-2_87

## 2  ITADS Overview

ITADS is an intelligent tutoring system for training U.S. Navy entry level Information Systems Technology (IT) support staff. The target audience for the ITS are the new recruits who attend the Navy's IT-A school and have limited on-the-job experience with troubleshooting fleet IT systems. The ITS is intended to serve as a bridge between schoolhouse training and on-the-job skills required on the fleet.

ITADS uses the problem-based learning approach to teach troubleshooting skills. The majority of its training is conducted in the context of real-world problems as encountered in a simulation environment. A training scenario presents a student with an IT trouble ticket that he/she must address following the Navy's six-step troubleshooting procedure [1].

The simulation consists of a dedicated virtual IT network of virtual machines (VMs) that is an exact representation of the Naval Shipboard IT network. Thus, the simulation is designed to provide real, hands-on experience of an IT watchstander's responsibilities. Each scenario has an associated VM network in which a fault has been introduced to reflect the training scenario. The student's task is to perform tests on the VM network to identify and fix the fault. ITADS automatically assesses performance and provides adaptive coaching and feedback. The assessments are also used to maintain a dynamic student model representing the mastery of the student on domain knowledge, skills and abilities (KSAs). The Tutor can function in either of two modes – Tutoring On and Tutoring Off. In the Tutoring On mode, the Tutor provides full intelligent tutoring capability. This includes monitoring and assessing student performance on simulation exercises as well as providing coaching, feedback, and an after-action review (AAR). In the Tutoring Off mode, the Tutor assesses student progress and performance on an exercise but does not provide coaching or feedback.

The main objective of ITADS is to teach troubleshooting skills. The Navy prescribes the following six-step troubleshooting procedure: 1. identify and replicate the reported problem, 2. establish a theory of a probable cause, 3. test the theory to determine the cause, 4. establish a plan of action to resolve the problem and implement the solution, 5. verify full system functionality and, if applicable, implement preventative measures, and 6. document findings, actions, and outcomes.

Given an IT troubleshooting problem in the form a symptom report (also called a trouble or service ticket), students are expected to form hypotheses about underlying faults. Based on a mental model of IT systems, they must select actions to perform in the VMs to test their hypothesis and observe and interpret the results of those actions. The refutation of candidate faults and the selection of a root cause are the most important inferences students must learn to make. Students adopt troubleshooting strategies based on their mental models and currently available information, perform actions based on their intentions, observe the results, interpret the results, and make inferences to refine their hypotheses. This cycle is repeated until they identify the fault.

Since training troubleshooting skills is an important objective for ITADS, assessing and coaching the knowledge supporting troubleshooting inferences is critical. When it comes to assessing student expertise and knowledge about the target system at a functional and system level, the inferences and strategies are at least as important as the actions performed. Unfortunately, inferences and strategies are not directly observable by the automated tutor. The problem, then, is how to augment the simulation-based tutor so it can elicit some useful aspects of the student's decision-making rationale, while keeping the focus on the troubleshooting process rather than making rationale dialogs the centerpiece of interaction. In developing ITADS, any solution with high module or content costs was eliminated from consideration, as this would have been inconsistent with the project's budget and objectives. Thus, we rejected designs requiring full natural language and speech processing.

A custom user interface panel was designed for rationale elicitation. Like the tutor developed by [3], ITADS presents rationales as a set of failure hypotheses that students update throughout an exercise. Figure 1 shows the user interface for hypothesis refinement called the Probably Causes Panel. The Probable Causes Panel is pre-populated with a set of hypotheses at the start of the exercise. The hypotheses are automatically generated from assessment model that establishes connections between observed system behavior and potential system faults [4]. The assessment model was developed with close guidance from SMEs. The pre-populated list of hypotheses includes distractors that can be generated from the model and also specified by subject matter experts (SMEs) using the ITADS Authoring Tool.

**Fig. 1.** Probable Causes Panel in the Tutor GUI

Students can refute a hypothesis singly or as a group using the red "x" button. They can assert or confirm a single hypothesis using the green "check-mark" button. Currently ITADS operates on a single-fault assumption, which limits the assertions to a single hypothesis. Groups of hypotheses can be expanded or collapsed as needed. This is a single-turn interaction in that the tutor provides feedback after every rationale update but does not follow up with additional probing. It is also an *ongoing* interaction because the panel remembers and displays the state of all considered hypotheses based on earlier actions. The student is free to choose the timing and extent of their rationale updates. Only one type of update is enforced and that is the assertion of their final problem diagnosis before students can move on to the fault repair phase.

Assessments of student performance are primarily based on Probable Causes Panel updates [4]. Simulation actions are indirectly assessed based on these updates. This gives students a greater degree of freedom to find alternate paths to a diagnosis since the tutor does not force them into any particular scripted action sequence.

For assessment of their reasoning process and system knowledge based on Probable Causes Panel updates, the tutor maintains a model relating simulator actions to fault hypotheses. When a student asserts or refutes a hypothesis, the tutor uses the model to check the consistency of the assertion (or refutation) with all the diagnostic information revealed to the student up to that point in the scenario (i.e., information given at the start of the scenario or revealed subsequently by student actions). An inconsistent hypothesis update is assessed as an incorrect inference. When a hypothesis is asserted, the tutor automatically scores the remaining hypotheses as refutations due to the single-fault assumption.

There is coaching available in the form of feedback and hints throughout the diagnosis task. ITADS provides process-oriented feedback wherein an incorrect assertion leads to a tutor-generated message about the last action that provides evidence against that assertion. This context-sensitive feedback is automatically generated from the assessment model. The Tutor provides hints that are generated using a greedy search approach for determining the best solution path from the current state. When a student finishes an exercise, the Tutor presents an after-action review (AAR). Here the student can review a summary of their overall performance in the exercise, their performance on primary learning objectives for the exercise, and receive a final exercise performance score as determined by the Tutor. The AAR can also include interactive, form-based dialogs between the ITS and the student to promote reflection.

The ability to control and maintain content without relying on outside contractors was an important project requirement. The ITADS system includes an authoring tool to enable end user organizations to modify and create scenarios. Users can create, edit, and delete training scenarios, and scaffolding content like hints and dialogs. The authoring tool provides an integrated development environment for creating and editing various kinds of content data using a set of incorporated custom tools.

## 3   ITADS Training Effectiveness Evaluation

We conducted a summative evaluation to study the learning gains resulting from ITADS. We conducted a controlled experiment with two independent groups of students drawn from a population representative of the target trainees.

- The experimental group went through a complete program of training with ITADS.
- The control group only went through the didactic lessons.

Both groups were administered a common post-test. The differences in post-test performance of the two groups provided derived measures for comparison and analysis in the evaluation of earning gains attributable to the use of ITADS.

The purpose of the evaluation was to study the added value that ITADS provides over their existing training program. Therefore, we did not provide the control group with alternative programs of training on the same content.

The post-test was performed using ITADS. The Tutor Off mode of ITADS system was designed for performance assessment without any coaching in the form of feedback or hints. The post-test was administered in the Tutoring Off mode. In this mode, students are essentially working in a VM network, with one additional requirement of having to assert their diagnosis. An additional 'sim-ism' is the simulated Q&A with users reporting the fault listed in the trouble tickets. However, the Q&A is easy to use and often is not a significant component of a scenario. Thus, the Tutoring Off mode is a fair replication of a real-world assessment of troubleshooting performance. The post-test consisted of six scenarios delivered in a fixed sequence to all students. The same post-test was used for both groups. The following measures of performance were collected during this post-test: Exercise scores, Exercise transcripts, and Exercise completion times.

The experimental group consisted of two batches with five students each. Students for the experimental group were selected from ongoing IT-A school classes. We planned for control group to have ten students who had completed the IT-A school training and were awaiting duty assignments. However, due to logistic and availability constraints, the evaluation was conducted with a control group of only five students. Participants in the experimental group spent ten days on the trainer, spread over nine weeks.

The control group received half a day of training on the use of ITADS (similar to the experimental group) and were given half a day to review didactic materials. They did not undergo any training with the ITADS simulations.

Assessment of student reaction was performed using surveys that were filled out by students at different stages of training. Additionally, a demographic questionnaire was administered at the beginning of the study. The control group was also administered a demographic questionnaire in the beginning and a satisfaction survey at the end of the segment.

To examine the hypothesis that ITADS is effective in teaching the knowledge and skills identified in the requirements, we compared the performance of the experimental and controls groups along these dimensions: 1. Post-test exercise scores, 2. Post-test exercise completion times, and 3. Successful completion rates on post-test exercises. On average the experimental group scored 19% higher than the control group. This difference is not statistically significant. In terms of post-test exercise completion times, on average the experimental group took an average of 18 min *less* than the control group to complete exercises, i.e. they were about 70% faster. This difference is statistically significant ($p < 0.001$).

Given the control group's unfamiliarity with the tutoring side of ITADS (i.e. scoring metrics, rationale updates), we felt that comparing exercise completion rates would be fairer than comparing scores. A student is said to have successfully completed a troubleshooting exercise when they have successfully diagnosed the problem, completed and verified the fix, and entered a log. Note that the tutor allows students to "give up" in the diagnosis phase and continue with the fix. Thus, it is possible for students to successfully complete one or the other phase but not both. We compared the number of exercises that were completed by the students in two groups. There were three measures of completeness: successfully completing each of the diagnosis and fix phases, and successfully completing both. Table 1 shows these completion rates.

**Table 1.** Comparison of exercise completion rates

| Average completion rate | Experimental group | Control group |
|---|---|---|
| Diagnosis phase | 85% | 63% |
| Fix phase | 82% | 53% |
| Both phases | 62% | 38% |

Analysis of the survey data showed that the trainees had a favorable reaction to ITADS. In particular, the trainees in the experimental group reacted very positively to the Probable Causes panel.

## 4 Conclusions

Training with ITADS significantly and substantially improved the performance of the experimental group in comparison to the control group. The impact was more pronounced and significant on exercise completion times and rates than on scores. The experimental group scored on average 19% higher than the control group on the Capstone tests, though this difference is not statistically significant. They also completed the exercises about 70% faster. Finally, the experimental group students successfully completed all phases of troubleshooting exercises 63% more often on average than the control group. Future studies will study how well learners retain this knowledge after transitioning out of the schoolhouse.

While ITADS was primarily developed as a cost-effective tool to address critical job skills, it was also intended as a demonstration that effective intelligent tutors can be developed that address real-world considerations of cost-effectiveness, fast schedules, and formal systems engineering processes. The ITADS system was successfully developed in twenty-six months from requirements to validation, following strict systems engineering procedures. The results of the training effectiveness study indicate that the ITS also leads to significantly improved performance among Navy IT recruits in troubleshooting tasks.

**Acknowledgments.** This work was performed under a contract awarded and administered by the U.S. Navy, Naval Air Warfare Center Training Systems Division (NAWCTSD) in Orlando, FL for the Navy's Center for Information Warfare Training (CIWT) IT A-School in Pensacola, FL.

## References

1. CISCO: IT Essentials 5.0, Chapter 6, Networks, Slides, pp. 63–69 (2012)
2. Folsom-Kovarik, J.T., Schatz, S., Nicholson, D.: Return on investment: a practical review of ITS student modeling techniques. M&S J. Winter Edn., 22–37 (2011)
3. Lajoie, S.P., Faremo, S.O.N.I.A., Gauthier, G.: Promoting self-regulation in medical students through the use of technology. Technol. Instr. Cognit. Learn. **3**(1/2), 81 (2006)
4. Jensen, R., Ramachandran, S., Domeshek, E., Tang, K., Marsh, J.: Simulation awareness: assessing performance with limited simulation instrumentation. Submitted to the Interservice/ Industry Training, Simulation, and Education Conference (I/ITSEC 2016) (2016)

# Simulated Dialogues with Virtual Agents: Effects of Agent Features in Conversation-Based Assessments

Jesse R. Sparks[✉], Diego Zapata-Rivera, Blair Lehman, Kofi James, and Jonathan Steinberg

Educational Testing Service, Princeton, NJ 08541, USA
{jsparks, dzapata, blehman, kjames, jsteinberg}@ets.org

**Abstract.** Pedagogical agents are widely employed in intelligent tutoring systems and game-based learning environments, but research suggests that learning benefits from virtual agents vary as a function of agent features (e.g., the form or register of agent dialogue) and student characteristics (e.g., prior knowledge). Students' responses to agent-based conversations provide useful evidence of students' knowledge and skills for assessment purposes; however, it is unclear whether these agent design features and student characteristics similarly influence students' interactions with agents in assessment (versus learning) contexts. In this paper, we explore relationships between agent features and student characteristics within a conversation-based assessment of science inquiry skills. We examined the effects of virtual agents' knowledge status (low vs. high) and language use (comparative vs. argumentative question framing) on agent perceptions (ratings) in a conversation-based assessment of scientific reasoning (i.e., using data to predict the weather). Preliminary results show that the effects of these features on students' perceptions of agents varied as a function of students' background characteristics, consistent with research on learning from agents. Implications for designing agent-based assessments will be discussed.

**Keywords:** Pedagogical agents · Conversation-based assessments
Task design

## 1 Introduction

Pedagogical agents are widely employed in intelligent tutoring systems and game-based learning environments. Researchers have argued that the instructional promise of these virtual agents lies in their ability to engage students in naturalistic, adaptive interactions that approximate human communication, thereby affording deeper learning [1, 2]. Deeper learning may result from agent interactions because learners perceive agents as though they are interactive conversational partners in authentic social contexts [3, 4].

A recent meta-analysis [5] found that the characteristics of virtual agents can affect students' learning outcomes, and that these characteristics vary widely across implementations despite some common features [1]. Specifically, agent features (e.g., the

© Springer International Publishing AG, part of Springer Nature 2018
C. Penstein Rosé et al. (Eds.): AIED 2018, LNAI 10948, pp. 469–474, 2018.
https://doi.org/10.1007/978-3-319-93846-2_88

agent's epistemic role, the surface form or register of agent dialogue), in addition to student characteristics (e.g., prior knowledge), can affect learning from agents [5, 6].

Conversation-based assessments (CBAs) are intended to provide students with multiple opportunities to demonstrate their knowledge and skills, using simulated, natural language conversations with virtual agents to elicit explanations about decisions that students make in scenario-based tasks, simulations, or games [7, 8]. Because CBAs share similar features with pedagogical agent interactions [1], including chat-like, written dialogues with animated conversational agents, it is important to examine the effects of agent and task features on students' interactions in CBA contexts.

In this paper, we examine the impact of two important aspects of authentic human conversations (*speaker identity* and *discourse content*) on students' interactions with a CBA measuring scientific reasoning and inquiry skills that included three natural language (typed) conversations with two virtual agents (a peer and a scientist; see [8]). We examined whether students' perceptions of the agents were affected by two task features: (a) virtual peer knowledge status (high vs. low topic knowledge) and (b) the format of an assessment question posed to the human student (compare notes vs. agree with peer's choice of note). In addition, we examined whether these perceptions varied as a function of student characteristics (e.g., school type, prior knowledge).

## 2   Methods

### 2.1   Participants

Two-hundred thirty-five students in grades 7 (n = 185) and 8 (n = 50) from one urban school (n = 152) and one rural school (n = 83) participated in the study. The overall sample was 48% female (n = 112), and included White (n = 186, 79%), Black (n = 22, 9%), Hispanic (n = 9, 4%), and Asian students (n = 1, 0.4%), with 17 (7%) identified as 'Other' ethnicity, as reported by their teachers, who provided demographics, including science grades. Over half (n = 124, 53%) of the students reported having previous instruction related to weather patterns. Within the urban school, over half (n = 79, 52%) of the students were identified as eligible for Free-Reduced Price Lunch (i.e., proxy for low socioeconomic status); science state test scores were also provided for these students.

### 2.2   Materials and Design

Participants completed three blocks of activities: pre-test, Weather CBA, and post-test.

**Pre-test Measures.** The pre-test included *self-report questions* (e.g., "Have you studied weather patterns?"; 50 items), a short *grit scale* ([9]; 8 items) and a *knowledge pre-test* (5 true/false and 2 open-ended items).

**Weather CBA.** The Weather CBA engages students in simulated scientific inquiry activities, which include (a) learning about thunderstorm formation and answering comprehension questions, (b) collecting simulated data from weather stations and providing justification for one's choices, and (c) drawing conclusions from the simulated data in the context of natural language (typed) conversations with agents: a peer (Art, a sixth grader) and a teacher/authority figure (Dr. Garcia, a scientist). The task measures several skills related to scientific reasoning: science knowledge, collecting data, analyzing data and identifying patterns, and making predictions from data [8].

*Introductory Conversation.* The virtual agents are introduced at the beginning of the Weather CBA in a conversation that included the peer knowledge manipulation. In the *high knowledge condition*, Art says "I learned about thunderstorms by reading a book in my science class," while the *low knowledge* Art states "I don't know much about thunderstorms." Students may respond differently to a high vs. low knowledge peer. Dr. Garcia was assumed to be a high knowledge character (this was not manipulated); ratings of the scientist therefore serve as a control on ratings of the virtual peer.

*Inquiry Conversations.* In the *Compare Notes* conversation, students are presented with two notes—one that they created after the simulated data collection, and one "created" by the virtual peer—and are asked to determine which note should be kept for making later predictions. There are two variants, depending on the quality of the student's notes. If the student created a note summarizing data across multiple stations (a note with "more data"), the peer's note included only one station; in contrast, if the student discussed one station ("less data"), the peer's note included multiple stations.

We manipulated question format in this conversation. In the *Compare* condition, Art asks students to "compare the two notes" and decide which one to keep for making predictions later; students must explain their choice of note. In the *Agree* condition, Art states his opinion that one note—whichever had more weather stations—should be kept for making predictions later. Students must explain why they do or do not they agree with Art's selection. In both conditions, students should choose the note with "more data." While follow-up questions and prompts from the agents vary slightly by condition (e.g., "Tell me again which note you think we should keep" vs. "Tell me again whether you agree with me"), the overall structure across conditions was identical.

In the *Evaluate Prediction* conversation, students evaluate Art's prediction about the likelihood of a thunderstorm; we did not manipulate this conversation. Students then make their own final prediction, providing supporting notes and a justification for why the evidence supports their prediction. All conversation and open-ended items were scored by two human raters (median $\kappa = .85$) for evidence of scientific reasoning, with each item worth between 1 and 3 points. Conversation items were also scored by an automated dialogue engine using regular expressions to score student input [7].

**Post-test Measures.** Students completed several post-test measures, including a *manipulation check* in which they rated (1 to 7) the Weather knowledge, general knowledge, expertise, and authority of both agents (8 items). Students also took a *knowledge post-test* (same as pre-test items), and rated their *perceptions of the task* (1 to 4; e.g., "I learned something new from interacting with Art/Dr. Garcia"; 32 items).

## 3  Results

Analyses of the data are ongoing. We are examining students' perceptions of the virtual agents, as a function of task features (Peer knowledge, Question format), and their relationships with student characteristics (e.g., school type, science grades, state test scores). Preliminary analyses revealed that question format influenced students' agent perceptions more than agent knowledge status did. However, consistent with research on learning from agents [5], the nature of these effects varied as a function of contextual variables, including students' background characteristics (e.g., urban vs. rural) and their performance, as measured by the Weather task, and by the pre- and post-test measures.

Correlations among students' agent perceptions (i.e., ratings), background characteristics, and performance measures were examined. Students' four ratings (1–7 for Weather knowledge, general knowledge, expertise, and authority) were averaged into a composite measure for each agent ($\alpha = .81$ for Art, $\alpha = .87$ for Dr. Garcia). The composite rating for Art positively correlated with school type ($\rho = .22$), but was negatively correlated with students' having 'A' grades in science class ($\rho = -.21$). For urban students, the composite rating for Art was negatively correlated with state science assessment scores ($r = -.25$). Across all students, composite ratings for Art were *negatively* correlated with inquiry task performance measures, including pre-test ($r = -.17$) and post-test ($r = -.14$) scores, scores on the Weather task background items ($r = -.24$), scores on the full Evaluate Prediction conversation ($r = -.13$ for automated scores; $r = -.21$ for human ratings), and scores on students' own final predictions ($r = -.15$).

In contrast, composite ratings for Dr. Garcia were *positively* correlated with students' self-reported weather knowledge ($r = .19$) and grit scores ($r = .19$), and with inquiry task performance measures, including pre-test ($r = .20$) and post-test ($r = .24$) scores, scores on the Weather task background items ($r = .20$), and scores on the Compare Notes ($r = .17$ for automated scores; $r = .30$ for human ratings) and Evaluate Prediction ($r = $ n.s. for automated scores; $r = .19$ for human ratings) conversations. Correlations with school type, or with state test scores (for the urban sample only), were not significant for Dr. Garcia.

## 4  Discussion and Implications

Learning technologies make considerable use of pedagogical agents to support students in building knowledge, but the specific features of agents, and their interactions with student characteristics, influence the quality of learning outcomes [5]. Agents are increasingly being used in assessment contexts, including large-scale assessments of constructs like collaborative problem solving [10]. In order to ensure that such assessments are fair and valid, research should examine the effects of task and agent features and student characteristics on students' experiences of and performances in these contexts.

In the current study, the multiple measures we administered attempted to capture key characteristics of the assessment, the virtual agents, and the participating students, because the interactions among these three factors are critical for designers of these kinds of technologies. Preliminary results are consistent with previous findings with learning agents, in that the interactions among agent-related task features (e.g., question format and agent knowledge status) and student characteristics (e.g., urban vs. rural or their level of task performance) influenced students' perceptions of agents within a conversation-based assessment. Notably, performance measures were positively correlated with student perceptions of the virtual scientist, but negatively correlated with perceptions of a virtual peer, such that students with higher inquiry skill (especially in the urban school) were more critical of the peer's expertise. These findings suggest a need for careful attention to the design of virtual agents that assume various epistemic roles [6, 11]. Implications of the preliminary findings are especially relevant for industry practitioners who wish to implement this kind of approach to dialogic assessment [7, 8]. We believe that this work can inform the design of so-called "caring assessments" [12], which take into account student-level characteristics and subsequently tailor the agent-based conversational interactions so that they can elicit fair and valid evidence of knowledge and skills from a wide variety of students.

# References

1. Johnson, W.L., Lester, J.C.: Face-to-face interaction with pedagogical agents, twenty years later. Int. J. Artif. Intell. Educ. **26**, 25–36 (2016)
2. Johnson, W.L., Rickel, J.W., Lester, J.C.: Animated pedagogical agents: face-to-face interaction in interactive learning environments. Int. J. Artif. Intell. Educ. **11**, 47–78 (2000)
3. Moreno, R., Mayer, R.E., Spires, H.A., Lester, J.C.: The case for social agency in computer-based teaching: Do students learn more deeply when they interact with animated pedagogical agents? Cogn. Instruct. **19**(2), 177–213 (2001)
4. Louwerse, M.M., Graesser, A.C., Lu, S., Mitchell, H.H.: Social cues in animated conversational agents. Appl. Cognitive. Psychol. **19**, 693–704 (2005)
5. Schroeder, N., Adesope, O., Gilbert, R.: How effective are pedagogical agents for learning? A meta-analytic review. J. Educ. Comput. Res. **49**(1), 1–39 (2013)
6. Baylor, A., Kim, Y.: Simulating instructional roles through pedagogical agents. Int. J. Artif. Intell. Educ. **15**, 95–115 (2005)
7. Zapata-Rivera, D., Jackson, T., Katz, I.R.: Authoring conversation-based assessment scenarios. In: Sottilare, R.A., Graesser, A.C., Hu, X., Brawner, K. (eds.) Design Recommendations for Intelligent Tutoring Systems Volume 3: Authoring Tools and Expert Modeling Techniques, pp. 169–178. U.S. Army Research Laboratory, Orlando (2015)
8. Liu, L., Steinberg, J., Qureshi, F., Bejar, I., Yan, F.: Conversation-based assessments: an innovative approach to measure scientific reasoning. Bullet. IEEE Tech. Committee Learn. Technol. **18**(1), 10–13 (2016)
9. Duckworth, A.L., Quinn, P.D.: Development and validation of the short grit scale (Grit-S). J. Pers. Assess. **91**(2), 166–174 (2009)
10. Fiore, S.M., Graesser, A., Greiff, S., Griffin, P., Gong, B., Kyllonen, P., Massey, C., O'Neil, H., Pellegrino, J., Rothman, R., Soulé, H., von Davier, A.A.: Collaborative problem solving: Considerations for the National Assessment of Educational Progress. National Center for Educational Statistics, Alexandria (2017)

11. Millis, K., Forsyth, C., Butler, H., Wallace, P., Graesser, A., Halpern, D.: Operation ARIES! A serious game for teaching scientific inquiry. In: Ma, M., Oikonomou, A., Lakhmi, J. (eds.) Serious Games and Edutainment Applications, pp. 169–196. Springer, London (2011). https://doi.org/10.1007/978-1-4471-2161-9_10

12. Zapata-Rivera, D.: Toward caring assessment systems. In: Adjunct Publication of the 25th Conference on User Modeling, Adaptation and Personalization (UMAP 2017), pp. 97–100. ACM, New York, NY, USA (2017)

# Adaptive Learning Based on Affect Sensing

Dorothea Tsatsou[1]([⊠]), Andrew Pomazanskyi[2], Enrique Hortal[3],
Evaggelos Spyrou[4], Helen C. Leligou[5], Stylianos Asteriadis[3], Nicholas Vretos[1],
and Petros Daras[1]

[1] Information Technologies Institute,
Centre for Research & Technology Hellas, Thessaloniki, Greece
{dorothea,vretos,daras}@iti.gr
[2] Nurogames, Cologne, Germany
andrew.pomazanskyi@nurogames.com
[3] University of Maastricht, Maastricht, The Netherlands
{enrique.hortal,stelios.asteriadis}@maastrichtuniversity.nl
[4] Institute of Informatics & Telecommunications,
National Centre for Scientific Research "Demokritos", Athens, Greece
espyrou@iit.demokritos.grs
[5] OTE Academy, Athens, Greece
leligou@gmail.com

**Abstract.** This paper introduces an end-to-end solution for dynamic adaptation of the learning experience for learners of different personal needs, based on their behavioural and affective reaction to the learning activities. Personal needs refer to what learner already know, what they need to learn, their intellectual and physical capacities and their learning styles.

## 1 Introduction

The emergence of new technologies has enabled the educational paradigm to shift from traditional classroom-based instruction to ubiquitous, highly personalised learning. Through the recognition of sensorial and performance cues, learning can adapt to each individual learner's preferences, situation and needs. Such cues may now be tracked seamlessly via the technological agents and digital content that materialise learning activities.

Moreover, the effectiveness of the learning process has been directly correlated with the learners' engagement to the learning activities [4], which increases when activities are tailored to the personal needs and emotional state of the learner [2]. As such, a major challenge is to provide personal mentors for learners and means for teachers' to amplify their awareness and progress monitoring capacities.

To this end, this paper outlines the novel ecosystem of the MaTHiSiS EU-funded project that pertains to an innovative modelling strategy for learning

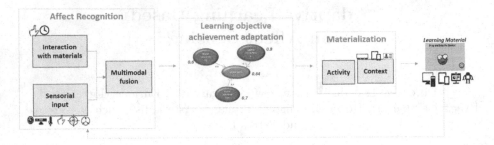

Fig. 1. The MaTHiSiS ecosystem's core workflow

experiences, multimodal affect recognition over a variety of learner types (with and without disabilities) and an on-the-fly adaptation strategy of the learning experience, as seen in Fig. 1.

## 2    Learning Experience Modeling

A novel framework for modeling learning experiences has been developed, comprising of (a) a graph-based representation of the learning objectives (i.e. *what to learn*) and (b) a knowledge-based schema of the learning activities (i.e. *what to do to learn*).

The graph-based modeling scheme provides educators the means and method to define re-usable, self-sustained and interoperable learning objectives, discretised into smaller learning goals, which represent competences, skills, or knowledge that they aim for their learners to acquire. Goals are interconnected in directed learning graphs, with different contribution degree (edge weights). Complex goals comprise the central-most nodes and atomic goals comprise leaf nodes that contribute to one or more complex goals. These atoms are competences that cannot be further reduced to more primitive notions.

Generic learning activities are attached to the atomic goals, while different materialisations for each activity can be defined based on contextual conditions (device used etc.). A Learning Actions Ontology has been engineered, based on educators and psychologists feedback, to represented under a holistic schema such abstract activities, but also parameters that affect their materialisation in the real world, such as the type of learner, the types of devices used during a learning session, the types of digital content, etc. Further details on the learning experience modeling strategy can be found in [9].

## 3    Affect Recognition During Learning

Achievement in a learning objective is maximised when the learner is engaged [4], i.e. when learner's skill and activity challenge levels are balanced comfortably and the learner feels neither frustrated nor bored.

The physical behaviour of a learner can be tracked through diverse sensing devices, such as cameras, microphones, gyroscopes, etc., and along with the learners' interactions with the digital content and devices they provide direct indications towards the learners' engagement, frustration and boredom.

In the case of the MaTHiSiS system, a key challenge was the different types of learners that it addresses, and subsequently the very diverse expressions of affect. Spanning from children to adults and from neurotypical learners to learners with learning and physical disabilities, both the unavailability of datasets, as well as the intricacies posed by the types of learners, mandated the creation of a new dataset, during extensive piloting phases. To this end, recordings of neurotypical children and adults, as well as children and teens in the autism spectrum and with multiple and profound disabilities, working on educational material (on desktop, mobile devices and in certain cases with an educational robot[1]) were annotated by their teachers and pedagogical experts-observers with affect state labels, in order to train machine learning algorithms for a multitude of modalities, outlined below.

*Facial Expression Analysis*: The graph-based method presented in [1] exploits the variation of interconnected facial landmark positions, to predict leaner affect per certain timeframes.

*Gaze Estimation*: A two-stream CNN method has been developed, fusing the spatial stream of the eye pupil with the temporal stream of the pupil's optical flow in a particular timeframe, in a 3D gaze vector. Based on gaze - affect label correlations in the dataset, the affect state of the learner is estimated.

*Skeleton Motion Analysis*: Through Slow Feature Analysis and Speed Relation Preserving Slow Feature Analysis (srpSFA), the geometrical structure of the moving skeletons of a learner is leveraged in order to extract features that capture the affective context of an action.

*Speech-Based Affect Recognition*: Audio signals are transformed to a sequence of feature vectors, classified through SVMs, based again on the labelled dataset. Experiments have indicated that this method may be language-independent [7].

*Inertial Sensor-Based Affect Recognition*: An affect recognition system which exploits the expression through 2D and 3D gesture using the accelerometer and gyroscope has been developed. These 2D but especially 3D descriptors contribute to emotion expression while interacting and using mobile devices.

*Interaction with Learning Material*: the Experience API (xAPI) [5] has been extended, in order to express prominent interactions of learners with educational materials, where time to complete a task, potential score, and type of interaction are employed in order to recognise behavioural affective cues of the learner.

All these channels are fused under an equally-weighted late multimodal fusion scheme, to result to an understanding of the overall affect of the learner at any given moment of the learning experience, since multi-channel fusion of affect states has already been proven to improve accuracy and reduce discrepancy in the recognition of affective states, in comparison to single-channel recognition [3].

---

[1] NAO robot.

# 4    Personalised Adaptation of the Learning Experience

While each teacher-defined learning graph applies to all learners, personalised instances of the graphs are assigned to each user, on which *weights* over the graph's nodes reflect each learner's achievement (or skill) level over each goal. This goal-oriented framework enables nonlinear training over the overall learning objective, as the system will promote learning activities, and level of challenge thereof, that train goals where the learner is weakest at, during each iteration of the learning experience.

Adaptation of the learning process relies on two axes: (a) the affect state of the learner while they are training in a specific atomic learning goal and (b) the learning graph structure and state of the personal graph instance in each iteration of the learning process. Content recommendation and learning process intervention based on student's affect has been pursued in [8] and [6] respectively, however not as means to fully guide the learning process itself or in direct combination with the learning experience model.

For the first part, once the affect of a learner is detected to be out of the flow state, the system automatically adjusts the skill level of the learner (atomic goal weight). If the affect state tends to boredom, the skill level is increased, so that the challenge level would ultimately be increased. In the case of anxiety detection, the skill is lowered, so that the challenge for the activities of this particular goal will be subsequently relaxed.

For the second step, graph-based update of the learning graph instance analyses the current goal weight change and previous state of the graph instance and (re)adapts all goals' weights, so that it reflects both (i) the contribution of the goals to the overall learning objective and (b) a smooth transition in knowledge acquisition. The latter ensures that there are no potential steep oscillations of goal weights from the previous adaptation step due to circumstantial conditions and that goal achievement score reflects the true progression of the learner.

Lastly, the generic learning activity selected based on the aforementioned 'weakest link' selection criterion is matched against the contextual situation of the learner (abilities, environment, device used) to result to the current appropriate materialisation of the activity.

Preliminary piloting observations have indicated the effectiveness of the platform towards (a) maintaining neurotypical and non-neurotypical learners engaged so that they retain their focus in the material they learn and (b) befittingly adapting the material (e.g. exercise/game) challenge level according to the learners' affect state, so that they are comfortable with the exercises taken up, thus successfully fulfilling them, with a direct correlation to increasing skill levels, while at the same time learners do not remain complacent about past achievements but are rather motivated to take up new/more skills.

# 5    Conclusions and Future Work

This paper presented the MaTHiSiS educational ecosystem and its main innovation arches, i.e. the novel learning experience modeling paradigm for learners with and without learning and physical disabilities, as well as the holistic affect-based adaptation of the learning process.

The system has been tested in extensive pilots with the core strengths and opportunities of the proposed solution brought to light. To this end, the personal mentoring capacities of the system, its applicability to any setting and device, the ability for teachers to re-use the learning experience model components and to monitor their students' progress and affect state, but most prominently its ability to maintain learners with or without disabilities engaged with the learning process are of the major strengths and innovation potentials of the platform. Future work will focus on enforcing a reliability factor during multimodal fusion to each affect recognition modality based on the type of learner.

**Acknowledgments.** This work has been supported by the European Commission under Grant Agreement No. 687772 MaTHiSiS.

# References

1. Antonaras, D., Pavlidis, C., Vretos, N., Daras, P.: Affect state recognition for adaptive human robot interaction in learning environments. In: 12th International Workshop on Semantic and Social Media Adaptation and Personalization (SMAP), pp. 71–75 (2017)
2. Athanasiadis, C., Hortal, E., Koutsoukos, D., Lens, C.Z., Asteriadis, S.: Personalized, affect and performance-driven computer-based learning. In: Proceedings of the 9th International Conference on Computer Supported Education, CSEDU, vol. 1 (2017)
3. D'Mello, S.K., Graesser, A.: Multimodal semi-automated affect detection from conversational cues, gross body language, and facial features. User Model. User Adapt. Interact. **20**(2), 147–187 (2010)
4. Hamari, J., Shernoff, D.J., Rowe, E., Coller, B., Asbell-Clarke, J., Edwards, T.: Challenging games help students learn: an empirical study on engagement, flow and immersion in game-based learning. Comput. Hum. Behav. **54**, 170–179 (2016)
5. Kevan, J.M., Ryan, P.R.: Experience API: flexible, decentralized and activity-centric data collection. Technol. Knowl. Learn. **21**(1), 143–149 (2016)
6. Mazziotti, C., Holmes, W., Wiedmann, M., Loibl, K., Rummel, N., Mavrikis, M., Hansen, A., Grawemeyer, B.: Robust student knowledge: adapting to individual student needs as they explore the concepts and practice the procedures of fractions. In: Workshop on Intelligent Support in Exploratory and Open-Ended Learning Environments Learning Analytics for Project Based and Experiential Learning Scenarios at the 17th International Conference on Artificial Intelligence in Education (AIED 2015), pp. 32–40 (2015)
7. Papakostas, M., Spyrou, E., Giannakopoulos, T., Siantikos, G., Sgouropoulos, D., Mylonas, P., Makedon, F.: Deep visual attributes vs. hand-crafted audio features on multidomain speech emotion recognition. Computation **5**(2), 26 (2017)
8. Santos, O.C., Saneiro, M., Salmeron-Majadas, S., Boticario, J.G.: A methodological approach to eliciting affective educational recommendations. In: IEEE 14th International Conference on Advanced Learning Technologies (ICALT), pp. 529–533. IEEE (2014)
9. Tsatsou, D., Vretos, N., Daras, P.: Modelling learning experiences in adaptive multi-agent learning environments. In: 9th International Conference on Virtual Worlds and Games for Serious Applications (VS-Games), pp. 193–200 (2017)

# Preliminary Evaluations of a Dialogue-Based Digital Tutor

Matthew Ventura[1]([✉]), Maria Chang[2], Peter Foltz[1], Nirmal Mukhi[2],
Jessica Yarbro[1], Anne Pier Salverda[1], John Behrens[1], Jae-wook Ahn[2],
Tengfei Ma[2], Tejas I. Dhamecha[2], Smit Marvaniya[2], Patrick Watson[2],
Cassius D'helon[2], Ravi Tejwani[2], and Shazia Afzal[2]

[1] Pearson Education, Pearson, USA
matthew.ventura@pearson.com
[2] IBM Research, Yorktown Heights, NY, USA

**Abstract.** IBM and Pearson have partnered to develop dialogue-based intelligent tutoring systems at an unprecedented scale. We leveraged the decades-long research in intelligent tutoring systems (specifically dialogue based tutoring systems) and advances in machine learning and natural language processing to create a Watson dialogue-based tutor (WDBT). WDBT is currently being used by hundreds of students across multiple institutions. This paper describes our plans for preliminary evaluations of WDBT. Our formal evaluations begin in Spring 2018 and we will present findings shortly thereafter.

**Keywords:** Intelligent tutoring systems · Dialogue Based Tutoring Systems
Scale

## 1 Introduction

In 2016, IBM and Pearson announced a partnership to develop dialogue-based intelligent tutoring systems at an unprecedented scale. Dialogue-based tutoring systems (DBTs) deliver a learning experiences through natural language dialogue, enabled by the classification of student natural language responses [1]. While DBTs have been shown to be effective and compelling, they are difficult to design and deploy at scale. Given Pearson's expertise in developing high-quality educational content and IBM's ability to deliver natural language processing and machine learning solutions at scale, this partnership is positioned to meet this challenge. As a result, we developed the Watson dialogue-based tutor (WDBT). This paper describes our approach for evaluating WDBT through in-class pilots and learning experiments.

## 2 Watson Dialogue Based Tutor

WDBT is influenced by the decades-long research in intelligent tutoring systems and DBTs in particular. WDBT takes an approach that is similar to the five-step tutoring in AutoTutor [1]: (1) tutor poses a question/problem, (2) student attempts to answer,

C. Penstein Rosé et al. (Eds.): AIED 2018, LNAI 10948, pp. 480–483, 2018.
https://doi.org/10.1007/978-3-319-93846-2_90

(3) tutor provides brief evaluation as feedback, (4) collaborative interaction to improve the answer, (5) tutor checks if student understands.

The design of Watson dialogue content is based off a *domain model* consisting of *learning objectives, enabling objectives* (sub-learning objectives that support the learning objective) and prerequisite relations among the learning objectives. In this sense, the domain model can be viewed as a formalization of the knowledge and skills in a textbook used in a course. The overall structure of the domain model is consistent across books which allows WDBT to scale to any domain model following our domain model format.

WDBT content consists of main questions, main answers, assertions (knowledge components of the main answer), and hint questions to elicit assertions, and fill in the blank (based off assertions). A dialogue manager controls the logic for when dialogue moves are delivered to a student. Given a learning objective, it begins by asking the student a main question. The student responses are classified by WDBT, which responds with appropriate feedback and a set of hint questions to cooperatively facilitate the ideal answer with the student. For main questions, the classifier matches the response to all the component assertions for the main answer. Additional dialogue moves also support question answering (i.e. answering questions asked by the student).

WBDT has a response classifier that classifies student answers. We implemented a supervised machine learning approach to classification requiring 35 scored student answers per question. The total number of questions (including main and hint questions) per book is around 600.

WDBT has a learner model, which estimates a student's proficiency over the course of the conversation. Proficiency is estimated for both learning and enabling objectives, allowing both a high-level and detailed view of student performance. This proficiency estimation is presented to students.

WDBT is integrated into a Pearson higher education courseware product called REVEL. REVEL is used by instructors to help teach courses. REVEL is lightweight primary consisting of e-text and multiple choice and writing assessments. Currently WDBT is optional in REVEL in select locations to provide support on more difficult learning objectives.

In our first phase of research we are building WDBT for 10 titles spanning developmental psychology, physiological psychology, abnormal psychology, sociology, communication, and government.

Table 1 displays what a typical conversation with WDBT looks like. WDBT always begins with a main question followed by hint questions in an attempt to elicit the main answer. If a student struggles on a learning objective WDBT will move down to an enabling objective and repeat the dialogue strategy. The student has the freedom to jump to any objective via a UI that displays both the objectives and chat window.

**Table 1.** Example WDBT session.

| Dialogue move | Text |
|---|---|
| Learning objective main question | Let's review this topic… Try answering this question: What are some variations in the definition of family? |
| Student answer | A family can be defined as individuals tied together by biological means, legal measures, and residency |
| Feedback on assertion covered by student | Wonderful. Kinship systems consist of the social links and boundaries, defined by biology and social custom, that establish who is related to whom. Let's take it a bit further |
| Learning objective hint question | How do social scientists define the family? |
| Student answer | Social scientists define the family as a group of people that reside together |
| Feedback with assertion covered by student | That looks partly correct. There's a little more to the answer. Let's work this out together |
| Fill in the blank hint | Can you fill in the missing word? Social scientists typically define family as a group of people who live together in a household and share biological and/or legal _____ |

## 3  Evaluation

The WDBT is currently being used by hundreds of students across multiple higher education institutions. These activities will enable us to collect feedback from students and gain insights into their potential learning. We have three primary ways of collecting data to drive the design off WDBT: user experience studies, in-class pilots, and learning experiments.

### 3.1  User Experience Studies

User experience studies investigate the learners' experiences with functional prototypes of WDBT. Written surveys and questionnaires enable learners to summarize their overall experiences with WDBT. Two important themes have emerged as a result of these studies. First, students want to see the scope of the dialogue experience. That is, students want to be able to visually see how many objectives will be covered in the dialogue. Second, students want to have some degree of control over the conversation. WDBT cannot always accurately identify the best objective to deliver when a student is struggling. Giving the student some control over their learning appears to increase engagement with WDBT.

### 3.2  In-Class Pilots

In-class pilots involve the use of WDBT by real students in real classes. We will be investigating learning in these pilots by comparing quiz scores paired with WDBT to quizzes scores not paired with WDBT. We also will manually annotate transcripts to identify strengths and weaknesses of the WDBT experience as well as misclassifications of natural language. We currently (Spring 2018) are running an in-class pilots for a sociology title and will report results on this pilot.

### 3.3    Learning Experiments

Learning experiments are quasi experimental studies comparing students using WDBT with a control group. These experiments allow us to more precisely measure learning gains. We have the potential to explore different features, such as updates to natural language classification models, learner models, dialogue strategies, and tone/language used by WDBT. Such experiments are necessary for understanding the potential impact of WDBT on learning and for discovering general strategies for tutoring that may be more helpful than others. We currently (Spring 2018) are running a learning experiment for a sociology title and will report results on this experiment.

## 4    Conclusion

In this paper we describe our approach for evaluating the Watson dialogue-based tutor (WDBT) in real classrooms and in more tightly controlled lab experiments. We anticipate that these evaluations will help us understand how effective WDBT is, as well as areas where it could be improved. Our formal evaluations begin in Spring 2018, enabling us to present our findings shortly thereafter.

**Acknowledgements.** This work was heavily supported by the broader teams at Pearson Education and IBM Research. We also thank the students and participants in our research for their invaluable feedback.

## Reference

1. Graesser, A.C.: Learning, thinking, and emoting with discourse technologies. Am. Psychol. **66**(8), 743–757 (2011)

# Young Researcher Papers

# Investigating Feedback Support to Enhance Collaboration Within Groups in Computer Supported Collaborative Learning

Adetunji Adeniran[✉]

University of Aberdeen, Aberdeen, Scotland
r01aba17@abdn.ac.uk

**Abstract.** Existing work and learning theories hold that collaborative learning has unique benefits to cognition due to knowledge sharing through interaction. This research assumes that if collaboration within learning groups can be enhanced, cognitive outcomes will be improved. I will investigate computational methods to provide real-time support to groups during joint problem-solving.

**Keywords:** Collaborative learning · Group interaction
Activity-state model · Shared-activity environment · Feedback support

## 1  Introduction and Related Work

Collaborative learning simply means learning together, for example in "joint problem-solving" (JPS) with learning as side effect [15]. Cognitive benefits of collaboration have been established in research e.g. [8,16,18,20] and much has been investigated to exploit these benefits for computer supported learning [1,6,9,10,12–15]. For example, hand position and head direction of learners was exploited and analyzed in [3] to identify differences in the process of JPS between-groups. [3] aimed to measure, collect, analyze and report "fiducial maker" and "face recognition" data of learners during JPS, to understand and optimize cognitive effects of collaboration. Findings in [3] were advanced in [4] where a "Nonverbal Indexes of Students' Physical Interactivity" (NISPI) framework was proposed to interpret the key indexes of quality JPS among learners that was conjectured in [3].

Similarly, learners' interactive activities (touches and physical interaction) around tabletops was captured in [11]; this data was analyzed to provided information to a "human teacher" about how best to support groups towards enhanced collaboration. Some other works towards optimization of learning through collaboration assumed that the best method to aid a group for enhanced

---

A. Adeniran—I am grateful for the advisory role of Prof. Judith Masthoff and Dr. Nigel Beacham and the support of TETFUND, Nigeria.

collaboration was to ensure the formation of cohesive groups from the start [2,7,21].They proposed different algorithms that will automatically form collaborative groups based on pre-collected characteristics' data of learners.

My research approach will build on [3,4,11] and other related work to propose real-time approach to advance the methods proposed in [2,7,21]. We will analyze activities within groups during the problem-solving process. The required data will be captured through a share-activity learning environment structured to trace activity-state transition patterns (ASTPs) during JPS. Our conjecture is that the analysis of the ASTP data of JPS process will provide information to a suitable computation mechanism that provides timely and appropriate feedback support to groups with the aim of enhancing collaboration in real-time. A diagrammatic representation of the framework is shown in Fig. 1.

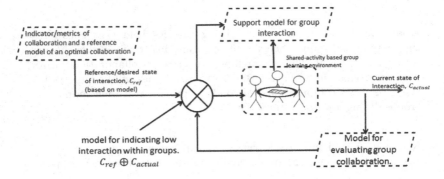

**Fig. 1.** Conceptual framework of research

## 2    Research Questions and Hypotheses

Based on my current literature review, preliminary work and research objective, the following hypotheses and associated research questions will be investigated:

1. Firstly, I hypothesize that solving a problem together in a group involves different "states" (e.g. start, propose solution, correct solution, discuss, accept, reject, end) of an individual's contributive activities (see Fig. 2), that each progressive solution involves the transition from one activity-state to another and thus forms an activity-state transition pattern (ASTP), and that the proposed shared-activity environment can be structured to capture ASTPs that make up the group's problem-solving process.
   (a) How do people collaborate to solve problems face-to-face?
   (b) Can we identify different "states" of activities within groups while they solve a learning task together?
   (c) How can we model, design and implement a group learning environment to capture ASTPs of a group's solution to learning task?
2. Secondly, I hypothesize that analysis of ASTPs can provide insight into the level of collaboration and problems that hinder effective collaboration within a group.

(a) Can the analysis of a group's ASTP provide information about how much groups have collaborated to solve a learning task?

(b) How can we identify triggers/inhibitors to collaboration based on an analysis of ASTPs produced from the group's problem solving process?

3. And lastly we hypothesize that appropriate feedback can enhance collaboration, that this feedback can be based on the indicated level and identified factors of group collaboration and that it can be provided in real-time employing a suitable computational mechanism.

(a) Can we determine feedback to groups that will enhance the triggers or mitigate the inhibitors of collaboration during group learning?

(b) What suitable computational method can be employed to provide appropriate feedback to enhance group collaboration in real-time?

(c) How can we validate the success of our feedback support mechanism?

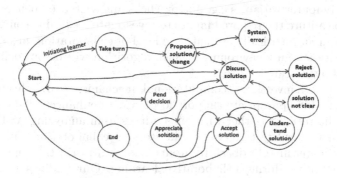

**Fig. 2.** Activity-state model: For joint problem-solving activities in group.

## 3   Methodology, Current and Future Work

My initial approach to achieve the objectives of these research is to identify and validate collaborative activity-states during JPS process through the following steps.

Firstly, we invited participants to solve a Sudoku puzzle in groups (triads) while we captured a video record of each groups' JPS process. We analyze the video data, to identify collaborative-states of learners JPS activities. In our current work, we pre-defined JPS activity-states by adapting "the collaborative learning conversation skill taxonomy" in [19]. Video of JPS process of each group was annotated based on these pre-defined states, using the Anvil video annotation research tool [5]. A preliminary result of this current study provides baseline information for further validation and re-definition of our conceptualized activity-state model (see Fig. 2) of JPS process. In further stages of this research, we will explore other techniques for example *Inter-Rater agreement and validating scheme* and *Human affect recording tool* in [17], to validate our hypothesized states of collaborative activities. Deliverable at this stage of my work will provide information for a design framework of a shared-activity environment that will capture ASTPs of groups during collaborative learning.

Secondly, to investigate and develop a model to evaluate collaboration within groups, I will build on existing work [3,4,9,10,12,13] and analysis of ASTP data to identify indicators of collaboration. I will validate this model with feedback from learners and evidence of knowledge gain during JPS. Computational methods and algorithms will be explored to automatically evaluate group collaboration during JPS in real-time. Video data of collaborating groups provides good information about the affective states of activities during JPS, it captures facial expressions and gestures that can help identifying varying states of learners activities [3,4]. However most CSCL systems do not capture video of JPS process, thus missing these facial expressions and gestures. Therefore, to achieve a real-time evaluation of collaboration during JPS, we have to resolve the activity-states into computer variables e.g. button clicks and sentence openers. This will enable us to capture the required inputs to investigate a suitable computer algorithm that can automatically evaluate the level of collaboration during JPS in a shared-activity learning environment. Such algorithm will be our deliverable at this stage of my research.

Finally, I will investigate computational mechanisms to indicate support needs and provide appropriate support feedback, to enhance collaboration. We will explore literature together with our findings from analyzing ASTPs during JPS, we aim to identify triggers or inhibitors to collaboration within groups. Also, we will determine feedback to groups that can instill the triggers or mitigate the inhibitors during collaborative learning. Our findings will assist us to develop a suitable algorithm that automates required support to groups. I envision a framework to integrate this group support algorithm into our shared-activity learning environment to support groups in real-time during JPS. We will validate the success of this research through a series of experiments and measure how much we are able to enhance collaboration within learning groups.

The expected novel contributions of this research include:

1. An algorithm for real-time evaluation of collaboration level of group during JPS in a shared-activity learning environment.
2. A real-time feedback group support algorithm, based on ASTPs during JPS activities to enhance collaboration.

# References

1. Alfonseca, E., Carro, R.M., Martín, E., Ortigosa, A., Paredes, P.: The impact of learning styles on student grouping for collaborative learning: a case study. User Model. User-Adap. Inter. **16**(3), 377–401 (2006)
2. Amarasinghe, I., Hernández Leo, D., Jonsson, A.: Towards data-informed group formation support across learning spaces (2017)

3. Cukurova, M., Luckin, R., Mavrikis, M., Millán, E.: Machine and human observable differences in groups' collaborative problem-solving behaviours. In: Lavoué, É., Drachsler, H., Verbert, K., Broisin, J., Pérez-Sanagustín, M. (eds.) EC-TEL 2017. LNCS, vol. 10474, pp. 17–29. Springer, Cham (2017). https://doi.org/10.1007/978-3-319-66610-5_2

4. Cukurova, M., Luckin, R., Millán, E., Mavrikis, M.: The nispi framework: analysing collaborative problem-solving from students' physical interactions. Comput. Educ. **116**, 93–109 (2018)

5. Kipp, M.: Anvil: The Video Annotation Research Tool, pp. 420–436. The Oxford handbook of corpus phonology (2014)

6. Kirschner, F., Paas, F., Kirschner, P.A., Janssen, J.: Differential effects of problem-solving demands on individual and collaborative learning outcomes. Learn. Instr. **21**(4), 587–599 (2011)

7. Lin, Y.-T., Huang, Y.-M., Cheng, S.-C.: An automatic group composition system for composing collaborative learning groups using enhanced particle swarm optimization. Comput. Educ. **55**(4), 1483–1493 (2010)

8. Liu, S., Joy, M., Griffiths, N.: Incorporating learning styles in a computer-supported collaborative learning model (2008)

9. Maldonado, R.M., Yacef, K., Kay, J., Kharrufa, A., Al-Qaraghuli, A.: Analysing frequent sequential patterns of collaborative learning activity around an interactive tabletop. In: Educational Data Mining 2011 (2010)

10. Martinez, R., Wallace, J.R., Kay, J., Yacef, K.: Modelling and identifying collaborative situations in a collocated multi-display groupware setting. In: Biswas, G., Bull, S., Kay, J., Mitrovic, A. (eds.) AIED 2011. LNCS (LNAI), vol. 6738, pp. 196–204. Springer, Heidelberg (2011). https://doi.org/10.1007/978-3-642-21869-9_27

11. Martinez Maldonado, R.: Analysing, visualising and supporting collaborative learning using interactive tabletops (2013)

12. Martinez-Maldonado, R., Dimitriadis, Y., Martinez-Monés, A., Kay, J., Yacef, K.: Capturing and analyzing verbal and physical collaborative learning interactions at an enriched interactive tabletop. Int. J. CSCL **8**(4), 455–485 (2013)

13. Martinez-Maldonado, R., Kay, J., Yacef, K.: An automatic approach for mining patterns of collaboration around an interactive tabletop. In: Lane, H.C., Yacef, K., Mostow, J., Pavlik, P. (eds.) AIED 2013. LNCS (LNAI), vol. 7926, pp. 101–110. Springer, Heidelberg (2013). https://doi.org/10.1007/978-3-642-39112-5_11

14. Meier, A., Spada, H., Rummel, N.: A rating scheme for assessing the quality of computer-supported collaboration processes. Int. J. CSCL **2**(1), 63–86 (2007)

15. Mühlenbrock, M.: Action Based Collaboration Analysis for Group Learning, no. 244. Ios Press (2001)

16. Newman, D.R., Webb, B., Cochrane, C.: A content analysis method to measure critical thinking in face-to-face and computer supported group learning. Interpers. Comput. Technol. **3**(2), 56–77 (1995)

17. Ocumpaugh, J.: Baker rodrigo ocumpaugh monitoring protocol (BROMP) 2.0 technical and training manual. Teachers College, Columbia University and Ateneo Laboratory for the Learning Sciences, New York, NY and Manila, Philippines (2015)

18. Savery, J.R., Duffy, T.M.: Problem based learning: an instructional model and its constructivist framework. Educ. Technol. **35**(5), 31–38 (1995)

19. Soller, A.: Supporting social interaction in an intelligent collaborative learning system. Int. J. Artif. Intell. Educ. (IJAIED) **12**, 40–62 (2001)
20. Suh, H., Lee, S.: Collaborative learning agent for promoting group interaction. ETRI J. **28**(4), 461–474 (2006)
21. Tanimoto, S.L.: The squeaky wheel algorithm: automatic grouping of students for collaborative projects. In: PALE Workshop, pp. 79–80. Springer-Verlag (2007)

# Supporting Math Problem Solving Coaching for Young Students: A Case for Weak Learning Companion

Lujie Chen[✉]

Carnegie Mellon University, Pittsburgh, PA, USA
lujiec@andrew.cmu.edu

**Abstract.** Solving challenging non-routine math problems often invites students to ride an "emotional roller coaster" to experience rich sets of emotions including confusion, frustration, surprise and joy. If done right, it stimulates young students' curiosity and interest in math and cultivate perseverance and resilience with long-term impact. Effective coaching needs to resolve an instance of "assistance dilemma [1]: making real time decisions on the right type of supports, be it cognitive, meta-cognitive or social, at the right time in order to maximize students' exposure to "productive struggles" while minimize unproductive ones. Though this ideal model of coaching is possible one-on-one basis, it is often not realistic in a regular classroom with high student-to-teacher ratio. In this thesis, I plan to explore a weak form of learning companion that can actively monitor students behavior to assist teacher to decide who to help and provides non-cognitive supports when teacher is not available.

**Keywords:** Math problem solving · Learning companion
Affective computing

## 1 Motivation

One of the ultimate goals of education is to prepare students to become mature problem solvers. Solving non-routine math problems for which no immediate solutions are available provides excellent practice opportunities. While early exposures to authentic problem solving experiences at elementary school level may stimulate students' curiosity and interest and nurture perseverance and resilience with long-term benefit, problem solving coaching is not a common practice in regular classroom. Indeed, effective coaching of problem solving at young age needs to resolve an instance of "assistance dilemma" [1]: making real time decision on the right kind of supports, be it cognitive, metacognitive or social, at the right time in order to maximize students' exposure to "productive struggles" while being watchful for unproductive ones. Though this type of ideal coaching is possible at one-on-one level, it is often not practical given the large

© Springer International Publishing AG, part of Springer Nature 2018
C. Penstein Rosé et al. (Eds.): AIED 2018, LNAI 10948, pp. 493–497, 2018.
https://doi.org/10.1007/978-3-319-93846-2_92

student-to-teacher ratios in a typical classroom. Due to the potential high cognitive load on the human teacher who is busy both with monitoring and offering help, it is unlikely that the support is optimal and personalized.

One possible solution is to have an intelligent agent as a teacher assistant who can actively monitor students' problem solving states, who alerts the teacher to offer help to those with genuine needs even without explicit help requests, who encourages those asking for premature help to try harder, who gently reminds on metacognitive strategies and who is empathetic, encouraging and cheerful. This vision is closely related to the idea of Learning companion [2]. However, due to the vast varieties of non-routine math problems and a large spaces of solutions paths, it is not feasible to build a step-based tutor [7] for any given math problems. Without such infrastructure or system to effectively and efficiently represent and interpreter students' cognitive states, the learning companion is "weak" in the sense that it can not provide the kind of cognitive supports as a human teacher do. On the other hand, while human teachers are capable of interpreting detailed cognitive signals (e.g. where the student is along the solution path) and providing relevant cognitive supports (e.g. giving hint, confirming a step or suggesting an alternative), they have limited bandwidth to perform multiple tasks of monitoring and interventions to a large number of students. Given the recent advances in affective computing, weak companion like this has the potential to provide valuable support to human teacher by exploiting machine's superior ability in processing and reasoning affective signals, and providing support within their reach.

In this thesis, I plan to investigate the feasibility of the "weak" learning companion as described above, from both technical and practical point of view. My exploration is mainly based on empirical models derived from student-teacher interactions from several multi-modal datasets. My collaboration with a local school provides authentic educational context for testing prototypes.

## 2   Proposed Solution

My proposed solution aims to answer two questions (1) *what* roles machine could assume given the current state of technology and the comparative advantage of machine comparing with human; (2) *How* the machine roles can be realized using models learned from student-teacher interaction data.

### 2.1   The Boundary of Roles Between Human and Machine

Figure 1 describes the hypothesized boundary of roles between human and machine in the context of group math problem solving coaching. This specification is inspired by my year-long observation of an elementary school math teacher's problem solving coaching sessions. On the left side of the table, I identify the inputs and outputs of the teacher as a decision maker. On the right side of the table, I assign roles given the comparative advantage between human and machine. For example, I observed human teacher's superior ability in processing

| Functions | | Description | Human | Machine |
|---|---|---|---|---|
| Sensing (Input) | Cognitive signals | General problem solving stages | | Y |
| | | Specific (e.g. where and why is stuck, if on the right path) | Y | |
| | Affective Signals | Real time tracking of affects (e.g. frustration, confusion, surprise, joy) | | Y |
| Support (output) | Cognitive | Problem specific and student specific hint, feedback or scaffolding | Y | |
| | Metacognitive | Hints on self monitoring or reflection | | Y |
| | Social | Support communicating growth mindset or empathy | | Y |

**Fig. 1.** The hypothesized role boundary between human and machine within context of math problem solving coaching.

cognitive signals and provide detailed cognitive supports, however, human is not as good as machine to carry out continuous monitoring of massive amount of affective signals from large number of students. In addition, machine may be able to assume some of the roles in providing non-cognitive supports (such as metacognitive coaching and social support), as suggested by an emerging body of research in affect aware tutor [5], metacognition tutor [6] and educational social robots.

## 2.2   How Machine Roles Can Be Realized

In this section, I will discuss a few ongoing studies with the goal to characterize students' general problem solving states and affective states from multi-modal signals and to model teacher's response to those signals. While the one-on-one coaching studies allow us to model student and teacher interactions in optimal scenarios, the group coaching study offers the opportunity to model behaviors in a more realistic context.

**One-on-One Coaching Studies.** In the first study, we collected 21 video recordings of problem solving coaching sessions between a third grade student and his parent tutor. We analyzed student's facial expressions, characterized his emotional profiles over time and validated the accuracy of the affect detection with promising results. An initial exploration of this dataset was presented as a full paper [3] at the Educational Data Mining conference in 2016 (nominated as exemplary paper). In a follow up paper [4] presented at the HRI4L (Human Robot Interaction for Learning) workshop in 2018, we discovered tutor's delayed response to student's negative affects, as compared with positive ones, consistent with tutor's intention to maximize student's exposure to struggle.

In a second ongoing study, we are collecting data from up to 10 parent-child pairs in their home environment with similar setup as in first study, however with an additional modality of child's pen traces recorded using a Smart Pen. We expect this extra data stream may find its value in modeling child's problem solving phases, complementing the existing affect signals from facial expressions, as a proxy measurement for student's engagement in the problem solving process. Those information will help the learning companion to determine the timing of the support on the assumption that the support is given only there is sufficient evidence that student has tried enough. The data collection is due to complete by the end of June 2018 and data analysis will be carried out in summer of 2018.

Based upon the detection models for moment-by-moment affective and cognitive states, the next step is to model tutor's response to those signals. The model inputs are such features as current problem solving stages, affect trends or accumulative time of non-actions and outputs are timing and types of support. This response model converts the moment-by-moment estimations into real time actionable information such as who needs what kind of support. From there, the model may proceed to decide whether to reach out to teacher for cognitive supports or to delegate to the agent for non-cognitive supports.

**Group Coaching Study.** In this study, we plan to collect video recordings of daily group coaching sessions with one teacher and seven 4th grade students over a month. In those sessions, the teacher has specific goal to delay cognitive support in order to maximize students' exposure to struggles, which offers great opportunity to get insights of how teacher determine the optimal amount of struggles. The teacher will also provide meta-cognitive coaching as necessary, which will inspired the design of agent in providing similar type of supports. We're in process of obtain IRB approval for this project, and data collection is to be finished by the end of May, and data analysis to be carried out during summer of 2018. A follow up of this study will be a prototype of the learning companion using real and simulated student data. We will involve teacher in the system design process. The end product will be a working prototype to be tested in classroom.

## 3   Contribution and Impact

This thesis aims to explore the data driven and model based design of a "weak" form of learning companion that can assist teachers to coach students in math problem solving sessions in brick-and-mortar classrooms. This work complements current research in affect sensitive and meta-cognitive tutors which are mainly situated in digital learning environment. This proposal is aligned with the framework of classroom orchestration system [8], both motivated by the goal of addressing teachers' cognitive load and giving teachers the ultimate control. While most of the orchestration examples focus on information flow from students to teachers via the realization of monitoring functions, my proposed work makes a step further, trying also explore to what extent machine could take over some of the intervention task from the teacher. If successful, those agents can be deployed in a real classrooms to improve the quality of math problem solving coaching.

**Acknowledgement.** The research reported here was supported in part by a training grant from the Institute of Education Sciences (R305B150008). Opinions expressed do not represent the views of the U.S. Department of Education.

# References

1. Koedinger, K.R., Pavlik, P., McLaren, B.M., Aleven, V.: Is it better to give than to receive? The assistance dilemma as a fundamental unsolved problem in the cognitive science of learning and instruction. In: Proceedings of the 30th Annual Conference of the Cognitive Science Society, pp. 2155–2160. Routledge, Austin (2008)
2. Kapoor, A., Mota, S., Picard, R.W.: Towards a learning companion that recognizes affect. In: AAAI Fall Symposium, pp. 2–4 (2001)
3. Chen, L., Li, X., Xia, Z., Song, Z., Morency, L.P., Dubrawski, A.: Riding an emotional roller-coaster: a multimodal study of young child's math problem solving activities. In: EDM, pp. 38–45 (2016)
4. Chen, L., Admoni, H., Dubrawski, A.: Toward a companion robot fostering perseverance in math - a pilot study. In: Human Robot Interaction for Learning Workshop (2018)
5. Woolf, B., Burleson, W., Arroyo, I., Dragon, T., Cooper, D., Picard, R.: Affect-aware tutors: recognising and responding to student affect. Int. J. Learn. Technol. 4(3–4), 129–164 (2009)
6. VanLehn, K., Burleson, W., Girard, S., Chavez-Echeagaray, M.E., Gonzalez-Sanchez, J., Hidalgo-Pontet, Y., Zhang, L.: The affective meta-tutoring project: lessons learned. In: Trausan-Matu, S., Boyer, K.E., Crosby, M., Panourgia, K. (eds.) ITS 2014. LNCS, vol. 8474, pp. 84–93. Springer, Cham (2014). https://doi.org/10.1007/978-3-319-07221-0_11
7. VanLehn, K.: The relative effectiveness of human tutoring, intelligent tutoring systems, and other tutoring systems. Educ. Psychol. 46(4), 197–221 (2011)
8. Dillenbourg, P.: Design for classroom orchestration. Comput. Educ. 69, 485–492 (2013)

# Improving Self-regulation by Regulating Mind-Wandering Through the Practice of Mindfulness

Wai Keung David Cheung[(✉)]

University College of London, London, UK
david.cheung.17@ucl.ac.uk

## 1  Introduction

Research on mind-wandering, self-regulation and mindfulness have mostly been undertaken independently of each other with little attempt to examine direct relationships between them. Although they seem to be related phenomena, there exists no unifying framework that helps to systematize all the current conceptualizations, definitions and current state of the art research on mind-wandering, self-regulation and mindfulness (MacKenzie et al. 2012). There exists no standardized definition of mind-wandering, self-regulation and mindfulness within each of the distinct area of research, let alone a universally agreed conceptualization that integrates all three phenomena. To reach a better understanding of the interconnectedness between mind-wandering, self-regulation and mindfulness, it is important that research attempts to converge our distinct understanding of these phenomena into a unifying theoretical framework.

## 2  Self-regulation and Mind-Wandering

Self-regulation is the psychological process by which people exercise control and direct their mental and physical resources to achieve a certain goal (Randall 2015). A number of theories and models of self-regulation have been postulated and generally concern one or more of the four components of a cybernetic-based model of self-regulation, organized in a linear feedback loop:

- Reference - the blueprint, a set standard, a goal, or an ideal,
- Input - assessment of one's present state measured against the reference in cognitive, affective or behavioral terms,
- Comparator - determination of any misalignment between the input and the reference, and
- Output - response as determined based on the measure of alignment between the input and the reference determined by the comparator.

Although self-regulation can take place at various levels of consciousness, ranging from non-conscious to metacognitive, meta-awareness of one's own physiological and

© Springer International Publishing AG, part of Springer Nature 2018
C. Penstein Rosé et al. (Eds.): AIED 2018, LNAI 10948, pp. 498–502, 2018.
https://doi.org/10.1007/978-3-319-93846-2_93

mental state, is found to be a critical component of self-regulatory processes (MacKenzie et al. 2012). Reduced meta-awareness is also posited as a causal link to the pervasive, familiar and relatable phenomenon of mind-wandering (Smallwood and Schooler 2015). Although lacking a standardised definition, mind-wandering is commonly characterised as being auto-generative in nature, independent from perception, dynamically unstable, temporally focused on either the past or the future, emotionally salient and pertaining to current interests or concerns (Smallwood and Schooler 2015). Given that mind-wandering accounts for as much as 46% of waking hours (Killingsworth and Gilbert 2010), this raises the question of how much mind-wandering impacts the self-regulatory abilities of students during learning. Furthermore, the mixed evidence showing both beneficial and adverse impact of mind-wandering (Mooneyham and Schooler 2013) raises a question as to whether mind-wandering can be regulated in order to maximise its benefits and minimise its negative impact on students' self-regulation and learning.

## 3   Mindfulness as a Tool for Self-regulation and Mind-Wandering

This paper posits that mindfulness can improve self-regulation by regulating mind-wandering. Mrazek et al. (2013) suggests that mindfulness and mind-wandering are opposing constructs with an inverse relationship, and proposes that mindfulness practice should be considered as a training for reducing mind-wandering. Jon Kabat-Zinn, the creator of the popular Mindfulness-Based Stress Reduction (MBSR) program, defines mindfulness as "the awareness that emerges through paying attention on purpose, in the present moment, and non-judgmentally to the unfolding of experience moment by moment" (Kabat-Zinn 2003, p. 145). Despite the nuances in understanding and practice, and a lack of unifying theoretical framework, a general consensus does exist amongst the main advocates of mindfulness on what they mean when they refer to mindfulness. The central components of mindfulness in the various major Buddhist schools of thought are clarity of awareness, non-conceptual and nondiscriminatory awareness, flexibility of awareness and attention, empirical stance towards reality, present-oriented consciousness, and stability or continuity of attention and awareness (Brown et al. 2007). These components of mindfulness are by no means distinct constructs and should be treated as mutually reinforcing.

## 4   My Research

My research aims to achieve four goals:

1. Define the causal relationship between mind-wandering and self-regulation,
2. Investigate whether mindfulness practice improves self-regulation by modulating mind-wandering,

3. Formulate a theoretical framework that explains and unifies the concepts of mind-wandering, mindfulness and self-regulation, and
4. Explore how traditional methodologies used in the study of mind-wandering, mindfulness and self-regulation can be improved by incorporating the use of artificial intelligence methods and techniques.

More specifically, my research questions are:

- Does mind-wandering affect learners' self-regulation, and if so, what are the underlying causal mechanisms?
- Does mindfulness practice improve self-regulation in learners by modulating unwanted mind-wandering?
- How can mindfulness, mind-wandering and self-regulation be unified under one theoretical framework?
- How can fully automated person-independent mind-wandering detection techniques be integrated in research on mindfulness, mind-wandering and self-regulation?

## 4.1    The Role of Artificial Intelligence in Research

Traditional methodologies used in studying experiences of inherently subjective nature share a number of limitations due to their over-reliance on subjective measures such as self-reports, post-hoc scales, experience and thought sampling using self or random probes, and neural or physiological correlates such as response time, response inhibition, or fMRI imaging. Such limitations include the notable difference in scales used in self-reports due to a lack of common theoretical framework, validity and reliability issues with self-report measures including the distinction between the total set of conscious experiences and its subset of experiences which can be reported, and the well-established fallibility of the mind in recalling lived experiences (Matthews et al. 2004; Wilson 2002; Lamme 2006; Loftus 2004; Porayska-Pomsta et al. 2018). Additionally, until scientists and philosophers of the mind are able to solve the hard problem of consciousness, i.e. how physical processes in the brain produce subjective conscious experiences, it is argued that even a full neurological mapping of subjective experiences falls short in providing a complete picture in our understanding of such inherently subjective experiences (Chalmers 1995).

In the past decade, there has been a growing interest in the use of Artificial Intelligence (AI) in educational research in various areas including intelligent and interactive technologies, modeling and representation of cognition, models of teaching and learning, and learning contexts and informal learning. A number of researchers are dedicating their efforts to devising smart technologies equipped with AI in order to support research in the study of subjective experiences in a more objective way that is less reliant on self-reports. Such efforts are being facilitated by an increasing number of more accessible, affordable and mobile technology that are available on the market. For instance, Bixler and D'Mello (2015) developed a fully automated user-independent detector of mind-wandering, which monitored eye gaze using an eye tracker during a reading task. Comparing the eye gaze data and participants' self-report on mind-wandering, their model predicted mind-wandering with an accuracy of up to 72%. Hutt et al. (2017) used eye trackers inside a uncontrolled classroom environment to detect mind-wandering when students were engaged with an intelligent tutor system (ITS). Despite constraints in the classroom such as noise, external distractions, and fidgeting by students, their model managed to predict mind-wandering with a moderate accuracy. Other smart systems being developed for user state detection include relying on physiological indicators such as facial features (Stewart et al. 2016), pitch recognition in speech detection, skin conductance, skin temperature, and prosodic and lexical features of spoken responses to ITS (Drummond and Litman 2010). One common criticism leveled at research focusing on the creation of new technologies is their over-emphasis on improving the predictive ability of the techniques, whilst lacking in theoretical grounding. Hence, how can the AI approach to detecting mind-wandering be improved by an integrated model of mind-wandering, self-regulation and mindfulness? How can such theoretical model in turn inform AI research in the field of mind-wandering?

## 4.2   Methodology

Participants will consist of students from an international secondary school in Hong Kong and will be assigned randomly to an experimental group and a control group. The former will undergo a standardized mindfulness training whilst the latter will undergo an active control such as a general Health Enhancement Program. Pre- and post-intervention measures of self-regulation and mind-wandering between the experimental group and the control group will be compared. To measure mind-wandering, a fully automated eye user-independent detector using eye-gaze in real classroom settings, and experience sampling techniques will be used. Measures of self-regulation will be triangulated from various methods including self-report, observation and objective measures. It is hoped that my study will help to clarify our understanding of the conceptual interconnectedness between mindfulness, mind-wandering and self-regulation, build upon the current literature and existing knowledge and serve as the basis to construct a tentative unifying theoretical framework.

## 5   Conclusion

My research hopes to advance the scientific body of knowledge by bringing convergence to our theoretical understanding of psychological processes underlying mind-wandering, self-regulation and mindfulness that are traditionally studied separately. It also seeks to contribute in practice to the field of education by helping learners improve their ability to achieve academic and developmental goals in their learning environments by modulating mind-wandering through the practice of mindfulness. Devising a unifying theoretical framework can also offer fresh fertile ground to develop new artificial intelligence techniques to help further our understanding of the human mind and help learners better achieve their goals.

# References

Bixler, R., D'Mello, S.: Automatic gaze-based user-independent detection of mind wandering during computerized reading. User Model. User Adap. Inter. **26**(1), 33–68 (2015). https://doi.org/10.1007/s11257-015-9167-1

Brown, K., Ryan, R., Creswell, J.: Mindfulness: theoretical foundations and evidence for its salutary effects. Psychol. Inq. **18**(4), 211–237 (2007)

Chalmers, D.: The puzzle of conscious experience. Sci. Am. **273**(6), 80–86 (1995)

Drummond, J., Litman, D.: In the zone: towards detecting student zoning out using supervised machine learning. In: Aleven, V., Kay, J., Mostow, J. (eds.) ITS 2010, Part II, pp. 306–308. Springer, Heidelberg (2010). https://doi.org/10.1007/978-3-642-13437-1_53

Hutt, S., Mills, C., Bosch, N., Krasich, K., Brockmole, J., D'Mello, S.: Out of the Fr-Eye-ing pan: towards gaze-based models of attention during learning with technology in the classroom. In: 25th Conference on User Modeling, Adaptation and Personalization, pp. 94–103. Association for Computing Machinery, Bratislava (2017)

Kabat-Zinn, J.: Mindfulness-based interventions in context: past, present, and future. Clin. Psychol. Sci. Pract. **10**(2), 144–156 (2003)

Killingsworth, M., Gilbert, D.: A wandering mind is an unhappy mind. Science **330**(6006), 932 (2010)

Lamme, V.: Towards a true neural stance on consciousness. Trends Cogn. Sci. **10**(11), 494–501 (2006)

Loftus, E.: Memories of things unseen. Curr. Dir. Psychol. Sci. **13**(4), 145–147 (2004)

MacKenzie, M., Mezo, P., Francis, S.: A conceptual framework for understanding self-regulation in adults. New Ideas Psychol. **30**(2), 155–165 (2012)

Matthews, G., Roberts, R., Zeidner, M.: TARGET ARTICLES: "Seven Myths About Emotional Intelligence". Psychol. Inq. **15**(3), 179–196 (2004)

Mooneyham, B., Schooler, J.: The cost and benefits of mind-wandering: a review. Can. J. Exp. Psychol. **67**(1), 11–18 (2013)

Mrazek, M., Franklin, M., Phillips, D., Baird, B., Schooler, J.: Mindfulness training improves working memory capacity and GRE performance while reducing mind wandering. Psychol. Sci. **24**(5), 776–781 (2013)

Porayska-Pomsta, K., Mavrikis, M., D'Mello, S., Conati, C., Baker, R.: Knowledge elicitation methods for affect modelling in education. Int. J. Artif. Intell. Educ. **22**(3), 107–140 (2018)

Randall, J.: Mind wandering and self-directed learning: testing the efficacy of self-regulation interventions to reduce mind wandering and enhance online training performance. Ph.D., Rice University (2015)

Smallwood, J., Schooler, J.: The science of mind wandering: empirically navigating the stream of consciousness. Annu. Rev. Psychol. **66**(1), 487–518 (2015)

Stewart, A., Bosch, N., Chen, H., Donnelly, P., D'Mello, S.: Where's your mind at? Video-based mind wandering detection during film viewing. In: 2016 Conference on User Modeling Adaptation and Personalization, pp. 295–296. Association for Computing Machinery, Halifax (2016)

Wilson, T.: Strangers to Ourselves: Discovering the Adaptive Unconscious, 1st edn. Harvard University Press, Cambridge (2002)

# Metacognitive Experience Modeling Using Eye-Tracking

Chou Ching-En[⊠]

UCL Knowledge Lab, UCL Institute of Education, London, UK
Joechou0929@gmail.com

**Abstract.** Metacognitive experience (ME) is one of the key facets of metacognition, which serves a critical cuing function in the process of self-regulated learning process. However, the study of ME is hindered by its subjective and implicit nature of and the challenges that are associated with accessing such experiences. In exploring such experiences, eye-tracking offers certain advantages over self-reporting methods. However, to date most studies tend to focus on utilizing eye-tracking to explore metacognitive skills (MS) rather than ME, with those that do explore ME also tending to require participants to self-report rather than relying on observation of possible behavioural indicators of such metacognitive processes. Based on previous works in this field, the research proposed is based on the hypothesis that eye-tracking data can provide a crucial objective measure of learners' implicit ME processes. The research will also investigate the extent to which such data can serve as the basis for automatically predicting the occurrence and intensity of ME during learning using machine learning, in a way that can support the delivery of adaptive domain-independent feedback in a variety of Intelligent Learning Environments (ILEs).

**Keywords:** Metacognition · Metacognitive experience · User modelling Eye-tracking

## 1 Introduction

Metacognition is a complex construct that comprises a number of interrelated components (Efklides 2009) such as *metacognitive knowledge* (MK), which refers the offline knowledge of cognition and *metacognitive skill* (MS), which supports the control of cognition and *metacognitive experience* (ME), which is the product of online cognition monitoring. A significant proportion of studies related to metacognition relates to the first two components, with ME having received relatively less attention to date. Following Efklides (2009), what may be responsible for this relative neglect of ME in current research is the fact that ME is much more elusive and complex in nature than the other two components insofar as it is both implicit and subjective in nature and reflective of both the affective and cognitive experiences. As such, to achieve the goals of any ongoing cognitive activities, ME can prompt the activation of MK retrieval and MS application. Given that ME is often implicit and tacit (*ibid*), traditional self-reporting methods may not fully capture the related processes. Eye-tracking has been proposed as an unobtrusive and real-time means for assessing metacognitive processes

© Springer International Publishing AG, part of Springer Nature 2018
C. Penstein Rosé et al. (Eds.): AIED 2018, LNAI 10948, pp. 503–507, 2018.
https://doi.org/10.1007/978-3-319-93846-2_94

(Veenman 2005). Building on the existing research in this area, the research presented proposes to explore the potential of eye-tracking in the research of ME.

## 2  Literature Review

### 2.1  The Role of Metacognitive Feeling in Learning

According to Efklides (2009), ME can be categorized in terms of metacognitive feelings (MF) and metacognitive judgment (MJ) (see Table 1 for examples). These online "experiences" are generated from the interaction between the object-level (i.e. information related to the task) and the meta-level (i.e. MK) information (Nelson and Narens 1990), or from the "interface between the person and the task" (Efklides 2009, p. 78). ME is critical to self-regulation of learning insofar as it serves to activate learners' retrieval of MK and the application of MS. For example, when a learner experiences a feeling of difficulty (FOD) during a learning task, s/he might seek information (as triggered and facilitated by MK retrieval and MS application) that could address such a feeling. However, although ME can help learners self-regulate, it is also subject to being influenced by multiple factors such as self-perception, self-efficacy and related affective experiences including: feeling of knowing (FOK), feeling of satisfaction (FOS), and feeling of confidence (FOC), each of which is tightly associated with different types of metacognitive judgements as listed in Table 1 (Flavell 1979; Efklides 2009).

**Table 1.** Examples of ME, Adapted from Efklides (2009)

| Category | Metacognitive Feelings (MFs) | Metacognitive judgments (MJs) |
|---|---|---|
| Examples | Tip-of-the-tongue phenomenon | Judgment of learning (JOL) |
| | Feeling of knowing (FOK) | Judgment of confidence (JOC) |
| | Feeling of confidence (FOC) | Estimate of effort (EOE) |
| | Feeling of difficulty (FOD) | Estimate of time (EOT) |
| | Feeling of satisfaction (FOS) | |
| | Feeling of familiarity (FOF) | |

Access to such metacognitive feelings seems critical to support the development of learners' metacognitive competencies and self-regulation in real-time adaptively, and to enhancing the educational benefit of adaptive feedback in intelligent learning environments (ILEs). For example, a tutoring system's ability to estimate and predict a learner's FOD can help the system calibrate the selection of learning tasks in terms of the level of difficulty that may be appropriate for the individual learners, whereas detection and/or predication of a feeling of familiarity (FOF) may help the system decide when to focus on students' consolidation of knowledge. Relying on an indepth model of ME, as proposed by Efklides, provides further potential for selecting and calibrating learning support. Specifically, understanding a student's experience of FOK, which is related to the tip-of-the-tongue phenomenon, may guide the selection of specific memory-jogging hints, FOC and FOS, which are related to the outcomes of task processing, may help in deciding that an explanation or different forms of instructions (including repeated instructions) are needed, whereas FOD and FOF, which can occur before and during task processing, may help the system decide on the specific timings of the feedback. Moreover, given that FOD is associated with negative affect while FOF is associated with positive affect (Efklides 2009) and the two can also be triggered by the fluency of task processing (Koriat 2007) may aid a targeted selection of the support strategies that specifically aim to address those factors. Because of their crucial role in ME, FOD and FOF provide the main focus for the research proposed.

## 2.2 Applying Eye-Tracking in Metacognitive Experience Research

Eye-tracking provides an unobtrusive tool for tracking visual behaviour information in real-time, which could reveal the implicit metacognitive processes associated with the different *metacognitive feelings* and *metacognitive judgements*. Although there exists an extensive body of research on eye-tracking and metacognition, many studies tend to focus on MS. Moreover, most studies conducted is the context reading skills (e.g. Kinnunen and Vauras 1995; Graesser et al. 2005) with significantly fewer focusing on ME. Exceptions include Paulus et al.'s (2013) study which explored children's judgment of confidence (JOC) during an image pairing activity where eye fixation for used to indicating the functioning of implicit JOC. However, the definition of implicit ME functioning adopted in Markus et al.'s research and similar studies, such as Thomas and Claudia (2010), differs from the definition adopted in the research proposed because in Markus et al.'s case participants are asked to explicitly report their JOC by choosing an item corresponding to their JOC on a scale provided. Here the eye-tracker data (in this case eye fixation) is recorded just before the item is clicked, meaning that the eye-tracking data acquired in that period might relate to the FOC evaluation process rather than to an implicit JOC. Eliciting ME functioning from participants by asking them to explicitly self-report requires explicit decision-making. Another related study is that by Chua and Solinger (2015), where they use eye-tracking to examine cue fluency (FOK and JOC), by collecting eye-tracking data before asking the participants to evaluate their level of FOK and JOC. However, in this work eye-tracking data is used to define cue fluency rather than determining the level of FOK and JOC. In contrast to both Markus et al.'s and Chua and Solinger's approaches, the research presented here explores implicit MEs during a learning task.

# 3 Methodology

## 3.1 Research Aims, Hypothesis and Questions, Initial Task and Participants

The research presented here aims to investigate whether and how well eye-tracking data can provide a meaningful access to implicit ME of learners during a learning task without requiring them to self-report. To ensure that the targeted ME can be observed, each targeted ME will be paired with a different activity which could potentially trigger the specific type of ME. As a result, it is assumed in the current proposal that the targeted ME can be triggered by the correspondent activities. For example, FOD has been related to task difficulty (e.g. Efklides 2009), and so a task whose objective difficulty can be manipulated may appropriate for exploring FOD. Similarly, following Whittlesea's and Rayner (1993) suggestion that FOF is attributed to the re-emergence of experienced stimulus, an item pairing activity could be used to trigger FOF.

Two overarching questions provide the focus for this research: **(1)** What are the distinguishable behavioural signifiers of different kinds of ME and different intensity of MEs?; **(2)** can the trained model generalize to different learning contexts? In other words, the ME user model may support the learning of different domains and delivery of adaptive support therein.

The initial task for exploring the construct of FOD is inspired by a match-three mobile game called Tower of Saviors (ToS) which requires the players to move a ball for 5 s at a time. Players have to plan the ball-moving path to reach the goal of dissolving as many sets of balls as possible. Obstacles that obstruct the path of ball-moving are used to manage the task difficulty. For exploring FOF, an item-paring task similar to Thomas and Claudia's (2010) will be adopted.

Students from primary school (aged 9–11) are the participants in the study proposed. Comparing to secondary school students, younger students need more metacognitive self-regulation support, especially that at this age they also face a demanding transition from primary to secondary level educational.

### 3.2   Procedure and Data Analysis

The participants will first get familiar with the basic rule and control of the tasks on a touch-screen laptop connected to a portable eye-tracker. Eye-tracking data along with screen and video recording of the interaction will be recorded. This data will be used in the later stimulated recall interview (SRI). For the FOD task, the game table will be refreshed randomly, while obstacles will be added through levelling game difficulty. Participants' level of FOD will be reported via a 4-point scale, ranging from 1 (not at all difficult) to 4 (very difficult). For the FOF-related task, participants will memorize the randomly picked portraits one at a time. A group of new and already shown portraits is then used for FOF elicitation, which will be followed by the FOF self-report.

Eye-tracking features will be selected based on Eivazi and Bednarik (2011) and will include mean and sum fixation duration, mean between fixation and total eye-movement path distance, number and rate (divided by the duration) of fixations, fixation position within the game, and pupil dilation. The SRI will explore other factors that may influence the target MEs (i.e. FOD and FOF) and will help the selection of eye-tracking features. Scale vector machine (SVM) method (e.g. Liang et al. 2007) will be explored as a way of constructing student's MEs model.

# 4  Conclusions

The current proposal will construct a user model of learners' level of FOD and FOF based on eye-tracking measurements. It will explore these MEs which are relatively less task-dependent compared to MS. The ultimate goal of the research is to investigate the extent to which such data can serve as the basis for automatically predicting the occurrence and intensity of MEs during learning using machine learning, in a way that can support the delivery of adaptive domain-independent feedback in a variety of ILEs.

# References

Efklides, A.: The role of metacognitive experiences in the learning process. Psicothema **21**, 76–82 (2009)

Eivazi, S., Bednarik, R.: Predicting problem-solving behavior and performance levels from visual attention data. In: 2nd Workshop on Eye Gaze in Intelligent Human Machine Interaction at IUI, pp. 9–16 (2011)

Chua, E.F., Esolinger, L.: Building metamemorial knowledge over time: insights from eye tracking about the bases of feeling-of-knowing and confidence judgments. Front. Psychol. **6**, 1206 (2015)

Flavell, J.H.: Metacognition and cognitive monitoring – a new area of cognitive-development inquiry. Am. Psychol. **34**(10), 906–911 (1979)

Graesser, A.C., Lu, S., Olde, B.A., Cooper-Pye, E., Whitten, S.: Question asking and eye tracking during cognitive disequilibrium: comprehending illustrated texts on devices when the devices break down. Mem. Cogn. **33**, 1235–1247 (2005)

Kinnunen, R., Vauras, M.: Comprehension monitoring and the level of comprehension in high- and low-achieving primary school children's reading. Learn. Instr. **5**, 143–165 (1995)

Koriat, A.: Metacognition and consciousness. In: Zelazo, P.D., Moscovitch, M., Thompson, E. (eds.) The Cambridge Handbook of Consciousness, pp. 289–325. Cambridge University Press, Cambridge (2007)

Liang, Y., Reyes, M.L., Lee, J.D.: Real-time detection of driver cognitive distraction using support vector machines. IEEE Trans. Intell. Transp. Syst. **8**(340), 350 (2007)

Paulus, M., Proust, J., Sodian, B.: Examining implicit metacognition in 3.5-year-old children: an eye-tracking and pupillometric study. Front. Psychol. **4**(145) (2013)

Nelson, T.O., Narens, L.: Metamemory: a theoretical framework and new findings. In: Bower, G. (ed.) The psychology of learning and motivation, vol. 26, pp. 125–141. Academic Press, New York (1990)

Roderer, T., Roebers, C.M.: Explicit and implicit confidence judgments and developmental differences in metamemory: an eye-tracking approach. Metacogn. Learn. **5**(3), 229–250 (2010)

Veenman, M.V.J.: The assessment of metacognitive skills: what can be learned from multimethod designs? In: Artelt, C., Moschner, B. (eds.) Lernstrategien und Metakognition: Implikationen für Forschung und Praxis, pp. 75–97. Waxmann, Berlin (2005)

Whittlesea, B., Rayner, K.: Illusions of familiarity. J. Exp. Psychol. Learn. Mem. Cogn. **19**(6), 1235–1253 (1993)

# Exploring the Meaning of Effective Exploratory Learner Behavior in Hands-on, Collaborative Projects Using Physical Computing Kits

Veronica Cucuiat[(✉)]

UCL Knowledge Lab, London WC1N 3QS, UK
v.cucuiat.14@ucl.ac.uk

**Abstract.** The present study aims to use learning analytics to explore the meaning of effective exploratory learning behavior in the context of practical, collaborative activities using physical computing kits. To find relevant ways of analysing the data which are strongly embedded in the learning context, four unique affordances of exploratory learning environments are identified from literature: responsive, social, open-ended and supportive. This paper proposes a set of data signifiers which may be used to generate visualisations into the ways in which the four affordances manifest themselves into the learning environment through the students' actions.

**Keywords:** Exploratory learning · Learning analytics · Responsive
Open-ended · Social · Supportive · Collaborative · Hands-on
Physical computing kits

## 1 Introduction

Education is increasingly moving away from static, instructionist, transmission-based teaching and learning methodologies in the direction of active, exploratory, growth-based tools and practices [1–3]. Exploratory learning environments intuitively allow for such learning to take place [2–4]. However, there is very little consensus over what a well-designed exploratory learning activity is and what are the practical implications of applying it in the classroom [3]. To advance our understanding of exploratory learning, it is important to study its origins and root any future analysis in the ideas which led to its conception. To that end, four key affordances unique to exploratory learning environments are identified from literature: responsive, open-ended, social and supportive.

The main question which this study intends to address is 'What does it mean for students to operate effectively as exploratory learners in the context of practical activities using physical computing kits?' What would it mean for a student to maximise the affordabilities - the responsiveness, the open-endedness, the social and supportive aspects of exploratory learning environments to, as a result, maximise their learnings? Importantly, rather than analysing what is an effective learner as an output, the focus of this study is what is an effective learner as a process.

© Springer International Publishing AG, part of Springer Nature 2018
C. Penstein Rosé et al. (Eds.): AIED 2018, LNAI 10948, pp. 508–512, 2018.
https://doi.org/10.1007/978-3-319-93846-2_95

## 2   Background

The fields of learning analytics and educational data mining have played a significant role in the understanding of exploratory environments using "continual and real-time assessment on student process and progress, in which the amount of formative feedback is radically increased" [3]. However, many studies apply exploratory learning simply as a different methodology to be plugged in-and-out of existing learning contexts. Whilst students conduct their learning through practical projects, the objectives and evaluations remain steeped in the limitations arising from content-focused, instructionist practices. For example, many studies will correlate exploratory behaviours to subject-specific knowledge measured through standardised tests [5–7] or classify students' actions according to one-dimensional performance labels [8–10]. Whilst these are important studies, highlighting the link between exploratory learning and more traditional ways of evaluating progress, they stop short of exposing new directions for designing and quantifying learning.

Educational theory shows us that evaluations against averaged-out standards across large pools of students are not effective measures of individual performance [11], context is important when designing learning activities and evaluating progress [11, 12], and ability is multidimensional and cannot be reduced to a single unit of measurement [11]. Novel data analysis methods allow us to move towards a more comprehensive way of evaluating performance, coping with the randomness and uniqueness of individual pathways and taking into account the social context. This study attempts to further advances in this direction, aiming to identify data signifiers based on students' actions, placed in the context of their environment, rooted in the four affordances unique to exploratory learning.

## 3   Methodology

For the proposed study, 18 children in Year 8 participated in a hands-on, collaborative, computationally-rich project over a school term. The project brief consists of building an 'intelligent' board game to be played as a fun way of revising for history lessons. Such 'intelligent' behaviour is to be achieved using the SAM Labs physical computing kits. The aim of the learning experience is to integrate SAM electronics, 3D printing and history knowledge into a coherent and engaging board game (Table 1). Given the

**Table 1.**  Breakdown of data collection

| Video | Audio | CCTV video | SAM labs app | Teacher input | Student input |
|---|---|---|---|---|---|
| Individual student | Individual student | Group | Individual action logs | Project design | Digital journal |
| | | | | Analysis interviews | Self-assessment |
| | | | | Student evaluation | Questionnaires |

wide spectrum of the analysis dimensions - responsive, social, open-ended and sup-portive - multiple data streams helped capture the learning experience in detail.

Data was collected over the course of a whole school term, in weekly two-hour sessions. Data signifiers are identified against the four exploratory learning affordances, in terms of actions in the physical environment as well as SAM Labs log entries. A starting point towards such a breakdown and coding schema is presented below.

### 3.1  Responsive

Feedback received promptly from the environment itself in response to pupils trying out their own theories, revealing inadequacies and mistakes in their beliefs is a fun-damental characteristic of an effective educational environment [1]. This is extracted from the data via the various actions students take which trigger feedback being returned to them by using the various tools available, and the ways in which they respond to the given feedback. A proposed breakdown of the events to be analysed is reproduced in Table 2.

**Table 2.** Breakdown of responsive data signifiers

| Event | Description |
|---|---|
| Discovery | Video & Audio: browse, try out new functionality, create new theories |
| | SAM: Add new blocks/connections never used before |
| Test | Video & Audio: implement an idea - SAM, 3D printing, prototype, draw |
| | SAM: Changes made throughout the project discarded by the end |
| Change | Video & Audio: modify implementation to match desired result |
| | SAM: Changes made throughout the project kept in final graph |

### 3.2  Open-Ended

Jean Piaget's idea that intelligence emerges from an evolutionary process in which many factors must have time to find their equilibrium, where different ideas must come together coherently and meaningful associations must be created in order for learners to identify with new concepts supports a view of education which is complex [13], influenced by a large number of parameters, some more correlated than others, and impossible to streamline across a large number of individuals [11] (Table 3). The open-ended nature of exploratory learning allows for knowledge to emerge in this way, and may be analysed within the context of the present case study via the following events.

**Table 3.** Breakdown of open-ended data signifiers

| Event | Description |
|---|---|
| New idea | Video & Audio: generate new ideas to implement in the game |
| | SAM: Novel uses of blocks/connections |
| Association | Video & Audio: explicit link to existing knowledge/experience |
| | SAM: Association with previous graph history changes |
| Adaptation | Video & Audio: modify idea to apply personally |
| | SAM: Adaptation of graphs within the classroom, similarity of components |

### 3.3  Social

Vygotsky argued that individual development cannot take place without considering the social and cultural context within which the learner is embedded in, asserting that higher mental processes originate in social processes [14] (Table 4). Thus, a proposed set of events analyzing the social interactions occurring in the context of the present case study is presented below.

**Table 4.**  Breakdown of social data signifiers

| Event | Description |
|---|---|
| Inspiration | Video & Audio: source of ideas: peers, teacher, discovery, feedback |
| | SAM: Adaptation of graphs within the video context of 'Inspiration' |
| Reach Out | Video & Audio: ask for help, showcase, proactively seek feedback |
| | SAM: Adaptation of graphs within the video context of 'Reaching Out' |
| Share | Video & Audio: proactively help others, share insights |
| | SAM: Adaptation of graphs within the video context of 'Share' |

### 3.4  Supportive

One of the primary theoretical bases for supporting students' learning is Vygotsky's zone of proximal development [14]. We turn to boundaries [15] as a useful concept in trying to find a balance between the open-endedness benefits of exploratory learning and relevant support. In the context of computationally-powered micro-worlds, building in relevant boundaries can provide effective support without disrupting the empowering freedom students require (Table 5). A potential way of visualizing the impact of such boundaries on the students' exploration may be observed through the following events.

**Table 5.**  Breakdown of supportive data signifiers

| Event | Description |
|---|---|
| Consolidate boundary | Video & Audio: efforts to work within the project boundaries |
| | SAM: Refinement of graph changes towards end state |
| Add boundary | Video & Audio: Actively refine towards more specific boundaries |
| | SAM: Restrict graph to specific blocks/branches |
| Remove boundary | Video & Audio: a set boundary is crossed/removed/broken |
| | SAM: Restrict graph to specific blocks/branches |

Based on the data signifiers presented above, the next stage of the research will design an individual learner profile as a visualisation into the ways in which the four dimensions manifest themselves into the learning environment through the students' actions. The visualisation will provide insights into the strategies that students employ in navigating exploratory learning.

**Acknowledgements.** This work has been supported by a Bloomsbury Consortium PhD studentship at UCL and Birkbeck, University of London.

# References

1. Perkinson, H.J.: Learning from Our Mistakes: A Reinterpretation of Twentieth-Century Educational Theory. Greenwood Press, Westport (1984)
2. Cukurova, M., Avramides, K., Spikol, D., Luckin, R., Mavrikis, M.: An analysis framework for collaborative problem solving in practice-based learning activities: a mixed-method approach. In: Proceedings of the Sixth International Conference on Learning Analytics and Knowledge, pp. 84–88 (2016)
3. Berland, M., Baker, R.S., Blikstein, P.: Educational data mining and learning analytics: applications to constructionist research. Technol. Knowl. Learn. **19**, 205–220 (2014)
4. Papert, S.: The Children's Machine. Rethinking School in the Age of the Computer. Basic Books, New York (1993)
5. Dong, Y., Giswas, Y.: An extended learner modeling method to assess students' learning behaviors. In: Proceedings of the 10th International Conference on Educational Data Mining (2017)
6. Käser, T., Hallinen, N.R,. Schwartz, D.L.: Modeling exploration strategies to predict student performance within a learning environment and beyond. In: Learning Analytics and Knowledge, pp. 13–17 (2017)
7. Kinnebrew, J.S., Gauch, B.C., Segedy, J.R., Biswas, G.: Studying student use of self-regulated learning tools in an open-ended learning environment. In: International Conference on Artificial Intelligence in Education (2015)
8. Bauer, A., Flatten, J., Popovic, Z.: Analysis of problem-solving behavior in open-ended scientific-discovery game challenges. In: Proceedings of the 10th International Conference on Educational Data Mining (2017)
9. Floryan, M., Dragon, T., Basit, N., Woolf, B.P.: Who needs help? Automating student assessment within exploratory learning environments. In: International Conference on Artificial Intelligence in Education (2015)
10. Frost, S., McCalla, G.: Exploring through simulation an instructional planner for dynamic open-ended learning environments. In: International Conference on Artificial Intelligence in Education (2015)
11. Rose, T.: The End of Average: How We Succeed in a World That Values Sameness. HarperOne, New York (2016)
12. Luckin, R.: Re-designing Learning Contexts: Technology-Rich, Learner-Centred Ecologies. Routledge, London (2010)
13. Piaget, J.: To Understand is to Invent. Penguin Books, New York (1976)
14. Vygotsky, L.S.: Thought and Language. MIT Press, Cambridge (1986)
15. Laurel, B.: Computers as Theatre. Addison-Wesley Professional, Upper Saddle River (1993)

# Multimodal Tutor for CPR

Daniele Di Mitri[✉]

Welten Institute, Research Centre for Learning, Teaching and Technology,
Open University of the Netherlands, Heerlen, Netherlands
`Daniele.Dimitri@ou.nl`

**Abstract.** This paper describes the design of an intelligent Multimodal Tutor for training people to perform cardiopulmonary resuscitation using patient manikins (CPR tutor). The tutor uses a multisensor setup for tracking the CPR execution and generating personalised feedback, including unobtrusive vibrations and retrospective summaries. This study is the main experiment of a PhD project focusing on multimodal data support for investigating practice-based learning scenarios, such as psychomotor skills training in the classroom or at the workplace. For the CPR tutor the multimodal data considered consist of trainee's body position (with Microsoft Kinect), electromyogram (with Myo armband) and compression rates data derived from the manikin. The CPR tutor uses a new technological framework, the Multimodal Pipeline, which motivates a set of technical approaches used for the data collection, storage, processing, annotation and exploitation of multimodal data. This paper aims at opening up the motivation, the planning and expected evaluations of this experiment to further feedback and considerations by the scientific community.

## 1 Background

Practical skills training, co-located group interactions, and tasks alternative to the classic desktop-based learning scenario represent still a big set of learning activities taking place in the classroom and at the workplace. In data-driven learning research, physical interactions are most of the time "offline moments", not captured by the data collection and not included in the datasets used for analysis. Bringing these moments into account requires extending the data collection from conventional data sources (e.g. data from the learning management system) to data "beyond learner-computer interaction". With the umbrella term *multimodal data* we refer to micro-level (1) learners behavioural data: i.e. motoric actions or physiological responses; (2) data of the learning situation such as learning context, environment and activity. The multimodal data collection can be achieved using wearable sensors, cameras or Internet of Things (IoT) devices. Several of these devices find direct application in the domain of learning [7].

There are several opportunities in using multimodal data with computerised methods. Multimodal data allow to bridge the gap between learners complex behavioural patterns with learning theories [8]. It does so by connecting sensor data to human-driven qualitative interpretations, like expert reports or teacher

C. Penstein Rosé et al. (Eds.): AIED 2018, LNAI 10948, pp. 513–516, 2018.
https://doi.org/10.1007/978-3-319-93846-2_96

assessments. The latter describe more qualitative and human-driven interpretations that sensors cannot directly observe, such as learning outcomes, cognitive aspects or affective states. For example, Ochoa and Chiluiza [6] collected multimodal data including video, audio and pen strokes with the aim to predict expertise. Multimodal data can also be used as historical evidence for the analysis and the description of the learning process [1]. Worsley and Blikstein [9] recorded video and audio from 13 students building simple structures with sticks and tape. From video data, they derived skeletal position and gesture movements and they translated the multimodal transcripts "action codes", task-specific patterns such as 'build', 'plan','test', 'adjust' and 'undo'. Finally, multimodal data can be used as the base to drive machine reasoning and adaptation during learning. This can be achieved with the design of intelligent computer agents empathic to the learners which work as an instructor in the box. Existing examples of multimodal ITS are AutoTutor [5] or the Affective Learning Companion [2].

Multimodal data have generally different formats, granularity and levels of abstractions. Dealing with such data raises a number of challenges including: (1) collecting the learning labels through reliable and unobtrusive annotation procedure; (2) designing a sensor fusion architecture for collecting and processing multi-sensor data; (3) finding a strategy to best represent and analyse the multimodal data; (4) produce insights that are valuable for the learner; (5) comply with the ethics and privacy regulation (e.g. the new European GDPR).

## 2  Proposed Approach

This PhD project aims to shed light on some of these challenges. Some of those were first encountered in the first experimental study "Learning Pulse", published in the LAK'17 proceedings, which aimed to predict learners' Flow, productivity and stress out of Fitbit data and self-reported questionnaires [3].

In this PhD project we also propose a theoretical model: the Multimodal Learning Analytics Model (MLeAM) [4]. MLeAM (left-hand Fig. 1) shows how multimodal data can produce feedback to the learner and help to classify similar experiments in the field. The MLeAM helps with the identification of meaningful modalities. At the same time the MLeAM illustrates how to formulate hypothesis and interpretations on the collected data through human annotations.

To provide technological support to the MLeAM, as part of this PhD project, we also propose the Multimodal Pipeline. The Pipeline is a chain of technical solutions for handling the multimodal tracking and to incorporate multimodal data for more accurate student modelling, learning analytics and intelligent machine tutoring. The Pipeline is composed by five steps: the collection, the storing, the processing, the annotation and the exploitation of multimodal data.

While writing this contribution, the technical implementation of the different steps of the Pipeline is being carried. We are creating a flexible system which can integrate multiple sensors and provide instantaneous feedback based on multimodal data. We plan to use this system for multiple use cases, including the scenario described in next section.

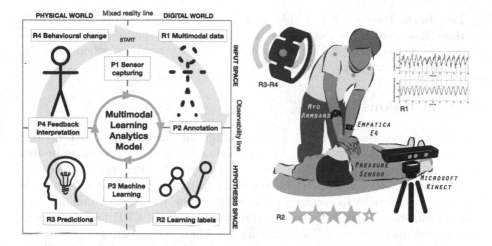

**Fig. 1.** L: Multimodal Learning Analytics Model. R: concept of the CPR tutor.

## 2.1   The Case of Cardiopulmonary Resuscitation

To provide a proof-of-concept of the MLeAM and the Multimodal Pipeline we decide to focus on a specific learning scenario, CPR training using manikins. CPR is a task that is usually trained singularly and has a clear procedure. The learning objectives are also well defined: e.g. the compressions should be around 120 per minute and 5 cm deep. CPR has also a strong practical significance, the cases of cardiopulmonary arrest are unfortunately very common, the more people are trained to do CPR the higher the chance of saving lives.

The experiment starts with an expert survey to be sent out to a network of CPR trainers. This survey aims to clarify the relevant feedback for learners doing CPR, with special focus on performing chest compressions. The experiment continues with a quantitative data collection which we summarise as follows.

1. **Sensor capturing**. The multimodal data sources considered for this experiment are (1) body position, specific jointures derived using Microsoft Kinect; (2) electro myogram data, collected using Myo armband; (3) physiological data as heart rate variability (HRV) and galvanic skin response (GSR) using an Empatica E4; (4) compression-rate and compression-depth using the wireless skill reporter of the Resusci Anne QCPR manikin.
2. **Annotation**. We focus on the chest compressions, assuming that the QCPR manikin already provides high-quality data. We use the manikin data as baseline. We label each compression (0.5 s) with an annotation tool to rate each compression either a binary scale or 5-points Likert scale.
3. **Machine learning**. We pre-process the data and extract only a number of informative attributes, depending on the number of available labels. Then we train multiple classifiers which can predict the labels given in step 2. For example, different classifiers can be trained for each individual learner, so to tackle the high inter-subject variability.

4. **Feedback**. The classifiers will be able to assess current performance on real-time. Based on this automatic and machine driven evaluation, we can generate haptic feedback pushing vibrations to the Myo armband when the CPR compressions are not correctly performed.

## 3   Conclusions

In this paper, we presented a PhD project background rationale and we described the planning of a Multimodal Tutor for CPR, a tutor able to generate predictions and to provide personalised feedback during CPR. This type of feedback is unobtrusive and could speed up the CPR training process. Describing this experiment we would to receive further feedback by the AIED community on the experimental design. We believe the development of CPR tutor is a relevant contribution for the AIED community. Although there are various studies using sensor data, these still represent a little portion of the AIED research. In addition, the CPR tutor will prove the concept of using multimodal data and validate the proposed models like MLeAM and the Multimodal Pipeline. We believe that these tools can be of great use for future learning research planning to use multimodal data.

## References

1. Blikstein, P.: Multimodal learning analytics. In: Proceedings of the Third International Conference on Learning Analytics and Knowledge - LAK 2013, p. 102 (2013)
2. Burleson, W.: Affective learning companions. Educ. Technol. **47**(1), 28 (2007)
3. Di Mitri, D., Scheffel, M., Drachsler, H., Börner, D., Ternier, S., Specht, M.: Learning pulse: a machine learning approach for predicting performance in self-regulated learning using multimodal data. In: LAK 2017 Proceedings of the 7th International Conference on Learning Analytics and Knowledge, pp. 188–197 (2017)
4. Di Mitri, D., Schneider, J., Specht, M., Drachsler, H.: From signals to knowledge. Modeling the emerging research field of multimodal data for learning (2018)
5. D'Mello, S., Jackson, T., Craig, S., Morgan, B., Chipman, P., White, H., Person, N., Kort, B., El Kaliouby, R., Picard, R.W., Graesser, A.: AutoTutor detects and responds to learners affective and cognitive states. IEEE Trans. Educ. **48**(4), 612–618 (2008)
6. Ochoa, X., Chiluiza, K., Méndez, G., Luzardo, G., Guamán, B., Castells, J.: Expertise estimation based on simple multimodal features. In: Proceedings of the 15th ACM International Conference on Multimodal Iteraction (ICMI 2013), pp. 583–590 (2013)
7. Schneider, J., Börner, D., van Rosmalen, P., Specht, M.: Augmenting the senses: a review on sensor-based learning support. Sensors **15**(2), 4097–4133 (2015)
8. Worsley, M.: Multimodal learning analytics as a tool for bridging learning theory and complex learning behaviors. In: 3rd Multimodal Learning Analytics Workshop and Grand Challenges, MLA 2014, pp. 1–4 (2014)
9. Worsley, M., Blikstein, P.: Towards the development of multimodal action based assessment. In: Proceedings of the Third International Conference on Learning Analytics and Knowledge - LAK 2013, pp. 94–101 (2013)

# Leveraging Educational Technology to Improve the Quality of Civil Discourse

Nicholas Diana[✉]

Carnegie Mellon University, Pittsburgh, PA 15213, USA
ndiana@cmu.edu

**Abstract.** The ability to critically assess the information we consume is vital to productive civil discourse. However, recent research indicates that Americans are generally not adept at, for instance, identifying if a news story is real or fake. We propose a three-part research agenda aimed at providing accessible, evidence-based technological support for critical thinking in civic life. In the first stage, we built an online tutoring system for teaching logical fallacy identification. In stage two, we will leverage this system to train crowd workers to identify potentially fallacious arguments. Finally, in stage three, we will utilize these labeled examples to train a computational model of logical fallacies. We discuss how our current research into instructional factors and Belief Bias has impacted the course of this agenda, and how these three stages help to realize our ultimate goal of fostering critical thinking in civil discourse.

**Keywords:** Cognitive tutors · Informal logical fallacies
Informal reasoning · Cognitive task analysis
Difficulty factors assessment · Ill-defined domains

## 1 Introduction

The recent rise of *fake news* on popular social media platforms has underscored the importance of critical thinking skills in informed civil discourse. Some estimates claim that Americans fall for fake news headlines approximately 75% of the time [5], and as reliance on social media as a primary new source increases, this problem may only get worse. One potential way to combat fake news is to embed support for key skills such as evidence evaluation and argument analysis into the media we consume. We propose that educational technology provides an opportunity for accessible, evidence-based instruction and support for these essential critical thinking skills, and describe our current and proposed research in this area.

## 2 Current and Proposed Work

Informal reasoning shares many of the challenges associated with other ill-defined domains (ambiguity, limited formal theories, etc.) [4]. To make the ill-defined

© Springer International Publishing AG, part of Springer Nature 2018
C. Penstein Rosé et al. (Eds.): AIED 2018, LNAI 10948, pp. 517–520, 2018.
https://doi.org/10.1007/978-3-319-93846-2_97

domain of informal reasoning more tractable, we focus on teaching informal fallacies. Informal fallacies are simply patterns of bad argumentation, where the premises of an argument fail to support the conclusion. More importantly, informal fallacies provide a semi-structured way to research how people reason about everyday arguments and the biases that may impact their logical reasoning. Our research agenda progresses towards this goal in three incremental stages.

## 2.1  Online Logical Fallacy Tutor

The first stage in exploring this space is to better understand how people learn to identify logical fallacies, and if educational technology can be an effective tool in teaching that skill. We have already taken some preliminary steps towards answering these questions by building and testing an online tutoring system designed to teach logical fallacy identification. The results of this initial foray are promising. First, our data suggest that a student's political beliefs may inhibit their ability to identify faulty logic in arguments that align with their own beliefs, a cognitive bias known as Belief Bias [3]. For example, liberal users have more difficulty identifying faulty logic in arguments with a liberal conclusion. This interaction between personal beliefs and our ability to identify faulty logic suggests that new solutions in this space may need to account for the user's beliefs in the instruction or intervention.

Our data also show clear evidence of learning. Specifically, we were interested in whether instruction that promoted deductive reasoning (e.g., definitions and explanations) was more effective than instruction that promoted inductive reasoning (e.g., seeing many examples of the fallacy). To test this, we conducted an Instructional Factors Analysis [2], and found that while users were able to learn a logical fallacy through inductive instruction (examples) alone, the deductive instruction (definitions and explanations) was more than twice as effective.

## 2.2  Crowdsourcing Logical Fallacy Detection

In addition to training citizens to identify logical fallacies themselves, we are also interested in ways that technology can support fallacy identification. It is likely the case that logical fallacies are easier to spot in the context of an online tutoring system simply because users are looking for them. In real life, we rarely expend so much energy thinking critically about each argument we read or hear (unless we fervently disagree with it), and real-world fallacies are often subtler than the illustrative examples given in textbooks [1]. Coupled with the pace of discourse in, for example, a presidential debate, logical fallacies are easy to miss, if youre not paying careful attention.

In this stage, we propose a system that helps users pay closer attention to specific pieces of discourse that might warrant some critical evaluation. We will leverage the online tutoring system we built previously to train or evaluate crowd workers. On the backend, our proposed system will break discourse content into digestible parts and then distribute the parts to crowd workers (trained using our tutoring system) who will flag any content that may contain a fallacy. On the frontend, a user reading an article with our service enabled may notice a section that has been highlighted, indicating the possibility of faulty logic. It is important here to note that our crowd workers are not simply labeling arguments as fallacious, but rather as potentially fallacious. There are two reasons for this choice. First, the presence of a logical fallacy does not necessarily invalidate an argument. If I were to say, The earth is round and youre crazy if you dont think so. Id be committing an Ad Hominem fallacy, but the earth is still round. In many cases, arguments containing logical fallacies are not invalid, just weak arguments. Second, and more importantly, by not passing a verdict we force the user to exercise their own critical thinking skills. In this way, our system (1) provides more opportunities for thinking critically about real-world discourse, and (2) scaffolds those opportunities with some degree of judgement about the discourse in question.

We can validate the performance of crowd workers by comparing their classifications against the classifications of other crowd workers, or to a smaller set of expert classified examples. Evaluating the impact of the system on a users critical thinking skills is more difficult. One possibility is asking users to report if they agree that a fallacy exists in the highlighted text. Once we have validated the high likelihood of a fallacys existence in that piece of text (using the methods mentioned previously), we could use user agreement as a rough proxy for critical thinking ability. Furthermore, while we would expect agreement to be lower for arguments that align with the users political orientation (due to the aforementioned Belief Bias), we might expect that agreement would increase on these types of arguments over time, as critical thinking skills improve.

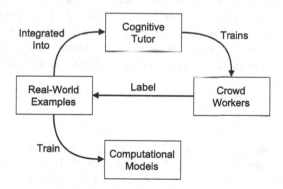

**Fig. 1.** Feedback loop relationship between the cognitive tutor and crowd workers. The real-world examples labeled by crowd workers can be used to both improve the cognitive tutor and train computational models. In addition to improving our tutoring system, we can also use those labeled examples to train a computational model of logical fallacies. We argue that machines may be able to recognize the possibility of a logical fallacy (using linguistic cues or similarity to prior labeled data). Once a potential fallacy is recognized, the machine will then prompt the human to assess the validity. This hybrid solution capitalizes on the computational strength of machines and the as-yet unparalleled power of human sense-making to improve fallacy identification.

## 2.3   Towards a Computational Model of Logical Fallacy Identification

The final goal of this work is to develop a computational model of logical fallacies. Achieving this goal requires overcoming several large challenges. First, to train a model to detect such a nuanced use of language will most likely require a large number of labeled examples. Furthermore, these examples will most likely have to be varied and authentic (perhaps unlike many of the purposefully illustrative examples used in textbooks). To solve this shortage of labeled examples, we propose using our cognitive tutor to train crowd workers to identify fallacies in real-world media sources (as described in the *Crowdsourcing* stage). High quality labels can then be automatically integrated into the tutor training system, increasing the number of potential examples crowd workers can use to achieve mastery. This increase in the number of examples may be especially important for fallacies that are most efficiently taught using inductive instruction. Figure 1 shows the feedback loop relationship between crowd workers and the cognitive tutor.

If we meet these challenges and are able to detect the markers of logical fallacies in real-world text, there are potential applications in media (both traditional and social), politics, and education. One could imagine a plugin for your favorite word processor that underlines a potential Appeal to Ignorance just as it would a misspelled word. Similarly, one could imagine how broadcasts of presidential debates in the future might be accompanied by a subtle notification anytime a candidate might be committing a Moral Equivalence fallacy.

Taken together, these projects represent an accessible, theory-driven way to impact the quality of civil discourse using educational technology. Just as technology has played an unfortunate role in amplifying fake news, so too will it play a role in combating those unreliable sources. We believe the most effective defense against this surge of misinformation are systems that both train citizens to be better critical thinkers and support that critical thinking in their everyday lives.

# References

1. Boudry, M., Paglieri, F., Pigliucci, M.: The fake, the flimsy, and the fallacious: demarcating arguments in real life. Argumentation **29**(4), 431–456 (2015)
2. Chi, M., Koedinger, K.R., Gordon, G.J., Jordon, P., VanLahn, K.: Instructional factors analysis: a cognitive model for multiple instructional interventions (2011)
3. Evans, J.S., Barston, J.L., Pollard, P.: On the conflict between logic and belief in syllogistic reasoning. Mem. Cogn. **11**(3), 295–306 (1983)
4. Lynch, C., Ashley, K., Aleven, V., Pinkwart, N.: Defining ill-defined domains; a literature survey. In: Proceedings of the Workshop on Intelligent Tutoring Systems for Ill-defined Domains at the 8th International Conference on Intelligent Tutoring Systems, pp. 1–10 (2006)
5. Silverman, C., Singer-Vine, J.: Most Americans who see fake news believe it, new survey says. BuzzFeed News (2016). https://www.buzzfeed.com/craigsilverman/fake-newssurvey

# Adapting Learning Activities Selection in an Intelligent Tutoring System to Affect

Chinasa Odo[✉]

University of Aberdeen, Kings Street, Aberdeen, UK
r01cro17@abdn.ac.uk

**Abstract.** My PhD focuses on adapting learning activities selection to learner affect in an intelligent tutoring system. The research aims to investigate the affective states considered for adapting learning activity selection, and how to adapt to these. It also seeks to know how learner's affective state can be obtained through tutor-learner interaction rather than via sensors or questionnaires. The research will use of a mixture of qualitative and quantitative methods to achieve these aims. This research will significantly contribute to the area of intelligent tutoring technology by providing more insights into how to adapt to affective states, and improve the delivery of learning. The result will lead to an algorithm for learning activity selection based on affect, which also incorporates other relevant learner characteristics, such as personalty, that moderate affect.

**Keywords:** Affective state · Learning activity selection
Personalization

## 1 Introduction

In recent times, affect is considered an important aspect in learning. Affective states are emotions or feelings expressed in the face, tone, or gesture which have a powerful and subconscious influence on how people think, behave, and deal with social information [6,9]. During learning, both positive and negative affect are expected in a learner. In a traditional learning environment, a human tutor uses the learners' observed affective state to adapt teaching strategies. However, different people learn differently and may well experience different affective states in the same learning context. Hence, the method a teacher adopts may not work well for every learner in a group. This has prompted a need for alternative solutions using computational methods. An intelligent tutoring system is a computer system aimed at providing customized instructions and feedback to learners [17]. Human tutors have the capability to observe most changes in affective state, but an intelligent tutoring system has the capability to recognize, respond and react to affect [16]. The intelligent tutoring system may respond to learners' affective state in real-time by providing personalized and contextual feedback. In my PhD, I am interested not just to respond to affective state (in the sense of providing for example emotional support), but

© Springer International Publishing AG, part of Springer Nature 2018
C. Penstein Rosé et al. (Eds.): AIED 2018, LNAI 10948, pp. 521–525, 2018.
https://doi.org/10.1007/978-3-319-93846-2_98

rather how learning acitivity selection can be adapted to affective state in the hope of not just gaining better learning outcomes but of postively influencing affective state.

## 2    Research Questions

My research will answer the following research questions:

1. Which affective states should be considered when adapting learning activity selection?
2. How can a learner's affective state and other relevant characteristics be obtained through tutor-learner interaction during learning (rather than via sensors or questionnaires)?
3. What is an effective algorithm for adapting learning activity selection to affective state?

## 3    Related Work

Several studies have investigated which student affective states are present during learning [1,10]. Their results revealed the affective states of confusion, frustration and anxiety as prominent during learning. Investigating facial features for affective state detection in learning environments [13] discovered the affective states of boredom, confusion, delight, flow, frustration, and surprise. Craig et al. [3] worked on the role that affective states play in learning from the perspective of a constructivist learning framework. They observed that frustration, boredom, flow, confusion, eureka and neutral affective states occurred during learning with AutoTutor. Several emotional models already exist such as the academic emotional model by Pekrun et al. in [7,15]

Affective states have been shown to influence learning. For example, Tyng et al's study [18] showed that emotional events are remembered more clearly, accurately and for longer periods of time than neutral events. They believe that affect has a strong influence particularly on attention and behaviour. Craig et al. [3] found significant relationships between learning and the affective states of boredom, flow and confusion. A pre- and post-test was used to explore the relationship between affect and learning using an animated pedagogical agent. [8] observed that system can hold a conversation with the learner using natural language and from the conversation, emotional experience can be tracked.

D'Mello et al. [4] investigated the reliability of a system detecting a learner's affective states in an attempt to augment an intelligent tutoring system with the ability to incorporate such states into its pedagogical strategies to improve learning. They believe that systems can be more than mere cognitive machines.

There is also previous work on learning activity selection. For example, a study investigating the impact of personality and cognitive efficiency on the selection of exercises for learners [14] showed how exercises can be selected based on learners' personality. Another study by [2] on a personalized e-learning system showed that applying Item Response Theory (IRT) to Web-based learning can achieve personalized learning and help learners to learn more effectively and efficiently. Additionally, there has been substantial research on so-called educational recommender system by [5,11,19] though, these tend to focus on learner interests and ability rather than affect.

## 4   Methodology, Current and Future Work

To answer Research Question 1, and get a first insight into Research Question 3, I will conduct qualitative research (focus groups, interviews) to supplement literature review, to discover how learners and teachers feel affective state should impact learning activity selection. I have developed scenarios to describe learners experiencing particular emotions. I have conducted 8 focus groups with learners which asked them about the emotions experienced during learning and used the scenarios to investigate how they felt activity selection should take the emotions described in the scenarios into account. The focus groups also provided insights into the relevant attributes of learning activities. For example, focus groups suggested to use activities in which the learner described in one scenario would work together with the learner described in another scenario. So, one possible adaptation regards the selection of activities that allow learners with complimentary affective states to work together. Follow-on interviews with teachers are planned.

The scenarios will need to be refined and validated to ensure they properly and only express a particular affective state and do not accidentally also express personality traits. I will use the validated scenarios to further investigate Research Question 3, conducting user studies to investigate how people adapt their selection of learning materials to a learner's affective state using the User-as-Wizard method by [12]. The scenarios are used to accurately portray a learner's effective state so that the participant can use this as part of their decision making. Based on the data, I will construct algorithms for automatic adaptation of learning material selection to affective state.

It is quite possible that other learner characteristics, in particular personality, may impact on how a learner's affective state needs to be taken into consideration (Research Question 2). Further qualitative studies will investigate this, followed by user studies. This is likely to modify the algorithm.

To investigate the effectiveness of the algorithm, I plan to first test it in a simple learning environment where a learner's affective state has been induced. I will need to consider on how exactly to do this (Research Question 3). This may be followed by testing it in real life. To do the latter, I require a simple and effective way of obtaining learner characteristics. I intend to base this on a dialogue (Research Question 3).

# References

1. Baker, R.S.J., Rodrigo, M.M.T., Xolocotzin, U.E.: The dynamics of affective transitions in simulation problem-solving environments. In: Paiva, A.C.R., Prada, R., Picard, R.W. (eds.) ACII 2007. LNCS, vol. 4738, pp. 666–677. Springer, Heidelberg (2007). https://doi.org/10.1007/978-3-540-74889-2_58

2. Cohn, M.A., Fredrickson, B.L., Brown, S.L., Mikels, J.A., Conway, A.M.: Happiness unpacked: positive emotions increase life satisfaction by building resilience. Emotion (Wash. D.C.) 9(3), 361–368 (2009). http://www.ncbi.nlm.nih.gov/pubmed/19485613

3. Craig, S.D., Graesser, A.C., Sullins, J., Gholson, B.: Affect and learning: an exploratory look into the role of affect in learning with AutoTutor. J. Educ. Media 29(3), 241–250 (2004)

4. D'Mello, S., Picard, R., Graesser, A.: Towards an affect-sensitive AutoTutor. IEEE Intell. Syst. 22(4), 53–61 (2007)

5. Drachsler, H., Verbert, K., Santos, O.C., Manouselis, N.: Panorama of recommender systems to support learning. In: Ricci, F., Rokach, L., Shapira, B. (eds.) Recommender Systems Handbook, pp. 421–451. Springer, Boston (2015). https://doi.org/10.1007/978-1-4899-7637-6_12

6. Forgas, J.P., Eich, E.: Affective influences on cognition mood congruence, mood dependence, and mood effects on processing strategies. In: Weiner, I.B. (ed.) Handbook of Psychology, Chap. 3, pp. 61–82. Wiley, New York (2012)

7. Goetz, T., Athan, N., Hall, C.: Emotion and Achievement in the Classroom. Routledge, New York (2013)

8. Graesser, A., D'Mello, S., Chipman, P., King, B., McDaniel, B.: Exploring relationships between affect and learning with AutoTutor. Int. J. Artif. Intell. Educ. 12(1), 257–279 (2001)

9. Kruglanski, A.W., Forgas, J.P.: Attitudes and attitude change frontier of social psychology. In: Crano, W.D., Prislin, R. (ed.) Frontiers of Social Psycology, Chap. 3. Psychology press Taylor and Francis group (2008)

10. Lehman, B., Matthews, M., D'Mello, S., Person, N.: What are you feeling? Investigating student affective states during expert human tutoring sessions. In: Woolf, B.P., Aïmeur, E., Nkambou, R., Lajoie, S. (eds.) ITS 2008. LNCS, vol. 5091, pp. 50–59. Springer, Heidelberg (2008). https://doi.org/10.1007/978-3-540-69132-7_10

11. Manouselis, N., Drachsler, H., Verbert, K., Duval, E.: Recommender Systems for Learning - An Introduction, 1st edn. Springer, New York (2012). https://doi.org/10.1007/978-1-4614-4361-2

12. Masthoff, J.: The user as wizard: a method for early involvement in the design and evaluation of adaptive systems. In: Fifth Workshop on User-Centred Design and Evaluation of Adaptive Systems, pp. 460–469 (2006)

13. McDaniel, B., D'Mello, S., King, B., Chipman, P., Tapp, K., Graesser, A., Edu, G.: Facial features for affective state detection in learning environments. In: Proceedings of the Annual Meeting of the Cognitive Science Society, vol. 29 (2007)

14. Okpo, J., Masthoff, J., Dennis, M., Beacham, N., Ciocarlan, A.: Investigating the impact of personality and cognitive efficiency on the selection of exercises for learners. In: Proceedings of the 25th Conference on User Modeling, Adaptation and Personalization - UMAP 2017, pp. 140–147 (2017)

15. Pekrun, R., Goetz, T., Titz, W., Perry, R.P.: Academic emotions in students' self-regulated learning and achievement: a program of qualitative and quantitative research. Educ. Psychol. 37(2), 91–106 (2002)

16. Picard, R.W.: Affective Computing. MIT Press, Cambridge (2000)
17. Psotka, J., Massey, L.D.L.D., Mutter, S.A.: Intelligent Tutoring Systems: Lessons Learned. L. Erlbaum Associates, Mahwah (1988)
18. Tyng, C.M., Amin, H.U., Saad, M.N.M., Malik, A.S.: The influences of emotion on learning and memory. Front. Psychol. **8**, 1454 (2017)
19. Verbert, K., Manouselis, N., Ochoa, X., Wolpers, M., Drachsler, H., Bosnic, I., Duval, E.: Context-aware recommender systems for learning: a survey and future challenges. IEEE Trans. Learn. Technol. **6**(1), 318–335 (2007)

# Investigation of Temporal Dynamics in MOOC Learning Trajectories: A Geocultural Perspective

Saman Zehra Rizvi[✉], Bart Rienties, and Jekaterina Rogaten

Institute of Educational Technology, The Open University, Milton Keynes, UK
{saman.rizvi, bart.rienties,
jekaterina.rogaten}@open.ac.uk

**Abstract.** Openness, scalability, and reachability are intrinsic features of MOOCs. However, research studies in MOOCs indicated low participation from some cultural clusters, mostly from less privileged strata of the world's population. The impeding factors are not only related to individual student characteristics, but also are related to structure and curriculum design. This proposed PhD thesis will address this stratification, performance and achievement gap. In a cross-module analysis on Open University MOOCs at FutureLearn, temporal predictive modelling was used to explore learners' background, regional belonging and behavioral patterns that contribute towards engagement, and overall performance. Later on, clustering and temporal process mining will be employed to observe end-to-end processes of learning. Behavioral traces and learning trajectories for different clusters of learners will be explored in a variety of MOOC Learning Designs (LD). The research findings aim to provide useful actionable insights on how adaptations in LD can make MOOCs more inclusive and diverse.

**Keywords:** Educational Data Mining (EDM)
Educational Process Mining (EPM) · Massive open online courses
Learning design · Cultural clusters

## 1 Introduction (The Problem)

Massive Open Online Courses (MOOCs) aim to provide learners an unlimited access to online courses through open access policy. Until recently, it was expected that these open, extensive online courses might help to address global disparity in education. However, so far international participation in leading MOOCs continue to present a form of *intellectual neo-colonialism,* in a way that the majority of active learners and mainstream MOOC providers belong to developed countries [1, 2].

As evidenced by both global studies in MOOCs as well as studies focused on geographical location within a particular country, there are strong regional, national, and cultural factors that influence success in online learning. In the literature there seems to be an emerging narrative of a global divide in MOOCs learning. In MOOCs 'significant disparities' existed for some ethnic and racial minorities. Similar

C. Penstein Rosé et al. (Eds.): AIED 2018, LNAI 10948, pp. 526–530, 2018.
https://doi.org/10.1007/978-3-319-93846-2_99

observations have been repeatedly reported for financial, social, or psychological barriers in MOOC learning in country-specific studies, or in those sampled for a particular region.

For this prevailing issues of retention and performance of learners from different regions, one method commonly used is introducing self-regulated nudges or general interventions. A number of random controlled trials have been used to address some impeding factors, such as learners' social identity threats and perceived course difficulty level. Although psychological dispositions can be changed, the overall efficacy of these interventions remained inconclusive [1, 3].

One way to approach this issue is by investigating the cognitive and pedagogical aspects. Learning Design (LD), in general, can be described as process of designing pedagogically informed learning activities to support learners while remaining aligned with the curriculum. The impact of LDs on learners' behavior, satisfaction and learning outcome, has been widely acknowledged [4]. Moreover, academic success and failure is partly hidden in learners' journeys, through their respective learning activities and in interactions with learning resources (e.g. video, audio, forum, quiz, reading material).

Open online learning generates voluminous log data. Therefore, the aim of this research is to examine to what extent learners' association with a country of particular cultural cluster influences their processual academic progress over time. This study will explore the potential roles of regional and cultural diversity on temporal learning choices in MOOCs. In particular, I will explore end-to-end learning processes to understand how different MOOC LDs impact, restrain or facilitate widening participation from all around the globe. I will also explore learners' decisions on whether to stay and continue learning in a MOOC, or else to drop out at a point-in-time after participating in a particular learning or assessment activity. This study will examine learners' journeys using processual nature of learning activities at three levels of granularity; activity type, week-wise performance, and dominant progression in individual activities.

Therefore, the main research questions are

**RQ1:** To what extent can main and dominating temporal learning paths be identified in a MOOC Learning Design (i.e. in a MOOC do significantly large subgroups of learners follow a particular learning path before dropping out)?

**RQ2.A:** To what extent does association with a cultural cluster impacts temporal learning paths in a MOOC Learning Design? (i.e. What temporal learning path learners from a cultural cluster follow, as they progress in a course)?

**RQ2.B:** To what extent are behavioral patterns (from RQ1 and RQ2.A) of cultural clusters dissimilar in different MOOC Learning Designs (i.e. Do cultural clusters progress differently in different Learning Designs)?

**RQ3:** With the help of descriptive and temporal process models from RQ1 and RQ2, how can we suggest meaningful, actionable insights from investigating the broader geocultural and pedagogical factors that may make MOOC learning more sustainable, diverse and inclusive?

## 2    Proposed Methodology

### 2.1    Data Sources

I intend to analyze four Open University FutureLearn MOOCs offered in 2017. All courses followed different LDs, each comprising a variety of categories: article, discussion, peer review, quiz, test, video/audio, and exercise. From the logs, I used following attributes for 16,757 learners; learners ID, week, learning activity type, learning activity and timestamps. To create cultural clusters, I plan to use data source from extended GLOBE study by [5], which employed statistical models to classify countries into 10 cultural groups based on cultural similarities and other factors such as racial/ethnic distribution, religious distribution, geographic proximity, language, and colonial heritage.

To meet the ethics standards, all datasets are anonymized by the FutureLearn before the release. As part of setting up the learner's account, FutureLearn attains consent of the learner to use this data to tailor their services to suit the learner.

### 2.2    Design and Methods

For behavioral mapping and modelling, I employed methods associated with Educational Data Mining (EDM) and Educational Process Mining (EPM). For predictive modelling (see Pilot Study1), I used decision tree based machine learning algorithm commonly used in EDM. However, EPM is traditionally used to observe end-to-end traces of learners' behavior. In Process Mining, the term *Variant* refers to a sequence of activities followed by significant number of cases. I focused on estimation and comparison of mean activity duration, and temporal learning pathways of dominant subgroup of learners (Variants). These subgroups followed particular learning trajectory or pathway in a MOOC. To construct process maps, I used *Disco* tool, which implements an extended and improved version of *Fuzzy Miner* algorithm [6]. This algorithm creates elaborative, uncomplicated process maps and can easily identify infrequent variants.

### 2.3    Current Status of Work and Future Work

**Pilot Study 1:** In this study, machine learning based predictive models were employed to dynamically predict learners' academic performance of 3,908 UK-based learners enrolled in four different online courses offered at The Open University, UK [7]. I examined whether, and how, six demographic characteristics (i.e., region of origin, multiple deprivation level, prior education, age group, gender, and disability) affected learning outcomes of assignments over time. It was reported that region of origin and socioeconomic indicator were most significant or important variables towards decision tree construction throughout. Model consistency was checked on the next course offering. Persistence of contribution of these two factors; *region of origin* and *deprivation level*, on academic outcome remained consistent when experiment was repeated on structurally different courses. This leads to the idea that change in LD can potentially influence academic performance of learners from different regions [Pilot Study 2, Main Study].

**Pilot Study 2 (Work in progress):** This study addressed **RQ1** by examining the processual nature of academic performance amongst FutureLearn MOOCs. Results suggested that learners' progress were linked with Learning Design (LD) and could be better understood by mapping end-to-end learning processes. In order to check consistencies and to validate the results, analyses were repeated on four MOOCs from different disciplines. (Some preliminary results will be presented as full paper at JURE 18 conference. I also plan to discuss some initial findings in next FLAN meeting with a title: Intertemporal Modelling of Learning Trajectories; a Validation Study of 4 MOOCs).

**Main Study (Future work):** My proposed main study will comprise of two phases. In Phase-I, I will answer RQ2 and will provide the bases to answer RQ3 by exploring how academic performance (which is processual in nature and is linked closely with LD) varies with cultural background. Hereby, I also aim to use clustering during preprocessing in order to find natural grouping in learners' population. In Phase-II, I will employ a mixed method approach to understand the underlying factors that contributed towards the results from Phase-I. Using observed end-to-end process of learning as a representation of learners' *plan of action*, I will try to explain why regional belonging or culture does (or doesn't) have an impact on processual nature of learning?

## 3   Unique Contribution

The presence of large number of underachieving, "inconsistent" MOOC learners raises a need for an in-depth, cross-national, dynamic behavioral analysis of 'active learning events', with a consideration of regional, social, and cultural belonging. As indicated above, while an emerging body of literature has found that large numbers of learners from across the globe are taking MOOCs, relatively few studies have actually measured and unpacked how learners from different cultural groups are engaging in MOOCs. In particular, while recent evidence seems to indicate that the way teachers design and implement online courses has a significant impact on engagement and retention, to the best of my knowledge no study has linked learning design with MOOCs. By linking learning design principles of MOOCs with actual engagements in learning activities for learners from countries all around the globe, this PhD thesis aims to better understand how we can design and implement effective MOOCs for ALL learners.

## References

1. Kizilcec, R.F., Halawa, S.: Attrition and achievement gaps in online learning. In: Proceedings of the Second (2015) ACM Conference on Learning @ Scale, pp. 57–66 (2015)
2. Kizilcec, R.F., Saltarelli, A.J., Reich, J., Cohen, G.L.: Closing global achievement gaps in MOOCs. Science **355**(6322), 251–252 (2017)
3. Baker, R., Evans, B., Dee, T.: A randomized experiment testing the efficacy of a scheduling nudge in a Massive Open Online Course (MOOC). AERA Open **2**(4), 2332858416674007 (2016)

4. Rienties, B., Toetenel, L.: The impact of learning design on student behaviour, satisfaction and performance: a cross-institutional comparison across 151 modules. Comput. Hum. Behav. **60**, 333–341 (2016)
5. Mensah, Y.M., Chen, H.-Y.: Global clustering of countries by culture–an extension of the GLOBE study (2013)
6. Günther, C.W., Van Der Aalst, W.M.: Fuzzy mining–adaptive process simplification based on multi-perspective metrics. In: International Conference on Business Process Management, pp. 328–343 (2007)
7. Rizvi, S., Rienties, B., Khoja, S.: The role of demographics in online learning; a decision tree based approach (2017). Submitted

# Sequence Based Course Recommender for Personalized Curriculum Planning

Chris Wong[✉] [ⓘ]

University of Sydney, Sydney, Australia
cwon7609@uni.sydney.edu.au

**Abstract.** Students in higher education need to select appropriate courses to meet graduation requirements for their degree. Selection approaches range from manual guides, on-line systems to personalized assistance from academic advisers. An automated course recommender is one approach to scale advice for large cohorts. However, existing recommenders need to be adapted to include sequence, concurrency, constraints and concept drift. In this paper, we propose the use of recent deep learning techniques such as Long Short-Term Memory (LSTM) Recurrent Neural Networks to resolve these issues in this domain.

**Keywords:** Recommender systems · Educational data mining
Study planning · Deep learning

## 1 Introduction

Students entering university face a myriad of choices when navigating their pathway through their degree. These choices influence student success defined as minimal completion time and maximized cumulative grade averages (GPA). Determining the optimal choice requires consideration of personal, institutional and external factors and could be described as a scheduling, graph navigation and optimization problem.

Personal factors include learner preparedness, failing courses, medical/employment pressures, social/friendship networks, credit transfer from prior study and financial reasons. Institutional factors include course constraints such as pre-requisites, course availability and enrolment quotas. External factors include regulatory and accreditation requirements.

Students often seek advice from academic advisers on appropriate course choices as there can be an overwhelming number of course-availability-sequence combinations. Explicit and Implicit knowledge about the choice may be present but not personalized in existing systems or web sites. Academic advisers often use experience and heuristics to determine an optimal pathway for these students. However, this could result in inconsistency of advice if there are multiple advisers and personal advice is not scalable with thousands of students.

© Springer International Publishing AG, part of Springer Nature 2018
C. Penstein Rosé et al. (Eds.): AIED 2018, LNAI 10948, pp. 531–534, 2018.
https://doi.org/10.1007/978-3-319-93846-2_100

## 1.1 Related Work

Many universities provide on-line enrolment systems which provide a pre-defined study plan template for enrolment. Enrolment planning tools may deal with constraints such as pre-requisites, course availability and recommended sequences.

The next level of advice comes from automated systems which range from grade prediction systems based on educational data mining [3, 6] and some which use classical recommender systems approaches such as Matrix Factorization and Random Forests [8].

Existing educational recommender systems advise students at many levels - from high level recommendations of career choices, degrees and majors to internal recommendations of learning objects within a course [1]. These systems use Collaborative Filtering (provides recommendations based on the student's profile and past/peer student choices), Content-based approaches (use past choices together with course meta-data), Association mining (popular clusters of courses) or combinations of these techniques [2].

Recent deep learning techniques based around Recurrent Neural Networks (RNN) have been used to provide recommendations using sequence predictions [4] and applied to learning analytics [9], student performance prediction [5] and contextual recommendations [7].

## 2    Proposed Solution

We will use deep learning techniques such as Long Short Term Memory (LSTM) RNN's to develop a sequence based course recommender because of the following challenges unique to this domain:

- Sequence and concurrency: Unlike classical recommender systems, a course recommender needs to supply a sequence of concurrent courses rather than a single item. The system must consider the historical sequencing of courses taken to provide the optimal recommendation.
- Constraints: A course recommender system will need to consider complex constraint issues including course timetabling, course availability, course quotas, curriculum constraints (pre-requisites, co-requisites, anti-requisites, admission rules) and degree rules such as core and optional course requirements.
- Context: Additional criteria may be required such as student career objectives, accreditation requirements, personal preferences and other situational constraints (such as scholarship restrictions and so on). We will NOT focus on personal factors due to a human ethics ruling.
- Concept drift: degree programs and courses continually evolve thus historical equivalence of courses must be considered by the recommender system. A course may also be a component of different degree/major programs which requires the system to adapt recommendations appropriately to the student's situation.

### 2.1 Methodology

The existing dataset consists of 10 years of student transcript records from the host university, totaling 2.1 million transcript results, 30 degrees, 14 majors, 400 + courses and 72000 graduation records. We will use a subset of the historical data for this research project consisting of undergraduate Engineering and IT students.

**Preliminary Experiment**

1. Initial data cleansing, wrangling and exploration of data will be used to select appropriate training and testing samples. This data will be k-anonymized and aggregated to form a non-confidential dataset as per the human ethics approved protocol. Attributes may include course, year/semester, grades/marks, degree/major and other non-identifying classification information such as gender etc.
2. Machine learning techniques (including clustering, ensembles and association rule learning) will be used to observe patterns which will then be used to implement a classical recommender. This will be applied to the training data set to provide a baseline for evaluation with the test dataset.
3. We then train a LSTM RNN on the training dataset and the model will be tuned and compared to the baseline evaluation. The objective function will be a hybrid of the estimated duration of the degree based on completed courses and the estimated Grade Point Average.
4. The model will be retrained every semester – this provides a sliding window of updated recommendations and is adjusted for concept drift as course content/identification may have changed in the interim. Concept drift adjustment will be via text mining course outlines and comparing new/old versions.

**Main Experiment**

We design and develop a prototype to use this RNN to recommend personalized curriculum to a pilot group of Engineering and IT students over a few semesters.

1. A qualitative survey/focus group/workshop will be conducted to create a baseline for the main experiment – this includes a course sequence planning workshop and will also create test cases for the recommender prototype.
2. Design of the recommendation presentation and explanation will be tested with this focus group.
3. This prototype will be used for the next several semesters to compare the interim and final transcript results of the pilot group. Each semester the RNN model will be re-trained on the current set of transcript results.
4. We then analyze these results against the remaining baseline Engineering and IT students.

## 3   Expected Contribution and Impact to AIED Community

There has been considerable literature on educational data science focused on grade prediction, student retention, personalized learning material selection, learner analytics and domain knowledge. This project focuses on the less investigated problem of curriculum planning for students and provides a novel approach to this domain using a synthesis of the following solutions:

- Using deep learning as a heuristic approach to the sequential recommendations [4]
- Using the recommender to provide a personalized pathway to completion using sequence, constraint and contextual parameters,
- The proposed recommender would be dynamically updated using a sliding window of student result data and would include concept drift adjustment based on course learning outcomes/topics [10]

# References

1. Burke, R., Abdollahpouri, H.: Educational recommendation with multiple stakeholders. In: 2016 IEEE/WIC/ACM International Conference on Web Intelligence Workshops (WIW), pp. 62–63. IEEE (2016)
2. Bydžovská, H.: Course enrollment recommender system. In: Proceedings of the 9th International Conference on Educational Data Mining, vol. 1, pp. 312–317 (2016)
3. Bydžovská, H., Popelinsky, L.: Predicting student performance in higher education. In: Proceedings of the International Workshop on Database Expert Systems Applications DEXA, pp. 141–145 (2013)
4. Devooght, R., Bersini, H.: Long and short-term recommendations with recurrent neural networks. In: Proceedings of the 25th Conference on User Modeling, Adaptation and Personalization - UMAP 2017, pp. 13–21 (2017)
5. Okubo, F. et al.: A neural network approach for students' performance prediction. In: Proceedings of the Seventh International Conference on Learning Analytics and Knowledge - LAK 2017, pp. 598–599. ACM Press, New York (2017)
6. Polyzou, A., Karypis, G.: Grade prediction with course and student specific models. In: Bailey, J., Khan, L., Washio, T., Dobbie, G., Huang, J., Wang, R. (eds.) PAKDD 2016. LNCS (LNAI), vol. 9651, pp. 89–101. Springer, Cham (2016). https://doi.org/10.1007/978-3-319-31753-3_8
7. Smirnova, E., Vasile, F.: Contextual sequence modeling for recommendation with recurrent neural networks. In: 2nd Workshop on Deep Learning for Recommender Systems (DLRS 2017), pp. 2–9. ACM Press, New York (2017)
8. Sweeney, M., et al.: Next-term student performance prediction: a recommender systems approach. In: International Conference on Educational Data Mining (2016)
9. Tang, S., et al.: Deep neural networks and how they apply to sequential education data. In: Proceedings of the Third (2016) ACM Conference on Learning @ Scale - L@S 2016, pp. 321–324. ACM Press, New York (2016)
10. Žliobaitė, I., Pechenizkiy, M., Gama, J.: An overview of concept drift applications. In: Japkowicz, N., Stefanowski, J. (eds.) Big Data Analysis: New Algorithms for a New Society. SBD, vol. 16, pp. 91–114. Springer, Cham (2016). https://doi.org/10.1007/978-3-319-26989-4_4

# Towards Improving Introductory Computer Programming with an ITS for Conceptual Learning

Franceska Xhakaj[✉] and Vincent Aleven[✉]

Human-Computer Interaction Institute, Carnegie Mellon University,
Pittsburgh, PA 15213, USA
{francesx, aleven}@cs.cmu.edu

**Abstract.** Computer programming is becoming important in almost every profession. However, programming is still difficult for students to learn. In this work, we focus on helping students acquire strong conceptual and procedural knowledge of programing. We propose to create a new Intelligent Tutoring System (ITS) that will support students in two types of conceptually-oriented activities: code tracing and code comprehension. Further, we propose to run a study to evaluate whether the ITS can support students' conceptual learning and transfer to procedural learning of computer programming.

**Keywords:** Conceptual learning · Procedural learning
Intelligent Tutoring Systems · Computer Science education

## 1   Introduction

Computer programming is a key skill set in many professions and STEM domains [8]. However, learning programming is hard, and typical introductory programming instruction may leave substantial room for improvement [5, 14]. Prior research in Computer Science education suggests that practice with conceptually-oriented activities (e.g., activities that emphasize knowledge of code constructs and code execution) can be very helpful in learning procedural knowledge (e.g., skills of generating code) [2, 9, 11]. Although this prior work shows promise, it does not take full advantage of current insights in the cognitive science and mathematics education literature on transfer between conceptual and procedural learning and how they mutually influence each other [10]. Nor have the conceptually-oriented approaches tested in prior CS education research taken advantage of the capabilities of advanced learning technologies, such as Intelligent Tutoring Systems (ITSs) [13]. We propose a program of research that capitalizes on insights from cognitive science and on advanced learning technologies to facilitate the learning of programming. The proposed research has two strands of work. First, we will create a new ITS building on our existing infrastructure (CTAT [1]). The new ITS will support students in two types of conceptually-oriented learning activities: code tracing and code comprehension. Second, we will conduct an experimental study that will test whether and how such an ITS can support conceptual learning and transfer to procedural learning in the area of computer programming.

© Springer International Publishing AG, part of Springer Nature 2018
C. Penstein Rosé et al. (Eds.): AIED 2018, LNAI 10948, pp. 535–538, 2018.
https://doi.org/10.1007/978-3-319-93846-2_101

## 2  The Intelligent Tutoring System: TiPs

Traditional instruction in programming targets conceptual knowledge with (video) lectures, textbook reading, programming exercises and with a "stepper" tool for stepping through code execution line-by-line. However, more highly interactive and adaptive instruction supported by ITSs may be more effective at helping students develop conceptual knowledge. In Fig. 1 we show an initial design of TiPs (Transfer in Programming system), the proposed ITS that will support two types of conceptually-oriented activities: code tracing (left) and code comprehension (right). TiPs will target common challenging topics in introductory computer programming [e.g., 3, 12] including variables, the assignment operation, conditional statements, loops, etc.

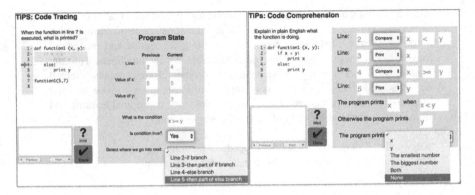

**Fig. 1.** Mockups of TiPs, the proposed ITS. Code tracing (left), code comprehension (right).

In code-tracing activities, the student tracks a program's changing internal state line-by-line (Fig. 1, left). The student generates and fills in the program state at each step of code execution, with support of feedback and hints from TiPs. TiPs simulates code execution by means of (1) a green arrow pointing to the current line, and (2) a greyed out area for code that is not relevant to the current step. TiPs will remove this scaffolding gradually as the student gains more competence. For each executed line, the student enters the line number, the values of the variables, and answers questions at the bottom. Once the student has correctly entered the current program state, TiPs dynamically changes the interface to let the student fill in the next state. This type of activity is likely to support acquisition of conceptual knowledge of code constructs and code execution, as it involves direct application of this kind of knowledge in the context of a piece of code. Past research suggests that code tracing can have beneficial effects for students, although it does not provide a fully rigorous demonstration of such effects on conceptual and in particular transfer to procedural knowledge of programming, as we plan to test in this work [4, 7, 15].

In code-comprehension activities, the student is asked to explain at a high level what the function of a given piece of code is (Fig. 1, right). In contrast to code tracing, the emphasis here is on being able to understand code at a higher level, without simulation of code execution. For each line, the student chooses from a drop-down menu what the construct in that line is doing. Once an instruction is selected, the appropriate values appear on the right for the student to fill in. The student then is prompted to explain what the code is doing, with the aid of the tutor as needed. Code-comprehension exercises may help students develop conceptual knowledge of how the individual constructs can work together to realize desired functionality. We know of no rigorous studies that showed that code-comprehension practice can foster conceptual or procedural knowledge. [6] found that tracing, explaining and writing code are statistically significantly correlated, but these results are correlational, not causal.

## 3  Proposed Study

We propose to run a study to find out whether three forms of conceptually-oriented activities (code tracing, code comprehension, or a combination), supported by an ITS, (1) enhance students' conceptual knowledge of code and (2) transfer to students' work on code-generation exercises (e.g., enhances the learning of programming skill). The study will examine transfer from conceptually to procedurally-oriented activities.

The study will have a 2 × 2 design with experimental factors code tracing and code comprehension. Students will be randomly assigned to conditions. Students in all conditions will do two blocks of activities. In the first block, students will engage in (1) code tracing, (2) code comprehension, (3) a combination, or (4) neither (they will engage in code generation). The code-tracing and code-comprehension activities will be supported by the proposed ITS. The second block will involve a sequence of code-generation exercises for all conditions. Before and after the first block, students will complete a pre- and post-test, to assess both conceptual and procedural knowledge of programming. The conceptual items will be based on existing literature and will contain code-tracing and code-comprehension exercises designed to measure conceptual transfer [3, 12]. The procedural items will involve writing code in the language that students are studying. We will create new problems for conceptual and procedural items that will contain known constructs, alone and combined in new ways. In addition, we will collect ITS log data that we will use to extract measures of the students' performance and knowledge growth in the tutor activities. We will conduct analyses to investigate how code-tracing and code-comprehension exercises affect students' conceptual and procedural knowledge of programming. We hypothesize that both these activities positively affect conceptual knowledge and outcomes in procedural learning from the code-generation activities. We hypothesize further that code comprehension is more effective in the presence of code tracing, as code tracing may be a step along the way to code comprehension [6].

## 4  Expected Contributions

If successful, the proposed research will generate new scientific knowledge about whether (1) an ITS that supports conceptually-oriented activities (code tracing and code comprehension) can enhance conceptual knowledge and transfer to procedural knowledge of computer programming, (2) which kind of conceptually-oriented activities are more effective in this regard. As a practical contribution, the research will yield a novel ITS that will support conceptually-oriented activities for learning programming. The results and findings could inform the design of other ITSs for introductory programming and of instruction beyond ITSs.

# References

1. Aleven, V., McLaren, B.M., Sewall, J., van Velsen, M., Popescu, O., Demi, S., Ringenberg, M., Koedinger, K.R.: Example-tracing tutors: intelligent tutor development for nonprogrammers. Int. J. Artif. Intell. Educ. **26**(1), 224–269 (2016)
2. Bayman, P., Mayer, R.E.: Using conceptual models to teach BASIC computer programming. J. Educ. Psychol. **80**(3), 291–298 (1988)
3. Caceffo, R., Wolfman, S., Booth, K.S., Azevedo, R.: Developing a computer science concept inventory for introductory programming. In: Proceedings of the 47th ACM Technical Symposium on Computing Science Education, pp. 364–369. ACM (2016)
4. Kumar, A. N.: A study of the influence of code-tracing problems on code-writing skills. In: Proceedings of the 18th ACM Conference on Innovation and Technology in Computer Science Education, pp. 183–188. ACM (2013)
5. Lahtinen, E., Ala-Mutka, K., Järvinen, H.M.: A study of the difficulties of novice programmers. ACM SIGCSE Bull. **37**(3), 14–18 (2005)
6. Lister, R., Fidge, C., Teague, D.: Further evidence of a relationship between explaining, tracing and writing skills in introductory programming. ACM SIGCSE Bull. **41**(3), 161–165 (2009)
7. Nelson, G.L., Xie, B., Ko, A.J.: Comprehension first: evaluating a novel pedagogy and tutoring system for program tracing in CS1. In: Proceedings of the 2017 ACM Conference on International Computing Education Research, pp. 2–11. ACM (2017)
8. Orsini, L.: Why Programming is the Core Skill of the 21st Century. https://readwrite.com/2013/05/31/programming-core-skill-21st-century/. Accessed 12 Dec 2017
9. Pennington, N., Nicolich, R., Rahm, J.: Transfer of training between cognitive subskills: is knowledge use specific? Cogn. Psychol. **28**(2), 175–224 (1995)
10. Rittle-Johnson, B., Siegler, R.S.: The relations between conceptual and procedural knowledge in learning mathematics: a review. In: The Development of Mathematical Skill, pp. 75–110. Psychology Press, Hove (1998)
11. Shih, Y.F., Alessi, S.M.: Mental models and transfer of learning in computer programming. J. Res. Comput. Educ. **26**(2), 154–175 (1993)
12. Tew, A.E.: Assessing fundamental introductory computing concept knowledge in a language independent manner. (Doctoral dissertation), Georgia Institute of Technology, Georgia, USA (2010)
13. VanLehn, K.: The relative effectiveness of human tutoring, intelligent tutoring systems, and other tutoring systems. Educ. Psychol. **46**(4), 197–221 (2011)
14. Watson, C., Li, F.W.: Failure rates in introductory programming revisited. In: Proceedings of the 2014 Conference on Innovation and Technology in Computer Science Education, pp. 39–44. ACM (2014)
15. Xie, B., Nelson, G.L., Ko, A.J.: An explicit strategy to scaffold novice program tracing. In: Proceedings of the 49th ACM Technical Symposium on Computer Science Education, pp. 344–349. ACM (2018)

# Workshops and Tutorials

# Flow Experience in Learning: When Gamification Meets Artificial Intelligence in Education

Ig Ibert Bittencourt[1] 🆔, Seiji Isotani[2(✉)] 🆔, Vanissa Wanick[3] 🆔,
and Ashok Ranchhod[3] 🆔

[1] Federal University of Alagoas, Maceio, Brazil
ig.ibert@ic.ufal.br
[2] University of Sao Paulo, Sao Paulo, Brazil
sisotani@icmc.usp.br
[3] University of Southampton, Southampton, UK
{v.w.vieira,a.ranchhod}@soton.ac.uk

**Abstract.** It is still very common that students become disengaged or bored during the learning process by using intelligent educational systems. On the other hand, there is a growing interest in gamification as well as its applications and implications in the field of Artificial Intelligence in Education since it provides an alternative to engage and motivate students, and thereby help students to reach flow state during the learning process. The term Gamification originated in the digital media industry, however, such a term only gained widespread acceptance after late 2010. Since then most of the research on gamification in educational systems was about conceptualization, modelling and impact of use. The goal of this workshop is to provide participants the opportunity to: (i) present and discuss the empirical studies of gamification in Intelligent Educational Systems; (ii) discuss and promote innovative initiatives in educational settings with the use of gamification; and iii) motivate and solidify the research on gamification of intelligent educational systems in order to leverage the development of such systems.

**Keywords:** Personalization · Intelligent tutoring systems · Game design

## 1 Introduction

Artificial Intelligence in Education (AIED) is an interdisciplinary field that integrates researchers with different backgrounds (Computer Science, Engineering, Education, Psychology, instructional design and others) but with a common goal: to use AI techniques to support personalized learning experiences where students can work mediated by technology and learn more effectively. The support of robust learning is a complex issue due to many factors (e.g., psychological, technological, personal, instructional, etc.) that affect learning processes and hence, the learning outcome. To tackle this problem, researchers in the field have always been innovative. Through the analysis of different learning settings, researchers have found ways to integrate major advances in Artificial Intelligence, Learning Sciences, Experimental Psychology,

© Springer International Publishing AG, part of Springer Nature 2018
C. Penstein Rosé et al. (Eds.): AIED 2018, LNAI 10948, pp. 541–543, 2018.
https://doi.org/10.1007/978-3-319-93846-2

Human-Computer Interaction and other areas to leverage the development of Intelligent Educational Systems. For teachers, an intelligent educational system offers better ways to create/reuse/share content, new methodologies and instruments to deploy effective learning activities and accurate tools (e.g. dashboards) to analyze students' progress throughout the learning process. For students, it allows for presenting the content in an intelligent and adaptive fashion, which enables the restructuring of learning content according to students' needs and stimulates the occurrence of deep and long-term understanding.

Nevertheless, it is still very common that students become disengaged or bored during the learning process when using intelligent educational systems [1]. To deal with that it would be interesting to investigate how to design environments that lead students to flow state, i.e. environments where students are fully immersed and engaged in the educational activity. In this direction, there is a growing interest in gamification as well as its applications and implications in the field of AIED since it provides an alternative to engage and motivate students during the process of learning [3, 5].

The term Gamification originated in the digital media industry, gained widespread acceptance after late 2010, and it refers to the use of game design elements such as mechanics, aesthetics, and game thinking in non-game contexts aimed at engaging people, motivating action, enhancing learning, and solving problems [2].

Indeed, gamification research has increase in significance in the past six years and shows no sign of slowing growth. The first wave of gamification research has predominantly consisted of (1) definitions, frameworks and taxonomies for gamification and game design elements; (2) technical papers describing systems, designs, and architectures; and (3) effect and user studies of gamified systems [4]. Such phenomenon also occurred in the context of education. Few studies presented empirical solutions and even fewer in the context of artificial intelligence in education [2].

If the first wave was held together by fundamental questions of "what?" and "why?", the current wave is asking differentiated questions around "how?", "when?", and "how and when not?"

Thus, the goal of this workshop is to provide participants the opportunity of: (i) present and discuss the empirical studies of gamification in Intelligent Educational Systems; (ii) discuss and promote innovative initiatives in educational settings with the use of gamification; and (iii) motivate and solidify the research on gamification of intelligent educational systems in order to leverage the development of such systems.

We are particularly interested in scientific and technological advances in the combination of gamification and intelligent educational systems that can help learners to achieve flow state. It is also on the scope of this workshop studies about gamifying intelligent educational systems and equipping gamified educational systems with AI techniques to improve learning experiences. The topics of interest include, but are not limited to: Quantitative studies on psychological and behavioral consequences of gamification design of intelligent educational systems; Qualitative studies that explore how gamification affects education; Novel approaches of designing gamified intelligent educational systems; Real-world Innovative solutions about gamification of intelligent educational systems; Theoretical contributions regarding societal impacts and ethical issues of gamification of intelligent educational systems; and so on.

During the workshop we intend to provide thought-provoking discussions about the quality of research on gamification and intelligent educational systems and we expect (i) to build a community of researchers and practitioners around the best practices for the implementation of gamification in intelligent systems in education; (ii) to understand game elements and/or game design thinking behind gamified strategies in the context of intelligent educational systems; (iii) to inform about the future of gamification and intelligent systems; and (iv) think about new propositions about how to integrate scientific impact into social and economic development through the research on gamification of intelligent educational systems.

## References

1. Baker, R.S., D'Mello, S.K., Rodrigo, M.M.T., Graesser, A.C.: Better to be frustrated than bored: the incidence, persistence, and impact of learners' cognitive–affective states during interactions with three different computer-based learning environments. Int. J. Hum Comput Stud. **68**(4), 223–241 (2010)
2. de Sousa Borges, S., Durelli, V.H., Reis, H.M., Isotani, S.: A systematic mapping on gamification applied to education. In: Proceedings of the 29th Annual ACM Symposium on Applied Computing, pp. 216–222. ACM, New York (2014)
3. Mohd Tuah, N., Wanick, V., Ranchhod, A., Wills, G.B.: Exploring avatar roles for motivational effects in gameful environments. EAI Endorsed Trans. Creative Technol. **17**(10), 1–11 (2017)
4. Nacke, L.E., Deterding, S.: The maturing of gamification research. Comput. Hum. Behav. **71**, 450–454 (2017)
5. Tenório, T., Bittencourt, I.I., Isotani, S., Pedro, A., Ospina, P.: A gamified peer assessment model for on-line learning environments in a competitive context. Comput. Hum. Behav. **64**, 247–263 (2016)

# 3rd International Workshop on Intelligent Mentoring Systems (IMS2018)

Vania Dimitrova[1(✉)], Art Graesser[2], Antonija Mitrovic[3],
David Williamson Shaffer[4], and Amali Weerasinghe[5]

[1] University of Leeds, Leeds LS2 9JT, UK
lncs@springer.com
[2] University of Memphis, Memphis, TN 38105, USA
lncs@springer.com
[3] University of Canterbury, Christchurch 8041, New Zealand
lncs@springer.com
[4] University of Wisconsin-Madison, Madison, WI 53706, USA
lncs@springer.com
[5] University of Adelaide, Adelaide, SA 5005, Australia
lncs@springer.com

**Abstract.** Mentoring constitutes an important aspect of professional development and lifelong learning, and Intelligent Mentoring Systems can expand the scope and accessibility by leveraging advances in digital learning environments and artificial intelligence. Intelligent Mentoring Systems form a new line of research, requiring interdisciplinary support to help bring invaluable experience and learning to a wide array of students in disparate fields. We are excited to invite the international community of AIED researchers and educators to discuss, evaluate, and plan the future of these systems. The workshop focuses around three broad themes – foundations, technology, and domains and contexts.

**Keywords:** Intelligent mentors · Digital learning environments
Learner modeling · Pedagogical agents

## 1 Motivation

Mentoring is crucial for professional development and lifelong learning. It is seen by organisations as the most cost-effective and sustainable method for developing talent, for building transferable skills, for increasing motivation and confidence, for assisting with transitions across formal and informal education, for learning across workplace contexts, and for continuous career development. Studies show that investment in virtual mentors can help companies build the skills, productivity, engagement, and loyalty of their workforces. The time is ripe for the emergence of a new breed of intelligent learning systems that provide mentor-like features.

© Springer International Publishing AG, part of Springer Nature 2018
C. Penstein Rosé et al. (Eds.): AIED 2018, LNAI 10948, pp. 544–546, 2018.
https://doi.org/10.1007/978-3-319-93846-2

- Virtual mentors would be able to facilitate self-actualisation, helping learners realise their full potential.
- They would require a multi-faceted learner experience modelling mechanisms to get sufficient understanding of the learner, his/her current situation, and relevance to past experiences by the same learner (or by other people).
- They would embed new pedagogic strategies for promoting reflection, self-awareness, self-regulation, and self-determination through interactive interventions (e.g. open learner models, interactive conversational agents, social spaces), as well as new knowledge models formed by establishing connections and associations.

Developing intelligent mentoring systems requires deep understanding of complex issues such as learner modeling, technological capabilities, and contextual understanding, among many others. To foster this understanding, we invite the international community of AIED researchers to contribute to and shape the discussion of this stream of research in a collaborative workshop.

This third edition of a workshop series will foster scientific discussion and sharing experience among researchers and practitioners to establish the state of the art and shape future directions around four main themes associated with intelligent mentoring systems – foundations, technology, and domains and contexts.

## 2  Themes

This workshop will provide a forum to shape new research direction that explores how to build on what is known about ITSs to develop lifelong virtual mentors, what are the opportunities and what new challenges have to be addressed. This includes:

- contextual understanding and broadening the scope of learner modelling (learning attitudes, cultural diversity, gender diversity, experience);
- support/scaffolding for metacognitive skills and contextualising self-regulated learning in the real world;
- integration of long term learner modelling with short-term, session-based learner modelling (macro vs micro level of learner modelling);
- methods/models that can be used for self-regulation and behaviour change;
- appropriate technologies (social spaces, digital media, pervasive systems, ebooks/hypertext); and
- techniques for intelligent support and crowdsourcing wisdom.

**Foundations.** *What are the key mentoring features; and what theories are they underpinned by?* Example topics include: main definitions (mentoring, coaching, advising); main mentoring features (contextual understanding, nudging, challenging, motivating); scope (difference between virtual mentors and virtual tutors); methodologies (design-based research, ecological validity, evaluation).

**Technology.** *What computational models are required to realise mentor-like features; and what are the opportunities and challenges brought by these models?* Example computational models include: social interaction spaces; situational simulations; open/interactive learner models; visualisations; interactive pedagogical agents; contextualised nudges; mobile assistants; cognitive computing; wearables and sensors.

**Domains and Contexts.** *What challenges are faced in traditional and emerging domains and contexts; and how mentor-like features can address these challenges?* Example domains/contexts include: peer mentoring; personalised assistants/buddies; social learning; flipped classroom; video-based learning; workplace learning; career advisors; transferable skills training.

## 3  IMS Workshop Series

The IMS workshop series aims to lay the foundations of a new research stream shaping intelligent learning environments that include mentor-like features. The workshops provide a forum to explore opportunities and challenges, identify relevant existing research, and point at new research avenues.

Web site: https://imsworkshop.wordpress.com/.

## 4  Program Committee

| | |
|---|---|
| Roger Azevedo | North Carolina State University, USA |
| Darina Dicheva | Winston-Salem State University, USA |
| Ben du Boulay | University of Sussex, USA |
| Paul Brna | University of Leeds, UK |
| Andrew J. Hampton | University of Memphis, USA |
| Mitsuru Ikeda | Japan Advanced Institute of Science and Technology |
| Tsukasa Hirashima | Hiroshima University, Japan |
| Styliani Kleanthous | University of Cyprus, Cyprus |
| Lydia Lau | University of Leeds, UK |
| Vanda Luengo | Université Pierre et Marie Curie, France |
| Moffat Mathews | University of Canterbury, New Zealand |
| Judith Masthoff | University of Aberdeen, UK |
| Alicja Piotrokowicz | University of Leeds, UK |
| Alexandra Polouvassilis | University of London, Birkbeck College |
| Vasile Rus | University of Memphis, USA |
| Tamsin Treasure-Jones | University of Leeds, UK |
| Diego Zapata-Rivera | Educational Testing Service, USA |
| Beverly Woolf | University of Massachusetts Amherst, USA |

# Hands-on with GIFT: A Tutorial on the Generalized Intelligent Framework for Tutoring

Benjamin Goldberg[1(✉)], Jonathan Rowe[2], Randall Spain[2], Brad Mott[2], James Lester[2], Bob Pokorny[3], and Robert Sottilare[1]

[1] U.S. Army Research Laboratory, Orlando, FL 32826, USA
{benjamin.s.goldberg.civ,
robert.a.sottilare.civ}@mail.mil
[2] North Carolina State University, Raleigh, NC 27695, USA
{jprowe,rdspain,bwmott,lester}@ncsu.edu
[3] Intelligent Automation, Inc., Rockville, MD 20855, USA
bpokorny@i-a-i.com

**Abstract.** In this tutorial, we showcase the Generalized Intelligent Framework for Tutoring (GIFT). GIFT is an open-source platform used to create, deliver, and analyze computer-based tutoring. The tutorial provided participants with hands-on experience using GIFT functions that support research and implementation of personalized learning experiences. Specifically, GIFT's adaptive course flow features are reviewed and demonstrated, with considerable time spent developing GIFT lessons and gaining familiarity with tools and authoring workflows.

**Keywords:** GIFT · Intelligent tutoring systems · Authoring
Personalized learning

## 1 Introduction

In this tutorial, participants learn how to create a computer-based tutoring system (CBTS) using the Generalized Intelligent Framework for Tutoring (GIFT). Developed by the U.S. Army Research Laboratory, GIFT is an open source, service-oriented framework that allows researchers, practitioners and instructional designers to develop, deliver, and evaluate CBTSs. GIFT is continually evolving and has more than 1,200 active users across 40 countries (https://gifttutoring.org). GIFT enables rapid creation of adaptive learning experiences that seamlessly interleave disparate instructional activities (e.g., multimedia, quizzes, simulations) by leveraging native components of the GIFT software as well as external training and simulation applications. GIFT's architecture is domain-agnostic, enabling it to be applied across a range of domains with diverse cognitive, affective, and psychomotor components [1].

The tutorial is broadly relevant to researchers in the AIED and Learning Sciences communities, and it serves three primary functions. First, it showcases recent developments in authoring and modeling functions supported by GIFT for building adaptive

© Springer International Publishing AG, part of Springer Nature 2018
C. Penstein Rosé et al. (Eds.): AIED 2018, LNAI 10948, pp. 547–550, 2018.
https://doi.org/10.1007/978-3-319-93846-2

lesson materials. Second, it introduces attendees to ongoing efforts to develop and extend GIFT's instructional capabilities, such as data-driven pedagogical models induced using reinforcement learning techniques. Third, the tutorial provides an open forum to discuss future directions for GIFT development.

## 2   Organization Plan

The tutorial centers on three experiences: (1) Building an adaptive lesson using the cloud-based GIFT Authoring Tool; (2) Taking an adaptive lesson in GIFT; and (3) Extracting log file data for analysis, evaluation, and model development. The goal is to demonstrate tools and workflows in GIFT to guide the configuration of a lesson with personalized content sequencing, feedback and remediation functionalities.

### 2.1   GIFT Authoring Tool Familiarization

In the first phase of the tutorial, participants learn how to build and configure a training course by assembling *course objects* using GIFT's authoring tool interface. Course objects provide a range of instructional features and are used to present text, images, videos, surveys, assessments, and training scenarios. Participants learn about the functionality of each course object by creating their own GIFT lessons and sequencing course objects in GIFT's authoring palette (Fig. 1).

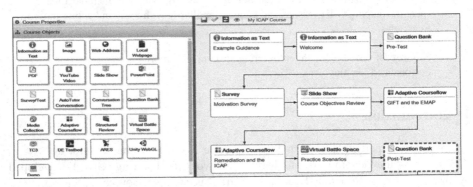

**Fig. 1.**   Available GIFT course objects (left) and a configured set of objects for a lesson (right).

### 2.2   GIFT's Adaptive Course Flow Course Object

In the second phase of the tutorial, participants learn about a distinctive type of course object: an *adaptive course flow object*. Adaptive course flow objects house GIFT's primary personalization functionalities, and they enable adaptive lesson flow based on learner model attributes [2]. This personalization is driven by GIFT's Engine for Management of Adaptive Pedagogy (EMAP), which is based on Merrill's Component Display Theory [2]. The EMAP organizes learning around four fundamental categories of learning: (1) **Rules**: Learning rules of a domain, (2) **Examples**: Seeing examples of the rules applied; (3) **Recall**: Recalling declarative and procedural information associated with the rules; and (4) **Practice**: Practicing the use of those rules in a novel context.

Participants are provided with instructional materials and programs (e.g., existing training environments and simulations) to configure an adaptive training course with the EMAP. Participants curate training content and add metadata for the Rules and Examples quadrants. They build Recall assessments using GIFT's survey interface, and they configure practice scenarios and assessment logic for the Practice quadrant.

Next, participants learn about recent additions to adaptive course flow object functionality inspired by Chi's ICAP framework for active learning [3]. The ICAP-inspired model in GIFT includes pedagogical strategies for selecting different variants of remedial activities, including activities that involve passive (e.g., reading), active (e.g., highlighting), and constructive (e.g., writing a summary) levels of student engagement. The ICAP-based remediation model is accompanied by a stochastic modeling framework that leverages Markov decision processes to formalize the task of selecting remediation for individual students [4]. These pedagogical strategies are induced using reinforcement learning techniques applied to observations of past student interactions with remediation content.

### 2.3   Lesson Delivery and Data Extraction

Following all authoring exercises, participants complete the lessons they have created, allowing them to experience how the course objects unfolded at runtime. After completing their own course, participants learn how to use the GIFT Event Reporting tool to extract student log data collected during a lesson. The Event Reporting Tool enables researchers to specify data types and formats needed for downstream research, evaluation, and model building activities.

## 3   Conclusions

In this tutorial, participants learn about GIFT's capabilities, tools and architecture, and they use these features to build their own adaptive courses. The purpose of the tutorial is to allow audience members to become familiar with GIFT, connect with the broader GIFT community, and learn how to use GIFT to support their own research interests.

## References

1. Sottilare, R., Brawner, K., Sinatra, A., Johnston, J.: An Updated Concept for a Generalized Intelligent Framework for Tutoring. US Army Research Lab, Orlando, FL (2017)
2. Goldberg, B., Hoffman, M., Tarr, R.: Authoring instructional management logic in GIFT using the EMAP. In: Sottilare, R., Graesser, A., Hu, X., Brawner, K. (eds.) Design Recommendations for ITS: Authoring Tools, vol. 3. US Army Research Laboratory (2015)

3. Chi, M.T.: Active-constructive-interactive: a conceptual framework for differentiating learning activities. Top. Cogn. Sci. **1**(1), 73–105 (2009)
4. Rowe, J., Mott, B., Lester, J., Pokorny, B., Peng, W., Goldberg, B.: Toward a modular reinforcement learning framework for tutorial planning in GIFT. In: Sottilare, R., Sinatra, A., (eds.) Proceedings of the 3rd Annual GIFT Users Symposium (2015)

# Ethics in AIED: Who Cares?

Wayne Holmes[1](✉) iD, Duygu Bektik[1] iD, Denise Whitelock[1] iD,
and Beverly Park Woolf[2]

[1] Institute of Educational Technology, The Open University, Milton Keynes, UK
wayne.holmes@open.ac.uk
[2] College of Information and Computer Sciences, University of Massachusetts,
Boston, USA

**Abstract.** The field of AIED raises far-reaching ethical questions with important implications for students and educators. However, most AIED research, development and deployment has taken place in what is essentially a moral vacuum (for example, what happens if a child is subjected to a biased set of algorithms that impact negatively and incorrectly on their school progress?). Around the world, virtually no research has been undertaken, no guidelines have been provided, no policies have been developed, and no regulations have been enacted to address the specific ethical issues raised by the use of Artificial Intelligence in Education. This workshop, *Ethics in AIED: Who Cares?*, was a first step towards addressing this critical problem for the field. It was an opportunity for researchers who are exploring ethical issues critical for AIED to share their research, to identify the key ethical issues, and to map out how to address the multiple challenges, towards establishing a basis for meaningful ethical reflection necessary for innovation in the field of AIED. The workshop was in three parts. It began with *Ethics in AIED: What's the problem?*, a round-table discussion introduced and led by Professor Beverly Woolf, one of the world's most accomplished AIED researchers. This was followed by *Mapping the Landscape*, in which participants each gave 'lightning' presentation on ethics in AIED research. The workshop concluded with *Addressing the Challenges*, a round-table discussion that agreed on a core list of ethical questions/areas of necessary research for the field of AIED, and identified next steps.

**Keywords:** Artificial intelligence in education · AIED · Ethics

## 1 Introduction

While the range of AI techniques and technologies researched in classrooms and discussed at conferences are extensive and growing, the ethical consequences are rarely fully considered (at least, there is very little published work considering the ethics). In fact, most AIED research, development and deployment has taken place in what is essentially a moral vacuum (for example, what happens if a child is subjected to a biased set of algorithms that impact negatively and incorrectly on their school progress?).

© Springer International Publishing AG, part of Springer Nature 2018
C. Penstein Rosé et al. (Eds.): AIED 2018, LNAI 10948, pp. 551–553, 2018.
https://doi.org/10.1007/978-3-319-93846-2

Around the world, virtually no research has been undertaken, no guidelines have been provided, no policies have been developed, and no regulations have been enacted to address the specific ethical issues raised by the use of Artificial Intelligence in Education. As a field (while we apply our university research regulations), we are working without any fully-worked out moral groundings specific to the field of AIED.

In fact, AIED techniques raise an indeterminate number of self-evident but as yet unanswered ethical questions. To begin with, concerns exist about the large volumes of data collected to support AIED (such as the recording of student competencies, emotions, strategies and misconceptions). Who owns and who is able to access this data, what are the privacy concerns, how should the data be analysed, interpreted and shared, and who should be considered responsible if something goes wrong?

However, while data raises major ethical concerns for the field of AIED, AIED ethics cannot be reduced to questions about data. Other major ethical concerns include the potential for bias (conscious or unconscious) incorporated into AIED algorithms and impacting negatively on the civil rights of individual students (in terms of gender, age, race, social status, income inequality...). But these particular AIED ethical concerns, centred on data and bias, are the 'known unknowns'. What about the 'unknown unknowns', the ethical issues raised by the field of AIED that have yet to be even identified?

AIED ethical questions include:

- What are the criteria for ethically acceptable AIED?
- How does the transient nature of student goals, interests and emotions impact on the ethics of AIED?
- What are the AIED ethical obligations of private organisations (developers of AIED products) and public authorities (schools and universities involved in AIED research)?
- How might schools, students and teachers opt out from, or challenge, how they are represented in large datasets?
- What are the ethical implications of not being able to easily interrogate how AIED deep decisions (using multi-level neural networks) are made?

Strategies are also needed for risk amelioration since AI algorithms are vulnerable to hacking and manipulation. Where AIED interventions target behavioural change (such as by 'nudging' individuals towards a particular course of action), the entire sequence of AIED enhanced pedagogical activity also needs to be ethically warranted. And finally, it is important to recognise another perspective on AIED ethical questions: in each instance, the ethical cost of inaction and failure to innovate must be balanced against the potential for AIED innovation to result in real benefits for learners, educators and educational institutions.

## 2   Workshop

The *Ethics in AIED: Who Cares?* workshop comprised:

Part 1   *Ethics in AIED: What's the problem?* (a round-table discussion, introduced and led by Professor Beverly Woolf).

Part 2   *Ethics in AIED: Mapping the Landscape* ('lightning' presentations on ethics in AIED research).
Part 3   *Ethics in AIED: Addressing the Challenges* (a round-table discussion, clarifying AIED ethical questions and areas of important research, and identifying next steps: an initial road map or targets).

## 3  Outcomes

As the first AIED workshop devoted to this key topic, *Ethics in AIED: Who Cares?* also served as community-building event. Participants were expected to leave with a clearer understanding of ethical issues central to AIED, and how they might contribute towards addressing the challenges. The workshop also aimed to help the AIED community begin to develop a shared understanding of the multiple challenges and points of contention around the ethics of AIED, that we can draw on when developing and researching AIED technologies. The ambition was for this to be the first of a series of meetings through which the community builds a firm ethical foundation for our work.

## References

Bektik, D.: Learning analytics for academic writing through automatic identification of meta-discourse. PhD thesis, The Open University (2017)

Bostrom, N., Yudkowsky, E.: The ethics of artificial intelligence. In: The Cambridge Handbook of Artificial Intelligence, pp. 316–334 (2014)

Luckin, R., Holmes, W., Forcier, L., Griffiths, M.: Intelligence Unleashed. An Argument for AI in Education. Pearson, London (2015)

Whitelock, D., Twiner, A., Richardson, J. T., Field, D., Pulman, S.: Feedback on academic essay writing through pre-emptive hints: moving towards 'advice for action'. Eur. J. Open, Distance E-learning **18**(1) (2015)

Woolf, B.: Building Intelligent Interactive Tutors: Student-Centered Strategies for Revolutionizing e-learning. Morgan Kaufmann, Burlington (2010)

# Workshop for Artificial Intelligence to Promote Quality and Equity in Education

Ronghuai Huang[1], Kinshuk[2], Yanyan Li[1], and TingWen Chang[1(✉)]

[1] Smart Learning Institute, Beijing Normal University, 12F, Block A, Jingshikeji Plaza, No. 12 South Xueyuan Rd, Haidian District, Beijing 100082, People's Republic of China
tingwenchang@bnu.edu.cn
[2] College of Information, University of North Texas, 1155 Union Circle, 311068, Denton, TX, USA

**Abstract.** The integration of technology in education is speeding up the reform of the education industry, and the innovative application of AI in education can provide the public with personalized, universal, life-long and quality educational services. It is clear that the field of AI will contribute to grow in terms of power and application areas. It would be a case of social negligence to overlook the potential applications of AI in the field of education and especially in addressing teacher shortages and providing basic education to many neglected populations around the world. This workshop is aimed at sharing the potential of AI to promote educational quality and equity for the benefit of society and all people. Therefore, during the workshop, we do hope to build a bridge of communication, create the learning opportunities of face-to-face communication with international renowned experts, and broaden the scope of AI and education research.

**Keywords:** Artificial intelligence · Quality and equity education
SDG

## 1 Introduction

The United Nation's seventeen sustainable development goals to transform the world by 2030 expressed in the United Nations Sustainable Development Goals (SDG) includes a focus on quality and equity in education to promote lifelong learning for everyone. Achieving this goal creates a requirement to resolve persistent problems, such as a lack of teachers in some places and many children not developing basic reading and math skills. The aim of SDG4 is 'Ensure inclusive and equitable quality education and promote lifelong learning opportunities for all [1]. Therefore, education must find ways of achieving this goal, responding to such challenges, taking into account multiple world views and alternative knowledge systems, as well as new frontiers in science and technology such as the advances in neurosciences and the developments in digital technology, such as AI [2, 3].

© Springer International Publishing AG, part of Springer Nature 2018
C. Penstein Rosé et al. (Eds.): AIED 2018, LNAI 10948, pp. 554–557, 2018.
https://doi.org/10.1007/978-3-319-93846-2

The integration of technology in education is speeding up the reform of the education industry, and the innovative application of AI in education can provide the public with personalized, universal, life-long and quality educational services [2, 4, 5]. The use of intelligent technology to accelerate the reform of the personnel training model, teaching methods, to build a new educational system, including intelligent learning and interactive learning. AI plays an important role in education, adaptive push and lifelong educational customization.

However, global education is still facing many difficulties and challenges, such as the unbalanced development of education, political instability, environmental degradation, natural disasters, natural resources competition, and the challenge of population structure, poverty and inequality. The arrival of the AI era, it is possible to solve these problems and challenges; however, it will also increase the gap between some underdeveloped areas and developed areas. Also, it brings new challenges for education, such as the role of educators/learners in the AI society, digital divide, knowledge gap, and also the economy gap between developing countries and developed countries [2, 3].

## 2 Background

The previous generation of AI in education involved intelligent tutoring systems that demonstrated some success in domains which were well-structured and, as a result, well-suited for automated teaching and feedback approaches. As it happens, the deficits involving early education, especially in rural and less developed areas, involved subject areas that are well-structured and suitable for automated support through targeted AI and adaptive technologies. Many examples of such AI applications in education already exist (see, for example, Mitchel Resnick's work with Scratch at the MIT Media Lab - https://www.media.mit.edu/people/mres/projects/). However, these advances have yet to make much impact in rural and less developed areas or used to target areas with limited teachers and teaching resources. The potential impact is significant and pushing innovative AI educational applications into such areas is one way to meet the objectives of SDG4 (Quality Education) [1].

Artificial intelligence brings new opportunities for social construction. AI technology can accurately perceive, forecast and warning of infrastructure and social security operation of the major trend, grasp the cognition and psychological changes, active decision reaction, will significantly improve the ability and level of social governance, has an irreplaceable role to effectively maintain social stability. The development of AI focuses on education, medical care, pension and other urgent needs of the people's livelihood; therefore, to accelerate the innovation of artificial intelligence applications can provide personalized, diversified, high-quality service for the public [4].

# 3  Workshop Description

## 3.1  Topical Themes

The Workshop will mainly focus on AI and Quality and Equity in Education. More specifically, it involves the following areas of emphasis and topical themes:

1. The state of AI technologies in education
2. AI educational success stories and cases
3. Adaptive technologies for a wide variety of individual learners
4. Implementing AI technologies in rural and less developed locations
5. Cost and implementation details of a variety of AI educational technologies
6. Digital technologies that can support and facilitate the implementation of AI in education
7. Implications of AI educational technologies for teachers and teacher training

## 3.2  Organization Plan

The target groups include researchers, educational leaders, educators, international organizations, policy makers at various levels, and enterprises engaged in AI.

The workshop invites 2–3 expert keynote speakers from China or the developed countries, one for each of proposed topical areas to provide presentations that focus on that particular theme and which will encourage further dialogue and elaboration. Each of the speakers will be asked to provide a position paper to be included in an edited volume based on the workshop. Furthermore, a round table discussions which will invited 4–6 experts will be transcribed and summarized for inclusion in the dieted volume as well.

## 3.3  Workshop Objectives

**Cooperation and sharing of resources.** Taking the summit as a focus, we will effectively advance project cooperation, promote smart development of education, achieve win-win cooperation and common development.

**Plan the future and build the blueprint.** To adapt to the development trend of The Times, and promote the sustainable development of artificial intelligence and education.

**Issued a declaration of meeting.** Through the related declaration on artificial intelligence and education, the development direction of artificial intelligence and education is led.

# References

1. SDG4. http://www.un.org/sustainabledevelopment/education/. accessed 10 Jan 2018
2. Preparing for the future of AI (2016). National Science and Technology Council, USA, Oct 2016

3. National Artificial Intelligence R&D Strategic Plan. National Science and Technology Council, USA (2016)
4. AI, Automation, and the Economy. National Science and Technology Council, USA (2016)
5. Human Brain Project. European Union (2017)

# 8th International Workshop on Personalization Approaches in Learning Environments PALE 2018

Milos Kravcik[1]([✉]), Olga C. Santos[2], Jesus G. Boticario[2], Maria Bielikova[3], Tomas Horvath[4], and Ilaria Torre[5]

[1] DFKI GmbH, Berlin, Germany
Milos.Kravcik@dfki.de
[2] aDeNu Research Group, UNED, Madrid, Spain
[3] Slovak University of Technology in Bratislava, Bratislava, Slovakia
[4] Eotvos Lorand University in Budapest, Budapest, Hungary
[5] DIBRIS, Genoa University, Genova, Italy

**Abstract.** Personalization is a well-established topic in education and there are more than 30 years of experience in adaptation and personalization approaches that use artificial intelligence. Bringing together methods, techniques and experiences is the motivation of PALE at AIED. Its aim is to share and discuss the new trends in current research, with specific focus on emerging approaches that exploit new data collection technologies to support multimodal personalization of learning.

**Keywords:** Personalization · Adaptive Learning Environments
Engagement · Context Awareness

## 1 Motivation

Personalization of learning is a wide-ranging educational strategy, which can apply artificial intelligence techniques in many different facets and processes. Basically, artificial intelligence techniques are used to comprehend the learners' peculiarities and to tailor the learning experience in a way that takes into account their individual differences and needs. Thus, artificial intelligence is used to model and infer the learners skills and goals, such as for automatic planning of adaptive learning paths, to match individual needs with learning materials and learning modalities, to name just a few.

Personalization is crucial to foster effective, active, efficient and satisfactory behavior in learning situations in an increasing and varied number of contexts which include informal learning scenarios that are being demanded in everyday life activities and lifelong learning settings, with more control on the learner side and more sensitivity towards context.

Personalization in learning environments is a long-term research area which evolves as new technological innovations appear and, thus, can take advantage of recent trends emerging from artificial intelligence and cognitive science

© Springer International Publishing AG, part of Springer Nature 2018
C. Penstein Rosé et al. (Eds.): AIED 2018, LNAI 10948, pp. 558–560, 2018.
https://doi.org/10.1007/978-3-319-93846-2

approaches for educational computing applications. Nowadays, there are new opportunities for building inter-operable personalized learning solutions that consider a wider range of data coming from varied learner situations and inter-action features (in terms of physiological and environmental sensors).

In such context of technological innovations, PALE aims to discuss how the combination of artificial intelligence, user modeling and personalization techniques is able to manage the increasing amount of information coming from the task at hand and its surrounding environment, in order to provide personalized learning support, which is sensitive to learners and their context. This covers many interrelated fields including intelligent tutoring systems, learning management systems, personal learning environments, serious games, agent-based learning environments, and informal workplace learning settings. Furthermore, we aim to cover the demanding need of personalized learning in wider contexts ranging from daily life activities to massive open on-line courses.

## 2  Objectives and Themes

PALE workshop at AIED 2018 is particularly focused on the enhanced sensitivity towards the management of big educational data coming from learners' interactions (e.g., multi-modal sensor detection of attention and affect) and technological deployment (including web, mobiles, tablets, tabletops), and how this wide range of situations and features might impact on modeling the learner interaction and context. In the current state-of-the-art it is not clear how the new information sources are to be managed and combined in order to enhance interaction in a way that positively impacts the learning process of essentially adaptive nature.

There are new open issues in this area which refer to the need of suitable user modeling that is able to understand both realistic learning environments cropping up in a wider range of situations and the needs of the learners within and across them. This requires enhancing the management of an increasing number of information sources (including wearables) and big data which ultimately are to provide a better understanding of every person's learning needs within different contexts and over short-, medium- and long-term periods of time. Hopefully, this will also increase the definition of standards for open learner models that support interoperability, enable the integration of an increasing amount of information sources coming from ambient intelligence devices to gather information not only about the learner interaction but the whole context of the learning experience, including affective state and engagement. The aim is to aid the combination of different external learning services into a personalized one and, in addition, to increase learners' understanding of their own needs.

Briefly, in summary, this workshop at AIED aims to give and share promising ideas to the following research question: *Which approaches can be followed to cater for the increasing amount of information available from immediate (e.g., in terms of wearable devices) to broader contexts in order to provide effective and personalized assistance in learning situations, bridging behavioral and computational learning?*

The main themes covered, but not limited, by the workshop include:

- User engagement in learning processes
- (Big) Data processing within and across learning situations
- Ambient intelligence
- Learner and context awareness
- Cognitive and meta-cognitive scaffolding
- Adaptive mobile learning
- Wearable devices for sensing and acting in ubiquitous learning scenarios
- Tracking technologies for accessible learning for all

## 3   PALE Workshop Series

PALE 2018 is a follow-up of seven previous editions. The focus of this workshop series is put on the different and complementary perspectives in which personalization can be addressed in learning environments (e.g., informal, workplace, lifelong, mobile, contextualized, and self-regulated learning). Previous editions have shown several important issues in this field, such as behavior and embodiment of pedagogic agents, suitable support of self-regulated learning, appropriate balance between learner control and expert guidance, design of personal learning environments, contextual recommendations at various levels of the learning process, tracking and reacting to affective states of learners, harmonization of educational and technological standards, big data processing for learning purposes, predicting student outcomes, adaptive learning assessment, and evaluation of personalized learning systems. Thus, PALE offers an opportunity to present and discuss a wide spectrum of issues and solutions. The format follows the Learning Cafe methodology to promote discussions on some of the open issues coming from the presented papers. Each Learning Cafe consists of brief presentations of the key questions posed and small group discussions with participants randomly grouped at tables. Each table is moderated by one expert in the topic under discussion (mostly the presenter of the paper who has addressed the issue) and participants change tables during the discussion with the aim to share ideas among the groups.

The first five editions of the PALE workshop led to the Special issue on User Modelling to Support Personalization in Enhanced Educational Settings in the International Journal of Artificial Intelligence in Education (IJAIED) [1].

## Reference

1. Santos, O.C., Kravcik, M., Boticario, J.G.: Preface to special issue on user modelling to support personalization in enhanced educational settings. Int. J. Artif. Intell. Educ. **26**(3), 809–820 (2016)

# Workshop on Authoring and Tutoring Methods for Diverse Task Domains: Psychomotor, Mobile, and Medical

Jason D. Moss[✉] and Paula J. Durlach

U. S. Army Research Laboratory, Orlando, FL 32826, USA
{Jason.D.Moss11.civ, Paula.J.Durlach.civ}@mail.mil

**Abstract.** Currently, intelligent tutoring systems are primarily used in conventional instructional environments, for the purpose of training predominantly cognitive and perceptual skills. This half-day workshop explored issues involved with applying intelligent tutoring methods to learning psychomotor or other types of skills not typically performed while sitting at a desk. Discussion during the workshop identified research questions, technical challenges, and the current state of the art with respect to creating and deploying intelligent tutoring methodology to support learning of diverse real world psychomotor tasks, such as the use of sensors, the creation of expert and assessment models, and provisions for feedback and remediation.

**Keywords:** Psychomotor · Learning · Models · Sensors

## 1 Workshop Overview

Currently, intelligent tutoring systems (ITS) are primarily used in conventional instructional environments, for the purpose of training predominantly cognitive and perceptual skills. This half-day workshop explored issues involved with applying intelligent tutoring methods to learning psychomotor or other types of skills not typically performed while sitting at a desk, such as marksmanship, golf, and dance. ITSs have been developed and used in various places including military, industry, and school (e.g., Anderson et al. 1990; Koedinger et al. 1997; Ritter et al. 2013; Sottilare 2015; Sottilare and LaViola 2015). The advantage of ITSs over traditional instruction is potential improvements in efficacy and effectiveness of training through adaptive feedback and content selection (e.g., Durlach and Ray 2011; Fletcher and Morrison 2012; Kulik and Fletcher 2016). With the advent of wearable devices, sensors, and the "internet of things" there is the potential to expand the use of ITS approaches from conventional instructional environments to more diverse task domains, such as psychomotor tasks and mobile activities. The workshop included papers about ongoing research and interactive discussion on the technical challenges, research questions, and current state of the art with regard to creating intelligent tutoring for tasks performed "in the wild." Some of these challenges included expert-model creation, task segmentation, performance assessment methods, and correctional feedback timing and form. The workshop is expected to include five presentations and dedicated time for discussion.

© Springer International Publishing AG, part of Springer Nature 2018
C. Penstein Rosé et al. (Eds.): AIED 2018, LNAI 10948, pp. 561–563, 2018.
https://doi.org/10.1007/978-3-319-93846-2

## 2 Workshop Presentations (in Order of Submission)

### 2.1 A Psychomotor Task Training in GIFT: Using a Physio-Cognitive Model for an Improved Understanding of the Domain and Learner Model

Jong W. Kim, Chris Dancy, and Robert A. Sottilare

### 2.2 An Approach for Supporting Dance Learning using Sensors

Augusto Dias Pereira dos Santos, Kalina Yacef, and Roberto Martinez-Maldonado

### 2.3 Authoring and Applying a Flexible and Data-Rich Intelligent Tutoring System

Keith T. Shubeck, Brent Morgan, Lijia Wang, Xiangen Hu, Art Graesser

### 2.4 Modelling physical activity behaviour in a health education system

Vincey Wing Sze Au, Kalina Yacef, Corinne Caillaud, Olivier Galy

### 2.5 What is distinctive about psychomotor skills training? A case study in ITS authoring challenges

Benjamin Bell, Elaine Kelsey, Debbie Brown and Benjamin Goldberg

## 3 Workshop Organizers

**Dr. Jason Moss** is a Research Psychologist for U.S. Army Research Laboratory in Orlando, FL. Prior to civilian service for the U.S. Army, he was a postdoctoral fellow in academia and a defense contractor. He has over 14 years of experience conducting military funded research and experimentation for the U.S. Navy and U.S. Army. His body of research has focused on human-machine interactions in virtual environments, training, and psychophysiological measures of workload. Dr. Moss received a Ph. D. in human factors psychology from Clemson University in 2008.

**Dr. Paula Durlach** has conducted and managed adaptive training research, as well as other projects, at U. S. Army and DoD organizations for more than ten years. Prior to that she did behavior research in both academia and industry. She is currently at the U.S. Army Research Lab, Simulation and Training Technology Center, in Orlando, FL. Dr. Durlach received a Ph.D. from Yale University in 1982.

# References

Anderson, J., Boyle, C., Corbett, A., Lewis, M.: Cognitive modeling and intelligent tutoring. Artif. Intell. **42**(1), 7–49 (1990)

Durlach, P., Ray, J.: Designing adaptive instructional environments: insights from empirical evidence. U. S. Army Research Institute, Technical report 1297, Arlington, VA (2011)

Fletcher, D., Morrison, J.: DARPA Digital Tutor: Assessment Data. Institute for Defense Analysis Document D-4686). Alexandria (2012)

Koedinger, K., Anderson, J., Hadley, W., Mark, M.: Intelligent tutoring goes to school in the big city. Int. J. Artif. Intell. Educ. **8**, 30–43 (1997)

Kulik, J., Fletcher, D.: Effectiveness of intelligent tutoring systems: a meta-analytic review. Rev. Educ. Res. **86**(1), 42–78 (2016)

Ritter, F., Yeh, K., Cohen, M., Weyhrauch, P., Kim, J., Hobbs, J.: Declarative to procedural tutors: a family of cognitive architecture-based tutors. In: Kennedy, B., Reitter, D., Amant, R. (eds.) Proceedings of the 22nd Annual Conference on Behavior Representation in Modeling and Simulation, pp. 1–6. BRIMS Society, Centerville (2013)

Sottilare, R.A.: Augmented cognition on the run: considerations for the design and authoring of mobile tutoring systems. In: Schmorrow, D., Fidopiastis, C. (eds.) AC 2015. LNCS, vol. 9183. Springer, Cham (2015)

Sottilare, R., LaViola, J.: Extending intelligent tutoring beyond the desktop to the psychomotor domain. In: Interservice/Industry Training, Simulation, and Education Conference (I/ITSEC) 2015, Orlando, FL (2015). Accessed 21 Nov 2016

# Assessment and Intervention During Team Tutoring Workshop

Anne M. Sinatra[1(⊠)] and Jeanine A. DeFalco[1,2]

[1] US Army Research Laboratory, Orlando, USA
{anne.m.sinatra.civ, jeanine.a.defalco.ctr}@mail.mil
[2] Oak Ridge Associated Universities, Oak Ridge, USA

**Abstract.** The "Assessment and Intervention during Team Tutoring" workshop covers the topic areas of assessment and intervention during team tutoring and collaborative learning in intelligent tutoring systems (ITSs). The development of team ITSs is a time-intensive and difficult task that includes technological, instructional and design based challenges. The goals of this workshop include providing a forum for researchers working in these up and coming areas to discuss the progress that they have made in team or collaborative tutoring, discuss the approaches that they have taken, and the challenges that they have encountered. After presentations of work in three topic areas: lessons learned from team ITSs, team assessment strategies and approaches, and collaborative learning/problem solving in ITSs, there will be an open discussion to identify commonalities and novelties in the approaches. This workshop is expected to be of interest to those in academia, government, and industry who are developing tutoring experiences for multiple learners. The expected outcomes of the workshop include an identification of team tutoring gaps/challenges in varying learning domains, approaches that have been successful or unsuccessful in meeting those challenges, and determining the next steps in approaches that AIED researchers can use for their own team tutor development.

**Keywords:** Team tutoring · Collaborative problem solving
Intelligent team tutoring systems

## 1 Introduction and Overview

### 1.1 Team Tutoring in Intelligent Tutoring Systems

The purpose of this workshop is to provide the AIED Community with an exploration of key issues surrounding assessment and intervention during team tutoring in intelligent tutoring systems (ITSs). Team Tutoring has been shown as an area of significant interest in the AIED community as multiple Journal of AIED articles were recently published in this topic area [1–3].

It is particularly challenging to create adaptive computer-based team and collaborative learning tutors. One of the reasons for this difficulty resides in accounting for technological and instructional challenges when designing ITSs for multiple distributed individuals to use simultaneously. As such, the goal of this workshop is to provide opportunities for discussion regarding approaches taken, challenges associated, and

C. Penstein Rosé et al. (Eds.): AIED 2018, LNAI 10948, pp. 564–566, 2018.
https://doi.org/10.1007/978-3-319-93846-2

techniques applied in addressing team tutoring. As there are a range of approaches and iterations that constitute team tutoring (e.g., team taskwork tutoring, teamwork tutoring, collaborative problem solving, etc.), this workshop is uniquely positioned to facilitate constructive and informative dialogue for interested stakeholders for the purposes of identifying relevant solutions.

## 1.2 The Generalized Intelligent Framework for Tutoring (GIFT) as an Example of a Team Tutoring Implementation

The US Army Research Laboratory (ARL) has been developing team tutoring capabilities in the Generalized Intelligent Framework for Tutoring (GIFT; www.gifttutoring.org) project. While GIFT [4] was initially implemented as an individual tutoring framework, both theoretical [4] and applied work [2, 5] has been done to ensure GIFT is applicable for use in team tutoring situations. In prior GIFT team research, a number of complex challenges have been identified. One such identified challenge includes transitioning individual learner's data, states, and performance to a team version that encompasses all individual performances as well as a team performance.

To contextualize and introduce the current challenges in team tutoring as identified by ARL researchers, the workshop organizers will provide an overview of the approaches used to date regarding incorporating team tutoring in GIFT. This will include detailing the background work conducted into the initial theoretical elements of team tutoring for GIFT (e.g., meta-analysis and identification of behavioral markers), as well as prior and ongoing approaches that have been used to incorporate team tutoring functionality into the architecture of GIFT. This introductory discussion of team tutoring and GIFT will be used as a jumping off point to frame one example of team tutoring in action that can then be compared and contrasted to other approaches employed by the community and attendees.

## 2  Themes of the Workshop

This workshop is made up of three main themes: (1) Team ITSs in action: Lessons learned from developing Team ITSs; (2) Team Assessment Strategies and Approaches in an ITS; (3) ITS based Collaborative Problem Solving and Learning. Papers that will be presented during the workshop include both empirical and theoretical papers covering topics including: communications in team tutoring; frameworks for teamwork assessment; considerations for assessment in team tasks; and case example approaches analyzing team tutoring problem solving processes. The presentations will be followed by open discussion reviewing commonalities and novelties in the approaches to team tutoring addressed in the workshop, as well as discussions to articulate research gaps.

# 3  Expected Outcomes

Much research has been conducted in regard to team training and the understanding of communication and performance within in-person teams [6]. However, there has been limited research in regard to applying these principles in ITSs, due in part to the complex challenges that are inherent to this field. Accordingly, this workshop is expected to contribute to the continued efforts of identifying optimal team tutoring paradigms in the following ways: (1) providing a forum to display the progress made in regard to all types of team and multi-learner ITSs; (2) discussing ways to overcome known challenges in team tutoring; (3) identifying theoretical frameworks for future team ITS research.

Outcomes of the workshop include an identification of challenges and research gaps that exist in team tutoring, and an initial discussion about approaches that have been used to overcome them. An additional outcome is expected to include the open discussion of team tutoring approaches in multiple domains, and the commonalities that exist between them that can be leveraged for future team tutoring development. In sum, the outcomes of this workshop are expected to be of interest to the AIED community, researchers working in the areas of team tutoring and collaborative learning, as well as GIFT developers actively working on designing a domain-independent framework for designing team ITSs.

**Acknowledgements.** The research described herein has been sponsored by the U.S. Army Research Laboratory. The statements and opinions expressed in this article do not necessarily reflect the position or the policy of the United States Government, and no official endorsement should be inferred.

# References

1. Fletcher, J.D., Sottilare, R.A.: Shared mental models in support of adaptive instruction for teams using the GIFT tutoring architecture. Int. J. Artif. Intell. Educ. 1–21 (2017)
2. Gilbert, S.B., Slavina, A., Dorneich, M.C., Sinatra, A.M., Bonner, D., Johnston, J., Holub, J., MacAllister, A., Winer, E.: Creating a team tutoring using GIFT. Int. J. Artif. Intell. Educ. 1–28 (2017)
3. Sottilare, R.A., Burke, C.S., Salas, E., Sinatra, A.M., Johnston, J.H., Gilbert, S.B.: Designing adaptive instruction for teams: a meta-analysis. Int. J. Artif. Intell. Educ. 1–40 (2017)
4. Sottilare, R., Brawner, K., Sinatra, A., Johnston, J.: An Updated Concept for a Generalized Intelligent Framework for Tutoring (GIFT). US Army Research Laboratory–Human Research & Engineering Directorate (ARL-HRED), Orlando (2017)
5. Bonner, D., Gilbert, S., Dorneich, M.C., Winer, E., Sinatra, A.M., Slavina, A., McAllister, A., Holub, J.: The challenges of building intelligent tutoring systems for teams. In: Proceedings of the Human Factors and Ergonomics Society Annual Meeting, vol. 60, issue 1, pp. 1981–1985. SAGE Publications, Los Angeles (2016)
6. Salas, E.: Team Training Essentials: A Research-Based Guide. Routledge (2015)

# Exploring Opportunities to Standardize Adaptive Instructional Systems (AISs)

Robert Sottilare[1]([✉]) [iD], Robby Robson[2], Avron Barr[3],
Arthur Graesser[4], and Xiangen Hu[4]

[1] Army Research Lab, Adelphi, USA
robert.a.sottilare.civ@mail.mil
[2] Eduworks, Corvallis, USA
[3] IEEE Learning Technologies Steering Committee
[4] University of Memphis, Memphis, USA

**Abstract.** This goal of the proposed workshop is to explore opportunities to standardize components and/or processes within a class of technologies called adaptive instructional systems (AISs) which include Intelligent Tutoring Systems (ITSs), intelligent media, and other learning tools and methods used to guide/optimize instruction for individual learners and teams. AISs use human variability (e.g., performance, preferences, affect) and other learner/team attributes along with instructional conditions to develop/select appropriate learning strategies (domain-independent policies) and tactics (tutor actions). Within AISs, the relationship of the learner(s) states/traits, environmental conditions (context within a learning experience), and AIS decisions is usually described by a machine learning algorithm which is used to select an action or set of actions to optimize one or more learning outcomes. Outcomes include: knowledge acquisition, skill development, retention, performance, and transfer of skills between the instructional environment and the work or operational environment where the skills learned during instruction may be applied. This workshop will present standardization opportunities and strategies with the goal of reducing the entry skills/time required to develop AISs, and promoting opportunities for reuse.

**Keywords:** Standards · Adaptive instructional systems (AISs)
Intelligent tutoring systems (ITSs) · Intelligent media
Reuse and interoperability

## 1 Introduction

In December 2017, the Learning Technologies Steering Committee (LTSC) under the auspices of the Institute for Electrical and Electronics Engineers (IEEE) formed a 6-month Standards Study Group to investigate the possible market need for standards across AISs. Several interactions with affiliated stakeholder communities point to broad interest in AIS standards. Discussions to date indicate opportunities to influence their affordability, their interoperability and reuse, making them more appealing to the masses. Standards in learner modeling, instructional strategies, and domain modeling have the potential to effect AIS design via machine-based reinforcement learning

C. Penstein Rosé et al. (Eds.): AIED 2018, LNAI 10948, pp. 567–569, 2018.
https://doi.org/10.1007/978-3-319-93846-2

strategies used to improve the accuracy and effectiveness of learner state predictions and instructional decisions by AISs. This workshop is relevant to communities researching and developing solutions including users of broadly used AIS technologies including, but not limited to the Cognitive Tutor [1], AutoTutor [2], the Generalized Intelligent Framework for Tutoring (GIFT) [3, 4], Dragoon [5], ASPIRE-Tutor [6], and the Total Learning Architecture (TLA) [7].

## 2  Target Audience

The target audience for this proposed workshop consists of researchers and practitioners within academia, industry, and government institutions interested in AIS standards and the associated goal of reducing time and cost to author, deliver, manage, and evaluate the effectiveness of adaptive instruction.

## 3  Organization Plan

The workshop is proposed in three sections or themes: (1) barriers to the adoption of AIS standards; (2) module level interoperability for AIS standards and reuse; knowledge and pedagogical strategies for AIS standards. The papers that will be presented during the workshop examine opportunities to solve AIS development problems (e.g., skill, time, and cost) and barriers to their adoption. Each briefing will be followed by open discussion reviewing the merits of the approaches presented during the workshop, and a final discussion panel will feature the workshop organizers to allow free flowing questions related to the motivations and potential of AIS standards.

## 4  Expected Outcomes

An important element of this workshop addresses the "why standards for AISs" question. The motivation behind AIS standards should be focused on how proposed standards can help current and future AIS developers bring their useful products to market. To develop AIS standards fairly and objectively, the organizers of this workshop have focused on presenting a sampling of approaches where the audience can engage in conversation on their merit (e.g., ability to promote/limit creativity).

The primary goal of this workshop is to increase the number of informed stakeholders who understand the potential of AIS standards and how they might influence their development. Standards can and should enable the streamlining and innovation of processes, decrease waste and development costs, increase the efficiency of research and development, reduce adopters' risks and integration costs, lower barriers to entry for innovative products, improve interoperability and reuse, expand markets, and support the development of new technologies and products.

**Acknowledgements**. A portion of the research described within this workshop has been sponsored by the U.S. Army Research Laboratory. The statements and opinions expressed in this article do not necessarily reflect the position or the policy of the United States Government, and no official endorsement should be inferred.

# References

1. Aleven, V.A., Koedinger, K.R.: An effective metacognitive strategy: learning by doing and explaining with a computer-based cognitive tutor. Cogn. Sci. **26**(2), 147–179 (2002)
2. Craig, S., Graesser, A., Sullins, J., Gholson, B.: Affect and learning: an exploratory look into the role of affect in learning with AutoTutor. J. Educ. Media **29**(3), 241–250 (2004)
3. Sottilare, R.A., Brawner, K.W., Goldberg, B.S., Holden, H.K.: The Generalized Intelligent Framework for Tutoring (GIFT). Concept Paper Released as Part of GIFT Software Documentation. US Army Research Laboratory–Human Research and Engineering Directorate (ARL-HRED). US Army Research Laboratory–Human Research and Engineering Directorate (ARL-HRED), Orlando (2012)
4. Sottilare, R., Brawner, K., Sinatra, A., Johnston, J.: An Updated Concept for a Generalized Intelligent Framework for Tutoring (GIFT). US Army Research Laboratory, Orlando, May 2017
5. Wetzel, J., VanLehn, K., Butler, D., Chaudhari, P., Desai, A., Feng, J., Samala, R.: The design and development of the dragoon intelligent tutoring system for model construction: lessons learned. Interact. Learn. Environ. **25**(3), 361–381 (2017)
6. Mitrovic, A., Martin, B., Suraweera, P., Zakharov, K., Milik, N., Holland, J., McGuigan, N.: ASPIRE: an authoring system and deployment environment for constraint-based tutors. Int. J. Artif. Intell. Educ. **19**(2), 155–188 (2009)
7. Folsom-Kovarik, J.T., Raybourn, E.M.: Total learning architecture (TLA) enables next-generation learning via meta-adaptation. In: Proceedings of the Interservice/Industry Training, Simulation, and Education Conference, Nov 2016

# Workshop: Design and Application of Collaborative, Dynamic, Personalized Experimentation

J. J. Williams[1]([⊠]), N. Heffernan[2]([⊠]), and O. Poquet[1]

[1] National University of Singapore, Singapore, Singapore
williams@comp.nus.edu.sg
[2] Worcester Polytechnic Institute, Worcester, USA
nth@wpi.edu

**Abstract.** The proposed workshop will focus on the design and application of randomized experimental comparisons, that investigate how components of digital problems impact students' learning and motivation. The workshop will demonstrate how randomized experiments powered by artificial intelligence can enhance personalized components of widely-used online problems, such as prompts for students to reflect, hints, explanations, motivational messages, and feedback. The participants will be introduced to dynamic experiments that reweight randomization to be proportional to the evidence that conditions are beneficial for future students and will consider the pros and cons of using such more advanced statistical methods to ensure research studies lead to practical improvement. The focus will be on real-world online problems that afford the application of randomized experiments; examples include middle school math problems (www.assistments.org), quizzes in on-campus university courses, activities in Massive Open Online Courses (MOOCs). The attendees will have the opportunity to collaboratively develop hypotheses and design experiments that could then be deployed, such as investigating the effects of different self-explanation prompts on students with varying levels of knowledge, verbal fluency, and motivation. This workshop aims to identify concrete, actionable ways for researchers to collect data and design evidence-based educational resources in more ecologically valid contexts.

## 1 Introduction

The adoption of digital technologies in education offers novel opportunities for bridging research and practice, as it lowers the barriers to conduct randomized comparisons in real-world settings. Currently many studies take place in laboratories, as classroom field experiments in physical environments are challenging to randomize at the student level. To address this challenge, the workshop aims to connect theories and approaches from the learning sciences with the improvement of ecologically valid educational resources, by designing randomized comparisons that can be deployed with students.

The workshop will investigate how to enhance components of digital problems to increase students' learning and motivation. The goal is to focus on components of

© Springer International Publishing AG, part of Springer Nature 2018
C. Penstein Rosé et al. (Eds.): AIED 2018, LNAI 10948, pp. 570–573, 2018.
https://doi.org/10.1007/978-3-319-93846-2

widely used online problems, like prompts for students to reflect [1, 2], hints, explanations, motivational messages, and feedback. The focus of the workshop will be real-world digital problems or activities for which it is actually possible to conduct the proposed experiments. These include problems on the www.assistments.org platform for middle school math, quizzes in on-campus university courses, and Massive Open Online Courses (MOOCs).

Components of online problems are especially germane because: (1) They are ubiquitous in a wide range of educational settings, topics, age groups. (2) There are immediate dependent measures of engagement (time spent on problems, repeated attempts) and learning (accuracy and time needed to solve future near and far transfer problems). (3) A wide range of variables can be experimentally investigated in enhancing online problems, through appropriate design of hints [3], explanations [4], and learning tips [5]. Despite the extant research that demonstrates that quality support in problems can benefit learning, there are many open questions about how to provide the best instructional support and feedback in interactive problems (see [6] for a review).

## 2 Dynamic Experimentation

A challenge that arises in conducting randomized comparisons is minimizing the chances that students are disadvantaged by receiving conditions that are bad for learning and maximizing the chances that data from experiments leads to practical improvements for future students. The workshop will introduce how to dynamically adapt experiments, by analyzing data in real-time and weighting randomization, so that the probability of assigning a student to a condition is proportional to the probability that the condition is best for them (leads to highest learning or engagement).

Algorithms that provide statistically principled trade-offs between experimenting and maximizing outcomes have been extensively studied in machine learning [7], website testing [8], and medical applications [9]. Workshop co-organizer Williams has implemented one of these algorithms, i.e. Thompson Sampling [10], into a system for experimentation on explanations in online problems [11], freely available at the URL www.josephjaywilliams.com/dynamicproblem. The Thompson Sampling algorithm used an adaptively weighted random policy that changed the probability of assigning different explanations by using data about students' ratings of how helpful explanations were for their learning. For example, the probability of receiving any one of four explanations was 25% for the first learner. But if the first twenty learners rated explanations three and four more highly than explanation one or two, the probability of the twenty-first learner receiving each explanation might be changed to 20%, 16%, 34%, 30%. This preserves random assignment and allows causal conclusions, while dynamically using the data collected to increase how many people receive higher rated explanations. A separate study with pre- and post- test measures of learning showed that using the system to identify highly rated explanations increased learning and transfer to accurately solving new math problems. Learning gains from these adaptive explanations did not differ significantly from high quality explanations written by a teacher. This is one example of the kinds of studies we hope workshop participants can design during the workshop, and then collaborate after the workshop.

## 3  Target Audience and Organizers

The workshop targets a broad group of researchers interested in randomized comparisons in digital educational environments, as well as university instructors and K12 teachers interested in collaborating on such studies.

Organizers of the workshop: **Joseph Jay Williams**, Assistant Professor, School of Computing, National University of Singapore (www.josephjaywilliams.com). **Neil Heffernan**, Professor, Learning Sciences Program & Computer Science, Worcester Polytechnic Institute (www.neilheffernan.net), Co-founder of www.assistments.org platform. **Oleksandra Poquet**, Postdoctoral Fellow, Institute for Applied Learning Sciences and Educational Technology, National University of Singapore.

## References

1. Williams, J.J., Lombrozo, T.: The role of explanation in discovery and generalization: evidence from category learning. Cogn. Sci. **34**, 776–806 (2010)
2. Chi, M.T.H., De Leeuw, N., Chiu, M.-H., Lavancher, C.: Eliciting self-explanations improves understanding. Cogn. Sci. **18**, 439–477 (1994)
3. Kardan, S., Conati, C.: In: Proceedings of the 33rd Annual ACM Conference on Human Factors in Computing Systems, pp. 3671–3680. ACM (2015). https://dl.acm.org/citation.cfm?doid=2702123.2702424
4. Wittwer, J., Renkl, A.: Why Instructional explanations often do not work: a framework for understanding the effectiveness of instructional explanations. Educ. Psychol. **43**, 49–64 (2008)
5. Berthold, K., Nückles, M., Renkl, A.: Do learning protocols support learning strategies and outcomes? The role of cognitive and metacognitive prompts. Learn. Instr. **17**, 564–577 (2007)
6. Shute, V.J.: Focus on formative feedback. Rev. Educ. Res. **78**, 153–189 (2008)
7. Langford, J., Zhang, T.: The epoch-greedy algorithm for contextual multi-armed bandits. http://hunch.net/ ∼ jl/projects/interactive/sidebandits/bandit.pdf
8. Li, L., Chu, W., Langford, J., Schapire, R.E.: In Proceedings of the 19th International Conference on World Wide Web, WWW 2010, pp. 661–670. ACM, New York (2010). http://doi.acm.org/10.1145/1772690.1772758
9. Murphy, S.A.: An experimental design for the development of adaptive treatment strategies. Stat. Med. **24**, 1455–1481 (2005)
10. Chapelle, O., Li, L.: An empirical evaluation of thompson sampling. In: Proceedings of the 24th International Conference on Neural Information Processing Systems, NIPS 2011, pp. 2249–2257. Curran Associates Inc., USA (2011). http://dl.acm.org/citation.cfm?id=2986459.2986710
11. Williams, J.J. et al.: AXIS: generating explanations at scale with learnersourcing and machine learning. In: Proceedings of the Third (2016) ACM Conference on Learning @ Scale, L@S 2016, pp. 379–388. ACM, New York, NY, USA (2016). http://doi.acm.org/10.1145/2876034.287604212

12. Williams, J., Rafferty, A., Tingley, D., Ang, A., Lasecki, W., Kim, J.: Enhancing online problems through instructor-centered tools for randomized experiments. In: Proceedings of CHI (2018), 36th Annual ACM Conference on Human Factors in Computing Systems (2018)
13. National Science Foundation: SI2-SSE. Adding Research Accounts to the ASSISTments Platform: Helping Researchers Do Randomized Controlled Studies with Thousands of Students. (1440753) $486,000. 2014–2016

# Author Index